ICELANDIC
Practical Dictionary
Icelandic-English/English-Icelandic

ICELANDIC
Practical Dictionary
Icelandic-English/English-Icelandic

Helga Hilmisdóttir

Hippocrene Books, Inc.
New York

For information, address:
HIPPOCRENE BOOKS, INC.
171 Madison Avenue
New York, NY 10016
www.hippocrenebooks.com

Library of Congress Cataloging-in-Publication Data

Names: Helga Hilmisdóttir, author.
Title: Icelandic practical dictionary : Icelandic-English/English-
Icelandic / Helga Hilmisdóttir.
Description: New York : Hippocrene Books, Inc., 2016.
Identifiers: LCCN 2016034674| ISBN 9780781813518 (pbk.) |
         ISBN 0781813514 (pbk.)
Subjects: LCSH: Icelandic language--Dictionaries--English. | English
  language--Dictionaries--Icelandic.
Classification: LCC PD2437 .H45 2016 | DDC 439/.69321--dc23
LC record available at https://lccn.loc.gov/2016034674

Printed in the United States of America.

CONTENTS

INTRODUCTION to ICELANDIC

Alphabet

The Icelandic alphabet contains 32 letters in the following order (the letters *c* and *z* occur in some names and foreign borrowings):

Aa Áá Bb (Cc) Dd Ðð Ee Éé Ff Gg Hh Ii Íí Jj
Kk Ll Mm Nn Oo Óó Pp Rr Ss Tt Uu Úú Vv
Yy Ýý Xx (Zz) Þþ Ææ Öö

Pronunciation and Reading Guide

In the following alphabet list, each letter has a short description of how to pronounce it. Note that some of the sounds and concepts have been simplified for ease of learning. Stress in Icelandic is always on the first syllable. Secondary stress or half-stress occurs in longer words.

Vowels in Icelandic can be either short or long. If a syllable has a short consonant, the vowel is long and vice versa. Thus, a long vowel is usually followed by one consonant, while a short vowel is usually followed by two.

Letter   Icelandic   English Equivalent

(Note: there are many letter combinations that change the pronunciation of letters, so also see Letter Combinations, pages x to xii.)

Vowels

A a	a	**a** like in f**a**ther
Á á	á	**ou** like in l**ou**d
E e	e	**e** like in l**e**t
É é	é	**ye** like in **ye**s
I i	i	**i** like in t**i**n *(the same sound as the y in Icelandic)*
Í í	í	**ee** like in s**ee** *(the same sound as the ý in Icelandic)*
O o	o	open **o** similar to **o** in m**o**re
Ó ó	ó	**o** like in l**o**w
U u	u	sound does not exist in English but can be approximated by saying *ee*-sound in *tee* with rounded lips; also similar to the *u*-sound in the French word *tu*
Ú ú	ú	**ou** like in y**ou**
Y y	yfsilon y	**i** like in t**i**n *(the same sound as the Icelandic letter i)*
Ý ý	yfsilon ý	**ee** like in t**ee** *(the same sound as the Icelandic letter í)*
Æ æ	æ	**i** like in d**i**ne
Ö ö	ö	**i** like in g**i**rl / **o** like in w**o**rker

Diphthongs

Au au	au	make this sound by starting out with an Icelandic ö-sound and then making an *ee*-sound. The sound is similar to the Yiddish interjection *oy!*.
Ei ei	ei	**ay** like in d**ay** and b**ay** or like Canadian interjection **eh!**
Ey ey	ey	sounds exactly the same as **ei** above

Consonants

B b	bé	**b** like in **b**ed (but it is unvoiced in Icelandic so sounds more like a **p**)
(Cc)	(sé)	**c** like in **c**ircus
D d	dé	**d** like in **d**og (but it is unvoiced in Icelandic so sounds more like a **t**:)
Ð ð	eð	voiced or unvoiced **th**-sound like in **th**is or **th**istle (*never used at the beginning of words*)
F f	eff	**f** like in so**f**a / **except** between two vowels it is pronounced as **v** like in **v**oice

G g	gé	after a, á, o, ó, u, ú: like **g** in **g**ood
		after e, i, í, y, ý, æ: like **g** in **g**ear
		before **t:** guttural sound like in German i**ch**
		    and Scottish lo**ch**
		between vowels, between *r* and ð, and as the
		    last sound of a word: voiced guttural sound
		in the combinations *agi, egi, ogi, ugi*:
		    the first vowel becomes diphthongized with
		    í and the **g** is pronounced as the English **y**
		    (agi>aíji, egi>eíji, ogi>oíji, ugi>uíji)
		in the word **Gu**ð '*God*': **gu** like in **Gu**atemala

H h	há	**h** as in **h**ouse in the combination **hv**: **qu** like in **qu**ick
J j	joð	**y** like in **y**es
K k	ká	**k** like in **k**ite after e, i, í, y, ý, æ: **k** like in **k**eep before **t:** guttural sound like in German i**ch** and Scottish lo**ch**
L l	ell	**l** like in **l**ate
M m	emm	**m** like in **m**ake
N n	enn	**n** like in **n**ose

P p	pé	**p** like in **p**an
R r	err	**r** in Icelandic is trilled or rolled like the Scottish or Spanish *r*-sounds
S s	ess	**s** like in **s**aw
T t	té	**t** like in **t**op
V v	vaff	**v** like in **v**ine
X x	ex	**x** like in fa**x**
Þ þ	þorn	**th** like in **th**istle (note that þ is always word- or syllable-initial)

Letter combinations

fl and *fn*

When the letter *f* is followed by either an *l* or an *n*, it is pronounced with a *p*-sound:

Word	**Pronunciation**
Keflavík	Keplavík
kartafla	kartapla
nafn	napn
stofna	stopna

ng and *nk*

The *n* in Icelandic is pronounced as in English, however, a special rule to remember is the environment of *ng* or *nk*. The *g* and *k* pull the *n* backwards, and the result is a palatalized *n* which is made by moving the tongue slightly back in the mouth and then sounding the *n*. In addition to the palatalization, the vowels *a, e, i, u, y,* ö change character. A summary of the vowel changes is given here:

Vowel	Icelandic		
a	á	banki>bánki	like **ou** in lo**u**d
e	ei	engill>eingill	like **ay** in d**ay**
i	í	fingur>fíngur	like **ee** in s**ee**
u	ú	lunga>lúnga	like **ou** in y**ou**
y	ý	syngur>sýngur	like **ee** in s**ee**
ö	au	löng>laung	like diphthong **au**

-pp, *-tt*, and *-kk*

When doubled, the sounds *p*, *t*, and *k* are pronounced with a breath of air before them. Thus, *pp* is pronounced close to *hp*, *tt* is pronounced *ht*, and *kk* is pronounced *hk*:

Word	Pronunciation
sokkur	so**hk**ur
stoppa	sto**hp**a
hattur	ha**ht**ur

-ll

Double *-l* is pronounced with a t-insertion, so that it becomes *tl*. Note that the t-insertion does not occur in loan-words such as *grilla* (*to barbecue*) and nicknames such as *Halli* or *Kalli* (short for *Haraldur* and *Karl*):

Word	Pronounciation
sæll	sæ**tl**
falla	fa**tl**a
pollur	po**tl**ur
hollur	ho**tl**ur

-nn

Double *-n* is also pronounced with a t-insertion, but only after accented vowels (á, é, í, ó, ú, ý) or the special letter combinations *au*, *ei*, and *ey*:

Word	Pronunciation	Word	Pronunciation
einn	eitn	finna	finna
fínn	fítn	kanna	kanna
bíll	bítl	bann	bann

T-insertion

The consonant clusters *sl, sn, rl,* and *rn* are pronounced respectively *stl, stn, rtl,* and *rtn*:

Word	Pronunciation
drasl	drastl
asni	astni
karl	kartl
horn	hortn

DICTIONARY USAGE GUIDE

For information on the key inflective forms, please consult the Icelandic-English section of the dictionary. The inflective forms are provided in parentheses, before the English equivalents. The inflectional ending of the entry word is indicated with a vertical line (e.g. **hest|ur**, **skemmtileg|ur**). No inflectional endings are indicated for words that have identical endings in all forms. Please note that the inflection of words may also affect the stem itself, e.g., with vowel shifts and assimilation. In such cases, longer forms of the words are shown in the dictionary.

The tilde (~) refers to the entry as a whole, while a dash (-) refers only to the stem.

Nouns

The main entry is usually in the nominative, singular, indefinite form, and any exceptions to this rule are noted in the dictionary. Each noun is assigned to one of three grammatical genders — masculine, feminine, and neuter — and they determine the inflectional category of the noun. The grammatical gender is shown after the main entry (*n masc*, *n fem*, and *n neu*).

Icelandic nouns have four cases: nominative, accusative, dative, and genitive. Each case has an indefinite and definite form in both singular and plural. In the dictionary, the following forms are provided: a) genitive singular, b) nominative plural, and c) genitive plural. All the forms are in the indefinite.

Íslending|ur *n masc* (-s, -ar, -a) Icelander

Adjectives

The majority of adjectives in Icelandic are inflected. The adjective is assigned the same gender, case, and number as the noun it describes. The entries in the dictionary are listed in the masculine-singular-indefinite form (also called strong adjectives). The feminine and neuter forms are shown in parentheses after the main entry:

> **skemmtileg|ur** *adj* (-, -t) fun, amusing

The comparative and superlative forms derive from the stem of the adjective. A few irregular comparatives and superlatives have a separate entry.

Pronouns

Pronouns decline in gender, number, and cases. A pronoun is either used with a noun or by itself. In the dictionary, pronouns are provided in the masculine-singular-nominative form. The feminine and neuter forms are provided in parentheses. Some of the most common pronouns, such as personal pronouns, have a separate entry for each case.

> **engin|n** *pron* (-, ekkert) nobody
> **mig** *pron acc* me

Numbers

Numbers 1 to 4 decline in gender and cases, and the grammatical form is determined by the gender of the noun it attributes. Each gender has its own entry in the nominative form. The accusative, dative, and genitive forms are provided in parentheses.

> **fjögur** *num neu* (-, fjórum, fjögurra) four

Cardinal numbers decline in gender and cases. The main entry is in the masculine form, and the feminine and neuter are provided in parentheses.

>   **fjórði** *num* (-a, -a) fourth

Verbs

Verbs conjugate according to person, number, tense, mood, and voice. They are divided into two main paradigms: strong and weak. The weak verbs are regular and mark the past tense with a dental suffix. Strong verbs are less common and more irregular (compared to English). They mark the past tense by using a vowel change.

Each entry for a weak verb provides the following forms: 1) infinitive, 2) 1st person present tense, 3) 1st person past tense singular, 4) past participle:

>   **tala** *v* (~, -ði, -ð)

Each entry for a strong verb provides the following forms: 1) infinitive, 2) 1st person present tense, 3) 1st person past tense singular, 4) 1st person past tense plural, and 5) past participle:

>   **far|a** *v* (fer, fór, fórum, -ið)

The perfect and past perfect is formed by using the verb *hafa* (have) followed by the past participle. The past participle is the last form provided in each verb entry.

Each verb has an indicative, subjunctive, and imperative mood. The indicative is the basic form and the other two categories do not in most cases have separate entries. However, some very common subjunctive forms and imperatives are listed with a reference to the main verb.

The middle voice is formed by using an *st*-ending (*kyssa* 'kiss', *kyssast* 'kiss each other'). Some verbs have a separate entry for the middle voice, in particular those that have a different semantic meaning in the active and the middle voice (*fara* 'go', *farast* 'perish').

Adverbs

Adverbs are generally non-inflected but do sometimes have a comparative and superlative form.

Prepositions

Prepositions are short, uninflected words that precede and describe a relation to a nominal phrase. Each preposition assigns particular cases. Some prepositions are followed by accusative and others by dative or genitive. The cases governed by each preposition is listed in the dictionary.

um *prep (+ acc)* about

Abbreviations

abbrev	abbreviation	*ling*	linguistics
acc	accusative	*lit*	literature
acc subj	subject in accusative	*masc*	masculine
adj	adjective	*math*	mathematics
adv	adverb	*mech*	mechanical
anat	anatomy	*med*	medical
arch	archaic	*mil*	military
art	article	*mus*	music
astro	astrology	*n*	noun
astron	astronomy	*N*	name
bio	biology	*neu*	neuter
chem	chemistry	*num*	number
colloq	colloquial	*obs*	obsolete
comp	computer	*ord*	ordinal number
compar	comparative	*phil*	philosophy
conj	conjunction	*phr*	phrase
dat	dative	*phys*	physics
dat subj	subject in the dative	*pl*	plural
defin art	definite article	*pref*	prefix
econ	economy	*prep*	preposition
excl	exclamation	*psych*	psychology
expr	expression	*recip*	reciprocal
fem	feminine	*refl*	reflective
fig	figurative	*sby*	somebody
form	formal language	*sg*	singular
geog	geography	*sth*	something
geol	geology	*superl*	superlative
inf	infinitive	*v*	verb
leg	legal	*vul*	vulgarity
indef	indefinite	*zool*	zoological

ICELANDIC-ENGLISH
DICTIONARY

A

AA-fund|ur *n masc* (-ar, -ir, -a)
Alcoholics Anonymous (AA)
meeting

AA-samtök|in *N neu* (-takanna)
Alcoholics Anonymous (AA)

AB-mjólk *n fem* (-ur) milk product
similar to buttermilk

að 1 *inf marker* to: **mig langar ~
læra íslensku** I would like to learn
Icelandic **2** *conj* that: **ég held ~
hann sé farinn** I think that he is
gone; **3** *prep + dat* to, towards:
förum ~ vatninu let's go towards
the lake; at [*with place name*]: **~
Hólum** at Hólar; **~ ári** in a year;
rauður ~ lit red colored; **íslenskur
~ ætt** of Icelandic decent; **4** *adv*
wrong: **hvað er ~?** what's wrong?

aðal- *pref* main, chief

aðalbláber *n neu* (-s, -, -ja) bilberry

aðalbygging *n fem* (-ar, -ar, -a) main
building

aðaldyr *n fem pl* (-a) front door

aðalgat|a *n fem* (-götu, -götur, -na)
main street

aðalinngang|ur *n masc* (-s, -ar, -a)
main entrance

aðal|l *n masc* (-s) nobility

aðallega *adv* mainly, largely, mostly,
principally

aðalpersón|a *n fem* (-u, -ur, -a) *lit*
protagonist, main character

aðalrétt|ur *n masc* (-ar, -ir, -a) main
course

aðalritar|i *n masc* (-a, -ar, -a)
secretary general

aðalsetning *n fem* (-ar, -ar, -a) *ling*
main clause

aðalsmað|ur *n masc* (-s, -menn,
-manna) aristocrat, nobleman

aðalsveld|i *n neu* (-is, ~, -a)
aristocracy

aðaltenging *n fem* (-ar, -ar, -a) *ling*
conjunction

aðdáand|i *n masc* (-a, aðdáendur,
aðdáenda) admirer, fan

aðdáun *n fem* (-ar) admiration

aðdáunarverð|ur *adj* (-, vert)
adorable

aðdráttarafl *n neu* (-s) attraction,
appeal

aðdráttarlins|a *n fem* (-u, -ur, -a)
telephoto lens

aðeins *adv* only, just, merely

aðfangadag|ur *n masc* (s, -ar, -a)
(Christmas) Eve; **~ jóla** Christmas
Eve

aðferð *n fem* (-ar, -ir, -a) method,
procedure, process, means

aðflutning|ur *n masc* (-s, -ar, -a)
immigration

aðgangaseyr|ir *n masc* (-ar) entrance
fee

aðgangsorð *n neu* (-s, -, -a) *comp*
password

aðgang|ur *n masc* (-s, -ar, -a) access,
admittance, entrance: **~ bannaður**
no entrance

aðgengi *n neu* (-s) access

aðgerð *n fem* (-ar, -ir, -a) *med*
operation

aðgerðadeild *n fem* (-ar, -ir, -a) *med*
operating suite

aðgerðahnapp|ur *n masc* (-s, -ar, -a)
comp function key

aðgerðalaus *adj* (-, -t) idle

aðgerðasinn|i *n masc* (-a, -ar, -a)
activist

aðgrein|a *v* (-i, -di, -t) separate

aðgreind|ur *adj* (-, -greint) separated

aðgöngumið|i *n masc* (-a, -ar, -a)
cover charge, entrance ticket

aðhald *n neu* (-s) restraint

aðil|i *n masc* (-a, -ar, -a) party *(participant in something)*

aðkom|a *n fem* (-u, -ur, -a) approach

aðlaga *v* (~, -ði, -ð) adapt; integrate

aðlagað|ur *adj* (aðlöguð, -) adapted; integrated

aðlaga|st *v refl* (~, -ðist, ~) adjust, adapt; integrate

aðleiðsl|a *n fem* (-u) *phil* induction

aðliggjandi *adj* surrounding

aðlög|un *n fem* (-unar, -laganir, -lagana) integration; adjustment

aðlögunarhæfni *n fem* (-) adaptability

aðsetur *n neu* (-s, -, -setra) residence

aðskilin|n *adj* (-, -skilið) separated, apart

aðskilj|a *v* (aðskil, aðskildi, aðskilið) separate

aðskilnað|ur *n masc* (-ar, -ir, -a) separation

aðstað|a *n fem* (-stöðu) facilities, location and technological resources for a certain type of activity

aðstoð *n fem* (-ar) aid, assistance, relief

aðstoða *v* (~, -ði, -ð) aid, assist

aðstoðarmað|ur *n masc* (-manns, -menn, -manna) assistant

aðstæð|ur *n fem pl* (-stæðna) circumstances

af 1 *adv* off: **farðu ~!** get off!; **2** *prep + dat* from, away from: **taktu bókina ~ henni** take the book from her; of **sopi ~ bjór** a sip of beer; **fullt ~ fólki** a lot of people; by: **hún var gagnrýnd ~ mörgum** she was criticized by many

af hverju *pron* why

afboða *v* (~, -ði, -ð) cancel

afboðað|ur *adj* (afboðuð, -) canceled

afbrigð|i *n neu* (-is, ~, -a) variety

afbrot *n neu* (-s, -, -a) crime, offense

afbrotamað|ur *n masc* (-manns, -menn, -manna) criminal

afferm|a *v* (-i, -di, t) unload

afgang|ur *n masc* (-s, -ar, -a) leftover, residue, surplus; *(coins)* change

Afgan|i *n masc* (-a, -ar/ir, -a) Afghan

Afganistan *N neu* (-/s) Afghanistan

afgansk|ur *adj* (afgönsk, -t) Afghan

afgerandi *adj* crucial

afglöp *n neu pl* (-a) malpractice

afgreiðsl|a *n fem* (-u, -ur, -na) customer service, front desk

afgreiðsluborð *n neu* (-s, -, -a) counter, reception desk

afgreiðslukass|i *n masc* (-a, -ar, -a) checkout

afgreiðslukon|a *n fem* (-u, -ur, -kvenna) *(female)* shop assistant

afgreiðslumað|ur *n masc* (-manns, -menn, -manna) cashier, clerk, *(male)* shop assistant

afgreiðslutím|i *n masc* (-a, -ar, -a) office hours, opening hours

afhend|a *v* (-i, -henti, -hent) hand over

afhending *n fem* (-ar, -ar, -a) handover

afhjúpa *v* (~, -ði, -ð) expose, disclose

afhjúp|un *n fem* (-unar, -anir, -ana) exposure, disclosure, revelation

afl|i *n masc* (-a, -ar, -a) grandfather

afkastamikil|l *adj* (-, -mikið) prolific

afklæð|ast *v* (-ist, afklæddist, -st) undress

afkomand|i *n masc* (-a, afkomendur, afkomenda) offspring

afkvæm|i *n neu* (is, ~, -a) progeny

afl *n neu* (-s, öfl, -a) power

afleggjar|i *n masc* (-a, -ar, -a) side road; *(plants)* cutting

afleiðing *n fem* (-ar, -ar, -a) consequence

afleysing *n fem* (-ar, -ar, -a) replacement

afleysingarmað|ur *n masc* (-manns, -menn, -manna) substitute employee

aflfræði *n fem* (-) *eng* mechanics

afmæl|i *n neu* (-is, ~, -a) birthday: **til hamingju með ~ ð!** happy birthday!; anniversary: **tíu ára brúðkaups ~** ten year wedding anniversary

afmælisveisl|a *n fem* (-u, -ur, -na) birthday party

afneita *v* (~, -ði, -ð) renounce

afneit|un *n fem* (-unar, -anir, -ana) renunciation

afpanta *v* (~, -ði, -ð) cancel (an order)

afrakstur *n masc* (-s) result; accomplishment

afreka *v* (~, -ði, -ð) accomplish

afrit *n neu* (-s, -, -a) copy; *comp* backup

afrita *v* (~, -ði, -ð) copy; *comp* backup

Afrík|a *N fem* (-u) Africa

Afríkumað|ur *n masc* (-manns, -menn, -manna) African person

afrísk|ur *adj* (-, t) African

afsaka *v* (~, -ði, -ð) apologize, pardon; ~ **sig** *refl* apologize

afsakaðu *interj (to one person)* excuse me, pardon me

afsakið *interj (to more than one person)* excuse me, pardon me

afsíðis *adv* aside

afskekkt|ur *adj* (-, -) remote

afskipt|i *n neu* (-is, ~, -a) intervention

afskráning *n fem* (-ar, -ar, -a) cancellation of registration; depreciation

afslappað|ur *adj* (-slöppuð, -) relaxing, easygoing

afslappandi *adj* relaxing

afslátt|ur *n masc* (-ar, afslættir, -a) discount, rebate

afslöppun *n fem* (-ar) relaxation

afstað|a *n fem* (-stöðu, -stöður, ~) attitude; position

afsteyp|a *n fem* (-u, -ur, -na/a) cast

afstýr|a *v* (-i, -ði, -t) prevent

afsökun *n fem* (-ar, afsakanir, afsakana) apology

afsönn|un *n fem* (-unar, -sannanir, -sannana) refutation

aftur *adv* again; back

aftur á bak *adv* backwards

afturbeygð|ur *adj ling* (-, beygt) reflexive

afturgang|a *n fem* (-göngu, -göngur, -gangna) living dead

afturhaldssegg|ur *n masc* (-s, -ir, -ja) reactionary, conservative

afturhurð *n fem* (-ar, -ir, -a) back door

afturkalla *v* (~, -ði, -ð) revoke

afturkallað|ur *adj* (-kölluð, -) revoked

afturköll|un *n fem* (-unar, -kallanir, -kallana) revocation

afturljós *n neu* (-s, -, -a) tail light

aftursæt|i *n neu* (-is, ~, -a) backseat

afþakka *v* (~, -ði, -ð) decline

afþíð|a *v* (-i, þíddi, þítt) defrost

afþreying *n fem* (-ar, -ar, -a) entertainment, recreation

afþurrkunarklút|ur *n masc* (-s, -ar, -a) dustcloth

afæt|a *n fem* (-u, -ur, -a/na) *bio* parasite; *slang* sponger

ag|i *n masc* (-a) discipline

agnarsmá|r *adj* (-, -tt) minuscule

akademí|a *n fem* (-u, -ur, -a) academy

akademísk|ur *adj* (-, -t) academic

akarn *n neu* (-s, akörn, -a) acorn

akker|i *n neu* (-is, ~, -a) anchor

akkúrat *adv* precisely

akrein *n fem* (-ar, -ar, -a) lane

akstur utan vega *phr* off road driving

akstursmæli|r *n masc* (-s, -ar, -a) odometer

aktyg|i *n neu* (-is, ~, -ja) harness

akur *n masc* (-s, akrar, akra) field

Akureyr|i *N fem* (-ar) Akureyri city

akurhæn|a *n fem* (-u, -ur, -a) *zool* partridge

ala *v* (el, ól, ólum, alið) foster; ~ **upp** raise

Alban|i *n masc* (-a, -ir, -a) Albanian person

Albaní|a *N fem* (-u) Albania

albansk|a *n fem* (-bönsku) Albanian language

albansk|ur *adj* (-bönsk, -t) Albanian

albatros *n masc* (-s, -ar, -a) albatross

albúm *n neu* (-s, -, -a) photo album

ald|a *n fem* (öldu, öldur, ~) wave

aldarafmæl|i *n neu* (-is, ~, -a) centenary
aldingarð|ur *n masc* (-s, -ar, -a) orchard
aldinkjöt *n neu* (-s) pulp in fruit
aldrað|ur *adj* (öldruð, -) elderly, old
aldrei *adv* never
aldur *n masc* (-s, aldrar, aldra) age
alfaalfa-spír|ur *n fem pl* (-a) alfalfa sprouts
algebr|a *n fem* (-u, -ur, -a) *math* algebra
Algeirsborg *N fem* (-ar) Algiers
algeng|ur *adj* (-, -t) common, prevalent
algjör *adj* (-, t) absolute, complete, total
algjörlega *adv* completely, purely, totally, absolutely
alheim|ur *n masc* (-s, -ar, -a) universe
alifugl *n masc* (-s, -ar, -a) *zool* fowl; poultry
alkóhól *n neu* (-s) alcohol
alkóhólism|i *n masc* (-a) alcoholism
alkóhólist|i *n masc* (-a, -ar, -a) alcoholic
allan sólarhringinn *phr* round-the-clock
all|ir *pron* (-ar, öll): all: **öll börnin fengu gjafir** all the children got gifts; everybody: ~ **fengu að fara** everybody got to go
allrahanda 1 *adj* all kinds; 2 *n neu* (~) ~ **krydd** allspice
alls ekki *phr* not at all
alls staðar *adv* everywhere
allsherjarverkfall *n neu* (-s, -föll, -a) general strike
allsnægt|ir *n fem pl* (-a) plenty
allt *adv* all
allt í einu *phr* suddenly
allt í lagi *phr* okay: **er ~ með þig?** are you okay?
alltaf *adv* always
alltumlykjandi *adj* omnipresent
all|ur *pron* (öll, -t) all, whole: **ég las alla bókina** I read the whole book

almannatrygging|ar *n fem pl* (-a) social security
almáttug|ur *adj* (-, t) omnipotent; *excl* Dear God!
almennilega *adv* properly
almennileg|ur *adj* (-, t) friendly, amicable
almennings- *pref* public
almenningsgarð|ur *n masc* (-s, -ar, -a) park
almenningsklósett *n neu* (-s, -, -a) public bathroom
almenningssalern|i *n neu* (-is, ~, -a) public bathroom
almenningssamgöng|ur *n fem pl* (-gangna) public transportation
almenningssím|i *n masc* (-a, -ar, -a) pay phone
almenning|ur *n masc* (-s) public
almennt *adv* generally, broadly
almenn|ur *adj* (-, t) common; general
almennur frídagur *phr* national holiday
almyrkv|i *n masc* (-a, -ar, -a) total eclipse
almætti *n neu* (-s) omnipotence
alnæmi *n neu* (-s) AIDS
Alparnir *N masc* (Alpanna) The Alps
Alríkislögregl|a Bandaríkjanna *n fem* (-u Bandaríkjanna) U.S. Federal Bureau of Investigation (FBI)
alræmd|ur *adj* (-, -ræmt) notorious
Alsír *N neu* (-s) Algeria
Alsíring|ur *n masc* (-s, -ar, -a) Algerian person
alsírsk|ur *adj* (-, t) Algerian
alskegg *n neu* (-s, -, -ja) full beard
altalandi *adj* fluent
altar|i *n neu* (-is, ~, -a) altar
altarisgang|a *n fem* (-göngu) communion
altaristafl|a *n fem* (-töflu, -töflur, -taflna) altar piece
alternator *n masc* (-s, -ar, -a) alternator
alvar|a *n fem* (alvöru) seriousness, for real: **í alvöru?** really?, seriously?

alvarlega *adv* seriously, severely

alvarleg|ur *adj* (-, t) serious, severe, acute

alveg *adv* totally: **hann er ~ brjálaður** he is totally crazy; quite: **ertu ~ viss?** are you quite sure?

alvöru- *pref* real, authentic: **þetta eru alvörupeningar** this is real money

Alþjóðaheilbrigðismálastofnun|in *N fem* (-arinnar) World Health Organization

alþjóðleg|ur *adj* (-, t) international

alþýð|a *n fem* (-u) common people, folk

alþýðu- *pref* folk

alþýðulist *n fem* (-ar, -ir, -a) folk art

alþýðutónlist *n fem* (-ar) folk music

alæt|a *n fem* (-u, -ur, -a/na) *bio* omnivore

Amerík|a *N fem* (-u) America: **frá Ameríku** from America

Ameríkan|i *n masc* (-a, -ar, -a) American person

amerísk|ur *adj* (-, t) American

amínósýr|a *n fem* (-u, -ur, -a) *bio* amino acids

amma *n fem* (ömmu, ömmur, ~) grandmother

ampúla *n fem* (-u, -ur, ~) *med* ampoule

ananas *n masc* (-s, -ar, -a) pineapple

anarkist|i *n masc* (-a, -ar, -a) anarchist

anatómí|a *n fem* (-u) *med* anatomy

and- *prefix* anti-

anda *v* (~, -ði, -ð) breathe

andagift *n fem* (-ar) inspiration

andanefj|a *n fem* (-u, -ur, ~) *zool* bottlenose whale

andardrátt|ur *n masc* (-s, -drættir, drætti) breath, respiration

andartak *n neu* (-s, -tök, -a) moment

andarung|i *n masc* (-a, -ar, -a) duckling

anddyr|i *n neu* (-is, ~, -a) foyer

and|i *n masc* (-a, -ar, -a) soul, spirit, psyche

andlag *n neu* (-s, -lög, -a) *ling* object

andlát *n neu* (-s, -, -a) death

andlátstilkynning *n fem* (-ar, -ar, -a) death notice

andlega *adv* spiritually, mentally

andleg|ur *adj* (-, -t) mental: **andleg veikindi** mental illness; spiritual: **andleg málefni** spiritual matters

andlit *n neu* (-i, -, -a) face

andlitsdrátt|ur *n masc* (-ar, -drættir, -drátta) facial features

andlitsmeðferð *n fem* (-ar, -ir, -a) facial treatment

andmæl|a *v* (-i, -ti, -t) oppose, object

andmæl|i *n neu* (-is, ~, -a) *leg* objection

Andorra *N neu* (-) Andorra

andrúmsloft *n neu* air; atmosphere

andskotans *interj vul* damn, hell

andspyrn|a *n fem* (-u) resistance

andspænis *prep + dat* opposite, facing: **~ dauðanum** facing death

andstað|a *n fem* (-stöðu) opposition

andstyggð *n fem* (-ar) repugnance

andstyggileg|ur *adj* (-, -t) repugnant, odious, repulsive

andstæð|a *n fem* (-u, -ur, -na) contrast, opposite

andstæðing|ur *n masc* (-s, -ar, -a) opponent

andstæð|ur *adj* (-, -stætt) opposite

andúð *n fem* (-ar) antipathy, repulsion

andvak|a *n fem* (-vöku, -vökur, ~) insomnia

andvana *adv* stillborn: **~ fæðing** still-birth

angandi *adj* having a strong smell (good or bad): **hún kom heim ~ af sígarettureyk** she came home reeking of cigarette smoke; **hann kom með ~ kaffi og nýbakað brauð** he brought nicely smelling coffee and fresh bread

angist *f* anxiety

Angóla *N fem* (-) Angola

angra *v* (~, -ði, -ð) annoy; trouble

anís *n masc* (-s) anise

anísfræ *n neu* (-s, -, -ja) aniseed
annað farrými *phr* second class;
tourist class
annað hvort ... eða *conj* either ... or:
ég ætla annað hvort að fara til
Íslands eða Færeyja I'm going
either to Iceland or Faroe Islands
annar 1 *pron* (önnur, annað) another;
2 *ord* (önnur, annað) second
annars *adv* alternatively
annars staðar *adv* elsewhere
anórakk|ur *n masc* (-s, -ar, -a) anorak
ansa *v* (~, -ði, -ð) answer, reply
ansi *adv* pretty, quite: það er ~ kalt í
dag it's pretty cold today
ansjós|a *n fem* (-u, -ur, -a) anchovy
Antillaeyj|ar *N fem pl* (-a) Antilles
(Caribbian Islands)
antílóp|a *n fem* (-u, -ur, -a) *zool*
antelope
ap|i *n masc* (-a, -ar, -a) *zool* monkey
app *n neu* (-s, öpp, -a) app
apótek *n neu* (-s, -, -a) pharmacy
appelsín|a *n fem* (-u, -ur, -a) orange
appelsínubörk|ur *n masc* (-barkar,
-berkir, -berki) orange peel
appelsínudjús *n masc* (-s, -ar, -a)
orange juice
appelsínugul|ur *adj* (-, -t) orange
appelsínuhúð *n fem* (-ar) cellulose
appelsínusaf|i *n masc* (-a, -ar, -a)
orange juice
appelsínuþykkni *n neu* (-s) extract
apríkós|a *n fem* (-u, -ur, -a) apricot
apríkósumauk *n neu* (-s, -, -a)
apricot jam
apríl *n masc* (-s) April
aprílgabb *n neu* (-s, -göbb, -a) April
Fool
Arab|i *n masc* (-a, -ar, -a) Arab
arabísk|a *n fem* (-u) the Arabic
language
arabísk|ur *adj* (-, -t) Arabic
arðbær *adj* (-, -t) profitable
arðræn|a *v* (-i, -di, -t) exploit
arðrán *n neu* (-s, -, -a) exploitation
arð|ur *n masc* (-s) profit; divide

arftak|i *n masc* (-a, -ar, -a) beneficiary
arf|ur *n masc* (-s) heritage
arfþeg|i *n masc* (-a, -ar, -a) beneficiary
Argentína *N fem* (-u) Argentina
argentínsk|ur *adj* (-, -t) Argentine
Argentínumað|ur *n masc* (-manns,
-menn, -manna) Argentinian
arin|n *n masc* (-s, arnar, arna)
fireplace
arkitekt *n masc* (-s, -ar, -a) architect
arkitektúr *n masc* (-s, -ar, -a)
architecture
armband *n neu* (-s, -bönd, -a) bracelet
Armen|i *n masc* (-a, -ar, -a) Armenian
Armení|a *N fem* (-u) Armenia
armensk|a *n fem* (-u) Armenian
language
armensk|ur *adj* (-, -t) Armenian
arm|ur *n masc* (-s, -ar, -a) arm
arnpáf|i *n masc* (-a, -ar, -a) *zool* macaw
arsenik *n neu* (-s) *chem* arsenic
Aserbaísjan *N neu* (-/s) Azerbaijan
Aser|i *n masc* (-a, -ar, -a) Azerbaijani
asersk|a *n fem* (-u) *(language)*
Azerbaijan
asersk|ur *adj* (-, -t) Azerbaijani
Así|a *N fem* (-u) Asia
asísk|ur *adj* (-, -t) Asian
Asíubú|i *n masc* (-a, -ar, -a) Asian
Asíumað|ur *n masc* (-manns, -menn,
-manna) Asian
ask|a *n fem* (ösku) ash
asnaleg|ur *adj* (-, -t) foolish
asn|i *n masc* (-a, -ar, -a) *zool* donkey;
slang idiot
aspartam *n neu* (-s) aspartame
aspas *n masc* (-) asparagus
astmakast *n neu* (-s, köst, -a) *med*
asthma attack
astm|i *n masc* (-a) *med* asthma
atburðarás *n fem* (-ar) course of
events
atburð|ur *n masc* (-ar, -ir, -a) incident
atferl|i *n neu* (-is, ~, -a) behavior
atferlisgreining *n fem* (-ar) *psych*
behavior analysis
athafnasam|ur *adj* (-söm, -t) busy

athuga v (~, -ði, -ð) check
athugasemd n fem (-ar, -ir, -a) comment; commentary
athug|un n fem (-unar, -anir, -ana) check
athygli n fem (~) attention
athyglisbrest|ur n masc (-s, -ir, -a) psych ADHD
athyglisverð|ur adj (-, -vert) interesting, remarkable
athöfn n fem (-hafnar, -hafnir, -hafna) act, ceremony
atkvæð|i n neu (-is, ~, -a) vote; ling syllable
Atlantshaf N neu (-s) Atlantic Ocean
atvik n neu (-s, -, -a) incident, occurrence
atviksorð n neu (-s, -, -a) ling adverb
atvinn|a n fem (-u, -ur, -a) work, job, profession
atvinnuauglýsing n fem (-ar, -ar, -a) job advertisement
atvinnulaus adj (-, -t) unemployed
atvinnuleyf|i n neu (-is, ~, -a) work permit
atvinnuleys|i n neu (-is) unemployment
atvinnuleysisbæt|ur n fem pl (-bóta) unemployment benefits
atvinnumað|ur n masc (-manns, -menn, -manna) professional
atvinnumiðl|un n fem (-unar, -anir, -ana) employment office
auðkenn|a v (-i, -di, -t) identify
auðkennandi adv identifying
auðkenning n fem (-ar, -ar, -a) identification
auðlind n fem (-ar, -ir, -a) resource
auðmjúk|ur adj (-, -t) humble
auðmýkt n fem (-ar) humility
auðn n fem (-ar, -ir, -a) desert
auðnutittling|ur n masc (-s, -ar, -a) zool redpoll
auðug|ur adj (-, -t) rich; wealthy
auð|ur 1 adj (-, autt) empty; blank; 2 n masc wealth
auðveldlega adv easily
auðveld|ur adj (-, -velt) easy

auðvitað adv of course
aug|a n neu (-a, -u, -na) eye
augabrún n fem (-ar, -ir/brýr, -a) eyebrow
augastein|n n masc (-s, -ar, -a) anat pupil
augljós adj (-, -t) obvious, apparent
augljóslega adv obviously
auglýs|a v (-i, -ti, -t) advertise, promote
auglýsing n fem (-ar, -ar, -a) promotion, advertisement; **sjónvarpsauglýsing** television commercial
auglýsingaherferð n fem (-ar, -ir, -a) ad campaign
auglýsingamarkað|ur n masc (-ar/s, -ir, -a) advertising business
auglýsingastof|a n fem (-u, -ur, -a) advertising company
augnablik n neu (-i, -, -a) moment
augnbaun n fem (-ar, -ir, -a) blackeyed pea
augnhár n neu pl eyelash
augnknöttur n masc (-knattar, -knettir, -knatta) anat eyeball
augnlækn|ir n masc (-is, -ar, -a) med optometrist
augnskol|un n fem (-unar, -anir, -ana) eyewash
augnskugg|i n masc (-a, -ar, -a) eyeshadow
augnskurðlækn|ir n masc (-is, -ar, -a) med opthalmologist
augnsýn n fem (-ar) view
auk prep + gen in addition to, besides: ~ **mín** besides me
auk þess adv furthermore, moreover, in addition
auka- pref additional, extra; spare
auk|a v (eyk, jók, ukum, aukið) increase
aukabúnað|ur n masc (-ar) extras, extra equipment
aukaefn|i n neu (-is, ~, -a) food additives
aukagjald n neu (-s, -gjöld, -a) extra charge; premium

aukahlut|ur *n masc* (-s, -ir, -a) extra
equipment
aukakostnað|ur *n masc* (-ar, -ir, -a)
surcharge
aukaleikar|i *n masc* (-a, -ar, -a)
extras in movies
aukarétt|ur *n masc* (-ar, -ir, -a) side
dish
aukasetning *n fem* (-ar, -ar, -a) *ling*
subordinate clause
aukasýning *n fem* (-ar, -ar, -a)
sideshow
aukatenging *n fem* (-ar, -ar, -a) *ling*
subjunction
aukning *n fem* (-ar, -ar, -a) increase
auming|i *n masc* (aumingja, auming-
jar, aumingja) looser; coward
aumkunarverð|ur *adj* (-, -vert)
pathetic, pitiful
aum|ur *adj* (-, -t) sore
aur *n masc* (-s, -ar, -a) mud; *colloq*
Icelandic pennies: **ég á ekki ~** I
don't have a penny

aurskriða *n fem* (-skriðu, -skriður, ~)
mudflow
austan *prep* + *gen* east of: **~ fjalls**
on the east side of the mountain
Austfirðir *n masc pl* (-fjarða)
The Icelandic East Fjords; **á**
Austfjörðum in the East Fjords
austur *adv* east
Austur-Kongó *N neu* (-s) Demo-
cratic Republic of the Congo
Austurland *N neu* (-s) East Iceland
austurlensk|ur *adj* (-, -t) oriental
Austurlönd nær *phr* Middle East
Austurríki *N neu* (-s) Austria
Austurríkismað|ur *n masc* (-manns,
-menn, -manna) Austrian
austurrísk|ur *adj* (-, -t) Austrian
Austur-Tímor *N neu* (-s) East Timor
(Timor-Leste)
avakadó *n masc* (-s, -ar, -a) avocado
axlabönd *neu pl* (-a) suspenders
Aþen|a *N fem* (-u) Athens

Á

á 1 *n fem* (ár, ár, áa) river, stream; **2** *prep* + *dat (location)* on, in: ~ **Íslandi** in Iceland, ~ **Akureyri** in Akureyri, **bókin er ~ borðinu** the book is on the table; *(time)* ~ **fimmtudögum** on Thursdays, ~ **jólunum** during Christmas; + *acc (movement towards)* **settu bókina** ~ **borðið** put the book on the table; *(time)* **á morgun** tomorrow; **á fimmtudag** on Thursday

á bak við *prep* + *acc* ~ **þig** behind

á eftir 1 *adv* later; **2** *prep* + *dat* after, behind: ~ **mér** after me, ~ **þér** after you

á hvolfi *adv* upside down

á milli 1 *adv* between; **2** *prep* + *gen* between

á móti 1 *adv* against, opposite; **2** *prep* + *dat* against: **ég er ~ þessu** I'm against this; across from: **ég sit ~ honum** I sit across from him

á meðan 1 *adv* meanwhile; **2** *conj* while: **bíddu ~ ég hringi** wait while I call

á móti *prep* + *dat*: against: **ég er ~ þessu** I'm against this; across: **hótelið er ~ kirkjunni** the hotel is across from the church

á sama hátt *adv* in the same way

á undan 1 *adv* ahead; **2** *prep* + *dat* before: **þú varst ~ mér** you were before me

ábatasam|ur *adj* (-söm, -t) lucrative

áberandi *adj* prominent, striking, notable

ábreið|a *n fem* (-u, -ur, -a) spread; *music* cover

áburð|ur *n masc* (-ar, -ir, -a) balm, creme; *bio* fertilizer

ábyrgð *n fem* (-ar, -ir, -a) guarantee, warranty; responsibility; liability

ábyrgðarpóst|ur *n masc* (-s, -ar, -a) registered mail

ábyrgj|ast *v* (ábyrgist, ábyrgðist, ábyrgst) guarantee

ábyrg|ur *adj* (-, -t) responsible, liable

áður *adv* before, previously

áður en *conj* before

áfall *n neu* (-s, -föll, -a) shock

áfangastað|ur *n masc* (-ar, -ir, -a) destination

áfast|ur *adj* (áföst, -) attached

áfellast *v* (áfellist, áfelltist, áfellst) reproach

áfengi *n neu* (-s,) alcohol

áfengissjúkling|ur *n masc* (-s, -ar, -a) alcoholic person

áfengissýki *n fem* (-) alcoholism

áfengisvandamál *n neu* (-s) alcoholism

áfengisverslun *n fem* (-ar, -verslanir, -verslana) liquor store: **hvar er næsta ~?** Where is the closest liquor store?

áfeng|ur *adj* (-, -t) alcoholic

áfengur drykkur *phr* alcoholic drink

áferð *n fem* (-ar, -ir, -a) texture

áforma *v* (~, -ði, -ð) plan

áflog *n neu pl* (-a) fighting

áfram *adv* forward: **haltu ~** continue, **farðu beint ~** go straight forward

áframhaldandi *adj* continuous, progressive

áframleigj|a *v* (leigi, leigði, leigt) sublet

áframsend|a *v* (-i, -i, -sent) forward (e-mail)

áfrýja *v* (~, -ði, -ð) appeal

áfrýj|un *n fem* (-unar, -anir, -ana) *leg* appeal

ágisk|un *n fem* (-unar, -anir, -ana) guess

áger|ast *v* (-ist, -ðist, -st) aggravate

ágóð|i *n masc* (-a) profit

ágreining|ur *n masc* (-s) dispute, disagreement

ágrip *n neu pl* (-s, -, -a) summary, abstract; resumé

ágúst *n masc* (-) August: **í ~** in August

ágætlega *adv* nicely

áhersl|a *n fem* (-u, -ur, -na) emphasis; *ling* emphasis, stress

áhlaup *n neu* (-s, -, -a) raid

áhorfand|i *n masc* (-a, áhorfendur, áhorfenda) audience, spectator, viewer

áhorfendapall|ur *n masc* (-s, -ar, -a) *sports* bleacher, stands

áhrif *n neu pl* (-a) influence, impact, impression, effect

áhrifamikil|l *adj* (-, -mikið) influential, effective, powerful

áhugamað|ur *n masc* (-mann, -menn, -manna) amateur; fan: **~ um fótbolta** a football fan

áhugamál *n neu* (-s, -, -a) hobby, pastime activity

áhugasam|ur *adj* (-söm, -t) interested, keen

áhugaverð|ur *adj* (-, -vert) interesting

áhug|i *n masc sg* (-a) interest

áhyggjufull|ur *adj* (-, -t) worried, concerned, alarmed

áhygg|jur *n fem pl* (-na) worry

áhætt|a *n fem sg* (-u) risk, venture, gamble

áhættulaus *adj* (-, -t) risk free

áhöfn *n fem* (-hafnar, -hafnir, -hafna) crew

ákafi *n masc* (-a) intensity, fervor

ákaflega *adv* very: **~ skemmtileg bók** a very enjoyable book

ákaf|ur *adj* (áköf, -t) intense, fervent, enticing

ákavít|i *n neu* (-s, ~, -a) aquavit

ákjósanleg|ur *adj* (-, -t) ideal

ákveð|a *v* (-, ákvað, ákváðum, -ið) decide, determine, resolve

ákveðin|n *adj* (-, ákveðið) determined, headstrong, resolute

ákveðni *n fem* (-) determination

ákvörð|un *n fem* (-unar, -kvarðanir, kvarðana) decision

ákærð|ur *adj* (-, ákært) *leg* sued; defendant

ál *n neu* (-s) aluminum

álag *n neu sg* (-s) pressure, stress

álagning *n fem* (-ar) levy; markup

álasa *v* (~, -ði, -ð) blame

álft *n fem* (-ar, -ir, -a) *zool* wild swan

álf|ur *n masc* (-a, -ar, -a) elf, fairy

ál|l *n masc* (-s, -ar, -a) *zool* eel

álit *n neu* (-s, -, -a) presumption, opinion

álitin|n *adj* (-, álitið) presumed

álít|a *v* (-, áleit, álitum, álitið) presume, consider

álpappír *n masc* (-s) aluminum foil

álykta *v* (~, -ði, -ð) resolve

álykt|un *n fem* (-unar, -anir, -ana) resolution; assumption

álög *n neu pl* (álaga) magic spell: **hún var undir álögum** she was under a magic spell

áminn|a *v* (-i, ti, -t) reprimand; remind

áminning *n fem* (-ar, -ar, -a) reminder, prompt; reprimand: **fyrsta ~** first reprimand

án *prep + gen* without: **~ þín** without you; **~ húsgagna** unfurnished; **~ þess að** without: **~ þess að borga** without paying

ánamaðk|ur *n masc* (-s, -ar, -a) *bio* (earth)worm

áningarstað|ur *n masc* (-ar, -ir, -a) picnic area

ánægð|ur *adj* (-, -t) satisfied

ánægj|a *n fem sg* (-u) pleasure, satisfaction

ánægjuleg|ur *adj* (-, -t) pleasing, satisfying

ár 1 *n neu* (-s, -, -a) year: **gleðilegt ~!** Happy New Year! 2 *n fem* **~** (-ar, -ar, -a) paddle; oar

árangur *n masc sg* (-s) achievement; result: **frábær ~** great achievement

árangurslaus *adj* (-, -t) unsuccessful
árangurslítil|l *adj* (-, -lítið) with little success
árangursrík|ur *adj* (-, -t) successful
áratug|ur *n masc* (-ar, -ir, -a) decade
árás *n fem* (-ar, -ir, -a) attack, assault, strike
árásargirni *n fem* (-) aggression
árásargjarn *adj* (-gjörn, -gjarnt) aggressive
árbakk|i *n masc* (-a, -ar, -a) riverbank
áreiðanlega *adv* surely
áreiðanleg|ur *adj* (-, -t) reliable, responsible
áreit|a *v* (-i, -ti, -t) harass
áreit|i *n neu* (-is, ~, -a) harassment
árekstur *n masc* (árekstrar/-s, árekstrar, árekstra) crash
árfjórðungslega *adv* quarterly
árgang|ur *n masc* (-s, -ar, -a) class
ármynn|i *n neu* (-is, ~, -a) *geog* delta
árita *v* (~, -ði, -ð) sign
áríðandi *adj* urgent, pressing, poignant
árlega *adv* annually
árleg|ur *adj* (-, -t) annual
áróður *n masc* (-s) propaganda
ársfjórðungsrit *n neu* (-s, -, -a) quarterly (publication)
ársfjórðung|ur *n masc* (-s, -ar, -a) quarter
ársskýrsla *n fem* (-skýrslu, -skýrslna) annual report
árstíð *n fem* (-ar, -ir, -a) season
árstíðarbundin|n *adj* (-, -bundið) seasonal
áræðni *n fem* (-) courage
ás *n masc* (-s, -ar, -a) hill; ace
ásaka *v* (~, -ði, -ð) accuse
ásamt *prep* + *dat* with, together with
ásetning|ur *n masc* (-s) intention, premeditation
ásigkomulag *n neu* (-s) condition
áskor|un *n fem* (-unar, -anir, -ana) challenge
áskrifand|i *n masc* (-a, áskrifendur, áskrifenda) subscriber
áskrift *n fem* (-ar, -ir, -a) subscription

ásláttarhljóðfær|i *n neu* (-is, ~, -a) *mus* percussion instruments
ást *n fem* (-ar, -ir, -a) love, affection
ástand *n neu* (-s) situation, state, status: **hvernig er ástandið?** How is the situation?
Ástand|ið *n neu def* (-sins) *refers to the situation when Icelandic women were romantically involved with British or American soldiers during WWII*
ástarævintýr|i *n neu* (-is, ~, -a) romance
ástarsamband *n neu* (-s, -sambönd, -a) love affair
Ástral|i *n masc* (-a, -ir, -a) Australian
Ástralí|a *N fem* (-u) Australia
ástralsk|ur *adj* (áströlsk, -t) Australian
ástríð|a *n fem* (-u, -ur, -a/na) passion
ástríðuávöxt|ur *n masc* (-ávaxtar, -vextir, -vaxta) passionfruit
ástríðufull|ur *adj* (-, -t) passionate
ástund|un *n fem* (-unar) pursuit; diligence
ástæð|a *n fem* (-u, -ur, -na) reason, motive
ásættanleg|ur *adj* (-, -t) acceptable
ásök|un *n fem* (-unar, -sakanir, -sakana) allegation
átakamikil|l *adj* (-, -mikið) dramatic
átakanleg|ur *adj* (-, -t) heartwrenching
átt *n fem* (-ar, -ir, -a) direction
átta *num* eight
áttatíu *num* eighty
áttavit|i *n masc* (-a, -ar, -a) compass
átthyrning|ur *n masc* (-s, -ar, -a) *math* octagon
áttund|i *ord* (-a, -a) eighth
áttræð|ur *adj* (-, -rætt) eighty years old
átján *num* eighteen
átjánd|i *ord* (-a, -a) eighteenth
ávallt *adv* always
ávan|i *n masc* (-a, -ar, -a) habit
ávarp *n neu* (-s, ávörp, -a) speech; term of address
ávarpa *v* (~, -ði, -ð) address

ávaxtagraut|ur *n masc* (-ar, -ar, -a)
fruit compote
ávaxtasaf|i *n masc* (-a, -ar, -a) fruit
juice
ávaxtasalat *n neu* (-s, -salöt, -a) fruit
salad
ávaxtasykur *n masc* (-s) *bio* fructose
ávaxtaþykkni *n neu* (-s) fruit syrup
áveit|a *n fem* (-u, -ur, -na) *eng*
irrigation
ávísanaheft|i *n neu* (-is, ~, -a)
checkbook
ávís|un *n fem* (-unar, -anir, -ana)
(monetary) check

ávíta *v* (~, -ði, -ð) reprimand, rebuke
ávít|ur *n fem pl* (-a) reproof
ávöxt|ur *n masc* (ávaxtar, ávextir,
ávaxta) fruit
áþreifanleg|ur *adj* (-, -t) concrete,
palpable
áætla *v* (~, -ði, -ð) estimate, project
áætl|un *n fem* (-unar, -anir, -ana)
plan, schedule
áætlunarferð|ir *n fem pl* (-a) shuttle
service
áætlunarflug *n neu* (-s, -, -a)
scheduled flight

B

babl *n neu* (-s) prattle
badminton *n neu* (-s) badminton
bað *n neu* (-s, böð, -a) bath
baða *v* (~, -ði, -ð) bathe
baðhandklæð|i *n neu* (-is, ~, -a) bath towel
baðherberg|i *n neu* (-is, ~, -ja) bathroom, restroom, washroom
baðhús *n neu* (-s, -, -a) spa
baðkar *n neu* (-s, -kör, -a) bathtub
baðker *n neu* (-s, -, -ja) bathtub
baðmull *n fem* (-ar) cotton
Bagdad *N fem* (-) Baghdad
Bahamaeyj|ar *N fem pl* (-a) The Bahamas
bak *n neu* (-s, bök, -a) back: **mér er illt í bakinu** I have a pain in my back
bak|a 1 *n fem* (böku, bökur, baka) pie: **eplabaka** apple pie; **2 baka** *v* (~, -ði, -ð) bake: ~ **köku** bake a cake
bakað|ur *adj* (bökuð, -) baked: **bökuð kartafla** baked potato
bakar|i *n masc* (-a, -ar, -a) baker
bakarí *n neu* (-s, -, -a) bakery
bakdyr *n fem pl* (-a) back door
bakgrunn|ur *n masc* (-s) background
bakhlið *n fem* (-ar, -ar, -a) backside, rear, reverse
bakhönd *n fem* (-handar, -hendur, -handa) backhand
bakka *v* (~, -ði, -ð) back; reverse
bakk|i *n masc* (-a, -ar, -a) tray
bakktakk|i *n masc* (-a, -ar, -a) *comp* backspace
bakpok|i *n masc* (-a, -ar, -a) backpack
bakterí|a *n fem* (-u, -ur, -a) bacteria
Bakú *N fem* (-) Baku
bakverk|ur *n masc* (-verkjar, -ir, -ja) backache

bakþank|i *n masc* (-a, -ar, -a) second thoughts
ballett *n masc* (-s, -ar, -a) ballet
balsamedik *n neu* (-s, -, -a) balsamic vinaigrette
bambus *n masc* (-s) *flora* bamboo
bambussprot|i *n masc* (-a, -ar, -a) *flora* bamboo shoot
bananabrauð *n neu* (-s, -, -a) banana bread
bananalýðveld|i *n neu* (-is, ~, -a) banana republic
banan|i *n masc* (-a, -ar, -a) banana
banaslys *n neu* (-s, -, -a) fatal accident
band *n neu* (-s, bönd, -a) string
bandamað|ur *n masc* (-mann, -menn, -manna) ally
Bandarík|in *N neu pl* (-janna) United States of America
Bandaríkjamað|ur *n masc* (-manns, -menn, -manna) American
bangs|i *n masc* (-a, -ar, -a) teddy bear
bank *n neu* (-s) knock, pat
banka *v* (~, -ði, -ð) knock
bankagjaldker|i *n masc* (-a, -ar, -a) bank teller
bankarán *n neu* (-s, -, -a) bank robbery
bankareikning|ur *n masc* (-s, -ar, -a) bank account
bankastarfsmað|ur *n masc* (-manns, -menn, -manna) bank employer
bank|i *n masc* (-a, -ar, -a) bank
bann *n neu* (-s, bönn, -a) prohibition, ban
banna *v* (~, -ði, -ð) ban, outlaw, prohibit
bannað|ur *adj* (bönnuð, -) prohibited, forbidden: **það er bannað að reykja hér** smoking is prohibited here
bar *n masc* (-s, -ir, -a) bar, pub, tavern
bara *adv* only, just, merely

barátt|a *n fem* (-u) struggle, battle
bardag|i *n masc* (-a, -ar, -a) fight, encounter
barkabólg|a *n fem* (-u) *med* laryngitis
barm|ur *n masc* (-s, -ar, -a) *anat* bosom
barn *n neu* (-s, börn, -a) child
barnabarn *n neu* (-s, -börn, -barna) grandchild
barnabók *n fem* (-ar, -bækur, -bóka) children's book
barnaföt *n neu pl* (-fata) childrenswear
barnagæsl|a *n fem* (-u) childcare
barnaherberg|i *n neu* (-s, ~, -ja) nursery
barnakerr|a *n fem* (-u, -ur, -a) baby stroller
barnalaug *n fem* (-ar, -ar, -a) kiddie pool
barnaleg|ur *adj* (-, -t) naive
barnalækn|ir *n masc* (-is, -ar, -a) *med* pediatrician
barnalæsing *n fem* (-ar, -ar, -a) child lock
barnamatseðil|l *n masc* (-seðils, -seðlar, -seðla) children's menu
barnamat|ur *n masc* (-ar, -ar, -a) baby food
barnapí|a *n fem* (-u, -ur, -a) babysitter
barnarúm *n neu* (-s, -, -a) children's bed
barnaskammt|ur *n masc* (-s, -ar, -a) children's portions
barnastól|l *n masc* (-s, -ar, -a) highchair; car seat; child bike seat; small chair for children
barokkstíl|l *n masc* (-s) Baroque style
barþjón|n *n masc* (-s, -ar, -a) bartender
basalt *n neu* (-s) *geol* basalt
basilik|a *n fem* (-u) basil
basmatihrísgrjón *n neu* (-s, -, -a) basmati rice
bass|i *n masc* (-a, -ar, -a) *mus* bass; **bassagítar** bass guitar; **kontrabassi** double bass

bat|i *n masc* (-a) recovery
batna *v* (~, -ði, -ð) improve
batterí *n neu* (-s, -, -a) *colloq* battery
baun *n fem* (-ar, -ir, -a) bean: **svartar ~ir** black beans; pea: **grænar ~ir** green peas; **gular ~ir** corn
baunapok|i *n masc* (-a, -ar, -a) bean bag
baunaspír|a *n fem* (-u, -ur, -a) bean sprout
baunasúp|a *n fem* (-u, -ur, -a) split pea soup
báðar leiðir *phr* round-trip
báð|ir *pron pl* (-ar, bæði) both
bál *n neu* (-s, -, -a) blaze
bálköst|ur *n masc* (-kastar, -kestir, -kasta) pyre
bár|a *n fem* (-u, -ur, -a) wave
básún|a *n fem* (-u, -ur, -a) *mus* trombone
bátalæg|i *n neu* (-is, ~, -ja) anchorage
bát|ur *n masc* (-s, -ar, -a) boat
beiðni *n fem* (-) request
beikon *n neu* (-s) bacon
bein *n neu* (-s, -, -a) bone
bein|a *v* (-i, -di, -t) direct
beinagrind *n fem* (-ar, -ur, -a) *anat* skeleton
beinbrot *n neu* (-s, -, -a) *med* bone fracture
beinlaus *adj* (-, -t) boneless
bein|n *adj* (-, -t) straight, direct: **beint flug** direct flight
beinskipting *n fem* (-ar) *mech* manual transmission
beint *adv* straight, directly: **farðu ~ heim** go straight home; **~ af býli** farm fresh
Beirút *N fem* (-) Beirut
beisk|ur *adj* (-, -t) bitter, pungent, tart
beitarfisk|ur *n masc* (-s, -ar, -a) tilapia
beitiland *n neu* (-s, -lönd, -a) pasture
beitt|ur *adj* (-, -) sharp, acute
beitukóng|ur *n masc* (-s, -ar, -a) *zool* whelk
bekk|ur *n masc* (-jar, -ir, -ja) bench;

kirkju~ pew; grade: **fyrsti** ~ first grade
Belgi *n masc* (-a, -ar, -a) Belgian
Belgi|a *N fem* (-u) Belgium
belgísk|ur *adj* (-, -t) Belgian
belgjurt *n fem* (-ar, -ir, -a) legumes
belgjurtafræ *n neu pl* (-s, -, -ja) leguminous seeds
Belgrad *N fem* (-) Belgrade
belt|i *n neu* (-is, ~, -a) belt
bend|a *v* (-i, benti, bent) point
bendil|l *n masc* (-s, bendlar, bendla) *comp* cursor
bending *n fem* (-ar, -ar, -a) gesture
bensín *n neu* (-s) gas, gasoline, petrol
bensíndæl|a *n fem* (-u, -ur, -na/a) gas pump
bensíngjöf *n fem* (-gjafar, -gjafir, -gjafa) *mech* accelerator
bensínmæl|ir *n masc* (-is, -ar, -a) gas meter
bensínstöð *n fem* (-var, -var, -va) gas station
bensíntank|ur *n masc* (-s, -ar, -a) gas tank
ber 1 *adj* (-, -t) naked, bare; **2** *n neu* (-s, -, -ja) berry: **bláber** blueberries
ber|a *v* (-, bar, bárum, borið) carry, bear; *(sheep)* give birth
berg *n neu* (-s) *geol* rock
bergmál *n neu* (-s) echo
bergmála *v* (~, -ði, -ð) echo
bergskrið|a *n fem* (-u, -ur, -a) rockslide
berj|ast *v* (berst, barðist, barist) fight, struggle, scramble: ~ **í bökkunum** struggle
berkjubólg|a *n fem* (-u) *med* bronchitis
berkl|ar *n masc pl* (-a) *med* tuberculosis
Berlín *N fem* (-ar) Berlin
berserksgang|ur *n masc* (-s) rampage
berserk|ur *n masc* (-s/jar, -ir, -ja) berserk
best|ur *adj superl* (-, -) best
betlar|i *n masc* (-a, -ar, -a) beggar

betr|i *adj compar* (~, -a) better: **betra veður** better weather
betrumbæt|a *v* (-i, ti, -t) improve, refine
beygingarending *n fem* (-ar, -ar, -a) *ling* inflectional suffix
beygingarmynd *n fem* (-ar, -ir, -a) *ling* inflectional form
beygj|a *n fem* (-u, -ur, ~) turn, bend
beygl|a *n fem* (-u, -ur, ~) dent *(on a car)*; bagel
beyglað|ur *adj* (beygluð, -) bent
beyki *n neu* (-s) *flora* beech
biblí|a *n fem* (-u, -ur, -a) Bible
bið *n fem* (-ar, -ir, -a) wait
biðj|a *v* (bið, bað, báðum, beðið) pray: ~ **fyrir** pray for; plead: ~ **um** request, ask for
biðj|ast *v refl* (biðst, baðst, báðumst, beðist) ask for oneself: ~ **afsökunar** apologize; ~ **vægðar** ask for mercy
biðla *v* (~, -ði, -ð) propose; beg
biðlist|i *n masc* (-a, -ar, -a) waiting list
biðskyld|a *n fem* (-u) *(for drivers)* yield
biðstof|a *n fem* (-u, -ur, -a) waiting room
bifreið *n fem* (-ar, -ar, -a) *form* automobile
bifreiðartrygging *n fem* (-ar, -ar, -a) car insurance
bikar *n masc* (-s, -ar, -a) trophy
bikiní *n neu* (-s, -, -a) bikini
bilað|ur *adj* (biluð, -) broken, not working; *slang* crazy
biljarð|ur *n masc* (-s) billiards
billeg|ur *adj* (-, -t) *colloq* cheap
bilstöng *n fem* (-stangar, -stangir, -stanga) *comp* spacebar
bind|a *v* (-i, batt, bundum, bundið) tie, bind
bind|i *n neu* (-is, ~, -a) **1** neck tie; **2** volume: **annað** ~ second volume
birgðageymsl|a *n fem* (-u, -ur, ~/-na) depot

birgðasal|i *n masc* (-a, -ar, -a) supplier

birgð|ir *n fem pl* (-a) supplies, provisions, stock

birki *n neu* (-s) *flora* birch

birkifræ *n neu* (-s, -, -ja) poppy seed

birt|a *v* (-i, -i, birt) get light: **það birti klukkan fimm** it gets light at five; publish

birt|ast *v* (-ist, -ist, birst) appear, emerge; ~ **aftur** reappear

biskup *n masc* (-s, -ar, -a) bishop

biskupa saga *n fem* (sögu) *lit* bishop's saga, Icelandic sagas about bishops and saints

bit *n neu* (-s, -, -a) bite

bit|i *n masc* (-a, -ar, -a) bite of something

bitur *adj* (-, -t) bitter

biturblöðung|ur *n masc* (-s, -ar, -a) *flora* aloe

biturlega *adv* bitterly

bíð|a *v* (-, beið, biðum, beðið) wait; hold on

bílaferj|a *n fem* (-u, -ur, -a) car ferry

bílageymsl|a *n fem* (-u, -ur, -na) parking garage

bílaleig|a *n fem* (-u, -ur, -a) car rental

bílaleigubíl|l *n masc* (-s, -ar, -a) rental car

bílapartasal|a *n fem* (-sölu, -sölur, -sala) junk yard

bílasal|a *n fem* (-sölu, -sölur, -na/~) car dealer (*store*)

bílasal|i *n masc* (-a, -ar, -a) car dealer (*sales person*)

bílastæð|i *n neu* (-is, ~, -a) parking lot; (*for one car*) parking space

bílaþvottastöð *n fem* (-var, -var, -va) (*the business*) car wash

bílaþvott|ur *n masc* (-ar/-s, -ar, -a) (*process*) car wash

bílbelt|i *n neu* (-is, ~, -a) seat belt

bílferð *n fem* (-ar, -ir, -a) car drive, car trip, car ride

bíl|l *n masc* (-s, -ar, -a) car

bíllykil|l *n masc* (-s, -lyklar, -lykla) ignition key

bílnúmer *n neu* (-s, -, -a) license plate number; **bílnúmeraplata** license plate

bílskúr *n masc* (-s, -ar, -a) garage

bílstjór|i *n masc* (-a, -ar, -a) driver, chauffeur

bíltúr *n masc* (-s, -ar, -a) drive: **fara í** ~ go for a drive

bílveiki *n fem* (~) *med* motion sickness

bílveik|ur *adj* (-, -t) *med* car sick

bíó *n neu* (-s, -, -a) movies: **fara í** ~ go to the movies; movie theater: **í hvaða ~i er myndin sýnd?** in which theater is the movie running?

bíóhús *n neu* (-s, -, -a) movie theater: **sýnd í öllum bíóhúsum borgarinnar** shown in all the movie theaters in the city

bíómið|i *n masc* (-a, -ar, -a) movie ticket

bíómynd *n fem* (-ar, -ir, -a) movie, film

bít|a *v* (-, beit, bitum, bitið) bite; graze

Bítlarnir *N masc* (Bítlanna) The Beatles

bjall|a *n fem* (bjöllu, bjöllur, -na/~) *mus* bell; *zool* beetle

bjarga *v* (~, -ði, -ð) save, rescue, retrieve

bjarga|st *v refl* (~, -ðist, ~) be saved

bjargvætt|ur *n masc* (-ar, -ir, -a) savior

bjartsýni *n fem* (-) optimism

bjartsýnismað|ur *n masc* (-mann, -menn, -manna) optimist

bjartsýn|n *adj* (-, -t) optimistic

bjart|ur *adj* (björt, -t) bright

bjánaleg|ur *adj* (-, -t) foolish

bján|i *n masc* (-a, -ar, -a) fool

bjálk|i *n masc* (-a, -ar, -a) wooden beam; **bjálkakofi** log house

bjóð|a *v* (býð, bauð, buðum, boðið) invite; offer; ~ **í** bid for; ~ **sig fram** volunteer; ~ **upp** auction

bjóð|ast *v refl* (býðst, bauðst, buðumst, boðist) offer to do something: ~

til að hjálpa offer to help; **~ til að borga** offer to pay

bjór *n masc* (-s, -ar, -a) beer, ale

bjórgerð *n fem* (-ar, -ir, -a) brewing house

bjórglas *n neu* (-s, -glös, -a) beer glass

bjórkrús *n fem* (-ar, -ir, -a) beer pint

björg|un *n fem* (-unar, -anir, -ana) rescue, salvage, save, redemption

björgunaraðgerð *n fem* (-ar, -ir, -a) rescue operation

björgunarbát|ur *n masc* (-s, -ar, -a) lifeboat

björgunarbelt|i *n neu* (-is, ~, -a) life belt

björgunarsveit *n fem* (-ar, -ir, -a) rescue team

björgunarvest|i *n neu* (-is, ~, -a) life jacket

björn *n masc* (bjarnar, birnir, bjarna) *zool* bear

blað *n neu* (-s, blöð, -a) paper; blade

blaðagrein *n fem* (-ar, -ar, -a) newspaper article

blaðaljósmyndar|i *n masc* (-a, -ar, -a) press photographer

blaðamannafund|ur *n masc* (-ar, -ir, -a) press conference

blaðbeðj|a *n fem* (-u, -ur, -a) chard

blaðdeig *n neu* (-s) filo dough

blaðr|a *n fem* (blöðru, blöðrur, ~) balloon; *med* bladder; blister; cyst

blaðselj|a *n fem* (-u) celery

blaðsíð|a *n fem* (-u, -ur, -na) page

blak *n neu* (-s) volleyball

bland|a *n fem* (blöndu, blöndur, -na/~) mixture, mix, blend; hybrid

blandað|ur *adj* (blönduð, -) mixed, assorted

blandar|i *n masc* (-a, -ar, -a) blender

blautbúning|ur *n masc* (-s, -ar, -a) *sports* wetsuit

blaut|ur *adj* (-, t) wet

blautþurrk|a *n fem* (-u, -ur, -na) wet wipe

Bláa lón|ið *N neu def* (-sins) The Blue Lagoon

bláber *n neu* (-s, -, -ja) blueberry

bláberjabak|a *n fem* (-böku, -bökur, baka) blueberry pie

blá|r *adj* (-, -tt) blue

blás|a *v* (blæs, blés, blésum, blásið) blow

bláskel *n fem* (-jar, -jar, -ja) *zool* blue mussel

blásturshljóðfær|i *n neu* (-is, ~, -a) *mus* wind instrument

blei|a *n fem* (-u, -ur, -a) diaper

bleikj|a *n fem* (-u, -ur, ~) *zool* char fish

bleik|ur *adj* (-, -t) pink

blek *n neu* (-s) ink

bless! *interj* bye!; **bless bless!** bye bye!

blessa *v* (~, -ði, -ð) bless

blessað|ur *adj* (blessuð, -) blessed; hi!, hello!: *(to a woman)* **blessuð!** hi!, *(to a man)* **blessaður!** hi!

blettatígur *n masc* (-s, -tígrar, -tígra) *zool* leopard

blett|ur *n masc* (-s, -ir, -a) spot

bleyja *n fem* (-u, -ur, ~) diaper

blindrahund|ur *n masc* (-s, -ar, -a) *zool* leader dog

blindraletur *n neu* (-s) Braille

blind|ur *adj* (-, blint) blind

blíðlega *adv* gently, softly

blíð|ur *adj* (-, blítt) gentle, soft, sweet, tender

blístra *v* (~, -ði, -ð) whistle

blístur *n neu* (-s) whistle

blokk *n fem* (-ar, -ir, -a) apartment building

blokkflaut|a *n fem* (-u, -ur, -na/~) *mus* recorder

blóð *n neu* (-s) blood

blóðappelsín|a *n fem* (-u, -ur, ~) blood orange

blóðberg *n neu* (-s) thyme

blóðflokk|ur *n masc* (-s, -ar, -a) *med* blood type

blóðgjaf|i *n masc* (-a, -ar, -a) *med* blood donor

blóðgjöf *n fem* (-gjafar, -gjafir, -gjafa) *med* blood transfusion

blóðleysi *n neu* (-s) *med* anemia

blóðmaur *n masc* (-s, -ar, -a) insect
tick
blóðpruf|a *n fem* (-u, -ur, ~) med
blood test
blóðsykur *n masc* (-s) med glucose
blóðtappamynd|un *n fem* (-unar,
-anir, -ana) med thrombosis
blóðtapp|i *n masc* (-a, -ar, -a) med
blood clot
blóðvatn *n neu* (-s) med serum
blóðvökv|i *n masc* (-a) med plasma
blóðþrýstingsmæl|ir *n masc* (-is, -ar,
-a) med blood pressure monitor
blóðþrýsting|ur *n masc* (-s) med
blood pressure
blóm *n neu* (-s, -, -a) flower
blómabúð *n fem* (-ar, -ir, -a) florist
(store), flower store
blómapott|ur *n masc* (-s, -ar, -a)
flower pot
blómaskeið *n neu* (-s, -, -a) heyday
blómkál *n neu* (-s) cauliflower
blómleg|ur *adj* (-, -t) lush
blómstra *v* (~, -ði, -ð) flourish, prosper
blórabögul|l *n masc* (-s, -bögglar,
-böggla) scapegoat
blót *n neu* (-s, -, -a) swearing; pagan
feast: **Þorrablót** midwinter feast
blóta *v* (~, -ði, -ð) swear; to do a
pagan ritual
blótsyrð|i *n neu* (-is, ~, -a) swear word
blund|ur *n masc* (-s, -ir, -a) doze, nap
blúnd|a *n fem* (-u, -ur, -na/~) lace
blúss|a *n fem* (-u, -ur, -na/~) blouse
blýant|ur *n masc* (-s, -ar, -a) pencil
blýlaus *adj* (-, -t) lead-free, unleaded
blæð|a *v* (-i, blæddi, blætt) bleed
blæj|a *n fem* (-u, -ur, ~) veil
blöndung|ur *n masc* (-s, -ar, -a)
mech carburetor
boð *n neu* (s, -, -a) invitation, offering, bid; party: **kvöldverðarboð**
dinner party
boða *v* (~, -ði, -ð) summon
boðhátt|ur *n masc* (-ar, -hættir,
hátta) *ling* imperative form
bog|i *n masc* (-a, -ar, -a) arch

Bogmað|urinn *n masc def* (Bog-
mannsins) *astro* Sagittarius
boll|a *n fem* (-u, -ur, -a) bun; punch
bollakak|a *n fem* (-köku, -kökur,
-na/~) cupcake
boll|i *n masc* (-a, -ar, -a) cup
bolludagur *n* Icelandic holiday, seven
weeks before Easter, celebrated by
eating buns with cream and jam
bol|ur *n masc* (-s, -ir, -a) long sleeve
shirt; t-shirt; tree trunk
boms|ur *n fem pl* (-a) waders
borð *n neu* (-s, -, -a) table; **um** ~ on
board
borða *v* (~, -ði, -ð) eat
borðbúnað|ur *n masc* (-ar) tableware
borðdúk|ur *n masc* (-s, -ar, -a)
tablecloth
borð|i *n masc* (-a, -ar, -a) ribbon, tape
borðspil *n neu* (-s, -, -a) board game
borðstof|a *n fem* (-u, -ur, -a) dining
room
borðtennis *n neu* (-s) ping-pong,
table tennis
borg *n fem* (-ar, -ir, -a) city
borga *v* (~, -ði, -ð) pay
borgaraleg|ur *adj* (-, -t) bourgeois,
civil
borgararéttind|i *n neu pl* (-a) civil
rights
borgar|i *n masc* (-a, -ar, -a) civilian
borgarskipulag *n neu* (-s) city
planning
borgarstjór|i *n masc* (-a, -ar, -a) mayor
borgarstjórn *n fem* (-ar, -ir, -a) city
council
Bosní|a og Hersegóvín|a *N neu* (-u
og -u) Bosnia and Herzegovina
bosnísk|ur *adj* (-, -t) Bosnian
Bosníumað|ur *n masc* (-manns, -menn,
-manna) Bosnian
botn *n masc* (-s, -ar, -a) bottom
botnfall *n neu* (-s) sediment
botnlangakast *n neu* (-s, -köst, -a)
med appendicitis
botnlang|i *n masc* (-a, -ar, -a) *(street)*
dead end; *med* appendix

box *n neu* (-, -, -a) box
boxa *v* (~, -ði, -ð) *sports* box
bók *n fem* (-ar, bækur, bóka) book
bóka *v* (~, -ði, -ð) book, reserve
bókabúð *n fem* (-ar, -búðir, -búða)
  bookstore
bókamerk|i *n neu* (-is, ~, -ja) bookmark
bókasafn *n neu* (-s, -söfn, -a) library
bókasafnsfræðing|ur *n masc* (-s, -ar,
  -a) librarian
bókfell *n neu* (-s) parchment paper
bókhaldar|i *n masc* (-a, -ar, -a)
  accountant
bókhveiti *n neu* (-s) buckwheat
bókmenntagagnrýnand|i *n masc*
  (-a, -gagnrýnendur, -gagnrýnenda)
  book reviewer
bókmenntir *n fem pl* (-a) literature
bókstaflega *adv* literally
bókstafleg|ur *adj* (-, -t) literal
bókstafstrú *n fem* (-ar) Orthodox
  religion
bók|un *n fem* (-unar, anir, -ana)
  reservation, booking
ból|a *n fem* (-u, -ur, -a) bubble; *med*
  pimple
bólg|a *n fem* (-u, -ur, -na/~) *med*
  swell, swelling, inflamation
bólgin|n *adj* (-, bólgið) swollen
bólgna *v* (~, -ði, -ð) swell
Bóliví|a *N fem* (-u) Bolivia
bólivísk|ur *adj* (-, -t) Bolivian
Bólivíumað|ur *n masc* (-manns,
  -menn, -manna) Bolivian
bóluefn|i *n neu* (-is, ~, -a) vaccine
bóluset|ja *v* (-, ti, -t) vaccinate
bólusetning *n fem* (-ar, -ar, -a) vaccination, immunization
bólusótt *n fem* (-ar) *med* small pox
bómull *n fem* (-ar) cotton
bómullarpinn|i *n masc* (-a, -ar, -a)
  cotton swab
bón *n neu* (-s) wax; **gólfbón** floor
  wax; **bílabón** car wax
bóndabaun *n fem* (-a, -ir, -a) fava bean
bóndabæ|r *n masc* (-jar, -ir, -ja)
  farmhouse

bónd|i *n masc* (-a, bændur, bænda)
  farmer
bónorð *n neu* (-s, -, -a) marriage
  proposal
bónus *n masc* (-s, -ar, -a) bonus
bót *n fem* (-ar, bætur, -a) patch
bótanísk|ur *adj* (-, -t) botanical
bragð *n neu* (-s, brögð, -a) flavor, taste
bragða *v* (~, -ði, -ð) taste
bragðbætt|ur *adj* (-, -) flavored
bragðdauf|ur *adj* (-, -t) flavorless
bragðefn|i *n neu* (-is, ~, -a) flavoring
bragðgóð|ur *adj* (-, -gott) delicious,
  tasty
bragðmikil|l *adj* (-, -mikið) tangy
bragðsterk|ur *adj* (-, -t) spicy, piquant
brandar|i *n masc* (-a, -ar, -a) joke
Brasil|a *N fem* (-u) Brasilia
brasilísk|ur *adj* (-, -t) Brazilian
Brasilíumað|ur *n masc* (-manns,
  -menn, -manna) Brazilian
Bratislava *N fem* (-) Bratislava
bratt|ur *adj* (brött, -) steep
brauð *n neu* (-s, ~, -a) bread; **rúg-**
  brauð rye bread; **heilhveitibrauð**
  multigrain bread
brauðboll|a *n fem* (-u, -ur, -a) bread
  bun
brauðhleif|ur *n masc* (-s, -ar, -a) loaf
  of bread
brauðhníf|ur *n masc* (-s, -ar, -a)
  breadknife
brauðmol|i *n masc* (-a, -ar, -a)
  breadcrumbs
brauðrist *n fem* (-ar, -ir, -a) toaster
brauðstöng *n fem* (-stangar, -stangir,
  -stanga) bread stick
brauðsúp|a *n fem* (-u, -ur, ~) bread
  soup
brauðtening|ur *n masc* (-s, -ar, -a)
  crouton
braut *n fem* (-ar, -ir, -a) *sports* track;
  astron orbit
brautartein|n *n masc* (-s, -ar, -a) rail
bráð *n fem* (-ar, -ir, -a) prey
bráðabirgða *adj* temporary, interim:
  til ~ temporarily

bráðamóttak|a *n fem* (-töku, -tökur, -taka) emergency room

bráðin|n *adj* (-, bráðið) molten

bráðna *v* (~, -ði, -ð) melt

bráðum *adv* soon, shortly

bráð|ur *adj* (-, brátt) acute

bregðast *v refl* (bregst, brást, brugðumst, brugðist) fail, let down; ~ **við** react

breidd *n fem* (-ar) width

breiddargráð|a *n fem* (-u, -ur, -a) *geog* latitude

breið|a *v* (-i, breiddi, breitt) spread; ~ **út** spread around

breið|ast *v refl* (-ist, breiddist, -st) spread; ~ **út** spread: **veiran breiddist hratt út** the virus spread fast

breiðband *n neu* (-s, -bönd, -a) broadband

breiðgat|a *n fem* (-götu, -götur, -gatna) avenue

breið|ur *adj* (-, breitt) broad, wide

brekk|a *n fem* (-u, -ur, -na) slope, hill

brell|a *n fem* (-u, -ur, -na) trick

bremsa *v* (~, -ði, -ð) brake

bremsuvökv|i *n masc* (-a, -ar, -a) brake fluid

brengla *v* (~, -ði, -ð) distort, scramble, confuse

brenglað|ur *adj* (brengluð, -) distorted; twisted

brenn|a *v* (-, brann, brunnum, brunnið) burn

brennandi *adj* burning

brennd|ur *adj* (-, brennt) burnt

brennidepil|l *n masc* (-s, -deplar, -depla) focus

brenninetl|a *n fem* (-u, -ur, -na) *flora* nettle

brennistein|n *n masc* (-s) *chem* sulphur

brennivín *n neu* (-s, ~, -a) Icelandic hard liquor with cumin flavor

bresk|ur *adj* (-, -t) British

brest|a *v* (-, brast, brustum, brostið) break

Bretland *N neu* (-s) Britain

breyt|a 1 *n fem* (-u, -ur, -na) parameter, variable; **2** *v* (-i, -ti, -tt) change, modify, alter

breyt|ast *v refl* (-ist, -tist, breyst) change, transform: ~ **í tröll** transform into a troll

breytileg|ur *adj* (-, -t) variable

breytileik|i *n masc* (-a) variation

breyting *n fem* (-ar, -ar, -a) change, transformation, alteration, transition

bréf *n neu* (-s, -, -a) letter

bréfasím|i *n masc* (-a, -ar, -a) fax machine

brim *n neu* (-s) waves; *sport* surf

brimbrettabrun *n neu* (-s) *sports* surfing

brimbrett|i *n neu* (-is, ~, -a) *sports* surfboard

bringa *n fem* (-u, -ur, -na) *anat* chest; *med* thorax; **kjúklingabringa** chicken fillet

brjálað|ur *adj* (brjáluð, -) crazy, mad

brjálæðing|ur *n masc* (-s, -ar, -a) lunatic

brjóst *n neu* (-s, -, -a) *anat* breast, bosom

brjóstahaldar|i *n masc* (-a, -ar, -a) bra

brjóstkass|i *n masc* (-a, -ar, -a) *anat* chest

brjóstsykur *n masc* (-s) bonbon

brjót|a *v* (brýt, braut, brutum, brotið) crush, smash; breach; ~ **saman** fold

brokka *v* (~, -ði, -ð) *(horses)* trot

brokkólí *n neu* (-s) broccoli

bronkítís *n neu* (-) *med* bronchitis

brons *n neu* (-) bronze

bros *n neu* (-s) smile

bros|a *v* (-i, -ti, -að) smile

brot *n neu* (-s, -, -a) fraction, fragment

brothljóð *n neu* (-s, -, -a) smash; cracking sound

brotin|n *adj* (-, brotið) crushed, broken

brotsjó|r *n masc* (-sjóar) *geog* surf
brottfararspjald *n neu* (-s, -spjöld, -a) boarding card
brottfarasal|ur *n masc* (-ar, -ir, -a) departure lounge
brottför *n fem* (-farar, -farir, -fara) departure
brottvís|un *n fem* (-unar, -anir, -ana) deportation
bróð|ir *n masc* (-ur, bræður, bræðra) brother
bróðurdótt|ir *n fem* (-ur, -dætur, -dætra) niece (the daughter of one's brother)
bróðurson|ur *n masc* (-ar, synir, sona) nephew (the son of one's brother)
brómber *n neu* (-s, -, -ja) marion-berry
brugghús *n neu* (-s, -, -a) brewery
brunabíl|l *n masc* (-s, -ar, -a) fire truck
brunabjall|a *n fem* (-björðu, -björllur, -na/~) fire alarm
brun|i *n masc* (-a, -ar, -a) fire, burning; *chem* oxidation
brunnin|n *adj* (-, brunnið) burned
brunn|ur *n masc* (-s, -ar, -a) fountain, well
Brussel *N fem* (-/s) Brussels
brú *n fem* (-ar, brýr, brúa) bridge
brúa *v* (~, -ði, -ð) bridge
brúð|a *n fem* (-u, -ur, -na/~) doll; puppet
brúðargjöf *n fem* (-gjafar, -gjafir, -gjafa) wedding present
brúðarmær *n fem* (-meyjar, -meyjar, -meyja) bridesmaid
brúðgum|i *n masc* (-a, -ar, -a) bridegroom
brúðkaup *n neu* (-s, -, -a) wedding
brúðkaupsafmæl|i *n neu* (-is, ~, -a) wedding anniversary
brúðkaupsferð *n fem* (-ar, -ir, -a) honeymoon
brúðkaupstert|a *n fem* (-u, -ur, -na/~) wedding cake

brúð|ur *n fem* (-ar, -ir, -a) bride
brún *n fem* (-ar, -ir, -a) edge, rim
brúnað|ur *adj* (brúnuð, -) caramelized: **brúnaðar kartöflur** carmelized potatoes
brún|n *adj* (-, -t) brown
bryðj|a *v* (bryð, bruddi, brutt) crunch
bryggj|a *n fem* (-u, -ur, -na/~) pier, dock
brynj|a *n fem* (-u, -ur, ~) armor
bryt|i *n masc* (-a, -ar, -a) purser
brytja *v* (~, -ði, -ð) chop
bræði *n fem* (-) rage
bröns *n masc* (-) *slang* brunch
budd|a *n fem* (-u, -ur, ~) purse
bugða|st *v* (~, -ðist, ~) wind: **áin ~ niður dalinn** the stream winds down the valley
bull *n neu* (-s) nonsense
bulla *v* (~, -ði, -ð) babble, to say nonsense
burðargjald *n neu* (-s, -gjöld, -a) postage: **~ greitt** postage paid
burðarmað|ur *n masc* (-manns, -menn, -manna) porter
burritó *n neu* (-s, ~, -a) burrito
bursta *v* (~, -ði, -ð) brush
buslulaug *n fem* (-ar, -ar, -a) baby pool
bux|ur *n fem pl* (-na) pants, trousers
bú|a *v* (bý, bjó, bjuggum, búið) reside; **~ til** create, make
bú|ast *v* (býst, bjóst, bjuggumst, búist) prepare; **~ við** anticipate, expect
Búdapest *N fem* (-) Budapest
búð *n fem* (-ar, -ir, -a) store
búðarhnupl *n neu* (-s) shoplifting
búðarhnuplar|i *n masc* (-a, -ar, -a) shoplifter
búðarkass|i *n masc* (-a, -ar, -a) cash register
búðing|ur *n masc* (-s, -ar, -a) pudding
búfræði *n fem* (-) agronomy
búin|n *adj* (-, búið) done, finished: **~ að borða** done eating
Búkarest *N fem* (-) Bucharest

Búlgar|i *n masc* (-a, -ar, -a) Bulgarian
Búlgarí|a *N fem* (-u) Bulgaria
búlgarsk|a *n fem* (-görsku) the
Bulgarian language
búlgarsk|ur *adj* (búlgörsk, -t)
Bulgarian
búningsklef|i *n masc* (-a, -ar, -a)
dressing room
búning|ur *n masc* (-s, -ar, -a) costume
búnt *n neu* (-s, -, -a) bundle
búr *n neu* (-s, -, -a) cage
búrhval|ur *n masc* (-s, -ir, -a) *zool*
sperm whale
búset|a *n fem* (-u) residence, housing
búsett|ur *adj* (-, -) living: ~ í Reykja-
vík resides in Reykjavík
búsvæð|i *n neu* (-is, ~, -a) habitat
búvísind|i *n neu pl* (-a) agronomy
bygg *n neu* (-s) barley
byggð|ur *adj* (-, byggt) built
bygging *n fem* (-ar, -ar, -a) building,
structure; construction
byggingarlist *n fem* (-ar) architecture
byggingavöruversl|un *n fem* (-unar,
-anir, -ana) hardware store
byggj|a *v* (byggi, byggði, byggt)
build, construct: ~ á base on;
fyrirbyggja prevent
bylgja|st *v* (~, -ðist, ~) wave
bylting *n fem* (-ar, -ar, -a) revolution
byltingarkennd|ur *adj* (-, -kennt)
revolutionary
byrði *n fem* (-) burden
byrja *v* (~, -ði, -ð) begin, start
byrjand|i *n masc* (-a, byrjendur,
byrjenda) beginner
byrjendabók *n fem* (-ar, -bækur, -a)
primer
byrj|un *n fem* (-unar, -anir, -ana)
beginning, start
byss|a *n fem* (-u, -ur, ~/-na) gun
byssukúl|a *n fem* (-u, -ur, -na) bullet

byssuskot *n neu* (-s, ~, -a) gunshot
býflug|a *n fem* (-u, -ur, -na) bee
býflugnabú *n neu* (-s, -, -a) beehive
býkúp|a *n fem* (-u, -ur, -na/~)
beehive
býl|i *n neu* (-is, ~, -a) farm: **beint af**
~ farm fresh
býsna *adv* quite; fairly
bæði. *See* **báðir**
bæði … og *prep* both … and: **sagan
er bæði sorgleg og fyndin** the
story is both sad and funny
bæjarstjór|i *n masc* (-a, -ar, -a) mayor
bæjarstjórn *n fem* (-ar, -ir, -a)
city/town council
bækling|ur *n masc* (-s, -ar, -a)
booklet, brochure, pamphlet
bæl|a *v* (-i, -di, -t) repress
bæn *n fem* (-ar, -ir, -a) prayer
bænaskrá *n fem* (-ar, -r, -a) petition
bændamarkað|ur *n masc* (-ar/s,
-ir, -a) produce market, farmers'
market
bæ|r *n masc* (-jar, -ir, -ja) town, city
bæt|a *v* (-i, -ti, -t) compensate; patch;
recoup; reform
bæt|ur *n fem pl* (bóta) compensation;
social benefits; patches
bökunarduft *n neu* (-s) baking
powder
bökunarform *n neu* (-s, -, -a) baking
pan
bökunarpappír *n masc* (-s) baking
sheet
bölsýni *n fem* (-) pessimism
bölsýnismað|ur *n masc* (-manns,
-menn, -manna) pessimist
bölsýn|n *adj* (-, bölsýnt) pessimistic
bölva *v* (~, -ði, -ð) swear
börk|ur *n masc* (barkar, berkir,
barka) peel, rind

C

camembertost|ur *n masc* (-s, -ar, -a)
camembert cheese
cayenne pipar *n masc* (-s) cayenne
pepper
chillipipar *n masc* (-s) chili pepper
chillisós|a *n fem* (-u, -ur, -a) chili
sauce

D

dagatal *n neu* (-s, -töl, -a) calendar
dagblað *n neu* (-s, -blöð, -a) newspaper
dagbók *n fem* (-ar, -bækur, -bóka) diary
dagheimil|i *n neu* (-is, ~, -a) day care
daglega *adv* daily
dagleg|ur *adj* (-, -t) daily
dagmamm|a *n fem* (-mömmu, -mömmur, -mamma) nanny
dagrenning *n fem* (-ar, -ar, -a) dawn
dagsetning *n fem* (-ar, -ar, -a) date
dagskrá *n fem* (-r, -r, -a) program, agenda
dagtím|i *n masc* (-a) daytime
dag|ur *n masc* (-s, -ar, -a) day
dal|ur *n masc* (-s, -ir, -a) valley; *econ* dollar
Damaskus *N fem* (-) Damascus
Dan|i *n masc* (-a, -ir, -a) Dane
Danmörk *N fem* (-merkur) Denmark
dans *n masc* (-, -ar, -a) dance
dansa *v* (~, -ði, -ð) dance
dansar|i *n masc* (-a, -ar, -a) dancer
danshreyfing|ar *n fem pl* (-a) choreography
danshöfund|ur *n masc* (-ar, -ar, -a) choreographer
dansk|a *n fem* (dönsku) Danish language
dansk|ur *adj* (dönsk, -t) Danish
dauðadá *n neu* (-s) coma
dauðadóm|ur *n masc* (-s, -ar, -a) death sentence
dauðadrukkin|n *adj* (-, -drukkið) dead drunk
Dauðahaf *N neu* (-s) Dead Sea
dauðhreinsað|ur *adj* (-hreinsuð, -) sterilized
dauð|i *n masc* (-a) death
dauðleg|ur *adj* (-, -t) mortal

dauf|ur *adj* (-, -t) bland
dá *v* (-i, -ði, -ð) admire, adore
dáin|n *adj* (-, dáið) dead
dáleið|a *v* (-i, -leiddi, -leitt) hypnotize
dáleiðsl|a *n fem* (-u) hypnotism
dálítið *adv* somewhat, a little bit
dálk|ur *n masc* (-s, -ar, -a) column
dánartíðni *n fem* (-) mortality rate
dánartilkynning *n fem* (-ar, -ar, -a) death notice
dásama *v* (~, -ði, -ð) praise
dásamleg|ur *adj* (-, -t) fantastic, wonderful
debitkort *n neu* (-s, -, -a) debit card
deig *n neu* (-s) batter, dough
deil|a 1 *n fem* (-u, -ur, -na) quarrel, argument, dispute; **2** *v* (-i, -di, -t) quarrel, argue, dispute; share
deild *n fem* (-ar, -ir, -a) division, league; *(university)* department; *(hospital)* ward
deildarmyrkv|i *n masc* (-a, -ar, -a) partial eclipse
deildarstjór|i *n masc* (-a, -ar, -a) department head
dekk *n neu* (-s, -, -ja) tire
dekra *v* (~, -ði, -ð) pamper
dell|a *n fem* (-u, -ur, -na/~) nonsense; craze, hype
demant|ur *n masc* (-s, -ar, -a) diamond
dempar|i *n masc* (-a, -ar, -a) *mech* shock absorber
depla *v* (~, -ði, -ð) blink
desember *n masc* (-) December
dett|a *v* (-, datt, duttum, dottið) fall, trip
deyfandi *adj med* anesthetic
deyfilyf *n neu* (-s, -, -ja) *med* anesthetic
deyfing *n fem* (-ar, -ar, -a) *med* anaesthesia

deyja *v* (dey, dó, dóum, dáið) die, pass away

dill *n neu* (-s) dill

dimm|a *n fem* (-u) darkness

dimm|ur *adj* (-, -t) dark

dindil|l *n masc* (-s, dindlar, dindla) tail on a lamb or goat

diplómat *n masc* (-s, -ar, -a) diplomat

dirf|ast *v* (-ist, -ðist, -st) dare

dirfsk|a *n fem* (-u) boldness, bravery

diskótek *n neu* (-s, -, -a) discotheque

disk|ur *n masc* (-s, -ar, -a) plate, dish; disc

dísarrunn|i *n masc* (-a, -ar, -a) *flora* lilac

dísil|l *n masc* (-s) diesel

dísilvél *n fem* (-ar, -ar, -a) *mech* diesel motor

djamm *n neu* (-s) *slang* partying

djarf|ur *adj* (djörf, -t) bold, daring

djass *n masc* (-) jazz

djassband *n neu* (-s, -bönd, -a) jazz band

djasssveit *n fem* (-ar, -ir, -a) jazz band

djasstónlist *n fem* (-ar) jazz music

djúphafsrækj|a *n fem* (-u, -ur, -na/~) prawn

djúpsteikt|ur *adj* (-, -) deep fried

djúpstæð|ur *adj* (-, -stætt) deep-seated

djúp|ur *adj* (-, -t) *(depth)* deep; *(emotion)* deep, profound

djús *n masc* (-s, -ar, -a) *colloq* juice

djöful|l *n masc* (-s, djöflar, djöfla) devil

djöfulsins *interj* *vul* darn!, hell!

doktor í hugvísindum *phr* Doctor of Philosophy (Ph.D.)

dollar|i *n masc* (-a, -ar, -a) dollar: **kanadískur** ~ Canadian dollar

dómar|i *n masc* (-a, -ar, -a) *leg* judge; *sports* referee

Dóminíkanska lýðveld|ið *N neu* (-isins) Dominican Republic

dómkirkj|a *n fem* (-u, -ur, -na) cathedral

dómshús *n neu* (-s, -, -a) courthouse

dómsmál *n neu* (-s, -, -a) legal case

dómssvæð|i *n neu* (-is, ~, -a) *leg* jurisdiction

dómstól|l *n masc* (-s, -ar, -a) *leg* court

dóm|ur *n masc* (-s, -ar, -a) *leg* judgement, sentence; the court

dónalega *adv* rudely

dónaleg|ur *adj* (-, -t) rude

dóp *n neu* (-s) narcotics, dope, illegal drugs

dópist|i *n masc* (-a, -ar, -a) drug abuser

dópsal|i *n masc* (-a, -ar, -a) drug dealer

dós *n fem* (-ar, -ir, -a) tin, can

dósamat|ur *n masc* (-ar) canned food

dósamjólk *n fem* (-ur) condensed milk

dósaopnar|i *n masc* (-a, -ar, -a) can opener

dósent *n masc* (-s, -ar, -a) associate professor

dót *n neu* (-s) stuff, thing

dótt|ir *n fem* (-ur, dætur, dætra) daughter

dótturdótt|ir *n fem* (-ur, dætur, dætra) granddaughter *(on the female side)*

dótturfyrirtæk|i *n neu* (-is, ~, -ja) subsidiary

dótturson|ur *n masc* (-ar, -synir, -a) grandson *(on the female side)*

draga *v* (dreg, dró, drógu, dregið) drag, pull; ~ **að sér** attract; ~ **andann** respire; ~ **frá** subtract, deduct; ~ **úr** reduce; ~ **út** extract

dragast *v refl* (dregst, drógst, drógust, dregist) be dragged; ~ **aftur úr** fall behind; ~ **saman** shrink, decrease

dragdrottning *n fem* (-ar, -ar, -a) drag queen

dram|a *n neu* (-a, drömu, ~) drama

dramatísk|ur *adj* (-, -t) dramatic

drang|ur *n masc* (-s, -ar, -a) *geol* stack

drapplitað|ur *adj* (-lituð, -/-litt) beige

draug|ur *n masc* (-s, -ar, -a) ghost, phantom, living dead

draumóramað|ur *n masc* (-manns, -menn, -manna) dreamer

draumór|ar *n masc pl* (-a) pipe dream

draum|ur *n masc* (-s, -ar, -a) dream

dráp *n neu* (-s, ~, drápa) killing

dráttarbíl|l *n masc* (-s, -ar, -a) tow truck

dráttarvél *n fem* (-ar, -ar, -a) tractor

dreggj|ar *n fem pl* (-a) sediment

dregil|l *n masc* (-s, dreglar, dregla) runner; *comp* touch pad

dreif|a *v* (-i, -ði, -t) distribute

dreifar|i *n masc* (-a, -ar, -a) spreader; *slang* a person from outside the capital area

dreifbýli *n neu* (-s) countryside

dreifð|ur *adj* (-, dreift) scattered, sparse

dreifing *n fem* (-ar) distribution

dreifingaraðil|i *n masc* (-a, -ar, -a) distributor

drek|i *n masc* (-a, -ar, -a) dragon

drekk|a *v* (-, drakk, drukkum, drukkið) drink

drekkandi *adj* drinkable

dreng|ur *n masc* (-s, -ir, -ja) boy, lad

drep|a *v* (-, drap, drápum, drepið) kill, slay, assassinate

drepsótt *n fem* (-ar, -ir, -a) pestilence

dreym|a *v + acc subj* (-i, -di, -t) dream: **mig dreymir** I dream

dropastein|n *n masc* (-s, -ar, -a) *geol* stalagmite

drop|i *n masc* (-a, -ar, -a) drop

drottin|n *n masc* (-s, -ar, -na) lord: **~ minn!** my lord!

drottna *v* (~, -ði, -ð) dominate

drottning *n fem* (-ar, -ar, -a) queen

drottnunargjarn *adj* (-gjörn, -t) possessive

drón|i *n masc* (-a, -ar, -a) drone

drukkna *v* (~, -ði, -ð) drown

drull|a *n fem* (-u) mud

drumb|ur *n masc* (-s, -ar, -a) log; *slang* a large and silent person

drusl|a *n fem* (-u, -ur, -na) rags; *colloq* tablecloth; *slang* slut

drykkj|a *n fem* (-u) drinking

drykkjarhæf|ur *adj* (-, -t) drinkable

drykkjumað|ur *n masc* (-manns, -menn, -manna) alcoholic, a person who drinks too much alcohol

drykk|ur *n masc* (-jar, -ir, -ja) drink, beverage

drög *n neu pl* (draga) sketch

duft *n neu* (-s) powder

dufthylk|i *n neu* (-is, ~, -ja) *comp* toner cartridge

dularfull|ur *adj* (-, -t) mysterious

dulnefn|i *n neu* (-is, ~, -a) pseudonym

dulræn|n *adj* (-, -t) mystic, psychic

dulspeki *n fem* (-) mysticism

durg|ur *n masc* (-s, -ar, -a) rude and insensitive person

dúett *n masc* (-s, -ar, -a) duet

dúf|a *n fem* (-u, -ur, -na) pigeon, dove

dúkk|a *n fem* (-u, -ur, -na/~) doll

dúr *n masc* (-s, -ar, -a) *mus* major: **í c ~** in C major

dúrr|a *n fem* (-u) *flora* sorghum

DVD-disk|ur *n masc* (-s, -ar, -a) DVD disc

DVD-spilar|i *n masc* (-a, -ar, -a) DVD player

dvelj|a *v* (dvel, dvaldi, dvalið) stay

dvelj|ast *v refl* (dvelst, dvaldist, dvalist) stay

dvöl *n fem* (dvalar, dvalir, dvala) stay

Dyflinni *N fem* (-ar) Dublin

dyggð *n fem* (-ar, -ir, -a) virtue

dyngj|a *n fem* (-u, -ur, -a) *geol* shield volcano

dyntótt|ur *adj* (-, -) capricious

dyr *n fem pl* (-a) door

dýf|a *n fem* (-u, -ur, ~) dip; dive

dýfing|ar *n fem pl* (-a) *sports* diving

dýn|a *n fem* (-u, -ur, -a) mattress

dýnamít *n neu* (-s) dynamite

dýpt *n fem* (-ar, -ir, -a) depth

dýr 1 *adj* (-, -t) expensive; **2** *n neu* (-s, -, -a) animal

dýragarð|ur *n masc* (-s, -ar, -a) zoo

dýralíf *n neu* (-s) wildlife

dýralækn|ir *n masc* (-is, -ar, -a) veterinarian

dýrð *n fem* (-ar, -ir, -a) glory

dýrka *v* (~, -ði, -ð) admire, adore, worship

dýrk|un *n fem* (-unar, -anir, -ana) worshipping

dýrleg|ur or **dýrðleg|ur** *adj* (-, -t) marvelous, gorgeous

dýrling|ur *n masc* (-s, -ar, -a) saint

dýrmæt|ur *adj* (-, -t) precious

dæl|a 1 *n fem* (-u, -ur, -na/~) pump: **bensín-** ~ gas pump; **2** *v* (-i, -di, -t) pump: ~ **vatni** pump water

dæm|a *v* (-i, -di, -t) sentence, judge

dæm|i *n neu* (-is, ~, -a) example

dæmigerð|ur *adj* (-, -gert) typical

dæmisag|a *n fem* (-sögu, -sögur, -sagna) parable

döðluplóm|a *n fem* (-u, -ur, -a) persimmon

dögg *n fem* (daggar, daggir, dagga) dew

dögurð|ur *n masc* (-ar, -ir, -a) brunch

dökkhærð|ur *adj* (-, -hært) brunet(te)

dökk|ur *adj* (-, -t) dark

dömubind|i *n neu* (-is, ~, -a) sanitary napkin

E

edik *n neu* (-s) vinegar

eða *conj* or

eðalstein|n *n masc* (-s, -ar, -a) jewel, gemstone, precious stone

eðl|a *n fem* (-u, -ur, -a) *zool* lizard

eðlileg|ur *adj* (-, -t) normal, regular

eðlisávísun *n fem* (-ar) instinct

eðlisfræði *n fem* (-) physics

eðlisfræðing|ur *n masc* (-s, -ar, -a) physicist

ef *conj* if

efa *v* (~, -ði, -ð) doubt

efasemd|ir *n fem pl* (-a) reservations, doubts

efa|st *v* (~, -ðist, -st) doubt

efl|a *v* (-i, -di, -t) reinforce

efling *n fem* (-ar, -ar, -a) reinforcement

efnafræði *n fem* (-) chemistry

efnafræðileg|ur *adj* (-, -t) chemical

efnafræðing|ur *n masc* (-s, -ar, -a) chemist

efnahagslægð *n fem* (-ar, -ir, -a) recession

efnahagsmál *n neu pl* (-a) economic issues

efnahagsreikning|ur *n masc* (-s, -ar, -a) balance sheet

efnahag|ur *n masc* (-s, -ir, -a) economy

efnahreins|un *n fem* (-unar, -anir, -ana) dry cleaning

efnaskipt|i *n neu* (-a) metabolism

efn|i *n neu* (-is, ~, -a) substance; material, fabric, cloth; matter, subject, topic: **rannsóknar~** research topic

efnileg|ur *adj* (-, -t) promising

efnisgrein *n fem* (-ar, -ar, -a) *ling* paragraph

efnislega *adv* substantially

efnisleg|ur *adj* (-, -t) material

efnisskrá *n fem* (-ar, -r, -a) program, repertoire

efnisyfirlit *n neu* (-s, -, -a) table of contents

efr|i *adj* (~, -a) *comp* upper: ~ **hæð** second floor; **á ~ hæð** upstairs

efst|ur *adj superl* (-, -) highest

eftir *prep* + *acc (temporal sequence)* after: ~ **skólann** after school; *(causality)* after: **ég var þreytt ~ ferðalagið** I was tired after the travel; *(creation)* by: **bók ~ vinsælan höfund** a book by a popular writer; + *dat (according to)* by: **fara ~ reglunum** go by the rules; *(fetching)* **fara ~** to get, **fara ~ mjólk** go get milk; *(movement along a surface)* along: ~ **ánni** along the river; **á ~** behind, after: **ég kem á ~ þér** I will come behind/after you

eftir á *adv* later on; ~ **að hyggja** in retrospect

eftirfarandi *adj* subsequent, following

eftirför *n fem* (-farar, -farir, -fara) pursuit

eftirherm|un *n fem* (-unar, -anir, -ana) impersonation

eftirköst *n neu pl* (-kasta) repercussion

eftirlaun *n neu pl* (-a) pension

eftirlit *n neu* (-s) surveillance; audit

eftirlitsstöð *n fem* (-var, -var, -va) checkpoint

eftirlíking *n fem* (-ar, -ar, -a) copy, imitation

eftirmál *n neu* (-s, -, -a) consequence

eftirmál|i *n masc* (-a, -ar, -a) *lit* afterword, epoch, postscript

eftirmynd *n fem* (-ar, -ir, -a) replica

eftirnafn *n neu* (-s, -nöfn, -a) last name, surname

eftirprent|un *n fem* (-unar, -anir, -ana) reproduction of an art work

eftirrétt|ur *n masc* (-ar, -ir, -a) dessert

eftirsjá *n fem* (-r) regret
eftirtekt *n fem* (-ar) attention, notice
eftirtektarverð|ur *adj* (-, -vert)
noticeable, noteworthy
egg *n neu* (-s, -, -ja) egg
eggaldin *n neu* (-s, -, -a) eggplant,
aubergine
eggja *v* (~, -ði, -ð) provoke
eggjakak|a *n fem* (-köku, -kökur,
-kakna/~) omelet
eggjaleiðar|i *n masc* (-a, -ar, -a) *anat*
fallopian tube
eggjarauð|a *n fem* (-u, -ur, ~/-na) yolk
eggjasker|i *n masc* (-a, -ar, -a) egg
slicer
eggjaskurn *n fem* (-ar, -ir, -a) egg
shell
eggjastokk|ur *n masc* (-s, -ar, -a)
anat ovary
egglos *n neu* (-s, -, -a) *med* ovulation
egó *n neu* (s) *psych* ego
Egyptaland *N neu* (-s) Egypt
Egypt|i *n masc* (-a, -ar, -a) Egyptian
eið|ur *n masc* (-s, -ar, -a) oath
eiga *v* (á, átti, átt) own: **ég á bíl**
I own a car; have: **ég á hund** I
have a dog; ~ **heima** live; ~ **skilið**
deserve; ~ **von á** expect
eigand|i *n masc* (-a, eigendur, eigenda)
owner, proprietor
eigingirni *n fem* (-) selfishness
eigingjarn *adj* (-gjörn, -t) selfish
eiginhagsmunasegg|ur *n masc* (-, -ir,
-ja) selfish person
eiginkon|a *n fem* (-u, -konur, -kvenna)
wife
eiginlega *adv* actually, basically,
practically
eiginleg|ur *adj* (-, -t) actual
eiginleik|i *n masc* (-a, -ar, -a) property
eiginmað|ur *n masc* (-manns, -menn,
-manna) husband
eiginn *pron* (eigin, eigið) own
eign *n fem* (-ar, -ir, -a) possession,
belonging, asset; acquisition
eignarfall *n neu* (-s, -föll, -a) *ling*
genitive case

eignarhlut|ur *n masc* (-ar, -ir, -a)
econ share
eigna|st *v* (~, -ðist, ~) acquire
eik *n fem* (-ar, -ur, -a) oak
eilíf|ur *adj* (-, -t) eternal, everlasting,
perpetual; **að eilífu** forever
eima *v* (~, -ði, -ð) distill
eimað|ur *adj* (eimuð, -) distilled
ein *num fem* (-a, -ni, nar) one
ein með öllu *phr* hot dog with all
toppings
einangra *v* (~, -ði, -ð) isolate
einangrað|ur *adj* (einangruð, -)
isolated
einangr|un *n fem* (-unar, -anir, -ana)
isolation
einangrunarherberg|i *n neu* (-s, -, -ja)
isolation room
einarð|ur *adj* (einörð, einart) dedicated
einbeit|a *v* (-i, -ti, -t) concentrate
einbeiting *n fem* (-ar) concentration
einbeitt|ur *adj* (-, -) resolute
einbú|i *n masc* (-a, -ar, -a) recluse
eind *n fem* (-ar, -ir, -a) *chem* particle
eindregið *adv* firmly
eineggja *adj bio* identical: ~ **tvíburar**
identical twins
einfaldlega *adv* simply
einfald|ur *adj* (einföld, -t) simple
eingöngu *adv* exclusively, purely
einhver *pron* (-, -t) somebody, someone: **það hringdi ~ í þig áðan**
somebody called you earlier;
some, any: **nennir ~ að hjálpa**
mér? can anyone help me?
einhvern tímann *adv* at some point
einhvern veginn *adv* in some way,
somehow
einhverra hluta vegna *adv* for some
reason
einhvers konar *adv* some kind of:
þetta er ~ ávöxtur this is some
kind of fruit
einhvers staðar *adv* somewhere:
hann er ~ úti he is somewhere
outside
einiber *n neu* (-s, -, -ja) juniper berries

eining *n fem* (-ar, -ar, -a) unit
einkaeign *n fem* (-ar, -ir, -a) private property
einkafyrirtæk|i *n neu* (-is, ~, -ja) private company
einkakennar|i *n masc* (-a, -ar, -a) tutor
einkaleyf|i *n neu* (-is, ~, -a) patent
einkalíf *n neu* (-s) private life
einkareikning|ur *n masc* (-s, -ar, -a) private account
einkasjúkrahús *n neu* (-s, -, -a) private hospital
einkaskól|i *n masc* (-a, -ar, -a) private school
einkatím|i *n masc* (-a, -ar, -a) tutorial
einkatölv|a *n fem* (-u, -ur, ~) personal computer (PC)
einkaumboð *n neu* (-s, -, -a) franchise
einkavæðing *n fem* (-ar) privatization
einkennandi *adj* characteristic, peculiar
einkenn|i *n neu* (-is, ~, -a) attribute, characteristic, feature; *med* symptom
einkennisbúning|ur *n masc* (-s, -ar, -a) uniform
einkirningasótt *n fem* (-ar) *med* infectious mononucleosis
einkunn *n fem* (-ar, -ir, -a) grade point: **meðaleinkunn** grade point average
einkunnagjöf *n fem* (-gjafar, -gjafir, -gjafa) assessment
einleikar|i *n masc* (-a, -ar, -a) *mus* soloist
einleik|ur *n masc* (-s) *mus* solo: **fiðlueinleikur** violin solo
einlæg|ur *adj* (-, -t) sincere, devoted
einmana *adv* lonely
einmitt *adv* exactly, precisely
ein|n 1 *pron* (-, eitt) alone, single, solo; **2** *num* (~, -um, -s) one
einnig *adv* also, too
einnota *adj* disposable
einok|un *n fem* (-unar, -anir, -ana) monopoly

einræða *n fem* (-u, -ur, -na/~) monologue
einræði *n neu* (-s) dictatorship
einræðisvald *n neu* (-s, -völd, -valda) autocracy
eins *adv* alike, the same; ~ **og** like: **hann er ~ og gamall maður** he is like an old man; ~ **og er** at the moment, currently
einskær *adj* (-, -t) sheer, pure
einslega *adv* privately
einstaka *adj* single, occurring now and then: **ég les bækur ~ sinnum** I read books every now and then
einstaklega *adv* singularly
einstakling|ur *n masc* (-s, -ar, -a) individual
einstak|ur *adj* (-stök, -t) singular, unique
einstefna *n fem* (-u) one-way traffic
einstefnuakstur *n masc* (-s) one-way traffic
einstefnugat|a *n fem* (-götu, -götur, -gatna) one-way street
einstæð|ur *adj* (-, stætt) single, unique
eintak *n neu* (-s, -tök, -a) specimen
eintal|a *n fem* (-tölu) *ling* singular number
einu sinni *phr* once: ~ **var** once upon a time
einungis *adv* only, just, merely
einvald|ur *n masc* (-s, -ar, -a) autocrat
einvörðungu *adv* only, purely
eirðarleysing|i *n masc* (-ja, -jar, -ja) a restless person, a person unwilling to stay in one place for long
eist|a *n neu* (-a, -u, -na) testicle
Eist|i *n masc* (-a, -ar, -a) Estonian
Eistland *N neu* (-s) Estonia
eistnesk|a *n fem* (-u) Estonian language
eitra *v* (~, -ði, -ð) poison
eitrað|ur *adj* (eitruð, -) poisonous, toxic
eitt *num neu* (~, einu, eins) one
eitthvað *pron* something; anything, any

eitthvað svoleiðis *phr* something like that

eitur *n neu* (~s, ~, eitra) poison, toxin, venom

eiturlyf *n neu* (-s, -, -ja) narcotics, drugs

eiturlyfjafík|ill *m masc* (-ils, -lar, -la) drug abuser

eiturlyfjasal|i *n masc* (-a, -ar, -a) drug dealer

eiturlyfjaviðskipt|i *n neu pl* (-a) drug trafficking

ekkert *pron neu* nothing

ekkert fleira *phr* that's all; is that all?

ekki *adv* not

ekki slæmt *phr* not bad

ekkil|l *n masc* (-s, ekklar, ekkla) widower

ekkj|a *n fem* (-u, -ur, ekkna) widow

ekr|a *n fem* (-u, -ur, ~) acre

ekta *adj* genuine; sterling

Ekvador *N neu* (-) Ecuador

El Salvador *N neu* (-) El Salvador

elda *v* (~, -ði, -ð) cook

eldabusk|a *n fem* (-u, -ur, -na) cook

eldamennsk|a *n fem* (-u) cooking

eld|ast *v* (-ist, eltist, elst) aging, getting older

eldavél *n fem* (-ar, -ar, -a) stove

eldfim|ur *adj* (-, -t) flammable

eldfjall *n neu* (-s, -fjöll, -a) *geol* volcano

eldfjallaask|a *n fem* (-ösku) *geol* volcanic ash

eldfjallaeyj|a *n fem* (-eyju, -eyjar, -eyja) *geol* volcanic island

eldfjallafræði *n fem* (-) *geol* volcanology

eldfjallasvæð|i *n neu* (-is, ~, -a) *geol* volcanic region

eldflaug *n fem* (-ar, -ar, -a) rocket

eldgos *n neu* (-s, -, -a) *geol* volcanic eruption

eldgosatímabil *n neu* (-s, -, -a) *geol* volcanic era

eldhús *n neu* (-s, -, -a) kitchen

eldhúsbekk|ur *n masc* (-jar/s, -ir, -ja) kitchen counter

eldhúsborð *n neu* (-s, -, -a) kitchen table

eldhúsbréf *n neu* (-s, -, -a) kitchen towel; tissue

eldhúskrók|ur *n masc* (-s, -ar, -a) kitchenette

eldhúsrúll|a *n fem* (-u, -ur, ~/-na) roll of kitchen towels; tissues

eldhúsverkfær|i *n neu* (-is, ~, -a) kitchen utensils

elding *n fem* (-ar, -ar, -a) lightning

eldivið|ur *n masc* (-ar) firewood

eldr|i *adj compar* (~, -a) older

eldri borgari *phr* senior citizen

eldsneyti *n neu* (-s) fuel

eldsneytismæl|ir *n masc* (-is, -ar, -a) *mach* gas meter, fuel gauge

eldsneytistank|ur *n masc* (-s, -ar, -a) *mach* gas tank, fuel tank

eldspýt|a *n fem* (-u, -ur, -na) match

eldstæð|i *n neu* (-s, -, -a) firepit

eldunaraðferð *n fem* (-ar, -ir, -a) method of cooking

eldunaraðstað|a *n fem* (-aðstöðu) cooking facilities

eld|ur *n masc* (-s, -ar, -a) fire

eldvegg|ur *n masc* (-jar/s, -ir, ja) *comp* firewall

eldvirkni *n fem* (-) *geol* volcanic activity

elg|ur *n masc* (-s, -ir, -a) elk, moose

elleft|i *ord* (-a, -a) eleventh

ellefu *num* eleven

ellilífeyr|ir *n masc* (-is) pension

elska *v* (~, -ði, -ð) love

elskhug|i *n masc* (-a, -ar, -a) lover

elst|ur *adj superl* (-, -) oldest

elt|a *v* (-i, -ti, -t) chase, follow, pursue

embættismað|ur *n masc* (-manns, -menn, -manna) governmental officer

en *conj (in contrasts)* but: **ég vildi fara en komst ekki** I wanted to go but couldn't; *(without contrast)* **ég er á leiðinni í afmæli til Sigga**

~ **hann á afmæli** I'm on my way
to Siggi's birthday party. He has
birthday today; *(in comparisons)*
than: **hún er eldri ~ hann** she is
older than him
enda 1 *v* (~, -ði, -ð) end; **2** *conj*
because (as we know): **ég tók mér
frí ~ var veðrið svo gott** I took a
vacation because (as we know) the
weather was so good
endajaxl *n masc* (-s, -ar, -a) wisdom
tooth
endalaus *adj* (-, -t) endless
endanleg|ur *adj* (-, -t) final, ultimate
endanleik|i *n masc* (-a) finality
end|ast *v* (-ist, entist, enst) last
endastöð *n fem* (-var, -var, -va)
terminal station
endaþarm|ur *n masc* (-s, -ar, -a)
anat rectum
endingartím|i *n masc* (-a) duration
end|ir *n masc* (-is, -ar, -a) end, ending
endunýjað|ur *adj* (-nýjuð, -) updated,
renovated
endurbót *n fem* (-bótar, bætur, bóta)
reform
endurbyggj|a *v* (-byggi, -byggði,
-byggt) rebuild, rehabilitate
endurbæt|a *v* (-i, ti, -t) reform
endurbætt|ur *adj* (-, -) improved,
updated
endurfæðing *n fem* (-ar, -ar, -a)
rebirth
endurgerð *n fem* (-ar, -ir, -a) remake,
reproduction, restoration
endurgjalda *v* (-geld, -galt, -guldum,
-goldið) reciprocate
endurgreið|a *v* (-i, -greiddi, -greitt)
reimburse
endurgreiðsl|a *n fem* (-u, -ur, -na)
refund, reimbursement, repayment
endurheimta *v* (~, -ði, -ð) reclaim,
recover, redeem, retrieve
endurhlaða *v* (-hleð, -hlóð, -hlóðum,
-hlaðið) recharge
endurhæf|a *v* (-i, -ði, -t) rehabilitate
endurhæfing *n fem* (-ar) rehabilitation

endurkast *n neu* (-s, -köst, -a)
reflection
endurkom|a *n fem* (-u, -ur, ~/-na)
return
endurkraf|a *n fem* (-kröfu, -kröfur,
-krafna) reclamation
endurlífga *v* (~, -ði, -ð) regenerate,
revive
endurlífg|un *n fem* (-unar, -anir, -ana)
revival
endurminning *n fem* (-ar, -ar, -a)
memories
endurminningar *n fem pl* (-a) memoir
endurnýja *v* (~, -ði, -ð) renew
endurnýj|un *n fem* (-unar, -anir, -ana)
renewal; replacement; rehabilitation; regeneration; recruitment
endurnærandi *adj* refreshing
endurprenta *v* (~, -ði, -ð) reprint
endurreisn *n fem* (-ar) regeneration;
renaissance: **endurreisnartímabilið** the Renaissance period
endurskinsmerk|i *n neu* (-is, ~, -ja)
reflector
endurskip|un *n fem* (-unar, -anir,
-ana) reinstatement
endurskoða *v* (~, -ði, -ð) audit; revise
endurskoðand|i *n masc* (-a, -endur,
-enda) auditor
endurskoð|un *n fem* (-unar, -anir,
-ana) revision
endursköp|un *n fem* (-sköpunar,
-skapanir, -skapana) reproduction
endurspegla *v* (~, -ði, -ð) mirror,
reflect
endur|tak|a *v* (-tek, -tók, -tókum,
-tekið) repeat
endurtalning *n fem* (-ar, -ar, -a) recount
endurtekin|n *adj* (-, -tekið) recurrent,
repeated
endurtekning *n fem* (-ar, -ar, -a)
recurrence, repetition
enduruppbygging *n fem* (-ar)
restoration
enduruppgerð|ur *adj* (-, -gert) rebuilt
endurvakning *n fem* (-ar) resurgence,
revival

endurvekj|a v (-vek, -vakti, -vöktum, -vakið) recapture; rekindle, start again

endurvinn|a v (-, -vann, -unnum, -unnið) recycle

endurvinnanleg|ur adj (-, -t) recyclable

endurvinnsl|a n fem (-u) recycling

eng|i n neu (-is, ~, -ja) meadow

engifer n neu (-s) ginger

engiferduft n neu (-s) ginger powder

engiferöl n neu (-s) ginger ale

engil|l n masc (-s, englar, engla) angel

engin|n pron (-, ekkert) nobody: ~ sá mig nobody saw me; no one: ~ skildi mig no one understood me

engisprett|a n fem (-u, -ur, -a) locust

England N neu (-s) England

Englending|ur n masc (-s, -ar, -a) English, a person from England

enn adv still, yet

enn fremur adv furthermore

enn|i n neu (-is, ~, -a) forehead

ennishol|a n fem (-u, -ur, -a) sinus

ennþá adv still, yet

ensím|i n neu (-is, ~, -a) bio enzyme

ensk|a n fem (-u) the English language

enskumælandi adj English-speaking

ensk|ur adj (-, -t) English

eplabak|a n fem (-böku, bökur, ~/-na) apple pie

eplamauk n neu (-s) applesauce

eplamús n fem (-ar) applesauce

eplasaf|i n masc (-a, -ar, -a) apple juice

epl|i n neu (-is, ~, -a) apple

erfðabreytt|ur adj (-, -) genetically modified: ~ matur genetically modified food

erfðaefn|i n neu (-is, ~, -a) DNA

erfðafræði n fem (-) genetics

erfðafræðilega adv genetically

erfðafræðileg|ur adj (-, -t) med genetic

erfðaskrá n fem (-r, -r, -a) testament

erfðavís|ir n masc (-is, -ar, -a) gene

erfiða v (~, -ði, -ð) plod

erfiðleik|ar n masc pl (-a) difficulty, adversity

erfið|ur adj (-, erfitt) difficult, hard, rough, tough

ergj|a v (ergi, ergði, ergt) aggravate, irritate

erind|i n neu (-is, ~, -a) stanza, verse

erkibiskup n masc (-s, -ar, -a) archbishop

erlendis adv abroad, overseas

erlend|ur adj (-, erlent) foreign

erm|i n fem (-ar, -ar, -a) sleeve

erótísk|ur adj (-, -t) erotic

ESB abbrev European Union (EU)

espa v (~, -ði, -ð) provoke

espressó n neu (-s) espresso

espressókann|a n fem (-könnu, -könnur, -kanna) espresso pot

evr|a n fem (-u, -ur, -a) econ Euro: tíu evrur ten Euros

Evrasíufleki n masc (-a, -ar, -a) geol the Eurasian plate

Evróp|a N fem (-u) Europe

evrópsk|ur adj (-, -t) European

Evrópubú|i n (-a, -ar, -a) European

eyð|a 1 n fem (-u, -ur, -a) blank; 2 v (-i, eyddi, eytt) delete; spend; waste

eyð|ast v refl (-ist, eyddist, eyðst) decay

eyðilagð|ur adj (eyðilögð, eyðilagt) destroyed

eyðilegging n fem (-ar) destruction, ruin

eyðileggj|a v (-legg, -lagði, -lagt) destroy, ruin, sabotage

eyðimörk n fem (-merkur/markar, -merkur, -marka) desert

eyðing n fem (-ar, -ar, -a) obliteration

eyðni n fem (-) AIDS

eyðsla n fem (-u) waste

eyðslusam|ur adj (-söm, -t) wasteful; prodigal

eyðslusemi n fem (-) prodigality

eyðublað n neu (-s, -blöð, -a) form

eyj|a n fem (-u, -ur, ~) island

eyr|a n neu (~, -u, -na) anat ear

eyrnabólg|a *n fem* (-u) *med* ear
infection
eyrnadrop|ar *n masc pl* (-a) *med*
ear drops
eyrnalokk|ur *n masc* (-s, -ar, -a)
earring
eyrnamerg|ur *n masc* (-s) ear wax
eyrnaskjól *n neu pl* (-s, -, -a)
earmuff
eyrnatapp|i *n masc* (-a, -ar, -a) ear
plug

eyrnaverk|ur *n masc* (-s, -ir, -ja)
med earache
Eystrasalt *N neu* (-salts) Baltic Sea
exi *n fem* (axar) axe, hatchet
Eþíópí|a *N fem* (-u) Ethiopia
eþíópsk|ur *adj* (-, -t) Ethiopian
Eþíópumað|ur *n masc* (-manns,
-menn, -manna) Ethiopian

É

ég *pron* I
él *n neu* (-s, ~, élja) snow, hail
ét|a *v* (-, át, átum, étið) *(animals)* eat
ét|ast *v refl* (-ast, ást, étist) be eaten

F

fað|ir *n masc* (föður, feður, feðra)
father
faðma *v* (~, -ði, -ð) hug, embrace
faðmlag *n neu* (-s, -lög, -a) hug,
embrace
fagmannleg|ur *adj* (-, -t) professional
fagna *v* (~, -ði, -ð) celebrate, rejoice
fagnað|ur *n masc* (-ar, -ir, -a)
celebration
fagott *n neu* (-s, -, -a) *mus* bassoon
fag|ur *adj* (fögur, -t) beautiful
fagurfræði *n fem* (-) aesthetics
fagurfræðileg|ur *adj* (-, -t) aesthetic
fall *n neu* (-s, föll, -a) fall, drop, fail;
ling case: **nefnifall** nominative
case
fall|a *v* (fell, féll, féllum, fallið) fall,
fail
fallega *adv* beautifully
falleg|ur *adj* (-, -t) beautiful
fallhlíf *n fem* (-ar, -ar, -a) parachute
fallhlífarstökk *n neu* (-s, -, -a) jump
with parachute
fallhlífastökkvar|i *n masc* (-a, -ar,
-a) sky diver
fallstökk *n neu* (-s, -, -a) sky diving
falsa *v* (~, -ði, -ð) forge
falsað|ur *adj* (fölsuð, -) false, forged
falsk|ur *adj* (fölsk, -t) insincere; *mus*
off tune
fangels|i *n neu* (-is, ~, -a) prison, jail
fangels|un *n fem* (-unar, -anir, -ana)
imprisonment, incarceration,
captivity
fang|i *n masc* (-a, -ar, -a) prisoner,
captive
fantasí|a *n fem* (-u, -ur, -a) *lit* fantasy
fant|ur *n masc* (-s, -ar, -a) rough person
far|a *v* (fer, fór, fórum, farið) go,
leave, depart; ~ **á hestbak** go
horseback riding; ~ **á puttanum**
hitchhike; ~ **frá** leave someone; ~
úr undress; *med* ~ **úr lið** dislocate
a joint
farangur *n masc* (-s) baggage
farangurshill|a *n fem* (-u, -ur, -na/~)
rack for baggage
farangursgeymsl|a *n fem* (-u, -ur,
-na) locker for baggage
farangursinnrit|un *n fem* (-unar,
-anir, -ana) baggage check-in
counter
farangurskerr|a *n fem* (-u, -ur, -a)
baggage cart
farangurskvitt|un *n fem* (-unar,
-anir, -ana) claim check
farangursmóttak|a *n fem* (-móttöku)
baggage claim area
fararstjór|i *n masc* (-a, -ar, -a) tour
guide
farartæk|i *n neu* (-is, ~, -ja) vehicle
far|ast *v* (ferst, fórst, fórumst, farist)
perish
farð|i *n masc* (-a, -ar, -a) make-up
farfugl *n masc* (-s, -ar, -a) *zool*
migrant bird
farfuglaheimil|i *n neu* (-is, ~, -a)
youth hostel, hostel
fargjald *n neu* (-s, -gjöld, -a) fare
farin|n *adj* (-, farið) gone
farm|ur *n masc* (-s, -ar, -a) cargo
farrým|i *n neu* (-is, ~, -a) travel class
farseðil|l *n masc* (-s, -seðlar, -seðla)
ticket
farsím|i *n masc* (-a, -ar, -a) cellphone,
mobile phone
farsæl|l *adj* (-, -t) successful
fartölv|a *n fem* (-u, -ur, -a) *comp*
laptop
farþeg|i *n masc* (-a, -ar, -a) passenger
fasan|i *n masc* (-a, -ar, -a) *zool*
pheasant

fas|i *n masc* (-a, -ar, -a) phase
fast *adv* firmly, tightly
fast|a *n fem* (föstu) Lent (time before Easter)
fasteign *n fem* (-ar, -ir, -a) real estate
fasteignasal|i *n masc* (-a, -ar, -a) real estate agent
fastheldni *n fem* (-) insistence
fast|ur *adj* (föst, -t) stuck
fat *n neu* (-s, föt, -a) big plate, platter
fat|a *n fem* (fötu, fötur, ~) bucket, pail
fatabúð *n* clothing store
fatageymsl|a *n fem* (-u, -ur, -a) cloakroom
fataheng|i *n neu* (-is, ~, -ja) cloak-room
fataskáp|ur *n masc* (-s, -ar, -a) wardrobe, closet
fatlað|ur *adj* (fötluð, -) disabled, handicapped
fatl|i *n masc* (-a, -ar, -a) *med* sling: **með hönd í fatla** with an arm in a sling
fatnað|ur *n masc* (-ar, -ir, -a) clothing
fax *n neu* (-, föx, -a) fax
faxa *v* (~, -ði, -ð) fax
faxtæk|i *n neu* (-is, ~, -ja) fax machine
fá *v* (fæ, fékk, fengum, fengið) get, gain, acquire; ~ **lánað** borrow
fáanleg|ur *adj* (-, -t) available
fáein|ir *pron pl* (-ar, -) a few
fáfnisgras *n neu* (-s, -grös, -a) tarragon
fágað|ur *adj* (fáguð, -) refined, sophisticated
fáir *pron pl* (fáar, fá) few
fálk|i *n masc* (-a, -ar, -a) *zool* falcon
fálma *v* (~, -ði, -ð) fumble
fámennisstjórn *n fem* (-ar, -ir, -a) oligarchy
fán|i *n masc* (-a, -ar, -a) flag
fáránleg|ur *adj* (-, -t) absurd, bizarre, ridiculous
fát *n neu* (-s) perplexity
fátækling|ur *n masc* (-s, -ar, -a) pauper
fátækrahverf|i *n neu* (-is, ~, -a) slum

fátækt *n fem* (-ar) poverty
fátæk|ur *adj* (-, -t) poor
febrúar *n masc* (-) February
fegurð *n fem* (-ar) beauty
fegurðarsamkeppn|i *n fem* (~, -ir, -a) beauty pageant
feimin|n *adj* (-, feimið) shy
feiti *n fem* (-) fat, oil; shortening
feit|ur *adj* (-, -t) fat
fel|a *v* (-, faldi, falið) hide
feld|ur *n masc* (-ar, -ir, -a) fur
fell|a *v* (-i, -di, -t) trip someone over; fail
felliglugg|i *n masc* (-a, -ar, -a) *comp* drop-down menu
femínism|i *n masc* (-a) feminism
femínist|i *n masc* (-a, -ar, -a) feminist
fen *n neu* (-s, -, -a/-ja) swamp, marsh
fenník|a *n fem* (-u, -ur, -a) fennel
ferð *n fem* (-ar, -ir, -a) journey, tour, ride, trip
ferðaáætl|un *n fem* (-unar, -anir, -ana) itinerary
ferðaávís|un *n fem* (-unar, -anir, -ana) traveler's check
ferðahandbók *n fem* (-ar, -bækur, -bóka) travel guide
ferðahóp|ur *n masc* (-s, -ar, -a) tour group
ferðalag *n neu* (-s, -lög, -a) trip, travel
ferðalang|ur *n masc* (-s, -ar, -a) traveler
ferðamað|ur *n masc* (-manns, -menn, -manna) tourist, traveler
ferðamannastað|ur *n masc* (-ar, -ir, -a) holiday resort, tourist attraction, place of interest
ferðamennsk|a *n fem* (-u) tourism; traveling
ferðaskrifstof|a *n fem* (-u, -ur, -a) travel agency
ferða|st *v* (~, -ðist, ~) travel
ferðatask|a *n fem* (-tösku, -töskur, -taska) suitcase
ferðavagg|a *n fem* (-vöggu, -vöggur, -vagga) portable crib

ferðaþjónust|a *n fem* (-u) tourist business

ferfald|ur *adj* (-föld, -falt) quadruple

ferhyrning|ur *n masc* (-s, -ar, -a) *math* quadrangle

ferj|a *n fem* (-u, -ur, -a) ferry

fern|a *n fem* (-u, -ur, -a) carton

ferning|ur *n masc* (-s, -ar, -a) *math* square

fern|ir *adj pl* (-ar, -) *(for plural words)* four: **fern skæri** four scissors; *(things that come in two)* four pairs: ~ **sokkar** four socks, **fern hjón** four couples

ferskj|a *n fem* (-u, -ur, ferskna/-a) peach

fersk|ur *adj* (-, -t) fresh

ferskvatn *n neu* (-i, -, -a) fresh water

fertugasti *ord* (-a, -a) fortieth

fertug|ur *adj* (-, -t) forty years old

fest|a *v* (-i, -i, -) fasten, attach

fest|ast *v refl* (-ist, -ist, -s) stick, get stuck; ~ **við** adhere

fé *n neu* (fjár) sheep; money

félag *n neu* (-s, félög, -a) company, club, organization, partnership

félag|i *n masc* (-a, -ar, -a) companion, partner, friend, member

félagsaðild *n fem* (-ar) membership

félagsfræði *n fem* (-) sociology

félagsfræðileg|ur *adj* (-, -t) sociological

félagsfræðing|ur *n masc* (-s, -ar, -a) sociologist

félagsheimil|i *n neu* (-is, ~, -a) clubhouse

félagslega *adv* socially

félagsleg|ur *adj* (-, -t) social: **félagsleg aðstoð** social support

félagslynd|ur *adj* (-, -lynt) social, sociable

félagsráðgjaf|i *n masc* (-a, -ar, -a) social worker

félagsskap|ur *n masc* (-ar) association, society, company: **í góðum félagsskap** in good company

félagsvísindi *n neu pl* social sciences

fiðl|a *n fem* (-u, -ur, -a) *mus* violin

fiðrild|i *n neu* (-is, ~, -a) butterfly

Filippseyjar *N fem pl* (-eyja) Philippines

filippseysk|ur *adj* (-, -t) Filipino

film|a *n fem* (-u, -ur, -a) *(for camera)* film

fimleikakon|a *n fem* (-u, -konur, -kvenna) *(female)* gymnast

fimleikamað|ur *n masc* (-manns, -menn, -manna) *(male)* gymnast

fimleik|ar *n masc pl* (-a) gymnastics

fimm *num* five

fimmhyrning|ur *n masc* (-s, -ar, -a) *math* pentagon

fimmtán *num* fifteen

fimmtándi *ord* (-a, -a) fifteenth

fimmti *ord* (-a, -a) fifth

fimmtíu *num* fifty

fimmtudag|ur *n masc* (-s, -ar, -a) Thursday

fimmtugasti *ord* (-a, -a) fiftieth

fimmtug|ur *adj* (-, -t) fifty years old

fim|ur *adj* (-, -t) nimble

fingur *n masc* (-s, -, fingra) finger

fingurgóm|ur *n masc* (-s, -ar, -a) fingertip

finn|a *v* (-, fann, fundum, fundið) find, notice, detect; ~ **upp** invent; ~ **fyrir** notice, feel; ~ **til** feel pain

finnast *v + dat subj* (finnst, fannst, fundist) find: **mér finnst ...** I find ...; learn: **honum finnst gaman að læra íslensku** he enjoys learning Icelandic; to be found: **þetta finnst aldrei** this will never be found

Finn|i *N masc* (-a, -ar, -a) Finn

Finnland *N neu* (-s) Finland

finnsk|a *n fem* (-u) the Finnish language

finnsk|ur *adj* (-, -t) Finnish

fiskabúr *n neu* (-s, -, -a) aquarium

Fiskarnir *n masc pl def* (-anna) *astro* Pisces

fiskborð *n neu* (-s, -, -a) fish counter

fiskbúð *n fem* (-ar, -ir, -a) fish store

fiskflak *n neu* (-s, -flök, -a) fish fillet

fiskiboll|a *n fem* (-u, -ur, -a) fishball

fiskihlaup *n neu* (-s, -, -a) fish jelly
fiskinet *n neu* (-s, -, -a) fishing net
fiskiofnæmi *n neu* (-s) fish allergy
fiskisoð *n neu* (-s) fish stock
fiskisós|a *n fem* (-u, -ur, -a) fish sauce
fiskstykk|i *n neu* (-is, ~, -ja) piece of fish
fit|a 1 *n fem* (-u, -ur, -a) fat; **2 fita** *v* (~, -ði, -ð) fatten
fitna *v* (~, -ði, -ð) put on weight
fitug|ur *adj* (-, -t) greasy, oily
fitusnauð|ur *adj* (-, -snautt) fat-free, low-fat
Fídjí *N neu* (-) Fiji
fídjísk|ur *adj* (-, -t) Fijian
fífa *n fem* (-u, -ur, -a) *flora* cotton grass
fífil|l *n masc* (-s, fíflar, fífla) *flora* dandelion
fígúr|a *n fem* (-u, -ur, -a) weird character
fíkj|a *n fem* (-u, -ur, ~) fig
fíkn *n fem* (-ar, -ir, -a) addiction
fíkniefnasal|i *n masc* (-a, -ar, -a) drug dealer
fíkniefn|i *n neu* (-is, ~, -a) narcotics, illegal drugs
Fílabeinsströnd|in *N fem* (-stranda-rinnar) Cote d'Ivoire, Ivory Coast
fílólóg *n masc* (-s, -ar, -a) philologist
fílólógí|a *n fem* (-u) philology
fílólógísk|ur *adj* (-, -t) philological
fínlega *adv* finely
fínleg|ur *adj* (-, -t) fine
fín|n *adj* (-, -t) fine, nice, dressed up
fjall *n neu* (-s, fjöll, -a) mountain
fjallahjól *n neu* (-s, -, -a) mountain bike
fjallaklifur *n neu* (-s, -, -klifa) mountain climbing, mountaineering
fjallaref|ur *n masc* (-s, -ir, -a) *zool* artic fox
fjallgang|a *n fem* (-göngu, -göngur, -gangna) mountain hike
fjallgarð|ur *n masc* (-s, -ar, -a) mountain range
fjallgöngubúnað|ur *n masc* (-ar) hiking gear

fjallgöngumað|ur *n masc* (-manns, -menn, -manna) mountaineer
fjallshrygg|ur *n masc* (-jar, -ir, -ja) ridge
fjandsamleg|ur *adj* (-, -t) hostile
fjandskap|ur *n masc* (-ar) hostility
fjar|a *n fem* (fjöru, fjörur, fjara) seashore
fjark|i *n masc* (-a, -ar, -a) number four
fjarlægð *n fem* (-ar, -ir, -a) distance
fjarlægj|a *v* (-lægi, -lægði, -lægt) remove
fjarlæg|ur *adj* (-, -t) distant, remote
fjarskipt|i *n neu pl* (-a) telecommunications
fjarstýring *n fem* (-ar, -ar, -a) remote control
fjarstæðukennd|ur *adj* (-, -kennt) absurd
fjarsýn|n *adj* (-, -t) far-sighted, long-sighted
fjarver|a *n fem* (-u) absence
fjarverandi *adj* absent
fjarvist *n fem* (-ar, -ir, -a) absence
fjarvistarsönn|un *n fem* (-unar, -sannanir, -sannana) alibi
fjárfest|a *v econ* (-i, -i, -) invest
fjárfesting *n fem* (-ar, -ar, -a) *econ* investment
fjárfest|ir *n masc* (-ar, -ar, -a) *econ* investor
fjárhagsáætl|un *n fem* (-unar, -anir, -ana) *econ* budget
fjárhagsleg|ur *adv* (-, -t) *econ* financial
fjárhag|ur *n masc* (-s) *econ* finance
fjárhald *n neu* (-s) *leg* guardianship
fjárhaldsmað|ur *n masc* (-manns, -menn, -manna) *leg* guardian, trustee
fjárhús *n neu* (-s, -, -a) sheepfold
fjárhættuspil *n neu* (-s, -, -a) gambling
fjárkúg|un *n fem* (-unar, -anir, -ana) blackmail
fjármagna *v* (~, -ði, -ð) *econ* finance, fund

fjármál *n neu pl* (-a) finance

fjármálaráðuneyti *n neu* (-s) *econ* treasury

fjármögn|un *n fem* (-unar, -magnanir, -magnana) *econ* funding

fjársjóð|ur *n masc* (-ar, -ir, -a) treasure: **fjársjóðaleit** treasure hunt

fjársvik *n neu pl* (-a) fraud

fjárvörsluaðil|i *n masc* (-a, -ar, -a) *leg* fiduciary

fjáröfl|un *n fem* (-unar, -aflanir, -aflana) fundraiser

fjólublá|r *adj* (-, -tt) purple

fjórar *num fem* (~, fjórum, fjögurra) four

fjórð|i *ord* (-a, -a) fourth

fjórðungsúrslit *n neu pl* (-s, -, -a) *sports* quarter final

fjórðung|ur *n masc* (-s, -ar, -a) quarter

fjórhjól *n neu* (-s, -, -a) quad bike

fjórhjóladrif *n neu* (-s, -, -a) four-wheel drive

fjórir *num masc* (fjóra, fjórum, fjögurra) four

fjórtán *num* fourteen

fjórtándi *ord* (-a, -a) fourteenth

fjós *n neu* (-s, -, -a) cowshed: **fjósakaffi** cowshed café

fjöð|ur *n masc* (fjaðrar, fjaðrir, fjaðra) feather; spring

fjögur *num neu* (~, fjórum, fjögurra) four

fjögurradyra *adj* four-door

fjölbreytileik|i *n masc* (-a) multiplicity

fjölbreytni *n fem* (-) variety

fjöldafund|ur *n masc* (-ar, -ir, -a) rally

fjöldamorð *n neu* (-s, -, -a) massacre

fjöld|i *n masc* (-a) multitude, great number: ~ **manns** a great number of people

fjölga *v* (~, -ði, -ð) increase something; ~ **sér** reproduce

fjölg|un *n fem* (-unar, -anir, -ana) reproduction

fjölkornabrauð *n neu* (-s, -, -a) multi-grain bread

fjölkvæni *n neu* (-s) polygamy

fjölleikahús *n neu* (-s, -, -a) circus

fjöllótt|ur *adj* (-, -) mountainous

fjölmarg|ir *pron* (-ar, -mörg) great many

fjölmiðil|l *n masc* (-miðils, -miðlar, -miðla) media

fjölskyld|a *n fem* (-u, -ur, -na) family

fjöltyngd|ur *adj* (-, -tyngt) polyglot

fjölþjóðleg|ur *adj* (-, -t) multinational

fjörð|ur *n masc* (fjarðar, firðir, fjarða) fjord, fiord

fjörfisk|ur *n masc* (-s) *med* tic

fjörkálf|ur *n masc* (-s, -ar, -a) romp

fjörleg|ur *adj* (-, -t) vital

fjörukál *n neu* (-s) sea kale

fjörutíu *num* forty

flag|a *n fem* (flögu, flögur, -na) chip, flake

flaggskip *n neu* (-s, -, -a) flagship

flambering *n fem* (-ar, -ar, -a) flambé

flask|a *n fem* (flösku, flöskur, -na) bottle

flass *n neu* (-, flöss, -a) flash

flassmyndatak|a *n fem* (-töku, -tökur, ~) flash photography

flatbrauð *n neu* (-s, -, -a) flatbread (Icelandic specialty)

flatfisk|ur *n masc* (-s, -ar, -a) flatfish

flat|ur *adj* (flöt, -t) flat; stale

flauel *n neu* (-s) velvet

flaut|a 1 *n fem* (-u, -ur, -na/~) *mus* flute; horn on a car; **2 flauta** *v* honk the horn

fleirtal|a *n fem* (-tölu) *ling* plural number

flekakenning *n fem* (-ar, -ar, -a) *geol* plate tectonics

flek|i *n masc* (-a, -ar, -a) *geol* plate: **flekar jarðarinnar** tectonic plates

flekklaus *adj* (-, -t) stainless

flens|a *n fem* (-u, -ur, -a) *med* flu

flest|ir *pron pl* (-ar, -) most

flett|a *v* (-i, -i, -) turn a page

fleygj|a *v* (fleygi, fleygði, fleygt) throw away

flink|ur *adj* (-, -t) skillful

flís *n fem* (-ar, -ar- a) splinter; tile
flísatöng *n fem* (-tangar, -tangir, -tanga) tweezers
fljót *n neu* (-s, -, -a) large river
fljót|a *v* (flýt, flaut, flutum, flotið) float
fljótandi *adj* (-, -) liquidy; floating
fljótfær *adj* (-, -t) rash
fljótt *adv* quickly, soon
fljót|ur *adj* (-, -t) fast, prompt, quick
fljúg|a *v* (flýg, flaug, flugum, flogið) fly
fljúgandi *adj* (-, -) flying
flogaveikisjúkling|ur *n masc* (-s, -ar, -a) *med* epileptic patient
flogaveik|ur *adj* (-, -t) *med* epileptic
flokka *v* (~, -ði, -ð) classify, sort
flokk|un *n fem* (-unar, -anir, -ana) classification
flokkunarstöð *n fem* (-var, -var, -va) sorting plant
flokk|ur *n masc* (-s, -ar, -a) group, category, class; political party; platoon
flott|ur *adj* (-, -) fine looking; cool
fló *n fem* (-ar, flær, -a) flea
flóamarkað|ur *n masc* (-ar/s, -ir, -a) flea market
flóð *n neu* (-s, -, -a) flood, torrent
flóðbylgj|a *n fem* (-u, -ur, -na) tsunami
fló|i *n masc* (-a, -ar, -a) bay
flókin|n *adj* (-, flókið) complicated; subtle
flórsykur *n masc* (-s) powdered sugar
flóttamað|ur *n masc* (-manns, -menn, -manna) refugee
flóttamannabúð|ir *n fem pl* (-a) refugee camp
flótt|i *n masc* (-a, -ar, -a) escape; refuge
flug *n neu* (-s, -, -a) flight; aviation
flug|a *n fem* (-u, -ur, -na) *(insect)* fly
flugbraut *n fem* (-ar, -ir, -a) runway
flugeld|ur *n masc* (-s, -ar, -a) fire cracker
flugfarartæk|i *n neu* (-is, ~, -ja) aircraft

flugfélag *n neu* (-s, -félög, -a) airline
flugfreyj|a *n fem* (-u, -ur, ~) stewardess
flugfreyjutask|a *n fem* (-tösku, -töskur, ~/na) *colloq* trolley bag
flugmað|ur *n masc* (-manns, -menn, -manna) pilot
flugmið|i *n masc* (-a, -ar, -a) airplane ticket
flugnúmer *n neu* (-s, -, -a) flight number
flugpóst|ur *n masc* (-s, -ar, -a) airmail
flugrút|a *n fem* (-u, -ur, -a) shuttle bus to airport
flugskeyt|i *n neu* (-is, ~, -a) missile
flugstöð *n fem* (-var, -var, -va) terminal
flugtak *n neu* (-s, -tök, -a) takeoff
flugunet *n neu* (-s, -, -a) mosquito net
flugupplýsing|ar *n fem pl* (-a) flight information
flugvallarskatt|ur *m* (-s, -ar, -a) airport tax
flugvél *n fem* (-ar, -ar, -a) airplane
flugþjón|n *n masc* (-s, -ar, -a) flight attendant
flus *n neu* (-s, -, -a) *(potato)* peel
flutningsmaður *n masc* (-manns, -menn, -manna) mover
flutning|ur *n masc* (-s, -ar, -a) performance, recital; portage; move
flúð|ir *n fem pl* (-a) whitewater, rapids
flúrljós *n neu* (-s, -, -a) strip lighting
flyðr|a *n fem* (-u, -ur, -a) *zool* flounder
flygil|l *n masc* (-s, flyglar, flygla) *mus* grand piano
flykkj|ast *v* (flykkist, flykktist, flykkst) crowd up
flysja *v* (~, -ði, -ð) peel
flytj|a *v* (flyt, flutti, flutt) move; recite; transplant; ~ **á milli** transport; ~ **inn** import, move in
flýj|a *v* (flý, flúði, flúið) flee
flýt|a *v* (-i, -ti, -t) hurry
flýti|r *n masc* (-s) hurry, rush
flæð|a *v* (-i, flæddi, flætt) flood
flækj| 1 *n fem* (-u, -ur, -a) twist; 2 *v* (flæki, flækti, flækt) entangle, complicate

flækjast *v refl* (flækist, flæktist, flækst) wander, roam, rove

flækt|ur *adj* (-, -) entangled, twisted

flöguberg *n neu* (-s) *geol* slate

fnyk|ur *n masc* (-s, -ir, -a) stink

folald *n neu* (-s, folöld, -a) *zool* foal

fordæm|i *n neu* (-is, ~, -a) precedent

forða *v* (~, -ði, -ð) rescue

fordóm|ar *n masc pl* (-a) prejudice, bias

fordrykk|ur *n masc* (-jar, -ir, -ja) aperitif

forða|st *v refl* (~, -ðist, ~) avoid

foreldr|i *n neu* (~s) parent; **foreldrar** *n masc pl* (-a) parents

forfað|ir *n masc* (-föður, -feður, -feðra) *(male)* ancestor

forgang|ur *n masc* (-s) priority

forkosning|ar *n fem pl* (-a) primary elections

forlagatrú *n fem* (-ar) fatalism

forleik|ur *n masc* (-s, -ir, -ja) *mus* prelude

forlög *n neu pl* (-laga) fate

form *n neu* (-s, ~, -a) shape; baking pan, oven pan

formað|ur *n masc* (-manns, -menn, -manna) chairman

formál|i *n masc* (-a, -ar, -a) foreword, preface, prologue

formlega *adv* formally

formleg|ur *adj* (-, -t) formal

formóð|ir *n fem* (-ur, -mæður, -mæðra) *(female)* ancestor

formsatrið|i *n neu* (-is, ~, -a) formality

formúl|a *n fem* (-u, -ur, -na/~) formula

forn *adj* (-, -t) ancient

fornafn *n neu* (-s, -nöfn, -a) *ling* pronoun

fornaldarsaga *n fem* (-sögu, -sögur, -sagna) *lit* legendary saga

fornbókabúð *n fem* (-ar, -ir, -a) antique bookstore, used-book store

fornensk|a *n fem* (-u) Old English

forngripaverslun *n fem* (-ar, -ir, -a) antique store

forngrip|ur *n masc* (-s, -ir, -a) antique item

forníslensk|a *n fem* (-u) Old Icelandic

fornleifafræði *n fem* (-) archeology

fornminj|ar *n fem pl* (-a) old relics

fornsag|a *n fem* (-sögu, -sögur, -sagna) saga

forréttind|i *n neu pl* (-a) advantage, prerogative, privilege

forrétt|ur *n masc* (-, -ir, -a) appetizer, first course

forrit *n neu* (-s, ~, -a) *comp* program

forrita *v* (~, -ði, -ð) *comp* program

forritar|i *n masc* (-a, -ar, -a) *comp* computer programmer

forræði *n neu* (-s) custody

forsal|a *n fem* (-sölu, -sölur, -salna) pre-order

forsend|a *n fem* (-u, -ur, -na) prerequisite, presupposition

forsetafrú *n fem* (-ar, -frúr, -frúa) first lady

forset|i *n masc* (-a, -ar, -a) president

forsetning *n fem* (-ar, -ar, -a) *ling* preposition

forsjóð|a *v* (-sýð, -sauð, -suðum, -soðið) precook

forskeyt|i *n neu* (-is, ~, -a) *ling* prefix

forstjór|i *n masc* (-a, -ar, -a) president; CEO

forstof|a *n fem* (-u, -ur, -a) entrance hall

forsætisráðherr|a *n masc* (-a, -ar, -a) prime minister

forstöðukon|a *n fem* (-u, -ur, -kvenna) matron

forstöðumað|ur *n masc* (-manns, -menn, -manna) *(administrator)* superintendent

forsöguleg|ur *adj* (-, -t) prehistoric, primeval

fortíð *n fem* (-ar, -ir, -a) past

fortíðarþrá *n fem* (-r) nostalgia

fortöl|ur *n fem pl* (-talna) persuasion

forver|i *n masc* (-a, -ar, -a) predecessor

forvitin|n *adj* (-, -vitið) curious

foryst|a *n fem* (-u) leadership

fosfór *n masc* (-s) *chem* phosphorous

foss *n masc* (-, -ar, -a) waterfall

fóðra *v* (~, -ði, -ð) *(for animals)* feed

fóður *n neu* (-s) feed
fókus *n masc* (-s/ar) focus
fókusera *v* (~, -ði, -ð) focus
fólk *n neu* (-s) people
fólksbíl|l *n masc* (-s, -ar, -a) car,
   automobile
fórn *n fem* (-ar, -ir, -a) sacrifice
fórnarlamb *n neu* (-i, -lömb, -a)
   victim
fóstbræðralag *n neu* (-s, -lög, -a)
   brotherhood
fóstbróð|ir *n masc* (-ur, bræður,
   bræðra) blood brother
fóstur *n neu* (-s, -, fóstra) *med* embryo
fósturbróð|ir *n masc* (-ur, bræður,
   bræðra) foster brother
fóstureyðing *n fem* (-ar, -ar, -a)
   abortion
fósturforeldr|i *n neu* (-s) foster parent;
   fósturforeldr|ar (-a) *n masc pl*
   foster parents
fósturjörð *n fem* (-jarðar, -jarðir,
   -jarða) homeland
fósturlát *n neu* (-s, -, -a) *med*
   miscarriage
fóstursyst|ir *n fem* (-ur, -ur, -ra)
   foster sister
fótboltaleik|ur *n masc* (-s, -ir, -ja)
   soccer game
fótboltaspil *n neu* (-i, -, -a) fussball
fótboltavöll|ur *n masc* (-vallar,
   -vellir, -valla) soccer field
fótbolt|i *n masc* (-a, -ar, -a) soccer;
   amerískur ~ American football
fótlegg|ur *n masc* (-jar, -ir, -ja) leg
fótspor *n neu* (-s, -, -a) step
fótstig *n neu* (-s, -, -a) pedal
fót|ur *n masc* (-ar, fætur, fóta) foot; leg
Frakkland *N neu* (-s) France
fram undan *adv* ahead
framagirni *n fem* (-) ambition
framagjarn *adj* (-gjörn, -t) ambitious
framandi *adj* exotic
frambjóðand|i *n masc* (-a, -bjóðendur,
   -bjóðenda) candidate in an election
framboð *n neu* (-s, -, -a) availability;
   candidacy

framburð|ur *n masc* (-ar) *ling* pro-
   nunciation; accent; *leg* statement,
   testimony
framdekk *n neu* (-s, -, -ja) front wheel
framfarasinn|i *n masc* (-a, -ar, -a)
   progressive
framfar|ir *n fem pl* (-a) improvement
framfót|ur *n masc* (-ar, fætur, fóta)
   foreleg
framfærslutuðning|ur *n masc* (-s)
   alimony
framför *n fem* (-farar, -farir, -fara)
   advance, development
framhandlegg|ur *n masc* (-jar/s, -ir,
   -ja) forearm
framhjá *prep* past
framhleypin|n *adj* (-, -hleypið)
   forward, pushy
framhlið *n fem* (-ar, -ar, -a) front side
framkalla *v* (~, -ði, -ð) develop (film)
framkom|a *n fem* (-u) behavior
framkvæm|a *v* (-i, -di, -t) carry out,
   perform, realize
framkvæmanleg|ur *adj* (-, -t)
   feasible
framkvæmd *n fem* (-ar, -ir, -a)
   implementation, accomplishment;
   performance; practice
framkvæmdastjór|i *n masc* (-a, -ar,
   -a) CEO
framkvæmdastjórn *n fem* (-ar, -ir, -a)
   administration, board of directors
framlag *n neu* (-s, framlög, -a)
   contribution, donation
framleið|a *v* (-i, -leiddi, -leitt) manu-
   facture, produce, fabricate
framleiðand|i *n masc* (-a, -leiðendur,
   -leiðenda) producer, maker
framleiðni *n fem* (~) productivity
framleiðsl|a *n fem* (-u) production,
   manufacturing
framlenging *n fem* (-ar, -ar, -a)
   extension
framlengingarsnúr|a *n fem* (-u, -ur,
   -a) extension cord
framlengj|a *v* (-lengi, -lengdi, -lengt)
   prolong

framljós *n neu* (-s, -, -a) headlight, front light

frammistað|a *n fem* (-stöðu) performance

framrúð|a *n fem* (-u, -ur, -a) windscreen, windshield

framseljanleg|ur *adj* (-, -t) transferable

framsetning *n fem* (-ar) presentation

framsækin|n *adj* (-, -sækið) progressive

framsæt|i *n neu* (-is, ~, -a) front seat

framtíð *n fem* (-ar, -ir, -a) future

framúrskarandi *adj* outstanding

framvind|a *n fem* (-u) progression

fransk|a *n fem* (frönsku) French language

franskbrauð *n neu* (-s, -, -a) white bread

fransk|ur *adj* (frönsk, -t) French; **franskar kartöflur** french fries

fras|i *n masc* (-a, -ar, -a) phrase

frauðbúðing|ur *n masc* (-s, -ar, -a) mousse

frá 1 *prep* + *dat* from: ~ **mér** from me; **2** *adv* away: **farðu ~!** go away!

frá því að *phr* since

frábær *adj* (-, -t) amazing, brilliant, magnificent, superb

frábrugðin|n *adj* (-, -brugðið) different

frádrátt|ur *n masc* (-ar) subtraction

fráhrindandi *adj* unfriendly; repellent

fráleit|ur *adj* (-, -t) ridiculous

frárennsl|i *n neu* (-is, ~, -a) suer

fráskilin|n *adj* (-, -skilið) divorced

frásögn *n fem* (-sagnar, -sagnir, -sagna) story; *lit* narrative

frátekin|n *adj* (-, -tekið) occupied, reserved, taken

frátengd|ur *adj* (-, -tengt) *comp* offline

frávís|un *n fem* (-unar, -anir, -ana) dismissal

frekar *adv* rather, pretty

frelsa *v* (~, -ði, -ð) free, emancipate

frelsi *n neu* (-s) freedom

frels|un *n fem* (-unar, -anir, -ana) release, emancipation

frem|ja *v* (-, framdi, framið) commit

fremr|i *adj compar* (-i, -a) superior

fremst|ur *adj superl* (-, -) foremost, first in line

fremur *adv* rather, somewhat

fresk|a *n fem* (-u, -ur, -na) fresco

fresta *v* (~, -ði, -ð) delay, postpone, procrastinate

frest|un *n fem* (-unar, -anir, -ana) procrastination, postponement

frest|ur *n masc* (-s, -ir, -a) delay; ~ **til að skila** deadline

freyðandi *adj* sparkling

freyðivín *n neu* (-s, -, -a) sparkling wine

fréttamað|ur *n masc* (-manns, -menn, -manna) journalist, reporter

fréttamennsk|a *n fem* (-u) journalism

fréttatilkynning *n fem* (-ar, -ar, -a) press release

frétt|ir *n fem pl* (-a) news

friða *v* (~, -ði, -ð) protect

friðað|ur *adj* (friðuð, -) protected: **friðað hús** listed building

friðsam|ur *adj* (-söm, -t) peaceful

friðsæl|l *adj* (-, -t) peaceful

frið|ur *n masc* (-ar) peace, tranquility, calmness

friðþæging *n fem* (-ar) atonement

frí *n neu* (-s, -, -a) vacation, holiday: **jólafrí** Christmas holiday, **helgarfrí** weekend off

frídag|ur *n masc* (-s, -ar, -a) day off: ~ **verkamanna** May Day, Labor Day

frík *n neu* (-s, -, -a) *slang* freak

frímerk|i *n neu* (~s, -, -ja) stamp

frímerkjasafn *n neu* (-s, -söfn, -a) stamp collection

frímið|i *n masc* (-a, -ar, -a) free ticket

fírskandi *adj* refreshing

frítím|i *n masc* (-a, -ar, -a) free time

frjáls *adj* (-, -t) free

frjálsar íþróttir *sports* track and field

frjálslega *adv* freely, relaxed

frjálsleg|ur *adj* (-, -t) relaxed

frjálslynd|ur *adj* (-, -t) liberal

frjókorn *n neu pl* (-s, -, -a) pollen

frjókornamæling *n fem* (-ar, -ar, -a) pollen count

frjókornaofnæmi *n neu* (-s) *med* pollen allergy

frjó|r *adj* (-, -tt) prolific

frjósam|ur *adj* (-söm, -t) fertile, prolific

frosin|n *adj* (-, frosið) frozen

frosk|ur *n masc* (-s, -ar, -a) frog

frost *n neu* (-s) frost

frostlög|ur *n masc* (-lagar) antifreeze

frostpinn|i *n masc* (-a, -ar, -a) ice pops

frostþurrkað|ur *adj* (-þurrkuð, -) freeze-dried

frum|a *n fem* (-u, -ur, -na) *bio* cell

frumbernsk|a *n fem* (-u) infantry

frumbygg|i *n masc* (-ja, -ar, -ja) native

frumefn|i *n neu* (-is, ~, -a) *chem* element

frumeind *n fem* (-ar, -ir, -a) *chem* atom

frumgerð *n fem* (-ar, -ir, -a) prototype

frumkvæði *n neu* (-s) initiative

frumkvöðul|l *n masc* (-s, -kvöðlar, -kvöðla) pioneer

frumlag *n neu* (-s, -lög, -a) *ling* subject

frumleg|ur *adj* (-, -t) original, unique

frummál *n neu* (-s, -, -a) *ling* source language

frummynd *n fem* (-ar, -ir, -a) original (painting)

frumraun *n fem* (-ar, -ir, -a) debut

frumskóg|ur *n masc* (-ar, -ar, -a) jungle

frumstæð|ur *adj* (-, -stætt) primitive; savage

frumsýning *n fem* (-ar, -ar, -a) premiere

frumtal|a *n fem* (-tölu, -tölur, -talna) *math* ordinal number

frú *n fem* (frúar, -r, -a) madam

frúktós|i *n masc* (-a) *bio* fructose

fryst|a *v* (-i, -i, -) freeze

frysting *n fem* (-ar) refrigeration

fryst|ir *n masc* (-is, -ar, -a) freezer

fræ *n neu* (-s, -, -ja) seed

fræð|a *v* (-i, fræddi, frætt) inform, educate

fræð|i *n neu pl* (-a) science

fræðigrein *n fem* (-ar, -ar, -a) discipline, study, subject

fræðileg|ur *adj* (-, -t) theoretical

fræðimað|ur *n masc* (-manns, -menn, -manna) scholar, researcher

fræðimennsk|a *n fem* (-u) scholarship

fræðirit *n neu* (-s, -, -a) nonfiction

fræðistörf *n neu pl* (-starfa) research

frægð *n fem* (-ar) fame, stardom

fræg|ur *adj* (-, -t) famous, renowned

frændhygli *n fem* (-) nepotism

frænd|i *n masc* (-a, frændur, frænda) uncle; nephew; male cousin (any male relative)

frændsystkin|i *n neu pl* (-a, ~, -a) cousin

frænk|a *n fem* (-u, -ur, -a) aunt; niece; female cousin (any female relative)

fröken *n fem* (-ar, -ar, -a) miss

frönskumælandi *adj* francophone

fugl *n masc* (-s, -ar, -a) bird

fuglaprik *n neu* (-s, -, -a) perch

fullkomin|n *adj* (-, -komið) perfect

fullkomlega *adv* perfectly; fully

fullkomn|un *n fem* (-unar, -anir, -ana) perfection

fullnæging *n fem* (-ar, -ar, -a) satisfaction; orgasm

fullnægja *v* (-nægi, -nægði, -nægt) satisfy

fullnægjandi *adj* sufficient, adequate

fullorðin|n *adj* (-, -orðið) adult

fullorðinsfræðsl|a *n fem* (-u) adult education

fullorðinstenn|ur *n fem pl* (-tanna) adult teeth

fulltrú|i *n masc* (-a, -ar, -a) representative, delegate, agent

full|ur *adj* (-, -t) drunk; full: **fullt fæði** full board, **fullt tungl** full moon

fullvalda *adj* sovereign: ~ **ríki** sovereign state

fullvissa *v* (~, -ði, -ð) reassure

fullþroskað|ur *adj* (-þroskuð, -) ripe

fundarherberg|i *n neu* (-is, ~, -ja) meeting room

fundarlaun *n neu pl* (-a) finder's reward

fundarstað|ur *n masc* (-ar, -ir, -a) meeting place

fund|ur *n masc* (-ar, -ir, -a) meeting

fur|a *n fem* (-u, -ur, -a) *flora* pine

furðulega *adv* strangely

furðuleg|ur *adj* (-, -t) peculiar; uncanny

furuhnet|a *n fem* (-u, -ur, -a) pine nut

fúkkalyf *n neu med* antibiotics

fúl|l *adj* (-, -t) foul; grumpy, in a bad mood

fúslega *adv* readily

fylgdarlið *n neu* (-s, -, -a) retinue

fylgismað|ur *n masc* (-manns, -menn, -manna) partisan

fylgja *v* (fylgi, fylgdi, fylgt) follow, pursue

fylgjand|i *n masc* (-a, -endur, -enda) follower

fylgni *n fem* (-) correlation

fylk|i *n neu* (-is, ~, -ja) *(US)* state; *(Canada)* province

fylkisstjór|i *n masc* (-a, -ar, -a) governor

fylkj|a *v* (fylki, fylkti, fylkt) rally

fyll|a *v* (-i, -ti, t) fill

fyllibytt|a *n fem* (-u, -ur, -na) drunkard

fylling *n fem* (-ar, -ar, -a) filling, stuffing

fyllt|ur *adj* (-, -) filled, stuffed

fyndin|n *adj* (-, fyndið) funny, comic, hilarious, humorous

fyrir 1 *adv* in the way; 2 *prep +
acc (time)* before: ~ **jól** before Christmas; *(beneficiary)* for: ~ **mig** for me; *(experience)* for: **þetta er erfitt ~ mig** this is difficult for me; *+ dat (obstacle)* in the way: **þú ert ~ mér** you are in my way; *(leadership)* on behalf of: **hann fer ~ hópnum** he speaks on behalf of the group; *(past tense)* ago: **þetta var ~ mörgum árum** this was many years ago

fyrir aftan 1 *adv* behind; 2 *prep + acc* behind: ~ **mig** behind me

fyrir framan 1 *adv* in the front; 2 *prep + acc* in front of

fyrir handan 1 *adv* on the other side; 2 *prep + acc* beyond

fyrir neðan 1 *adv* below; 2 *prep + acc* underneath, below

fyrir ofan 1 *adv* above; 2 *prep + acc* above

fyrir utan 1 *adv* outside; 2 *prep + acc* apart from

fyrirboð|i *n masc* (-a, -ar, -a) sign, foreshadowing, omen

fyrirbyggjandi *adj* preventive

fyrirbær|i *n neu* (-is, ~, -a) phenomenon

fyrirfram *adv* beforehand, in advance

fyrirframgreiðsl|a *n fem* (-u, -ur, -na) advance payment

fyrirgef|a *v* (-, -gaf, -gáfum, -gefið) forgive, pardon

fyrirgefðu *interj* I´m sorry

fyrirgefning *n fem* (-ar) forgiveness

fyrirhyggj|a *n fem* (-u) foresight

fyrirhyggjusam|ur *adj* (-söm, -t) provident

fyrirlesar|i *n masc* (-a, -ar, -a) speaker, lecturer

fyrirlestrarsal|ur *n masc* (-ar, -ir, -a) lecture hall, auditorium

fyrirlestur *n masc* (-s, -lestrar, -lestra) lecture

fyrirlitleg|ur *adj* (-, -t) despicable

fyrirmynd *n fem* (-ar, -ir, -a) model, ideal

fyrirrennar|i *n masc* (-a, -ar, -a) forerunner

fyrirskipa *v* (~, -ði, -ð) prescribe

fyrirskip|un *n fem* (-unar, -anir, -ana) order

fyrirspurn *n fem* (-ar, -ir, -a) inquiry

fyrirstað|a *n fem* (-stöðu, -stöður, -staða) obstacle

fyrirsæt|a *n fem* (-u, -ur, -a) model

fyrirsögn *n fem* (-sagnar, -sagnir, -sagna) heading

fyrirtæk|i *n neu* (-is, ~, -ja) company, firm
fyrirvar|i *n masc* (-a, -ar, -a) reservation
fyrirvinn|a *n fem* (-u, -ur, -a) breadwinner
fyrr *adv* earlier
fyrri *adj compar* (-i, -a) previous, past
fyrrum *adv* formerly
fyrrverandi *adj* former, previous
fyrst *adv* first; since
fyrst|i *ord* (-a, -a) first: **fyrsti klassi** first class, **fyrsta flokks** first-rate, **fyrsta sæti** first place
fyrst|ur *adj* (-, -) first: **ég var fyrst(ur)!** I was first!
fýl|l *n masc* (-s, -ar, -a) *zool* fulmar (an Icelandic sea bird)
fýl|a *n fem* (-u, -ur, -na) stink; bad mood: **vera í fýlu** be in a bad mood
fædd|ur *adj* (-, fætt) born
fæð|a 1 *n fem* nutrients (-u); **2** *v* (-i, fæddi, fætt) give birth (to)
fæðing *n fem* (-ar, -ar, -a) birth
fæðingarblett|ur *n masc* (-s, -ir, -a) birthmark, mole
fæðingarstof|a *n fem* (-u, -ur, ~) *med* delivery room
fæðingartíðni *n fem* (-) birthrate
fæðingarvottorð *n neu* (-s, ~, -a) birth certificate
fæðingastað|ur *n masc* (-ar, -ir, -a) place of birth
fæðubótarefn|i *n neu* (-is, ~, -a) dietary supplement
fæðuofnæmi *n neu* food allergy
fæðupíramíd|i *n masc* (-a, -ar, -a) food pyramid
fægiskófl|a *n fem* (-u, -ur, -na) dustpan

fæl|a *v* (-i, -di, -t) scare, chase away
fær *adj* (-, -t) accomplished, skillful
fær|a *v* (-i, -ði, -t) move, transfer, carry over; deliver, bring; ~ **sig** move oneself
færanleg|ur *adj* (-, -t) movable, mobile
fær|ast *v refl* (-ist, -ðist, -st) move by itself, shift
Færeying|ur *n masc* (-s, -ar, -a) Faroese (person from The Faroe Islands)
Færeyj|ar N *fem pl* (-eyja) Faroe Islands
færeysk|a *n fem* (-u) the Faroese language
færeysk|ur *adj* (-, -t) Faroese
færni *n fem* (-) fluency, skill
færsluhnapp|ur *n masc* (-s, -ar, -a) *comp* enter
fætur. *See* **fótur**
föðurbróð|ir *n masc* (-ur, -bræður, -bræðra) uncle
föðurforeldr|ar *n masc pl* (-a) paternal grandparents
föðurland *n neu* (-s, -lönd, -a) fatherland; long johns
föðurlandsvin|ur *n masc* (-ar, -ir, -a) patriot
föðursyst|ir *n fem* (-ur, -ur, ra) paternal aunt
föls|un *n fem* (-unar, -anir, -ana) forgery
föl|ur *adj* (-, -t) pale
föstudag|ur *n masc* (-s, -ar, -a) Friday
föt *n neu pl* (fata) clothes
fötl|un *n fem* (-unar, -anir, -ana) disability, handicap

G

gabb *n neu* (-s) trick

gabba *v* (~, -ði, -ð) fool, trick

gaffal|l *n masc* (-s, gafflar, gaffla) fork

gagn *n neu* (-s) utility

gagnagrunn|ur *n masc* (-s, -ar, -a) database

gagnaug|a *n neu* (-a, -u, -na) temple

gagnfræðaskól|i *n masc* (-a, -ar, -a) junior high school

gagnkvæm|ur *adj* (-, -t) reciprocal

gagnkynhneigð|ur *adj* (-, -hneigt) heterosexual

gagnleg|ur *adj* (-, -t) beneficial; practical, useful

gagnrýn|a *v* (-i, -di, -t) review; criticize

gagnrýnand|i *n masc* (-a, -endur, -enda) critic

gagnrýni *n fem* (-) criticism; review

gagnrýnin|n *adj* (-, -rýnið) critical

gagnslaus *adj* (-, -t) useless

gagnstæð|ur *adj* (-, -stætt) opposite

gagnstætt *adv* contrary

gagntak|a *v* (-tek, -tók, -tókum, -tekið) preoccupy

gagntekin|n *adj* (-, -tekið) thrilled

gagnvart *prep + dat* towards: **þetta er ósanngjarnt ~ henn**i this was unfair towards her

gagnvirk|ur *adj* (-, -t) interactive

galdramað|ur *n masc* (-manns, -menn, -manna) wizard

galdranorn *n fem* (-ar, -ir, -a) witch

galdur *n masc* (-s, galdrar, galdra) witchcraft, magic

gallabuxnaefn|i *n neu* (-is, ~, -a) denim

gallabux|ur *n fem pl* (-na) jeans

gallað|ur *adj* (gölluð, -) faulty

gallblaðr|a *n fem* (-blöðru, -blöðrur, ~) *anat* gall bladder

gallerí *n neu* (-s, -, -a) gallery

gall|i *n masc* (-a, -ar, -a) fault; outfit

gallon *n neu* (-s, -, -a) gallon

gals|i *n masc* (-a) playfulness

gamaldags *adj* archaic, old-fashioned

gamaleikrit *n neu* (-s, -, -a) *(theater)* comedy

gamal|l *adj* (gömul, -t) old: **gamli bærinn** the old town center; *slang* **(þau) gömlu** my parents

gamanmynd *n fem* (-ar, -ir, -a) comedy film

gamansem|i *n fem* (-) pleasantry

Gambía *N fem* (-u) The Gambia

gamlárskvöld *n neu* (-s, -, -a) New Year's Eve

gaml|i *adj weak* (-a, -a) the old one; *slang*, dad; buddy; **gamla** mom

Gana *N neu* (-) Ghana

gang|a 1 *n fem* (göngu, göngur, gangna) walk, walking; **2 ganga** *v* (geng, gekk, gengum, gengið) walk, hike; ~ **fram af** shock; ~ **í gegnum** live through, undergo

gangandi *adj* walking; ~ **vegfarandi** pedestrian

gang|ast *v refl* (gengst, gekkst, gengist) ~ **undir** undergo, go through; ~ **við barninu** confirm that you are the father of the child

gangbraut *n fem* (-ar, -ir, -a) pedestrian crossing

gangráð|ur *n masc* (-s, -ar, -a) *med* pacemaker

gangstétt *n fem* (-ar, -ir, -a) pavement, sidewalk

gangstéttarbrún *n fem* (-ar, -ir, -a) curb

gang|ur *n masc* (-s, -ar, -a) aisle: **sæti við ganginn** an aisle seat; hall, hallway: **fram á gangi** out in the hallway

Ganverj|i *n masc* (-a, -ar, -a)
Ghanaian

ganversk|ur *adj* (-, -t) Ghanaian

gardín|a *n fem* (-u, -ur, -a) curtain

garðasól *n fem* (-ar, -ir, -a) *flora*
Iceland poppy

garðskál|i *n masc* (-a, -ar, -a) pavilion

garð|ur *n masc* (-s, -ar, -a) garden,
yard

garðyrkj|a *n fem* (-u) gardening

garðyrkjusal|a *n fem* (-sölu, -sölur,
-sala) garden center

garn *n neu* (-s) yarn

gas *n neu* (-s, gös, -a) gas *(not
gasoline)*

gasgrím|a *n fem* (-u, -ur, -na) gas mask

gaskút|ur *n masc* (-s, -ar, -a) gas
bottle

gasmæl|ir *n masc* (-is, -ar, -a) gas
gauge, gas meter

gat *n neu* (-s, göt, -a) hole, tear

gat|a *n fem* (götu, götur, -na) street

gatamapp|a *n fem* (-möppu, -möppur,
~) ring binder

gatar|i *n masc* (-a, -ar, -a) paper punch

gatnamót *n neu pl* (-a) intersection

gaur *n masc* (-s, -ar, -a) *slang* guy,
dude, fellow

gáf|a *n fem* (-u, -ur, -na) gift

gáfað|ur *adj* (gáfuð, -) intellectual,
intelligent, clever, smart, wise

gáfumenn|i *n masc* (-is, -i, -a)
intellectual

gáf|ur *n fem pl* (-na) intelligence

gámaskip *n neu* (-s, -, -a) container
ship

gám|ur *n masc* (-s, -ar, -a) container

gát|a *n fem* (-u, -ur, -na) puzzle, riddle

gedd|a *n fem* (-u, -ur, ~) pike

geðflækj|a *n fem* (-u, -ur, ~) neurosis

geðjast *v refl* + *dat subj* (~, geðjaðist,
~) like: **mér ~ ekki að þessu** I
don't like this

geðklofasjúkling|ur *n masc* (-s, -ar,
-a) *med* schizophrenic

geðklof|i *n masc* (-a) *med* schizo-
phrenia

geðlækning|ar *n fem pl* (-a)
psychiatry

geðlækn|ir *n masc* (-is, -ar, -a)
psychiatrist

geðræn|n *adj* (-, -t) psychic

geðshræring *n fem* (-ar, -ar, -a) emotional affect; **vera í ~u** to be upset

geðsjúkling|ur *n masc* (-s, -ar, -a)
psychopath

geðug|ur *adj* (-, -t) sympathetic, nice,
friendly

geðveik|ur *adj* (-, -t) mentally ill

gef|a *v* (gef, gaf, gáfum, gefið) give;
deal; ~ **í skyn** imply; ~ **út** issue,
publish

gefin|n *adj* (-, gefið) given; **að því
gefnu að** provided that

gefandi *n masc* (-a, -endur, -enda)
donor

gef|ast *v* (gefst, gafst, gefist) ~ **upp**
submit, surrender; ~ **vel** works well

geggjað|ur *adj* (geggjuð, -) crazy;
slang awesome

gegn *prep* + *dat* against: **fótboltaleikur ~ Póllandi** a soccer game
against Poland

gegndarlaus *adj* (-, -t) profuse

gegnheil|l *adj* (-, -t) solid; massive

gegnsýr|a *v* (-i, ði, -t) pervade

gegnsæ|r *adj* (-, -tt) transparent

gegnt *prep* across from: **klósettið er
~ stiganum** the bathroom is across
from the stairs

gegnum *prep* + *acc* through, via:
~ **gluggann** through the window,
ég flýg í ~ Þýskaland I will fly
through Germany

geimfar|i *n masc* (-a, -ar, -a) astronaut

geim|ur *n masc* (-s, -ar, -a) space

geimver|a *n fem* (-u, -ur, ~) alien,
extraterrestrial

geimvísindamað|ur *n masc* (-manns,
-menn, -manna) astronomer

geimvísind|i *n neu* (-a) astronomy

geirfugl *n masc* (-s, -ar, -a) *zool*
great auk

geir|i *n masc* (-a, -ar, -a) sector; clove

geirvart|a *n fem* (-vörtu, -vörtur, -vartna) nipple

geisla *v* (~, -ði, -ð) radiate

geislabaug|ur *n masc* (-s, -ar, -a) nimbus

geisladisk|ur *n masc* (-s, -ar, -a) CD

geislandi *adj* radiant

geislaspilar|i *n masc* (-a, -ar, -a) CD player

geislavirk|ur *adj* (-, -t) radioactive

geisl|i *n masc* (-a, -ar, -a) ray, beam

geisl|un *n fem* (-unar, -anir, -ana) radiation

geispa *v* (~, -ði, -ð) yawn

geisp|i *n masc* (-a, -ar, -a) yawn

geit *n fem* (-ar, -ur, -a) goat

geitakjöt *n neu* (-s) goat meat

geitaost|ur *n masc* (-s, -ar, -a) goat cheese

geitung|ur *n masc* (-s, -ar, -a) wasp

gelatín *n neu* (-s) gelatin

geld|ur *adj* (-, gelt) sterilized

gelt *n neu* (-s) bark

generalpruf|a *n fem* (-u, -ur, -a) dress rehearsal

geng|i *n neu* (-is, ~, -a) exchange rate

Georgí|a *N fem* (-u) Georgia

georgísk|ur *adj* (-, -t) Georgian

ger *n neu* (-s) yeast: **þurr~** dry yeast; **~laus** unleavened

ger|a *v* (-i, -ði, -t) do, accomplish; practice; **~ grein fyrir** account for; **~ ráð fyrir** assume, expect; **~ sér upp** pretend; **~ upp** rebuild, renovate; **~ við** repair; **~ sér upp** fake

ger|ast *v refl* (-ist, -ðist, -st) happen

gerð *n fem* (-ar, -ir, -a) sort, type

gerð|ur *adj* (-, gert) made

gerilsneydd|ur *adj* (-, -sneytt) pasteurized

gerja *v* (~, -ði, -ð) ferment

gerlaus *adj* (-, -t) unleavened

germansk|ur *adj* (germönsk, -t) Germanic, Teutonic

gerp|i *n neu* (-is, ~, -a) *slang* asshole, idiot

gervi- *pref* fake; synthetic

gerviefn|i *n neu* (-is, ~, -a) synthetic material

gervihnattadisk|ur *n masc* (-s, -ar, -a) satellite disc

gervihnattasjónvarp *n neu* (-s, -sjónvörp, -a) satellite TV

gervihnött|ur *n masc* (-hnattar, -hnettir, -hnatta) satellite

gestgjaf|i *n masc* (-a, -ar, -a) host

gestrisni *n fem* (-) hospitality

gest|ur *n masc* (-s, -ir, -a) guest, visitor

get|a *n fem* (-u) ability, capability, capacity; **2** *v* (get, gat, gátum, getið) able to, can: **ég get hjálpað þér** I can help you

getgát|a *n fem* (-u, -ur, -na) guesses

getnaðarlim|ur *n masc* (-s, -ir, -a) penis

getnaðarvarnarpill|a *n fem* (-u, -ur, -a) contraceptive

getnaðarvörn *n fem* (-varnar, -varnir, -varna) contraception

geyma *v* (-i, -di, -t) store, keep, preserve, reserve

geymsl|a *n fem* (-u, -ur, -na) storage space, repository

gifs *n neu* (-is, ~, -a) *med* plaster: **með höndina í ~i** with the arm in plaster

gift|a *v* (-i, -i, -) marry

gift|ast *v refl* (-ist, -ist, gifst) get married

gift|ur *adj* (-, -) married

gigt *n fem* (-ar) *med* rheumatism, arthritis

gigtarsjúkling|ur *n masc* (-s, -ar, -a) *med* rheumatic, arthritic

gigtveik|ur *adj* (-, -t) *med* rheumatic

gil *n neu* (-s, -, -ja) ravine, wadi

gild|i *n neu* (-is, ~, -a) significance, value

gildistím|i *n masc* (-a) expiration date

gildr|a *n fem* (-u, -ur, -a) trap

gild|ur *adj* (-, gilt) valid; thick

gimstein|n *n masc* (-s, -ar, -a) jewel, gem

gin *n neu* (-s, -, -a) gin: **~ og tónik** gin and tonic

girðing *n fem* (-ar, -ar, -a) fence

girn|ast *v refl* (-ist, -dist, -st) desire
girnd *n fem* (-ar, -ir, -a) desire
gisin|n *adj* (-, gisið) sparse
giska *v* (~, -ði, -ð) guess
gist|a *v* (-i, -i-, -t) stay overnight
gistiheimil|i *n neu* (-is, ~, -a)
  guesthouse
gisting *n fem* (-ar, -ar, -a)
  accommodations
gíg|ur *n masc* (-s, -ir/ar, -a) *geol* crater
gífurlega *adv* terribly, awfully, very
gífurleg|ur *adj* (-, -t) large, very big
gín|a *n fem* (-u, -ur, -a) mannequin
Gíne|a *N fem* (-u) Guinea
Gínea-Bissaú *N neu* (-) Guinea-Bissau
gír *n masc* (-s, -ar, -a) gear
gíraff|i *n masc* (-a, -ar, -a) giraffe
gírkass|i *n masc* (-a, -ar, -a) *mech*
  transmission
gírstöng *n fem* (-stangar, -stangir,
  -stanga) *mech* gearshift lever, shift
  stick
gísl *n neu* (-s, -ar, -a) hostage
gítar *n masc* (-s, -ar, -a) guitar
gítarleikar|i *n masc* (-a, -ar, -a)
  guitarist
gjafavöruversl|un *n fem* (-unar, -anir,
  -ana) gift shop
gjafmildi *n fem* (-) generosity
gjafmild|ur *adj* (-, -milt) generous
gjald *n neu* (-s, gjöld, -a) fee
gjalda *v* (~, -ði, -ð) pay; return
gjaldeyrisafgreiðsl|a *n fem* (-u, -ur,
  -na) *econ* currency exchange
gjaldfallin|n *adj* (-, -fallið) *econ* due,
  payable; overdraw
gjaldmiðil|l *n masc* (-s, -miðlar,
  -miðla) *econ* currency
gjaldþrot *n neu* (-s, -, -a) bankruptcy
gjaldþrota *adj* bankrupt
gjá *n fem* (-r, -r, -a) rift
gjóa *v* (~, -ði, -ð) ogle
gjöf *n fem* (gjafar, gjafir, gjafa) gift,
  present
gjörðu svo vel *phr* here you are
gjöreyð|a *v* (-i, -eyddi, -eytt)
  annihilate

gjöreyðileggj|a *v* (-legg, -lagði, -lagt)
  annihilate
gjöreyðing *n fem* (-ar) annihilation
gjörgæsl|a *n fem* (-u) *med* intensive
  care
gjörgæsludeild *n fem* (-ar, -ir, a)
  med intensive care unit
gjörsamlega *adv* completely
gjörv|i *n masc* (-a, -ar, -a) *comp*
  processor
glaðlega *adv* cheerfully
glaðleg|ur *adj* (-, -t) cheerful
glað|ur *adj* (glöð, glatt) glad, happy,
  delighted
glampa *v* (~, -ði, -ð) flash, reflect
  light
glannaleg|ur *adj* (-, -t) reckless
glansandi *adj* shiny
glappaskot *n neu* (-s, -, -a) lapse,
  mistake
glata *v* (~, -ði, -ð) lose
gleði *n fem* (-) joy, delight
gler *n neu* (-s, ~, -ja) glass
gleraugnaversl|un *n fem* (-unar, -anir,
  -ana) *med* optician
gleraug|u *n neu pl* (-na) eyeglasses
glerung|ur *n masc* (-s) enamel
glervör|ur *n fem pl* (-vara) glassware
gleym|a *v* (-i, -di, -t) forget
gleymin|n *adj* (-, gleymið) forgetful;
  oblivious
gleymmérei *n fem* (-ar, -ar, -a) *flora*
  forget-me-not
gleymsk|a *n fem* (-u) oblivion
gleyp|a *v* (-i, -ti, -t) swallow; devour
glitrandi *adj* sparkling
glím|a *n fem* (-u, -ur, -na) wrestling
gljá|i *n masc* (-a, -ar, -a) wax, polish;
  glaze
gljúfur *n neu* (-s, ~, gljúfra) ravine,
  gorge
glóðarsteiking *n fem* (-ar) barbecue
glóðarsteikj|a *v* (-steiki, -steikti,
  -steikt) barbecue
glós|a *n fem* (-u, -ur, -na) gloss,
  glossing; note; **2 glósa** *v* (~, -ði,
  -ð) gloss; take notes

glósubók *n fem* (-ar, -bækur, -bóka) notebook
gluggahler|i *n masc* (-a, -ar, -a) shutter
gluggasæt|i *n neu* (-s, ~, -a) window seat
gluggatjöld *n neu pl* (-tjalda) curtains
glugg|i *n masc* (-a, -ar, -a) window
glúkós|i *n masc* (-a) *chem* glucose
glúten *n neu* (-s) gluten
glútenlaus *adj* (-, -t) gluten-free
glútenofnæmi *n neu* (-s) *med* gluten allergy
glýseról *n neu* (-s) *chem* glycerin
glæpamað|ur *n masc* (-manns, -menn, -manna) criminal
glæparannsókn *n fem* (-ar, -ir, -a) crime investigation
glæpasag|a *n fem* (-sögu, -sögur, -sagna) *lit* crime novel
glæpsamleg|ur *adj* (-, -t) felony
glæp|ur *n masc* (-s, -ir, -a) crime
glær|a *n fem* (-u, -ur, -a) slide
glæsileg|ur *adj* (-, -t) elegant, classy
glæsileik|i *n masc* (-a) elegance
glögg *n neu* (-s) mulled wine (Scandinavian winter drink)
gnægð *n fem* (-ar, -ir, -a) affluence
goð *n neu* (-s, -, -a) a heathen god
goðafræði *n fem* (-) mythology
goðsögn *n fem* (-sagnar, -sagnir, -sagna) myth
goðsöguleg|ur *adj* (-, -t) mythical
gogg|ur *n masc* (-s, -ar, -a) beak
gol|a *n fem* (-u) breeze
golf *n neu* (-s) *sports* golf
golfbíl|l *n masc* (-s, -ar, -a) golf cart
golfklúbb|ur *n masc* (-s, -ar, -a) golf club
golfkylf|a *n fem* (-u, -ur, -a) golf club
golfvöll|ur *n masc* (-vallar, -vellir, -valla) golf course
gorm|ur *n masc* (-s, -ar, -a) spring (coil)
gos *n neu* (-s, -, -a) soft drink; volcanic eruption
gosbrunn|ur *n masc* (-s, -ar, -a) water fountain

goshver *n masc* (-s, -ir, -a) *geol* geyser
gott *n neu* (-s) candy, sweets
góða ferð *phr* bon voyage!
góðgerðamál *n neu* (-s, -, -a) charity
góðgæt|i *n neu* (~s) delicacy
góðkynja *adj* benign
góðmennsk|a *n fem* (-u) kindness
góð|ur *adj* (-, gott) good, kind
góðviljað|ur *adj* (-viljuð, -) benevolent
gól *n neu* (-s, -, -a) clamor
gólf *n neu* (-s, -, -a) floor
gólfhæð *n fem* (-ar, -ir, -a) headroom
gólftepp|i *n neu* (-is, ~, -a) carpet
góm|ur *n masc* (-s, -ar, -a) *anat* gum
graðfol|i *n masc* (-a, -ar, -a) *zool* stud
graf *n neu* (-s, gröf, -a) graph
graf|a *v* (gref, gróf, grófum, grafið) dig; bury
grafhýs|i *n neu* (-is, ~, -a) mausoleum
grafísk|ur *adj* (-, -t) graphic: **grafísk hönnun** graphic design, **grafísk list** graphic art
grafreit|ur *n masc* (-s, -ir, -a) graveyard
graftarból|a *n fem* (-u, -ur, -a) pimple
gramm *n neu* (-s, grömm, -a) gram
granat *n neu* (-s) *geol* garnet
granatepl|i *n neu* (-is, ~, -a) pomegranate
grandskoða *v* (~, -ði, -ð) scrutinize, examine carefully
grann|ur *adj* (grönn, -t) slim, thin
granóla *n neu* (-) granola
gras *n neu* (-s, grös, -a) grass
grasagarð|ur *n masc* (-s, -ar, -a) botanical garden
grasalækning|ar *n fem pl* (-a) *med* homeopathy
grasate *n neu* (-s) herbal tea
grashokkí *n neu* (-s) *sports* field hockey
grasker *n neu* (-s, -, -ja) pumpkin; squash
graslauk|ur *n masc* (-s, -ar, -a) chive
grasæt|a *n fem* (-u, -ur, -a) herbivore
graut|ur *n masc* (-ar, -ar, -a) porridge:

hafragrautur oatmeal porridge; pudding: **hrísgrjónagrautur** rice pudding

gráð|a *n fem* (-u, -ur, -a) degree, rank

gráhærð|ur *adj* (-, -t) gray-haired

gráháf|ur *n masc* (-s, -ar, -a) *zool* crayfish

grá|r *adj* (-, -tt) *color* gray

grát|a *v* (græt, grét, grétum, grátið) cry

greidd|ur *adj* (-, greitt) paid

greið|a *n fem* (-u, -ur, -a) comb; **2** *v* (-i, greiddi, greitt) comb

greið|i *n masc* (-a, -ar, -a) favor

greiðsl|a *n fem* (-u, -ur, -na) payment

greiðslufær *adj* (-, -t) solvent

greiðslukort *n neu* (-s, -, -a) bank card; credit card

greiðslukortanúmer *n neu* (-s, -, -a) card number

grein *n fem* (-ar, -ar, -a) article; branch; subject; field

grein|a *v* (-i, -di, -t) notice; analyze

greinamerk|i *n neu* (-is, ~, -ja) punctuation

greinand|i *n masc* (-a, -endur, -enda) analyst

greinarmerkjasetning *n fem* (-ar, -ar, -a) punctuation

greinast *v refl* be diagnosed with

greinilega *adv* clearly, notably, distinctly

greining *n fem* (-ar, -ar, -a) analysis

grein|ir *n masc* (-is, -ar, -a) *ling* article

greip *n neu* (-s) grapefruit

Grenada *N fem* (-) Grenada

grenadísk|ur *adj* (-, -t) Grenadian

greni *n neu* (-s, -, -a) *flora* spruce

griðarstað|ur *n masc* (-ar, -ir, -a) asylum, sanctuary

Grikk|i N *masc* (-ja, -ir, -ja) Greek

grikkjasmár|i *n masc* (-a, -ar, -a) fenugreek

Grikkland *N neu* (-s) Greece

grill *n neu* (-s, -, -a) barbecue, grill

grilla *v* (~, -ði, -ð) barbecue, grill

grillað|ur *adj* (grilluð, -) grilled:

grillaðar pylsur grilled sausages, ~ **fiskur** grilled fish, ~ **ostur** grilled cheese

grillkol *n neu* (-s, -, -a) charcoal

grillolí|a *n fem* (-u, -ur, -a) grilling oil

grimmd *n fem* (-ar) cruelty

grimm|ur *adj* (-, -t) cruel

grindhval|ur *n masc* (-s, -ir, -a) *zool* pilot whale

grindverk *n neu* (-s, -, -a) fence

gripahús *n neu* (-s, -, -a) stable

grisjurúll|a *n fem* (-u, -ur, -a) *med* gauze roller bandage

grím|a *n fem* (-u, -ur, -na) mask

grín *n neu* (-s) joke

grína|st *v refl* (~, -ðist, ~) joke: **ertu að ~?** are you joking?

grínatrið|i *n neu* (-is, ~, -a) sketch

grínist|i *n masc* (-a, -ar, -a) comedian

grínmynd *n fem* (-ar, -ir, -a) comedy film

gríp|a *v* (-, greip, gripum, gripið) grab

grísk|a *n fem* (-u) Greek language

grísk|ur *adj* (-, -t) Greek

grjónagrat|ur *n masc* (-ar, -ar, -a) rice pudding

grjót *n neu* (-s, -, -a) rock, stone

grjótskrið|a *n fem* (-u, -ur, -a) rock slide

gró|a *v* (græ, greri, greru, gróið) *(vegetation)* grow; heal

gróð|i *n masc* (-a) profit, return, dividend, win

gróð|ur *n masc* (-s/gróðrar) vegetation

gróðurhús *n neu* (-s, -, -a) greenhouse

gróðurhúsaáhrif *n neu pl* (-a) greenhouse effect

gróðursetj|a *v* (-set, -setti, -sett) *flora* plant

gróflega *adv* roughly, severely

gróf|ur *adj* (-, -t) rough, rustic, coarse

gruna *v* (~, -ði, -ð) suspect

grunað|ur *adj* (grunuð, -) suspected

grundvallaratrið|i *n neu* (-is, ~, -a) basics, basic facts

grunnhyggin|n *adj* (-, -hyggið) shallow

grunnskól|i *n masc* (-a, -ar, -a) primary school, elementary school
grunn|ur 1 *adj* (-, -t) shallow; **2** *n masc* (-s, -ar, -a) foundation, base
grunnvatnsborð *n neu* (-s) *geol* water table
grunsamleg|ur *adj* (-, -t) suspicious
grun|ur *n masc* (-s) suspicion
grúpp|a *n fem* (-u, -ur, ~) *colloq* band
grýtt|ur *adj* (-, -) rocky
græð|a *v* (-i, græddi, grætt) benefit, make money, earn; heal
Grænhöfðaeyj|ar *N fem pl* (-a) Cape Verde
grænkál *n neu* (-s) kale; collards
Grænland *N neu* (-s) Greenland
Grænlandshaf *N neu* (-s) Greenland Sea
Grænlending|ur *n masc* (-s, -ar, -a) Greenlander
grænlensk|a *n fem* (-u) Inuktitut (Inuit language)
grænmeti *n neu* (~s) vegetable
grænmetisæt|a *n fem* (-u, -ur, -a) vegetarian
grænmetisborgar|i *n masc* (-a, -ar, -a) vegetarian burger
grænmetisrétt|ur *n masc* (-ar, -ir, -a) vegetarian dish
grænmetissal|i *n masc* (-a, -ar, -a) greengrocer
græn|n *adj* (-, -t) green: **græn paprika** green pepper, **grænar ertur** green peas, **grænt te** green tea
gröf *n fem* (grafar, grafir, grafa) grave
gröft|ur *n masc* (graftar, greftir, grafta) *med* pus
gubba *v* (~, -ði, -ð) throw up, vomit
guð *n masc* (-s, -ir, -a) God
guðdóm|ur *n masc* (-s) deity
guðfræði *n fem* (-) theology
guðfræðing|ur *n masc* (-s, -ar, -a) theologist
guðhrædd|ur *adj* (-, -hrætt) pious
guðþjónust|a *n fem* (-u, -ur, ~) mass, church service
guf|a 1 *n fem* (-u, -ur, -a) steam,

vapor; **2 gufa** *v* (~, -ði, -ð) steam; **~ upp** vaporize; disappear
gufubað *n neu* (-s, -böð, -a) steam bath, sauna
gufuhver *n masc* (-s, -ir, -a) *geol* hot spring; fumarole
gufusoðin|n *adj* (-, -soðið) steamboiled
gufustraujárn *n neu* (-s, -, -a) steam iron
gufusuðupott|ur *n masc* (-s, -ar, -a) steam cooker
gulbrún|n *adj* (-, -t) *color* tan
gull *n neu* (-s, -, -a) *chem* gold; precious things; **gullið mitt** darling
gullgerðarlist *n fem* (-ar) alchemy
gullhúð *n fem* (-ar, -ir, -a) goldplate
gullinrót *n fem* (-ar) turmeric
gulllitað|ur *adj* (-lituð, -) *color* gold
gullnám|a *n fem* (-u, -ur, -a) gold mine
gullsmið|ur *n masc* (-s, -ir, -a) goldsmith
gullverðlaun *n neu pl* (-a) gold medal
gulróf|a *n fem* (-u, -ur, -na) rutabaga
gulrót *n fem* (-ar, -rætur, -róta) carrot
gulrótarkak|a *n fem* (-köku, -kökur, -kakna) carrot cake
gul|ur *adj* (-, -t) *color* yellow
gust|ur *n masc* (-s, -ir, -a) gust
gúllas *n neu* (-) goulash
gúmmí *n neu* (-s) rubber
gúrk|a *n fem* (-u, -ur, -na) cucumber
Gvæjana *N neu* (-s) Guyana
gvæjansk|ur *adj* (gvæjönsk, -t) Guyananese
Gvatemala *N neu* (-) Guatemala
Gvatemalsk|ur *adj* (-ölsk, -alst) Guatemalan
gyðingahátíð *n fem* (-ar, -ir, -a) Jewish holiday
gyðing|ur *n masc* (-s, -ar, -a) Jew, Jewish
gyllt|ur *adj* (-, -) golden
gæði *n neu pl* (-a) quality
gæludýr *n neu* (-s, -, -a) pet
gæludýraversl|un *n fem* (-unar, -anir, -ana) pet shop

gælunafn *n neu* (-s, -nöfn, -a)
    nickname
gær *adv* yesterday; **í ~** yesterday
gærdag|ur *n masc* (-s,-ar, -a)
    yesterday
gæs *n fem* (-ar, -ir, -a) goose
gæsahúð *n fem* (-ar, -ir, -a) goose
    bumps
gæsalif|ur *n fem* (-rar, -rar, -ra)
    goose liver
gæsalöpp *n fem* (-lappar, -lappir,
    -lappa) *ling* quotation mark
gæt|a *v* (-i, -ti, -t) mind, take care of
gæti. *See* **geta**
göfuglynd|ur *adj* (-, -lynt) of noble
    character
göfug|ur *adj* (-, -t) noble
gögn *n neu pl* (gagna) data
göng *n neu pl* (ganga) underpass;
    tunnel

göngubraut *n fem* (-ar, -ir, -a)
    pedestrian crossing
göngubrú *n fem* (-ar, -brýr, -brúa)
    footbridge
göngudeild *n fem* (-ar, -ir, -a) *med*
    ambulatory care unit, out-patient
    department
gönguferð *n fem* (-ar, -ir, -a) walk
gönguleið *n fem* (-ar, -ir, -a) hiking
    route, walking route
göng|ur *n fem pl* (gangna) roundup
    of the sheep in October
gönguskíð|i *n neu* (-is, ~, -a) cross-
    country skiing
gönguskó|r *n masc* (-s, ~, -a) hiking
    boot
göngustíg|ur *n masc* (-s, -ar, -a)
    footpath

H

ha *interj* what?, huh?
Haag *N fem* (-) The Hague
haf|a *v* (hef, -ði, -t) have: ~ **áhuga á** to
  have interest in, ~ **tíma** have time;
  ~ **áhrif á** affect; ~ **efni á** afford
hafgol|a *n fem* (-u, -ur, -a) sea breeze
hafna *v* (~, -ði, -ð) reject; *(in a*
  competition) to come in: **að hafna**
  í þriðja sæti to come in third place
hafnabolt|i *n masc* (-a, -ar, -a) baseball
hafnarbakk|i *n masc* (-a, -ar, -a)
  harbor front
hafnarsvæð|i *n neu* (-is, ~, -a) harbor
  area
haframjöl *n neu* (-s) oatmeal
hafr|ar *n masc pl* (-a) oats
haf *n neu* (-s, höf, -a) sea, ocean
haga *v* (~, -ði, -ð) organize, arrange;
  ~ **sér vel/illa** behave well/badly
hagfræði *n fem* (-) economics
hagfræðing|ur *n masc* (-s, -ar, -a)
  economist
hagkerf|i *n neu* (-is, ~, -a) economy
haglabyss|a *n fem* (-u, -ur, -a) shotgun
haglél *n fem* (-éls, -él, -élja) hail
hagnað|ur *n masc* (-ar) profit, return
hagnýt|ur *adj* (-, -tt) functional;
  practical
hagsýni *n fem* (-) prudence
hagsýn|n *adj* (-, -t) economical;
  prudent
hagsæld *n fem* (-ar) economic success
Haítí *N neu* (-) Haiti
haítíbú|i *n masc* (-a, -ar, -a) Haitian
hak|a *n fem* (höku, hökur, ~) *anat* chin
hakk *n neu* (-s) minced meat
hakka *v* (~, -ði, -ð) mince
hakkað|ur *adj* (hökkuð, -) minced
hala *v* (~, -ði, -ð) *comp* ~ **niður**
  download
halda *v* (held, hélt, héldum, haldið)

hold; think, believe, assume: **ég**
  held ekki I don't think so; ~ **áfram**
  continue, carry on; ~ **fram** claim;
  ~ **veislu** throw a party
hal|i *n masc* (-a, -ar, -a) tail
halla *v* (~, -ði, -ð) lean, slope, tilt
hall|i *n masc* (-a, -ar, -a) slope
halló *interj* hello
hallsvepp|ur *n masc* (-s, -ir, -a) truffle
hallærisleg|ur *adj* (-, -t) awkward,
  out of fashion
hamar *n masc* (-s, hamrar, hamra)
  hammer; cliff
hamborgarabrauð *n neu* (-s, -, -a)
  hamburger bun
hamborgarakjöt *n neu* (-s) hamburger steak
hamborgar|i *n masc* (-a, -ar, -a)
  hamburger
hamfar|ir *n fem pl* (-a) disaster
hamingj|a *n fem* (-u) happiness;
  til hamingju! congratulations!
hamingjuósk|ir *n fem pl* (-a)
  congratulations
hamingjusam|ur *adj* (-söm, -samt)
  happy
hamingjusöm egg *n neu pl* free-
  range eggs
hamra *v* (~, -ði, -ð) pound, hit with
  a hammer
hamskipt|i *n neu* (-is, ~, -a)
  transformation
hamstur *n masc* (-s, hamstrar, hamstra)
  hamster
hana *pron acc* her
hanastél *n neu* (-s, -, -a) cocktail
handa *prep + dat* for: ~ **þér** for you,
  ég er með mat ~ öllum I have
  food for everyone
handahófskennd|ur *adj* (-, -kennt)
  random

handakrik|i *n masc* (-a, -ar, -a) *anat* armpit

handan 1 *adv* on the other side: **raddir að** ~ voices from the other side; **2** *prep* + *gen* on the other side: ~ **götunnar** on the other side of the street

handavinn|a *n fem* (-u) handicrafts

handbolt|i *n masc* (-a, -ar, -a) handball

handbrems|a *n fem* (-u, -ur, -a) handbrake

handfang *n neu* (-s, -föng, -a) handle

handfarangur *n masc* (-s) carry-on baggage

handfjatla *v* (~, -ði, -ð) handle

handfrjáls *adj* (-, -t) hands-free; **handfrjáls búnaður** headset kit

handföng *n neu pl* (-fanga) handles

handgerð|ur *adj* (-, -t) handmade

handjárn *n neu* (-s, -, -a) handcuffs

handklæð|i *n neu* (-is, ~, -a) towel

handlegg|ur *m* (-s, -ir, -ja) *anat* arm

handrið *n neu* (-s, -, -a) railing

handrit *n neu* (-s, -, -a) manuscript

handritafræð|i *n neu pl* (-a) manuscript studies

handsaumað|ur *adj* (-saumuð, -) handsewn

handtak|a *n fem* (-töku, -tökur, ~) arrest

handtask|a *n fem* (-tösku, -töskur, -taska) handbag, purse

handtekin|n *adj* (-, -tekið) arrested

handverk *n neu* (-s, -, -a) craft

handverksmað|ur *n masc* (-manns, -menn, -manna) artisan

handverksversl|un *n fem* (-unar, -anir, -anir) craft store

handverksvör|ur *n fem pl* (-vara) crafts

handþeytar|i *n masc* (-a, -ar, -a) hand mixer

handþvott|ur *n masc* (-ar/s, -ar, -a) hand wash

hang|a *v* (heng, hékk, hengum, -ið) hang; idle, waste time: ~ **í tölvunni** waste time on the computer

hangsa *v* (~, -ði, -ð) waste time, spend time without doing anything specific

han|i *n masc* (-a, -ar, -a) *zool* rooster

hann *pron nom/acc* he, him

hanna *v* (~, -ði, -ð) design

hannað|ur *adj* (hönnuð, -) designed

hans *pron gen* his

hansk|i *n masc* (-a, -ar, -a) glove

happadrætt|i *n neu* (-is, ~, -a) raffle

harðbrjósta *adj* pitiless

harðfisk|ur *n masc* (-s, -ar, -a) stock fish (Icelandic specialty)

harðlífi *n neu* (-s) constipation

harðneskj|a *n fem* (-u) harshness, rigor

harðsoðin|n *adj* (-, -soðið) hard-boiled: **harðsoðið egg** hard-boiled egg

harð|ur *adj* (hörð, hart) hard, tough, severe, rigorous; ~ **diskur** hard disc

hark|a *n fem* (hörku) harshness, rigor

harma *v* (~, -ði, -ð) regret

harmleik|ur *n masc* (-s, -ir, -a) tragedy

harp|a *n fem* (hörpu, hörpur, -na) *mus* harp

hasarmynd *n fem* (-ar, -ir, -a) action movie

hass *n neu* (-) hashish

hastarleg|ur *adj* (-, -t) acute

hata *v* (~, -ði, -ð) hate

hatt|ur *n masc* (-s, -ar, -a) hat

hatur *n neu* (-s) hatred

haug|ur *n masc* (-s, -ar, -a) mound, pile

hauk|ur *n masc* (-s, -ar, -a) *zool* hawk

haust *n neu* (-s, -, -a) autumn, fall

hausverk|ur *n masc* (-jar, -ir, -ja) headache

Hawaiibú|i *N masc* (-a, -ar, -a) Hawaiian

háð *n neu* (-s) *lit* irony

hádeg|i *n neu* (~s, ~) noon, midday; lunchtime; **eftir** ~ in the afternoon

hádegismat|ur *n masc* (-ar, -ar, -a) lunch

hádegisverð|ur *n masc* (-ar, -ir, -a) lunch

háðsádeil|a *n fem* (-u, -ur, -na) satire
háðsk|ur *adj* (-, -t) ironic
háð|ur *adj* (-, -) addicted
háf|ur *n masc* (-s, -ar, -a) kitchen fan;
butterfly net; *zool* dogfish
háhitasvæð|i *n neu* (-is, ~, -a) *geol*
geothermal area
háhyrning|ur *n masc* (-s, -ar, -a)
zool killer whale
háhýs|i *n neu* (-is, ~, -a) high-rise build-
ings, skyscrapers; condominiums
hákarl *n masc* (-s, -ar, -a) shark
hálendi *n neu* (-s) highland; interior
hálfbaun|ir *n fem pl* (-a) split peas
hálfbróð|ir *n masc* (-bróður, -bræður,
-bræðra) half-brother
hálfsyst|ir *n fem* (-ur, -ur, -ra) half-
sister
hálf|ur *adj* (-, -t) half: **hálft fæði**
half-board
hálfvirði *n neu* (-s) half price
háljós *n neu* (-s, -, -a) high-beam
lights
háls *n masc* (-, -ar, -a) throat
hálsbólg|a *n fem* (-u, -ur, -na) *med*
sore throat
hálskirtil|l *n masc* (-s, -kirtlar, -kirt-
la) *anat* tonsils
hálskirtlabólg|a *n fem* (-u) *med*
tonsillitis
hálsmen *n neu* (-s, -, -a) necklace
hámark *n neu* (-s) maximum
hámarka *v* (~, -ði, -ð) maximize
hápunkt|ur *n masc* (-s, -ar, -a) peek,
highlight
há|r 1 *adj* (-, -tt) tall; high; loud; **2** *n
neu* (-s, -, -a) hair
hárblásar|i *n masc* (-a, -ar, -a) hair
dryer
hárblást|ur *n masc* (-s, -blástrar,
-blástra) blow-dry
hárburst|i *n masc* (-a, -ar, -a) hairbrush
hárfroð|a *n fem* (-u, -ur, -a) hair
mousse
hárgreiðsl|a *n fem* (-u, -ur, -na) hairdo
hárgreiðslukon|a *n fem* (-u, -ur,
-kvenna) hairdresser

hárgreiðslumað|ur *n masc* (-manns,
-menn, -manna) barber
hárgreiðslustof|a *n fem* (-u, -ur, -a)
hair salon
hárlit|ur *n masc* (-ar, -ir, -a) hair color
hárnákvæm|ur *adj* (-, -t) subtle;
very precise
hárnæring *n fem* (-ar, -ar, -a) hair
conditioner
hársprey *n neu* (-s) hair spray
hársvörð|ur *n masc* (-varðar, -sverðir,
-svarða) *anat* scalp
hárþurrk|a *n fem* (-u, -ur, -na) blow
drier
hárúð|i *n masc* (-a, -ar, -a) hair spray
háset|i *n masc* (-a, -ar, -a) sailor
hásin *n fem* (-ar, -ar, -a) *anat* tendon
háskólamenntað|ur *adj* (-menntuð, -)
university educated
háskólaráð *n neu* (-s, -, -a) university
senate
háskól|i *n masc* (-a, -ar, -a) university,
college
háslétt|a *n fem* (-u, -ur, -na) *geog*
plateau
háspenn|a *n fem* (-u, -ur, -a) high
voltage
háspennulín|a *n fem* (-u, -ur, -a)
high voltage line
hástafalás *n masc* (-s, -ar, -a) *comp*
caps lock
hástafalykil|l *n masc* (-s, -lyklar,
-lykla) *comp* shift key
hásumar *n neu* (-s, -sumur, -sumra)
middle of the summer
hátalar|i *n masc* (-a, -ar, -a) loud-
speaker
hátíð *n fem* (-ar, -ir, -a) feast, festival
hátíðarhöld *n neu pl* (-halda)
festivities
hátíðarklæðnað|ur *n masc* (-ar)
formal wear
hátind|ur *n masc* (-s, -ar, -a) summit,
pinnacle, peak
hátta *v* (~, -ði, -ð) undress; **~ sig**
undress
háttsett|ur *adj* (-, -) high-ranked

hátt|ur *n masc* (-ar, hættir, hátta) way to do something; *ling* mode

háttvís *adj* (-, -t) polite

hátækni *n fem* (-) high-tech

hávað|i *n masc* (-a, -ar, -a) noise

hávaxin|n *adj* (-, -vaxið) tall

hávær *adj* (-, -t) loud

hebresk|a *n fem* (-u) Hebrew language

hebresk|ur *adj* (-, -t) Hebrew

hefð *n fem* (-ar, -ir, -a) tradition; practice

hefðarklerk|ur *n masc* (-s, -ar, -a) prelate

hefðarmað|ur *n masc* (-manns, -menn, -manna) aristocrat

hefðbundin|n *adj* (-, -bundið) conventional, routine

hefja *v* (hef, hóf, hófum, hafið) start, instigate, launch

hefn|a *v* (-i, -di, -t) revenge, retaliate; *refl* ~ **sín** revenge

hefnd *n fem* (-ar, -ir, -a) revenge, retaliation

heft|a *v* **1** (-i, -i, -t) hold back, stop, retard; depress; **2** (~, -aði, að) staple

heftar|i *n masc* (-a, -ar, -a) stapler

heftiplást|ur *n masc* (~s, -rar, -ra) adhesive tape; sticking plaster

hegða *v* (~, -ði, -ð) ~ **sér** *refl* behave

hegð|un *n fem* (-unar, -anir, -ana) behavior, conduct, manner

heiðarleg|ur *adj* (-, -t) honest

heiðra *v* (~, -ði, -ð) honor

heið|ur *n masc* (-s) honor, respect

heilag|ur *adj* (heilög, -t) holy, sacred

heilahimnubólg|a *n fem* (-u) *med* meningitis

heilahristing|ur *n masc* (-s) *med* brain concussion

heilaskað|i *n masc* (-a, -ar, -a) *med* brain damage

heilaþvott|ur *n masc* (-ar/s, -ar, -a) brainwashing

heilbrigð|ur *adj* (-, -brigt) healthy, sound, well

heild *n fem* (-ar, -ir, -a) total, whole

heildarsýn *n fem* (-ar) vision

heildarupphæð *n fem* (-ar, -ir, -a) sum, total amount

heilhveiti *n neu* (-s) whole wheat

heil|i *n masc* (-a, -ar, -a) *anat* brain

heil|l *adj* (-, -t) whole, full, in one piece; healthy, sound and safe

heilla *v* (~, -ði, -ð) charm, allure; impress

heillað|ur *adj* (heilluð, -) fascinated

heillagrip|ur *n masc* (-s, -ir, -a) lucky charm

heillandi *adj* fascinating, charming

heils|a **1** *n fem* (-u) health; **2 heilsa** *v* (~, -ði, -ð) greet

heilsubúð *n fem* (-ar, -ir, -a) health-food store

heilsudrykk|ur *n masc* (-jar, -ir, -ja) elixir

heilsufæði *n neu* (-s) health food

heilsugæsl|a *n fem* (-u) health care

heilsugæslustöð *n fem* (-var, -var, -va) health clinic, health center

heilsuhæl|i *n neu* (-is, ~, -a) sanatorium

heilsulind *n fem* (-ar, -ir, -a) spa

heilsutengd|ur *adj* (-, -t) health related: **heilsutengd ferðaþjónusta** wellness tourism

heim *adv* home: **fara** ~ go home

heima *adv* home: **vera** ~ be at home

heimagerð|ur *adj* (-, -gert) homemade

heimamað|ur *n masc* (-manns, -menn, -manna) local person

heiman *adv* **að** ~ from home; **fara að** ~ leave home

heimanmund|ur *n masc* (-ar) dowry

heimasíð|a *n fem* (-u, -ur, -na) *comp* homepage

heimavinn|a *n fem* (-u, -ur, -a) homework

heimavinnandi *adj* works at home: ~ **húsmóðir** homemaker

heimavist *n fem* (-ar, -ir, -a) dormitory

heimild *n fem* (-ar, -ir, -a) reference, source; *leg* warrant

heimildarmynd *n fem* (-ar, -ir, -a) documentary

heimildaskrá *n fem* (-ar, -r, -a) list of references

heimil|i *n neu* (-is, ~, -a) residence, home

heimilisfang *n neu* (-s, -föng, -a) street address

heimilisfólk *n neu* (-s) people in the household

heimilishald *n neu* (-s) housekeeping

heimilislaus *adj* (-, -t) homeless

heimilislækn|ir *n masc* (-is, -ar, -a) *med* general practicioner, family doctor

heimilismat|ur *n masc* (-ar) home-style cooking

heimilisstörf *n pl* housework, chores

heimilistæk|i *n neu* (-is, ~, -ja) domestic appliances

heimsálf|a *n fem* (-u, -ur, -a) continent

heimsborgar|i *n masc* (-a, -ar, -a) world citizen

heimsbókmennt|ir *n fem pl* (-a) *lit* world literature, classics

heimsk|a *n fem* (-u) stupidity

heimskautaref|ur *n masc* (-s, -ir, -a) *zool* artic fox

heimskautasug|a *n fem* (-u, -ur, a) *zool* lamprey

heimskautsbaug|ur *N masc* (-s, -ar, -a) Arctic Circle

heimskuleg|ur *adj* (-, -t) stupid, senseless

heimsk|ur *adj* (-, -t) stupid, dumb, ignorant

heimsókn *n fem* (-ar, -ir, -a) visit

heimspeki *n fem* (-) philosophy

heimspeking|ur *n masc* (-s, -ar, -a) philosopher

heimsskautabaug|ur *n masc* (-s, -ar, -a) *geog* polar circle

heimsveld|i *n neu* (-is, ~, -a) empire

heimsækj|a *v* (-sæki, -sótti, -sótt) visit

heim|ur *n masc* (-s, -ar, -a) world

heit *n neu* (-s, -, -a) promise

heit|a *v* (-i, hét, hétum, heitið) named: **ég heiti Anna** my name is Anna; promise: **ég heiti því að ...** I promise that ...

heit|ur *adj* (-, -t) warm

heldur 1 *adj* holds, is solid and strong: **ísinn er ekki ~** the ice is not safe; **2** *adv* rather: **ég vil ~ vera heima** I would rather stay home, **það er ~ kalt í dag** it's rather cold today; neither: **ekki ég ~ me** neither; **3** *conj* but: **hann er ekki frá Íslandi ~ er hann frá Svíþjóð** he's not from Iceland but from Sweden

heldur betur *adv* certainly, I would say so!

heldur en *conj* than: **ég er eldri ~ en hann** I'm older than him

helga *v* (~, -ði, -ð) devote; sanctify

helg|i *n fem* (-ar) weekend: **góða ~!** have a nice weekend!, **um helgina** during the weekend

helgidóm|ur *n masc* (-s, -ar, -a) sanctuary, shrine

helgisið|ur *n masc* (-ar, -ir, -a) ritual

helgispjöll *n neu pl* sacrilege

heljarmikil|l *adj* (-, -mikið) very big

hell|a 1 *n fem* (-u, -ur, -na) paving stone; **2** *v* (-i, -ti, -t) pour; **~ niður** spill

hell|ir *n masc* (-is, -ar, -a) *geol* cave

helming|ur *n masc* (-s, -ar, -a) half

Helsingfors *N fem* (-) Helsinki

helst *adv* principally, primarily: **hvað er ~ í fréttum?** what is the most important news?; preferably: **ég vil ~ ekki fara** I prefer not to go

heltak|a *v* (-tek, -tók, -tókum -tekið) obsess

helvíti *n neu* (-s) hell

helvítis *interj vul* hell!

hend|a *v* (-i, ti, -t) throw: **~ bolta** throw a ball, **~ í ruslið** throw in the garbage

hengilás *n masc* (-s, -ar, -a) padlock

hengirúm *n neu* (-s, -, -a) hammock

hennar *pron gen* hers

hentug|ur *adj* (-, -t) suitable

heppin|n *adj* (-, heppið) lucky
heppna|st *v* (~, ðist, ~) succeed
heppni *n fem* (-) luck
her *n masc* (-s, -ir, -ja) army
herberg|i *n neu* (-is, ~, -a) room: ~
  með sturtu a room with a shower
herbergisfélag|i *n masc* (-a, -ar, -a)
  roommate
herbergisnúmer *n neu* (-s, -, -a)
  room number
herbergisþjón|n *n masc* (-s, -ar, -a)
  valet
herbergisþjónust|a *n fem* (-u) room
  service
herðablað *n neu* (-s, -blöð, -a) *anat*
  shoulder blade, scapula
herðatré *n neu* (-s, -, -trjáa) clothes
  hanger
herm|a *v* (-i, -di, -t) imitate: ~ **eftir**
  impersonate
hermað|ur *n masc* (-manns, -menn,
  -manna) soldier
hernám *n neu* (-s) occupation by a
  foreign army
herra *n masc* (-, -r, -) mister
herramað|ur *n masc* (-manns, -menn,
  -manna) gentleman
hersveit *n fem* (-ar, -ir, -a) regiment
hertog|i *n masc* (-a, -ar, -a) duke
herþjónust|a *n fem* (-u, -ur, -a)
  military service
heslihnet|a *n fem* (-u, -ur, -a) hazelnut
hestabaun *n fem* (-ar, -ir, -a) broad
  bean
hestamennsk|a *n fem* (-u) horseback
  riding
hesthús *n neu* (-s, -, -a) stable
hest|ur *n masc* (-s, -ar, -a) horse;
  íslenski hesturinn the Icelandic
  horse
hetj|a *n fem* (-u, -ur, ~) hero
hett|a *n fem* (-u, -ur, ~) hood; *anat*
  diaphragm
hettupeys|a *n fem* (-u, -ur, -a) hooded
  sweater
hettusótt *n fem* (-ar) *med* mumps
hey *n neu* (-s) hay

heymæði *n neu* (-s) hay fever
heyr|a *v* (-i, -ði, -t) hear
heyrðu *excl* listen; oh
heyrn *n fem* (-ar, -ir, -a) hearing
heyrnarlaus *adj* (-, -t) deaf
heyrnarmæling *n fem* (-ar, -ar, -a)
  hearing test
heyrnartæk|i *n neu* (-is, ~, -ja)
  hearing aid
heyrnartól *n neu pl* (-a) headphones
hér *adv* here
hér um bil *adv* circa
hérað *n neu* (-s, héruð, -a) *administrative area in Iceland comparable
  to a county*
hér|i *n masc* (-a, -ar, -a) *zool* hare
hérna *adv* here
hið. *See* hinn
hika *v* (~, -ði, -ð) hesitate
hikst|i *n masc* (-a, -ar, -a) hiccup
hill|a *n fem* (-u, -ur, -na) shelf
himinblá|r *adj* (-, -tt) sky-blue
himin|n *n masc* (-s, himnar, himna)
  sky; heaven
himn|a *n fem* (-u, -ur, ~) *bio*
  membrane
hindber *n neu* (-s, -, -ja) raspberry
hindra *v* (~, -ði, -ð) prevent, obstruct
hindr|un *n fem* (-unar, -anir, -ana)
  obstacle, obstruction, prevention
hingað *adv* to here: **komdu** ~ come
  here
hin|n *pron* (-, hitt) the other: ~
  nemandinn the other student,
  hinum megin on the other side; **2**
  defin art (-, hið) [*used only in old
  or formal language*]: **Hið íslenska
  bókmenntafélag** The Icelandic
  Literary Society
hirðuleysi *n neu* (-s) carelessness,
  neglect
hirsi *n neu* (-s) millet
hismi *n neu* (-s) husk
hissa *adj* surprised, amazed
hita *v* (~, -ði, -ð) heat, warm; ~ **upp**
  re-heat
hitabrús|i *n masc* (-a, -ar, -a) thermos

hitaeiningasnauð|ur *adj* (-, -snautt)
  low-calorie
hitamæl|ir *n masc* (-is, -ar, -a)
  thermometer
hitasótt *n fem* (-ar, -ir, -a) *med* fever
hitastig *n neu* (-s, -, -a) temperature
hitaveit|a *n fem* (-u, -ur, -na) central
  heating
hit|i *n masc* (-a) heat; *med* temperature;
  med **vera með hita** have a fever
hitt. *See* **hinn**
hitt|a *v* (-i, -i, -t) meet, encounter;
  hit a target
HIV-jákvæð|ur *adj* (-, -kvætt) HIV-
  positive
híð|i *n neu* (-is, ~, -a) bear cave;
  leggjast í ~ go into hibernation
hjal *n neu* (-s) prattle
hjala *v* (~, -ði, -ð) prattle
hjart|a *n neu* (-a, hjörtu, -na) *anat*
  heart
hjartaáfall *n neu* (-s, -föll, -a) *med*
  heart attack
hjartabil|un *n fem* (-unar, -anir, -ana)
  med heart failure
hjartakveis|a *n fem* (-u) *med* angina
hjartaöng *n fem* (-angar) *med* angina
hjartslátt|ur *n masc* (-ar) *med*
  heartbeat
hjartveik|i *n fem* (-) *med* heart
  condition
hjá *prep* + *dat (approximate location)* by: **hittumst ~ styttunni af
  Jóni Sigurðssyni** let's meet by the
  statue of Jón Sigurðsson; **rétt ~**
  close by; *(person)* at, with: **~ mér**
  at my place, with me, **~ pabba
  og mömmu** at my parent's place,
  with my parents; **ég vinn ~ ríkinu**
  I work for the government; among:
  þetta er vinsælt ~ ferðamönnum
  this is popular among tourists
hjákon|a *n fem* (-u, -ur, -kvenna)
  mistress, lover
hjáleið *n fem* (-ar, -ir, -a) bypass
hjálm|ur *n masc* (-s, -ar, -a) helmet
hjálp *n fem* (-ar) help, relieve, aid

hjálpa *v* (~, -ði, -ð) help, aid
hjálparsögn *n fem* (-sagnar, -sagnir,
  -sagna) *ling* auxiliary; modal verb
hjálpartæk|i *n neu* (-is, ~, -ja) aid
hjálpleg|ur *adj* (-, -t) helpful
hjátrú *n fem* (-ar) superstition
hjátrúarfull|ur *adj* (-, -t) superstitious
hjól *n neu* (-s, -, -a) bicycle; wheel
hjóla *v* (~, -ði, -ð) bike
hjólabrett|i *n neu* (-is, ~, -a) skate-
  board
hjólahjálm|ur *n masc* (-s, -ar, -a)
  cycling helmet
hjólalás *n masc* (-s, -ar, -a) cycle lock
hjólastíg|ur *n masc* (-s, -ar, -a)
  bicycle path
hjólastól|l *n masc* (-s, -ar, -a)
  wheelchair
hjólbarð|i *n masc* (-a, -ar, -a) tire
hjólfar *n neu* (-s, -för, -a) tire track
hjólhýs|i *n neu* (-is, ~, -a) caravan
hjólkopp|ur *n masc* (-s, -ar, -a)
  hubcap
hjólreiðarmað|ur *n masc* (-manns,
  -menn, -manna) bicyclist
hjónaband *n neu* (-s, -bönd, -a)
  marriage
hjónaherberg|i *n neu* (-is, ~, -a)
  master bedroom
hjúkrunarfræði *n fem* (-) nursing
hjúkrunarfræðing|ur *n masc* (-s,
  -ar, -a) nurse
hjúkrunarheimil|i *n neu* (-is, ~, -a)
  nursing home
hjúpa *v* (~, -ði, -ð) coat
hjúskaparstað|a *n fem* (-stöðu)
  marital status
hjúskap|ur *n masc* (-ar) marriage
hjörð *n fem* (hjarðar, hjarðir, hjarða)
  herd
hjört|ur *n masc* (hjartar, hirtir, hjarta)
  zool deer
hlað *n neu* (-s, hlöð, -a) courtyard
hlað|a *n fem* (hlöðu, hlöður, -na) barn
hlað|a *v* (hleð, hlóð, hlóðum, hlaðið)
  load
hlakka *v* (~, -ði, -ð) **~ til** look forward to

hlass *n neu* (-, hlöss, -a) load, cargo

hlaup *n neu* (-s, -, -a) run, running; jelly; jello

hlaupar|i *n masc* (-a, -ar, -a) runner

hlaupaskó|r *n masc* (-s, ~, -a) jogging shoes

hlátur *n masc* (-s, hlátrar, hlátra) laugh, laughter

hleif|ur *n masc* (-s, -ar, -a) loaf

hlekk|ur *n masc* (-s/jar, -ir, -ja) link

hlera *v* (~, -ði, -ð) eavesdrop, listen without permission

hlé *n neu* (-s, -, -a) pause, break, interval, intermission, recess

hlébarð|i *n masc* (-a, -ar, -a) *zool* panther

hlið 1 *n fem* (-ar, -ar, -a) side; **2** *n neu* (-s, -, -a) gate

hliðargat|a *n fem* (-götu, -götur, -gatna) side street

hlíf *n fem* (-ar, -ar, -a) shield

hlífðargleraug|u *n neu pl* (-na) safety glasses, goggles

hljóð *n neu* (-s, -, -a) sound

hljóðbók *n fem* (-ar, -bækur, -a) audiobook

hljóðfær|i *n neu* (-is, ~, -a) musical instrument

hljóðfræði *n fem* (-) *ling* phonetics

hljóðlátlega *adv* quietly

hljóðlát|ur *adj* (-, -t) quiet

hljóðnem|i *n masc* (-a, -ar, -a) microphone

hljóðrita *v* (~, -ði, -ð) transcribe

hljóðstyrk|ur *n masc* (-s) volume, loudness

hljóð|ur *adj* (-, hljótt) quiet

hljóðvarp *n neu* (-s, -vörp, -a) *ling* umlaut; sound shift

hljóðver *n neu* (-s, -, -a) recording studio

hljóma *v* (~, -ði, -ð) sound, resound

hljómfall *n neu* (-s, -föll, -a) *ling* prosody

hljómplat|a *n fem* (-plötu, -plötur, -platna) vinyl record

hljómskál|i *n masc* (-a, -ar, -a) pavilion

hljómsveit *n fem* (-ar, -ir, -a) band, orchestra

hljóm|ur *n masc* (-s, -ar, -a) sound; ring; *mus* accord

hljót|a *v* (hlýt, hlaut, hlutum, hlotið) get, acquire; must: **það hlýtur að fara að rigna bráðum** it must start raining soon

hlusta *v* (~, -ði, -ð) listen

hlustand|i *n masc* (-a, -endur, -enda) listener

hlustunarpíp|a *n fem* (-u, -ur, -na) stethoscope

hlutabréf *n neu* (-s, -, -a) *econ* shares, stocks

hlutabréfahaf|i *n masc* (-a, -ar, -a) *econ* stockholder

hlutabréfaviðskipt|i *n neu pl* (-a) *econ* stock trading

hlutafélag *n neu* (-s, -félög, -a) *econ* corporation

hlutastarf *n neu* (-s, -störf, -a) part-time job

hlutfall *n neu* (-s, -föll, -a) proportion, ratio, rate; **hlutföll** dimensions

hlutfallslega *adv* relatively

hlutfallsleg|ur *adj* (-, -t) proportional, relative

hluthaf|i *n masc* (-a, -ar, a) *econ* shareholder

hlut|i *n masc* (-a, -ar, -a) part, share, component, section, portion

hlutlaus *adj* (-, -t) neutral

hlutlæg|ur *adj* (-, -t) objective

hlut|ur *n masc* (-ar, -ir, -a) thing, item

hlutverk *n neu* (-s, -, -a) role, part, function

hlú|a *v* (-i, -ði, -ð) ~ **að** tend to, take care of

hlynsíróp *n neu* (-s) maple syrup

hlyn|ur *n masc* (-s, -ir, -a) *flora* maple

hlýð|a *v* (-i, hlýddi, hlýtt) obey

hlýj|a *n fem* (-u) warmth

hlýnun *n fem* (-ar) warming: ~ **jarðar** global warming

hlægileg|ur *adj* (-, -t) comical, funny, laughable

hnakk|i *n masc* (-a, -ar, -a) *anat* neck, nape

hnakk|ur *n masc* (-s, -ar, -a) saddle

hnapp|ur *n masc* (-s, -ar, -a) button

hnattræn|n *adj* (-, -t) global

hnattvæðing *n fem* (-ar) globalization

hnefaleik|ar *n masc pl* (-a) boxing

hnef|i *n masc* (-a, -ar, -a) fist

hneigð *n fem* (-ar, -ir, -a) incline, tendency

hnet|a *n fem* (-u, -ur, ~) nut

hnetusmjör *n neu* (-s) peanut butter

hneyksl|i *n neu* (-is, ~, -a) scandal

hné *n neu* (-s, -, hnjáa) *anat* knee

hnigna *v* (~, -ði, -ð) decline

hnignun *n fem* (-ar) decline

hnit *n neu* (-s, -, -a) coordinate

hnitmiðað|ur *adj* (-miðuð, -) brief and to the point

hnífapör *n neu pl* (-para) cutlery, utensils

hníf|ur *n masc* (-s, -ar, -a) knife

hnís|a *n fem* (-u, -ur, -a) porpoise

hnoða *v* (~, -ði, -ð) knead

hnossgæt|i *n neu* (-is, ~, -a) delicacy

hnupla *v* (~, -ði, -ð) steal, pilfer, shoplift

hnúðkál *n neu* (-s) kohlrabi

hnúfubak|ur *n masc* (-s, -ar, -a) *zool* humpback whale

hnút|ur *n masc* (-s, -ar, -a) knot; *med* node

hnykklækn|ir *n masc* (-is, -ar, -a) chiropractor

hnýs|ast *v* (-ist, tist, -t) pry

hnöttótt|ur *adj* (-, -) round, globe-shaped

hol|a *n fem* (-u, -ur, -na) hole

hold *n neu* (-s, -, -a) flesh

Holland *N neu* (-s) The Netherlands

Hollending|ur *n masc* (-s, -ar, -a) Dutch

hollensk|a *n fem* (-u) Dutch language

hollensk|ur *adj* (-, -t) Dutch

holl|ur *adj* (-, -t) wholesome

hommabar *n masc* (-s, -ir, -a) gay bar

hommastað|ur *n masc* (-ar, -ir, -a) gay club

homm|i *n masc* (-a, -ar, -a) homosexual male

Hondúras *N neu* (-s) Honduras

honum *pron dat* him

hopp *n neu* (-s, -, -a) jump

hoppa *v* (~, -ði, -ð) jump

horað|ur *adj* (horuð, -) skinny

horf|a *v* (-i, -ði, -t) watch, look

horf|ur *n fem pl* (-a) prospect

horn *n neu* (-s, -, -a) corner; *math* angle; *bio* antler; *mus* french horn

hornklof|i *n masc* (-a, -ar, -a) bracket

hornstein|n *n masc* (-s, -ar, -a) cornerstone

hógvær *adj* (-, -t) modest

hól|l *n masc* (-s, -ar, -a) hill

hólótt|ur *adj* (-, -) with many hills, hilly

hóp|ur *n masc* (-s, -ar, -a) group, party

hópverkefn|i *n neu* (-is, ~, -a) group activity

hósta *v* (~, -ði, -ð) *med* cough

hóstasaft *n neu* (-s) cough medicine

hóta *v* (~, -ði, -ð) threaten

hótel *n neu* (-s, -, -a) hotel

hótelíbúð *n fem* (-ar, -ir, -a) suite

hót|un *n fem* (-unar, -anir, -ana) threat

hraðamæl|ir *n masc* (-is, -ar, -a) speedometer

hraðatakmark *n neu* (-s, -mörk, -marka) speed limit

hraðbank|i *n masc* (-a, -ar, -a) cash dispenser, ATM

hraðbraut *n fem* (-ar, -ir, -a) highway, motorway

hraðferð *n fem* (-ar, -ir, -a) express route

hrað|i *n masc* (-a, -ar, -a) speed

hraðlest *n fem* (-ar, -ir, -a) intercity train

hraðsending *n fem* (-ar, -ar, -a) express delivery

hraðsuðuketil|l *n masc* (-s, -katlar, -katla) water boiler

hrað|ur *adj* (hröð, hratt) fast, quick, rapid

hrafn *n masc* (-s, -ar, -a) raven

hraka *v* (~, -ði, -ð) relapse
hramm|ur *n masc* (-s, -ar, -a) bear paw; *colloq* large hand
hrasa *v* (~, -ði, -ð) trip over
hratt *adv* fast, rapidly
hraun *n neu* (-s, -, -a) *geol* lava
hraunbreið|a *n fem* (-u, -ur, -a) *geol* lava field
hraungos *n neu* (-s, -, -a) *geol* effusive volcano
hraunrennsli *n neu* (-s) *geol* lava stream
hraust|ur *adj* (-, -) healthy, in good shape
hrá|r *adj* (-, -tt) raw
hrásalat *n neu* (-s, salöt, -a) coleslaw
hreiður *n neu* (-s, -, hreiðra) nest
hreim|ur *n masc* (-s, -ar, -a) accent
hreindýr *n neu* (-s, -, -a) *zool* reindeer
hreindýrakjöt *n neu* (-s) venison
hreindýramos|i *n masc* (-a, -ar, -a) *flora* reindeer lichen
hreinlát|ur *adj* (-, -t) hygienic
hreinleik|i *n masc* (-a) purity
hrein|n *adj* (-, -t) clean: **hreint herbergi** clean room; pure: **hreint vatn** pure water; sterling: **hreint silfur** sterling silver; solid: ~ **og beinn** straight forward
hreinsa *v* (~, -ði, -ð) clean, clear, purge, purify, rid
hreinsað|ur *adj* (hreinsuð, -) refined
hreinskilin|n *adj* (-, -skilið) frank, outspoken
hreinskilningslega *adv* openly, honestly
hreinstefnumað|ur *n masc* (-manns, -menn, -manna) purist
hreins|un *n fem* (-unar, -anir, -ana) cleaning, purification, purge
hreinsunareld|ur *n masc* (-s, -ar, -a) purgatory
hreinsunarstöð *n fem* (-var, -var, -va) refinery
hreintrúarmað|ur *n masc* (-manns, -menn, -manna) puritan
hrekj|a *v* (hrek, hrakti, hrakið) rebut, refute, repel

hrekkjavak|a *n fem* (-vöku) Halloween
hrekk|ur *n masc* (-s, -ir, -ja) prank
hreppstjór|i *n masc* (-a, -ar, -a) the leader of a "*hreppur*"
hrepp|ur *n masc* (-s, -ir, -a) smallest administrative unit in Iceland
hress *adj* (-, -t) healthy; happy, in a good mood
hressa *v* (-i, -ti, -t) make somebody feel better
hressandi *adj* refreshing
hress|ast *v refl* (-ist, -tist, -t) getting better, recovering
hressing *n fem* (-ar, -ar, -a) refreshments
hreyfanleg|ur *adj* (-, -t) mobile
hreyfanleik|i *n masc* (-a, -ar, -a) mobility
hreyfihamlað|ur *adj* (-hömluð, -) disabled
hreyfihöml|un *n fem* (-unar, -anir, -ana) disability
hreyfimynd *n fem* (-ar, -ir, -a) animation
hreyfing *n fem* (-ar, -ar, -a) motion, movement, activity
hreyfingarlaus *adj* (-, -t) still
hreykin|n *adj* (-, hreykið) proud
hreysti *n fem* (-) wellness; *sports* fitness
hrifin|n *adj* (-, hrifið) impressed; infatuated
hrifning *n fem* (-ar) awe; crush
hrifsa *v* (~, -ði, -ð) grab
hrikalega *adv* tremendously
hrikaleg|ur *adj* (-, -t) tremendous; scary
hringing *n fem* (-ar, -ar, -a) ring, ringtone
hringj|a *v* (hringi, hringdi, hringt) make a phone call; ring a bell
hringla *v* (~, -ði, -ð) rattle
hringlótt|ur *adj* (-, -) round, circular
hringorm|ur *n masc* (-s, -ar, -a) ringworm
hringrás *n fem* (-ar, -ir, -a) circulation

hringtorg *n neu* (-s, -, -a) roundabout
hring|ur *n masc* (-s, -ir/ar, -ja/a) circle, ring
hrist|a *v* (-i, -i, -t) shake
hristing|ur *n masc* (-s, -ar, -a) shake, milkshake
hríð|ir *n fem pl* (-a) *med* labor pain
hríf|a 1 *n fem* (-u, -ur, ~) rake; **2** *v* (-, hreif, hrifum, hrifið) thrill, charm, impress
hrífandi *adj* charming; impressive
hrím *n neu* (-s) rime, frost
hrímað|ur *adj* (hrímuð, -) frosted
hrísgrjón *n neu* (-s, -, -a) rice
hrísl|a *n fem* (-u, -ur, -na) *flora* sapling
hrjúf|ur *adj* (-, -t) coarse, rough
hrogn *n neu pl* (-s, -, -a) fish roe
hrok|i *n masc* (-a) arrogance
hroll|ur *n masc* (-s) shivers
hrossagauk|ur *n masc* (-s, -ar, -a) *zool* snipe
hrott|i *n masc* (-a, -ar, -a) ruffian, brute
hróp *n neu* (-s, -, -a) shout, cry
hrópa *v* (~, -ði, -ð) shout
hrós *n neu* (-s, -, -a) praise
hrósa *v* (~, -ði, -ð) praise
hrufla *v* (~, -ði, -ð) scrape
hrufla|st *v refl* (~, -ðist, ~) get a surface wound
hrun *n neu* (-s, -, -a) collapse
hrúg|a *n fem* (-u, -ur, -na) pile
hrúga|st *v refl* (~, ðist, ~) something building piles; ~ **upp** pile up
hrút|ur *n masc* (-s, -ar, -a) *zool* ram
Hrút|urinn *n masc def* (-sins) *astro* Aries
hryðjuverkaárás *n fem* (-ar, -ir, -a) terror attack
hryðjuverkamað|ur *n masc* (-manns, -menn, -manna) terrorist
hryggjarlið|ur *n masc* (-ar, -ir, -a) *anat* vertibra
hrygg|ur 1 *adj* (-, -t) saddened; **2** *n masc* (-jar, -ir, -ja) *anat* spinal column; *(meat)* saddle
hryllileg|ur *adj* (-, -t) terrible

hryllingsmynd *n fem* (-ar, -ir, -a) horror film
hrylling|ur *n masc* (-s) horror
hrynj|a *v* (-, hrundi, hrunið) collapse
hrynjandi *n fem* (-) rhythm
hræð|a *v* (-i, hræddi, hrætt) frighten, scare, alarm
hræð|ast *v refl* (-ist, hræddist, hræðst) fear
hrædd|ur *adj* (-, hrætt) afraid, scared, frightened
hræðilega *adv* awfully, terribly
hræðileg|ur *adj* (-, -legt) awful, horrible, terrible
hræðsl|a *n fem* (-u) fear
hræðslupúk|i *n masc* (-a, -ar, -a) coward
hrær|a *v* (-i, -ði, -t) stir, scramble
hrærð|ur *adj* (-, hrært) scrambled: **hrærð egg** scrambled eggs; touched emotionally
hrærivél *n fem* (-ar, -ar, -a) mixer
hrökkbrauð *n neu* (-s, -, -a) crisp bread
hugað|ur *adj* (huguð, -) brave
hugarflug *n neu* (-s) imagination
hugboð *n neu* (-s, -, -a) premonition
hugbúnað|ur *n masc* (-ar) *comp* software
hugfangin|n *adj* (-, -fangið) fascinated
hugga *v* (~, -ði, -ð) soothe, comfort
huglæg|ur *adj* (-, -t) subjective; abstract
hugleið|a *v* (-i, -leiddi, -leitt) meditate
hugleiðsl|a *n fem* (-u) meditation
hugmynd *n fem* (-ar, -ir, -a) idea, notion, concept, conception
hugmyndarík|ur *adj* (-, -t) imaginative
hugsa *v* (~, -ði, -ð) think
hugsandi *adj* thinking
hugsanlega *adv* possibly
hugsanleg|ur *adj* (-, -t) possible, potential
hugsjón *n fem* (-ar, -ir, -a) ideal
hugsjónamað|ur *n masc* (-manns, -menn, -manna) idealist
hugsjónamennsk|a *n fem* (-u) idealism

hugs|un *n fem* (-unar, -anir, -ana) thought

hugtak *n neu* (-s, -tök, -a) *ling* term

hug|ur *n masc* (-ar, -ir, -a) mind

hugverk *n neu* (-s, -, -a) intellectual property

hugverkaþjófnað|ur *n masc* (-ar, -ir, -a) copyright infringement

hugvísind|i *n neu pl* (-a) humanities: **hugvísindadeild** faculty of humanities

huldufólk *n neu* (-s) hidden people, elves

humar *n masc* (-s, humrar, humra) lobster

humarhal|i *n masc* (-a, -ar, -a) scampi

humarsúp|a *n fem* (-u, -ur, -na) lobster bisque

hunang *n neu* (-s) honey

hunangsflug|a *n fem* (-u, -ur, -na) bumblebee

hundabit *n neu* (-s, -, -a) dog bite

hundakof|i *n masc* (-a, -ar, -a) kennel

hundrað *num* (*pl* hundruð) hundred: ~ **krónur** hundred krónas

hundraðasti *ord* (-a, -a) hundredth

hund|ur *n masc* (-s, -ar, -a) dog

hungrað|ur *adj* (hungruð, -) hungry

hunangssinnep *n neu* (-s) honey mustard

hungur *n neu* (-s) hunger

hungursneyð *n fem* (-ar, -ir, -a) famine

hurð *n fem* (-ar, -ir, -a) door

húð *n fem* (-ar, -ir, -a) skin

húðflúr *n neu* (-s, -, -a) tattoo

húf|a *n fem* (-u, -ur, ~) hat

húmmus *n neu* (-s) hummus

hún *pron* she

húrra *interj* hooray

hús *n neu* (-s, -, -a) house: ~ **til leigu** house for rent; **í boði ~sins** on the house

húsamálar|i *n masc* (-a, -ar, -a) painter

húsbíl|l *n masc* (-s, -ar, -a) camper

húsbóndavald *n neu* (-s, -völd, -a) authority

húsbónd|i *n masc* (-a, -ar, -a) master

húsbúnað|ur *n masc* (-ar) home furnishings

húsdýr *n neu* (-s, -, -a) domestic animal

húseigand|i *n masc* (-a, -endur, -enda) house owner

húsfreyj|a *n fem* (-u, -ur, ~) house mistress

húsgagn *n neu* (-s, -gögn, -a) piece of furniture

húsleitarheimild *n fem* (-ar, -ir, -a) *leg* search warrant

húsmóð|ir *n fem* (-ur, -mæður, -mæðra) housewife

húsmun|ir *n masc pl* (-a) household goods

hvað *pron* what: ~ **er þetta?** what is this?; ~ **sem er** anything; ~ **um það** anyway

hvaða *pron* which

hvaðan *pron* where from: ~ **ertu?** where are you from?

hvalasafn *n neu* (-s, -söfn, -a) whale museum

hvalaskoð|un *n fem* (-unar, -anir, -ana) whale watching

hvalaskoðunarferð *n fem* (-ar, -ir, -a) whale watching trip

hval|ur *n masc* (-s, -ir, -a) *zool* whale

hvar *pron* where: ~ **er pósthúsið?** where is the post office?; ~ **sem er** wherever

hvarf *n neu* (-s, hvörf, -a) disappearance; *chem* reaction

hvass *adj* (hvöss, -t) acute; windy; talking in a strict voice

hvassviðri *n neu* (-s) stormy weather

hvat|i *n masc* (-a, -ar, -a) incentive

hvatning *n fem* (-ar, -ar, -a) motivation, stimulus, encouragement

hveiti *n neu* (-s) flour; wheat

hveitideig *n neu* (-s) pastry

hvelfing *n fem* (-ar, -ar, -a) vault, arch, dome

hvell|ur *n masc* (-s, -ir, -a) bang

hvenær *pron* when: ~ **fer rútan?** when does the bus leave?

hver 1 *n masc* (-s, -ir, -a) *geog* hot
spring; **2** *pron* who: ~ **er þetta?**
who is this?; ~ **fyrir sig** each for
himself; ~ **í sínu lagi** separately
hver annan *pron* each other
hverf|a *v* (-, hvarf, hurfum, horfið)
disappear
hvergi *pron* nowhere: **ég sé hann ~**
I don't see him anywhere (literally:
I see him nowhere)
hvernig *pron* how: ~ **smakkast?**
how is the food?
hvers vegna *pron* why: ~ **ákvaðstu**
að koma hingað? why did you
decide to come here?
hversdagsleg|ur *adj* (-, -t) casual,
everyday, mundane
hversu *pron (about quantity)* how: ~
lengi bjóstu í Kanada how long
did you live in Canada?
hvert *pron* where to: ~ **ertu að fara?**
where are you going to?
hvet|ja *v* (-, hvatti, hvatt) motivate,
cheer, urge, prompt, stimulate,
encourage; ~ **til mótmæla** prompt
a demonstration
hvið|a *n fem* (-u, -ur, ~) gust of wind
hvirfilbyl|ur *n masc* (-s/jar, -jir, -ja)
tornado
hví *pron arch* why
hvíl|a *v* (-i, -di, -t) rest
hvíl|ast *v refl* (-ist, -dist, -st) rest oneself
hvílíkur *pron* (-, -t) such: ~ **léttir**
such a relief
hvíld *n fem* (-ar, -ir, -a) rest
hvísl *n neu* (-s) whisper
hvísla *v* (~, -ði, -ð) whisper
hvít|a *n fem* (-u, -ur, -a) protein
Hvíta-Rússland *N neu* (-s) Belarus
hvítasunn|a *n fem* (-u) Whitsun
hvítasunnudag|ur *n masc* (-s, -ar, -a)
Whit Sunday
hvítkál *n neu* (-s) white cabbage
hvítkálssalat *n neu* (-s, -salöt, -a) slaw
hvítlauksduft *n neu* (-s) garlic powder
hvítlauksgeir|i *n masc* (-a, -ar, -a)
clove of garlic

hvítlauksmajónes *n neu* (-s) garlic
mayonnaise
hvítlaukssós|a *n fem* (-u, -ur, ~)
garlic sauce
hvítlauk|ur *n masc* (-s, -ar, -a) garlic
Hvít-Rúss|i *n masc* (-a, -ar, -a)
Belarusian
hvítuefni *n neu* (-s) *bio* protein
hvít|ur *adj* (-, -t) *color* white: **Hvíta**
húsið The White House; ~ **fiskur**
whitefish; **hvítt kjöt** white meat
hvítvín *n neu* (-s, -, -a) white wine
hvolp|ur *n masc* (-s, -ar, -a) puppy
hvor *pron* which of two: ~ **ætlar að**
byrja which one begins?; both,
two: **þið fáið klukkutíma ~** you
both get one hour each
hvorki ... né *conj* neither ... nor:
hvorki hann né hún ætluðu að
fara neither he nor she were going
hvort. See **hvor**
hvort 1 *pron* See **hvor**; **2** *conj*
whether: **hún spurði ~ hann væri**
frá Íslandi she asked whether he
was from Iceland
hvort ... eða *conj* which one: **hvort**
viltu rauðvín eða hvítvín? which
one would you like, red wine or
white wine?
hvorugkyn *n neu* (-s) *ling* neuter
gender
hvorug|ur *pron* (-, -t) neither one
hvönn *n fem* (hvannar, hvannir,
hvanna) *flora* angelica (herb)
hyl|ja *v* (-, huldi, hulið) cover, hide
hylk|i *n neu* (-is, ~, -ja) capsule
hýð|i *n neu* (-is, ~, -a) peel; bear cave
hýen|a *n fem* (-u, -ur, -a) *zool* hyena
hæð *n fem* (-ar, -ir, -a) height, altitude;
floor: **fyrsta ~** ground floor
hæðarmæl|ir *n masc* (-is, -ar, -a)
altimeter
hæðótt|ur *adj* (-, -) hilly
hæfileikarík|ur *adj* (-, -t) talented
hæfileik|i *n masc* (-a, -ar, -a) talent,
ability
hæfni *n fem* (-) qualification

hæf|ur *adj* (-, -t) qualified
hægðalyf *n neu pl* (-ja) *med* laxative
hægð|ir *n fem pl* (-a) *med* stool
hægfara *adj* slow
hægt. *See* **hægur**
hæg|ur *adj* slow: ~ **vindur** slow
wind; **hafa sig hægan** take it easy;
hægt og hljótt quietly
hægt *adj* possible: **það er ekki** ~ it's
not possible
hægvirk|ur *adj* (-, -t) slow
hækj|a *n fem* (-u, -ur, ~) crutch
hækk|un *n fem* (-unar, -anir, -ana)
rise
hæl|l *n masc* (-s, -ar, -a) heel; peg, pin
hæn|a *n fem* (-u, -ur, -a) hen
hænsnakof|i *n masc* (-a, -ar, -a) hen
house
hæstastig *n neu* (-s) *ling* superlative
hæstirétt|ur *n masc* (-ar) supreme
court
hætt|a 1 *n fem* (-u, -ur, ~) danger,
hazard, peril, threat, risk: **hætta
á snjóflóði** risk of an avalanche;
2 *v* (-i, -i, -) end, stop, quit: ~ **að
reykja** quit smoking; ~ **við** abort;
risk; **ég hætti mér ekki þangað** I
don't dare to go there
hættuleg|ur *adj* (-, -t) dangerous,
harmful, threatening
höfða *v* (~, -ði, -ð) ~ **til** appeal to
Höfðaborg *N fem* (-ar) Cape Town
höfðing|i *n masc* (-ja, -jar, -ja)
chieftain
höfn *n fem* (hafnar, hafnir, hafna)
harbor, port
höfn|un *n fem* (-unar, hafnanir, hafnana)
rejection

höfrung|ur *n masc* (-s, -ar, -a)
dolphin
höfuðborg *n fem* (-ar, -ir, -a) capital
city
höfuðkúp|a *n fem* (-u, -ur, -na) *anat*
skull
höfuðverk|ur *n masc* (-jar, -ir, -ja)
med headache
höfundalaun *n neu* (-a) royalties
höfundarréttarlög *n neu pl* (-laga)
leg copyright law
höfundarrétt|ur *n masc* (-ar, -ir, -a)
leg copyright
höfund|ur *n masc* (-ar, -ar, -a) author,
writer
högg *n neu* (-s, -, -a) hit, blow, punch,
strike, stroke
höggmynd *n fem* (-ar, -ir, -a) statue,
sculpture
höggþétt|ur *adj* (-, -) shockproof
högg|va *v* (hegg, hjó, huggum, hog-
gið) chop
höll *n fem* (hallar, hallir, halla) palace
hömlulaus *adj* (-, -t) rampant
höml|ur *n fem pl* (hamla) constraint,
restriction
hönd *n fem* (handar, hendur, handa)
anat hand
hönnuð|ur *n masc* (-ar, -ir, -a) designer
hönn|un *n fem* (-unar, hannanir,
hannana) design
hör *n neu* (-s) flax, linen
hörfa *v* (~, -ði, -ð) retreat, recede
hörmung *n fem* (-ar, -ar, -a) calamity
hörpudisk|ur *n masc* (-s, -ar, -a)
scallops
hörpuskel *n fem* (-jar, -jar, -ja) shell

I

iðgjald *n neu* (-s, -gjöld, -a) premium
iðnaðarhverf|i *n neu* (-is, ~, -a)
    industrial district
iðnað|ur *n masc* (-ar, -ir, -a) industry
iðnskól|i *n masc* (-a, -ar, -a) trade
    school
iðra|st *v* (-, ðist, ~) repent, regret
iðrun *n fem* remorse
igla *n fem zool* leech
illgirni *n fem* spite, malice
illgjarn *adj* (-gjörn, -t) malicious
illgres|i *n neu* (-is, ~, -a) weed
illilega *adv* badly
illkynjað|ur *adj* (-kynjuð, -) *med*
    malignant
illsk|a *n fem* (-u) evilness
illúðleg|ur *adj* (-, -t) evil
ill|ur *adj* (-, -t) angry; evil
illviðrasam|ur *adj* (-söm, -t) stormy:
    ~ **vetur** a stormy winter
ilmandi *adj* fragrant
ilmsterk|ur *adj* (-, -t) aromatic
ilm|ur *n masc* (-s, -ir, -a) aroma,
    good smell
ilmvatn *n neu* (-s, -vötn, -a) perfume
ilskó|r *n masc* (-s, ~, -a) flip-flops
Indland *N neu* (-s) India
Indlandshaf *N neu* (-s) Indian Ocean
Indónesía *N fem* (-u) Indonesia
indónesísk|ur *adj* (-, -t) Indonesian
Indverj|i *n masc* (-a, -ar, -a) Indian
    (a person from India)
indversk|ur *adj* (-, -t) Indian
indæl|l *adj* (-, -t) lovely, pleasant, nice
inflúens|a *n fem* (-u) *med* influenza
inkanjálafræ *n neu* (-s, -, -ja) quinoa
inn *adv* in: **komdu** ~ come in; *prep*
    in, through: **fara** ~ **ganginn** walk
    through the corridor
inn í *prep* into: **fara** ~ **búðina** go
    into the store

innan 1 *adv* on the inside; **2** *prep*
    + *gen* within, from the inside: ~
    flokksins within the party
innanhússhönnuð|ur *n masc* (-ar,
    -ir, -a) interior designer
innanhússhönn|un *n fem* (-unar,
    -hannanir, -ana) interior design
innanríkisráðherra *n masc* (~, -r, ~)
    secretary of state
innantóm|ur *adj* (-, -t) meaningless,
    empty: **innantóm orð** empty words
innblást|ur *n masc* (-s, -blástrar,
    -blástra) inspiration
innborg|un *n fem* (-unar, -anir, -ana)
    deposit
innfædd|ur *adj* (-, -fætt) native
innflutning|ur *n masc* (-s) import
innflytjand|i *n masc* (-a, -endur, -enda)
    importer; immigrant
inngang|ur *n masc* (-s, -ar, -a)
    entrance
innherjaviðskipt|i *n neu pl* (-a)
    insider trading
inni *adv* in; inside, indoors
innifalin|n *adj* (-, -falið) inclusive
innihald *n neu* (-s) ingredient, content
innilaug *n fem* (-ar, -ar, -a) indoor
    pool
innileg|ur *adj* (-, -t) sincere
innilokað|ur *adj* (-lokuð, -) confined
inniskó|r *n masc* (-s, ~, -a) slippers
innkaup *n neu pl* (-a) shopping;
    purchase
innkaupakarf|a *n fem* (-körfu, -kör-
    fur, -karfa) shopping basket
innkaupakerr|a *n fem* (-u, -ur, -a)
    shopping cart
innkaupavagn *n masc* (-s, -ar, -a)
    shopping cart
innkom|a *n fem* (-u) entering
innlögn *n fem* (-lagnar) input

innmat|ur *n masc* (-ar) *a food made out of organs and intestines*
innrás *n fem* (-ar, -ir, -a) intrusion
innrásarmað|ur *n masc* (-manns, -menn, -manna) intruder
innri *adv* inner
innrit|un *n fem* (-unar, -anir, -ana) admission
innsetning *n fem* (-ar, -ar, -a) installation

innskráning *n fem* (-ar, -ar, -a) admission
innstung|a *n fem* (-u, -ur, -na) socket, electrical outlet
innvið|ir *n masc pl* (-a) infrastructure
innvortis *adv* internal: ~ **blæðing** internal bleeding
insúlín *n neu* (-s) *med* insulin
internet *n neu* (-s) Internet

Í

í *prep + dat (location)* in: ~ **Reykja-vík** in Reykjavík, ~ **búðinni** in the store; *(lifespan)* ~ **ellinni** during old age; *(body parts)* **heilinn ~ mér** my brain; *+ acc (movement to)* to: **ég ætla ~ búðina** I'm going to the store, **fara ~ skólann** going to school; *(stretch of time)* for: **ég er á Íslandi ~ fimm daga** I'm in Iceland for five days

í bak og fyrir *adv* thoroughly
í bili *adv* for a while
í bráð *adv* soon
í burtu *adv* away
í gegn *adv* through
í kring *adv* around
í kringum *prep + acc* around: ~ **jólatréð** around the Christmas tree
í laumi *adv* secretly, in secret
í rauninni *phr* actually
íbúafjöld|i *n masc* (-a, -ar, -a) population
íbúð *n fem* (-ar, -ir, -a) apartment, flat
íbúðarhús *n neu* (-s, -, -a) residence
íbú|i *n masc* (-a, -ar, -a) inhabitant, resident, occupant
ídýf|a *n fem* (-u, -ur, ~) dip
íðorð *n neu ling* terminology
ígerð *n fem* (-ar, -ir, -a) *med* sepsis
ígræðsl|a *n fem* (-u, -ur, -na) *med* transplant
ígulker *n neu* (-s, -, -a/ja) *zool* sea urchin
íhaldsmað|ur *n masc* (-manns, -menn, -manna) conservative person
íhaldssam|ur *adj* (-söm, -t) conservative
íhuga *v* (~, -ði, -ð) consider, ponder
íhugun *n fem* (-ar) reflection
íkorn|i *n masc* (-a, -ar, -a) *zool* squirrel
íkveikj|a *n fem* (-u, -ur, ~) arson

ímynd *n fem* (-ar, -ir, -a) image
ímynda sér *v refl* (~, -ði, -ð) imagine, fancy
ímyndað|ur *adj* (ímynduð, -) imaginary
ímynd|un *n fem* (-unar, -anir, -ana) imagination
ímyndunarafl *n neu* (-s) fantasy
Írak *N neu* (-s) Iraq
írak|i *n masc* (-a, -ar, -a) Iraqi
Íran *N neu* (-s) Iran
íransk|ur *adj* (írönsk, -t) Iranian
Ír|i *n masc* (-a, -ar, -a) Irish person
Írland *N neu* (-s) Ireland
íróní|a *n fem* (-u) *lit* irony
írsk|a *n fem* (-u) Irish language
írsk|ur *adj* (-, -t) Irish
ís *n masc* (-s, -ar, -a) ice; ice cream
ísbjörn *n masc* (-bjarnar, -birnir, -bjarna) *zool* polar bear
ísbrauð *n neu* (-s, -, -a) ice cream cone
ísbrjót|ur *n masc* (-s, -ar, -a) ice-breaker
ísbúð *n fem* (-ar, -ir, -a) ice cream parlor
íshokkí *n neu* (-s) ice hockey
íshokkískaut|i *n masc* (-a, -ar, -a) hockey skate
ísing *n fem* (-ar) glazed frost
ísjak|i *n masc* (-a, -ar, -a) iceberg
ískex *n neu* (-, -, -a) wafer
ískra *v* (~, -ði, -ð) screech
ískur *n neu* (-s) screech
Íslamabad *N neu* (-) Islamabad
íslamsk|ur *adj* (íslömsk, -t) Islamic
Ísland *N neu* (-s) Iceland
Íslendingasag|a *n fem* (-sögu, -sö-gur, -sagna) *lit* Saga of Icelanders
Íslending|ur *n masc* (-s, -ar, -a) Icelander

íslensk|a *n fem* (-u) Icelandic
language
íslensk|ur *adj* (-, -t) Icelandic:
íslensk fræði Icelandic studies
íspinn|i *n masc* (-a, -ar, -a) popsicle
Ísrael *N neu* (-s) Israel
ísraelsk|ur *adj* (-, -t) Israeli
Ísraelsmað|ur *n masc* (-manns,
-menn, -manna) Israeli
ísskáp|ur *n masc* (-s, -ar, -a)
refrigerator
íste *n neu* (-s) iced tea
ístert|a *n fem* (-u, -ur, -na) ice cream
cake
Ítal|i *n masc* (-a, -ir, -a) Italian
Ítalí|a *N fem* (-u) Italy
ítalsk|a *n fem* (ítölsku) Italian
language
ítalsk|ur *adj* (ítölsk, -t) Italian
ítarlega *adv* thoroughly
ítarleg|ur *adj* (-, -t) thorough,
detailed
ítreka *v* (~, -ði, -ð) reaffirm, reiterate
ítrek|un *n fem* (-unar, -anir, -ana)
reiteration, reminder

íþrótt *n fem* (-ar, -ir, -a) sports
íþróttabúð *n fem* (-ar, -ir, -a) sports
store
íþróttafélag *n neu* (-s, -félög, -a)
sports club
íþróttaföt *n neu pl* (-fata) sportswear
íþróttahús *n neu* (-s, -, -a) sports hall
íþróttaleikvang|ur *n masc* (-s, -ar, -a)
sports stadium
íþróttamað|ur *n masc* (-manns,
-menn, -manna) athlete
íþróttapeys|a *n fem* (-u, -ur, -a)
sweatshirt
íþróttasal|ur *n masc* (-ar, -ir, -a)
sports hall
íþróttaskó|r *n masc* (-s, ~, -a) sneaker
íþróttavöll|ur *n masc* (-vallar, -vellir,
-valla) playing field
íþróttavör|ur *n fem pl* (-vara)
sporting goods
íþyngj|a *v* (íþyngi, íþyngdi, íþyngt)
burden

J

jaðartilfell|i *n neu* (-is, ~, -a) border-line case

jaðartónlist *n fem* (-ar) underground music, alternative music

jafn *adj* (jöfn, -t) equal, even; smooth

jafna *v* (~, -ði, -ð) even out, equal, tie

jafnaðarmað|ur *n masc* (-manns, -menn, -manna) Social Democrat

jafna|st *v refl* (~, ðist, ~) evens out; ~ **á við** matches

jafngild|a *v* (-i, -gilti, -gilt) equal, correspond

jafning|i *n masc* (-a, -jar, -ja) peer

jafnrétti *n neu* (-s) equal rights

jafnræði *n neu* (-s) equality

jafnvel *adv* even

jafnvægi *n neu* (-s) balance, equity

jakk|i *n masc* (-a, -ar, -a) jacket

jalapenjó *n neu* (-s, -, -a) jalapeno

Jamaík|a *N fem* (-u) Jamaica

janúar *n masc* (-) January

Japan *N neu* (-s) Japan

Japan|i *n masc* (-a, -ir/-ar, -a) Japanese person

japansk|a *n fem* (japönsku) Japanese language

japansk|ur *adj* (japönsk, -t) Japanese

jarðaber *n neu* (-s, -, -ja) strawberry

jarðaberjaís *n masc* (-s, -ar, -a) strawberry ice cream

jarðarför *n fem* (-farar, -farir, -a) funeral

jarðeðlisfræð|i *n neu* (-a) geophysics

jarðfræði *n fem* (-) geology

jarðfræðileg|ur *adj* (-, -t) geological

jarðfræðing|ur *n masc* (-s, -ar, -a) geologist

jarðgöng *n neu pl* tunnel

jarðhitasvæð|i *n neu* (-is, ~, -a) *geol* geothermal area

jarðhnet|a *n fem* (-u, -ur, ~) peanut

jarðhnetuolí|a *n fem* (-u, -ur, -a) peanut oil

jarðhnetusmjör *n neu* (-s) peanut butter

jarðhæð *n fem* (-ar, -ir, -a) ground floor

jarðskjálftamæl|ir *n masc* (-is, -ar, a) *geol* seismograph

jarðskjálft|i *n masc* (-a, -ar, a) *geol* earthquake

jarðskorpuhreyfing|ar *n fem pl* (-a) *geol* continental drift

jarðveg|ur *n masc* (-s/ar, -ir, -a) soil

jarl *n masc* (-s, -ar, a) earl

jasmín|a *n fem* (-u, -ur, -a) *flora* jasmine

jaxl *n masc* (-s, -ar, a) molar (tooth)

já *adv* yes

jákvæð|ur *adj* (-, -kvætt) positive

járn *n neu* (-s, ~, -a) iron

járna *v* (~, -ði, -ð) shoe a horse

járnbraut *n fem* (-ar, -ir, -a) rail

járnbrautarstöð *n fem* (-var, -var, -va) railway station

játning *n fem* (-ar, -ar, -a) confession

Jemen *N neu* (-s) Yemen

jemensk|ur *adj* (-, -t) Yemeni

jepp|i *n masc* (-a, -ar, a) jeep, all-terrain vehicle

Jerúsalem *N fem* (-) Jerusalem

jiddísk|a *n fem* (-u) Yiddish

joð *n neu* (-s) *chem* iodine

jóga *n neu* (-) yoga

jógúrt *n fem* (-ar, -ir, -a) yogurt

jól *n neu pl* (-a) Christmas

jólaboð *n neu* (-s, -, -a) Christmas party

jóladag|ur *n masc* (-s, -ar, a) Christmas Day

jólafrí *n neu* (-s, -, -a) Christmas holiday

jólagjöf *n fem* (-gjafar, -gjafir, -gjafa) Christmas gift

jólakort *n neu* (-s, -, -a) Christmas card

jólaskraut *n neu* (-s) Christmas decoration

jólatré *n neu* (-s, -, -trjáa) Christmas tree

jón *n fem* (-ar, -ir, -a) *chem* ion

Jórdan *N neu* (-s) Jordan

Jórdan|i *n masc* (-a, -ar, a) Jordanian

jórdansk|ur *adj* (-dönsk, -t) Jordanian

jurt *n fem* (-ar, -ir, -a) plant

jurtate *n neu* (-s) herbal tea

jú *adv* yes

júdó *n neu* (-s) judo

júlí *n masc* (-) July

júní *n masc* (-) June

jæja *interj* well, oh well

jöklasalat *n neu* (-s) iceberg lettuce

jökulá *n fem* (-ár, -ár, -a) *geog* glacier river

jökulhlaup *n neu* (-s, -, -a) *geol* glacier burst

jökulkald|ur *adj* (-köld, -kalt) frigid

jökul|l *n masc* (-s, jöklar, jökla) *geol* glacier

jökulsprung|a *n fem* (-u, -ur, -na) *geol* crevasse

jörð *n fem* (jarðar, jarðir, jarða) earth

jötun|n *n masc* (-s, jötnar, jötna) giant

K

kabarett *n masc* (-s, -ar, -a) cabaret
Kabúl *N fem* (-) Kabul
kaðal|l *n masc* (kaðals, kaðlar, kaðla) rope
kafar|i *n masc* (-a, -ar, -a) scuba diver
kafbát|ur *n masc* (-s, -ar, -a) submarine
kaffi *n neu* (-s) coffee
kaffiboll|i *n masc* (-a, -ar, -a) coffee cup
kaffifífil|l *n masc* (-s, -fíflar, -fífla) *flora* chicory
kaffihús *n neu* (-s, -, -a) café
kaffikann|a *n fem* (-könnu, -könnur, -kanna) coffee pot
kaffikrús *n fem* (-ar, -ir, -a) coffee mug
kaffipok|i *n masc* (-a, -ar, -a) coffee filter
kaffiterí|a *n fem* (-u, -ur, -a) cafeteria
kaffitím|i *n masc* (-a, -ar, -a) coffee break
kaffivél *n fem* (-ar, -ar, -a) coffeemaker
kafl|i *n masc* (-a, -ar, -a) *lit* chapter; *mus* movement
kafna *v* (~, -ði, -ð) choke
Kairó *N fem* (-) Cairo
kakkalakk|i *n masc* (-a, -ar, -a) cockroach
kakó *n neu* (-s) cocoa, hot chocolate
kaktus *n masc* (-s, -ar, -a) cactus
kaldhæðni *n fem* (-) *lit* sarcasm
kald|ur *adj* (köld, kalt) cold
kalkstein|n *n masc* (-s, -ar, -a) *geol* limestone
kalkún|i *n masc* (-s, -ar, -a) *zool* turkey
kall *n neu* (-s, köll, -a) shout
kalla *v* (~, -ði, -ð) call, shout; ~ **upp** page
kalorí|a *n fem* (-u, -ur, -a) calorie
kalsíum *n neu* (-s) *chem* calcium
Kambódí|a *N fem* (-u) Cambodia

Kamerún *N neu* (-s) Cameroon
kamill|a *n fem* (-u, -ur, -a) chamomile
kampavín *n neu* (-s, -, -a) champagne
Kanada *N neu* (-) Canada
Kanadabú|i *n masc* (-a, -ar, -a) Canadian
Kanadamað|ur *n masc* (-manns, -menn, -manna) Canadian
kanadísk|ur *adj* (-, -t) Canadian
Kan|i *n masc* (-a, -ar, -a) *slang* American
kanil|l *n masc* (-s) cinnamon
kanilsnúð|ur *n masc* (-s/ar, -ar, -a) cinnamon bun
kanín|a *n fem* (-u, -ur, -a) rabbit
kann|a 1 *n fem* (könnu, könnur, kanna) jug, pitcher; **2 kanna** *v* (~, -ði, -ð) survey
kannski *adv* maybe, perhaps
kanslar|i *n masc* (-a, -ar, -a) chancellor
kantalúpmelón|a *n fem* (-u, -ur, -a) cantaloupe
kantarell|a *n fem* (-u, -ur, -a) chantarelle
kant|ur *n masc* (-s, -ar, -a) curb; edge
kapalsjónvarp *n neu* (-s, -vörp, -a) cable TV
kapell|a *n fem* (-u, -ur, -na) chapel
kapers *n neu* (-) capers
kappakstur *n masc* (-s) car race
kappræð|ur *n fem pl* (-na) debate
karafl|a *n fem* (-u, -ur, -a/-na) carafe
karakter *n masc* (-s, -ar, -a) character
karamell|a *n fem* (-u, -ur, -a) caramel, toffee; fudge
karamellusós|a *n fem* (-u, -ur, -a) caramel sauce
karate *n neu* (-s) karate
kardimomm|a *n fem* (-u, -ur, -a) cardamom

karf|a *n fem* (körfu, körfur, karfa) basket
karf|i *n masc* (-a, -ar, -a) *zool* redfish
Karíbahaf *N neu* (-s) Caribbean Sea
karlaklósett *n neu* (-s, -, -a) mens' restroom
karlasnyrting *n fem* (-ar, -ar, -a) mens' restroom
karlkyn *n neu* (-s) male
karlmannaföt *n neu pl* (-fata) menswear
karlmannleg|ur *adj* (-, -t) masculine
karrí *n neu* (-s) curry
kart|a *n fem* (körtu, körtur, -na) *zool* toad
kartafl|a *n fem* (-öflu, -öflur, -afla) potato
kartöfluflag|a *n fem* (-flögu, -flögur, -na) potato chip
kartöflugratín *n neu* (-s, -, -a) potatoes au gratin
kartöflustapp|a *n fem* (-stöppu, -stöppur, -stappa) mashed potatoes
kartöflusúp|a *n fem* (-u, -ur, -na) potato soup
Kasakstan *N neu* (-s) Kazakhstan
Kasakstan|i *n masc* (-a, -ar, -a) Kazakhstani
kasjúhnet|a *n fem* (-u, -ur, ~) cashew
kassavarót *n fem* (-ar, -rætur, -a) cassava
kassett|a *n fem* (-u, -ur, -a) cassette, tape
kass|i *n masc* (-a, -ar, -a) box
kast *n neu* (-s, köst, -a) pitch, throw; fit, tantrum: **hann fékk ~** he had a trantrum
kasta *v* (~, -ði, -ð) throw, toss, pitch; **~ upp** throw up
kastal|i *n masc* (-a, -ar, -a) castle
kastaníuhnet|a *n fem* (-u, -ur, -a) chestnut
katalónsk|a *n fem* (-u) Catalan language
Katar *N neu* (-s) Qatar
Katar|i *n masc* (-a, -ar, -a) Qatari
katarsk|ur *adj* (katörsk, -t) Qatari

kattarmint|a *n fem* (-u) *flora* catmint
kaup *n neu* (-s, -, -a) pay, salary, wage; *(in plural)* purchase
kaup|a *v* (-i, keypti, keypt) purchase, buy; **~ inn** shop
kaupand|i *n masc* (-a, -endur, -enda) buyer
kauphöll *n fem* (-hallar, -hallir, -halla) *econ* stock exchange
kaupmað|ur *n masc* (-manns, -menn, -manna) grocer
Kaupmannahöfn *N fem* (-hafnar) Copenhagen
kaupmál|i *n masc* (-a, -ar, -a) *leg* prenuptial agreement
kavíar *n masc* (-s) caviar
kaþólsk|ur *adj* (-, -t) Catholic
káet|a *n fem* (-u, -ur, -a) cabin on boat
kál *n neu* (-s) cabbage
kálfakjöt *n neu* (-s) veal
kálf|i *n masc* (-a, -ar, -a) calf muscle
kálf|ur *n masc* (-s, -ar, -a) calf
kálsúp|a *n fem* (-u, -ur, -na) cabbage soup
kámug|ur *adj* (-, -t) sticky; messy
káp|a *n fem* (-u, -ur, -a) *(for women)* overcoat
káss|a *n fem* (-u, -ur, -a) stew
kát|ur *adj* (-, -t) glad
kebab *n neu* (-s) kebab
keðj|a *n fem* (-u, -ur, ~) chain
Keflavíkurflugvöll|ur *n masc* (-vallar, -vellir, -valla) Keflavik airport
keil|a *n fem* (-u) *bio* tusk; *sports* bowling
keilukúl|a *n fem* (-u, -ur, -na) bowling ball
keim|ur *n masc* (-s) savor
keisarynj|a *n fem* (-u, -ur, ~) empress
kekkja|st *v refl* (~, -ðist, ~) clot
kekkjótt|ur *adj* (-, -) clotted
Kenía *N fem* (-) Kenya
Keníamað|ur *n masc* (-manns, -menn, -manna) Kenyan
kenísk|ur *adj* (-, -t) Kenyan
kenn|a *v* (-i, -di, -t) teach; **~ um** blame

kennaraborð *n neu* (-s, -, -a)
teacher's desk
kennarastof|a *n fem* (-u, -ur, -a)
teacher's room
kennaratafl|a *n fem* (-töflu, -töflur,
-taflna) whiteboard
kennar|i *n masc* (-a, -ar, -a) teacher
kennileit|i *n neu* (-is, ~, -a) landmark
kenning *n fem* (-ar, -ar, -a) theory
kennsl|a *n fem* (-u) teaching
kennslufræði *n fem* (-) pedagogy
kennslustof|a *n fem* (-u, -ur, -a)
classroom
kennslustund *n fem* (-ar, -ir, -a) lesson
kepp|a *v* (-i, -ti, -t) compete
keppinaut|ur *n masc* (-s/ar, -ar, -a)
rival
keppn|i *n fem* (-i, -ir, -a) competition,
race
keramík *n neu* (-s) ceramics
kerf|i *n neu* (-is, ~, -a) system
kerfil|l *n masc* (-s, kerflar, kerfla)
flora chervil
kerfisbundið *adv* systematically
kerfisbundin|n *adj* (-, -bundið)
systematic
kerr|a *n fem* (-u, -ur, -a) stroller; cart
kert|i *n neu* (-is, ~, -a) candle
ketil|l *n masc* (-s, katlar, katla) boiler
kettling|ur *n masc* (-s, -ar, -a) kitten
kex *n neu* (-, -, -a) biscuit, cookie
keyr|a *v* (-i, -ði, -t) drive
keyrsl|a *n fem* (-u, -ur, -na) driving
kilj|a *n fem* (-u, -ur, -a) paperback
kind *n fem* (-ar, -ir, -a) sheep
kindakjöt *n neu* (-) mutton
kinn *n fem* (-ar, -ar, -a) *anat* cheek
kinnhol|a *n fem* (-u, -ur, -a) *anat*
sinus
kipp|a *n fem* (-u, -ur, ~) bundle; six
pack
kirkj|a *n fem* (-u, -ur, kirkna) church
kirkjugarð|ur *n masc* (-s, -ar, -a)
cemetery
kirkjutónlist *n fem* (-ar) sacred
music, church music, hymn
kirsuber *n neu* (-s, -, -ja) cherry

kirsuberjabak|a *n fem* (-böku,
-bökur, -baka) cherry pie
kirsuberjalíkjör *n masc* (-s, -ar, -a)
cherry liquor
kirsuberjatómat|ur *n masc* (-s, -ar,
-a) cherry tomato
kirtil|l *n masc* (-s, kirtlar, kirtla) *bio*
gland
kis|a *n fem* (-u, -ur, -a) *colloq* kitty
kis|i *n masc* (-a, -ar, -a) *colloq* kitty
kist|a *n fem* (-u, -ur, -na) trunk
kík|ir *n masc* (-is, -jar, -ja) binoculars
kík|ja *v* (-i, -ti, -t) look, peek
kíló *n neu* (-s, -, -a) kilogram
kílóbæt|i *n neu* (-is, ~, -a) kilobyte
kílógramm *n neu* (-s, -grömm, -a)
kilogram
kílómetr|i *n masc* (-a, -ar, -a) kilometer
Kína *N neu* (-) China
kínakál *n neu* (-s) Chinese cabbage,
pe-tsai cabbage
kínóa *n neu* (-) quinoa
Kínverj|i *N masc* (-a, -ar, -a) Chinese
person
kínversk|ur *adj* (-, -t) Chinese
Kírgistan *N neu* (-s) Kyrgyzstan
kírgistansk|ur *adj* (kírgistönsk, -t)
Kyrgyzstani
kírópraktor *n masc* (-s, -ar, -a) *med*
chiropractor
kíví *n masc* (-s, -ar, -a) kiwi
kjafta *v slang* (~, -ði, -ð) talk, chat
kjaftasag|a *n fem* (-sögu, -sögur,
-sagna) hearsay, rumor
kjaft|ur *n masc* (-s, -ar, -a) animal's
mouth
kjaftæði *n neu* (-s) rubbish, unseri-
ous talk
kjallar|i *n masc* (-a, -ar, -a) basement
kjarkur courage
kjarnaofn *n masc* (-s, -ar, -a) nuclear
reactor
kjarn|i *n masc* (-a, -ar, -a) core,
kernel, nucleus
kjarnork|a *n fem* (-u) nuclear energy
kjarnorkusprengj|a *n fem* (-u, -ur, ~)
nuclear bomb

kjarnorkustöð *n fem* (-var, -var, -va)
nuclear power station

kjarnorkutilraun|ir *n fem pl* (-a)
nuclear testing

kjarnorkuvopn *n neu* (-s, -, -a)
nuclear weapon

kjarr *n neu* (-s, kjörr, -) brushwood

kjálk|i *n masc* (-a, -ar, -a) *anat* jaw

kjánaleg|ur *adj* (-, -t) silly

kjól|l *n masc* (-s, -ar, -a) dress, gown

kjós|a *v* (kýs, kaus, kusum, kosið)
elect, vote

kjósand|i *n masc* (-a, -endur, -enda)
voter

kjúklingabaun *n fem* (-ar, -ir, -a)
chickpea

kjúklingabring|a *n fem* (-u, -ur, -na)
chicken breast

kjúklingasúp|a *n fem* (-u, -ur, -na)
chicken soup

kjúklingavæng|ur *n masc* (-s, -ir,
-ja) chicken wing

kjúkling|ur *n masc* (-s, -ar, -a) chicken

kjöl|ur *n masc* (kjalar, kilir, kjala)
keel; *(of a book)* spine

kjörbúð *n fem* (-ar, -ir, -a) grocery
store; convenience store

kjörbýl|i *n neu* (-is, -, -a) *geog*
natural habitat

kjörklef|i *n masc* (-a, -ar, -a) polling
booth

kjörseðil|l *n masc* (-s, -seðlar, -seðla)
ballot

kjörstað|ur *n masc* (-ar, -ir, -a)
polling station

kjöt *n neu* (-s) meat: **nautakjöt** beef;
lambakjöt lamb; **svínakjöt** pork

kjötálegg *n neu* (-s, -, -ja) cold cuts

kjötboll|a *n fem* (-u, -ur, -a) meatball

kjöthakk *n neu* (-s) minced meat

kjöthleif|ur *n masc* (-s, -ar, -a)
meatloaf

kjötkveðjuhátíð *n fem* (-ar, -ir, -a)
carnival

kjötsneið *n fem* (-ar, -ar, -a) slice
of meat

kjötsoð *n neu* (-s) meat stock

klaga *v* (~, -ði, -ð) complain; report

klak|i *n masc* (-a, -ar, -a) ice

klapp *n neu* (-s, klöpp, -a) clap,
clapping; pat

klappa *v* (~, -ði, -ð) clap; pat: ~
hundinum pat the dog

klarinett|a *n fem* (-u, -ur, ~) clarinet

klas|i *n masc* (-a, -ar, -a) cluster

klassík *n fem* (-ur) classic

klassísk|ur *adj* (-, -t) classic

klaufaleg|ur *adj* (-, -t) awkward

klaustur *n neu* (-s, -, klaustra) abbey,
monastery, convent

kláðamaur *n masc* (-s) *med* scabies

kláf|ur *n masc* (-s, -ar, -a) gondola

klár *adj* (-, -t) smart, wise, sharp

klára *v* (~, -ði, -ð) complete, finish

klef|i *n masc* (-a, -ar, -a) cell

klein|a *n fem* (-u, -ur, ~) Icelandic
twisted doughnut

kleinuhring|ur *n masc* (-s, -ir/ar,
-ja/a) doughnut

klementín|a *n fem* (-u, -ur, ~)
clementine

klemm|a *n fem* (-u, -ur, ~) peg for
laundry

klerk|ur *n masc* (-s, -ar, -a) parson

klettabog|i *n masc* (-a, -ar, -a) *geol*
natural arch

Klettafjöll *N neu pl* (-fjalla) Rocky
Mountains

klettasalat *n neu* (-s) rocket salad,
arugula

klettaströnd *n fem* (-strandar, -strandir,
-stranda) *geol* shore cliff

klett|ur *n masc* (-s, -ar, -a) *geol* cliff,
rock

klifra *v* (~, -ði, -ð) climb

klifur *n neu* (-s) climbing, climb

klifurjurt *n fem* (-ar, -ir, -a) vine

klikkað|ur *adj* (klikkuð, -) crazy

klippar|i *n masc* (-a, -ar, -a) barber,
hairdresser

klipping *n fem* (-ar, -ar, -a) haircut

klipp|ur *n fem pl* (-a) shears

klíð *n neu* (-s) bran

klíp|a 1 *n fem* (-u, -ur, -na) pinch; **2** *v*

(-i, kleip, klipum, klipið) pinch

klístrað|ur *adj* (klístruð, -) sticky

kljúf|a *v* (klýf, klauf, klufum, klofið) split

kloss|i *n masc* (-a, ar, -a) clog

klóna *v* (~, -ði, -ð) clone

klón|un *n fem* (-unar, -anir, -ana) cloning

klór *n masc* (-s) bleach, chlorine

klósett *n neu* (-s, -, -a) lavatory, toilet

klósettpappír *n masc* (-s) toilet paper

klukk|a *n fem* (-u, -ur, -na) clock

klukkustund *n fem* (-ar, -ir, -a) hour

klukkutím|i *n masc* (-a, -ar, -a) hour

klúbb|ur *n masc* (-s, -ar, -a) club

klút|ur *n masc* (-s, -ar, -a) scarf

klæð|a *v* (-i, klæddi, klætt) suit, look good on someone; dress, put on clothes

klæðaburð|ur *n masc* (-ar, -ir, -a) way of dressing

klæð|ast *v refl* (-ist, klæddist, klæðst) wear

klæðnað|ur *n masc* (-ar) clothing

klæðsker|i *n masc* (-a, -ar, -a) tailor

klæðskipting|ur *n masc* (-s, -ar, -a) transvestite

klæja *v + acc subj* (~, -ði, -ð) itch: **mig klæjar** I'm itching

klöngra|st *v* (~, -ðist, ~) scramble

klöpp *n fem* (klappar, klappir, klappa) *geol* rock

knap|i *n masc* (-a, -ar, -a) jockey

knipp|i *n neu* (-is, ~, -a) bunch

knýj|a *v* (kný, knúði, knúið) propel

knæp|a *n fem* (-u, -ur, -a) pub

koddaver *n neu* (-s, -, -a) pillowcase

kodd|i *n masc* (-a, -ar, -a) pillow

koffín *n neu* (-s) caffeine

koffínlaus *adj* (-, -t) caffeine-free

kof|i *n masc* (-a, -ar, -a) cottage, cabin, hut, shed

kokk|ur *n masc* (-s, -ar, -a) cook, chef

kokteil|l *n masc* (-s, -ar, -a) cocktail

kol *n neu* (-s, -, -a) coal

kolefn|i *n neu* (-is, ~, -a) carbon

kolkrabb|i *n masc* (-a, -ar, -a) octopus, cuttlefish

koll|a *n fem* (-u, -ur, -na) mug, beer mug

koll|ur *n masc* (-s, -ar, -a) stool

kolsýrð|ur *adj* (-, -sýrt) carbonated

kom|a 1 *n fem* (-u, -ur, -a) arrival; **2** *v* (kem, kom, komum, komið) come, arrive; **~ á óvart** surprise; **~ fram** perform; **~ fyrir** occur; **~ í verk** accomplish; **~ með** bring; **~ upp** appear, arise, establish; **~ við** touch

kom|ast *v refl* (kemst, -st, -ist) able to go: **ég kemst ekki í dag** I'm not able to go today; **~ af** survive

komm|a *n fem* (-u, -ur, -a) comma

kommóð|a *n fem* (-u, -ur, -a) dresser, chest of drawers

kommúnism|i *n masc* (-a) communism

kommúnist|i *n masc* (-a, -ar, -a) communist

kon|a *n fem* (-u, -ur, kvenna) woman

Kongóbú|i *n masc* (-a, -ar, -a) Congolese

konsert *n masc* (-s, -ar, -a) *mus* concerto

kontrabass|i *n masc* (-a, -ar, -a) *mus* double bass

konungasaga *n fem* (-sögu, -sögur, -sagna) *lit* king's saga

konungleg|ur *adj* (-, -t) royal, regal

konungsfólk *n neu* (-s) royalty

konungsrík|i *n neu* (-is, ~, -ja) kingdom

konungsveld|i *n neu* (-is, ~, -a) monarchy

konung|ur *n masc* (-s, -ar, -a) king

kopar *n masc* (-s) copper

kork|ur *n masc* (-s, -ar, -a) cork

korn *n neu* (-s, -, -a) grain

kornflex *n neu* (-) cornflakes

kornhæn|a *n fem* (-u, -ur, -a) *zool* quail

kornótt|ur *adj* (-, -) granulated

kort *n neu* (-s, -, -a) card

kortanúmer *n neu* (-s, -, -a) card number

kosningabarátt|a *n fem* (-u, -ur, -a) election campaign

kosning|ar *n fem pl* (-a) elections

koss *n masc* (-, -ar, -a) kiss
kostaboð *n neu* (-s, -, -a) bargain
kostnað|ur *n masc* (-ar) cost, expense
kost|ur *n masc* (-s, -ir, -a) advantage; alternative; **að öðrum kosti** otherwise, alternatively
kotasæl|a *n fem* (-u) cottage cheese
kóð|i *n masc* (-a, -ar, -a) code
kók *n neu/fem* coke *(cola soda)*: **ég ætla að fá eina ~** I would like to have a coke, please
kókaín *n neu* (-s) cocaine
kókoshnet|a *n fem* (-u, -ur, -a) coconut
kókoshnetumjólk *n fem* (-ur) coconut milk
kókoshneturjóm|i *n masc* (-a) coconut cream
kókossmjör *n neu* (-s) coconut butter
Kólumbí|a *N fem* (-u) Colombia
kólumbísk|ur *adj* (-, -t) Colombian
Kólumbíumað|ur *N masc* (-manns, -menn, -manna) Colombian person
kónguló *n fem* (-ar, -lær, -lóa) spider
kóng|ur *n masc* (-s, -ar, -a) king
kóp|ur *n masc* (-s, -ar, -a) *zool* seal pup
kór *n masc* (-s, -ar, -a) choir
Kóre|a *N fem* (-u) Korea
kóresk|a *n fem* (-u) Korean language
kóresk|ur *adj* (-, -t) Korean
Kóreumað|ur *n masc* (-manns, -menn, -manna) Korean
kóríander *n masc* (-s) coriander, cilantro
kórón|a *n fem* (-u, -ur, -a) crown
kósher *adj* kosher
Kósóvó *N neu* (-) Kosovo
kótilett|a *n fem* (-u, -ur, -a) cutlet, chop
krá *n fem* (-r, -r, -a) pub, bar, tavern
krabbamein *n neu* (-s, -, -a) *med* cancer
krabb|i *n masc* (-a, -ar, -a) crab
Krabb|inn *N masc def* (-ans) *astro* Cancer
kraf|a *n fem* (kröfu, kröfur, krafna) demand
kraftlyfting|ar *n fem pl* (-a) weight-lifting

kraftmikil|l *adj* (-, -mikið) powerful
kraft|ur *n masc* (-s, -ar, -a) power, energy
krakk|i *n masc* (-a, -ar, -a) kid
krampaflog *neu* (-s, -, -a) *med* spasm, seizure
kramp|i *n masc* (-a, -ar, -a) *med* spasm, seizure
kranabjór *n masc* (-s, -ar, -a) beer on tap
kran|i *n masc* (-a, -ar, -a) tap, faucet: **á krana** on tap
krapís *n masc* (-s, -ar, -a) sorbet, sherbet, sherbert
krák|a *n fem* (-u, -ur, -a) *zool* crow
kredit *n neu* (-s) credit
kreditkort *n neu* (-s, -, -a) credit card
krefj|a *v* (kref, krafði, krafið) demand
krefj|ast *v refl* (krefst, krafðist, krafist) demand
kreista *v* (-i, -i, -t) squeeze
krem *n neu* (-s, -, -a) lotion
kremj|a *v* (krem, kramdi, kramið) crush, squish
krepp|a *n fem* (-u, -ur, ~) *econ* recession, depression
krimm|i *n masc* (-a, -ar, -a) *slang* criminal; crime novel
kringluleit|ur *adj* (-, -t) round-faced
kringum *prep + acc* around: **~ húsið** around the house
kristal|l *n masc* (-s, -ar, -a) *geol* crystal
kristallað|ur *adj* (kristölluð, -) crystallized
kristin|n *adj* (-, kristið) Christian
Kristur *N masc* (-s) Christ
krí|a *n fem* (-u, -ur, ~) *zool* tern
krís|a *n fem* (-u, -ur, ~) crisis
krjúpa *v* (krýp, kraup, krupum, kropið) kneel
kropp|ur *n masc* (-s, -ar, -a) body
kross *n masc* (-, -ar, -a) cross
krossgát|a *n fem* (-u, -ur, -a) crossword puzzle
Króat|i *n masc* (-a, -ar, -a) Croatian person
Króatí|a *N fem* (-u) Croatia

króatísk|a *n fem* (-u) Croatian language
króatísk|ur *adj* (-, -t) Croatian
krókaleið *n fem* (-ar, -ir, -a) detour
krók|ur *n masc* (-s, -ar, -a) hook; alcove
krónísk|ur *adj* (-, -t) chronic
krónublað *n neu* (-s, -blöð, -a) *flora* petal
krukk|a *n fem* (-u, -ur, -na) pot, jar
krull|a 1 *n fem* (-u, -ur, -a) curl; *sports* curling; **2 krulla** *v* (~, -ði, -ð) curl; *sports* play curling
krullað|ur *adj* (krulluð, -) curly
krús *n fem* (-ar, -ir, -a) jar
krydd *n neu* (-s, -, -a) seasoning, spice
krydda *v* (~, -ði, -ð) season (food)
kryddað|ur *adj* (krydduð, -) spicy, hot
kryddjurt *n fem* (-ar, -ir, -a) herb
kryddjurtabland|a *n fem* (-blöndu, blöndur, blanda) mixed herbs
krýn|a *v* (-i, -di, -t) crown
krækj|a *v* (kræki, krækti, krækt) hook
krækling|ur *n masc* (-s, -ar, -a) blue mussel
kröftug|ur *adj* (-, -t) powerful, forceful
kröfugang|a *n fem* (-göngu, -göngur, -na) demonstration, march
kröfuhaf|i *n masc* (-a, -ar, -a) *econ* creditor
kuldahroll|ur *n masc* (-s) chills
kuldakast *n neu* (-s, -köst, -a) cold spell
kuldalega *adv* coldly
kuldaleg|ur *adj* (-, -t) chilly
kuld|i *n masc* (-a, -ar, -a) cold, chill
kunn|a *v* (kann, kunni, kunnum, kunnað) can
kunnátt|a *n fem* (-u) skill, expertise
kunnger|a *v* (-i, -ði, -t) proclaim
kunning|i *n masc* (-ja, -jar, -ja) acquaintance
kunningjahóp|ur *n masc* (-s, -ar, -a) circle of friends
kunnugleg|ur *adj* (-, -t) familiar

kurteis *adj* (-, -t) polite
kurteisi *n fem* (-) politeness, courtesy
kurteisislega *adv* politely
Kúb|a *N fem* (-u) Cuba
Kúbverj|i *n masc* (-a, -ar, -a) Cuban person
kúbverskur *adj* Cuban
kúga *v* (~, -ði, -ð) oppress, repress; blackmail
kúgar|i *n masc* (-a, -ar, -a) oppressor
kúg|un *n fem* (-unar, -anir, -ana) repression, oppression; blackmailing
kúlufisk|ur *n masc* (-s, -ar, -a) *zool* blowfish
kúmen *n neu* (-s) cumin; caraway
kúmenfræ *n neu pl* (-s, -, -ja) caraway seeds
kúpling *n fem* (-ar, -ar, -a) clutch
kúr *n masc* (-s, -ar, -a) diet
kúrbít|ur *n masc* (-s, -ar, -a) zucchini
kúren|a *n fem* (-u, -ur, -a) sultana
kúrkúm|a *n fem* (-u) turmeric
kúskús *n neu* (-s) couscous
Kúveit *N neu* (-) Kuwait
Kúveitbú|i *n masc* (-a, -ar, -a) Kuwaiti *(person)*
kvalalost|i *n masc* (-a) sadism
kvarta *v* (~, -ði, -ð) complain
kvartett *n masc* (-s, -ar, -a) quartet
kveðj|a *n fem* (-u, -ur, ~) greeting; say goodbye
kveikiþráð|ur *n masc* (-ar, -þræðir, -a) fuse
kveikj|a *v* (kveiki, kveikti, kveikt) light, turn on, ignite
kveikjar|i *n masc* (-a, -ar, -a) lighter
kveinstaf|ir *n masc pl* (-a) lamentation
kvelj|a *v* (kvel, kvaldi, kvalið) agonize
kvendýr *n neu* (-s, -, -a) female animal
kvenföt *neu pl* (-fata) women's clothing
kvenhetj|a *n fem* (-u, -ur, -a) heroin
kvenleg|ur *adj* (-, -t) feminine
kvenmað|ur *n masc* (-manns, -menn, -manna) woman
kvennaklósett *n neu* (-s, -, -a) ladies' restroom

kvennasnyrting *n fem* (-ar, -ar, -a) ladies' restroom

kvenréttindastefn|a *n fem* (-u) feminism

kvensjúkdómafræði *n fem* (-) *med* gynecology

kvensjúkdómalækn|ir *n masc* (-is, -ar, -a) *med* gynecologist

kviðarhol *n neu* (-s, -, -a) *anat* abdomen

kviðdóm|ur *n masc* (-s, -ar, -a) *leg* jury

kviðslit *n neu* (-s, -, -a) *med* hernia

kvið|ur *n masc* (-ar, -ir, -a) *anat* abdomen

kvik|a *n fem* (-u, -ur, -na) *geol* magma

kvikasilfur *n neu* (-s) *chem* mercury, quicksilver

kvikmynd *n fem* (-ar, -ir, -a) film, movie

kvikmynda *v* (~, -ði, -ð) shoot a film/movie

kvikmyndagerðalist *n fem* (-ar, -ir, -a) cinema

kvikmyndahús *n neu* (-s, -, -a) movie theater

kvikmyndasal|ur *n masc* (-s, -ir, -a) movie theater

kvikmyndaver *n neu* (-s, -, -a) film/movie studio

kviksand|ur *n masc* (-s, -ar, -a) *geog* quicksand

kvikuhólf *n neu* (-s, -, -a) *geol* magma chamber

kvist|ur *n masc* (-s, -ir, -a) stick, twig

kvitt|un *n fem* (-unar, -anir, -ana) receipt

kvíg|a *n fem* (-u, -ur, -na) *zool* heifer *(a young cow)*

kvótakóng|ur *n masc* (-s, -ar, -a) *a person who has made a fortune by owning fish quota*

kvót|i *n masc* (-a, -ar, -a) quota: **þorskkvóti** quota for cod

kvæði *n neu* (-s, -, -a) poem

kvöl *n fem* (kvalar, kvalir, kvala) agony, suffering

kvöld *n neu* (-s, -, -a) evening

kvöldmat|ur *n masc* (-ar, -ar, -a) dinner, supper

kvört|un *n fem* (-unar, -anir, -ana) complaint

kvörtunarefn|i *n neu* (-is, ~, -a) grievance

kylf|a *n fem* (-u, -ur, -a) mallet, club

kyn *n neu* (-s, -, -ja) gender

kynæsandi *adj* (-, -) sexy

kyndil|l *n masc* (-s, kyndlar, kyndla) torch

kynding *n fem* (-ar, -ar, -a) heating

kynfær|i *n neu* (-is, ~, -a) *anat* genitals

kynferðislega *adv* sexually

kynferðisleg|ur *adj* (-, -t) sexual

kyngj|a *v* (kyngi, kyngdi, kyngt) swallow

kynhneigð *n fem* (-ar, -ir, -a) sexuality

kynjamisrétti *n neu* (-s) sexism

kynlíf *n neu* (-s) sex

kynn|a *v* (-i, -ti, -t) introduce, present

kynn|ast *v refl* (-ist, -tist, -st) get to know

kynning *n fem* (-ar, -ar, -a) introduction, presentation, promotion

kynningarbæklingu|ur *n masc* (-s, -ar, -a) information brochure, pamphlet

kynn|ir *n masc* (-is, -ar, -a) announcer

kynsjúkdóm|ur *n masc* (-s, -ar, -a) sexually transmitted disease, veneral disease

kynslóð *n fem* (-ar, -ir, -a) generation

kynþáttafordóm|ar *n masc pl* (-a) racism

kynþátt|ur *n masc* (-ar, -þættir, -þátta) race (of people)

kynþokkafull|ur *adj* (-, -t) sexy

kynþroskaald|ur *n masc* (-s) age of puberty

kynþroskaskeið *n neu* (-s, -, -a) puberty

kyrr *adj* (-, -t) still

Kyrrahaf *N neu* (-s) Pacific Ocean

kyrrð *n fem* (-ar) quiet, tranquility, repose

kyrrlát|ur *adj* (-, -t) placid

kyrrstað|a *n fem* (-stöðu, -stöður, -staðna) stagnation

kyss|a *v* (-i, -ti, -t) kiss

kyss|ast *v refl* (-ist, -tist, -t) kiss each other

kýl|a *v* (-i, -di, -t) punch

Kýpur *N neu* (-s) Cyprus

Kýpverji *n masc* (-a, -ar, -a) Cypriot *(person)*

kýr *n fem* (~, ~, kúa) *zool* cow

kæf|a *n fem* (-u) paté: **kindakæfa** sheep paté, **lifrarkæfa** liver paté

kæl|a *v* (-i, -di, -t) chill, cool; ~ **sig** *refl* cool down

kæld|ur *adj* (-, kælt) chilled, cooled down

kæling *n fem* (-ar, -ar, -a) refrigeration, cooling

kæl|ir *n masc* (-is, -ar, -a) refrigerator

kæliskáp|ur *n masc* (-s, -ar, -a) refrigerator

Kænugarð|ur *N masc* (-s) Kiev

kær *adj* (-, -t) dear: **kæri Jón** dear Jón, **kæra Hanna** dear Hanna

kær|a *v* (-i, -ði, -t) report; charge, sue

kærar þakkir *phr* thanks

kærast|a *n fem* (-u, -ur, -a) girlfriend

kærast|i *n masc* (-a, -ar, -a) boyfriend

kærleik|ur *n masc* (-s, -ar, -a) love, affection

kærulaus *adj* (-, -t) careless, relaxed

kæruleysisleg|ur *adj* (-, -t) nonchalant

köfnunarefn|i *n neu* (-is, ~, -a) *chem* nitrogen

köfun *n fem* (-ar) scuba diving

köfunarbúnað|ur *n masc* (-ar) equipment for scuba diving

köfunartæk|i *n neu pl* (-ja) equipment for scuba diving

kökk|ur *n masc* (kakkar/-s, kekkir, kakka) *med* clot, lump

kökukefl|i *n neu* (-is, ~, -a) rolling pin

kökukrem *n neu* (-s, ~, -a) frosting, icing

köngul|l *n masc* (-s, könglar, köngla) *flora* cone

könguló *n fem* (-ar, -lær, -a) spider

könn|un *n fem* (-unar, kannanir, kannana) survey

körfubolt|i *n masc* (-a, -ar, -a) *sports* basketball

kött|ur *n masc* (kattar, kettir, katta) cat

L

laða *v* (~, -ði, -ð) ~ **að** attract

lag *n neu* (-s, lög, -a) song, tune; layer

laga *v* (~, -ði, -ð) fix, adjust; ~ **til** tidy

lagasmið|ur *n masc* (-s, -ir, -a) songwriter

laga|st *v refl* (~, -ðist, ~) get better

lagfær|a *v* (-i, -ði, -t) fix, restore

lagkak|a *n fem* (-köku, -kökur, -na) multi-tiered cake

lagleg|ur *adj* (-, -t) pretty

laglín|a *n fem* (-u, -ur, ~) melody

lak *n neu* (-s, lök, -a) sheet

lakk *n neu* (-s, lökk, -a) lacquer

lakka *v* (~, -ði, -ð) lacquer; ~ **neglurnar** polish nails

lakkrís *n masc* (-s, -ar, -a) licorice

laktós|i *n masc* (-a) lactose

laktósofnæmi *n neu* (-s) *med* lactose allergy

laktósóþol *n neu* (-s) *med* lactose intolerance

lama *v* (~, -ði, -ð) paralyze

lamadýr *n neu* (-s, -, -a) llama

lamb *n neu* (-s, lömb, -a) *zool* lamb

lambahrygg|ur *n masc* (-jar, -ir, -ja) saddle of lamb

lambakjöt *n neu* (-s) lamb (meat)

lambasalat *n neu* (-s) corn salad

lambhúshett|a *n fem* (-u, -ur, ~) balaclava

lampastæð|i *n neu* (-is, ~, -a) socket for a light bulb

lamp|i *n masc* (-a, -ar, -a) lamp

land *n neu* (-s, lönd, -a) land, country

landafræði *n fem* (-) geography

landakort *n neu* (-s, -, -a) map

landamæravörð|ur *n masc* (-varðar, -verðir, -varða) border guard

landamær|i *n neu* (-is, ~, -a) border

landareign *n fem* (-ar, -ir, -a) land property

landbúnað|ur *n masc* (-ar) farming, agriculture

landfræðing|ur *n masc* (-s, -ar, -a) geographer

landgrunn *n neu* (-s, -, -a) *geog* continental shelf

landhelgi *n fem* (-) territorial waters

landhelgisgæsl|a *n fem* (-u) coast guard

landmælingar *n fem pl* (-a) *geog* survey

landnám *n neu* (-s) settlement

landnem|i *n masc* (-a, -ar, -a) pioneer, settler

landsframleiðsl|a *n fem* (-u) *econ* Gross Domestic Product (GDP)

landslag *n neu* (-s) landscape, scenery

landsnúmer *n neu* (-s, -, -a) country code

landspild|a *n fem* (-u, -ur, -na) piece of land

landstjór|i *n masc* (-a, -ar, -a) governor-general

landvistarleyf|i *n neu* (-is, ~, -a) residence permit

landvörð|ur *n masc* (-varðar, -verðir, -varða) park ranger

langa *v + acc subj* (~, -ði, -ð) want: **mig langar í ís** I want ice cream

langlíf|i *n neu* (-is) longevity

langlínusímtal *n neu* (-s, -töl, -a) long-distance call

langreyð|ur *n fem* (-ar, -ar, -a) *zool* fin whale

langskip *n neu* (-s, -, -a) *arch* longship

langtíma *adj* long-term: ~ **bílastæði** long-term parking

langtímaspá *n fem* (-r, -r, -a) long-term weather forecast

lang|ur *adj* (löng, -t) long, extended: ~ **laugardagur** Saturday with

extended opening hours; **löng hrísgrjón** long-grain rice
langvarandi *adj* long-term
Laós *N neu* (-) Laos
lasagna *n neu* (-) lasagna
lasin|n *adj* (-, lasið, -) ill, sick, ailing
lasleik|i *n masc* (-a) sickness
lat|ur *adj* (löt, -t) lazy
laufblað *n neu* (-s, -blöð, -a) leaf
laugardag|ur *n masc* (-s, -ar, -a) Saturday
laukhring|ur *n masc* (-s, -ir, -ja) onion ring
lauksúp|a *n fem* (-u, -ur, -na) onion soup
lauk|ur *n masc* (-s, -ar, -a) onion
lauma *v* (~, -ði, -ð) sneak
lauma|st *v* (~, -ðist, ~) sneak, prowl
laun *n neu pl* (-a) pay, income, wage, salary
launa *v* (~, -ði, -ð) recompense, reward, return
launaseðil|l *n masc* (-s, -seðlar, -seðla) pay slip
laus *adj* (-, -t) free, loose; vacant
lausagang|a *n fem* (-göngu, -göngur, -na) roaming free; **lausaganga hunda bönnud** dogs not on leash forbidden
lauslega *adv* loosely
lausleg|ur *adj* (-, -t) approximate; **í lauslegri þýðingu** in free translation
lausnargjald *n neu* (-s, -gjöld, -a) bail bond; ransom
lautarferð *n fem* (-ar, -ir, -a) picnic
lax *n masc* (~, -ar, -a) *zool* salmon
laxaborr|i *n masc* (-a, -ar, -a) *zool* bass
laxerandi *adj med* purgative
lágfiðl|a *n fem* (-u, -ur, ~) *mus* viola
láglendi *n neu* (-s) *geog* lowland
lágmark *n neu* (-s, -mörk, -a) minimum
lágmarksverð *n neu* (-s, -, -a) minimum charge
lág|ur *adj* (-, -t) low
lágvær *adj* (-, -t) quiet

lán *n neu* (-s, -, -a) loan
lána *v* (~, -ði, -ð) lend
lánardrottin|n *n masc* (-s, -drottnar, -drottna) lender
lántakand|i *n masc* (-a, -endur, -enda) borrower
lárétt|ur *adj* (-, -) horizontal
lárper|a *n fem* (-u, -ur, -a) avocado
lárviðarlauf *n neu* (-s, -, -a) bay leaf
lárvið|ur *n masc* (-ar, -ir, -a) laurel
lás *n masc* (-s, -ar, -a) lock
lát|a *v* (læt, lét, létum, látið) let; **~ í ljós** display, show, express; **~ undan** give in
látast *v* (læst, lést, létumst, látist) pretend; die: **hann lést í slysi** he died in an accident
látbragðsleik|ur *n masc* (-s, -ir, -ja) pantomime
látin|n *adj* (-, látið) dead; let: **~ fara** let go; forced: **~ syngja** forced to sing
látún *n neu* (-s) brass
leðj|a *n fem* (-u) mud, slime
leður *n neu* (-s) leather
leðurblak|a *n fem* (-blöku, -blökur, blakna) *zool* bat
Leðurblökumað|urinn *N masc def* (-mannsins) Batman
leðurjakk|i *n masc* (-a, -ar, -a) leather jacket
leðurvör|ur *n fem pl* (-vara) leather goods
leggings *n fem pl* (-) *colloq* leggings
leggj|a *v* (legg, lagði, lagt) lay; park; **~ áherslu á** stress; **~ saman** add; **~ til** suggest
leggj|ast *v refl* (leggst, lagðist, lagst) lie down
leggöng *n neu pl* (-ganga) *anat* vagina
legstein|n *n masc* (-s, -ar, -a) gravestone
legstrok *n neu* (-s, -, -a) *med* pap smear
leið *n fem* (-ar, -ir, -a) way, route, passage; **á leiðinni** on the way
leið|a *v* (-i, leiddi, leitt) lead, hold hand; **~ til** result in

leiðandi *adj* leading

leiðar|i *n masc* (-a, -ar, -a) editorial

leiðarstjarn|a *n fem* (-stjörnu, -stjörnur, ~) lodestar

leiðarvís|ir *n masc* (-is, -ar, -a) manual

leið|ast 1 *v* (-ist, leiddist, -st) hold hands; 2 *v* + *dat subj* to be bored: **mér leiðist** I'm bored

leiðbein|a *v* (-i, -di, -t) instruct, supervise

leiðbeinand|i *n masc* (-a, -endur, -enda) instructor

leiðbeiningabækling|ur *n masc* (-s, -ar, -a) instruction manual

leiðbeining|ar *n fem pl* (-a) instructions

leið|i 1 *n masc* (-a) sadness; 2 *n neu* (-is, ~, -a) gravestone

leiðinleg|ur *adj* (-, -t) boring

leiðrétt|a *v* (-i, -i, -) correct, rectify

leiðrétting *n fem* (-ar, -ar, -a) correction, rectification

leiðsögn *n fem* (-sagnar) guidance; ~ **á hljóðbandi** audio-guide

leiðsögumað|ur *n masc* (-manns, -menn, -manna) tour guide

leiðtog|i *n masc* (-a, -ar, -a) leader

leið|ur *adj* (-, leitt) *(about feelings)* sad, sorry

leif|ar *n fem pl* (-a) leftovers, residue, relics

leiftur *n neu* (-s, -, leiftra) flash, flicker

leig|a *n fem* (-u, -ur, -na) rent; lease

leigj|a *v* (leigi, leigði, leigt) hire, lease, rent

leigjand|i *n masc* (-a, -endur, -enda) tenant

leigubíl|l *n masc* (-s, -ar, -a) taxi, cab

leiguflug *n neu* (-s, -, -a) charter flight

leigusal|i *n masc* (-a, -ar, -a) landlord

leik|a *v* (-, lék, lékum, leikið) act, play

leikar|i *n masc* (-a, -ar, -a) actor

leikfang *n neu* (-s, -föng, -a) toy

leikfangaversl|un *n fem* (-unar, -anir, -ana) toy store

leikhús *n neu* (-s, -, -a) theater

leikjasal|ur *n masc* (-s, -ir, -a) game room

leikkon|a *n fem* (-u, -ur, -kvenna) actress

leiklist *n fem* (-ar) acting, art of drama/theater

leiklistarkennar|i *n masc* (-a, -ar, -a) drama teacher

leikmaõ|ur *n masc* (-manns, -menn, -manna) lay person; *sports* player

leikmun|ur *n masc* (-ar, -ir, -a) props

leikn|i *n fem* (-) ability, facility

leikrit *n neu* (-s, -, -a) play *(theater)*

leikskólakennar|i *n masc* (-a, -ar, -a) kindergarten teacher

leikskól|i *n masc* (-a, -ar, -a) daycare

leikstjór|i *n masc* (-a, -ar, -a) director of a play or film/movie

leiksvæð|i *n neu* (-is, ~, -a) play area, playground

leiktjöld *n neu pl* (-tjalda) theater curtains

leik|ur *n masc* (-s, -ir/ar, -ja/a) game

leikvöll|ur *n masc* (-vallar, -vellir, -valla) playground

leir *n masc* (-s) clay, playdough

leira *v* (~, -ði, -ð) play with playdough

leirhver *n masc* (-s, -ir, -a) *geol* solfatara

leirkeragerð *n fem* (-ar, -ir, -a) pottery

leirkerasmið|ur *n masc* (-s, -ir, -a) potter

leirkeravinnustof|a *n fem* (-u, -ur, -a) pottery (workshop to make pottery)

leist|i *n masc* (-a, -ar, -a) sock

leit *n fem* (-ar, -ir, -a) search, pursuit, quest

leita *v* (~, -ði, -ð) search

leitarflokk|ur *n masc* (-s, -ar, -a) search party

leitarvél *n fem* (-ar, -ar, -a) *comp* search engine

lek|a *v* (-, lak, lákum, lekið) drip, leak

lekand|i *n masc* (-a) *med* gonorrhea

lek|i *n masc* (-a, -ar, -a) leak

lektor *n masc* (-s, -ar, -a) lecturer, assistant professor

lemj|a *v* (lem, lamdi, lamið) hit

lemstra *v* (~, -ði, -ð) mutilate

lend *n fem* (-ar, -ar, -a) loin

lend|a *v* (-i, lenti, lent) land

lengd *n fem* (-ar, -ir, -a) length

lengdarbaug|ur *n masc* (-s, -ar, -a) *geog* meridian

lengdargráð|a *n fem* (-u, -ur, ~) *geog* longitude

lengra *adv compar* farther

lengr|i *adj compar* (-i, -a) farther

lengst|ur *adj superl* (-, -) farthest

lerki *n neu* (-s) *flora* larch

les|a *v* (-, las, lásum, -ið) read

lesand|i *n masc* (-a, -endur, -enda) reader

lesbí|a *n fem* (-u, -ur, -a) lesbian

lesbísk|ur *adj* (-, -t) lesbian

lesefni *n neu* (-is, ~, -a) reading, material for reading

lesin|n *adj* (-, lesið) read; *n* a person who has read much

lesstof|a *n fem* (-u, -ur, -a) study *(a room to read)*

lest *n fem* (-ar, -ir, -a) train

lestarstöð *n fem* (-var, -var, -va) train station

lestur *n masc* (-s, lestrar, lestra) reading

Lettland *N neu* (-s) Latvia

lettnesk|a *n fem* (-u) Latvian language

lettnesk|ur *adj* (-, -t) Latvian

letur *n neu* (-s, -, letra) font, script

leyf|a *v* (-i, -ði, -t) allow, authorize, permit

leyfð|ur *adj* (-, leyft) permitted, allowed, authorized

leyfi *n neu* (-is, ~, -a) permit: **atvinnu-leyfi** work permit, **landvistarleyfi** residence permit; license, permission, sanction; vacation, holiday: **jólaleyfi** Christmas Holiday

leyfileg|ur *adj* (-, -t) allowed, permitted

leyfishaf|i *n masc* (-a, -ar, -a) license holder

leyndardóm|ur *n masc* (-s, -ar, -a) secret

leyndarmál *n neu* (-s, -, -a) secret

leynileg|ur *adj* (-, -t) secret

leyninafn *n neu* (-s, -nöfn, -a) alias

leys|a *v* (-i, -ti, -t) resolve, solve; untie; ~ **upp** dissolve

leysigeisl|i *n masc* (-a, -ar, -a) laser beam

leysiprentar|i *n masc* (-a, -ar, -a) laser printer

leys|ir *n masc* (-is, -ar, -a) laser

léleg|ur *adj* (-, -t) not good, poorly done

lénsskipulag *n neu* (-s) feudal system

létt|a *v* (-i, -i, -) ease

létt|ast *v refl* (-ist, -ist, lést) lose weight

léttbjór *n masc* (-s, -ar, -a) light beer

léttilega *adv* lightly, easily

létt|ir *n masc* (-is) ease, alleviation, relief

léttmjólk *n fem* (-ur) low-fat milk

léttsaltað|ur *adj* (-söltuð, -) lightly salted

léttskýjað|ur *adj* (-skýjuð, -) fair sky

Lichtenstein *N neu* (-s) Liechtenstein

Lichtensteinbú|i *n masc* (-a, -ar, -a) Liechtensteiner *(person)*

lið *n neu* (-s, -, -a) team

liðin|n *adj* (-, liðið) passed: **liðin tíð** time that has passed; **lífs eða ~** dead or alive

liðsforing|i *n masc* (-ja, -jar, -ja) *mil* lieutenant

lið|ur *n masc* (-ar/s, -ir, -a) *anat* joint; point in a plan: **fyrsti ~ á dagskrá** first point on the agenda

líf|a *v* (-i, -ði, -að) live

lifandi *adj* alive, living

lifibrauð *n neu* (-s, -, -a) livelihood

lifrarpyls|a *n fem* (-u, -ur, -na) liverwurst

lifur *n fem* (lifrar, lifrar, lifra) liver

liggj|a *v* (ligg, lá, lágum, legið) lie (down); ~ **í bleyti** soak

lilj|a *n fem* (-u, -ur, -a) *flora* lily

lillablá|r *adj* (-, -tt) *color* lilac

limlesting *n fem* (-ar, -ar, -a) mutilation

lim|ur *n masc* (-s, -ir, -a) *anat* penis
lina *v* (~, -ði, -ð) relieve
linditré *n neu* (-s, -, -trjáa) *flora* linden tree
linkind *n fem* (-ar) leniency
lins|a *n fem* (-u, -ur, -a) lens, optical lense, contact lens
linsubaun *n fem* (-ar, -ir, -a) lentil
linsulok *n neu* (-s, -, -a) lens cap
lin|ur *adj* (-, -t) soft
lirf|a *n fem* (-u, -ur, -a) caterpillar
Lissabon *N fem* (-) Lisbon
list *n fem* (-ar, -ir, -a) art
listagallerí *n neu* (-s, -, -a) art gallery
listakon|a *n fem* (-u, -ur, -kvenna) *(female)* artist
listamað|ur *n masc* (-manns, -menn, -manna) artist
listasafn *n neu* (-s, -söfn, -a) art museum
listaverk *n neu* (-s, -, -a) artwork
listdansskaut|i *n masc* (-a, -ar, -a) dance skates
listgrein *n fem* (-ar, -ar, -a) art form
list|i *n masc* (-a, -ar, -a) list
listilega *adv* skillfully
listmálar|i *n masc* (-a, -ar, -a) painter, visual artist
listræn|n *adj* (-, -t) artistic
listvefnað|ur *n masc* (-ar, -ir, -a) tapestry
lita *v* (~, -ði, -ð) color, dye, stain
litað|ur *adj* (lituð, -) stained; **litað gler** stained glass
litarefn|i *n neu* (-is, ~, -a) coloring substance
litarhaft *n neu* (-s, -höft, -a) complexion
litaspjald *n neu* (-s, -spjöld, -a) palette
litbrigð|i *n neu* (-is, ~, -a) color shade
Litháen *N neu* (-s) Lithuania
Lithá|i *n masc* (-a, -ar, -a) Lithuanian *(person)*
litháísk|a *n fem* (-u) Lithuanian language
litháísk|ur *adj* (-, -t) Lithuanian
litkatré *n neu* (-s, -, -trjáa) lychee

litning|ur *n masc* (-s, -ar, -a) *bio* chromosome
litróf *n neu* (-s, -, -a) color spectrum
lit|un *n fem* (-unar, -anir, -ana) coloring
lit|ur *n masc* (-ar, -ir, -a) color, dye, stain
Líbanon *N neu* (-s) Lebanon
líbansk|ur *adj* (líbönsk, -t) Lebanese
Líberí|a *N fem* (-u) Liberia
Líbí|a *n fem* (-u) Libya
líbísk|ur *adj* (-, -t) Libyian
líf *n neu* (-s, -, -a) life
lífbein *n neu* (-s, -, -a) *anat* pubis
lífeyrisþeg|i *n masc* (-a, -ar, -a) retiree
líffærafræði *n fem* (-) anatomy
líffær|i *n neu* (-is, ~, -a) *anat* organ
líffræði *n fem* (-) biology
líffræðileg|ur *adj* (-, -t) biological; **~ fjölbreytileiki** biodiversity
lífræn|n *adj* (-, -t) organic: **lífræn ræktun** organic farming; **lífrænt sorp** compost
lífshættulega *adv* fatally
lífsnauðsynleg|ur *adj* (-, -t) vital
lífsregl|a *n fem* (-u, -ur, -na) precept
lífstíl|l *n masc* (-s, -ar, -a) lifestyle
líftækni *n fem* (-) biotechnology
lífver|a *n fem* (-u, -ur, -a) organism
lífvörð|ur *n masc* (-varðar, -verðir, -varða) lifeguard
líka *adv* also, too
líkam|i *n masc* (-a, -ar, -a) *anat* body
líkamlega *adv* physically
líkamsbygging *n fem* (-ar, -ar, -a) body build, figure
líkamsrækt *n fem* (-ar) workout
líkamsræktarkon|a *n fem* (-u, -ur, -kvenna) *(female)* bodybuilder
líkamsræktarmað|ur *n masc* (-manns, -menn, -manna) *(male)* bodybuilder
líkamsræktarstöð *n fem* (-var, -var, -va) gym
líkamsstað|a *n fem* (-stöðu, -stöður, -staða) body posture
líkamsvef|ur *n masc* (-jar, -ir, -ja) *bio* biological tissue

líkind|i *n neu pl* (-a) similarity; *math* probability

líkj|ast *v* (líkist, líktist, líkst) look like, resemble

líkjör *n masc* (-s, -ar, -a) liqueur

líklega *adv* probably, persumably, likely

líkleg|ur *adj* (-, -t) likely, probable

lík|ur 1 *adj* (-, -t) similar, looks like; **2** *n fem pl* (-a) odds

lím *n neu* (-s, -, -a) glue, paste

Líma *N fem* (-) Lima

lím|a *v* (-i, -di, -t) glue

límabaun *n fem* (-ar, -ir, -a) lima bean

límband *n neu* (-s, -bönd, -a) tape

límmið|i *n masc* (-a, -ar, -a) sticker

límón|a *n fem* (-u, -ur, -a) lime

límónaði *n neu* (-s) lemonade

límósín|a *n fem* (-u, -ur, -a) limousine

lín *n neu* (-s) linen

lín|a *n fem* (-u, -ur, -a) line, row

línuleg|ur *adj* (-, -t) linear

línurit *n neu* (-s, -, -a) line chart

lít|a *v* (-, leit, litum, litið) look

lítil|l *adj* (-, lítið) little, small

lítillát|ur *adj* (-, -t) humble

lítilvæg|ur *adj* (-, -t) insignificant

lítr|i *n masc* (-a, -ar, -a) liter

ljóð *n neu* (-s, -, -a) *lit* poem, verse

ljóðagerð *n fem* (-ar) *lit* poetry

ljóðlín|a *n fem* (-u, -ur, ~) *lit* verse

ljóðlist *n fem* (-ar) *lit* poetics

ljóðræn|n *adj* (-, -t) *lit* lyrical

ljóðskáld *n neu* (-s, ~, -a) *lit* poet

ljóm|i *n masc* (-a) radiance

ljón *n neu* (-s, -, -a) *zool* lion

Ljón|ið *n neu def* (-sins) *astro* Leo

ljós *n neu* (-s, -, -a) light

ljósaper|a *n fem* (-u, -ur, ~) lightbulb

ljóshærð|ur *adj* (-, -hært) blonde

ljósk|a *n fem* (-u, -ur, ~) *slang* blonde

ljósmóð|ir *n fem* (-ur, -mæður, -mæðra) *med* midwife

ljósmynd *n fem* (-ar, -ir, -a) photo

ljósmynda *v* (~, -ði, -ð) take a photo

ljósmyndar|i *n masc* (-a, -ar, -a) photographer

ljósmyndasjálfsal|i *n masc* (-a, -ar, -a) photo booth

ljósmyndaversl|un *n fem* (-unar, -anir, -ana) photo store

ljósmynd|un *n fem* (-unar, -anir, -ana) *(the art)* photography

ljósrit *n neu* (-s, -, -a) photocopy

ljósrita *v* (~, -ði, -ð) photocopy

ljósritunarvél *n fem* (-ar, -ar, -a) photocopier

ljót|ur *adj* (-, -t) ugly

Ljúblan|a *N fem* (-) Ljubljana

ljúffeng|ur *adj* (-, -t) delicious, savory

ljúf|ur *adj* (-, -t) sweet, kind: **mjög ~ maður** a very sweet guy

ljúg|a *v* (lýg, laug, lugum, logið) lie, tell a lie

ljúk|a *v* (lýk, lauk, lukum, lokið) finish

loddar|i *n masc* (-a, -ar, -a) scammer

loðfeld|ur *n masc* (-ar, -ir, -a) fur coat

loðfíl|l *n masc* (-s, -ar, -a) *zool* mammoth

loðhúf|a *n fem* (-u, -ur, -a) shapka *(hat)*

loðin|n *adj* (-, loðið) furry, hairy

lofa *v* (~, -ði, -ð) promise

lofnarblóm *n neu* (-s, -, -a) *flora* lavender

loforð *n neu* (-s, -, -a) promise

lofsamleg|ur *adj* (-, -t) laudable

lofsverð|ur *adj* (-, -t) praiseworthy

lofsyngj|a *v* (-syngur, -söng, -syngjum, -sungið) praise

loft *n neu* (-s, -, -a) air; ceiling

loftbelg|ur *n masc* (-s/jar, -ir, -ja) air balloon

loftból|a *n fem* (-u, -ur, -na) water bubbles

lofthræðsl|a *n fem* (-u) *med* vertigo

loftpúð|i *n masc* (-a, -ar, -a) airbag

loftræstikerf|i *n neu* (-is, ~, -a) air conditioning

loftræsting *n fem* (-ar, -ar, -a) air conditioning

loftræstitæk|i *n neu* (-is, ~, -ja) ventilator

loftræst|ur *adj* (-, -) air-conditioned

loftslag *n neu* (-s) climate

loftþrýstivog *n fem* (-ar, -ir, -a) barometer

loga *v* (~, -ði, -ð) flame

logandi *adj* (-, -) fiery, in flames; ~ **hræddur** very scared

log|i *n masc* (-a, -ar, -a) flame

logn *n neu* (-s) calm, no wind

logna|st *v* (~, -ðist, ~) ~ **út af** fall asleep

lok *n neu* (-s, -, -a) lid: **pott~** pot lid; end: ~ **myndarinnar** end of the movie; **að ~um** finally, in the end

loka *v* (~, -ði, -ð) close, shut

lokað|ur *adj* (lokuð, -) closed, shut

lokka *v* (~, -ði, -ð) tempt

lokkandi *adj* (-, -,) tempting

loksins *adv* finally

lopapeys|a *n fem* (-u, -ur, -a) *Icelandic wool sweater*

lop|i *n masc* (-a, -ar, -a) *wool made from the fleece of Icelandic sheep*

lopp|a *n fem* (-u, -ur, -a) paw

losa *v* (~, -ði, -ð) detach, unload, rid

lost|i *n masc* (-a, -ar, -a) lust

los|un *n fem* (-unar, -anir, -ana) release

lot|a *n fem* (-u, -ur, -a) sequence

lotning *n fem* (-ar) reverence

lotterí *n neu* (-s, -, -a) lottery

ló|a *n fem* (-u, -ur, -a) *zool* golden plover

lóð *n fem* (-ar, -ir, -a) site, lot

lóðrétt|ur *adj* (-, -) vertical

lófalesar|i *n masc* (-a, -ar, -a) palmist

lófalestur *n masc* (-s, -lestrar, -lestra) palmistry

lóf|i *n masc* (-a, -ar, -a) *anat* palm

lón *n neu* (-s, -, -a) lagoon: **Bláa lónið** The Blue Lagoon

lótusfræ *n neu* (-s, -, -ja) lotus seed

lugnabólg|a *n fem* (-u) *med* pneumonia

lukkudýr *n neu* (-s, -, -a) mascot

lund *n fem* (-ar, -ir, -a) tenderloin

lundabúð *n fem* (-ar, -ir, -a) *slang* souvenir shop

lund|i *n masc* (-a, -ar, -a) *zool* puffin

Lundún|ir *N masc pl* (-a) London

lung|a *n neu* (-a, -u, -na) *anat* lung

lúð|a *n fem* (-u, -ur, -a) halibut, sole

lúð|i *n masc* (-a, -ar, -a) *slang* looser, unattractive and uncharming person

lúff|a *n fem* (-u, -ur, ~) thick mitten

lúpín|a *n fem* (-u, -ur, -a) *flora* lupin

lús *n fem* (-ar, lýs, -a) louse

Lúxemborg *N fem* (-ar) Luxembourg

lúxus *n masc* (-s) luxury

lúxusvar|a *n fem* (-vöru, -vörur, ~) luxury goods

lyf *n neu* (-s, -, -ja) drug, medicine

lyfjabið|a *n fem* (-u, -ur, ~) *med* ampoule

lyfjabúð *n fem* (-ar, -ir, ~) pharmacy

lyfjadá *n fem* (-s, -, -a) *med* medically induced coma

lyfjameðferð *n fem* (-ar, -ir, -a) *med* medication

lyfjaofnæmi *n neu* (-s) *med* drug allergy

lyfjaskammt|ur *n masc* (-s, -ar, -a) *med* dosage

lyfjaversl|un *n fem* (-unar, -anir, -ana) pharmacy

lyfleys|a *n fem* (-u) *med* placebo

lyfseðil|l *n masc* (-s, -seðlar, -seðla) *med* prescription

lyft|a 1 *n fem* (-u, -ur, -a) elevator, lift; **2** *v* (-i, -i, -t) lift, raise

lyftupass|i *n masc* (-a, -ar, -a) lift pass

lygar|i *n masc* (-a, -ar, -a) liar

lyg|i *n fem* (-i, ar, -a) lie, falsehood

lykil|l *n masc* (-s, lyklar, lykla) key

lykilnúmer *n neu* (-s, -, -a) key number

lykilorð *n neu* (-s, -, -a) password

lyklaborð *n neu* (-s, -, -a) *comp* keyboard

lyklakippuhring|ur *n masc* (-s, -ir/ ar, -ja/a) key ring

lyklasmið|ur *n masc* (-s, -ir, -a) key cutter

lykt *n fem* (-ar, -ir, -a) smell, odor

lykta *v* (~, -ði, -ð) smell, stink

lymsk|ur *adj* (-, -t) cunning

lyndiseinkunn *n fem* (-ar, -ir, -a) character of a person

lystarstol *n neu* (-s) *med* anorexia
lystaukandi *adj* (-, -) appetizing
lystisnekkj|a *n fem* (-u, -ur, ~) yacht
lýðveld|i *n neu* (-is, ~, -a) republic
lýs|a *v* (-i, -ti, -t) describe, portray;
shine, glow; whiting; ~ **yfir** declare
lýsing *n fem* (-ar, -ar, -a) description;
illumination, lighting
lýsingarhátt|ur *n masc* (-ar, -hættir,
-hátta) *ling* participle: ~ **nútíðar**
present participle, ~ **þátíðar** past
participle
lýsingarorð *n neu* (-s, -, -a) *ling*
adjective
læð|ast *v* (-ist, læddist, -st) sneak
lækka *v* (~, -ði, -ð) lower, sink
lækk|un *n fem* (-unar, -anir, -ana)
decline, reduction
lækna *v* (~, -ði, -ð) cure
læknað|ur *adj* (læknuð, -) cured
læknakandídat *n masc* (-s, -ar, -a)
*graduated medical students before
they aquire their medical license*
læknastof|a *n fem* (-u, -ur, -a) doctor's
office
lækning *n fem* (-ar) *med* cure, remedy
lækn|ir *n masc* (-is, -ar, -a) doctor,
physician
læknisskoð|un *n fem* (-unar, -anir,
-ana) medical examination
læk|ur *n masc* (-jar, -ir, -ja) stream,
rivulet
lær|a *v* (-i, -ði, -t) learn, study
lær|i *n neu* (-is, -i, -a) *anat* thigh
lærling|ur *n masc* (-s, -ar, -a)
apprentice
læs|a *v* (-i, -ti, -t) lock
læti *n neu pl* (-láta) fuss
lævirk|i *n masc* (-ja, -jar, -ja) lark
lævís *adj* (-, -t) sly
lög *n neu pl* (laga) law: ~ **og regla**
law and order

lögboðin|n *adj* (-, -boðið) *leg*
statutory
lögbrot *n neu* (-s, -, -a) *leg* breech
of law
lögfræðing|ur *n masc* (-s, -ar, -a)
lawyer, attorney
lögg|a *n fem* (-u, -ur, -a) *slang* cop
löggild|a *v* (-i, -gilti, -gilt) validate
löggilt|ur *adj* (-gilt, -) authorized:
~ **þýðandi** authorized translator;
certified: ~ **bókhaldari** certified
accountant
löggjaf|i *n masc* (-a, -ar, -a) legislator
löggjöf *n fem* (-gjafar) legislation
löglega *adv* legally
lögleg|ur *adj* (-, -t) legal
lögleiðing *n fem* (-ar) legalization
lögmað|ur *n masc* (-manns, -menn,
-manna) *leg* advocate
lögregl|a *n fem* (-u, -ur, -na) police
lögreglubíl|l *n masc* (-s, -ar, -a)
police car
lögreglumað|ur *n masc* (-manns,
-menn, -manna) policeman
lögreglustjór|i *n masc* (-a, -ar, -a)
sheriff
lögreglustöð *n fem* (-var, -var, -va)
police station
lögregluþjón|n *n masc* (-s, -ar, -a)
policeman
lögsækj|a *v* (-i, -sótti, -sótt) *leg*
prosecute
lögsókn *n fem* (-ar, -ir, -a) *leg*
prosecution
lög|un *n fem* (-unar, -anir, -ana)
shape
lömun *n f sing* (-ar) paralysis
löng. *See* **lang|ur.**
löng|un *n fem* (-unar, -anir, -ana)
longing, craving

M

m.fl. (= með fleirum) *abbrev* and more
Madagaskar *N neu* (-) Madagascar
Madríd *N fem* (-/ar) Madrid
maðk|ur *n masc* (-s, -ar, -a) worm
mað|ur *n masc* (-manns, -menn, -manna) human being, man
magabólg|a *n fem* (-u, -ur, -na) *med* gastritis
magakveis|a *n fem* (-u, -ur, -a) *med* stomachache
magapín|a *n fem* (-u) *colloq* stomach-ache
magasár *n neu* (-s, -, -a) *med* gastric ulcer
magasýr|a *n fem* (-u, -ur, -a) *med* stomach acid
magaverk|ur *n masc* (-jar, -ir, -ja) stomachache
mag|i *n masc* (-a, -ar, -a) *anat* stomach
magn *n neu* (-s) magnitude, quantity
magna *v* (~, -ði, -ð) amplify
magnar|i *n masc* (-a, -ar, -a) amplifier
magnesíum *n neu* (-s) *chem* magnesium
magur *adj* (mögur, -t) lean, skinny
maí *n masc* (-) May
maís *n masc* (-s) corn
maísbrauð *n neu* (-s, -, -a) cornbread
maísflög|ur *n fem pl* (-flaga) corn-flakes
maískólf|ur *n masc* (-s, -ar, -a) corncob
maísmjöl *n neu* (-s) cornmeal, cornflour
maíssterkj|a *n fem* (-u) cornstarch
maizenamjöl *n neu* (-s) cornstarch
majónes *n neu* (-) mayonnaise
majóran *n neu* (-s) marjoram
Makedóní|a *N fem* (-u) Macedonia
makedónsk|ur *adj* (-, -t) Macedonian

mak|i *n masc* (-a, -ar, -a) spouse
makkarón|a *n fem* (-u, -ur, -a) macaroni
makkarónukak|a *n fem* (-köku, -kökur, -na) macaroon
makríl|l *n masc* (-s, -ar, -a) mackerel; **reyktur** ~ smoked mackerel
mala *v* (~, -ði, -ð) grind
malað|ur *adj* (möluð, -) ground: **malað kaffi** ground coffee, ~ **pipar** ground pepper
malarí|a *n fem* (-u) *med* malaria
Malasí|a *N fem* (-u) Malaysia
Malaví *N neu* (-) Malawi
malavísk|ur *adj* (malavísk, -t) Malaysian
Maldív|ur *N fem pl* (-a) Maldives
Malí *N neu* (-) Mali
malla *v* (~, -ði, -ð) simmer
malt *n neu* (-s) malt
Malt|a *N fem* (-Möltu) Malta
mamm|a *n fem* (mömmu, mömmur, mamma) *colloq* mom
mammút|ur *n masc* (-s, -ar, -a) *zool* mammoth
mandarín|a *n fem* (-u, -ur, -a) mandarin orange
mandl|a *n fem* (möndlu, möndur, ~) almond
mangó *n neu* (-s, -, -a) mango
Manila *N fem* (-) Manila
mannasið|ir *n masc pl* (-a) manners
manndráp *n neu* (-s, -, -a) homicide, manslaughter
manneskja *n fem* (-u, -ur, -a) human being
mannfjöld|i *n masc* (-a) population
mannfræði *n fem* (-) anthropology
mannfræðing|ur *n masc* (-s, -ar, -a) anthropologist
mannfækkun *n fem* (-ar) depopulation

mannkynssag|a *n fem* (-sögu) history of mankind
mannkærleik|ur *n masc* (-s, -ar, -a) philanthropy
mannleg|ur *adj* (-, -t) human
mannlýsing *n fem* (-ar, -ar, -a) *lit* description of a human being
mannmergð *n fem* (-ar) crowd
mannorð *n neu* (-s) reputation
mannrán *n neu* (-s, -, -a) abduction
mannréttind|i *n neu pl* (-a) human rights
mannræfil|l *n masc* (-s, -ræflar, -ræfla) loser, a pathetic person
mannræning|i *n masc* (-ja, -jar, -ja) kidnapper
manntal *n neu* (-s, -töl, -a) census
manntalsskrifstof|a *n fem* (-u, -ur, -a) registry office
manntjón *n neu* (-s) casualities
mannver|a *n fem* (-u, -ur, -a) human being
mannvin|ur *n masc* (-ar, -ir, -a) philanthropist
mansal *n neu* (-s) human trafficking
mapp|a *n fem* (möppu, möppur, -a) folder, ring binder, portfolio
mar *n neu* (-s) bruise
maraþon *n neu* (-s, -, -a) marathon
marens *n masc* (-, -ar, -a) meringue
marenstert|a *n fem* (-u, -ur, -na) meringue cake
margbrotin|n *adj* (-, -brotið) complex, complicated
margfalda *v* (~, -ði, -ð) multiply
margfald|ur *adj* (-föld, -falt) multiple
margföld|un *n fem* (-unar, -anir, -ana) multiplication
marg|ir (-ar, mörg) *pron* many
marglit|ur *adj* (-, -t) colorful
marglytt|a *n fem* (-u, -ur, ~) jellyfish
margmiðlun *n fem* (-ar) multimedia
margþætt|ur *adj* (-, -) complex
margvísleg|ur *adj* (-, -t) of many kinds
marijúana *n neu* (-) marijuana, weed
marínerað|ur *adj* (maríneruð, -) marinated

marínering *n fem* (-ar, -ar, -a) marinade
maríuerl|a *n fem* (-u, -ur, ~) *zool* white wagtail
markaðssetning *n fem* (-ar) *econ* marketing
markaðsverð *n neu* (-s) *econ* market price
markað|ur *n masc* (-ar/s, -ir, -a) market, marketplace
markmál *n neu* (-s, -, -a) target language
markmið *n neu* (-s, -, -a) aim, goal
markviss *adj* (-, -t) systematical, resolute
markvörð|ur *n masc* (-varðar, -verðir, -varða) *sports* goalkeeper
marmar|i *n masc* (-a, -ar, -a) marble
marmelaði *n neu* (-s) marmalade
Marokkó *N neu* (-) Morocco
Marokkómað|ur *n masc* (-manns, -menn, -manna) Moroccan *(person)*
marokkósk|ur *adj* (-, -t) Moroccan
mars *n masc* (-) *(month)* March; *(walk)* march
Mars *N masc* (-) Mars
marsera *v* (~, -ði, -ð) march
marsipan *n neu* (-s) marzipan
marsvín *n neu* (-s, -, -a) guinea pig
martröð *n fem* (-traðar, -traðir, -traða) nightmare
maskar|i *n masc* (-a, -ar, -a) mascara
mat *n neu* (-s) evaluation
mata *v* (~, -ði, -ð) feed
mata|st *v refl* (~, -ðist, ~) eat
mataræði *n neu* (-s) diet
matarbit|i *n masc* (-a, -ar, -a) bite of food
matarbúr *n neu* (-s, -, -a) pantry
matareitr|un *n fem* (-unar, -anir, -ana) food poisoning
matarfeit|i *n fem* (-) grease
matargerðarlist *n fem* (-ar) gastronomy
matarhátíð *n fem* (-ar, -ir, -a) food festival
matarinnkaup *n neu* (-s, -, -a) grocery shopping

matarlit|ur *n masc* (-ar, -ir, -a) food coloring

matarlyst *n fem* (-ar) appetite

matarmenning *n fem* (-ar) food culture

matarskammt|ur *n masc* (-s, -ar, -a) food portion

matarsód|i *n masc* (-a) baking soda

matarúthlutunarröð *n fem* (-raðar, -raðir, -raða) breadline

matjurtagarð|ur *n masc* (-s, -ar, -a) vegetable garden

matreiðslubók *n fem* (-ar, -bækur, -bóka) cookbook

matreiðslumað|ur *n masc* (-manns, -menn, -manna) chef, cook

matseðil|l *n masc* (-s, -seðlar, -seðla) menu

matskeið *n fem* (-ar, -ar, -a) tablespoon

matsölustað|ur *n masc* (-ar, -ir, -a) restaurant; deli

mat|ur *n masc* (-ar, -ar, -a) food

matvælaþjónust|a *n fem* (-u) catering service

mauk *n neu* (-s, -, -a) compote; puree

maula *v* (~, -ði, -ð) munch

maur *n masc* (-s, -ar, -a) ant

mál *n neu* (-s, -, -a) issue, problem: ekkert ~ no problem; drinking cup; measuring cup; *leg* case; mér er ~ I need to pee; í stuttu máli in sum

mála *v* (~, -ði, -ð) paint

málaferl|i *n neu pl* (-a) *leg* court process

málamiðl|un *n fem* (-unar, -anir, -ana) compromise

málaralist *n fem* (-ar) *(art)* painting

málarekstur *n masc* (-s, -rekstrar, -rekstra) *leg* proceeding

málaskrá *n fem* (-r, -r, -a) *leg* docket

málband *n neu* (-s, -bönd, -a) tape measure

málfar *n neu* (-s) language, way of talking

málflutningsmað|ur *n masc* (-manns, -menn, -manna) *leg* advocate, solicitor

málfrelsi *n neu* (-s) freedom of speech

málfræði *n fem* (-) grammar

málhreinsunarmað|ur *n masc* (-manns, -menn, -manna) purist

mállaus *adj* (-, -t) speechless

mállýsk|a *n fem* (-u, -ur, -na) dialect

málmgrýti *n neu* (-s) *geol* ore

málm|ur *n masc* (-s, -ar, -a) metal

málning *n fem* (-ar) paint

málsgrein *n fem* (-ar, -ar, -a) *ling* sentence

málshátt|ur *n masc* (-ar, -hættir, -hátta) *ling* proverb

málsókn *n fem* (-ar, -ir, -a) *leg* lawsuit

málstof|a *n fem* (-u, -ur, -a) seminar, workshop

málsækjand|i *n masc* (-a, -endur, -enda) *leg* plaintiff

máltíð *n fem* (-ar, -ir, -a) meal

málverk *n neu* (-s, -, -a) painting

málvísindamað|ur *n masc* (-manns, -menn, -manna) linguist

málvísind|i *n neu* (-a) linguistics

mánaðarlega *adv* monthly

mánaðarleg|ur *adj* (-, -t) monthly

mánudag|ur *n masc* (-s, -ar, -a) Monday

mánuð|ur *n masc* (mánaðar, -ir, -a) month

Máritaní|a *N fem* (-u) Mauritania

Máritíus *N neu* (-) Mauritius

más *n neu* (-s) *med* wheezing

mása *v* (~, -ði, -ð) pant

máttfarin|n *adj* (-, -farið) exhausted

máttlítil|l *adj* (-, -lítið) weak

mátt|ur *n masc* (-ar, mættir, mátta) power, energy

mát|un *n fem* (-unar, -anir, -ana) fitting

mátunarklef|i *n masc* (-a, -ar, -a) fitting room

máv|ur *n masc* (-s, -ar, -a) seagull

með *prep* + *acc (accessories, sth or sby brought along)* with: ~ gler-augu with glasses, ég kem ~ hann I'll bring him; *(together)* + *dat* with: **ég kem ~ honum** I'll come with him; *(tools)* with: **klippa ~ skærum** cut with scissors; *(content)* of: **kassi ~ mynda** box of photos; *(time)* during: **kólnar ~ kvöldinu** gets colder during the course of the evening

meðal 1 *n neu* (-s, meðöl, -a) medicine, drug; **2** *prep + gen* among, one of: **~ Íslendinga** among Icelanders, **~ annars** among others

meðaljón *n masc* (-s, -ar, -a) John Doe, average person

meðalmaðu|ur *n masc* (-manns, -menn, -manna) average person

meðalmennsk|a *n fem* (-u) mediocrity

meðaltal *n neu* (-s, -töl, -a) average

meðaumkun *n fem* (-ar) pity

meðeigand|i *n masc* (-a, -endur, -enda) co-owner

meðferð *n fem* (-ar, -ir, -a) *med* therapy; **áfengismeðferð** rehabilitation

meðfram *prep* alongside; *prep + dat* along: **~ ánni** along the river

meðfædd|ur *adj* (-, -fætt) innate: **~ hæfileiki** natural talent

meðfærileg|ur *adj* (-, -t) amenable

meðgang|a *n fem* (-göngu) pregnancy

meðlim|ur *n masc* (-s, -ir, -a) member

meðmæl|i *n neu pl* (-a) recommendation

meðvitað|ur *adj* (-vituð, -) conscious, aware

meðvitund *n fem* (-ar) conciousness, awareness

meðvitundarlaus *adj* (-, -t) *med* unconscious

mega *v* (má, mátti, máttum, megað) may, can: **má ég fara í bíó?** can I go to the movies?

megabæt|i *n neu* (-is, ~, -a) *comp* megabyte

megin *adv* side: **báðum ~** on both sides

meginregl|a *n fem* (-u, -reglur, -na) principle

megr|un *n fem* (-unar, -anir, -ana) diet

meidd|ur *adj* (-, meitt) hurt, injured

meið|a *v* (-i, meiddi, meitt) hurt, injure

meiðsl *n neu pl* (-a) injury

meiðyrð|i *n neu* (-is, ~, -a) *leg* libel

meinsær|i *n neu* (-is, ~, -a) *leg* perjury

meir|i *adj compar* (~, -a) *used as an emphasis*; **~ vitleysan!** what nonsense!; **þú ert nú ~ lygarinn!** you are such a liar!

meira *adv compar* more; **~ að segja** even; **~ og ~** more and more

meiriháttar *adj* major: **~ breytingar** major changes

meirihlut|i *n masc* (-a, -ar, -a) majority

meistaraverk *n neu* (-s, -, -a) masterpiece

melasól *n fem* (-ar, -ir, -a) *flora* arctic poppy

melóna *n fem* (-u, -ur, ~) melon

melt|a *v* (-i, -i, -t) digest

meltingarfær|i *n neu* (-is, ~, -a) *anat* digestive system

meltingartruflan|ir *n fem pl* (-a) *med* indigestion

meltingarveg|ur *n masc* (-ar/s, -ir, -a) *anat* digestive system

menga *v* (~, -ði, -ð) pollute

mengun *n fem* (-ar) pollution

menj|ar *n fem pl* (-a) remains, relics

menning *n fem* (-ar) culture

menningarleg|ur *adj* (-, -t) cultural

menningarmál *n neu pl* (-s, -, -a) cultural issues

mennta *v* (~, -ði, -ð) educate

menntað|ur *adj* (menntuð, -) educated

menntafólk *n neu* (-s) educated people

menntamað|ur *n masc* (-manns, -menn, -manna) educated person

menntaskól|i *n masc* (-a, -ar, -a) high school; college; upper secondary school for 16-20-year-old students

menntun *n fem* (-ar) education

mentól *n neu* (-s) menthol

mér *pron dat* me: **ekki gleyma ~!**
don't forget me!

merg|ur *n masc* (-jar) marrow

merj|a *v* (mer, marði, marið) bruise

merk|i *n neu* (-is, ~, -ja) sign, mark,
signal, symbol; suggestion; token

merkimið|i *n masc* (-a, -ar, -a) tag

merking *n fem* (-ar, -ar, -a) meaning,
sense, significance; label

merkingafræði *n fem* (-) *ling* semantics

merkingafræðileg|ur *adj* (-, -t) *ling*
semantic

merkipenn|i *n masc* (-a, -ar, -a)
marker

merkisstað|ur *n masc* (-ar, -ir, -a)
show place; point of interest

merkj|a *v* (merki, merkti, merkt)
label, mark

merkt|ur *adj* (-, -) labeled, marked

mess|a *n fem* (-u, -ur, ~) mass

met|a *v* (-, mat, mátum, metið) rate,
assess, value

metnaðargirni *n fem* (-i) ambition

metnaðargjarn *adj* (-gjörn, -t)
ambitious

metnað|ur *n masc* (-ar) ambition

metr|i *n masc* (-a, -ar, -a) meter

metta *v* (~, -ði, -ð) saturate

mettað|ur *adj* (mettuð, -) saturated

Mexíkó *N neu* (-/s) Mexico

Mexíkóborg *N fem* (-ar) Mexico City

Mexíkófló|i *N masc* (-a) Gulf of
Mexico

Mexíkó|i *n masc* (-a, -ar, -a) Mexican
(person)

Meyj|an *n fem def* (-unnar) *astro* Virgo

miða *v* (~, -ði, -ð) aim

Mið-Afríkurík|i *n neu* (-is, ~, -ja)
Central African Republic

miðaldabókmennt|ir *n fem pl* (-a)
medieval literature

miðaldasag|a *n fem* (-sögu, -sögur,
-sagna) medieval history

Mið-Ameríka *N fem* (-u) Central
America

mið-amerísk|ur *adj* (-, -t) Central
American

miðasal|a *n fem* (-sölu, -sölur, -na)
ticket counter

miðaverð *n neu* (-s) ticket price

miðbæ|r *n masc* (-jar, -ir, -ja) center
of town, downtown

miðbaug|ur *n masc* (-s, -ar, -a) *geog*
equator

mið|i *n masc* (-a, -ar, -a) tag; ticket:
~ á biðlista standby ticket, **~
báðar leiðir** round-trip ticket

miðil|l *n masc* (-s, miðlar, miðla)
medium, fortuneteller, psychic;
fjöl~ mass medium

miðj|a *n fem* (-u, -ur, ~) middle

Miðjarðarhaf *N neu* (-s) Mediterranean Sea

miðla *v* (~, -ði, -ð) carry on a message; **~ málum** mediate

miðlar|i *n masc* (-a, -ar, -a) *econ*
broker

miðnætti *n neu* (-s) midnight

miðpunkt|ur *n masc* (-s, -ar, -a)
centerpoint

miðstöð *n fem* (-var, -var, -va) center

miðstöðvarketil|l *n masc* (-s, -katlar,
-katla) furnace

miðstöðvarofn *n masc* (-s, -ar, -a)
radiator

miðvikudag|ur *n masc* (-s, -ar, -a)
Wednesday

mig *pron acc* me: **hún borgar fyrir
~** she pays for me

mikið 1 *pron neu* great; **2** *adv* much:
borða of ~ each too much

mikill *pron* great: **hún er ~ listamaður** she is a great artist

mikilvægi *n neu* (-s) importance

mikilvæg|ur *adj* (-, -t) important

Miklagljúfur *N neu* (-s) Grand Canyon

milda *v* (~, -ði, -ð) soften

mild|ur *adj* (-, milt) gentle, mild

milli *prep* + *gen* between: **~ mín og
þín** between me and you, **~ Akur-
eyrar og Reykjavíkur** between
Akureyri and Reykjavik

millifærsl|a *n fem* (-u, -ur, -na) bank
transfer

milligramm *n neu* (-s, -grömm, -a) milligram

millilandasímtal *n neu* (-s, -töl, -a) international call

millilend|a *v* (-i, -lenti, -lent) stop over (between flights)

millilending *n fem* (-ar, -ar, -a) flight transfer

millimetr|i *n masc* (-a, -ar, -a) millimeter

millipils *n neu* (-, -, -a) petticoat

milliríkjasamning|ur *n masc* (-s, -ar, -a) international treaty

milliveg|ur *n masc* (-ar/s, -ir, -a) compromise

milljarð|ur *n masc* (-s, -ar, -a) billion

milljón *n fem* (-ar, -ir, -a) million

milljónamæring|ur *n masc* (-s, -ar, -a) millionaire

milt|a *n neu* (-a, -u, -na) *anat* spleen

minjagripaversl|un *n fem* (-unar, -anir, -ana) souvenir shop

minjagrip|ur *n masc* (-s, -ir, -a) souvenir

mink|ur *n masc* (-s, -ar, -a) mink

min|n *pron* (mín, mitt) my: **pabbi ~** my dad

minn|a **1** *v* (-i, -ti, -t) **~ á** remind; **2** *adv* less

minn|ast *v* (-ist, -tist, -st) recollect

minn|i **1** *adj compar* (-i, -a) smaller, minor: **~ háttar slys** minor accident; **2** *n neu* memory

minnihlut|i *n masc* (-a, -ar, -a) minority

minning *n fem* (-ar, -ar, -a) memory, recollection

minningarathöfn *n fem* (-hafnar, -hafnir, -hafna) commemoration

minningargrein *n fem* (-ar, -ar, -a) obituary

minningarsjóð|ur *n masc* (-s, -ir, -a) memorial fund

minnisblað *n neu* (-s, -blöð, -a) memo

minnismerk|i *n neu* (-is, ~, -ja) monument

minnismið|i *n masc* (-a, -ar, -a) note to remind

minnispunkt|ur *n masc* (-s, -ar, -a) note

minnistap *n neu* (-s) *med* amnesia

minnisvarð|i *n masc* (-a, -ar, -a) monument

minnka *v* (~, -ði, -ð) reduce

minnst|ur *adj superl* (-, -) smallest

Minsk *N fem* (-) Minsk

mint|a *n fem* (-u, -ur, -na) mint *(herb)*

mirr|a *n fem* (-u) myrrh

mislíka *v* (~, -ði, -ð) dislike

misling|ar *n masc pl* (-a) *med* measles

mismuna *v* (~, -ði, -ð) discriminate

mismunandi *adj* of different sorts

mismunun *n fem* (-ar) discrimination

mismun|ur *n masc* (-ar) difference

misnotkun *n fem* (-ar) addiction; abuse

misreikna *v* (~, -ði, -ð) miscalculate

miss|a *v* (-i, -ti, -t) loose, drop

misser|i *n neu* (-is, ~, -a) term; **undanfarin ~** recent years

misskilin|n *adj* (-, -skilið) misunderstood

misskilning|ur *n masc* (-s) misconception, misunderstanding

mistak|ast *v* (-tekst, -tókst, -tókst, -tekist) fail: **tilraunin mistókst** the experiment was a failure, **mér mistókst** I failed

mistur *n neu* (-s) vapor

mistök *n neu pl* (-taka) mistake, failure

misþyrm|a *v* (-i, -di, -t) torture

misþyrming *n fem* (-ar) torture

mitt *pron neu* my **barnið ~** my child

mitt|i *n neu* (-is, ~, -a) *anat* waist

mígreni *n neu* (-s) migraine

Míkrónesí|a *N fem* (-u) Federated States of Micronesia

míl|a *n fem* (-u, -ur, -na) mile

mín *pron fem* mine, my: **mamma ~** my mom

míníbar *n masc* (-s, -ir, -a) minibar

mínút|a *n fem* (-u, -ur, -na) minute

mjaldur *n masc* (-s, mjaldrar, mjaldra) *zool* beluga whale, white whale

Mjanmar *N neu* (-) Myanmar (Burma)
mjólk *m fem* (-ur) milk
mjólkurbú *n neu* (-s, -, -a) dairy
mjólkurhristing|ur *n masc* (-s, -ar, -a) milkshake
mjólkurlaus *adj* (-, -t) dairy-free
mjólkursykur *n masc* (-s) *bio* lactose
mjólkursykursóþol *n neu* (-s) *med* lactose intolerance
mjólkurvör|ur *n fem pl* (-vara) dairy products
mjó|r *adj* (-, -tt) slim, thin, skinny
mjúklega *adv* smoothly, softly
mjúk|ur *adj* (-, -t) soft, smooth; tender
mjöðm *n fem* (mjaðmar, mjaðmir, mjaðma) *anat* hip
mjöð|ur *n masc* (mjaðar, miðir, mjaða) mead
mjög *adv* very
mjölbanan|i *n masc* (-a, -ar, -a) plantain
moka *v* (~, -ði, -ð) shovel
Moldaví|a *N fem* (-u) Moldova
moldvarp|a *n fem* (-vörpu, -vörpur, ~) *zool* mole
mol|i *n masc* (-a, -ar, -a) little piece
moll *n masc* (-s, -ar, -a) *mus* minor
mulleleg|ur *adj* (-, -t) muggy
molna *v* (~, -ði, -ð) crumble
Mongól|i *n masc* (-a, -ar, -a) Mongolian *(person)*
Mongólí|a *N fem* (-u) Mongolia
mongólsk|a *n fem* (-u) Mongolian language
mongólsk|ur *adj* (-, -t) Mongolian
Monróvía *N fem* (-u) Monrovia
monthan|i *n masc* (-a, -ar, -a) person that shows off
moppa 1 *n fem* (-u, -ur, -a) mop; **2** *v* (~, -ði, -ð) mop
morð *n neu* (-s, -, -a) assassination, murder
morðing|i *n masc* (-ja, -jar, -ja) assassin, murderer
morfín *n neu* (-s) *med* morphine
morgunkorn *n neu* (-s, -, -a) cereal
morgunmat|ur *n masc* (-ar, -ar, -a) breakfast

morgun|n *n masc* (-s, morgnar, morgna) morning
morgunverðarhlaðborð *n neu* (-s, -, -a) breakfast buffet
morgunverð|ur *n masc* (-ar, -ir, -a) breakfast
mortadella-pyls|a *n fem* (-u, -ur, -a) mortadella
mortél *n neu* (-s, -s, -a) mortar
mos|i *n masc* (-a, -ar, -a) *flora* moss
mosk|a *n fem* (-u, -ur, -na) mosque
moskítóbit *n neu* (-s, -, -a) mosquito bite
moskítóflug|a *n fem* (-u, -ur, -na) mosquito
Moskv|a *N fem* (-u) Moscow
mott|a *n fem* (-u, -ur, -a) mat, rug
mozzarella-ost|ur *n masc* (-s, -ar, -a) mozzarella
módel *n neu* (-s, -, -a) model
módem *n neu* (-s, -, -a) *comp* modem
móðga *v* (~, -ði, -ð) insult, offend
móðgandi *adj* insulting, offensive
móðg|un *n fem* (-unar, -anir, -ana) insult
móð|ir *n fem* (-ur, mæður, mæðra) mother
móðurbróð|ir *n masc* (-bróður, -bræður, -bræðra) maternal uncle
móðurforeldr|ar *n masc pl* (-a) maternal grandparent
móðurhlutverk *n neu* (-s) motherhood
móðurlíf *n neu* (-s) womb
móðurmál *n neu* (-s, -, -a) mother tongue
móðursjúk|ur *adj* (-, -t) hysterical
móðursyst|ir *n fem* (-ur, -ur, -ra) maternal aunt
móðursýki *n fem* (-) hysteria
Mónakó *N neu* (-/s) Monaco
mórber *n neu* (-s, -, -ja) *flora* mulberry
mósaík *n fem* (-ur) mosaic
mót *n neu* (-s, -, -a) form
móta *v* (~, -ði, -ð) shape
mótald *n neu* (-s, mótöld, -a) *comp* modem
mótefni *n neu* (-s, -, -a) *med* antibody

móteitur *n neu* (-s) *med* antidote

móti. *See* **á móti**

mótmæl|a *v* (-i, -ti, -t) demonstrate, protest

mótmæland|i *n masc* (-a, -endur, -enda) demonstrant, protestant

mótmæli *n neu pl* (-a) demonstration, protest

mótor *n masc* (-s, -ar, -a) *mech* motor

mótorbát|ur *n masc* (-s, -ar, -a) motorboat

mótorhjól *n neu* (-s, -, -a) motorbike

mótspyrn|a *n fem* (-u, -ur, ~) resistance

móttak|a *n fem* (-töku, -tökur, ~) reception, lobby

móttakand|i *n masc* (-a, -endur, -enda) receiver, recipient

mottó *n neu* (-s, -, -a) motto

móttökustjór|i *n masc* (-a, -ar, -a) receptionist

mótun *n fem* (-ar) formation

muldra *v* (~, -ði, -ð) mumble

muldur *n neu* (-s) murmur

mun|a *v* (man, mundi, munað) remember, recollect

munaðarleysing|i *n masc* (-ja, -jar, -ja) orphan

munaðarleysingjahæl|i *n neu* (-is, ~, -a) orphanage

mundi. *See* **munu**

mungbaun *n fem* (-ar, -ir, -a) mung beans

munnangur *n neu* (-s) *med* mouth ulcer

munnbit|i *n masc* (-a, -ar, -a) bite-size

munnfyll|i *n neu* (-is, ~, -a) mouthful

munnlega *adv* orally

munnleg|ur *adj* (-, -t) oral, verbal

munnþurrk|a *n fem* (-u, -ur, -a) napkin

munntóbak *n neu* (-s) chewing tobacco

munn|ur *n masc* (-s, -ar, -a) mouth

munnvatn *n neu* (-s) saliva

munstur *n neu* (-s, -, munstra) pattern

mun|u *v* (mun *only in present tense*) will, shall

mun|ur *n masc* (-ar, -ir, -a) difference; object

muster|i *n neu* (-is, ~, -a) temple *(religious)*

múff|a *n fem* (-u, -ur, -a) muffin

múldýr *n neu* (-s, -, -a) mule

múltuber *n neu* (-s, -, -ja) cloudberry

múmí|a *n fem* (-u, -ur, ~) mummy

múrstein|n *n masc* (-s, -ar, -a) brick

mús *n fem* (-ar, mýs, -a) *zool* mouse

músikalsk|ur *adj* (-ölsk, -t) musical

múskat *n neu* (-s) nutmeg

múslí *n neu* (-s) muesli

múslim|i *n masc* (-a, -ar, -a) Muslim

múta *v* (~, -ði, -ð) bribe

mygl|a 1 *n fem* (-u) mold; **2 mygla** *v* (~, -ði, -ð) get moldy

myglað|ur *adj* (mygluð, -) moldy

mygluost|ur *n masc* (-s, -ar, -a) blue cheese

mylsn|a *n fem* (-u, -ur, ~) crumb

mynd *n fem* (-ar, -ir, -a) picture, photo, image; movie; painting

mynda *v* (~, -ði, -ð) take a photo

myndarleg|ur *adj* (-, -t) handsome, attractive

myndavél *n fem* (-ar, -ar, -a) camera

myndavélatask|a *n fem* (-tösku, -töskur, -taska) camera bag

myndbandsupptökuvél *n fem* (-ar, -ar, -a) video recorder

myndbygging *n fem* (-ar) composition of a picture

myndhöggvar|i *n masc* (-a, -ar, -a) sculptor

myndlesar|i *n masc* (-a, -ar, -a) optical scanner

myndlíking *n fem* (-ar, -ar, -a) *lit* metaphor

myndmál *n neu* (-s, -, -a) *lit* metaphor

myndræn|n *adj* (-, -t) figurative

myndskeið *n neu* (-s, -, -a) film clip

myndskreyt|a *v* (-i, -ti, -t) illustrate

myndskreyting *n fem* (-ar, -ar, -a) illustration

mynd|un *n fem* (-unar, -anir, -ana) formation

mynt *n fem* (-ar, -ir, -a) coin
myntsafn *n neu* (-s, -söfn, -a) coin
  collection
myrð|a *v* (-i, -ti, -t) murder
myrkv|i *n masc* (-a, -ar, -a) eclipse:
  tungl~ eclipse of the moon
mys|a *n fem* (-u) whey
mýr|i *n fem* (-ar, -ar, -a) marsh, moor,
  swamp
mjölv|i *n masc* (-a) starch
mæla *v* (-, -di, -t) measure; ~ **með**
  recommend
mælaborð *n neu* (-s, -, -a) panel
mæland|i *n masc* (-a, -endur, -enda)
  speaker
mælieining *n fem* (-ar, -ar, -a)
  measurement
mælikvarð|i *n masc* (-a, -ar, -a) scale
mæling *n fem* (-ar, -ar, -a) measurement
mælsk|a *n fem* (-u) eloquence
mælskulist *n fem* (-ar) rhetorics
mælsk|ur *adj* (-, -t) eloquent
mæn|a *n fem* (-u, -ur, ~) *anat* spinal
  cord

mær *n fem* (meyjar, meyja) maid
mæt|a *v* (-i, -ti, -t) attend, show up,
  meet
mögulega *adv* possibly
möguleg|ur *adj* (-, -t) possible,
  potential
möguleik|i *n masc* (-a, -ar, -a) pos-
  sibility, potential
mölflug|a *n fem* (-u, -ur, -na) moth
mölva *v* (~, -ði, -ð) smash
möndludrop|ar *n masc pl* (-a)
  almond extract
möndlumjólk *n fem* (-ur) almond
  milk
möndluolí|a *n fem* (-u, -ur, -a)
  almond oil
möndlusmjör *n neu* (-s) almond
  butter
mörgæs *n fem* (-ar, -ir, -a) penguin
mörk *n neu pl* (marka) boundary

N

nachos-flög|ur *n fem* (-flagna) nachos
nafl|i *n masc* (-a, -ar, -a) *anat* navel;
  ~ **alheimsins** center of the universe
nafn *n neu* (-s, nöfn, -a) name
nafnhátt|ur *n masc* (-ar, -hættir,
  -hátta) *ling* infinitive
nafnlaus *adj* (-, -t) anonymous
nafnleysi *n neu* (-s) anonymity
nafnorð *n neu* (-s, -, -a) *ling* noun
nafnspjald *n neu* (-s, -spjöld, -a)
  name card
naggrís *n fem* (-ar, -ir, -a) guinea pig
naglasnyrting *n fem* (-ar) manicure
naglastof|a *n fem* (-u, -ur, -a) nail
  salon
nagl|i *n masc* (-a, -ar, -a) *(tool)* nail
nakin|n *adj* (-, nakið) naked
Namibí|a *N fem* (-u) Namibia
nammi *n neu* (-s) sweets
nart *n neu* (-s) nibble
narta *v* (~, -ði, -ð) nibble
nashyrning|ur *n masc* (-s, -ar, -a)
  zool rhinoceros
nasl *n neu* (-s) snack
natríum *n neu* (-s) sodium
natrón *n neu* (-s) baking soda
nauðga *v* (~, -ði, -ð) rape
nauðgar|i *n masc* (-a, -ar, -a) rapist
nauðg|un *n fem* (-unar, -anir, -ana)
  rape
nauðsyn *n fem* (-jar, -jar, -ja) need,
  necessity
nauðsynlega *adv* necessarily,
  essentially
nauðsynleg|ur *adj* (-, -t) necessary,
  essential, imperative
nauðug|ur *adj* (-, -t) forced
naut *n neu* (-s, -, -a) *zool* bull
nautakjöt *n neu* (-s) beef
nautgrip|ur *n masc* (-s, -ir, -a)
  kettle; cattle

Naut|ið *n neu* (-sins) *astro* Taurus
ná *v* (næ, -ði, -ð) reach, extend to
náða *v* (~, -ði, -ð) *leg* pardon
náð|un *n fem* (-unar, -anir, -ana) *leg*
  pardon
nágrannarík|i *n neu* (-is, ~, -ja)
  border state
nágrann|i *n masc* (-a, -ar, -a) neighbor
nágrenni *n neu* (-s) surroundings,
  neighborhood
náhval|ur *n masc* (-s, -ir, -a) *zool*
  narwhal
náin|n *adj* (-, náið) intimate
nákvæmlega *adv* precisely
nákvæmni *n fem* (-) precision
nákvæm|ur *adj* (-, -t) exact, accurate,
  precise, detailed
nál *n fem* (-ar, -ar, -a) needle
nálarstung|a *n fem* (-u, -ur, -a)
  acupuncture
nálga|st *v refl* (~, -ðist, ~) approach
nálg|un *n fem* (-unar, anir, -ana)
  approach
nálægð *n fem* (-ar) proximity
nálægt *adv* near
nálæg|ur *adj* (-, -t) close, near,
  approximate
námsefn|i *n neu* (-is, ~, -a) study
  material
námsgrein *n fem* (-ar, -ar, -a) school
  subject
námskeið *n neu* (-s, -, -a) course
námsstyrk|ur *n masc* (-s, -ir, -ja)
  grant, scholarship
nánari *adv compar* further: ~
  upplýsingar further information;
  closer
nánast *adv* practically, almost: **þetta
  er ~ búið** it's almost finished
nánd *n fem* (-ar, -ir, -a) intimacy
nár|i *n masc* (-a, -ar, -a) *anat* groin

náttborð *n neu* (-s, -, -a) night table

náttföt *n neu pl* (-fata) pajamas

náttúr|a *n fem* (-u, -ur, -a) nature

náttúrulega *adv* naturally

náttúruleg|ur *adj* (-, -t) natural

náttúrustíg|ur *n masc* (-s, -ar/ir, -a) nature trail

náttúruvernd *n fem* (-ar) nature conservation

náttúruverndarsvæð|i *n neu* (-is, ~, -a) conservation area, nature reserve

náttúruvísind|i *n neu* (-a) natural sciences

náung|i *n masc* (-a, -ar, -a) fellow, guy

né *adv* nor; **hvorki ... né ...** neither ... nor ...

neðan 1 *adv* að ~ below: **hér að ~** here below; **fyrir ~** below: **hann býr fyrir ~** he lives below **2** *prep* + *gen* below: **~ brúar** below the bridge

neðanjarðar *adv* underground

neðanjarðarlest *n fem* (-ar, -ir, -a) subway

neðansjávar *adv* underwater

neðri *adv compar* lower; **~ hæð** downstairs

nef *n neu* (-s, -, -a) *anat* nose

nefhol|a *n fem* (u, -ur, ~) *anat* nasal sinus

nefn|a *v* (-i, -di, -t) mention, call, name

nefnd *n fem* (-ar, -ir, -a) commission, committee

nefndarfund|ur *n masc* (-ar, -ir, -a) council meeting

nefrennsli *n neu* (-s, -, -a) runny nose

negl|a *v* (-i, -di, -t) nail

nei *adv* no

neikvæð|ur *adj* (-, -kvætt) negative; **neikvæður vöruskiptajöfnuður** *econ* trade gap

nein|n *pron* (-, neitt) anyone; anything: **ég sá ekki neitt** I didn't see anything

neins staðar *adv* anywhere, nowhere

neita *v* (~, -ði, -ð) deny, refuse

neitt. *See* **neinn**

neit|un *n fem* (-unar, -anir, -ana) refusal

neitunarvald *n neu* (-s) veto

nektarín|a *n fem* (-u, -ur, -a) nectarine

nektarströnd *n fem* (-strandar, -strendur, -stranda) nudist beach

nema *conj* unless, except, except if

nemand|i *n masc* (-a, -endur, -enda) student, pupil

nem|i *n masc* (-a, -ar, -a) student; receptor

Nepal *N neu* Nepal

Nepal|i *n masc* (-a, -ar/ir, -a) Nepali *(person)*

nepalsk|ur *adj* (nepölsk, -t) Nepali

Neptúnus *N masc* (-ar) Neptune

nes *n neu* (-s, ~, -ja) peninsula

nesti *n neu* (-s) packed lunch

nestisbox *n neu* (-, -, -a) lunch box

net *n neu* (-s, -, -a) net; network

netfang *n neu* (-s, -föng, -a) e-mail address

netkaffihús *n neu* (-s, -, -a) Internet café

netleik|ur *n masc* (-s, -ir, -ja) *comp* online game

netnotand|i *n masc* (-a, -endur, -enda) *comp* Internet user

nettálm|i *n masc* (-a, -ar, -a) *comp* firewall

netþjónust|a *n fem* (-u, -ur, ~) *comp* Internet service provider

netversl|un *n fem* (-unar, -anir, -ana) e-commerce, webstore

netviðskipt|i *n neu pl* (-a) e-business

neyð *n fem* (-ar, -ir, -a) emergency

neyð|a *v* (-i, -ddi, -tt) force

neyðarbíl|l *n masc* (-s, -ar, -a) ambulance

neyðarmóttak|a *n fem* (-töku, -tökur, ~) *med* emergency room

neyðarpill|a *n fem* (-u, -ur, -a) *med* morning-after pill

neysl|a *n fem* (-u) consumption

neytand|i *n masc* (-a, -endur, -enda) consumer

niður 1 *n masc* (-ar) murmur, soft
noise; **2** *adv* down
niðurbrot *n neu* (-s, -, -a) breakdown
niðurfall *n neu* (-s, -föll, -a) drain
niðurgang|ur *n masc* (-s) diarrhea
niðurlæging *n fem* (-ar) humiliation
niðurlægj|a *v* (-lægi, -lægði, -lægt)
humiliate
niðurnídd|ur *adj* (-, -nítt) rundown,
slummy
niðurskorin|n *adj* (-, -skorið) chopped;
sliced
niðurskurð|ur *n masc* (-ar)
retrenchment
niðursneidd|ur *adj* (-, -sneitt) sliced;
niðursneitt kjötálegg coldcuts
niðurstað|a *n fem* (-stöðu, -stöður, ~)
result, findings, conclusion
Níger *N neu* (-s) Niger
Nígería *N fem* (-u) Nigeria
nígerísk|ur *adj* (-, -t) Nigerian
Nígeríumað|ur *n masc* (-manns,
-menn, -manna) Nigerian *(person)*
níhílism|i *n masc* (-a) nihilism
níkaragsk|ur *adj* (níkarösk, -t)
Nicaraguan
Níkaragva *N neu* (-) Nicaragua
Níkaragvamað|ur *n masc* (-manns,
-menn, -manna) Nicaraguan *(person)*
nikótín *n neu* (-s) nicotine
níp|a *n fem* (-u, -ur, -na) parsnip
níræð|ur *adj* (-, nírætt) ninety-years-
old
nísk|a *n fem* (-u) stinginess
nísk|ur *adj* (-, -t) stingy
nítján *num* nineteen
nítjánd|i *ord* (-a, -a) nineteenth
nítugast|i *ord* (-a, -a) ninetieth
níu *num* nine
níund|i *ord* (-a, -a) ninth
níutíu *num* ninety
njósnar|i *n masc* (-a, -ar, -a) spy
njót|a *v* (nýt, naut, nutum, notið)
enjoy
nokkur *pron* (-, -t) *(quantity)* some,
several, a few: **ég á nokkrar
krónur** I have a few krónas; *(in*

questions) any, anyone: **getur ~
sagt mér hvar hann er?** can anyone tell me where he is?; *(absence
of a quality)* any, anything: **hann
hefur ekki nokkurt vit á þessu!**
he doesn't know anything about
this!
nokkurs staðar *adv* anywhere
norðan 1 *adv* north: **fyrir ~ up**
north; **2** *prep + gen* ~ **ár** north of
the river
norðaustur *adv* northeast
norður 1 *n neu* (-s) north: **norðrið**
the north; **2** north: **keyra ~** drive
north
Norður-Ameríka *N fem* (-u) North
America
Norður-Ameríkuflek|i *n masc* (-a,
-ar, -a) *geol* North American Plate
Norðurheimskautabaug|ur *N masc*
(-s) *geog* Arctic Circle
Norður-Írland *N neu* (-s) Northern
Ireland
Norður-Íshaf *N neu* (-s) Arctic Ocean
Norður-Kórea *N fem* (-u) North
Korea
Norðurland *N neu* (-s) north Iceland
Norðurlandaráð *N neu* (-s) Nordic
Council
norðurljós *n neu pl* (-a) Aurora
Borealis
Norðurlönd *N neu pl* (-landa) Scan-
dinavia (includes Iceland, Faeroe
Islands, and Greenland)
Norðurpól|linn *N masc* (-sins) North
Pole
Norðursjó|r *N masc* (-sjávar) North
Sea
Norðurskaut *N neu* (-s) Arctic
norðvestur *adv* northwest
Noreg|ur *N masc* (-s) Norway
norm *n neu* (-s, -, -a) norm
Norðmað|ur *n masc* (-manns, -menn,
-manna) Norwegian *(person)*
norn *n fem* (-ar, -ir, -a) witch
norræn|n *adj* (-, -t) Nordic, Norse:
norræn fræði Nordic studies,

norræn goðatrú Norse mythology, Norse paganism; **norræn tungumál** North-Germanic languages, Scandinavian languages; **Norræna ráðherranefndin** The Nordic Council of Ministers; **norrænar tungur** Scandinavian languages; **norrænir menn** Scandinavian people

norræn|a *n fem* (-u) Old Norse

norsk|a *n fem* (-u) Norwegian language

norsk|ur *adj* (-, -t) Norwegian

nota *v* (~, -ði, -ð) use

nota|st *v refl* (~, -ðist, ~) ~ **við** use

notað|ur *adj* (notuð, -) secondhand, used

notalega *adv* pleasantly

notaleg|ur *adj* (-, -t) pleasant

notand|i *n masc* (-a, -endur, -enda) user

notendanafn *n neu* (-s, -nöfn, -a) *comp* username, login

notkun *n fem* (-ar) usage

nóg *adv* enough: **ertu með ~ af peningum?** do you have enough money?

nóg|ur *adj* (-, -) enough, sufficient-

nótnastatíf *n neu* (-s, -, -a) music stand

nótt *n fem* (nætur, nætur, -a) night

nóvember *n masc* (-) November

nudd *n neu* (-s) massage

nudda *v* (~, -ði, -ð) massage, rub

nuddar|i *n masc* (-a, -ar, -a) masseur

nudda|st *v refl* (~, -ðist, ~) rub against

nunn|a *n fem* (-u, -ur, ~) nun

nunnuklaustur *n neu* (-s, -, -klaustra) nunnery, convent

nú *adv* **1** now: ~ **förum við** now we will leave; ~ **á dögum** *phr* nowadays; ~ **þegar** already; **2** *interj (between subtopics)* now; *(marking surprise)* oh

núðl|a *n fem* (-u, -ur, ~) noodle

núðlusúp|a *n fem* (-u, -ur, -na) noodle soup

núggat *n neu* (-s) nougat

núliðin tíð *n fem* (-ar) *ling* present perfect

núll *num neu* (-s, -, -a) zero

númer *n neu* (-s, -, -a) number

númeraplat|a *n fem* (-plötu, -plötur, -na) number plate

núna *adv* now

nútíð *n fem* (-ar) *ling* present tense

nútímafimleik|ar *n masc pl* (-a) rhythmic gymnastics

nútímaleg|ur *adj* (-, -t) modern

nútím|i *n masc* (-a) present time

núverandi *adj* current, present: ~ **forseti** current president

núvitund *n fem* (-ar) mindfulness

nýbreytni *n fem* (-) novelty

nýbú|i *n masc* (-a, -ar, -a) immigrant

Nýfundnaland *N neu* (-s) Newfoundland

Nýja Delhi *N fem* (-) New Delhi

Nýja Sjáland *N neu* (-s) New Zealand

nýjársdag|ur *n masc* (-s) New Year's Day

nýjung *n fem* (-ar, -ar, -a) innovation

nýlega *adv* recently, newly

nýleg|ur *adj* (-, -t) recent

nýlend|a *n fem* (-u, -ur, -na) colony, settlement

nýlið|i *n masc* (-a, -ar, -a) recruit

nýmjólk *n fem* (-ur) milk

ný|r *adj* (-, -tt) new: **nýjar kartöflur** new potatoes

nýr|a *n neu* (-a, -u, -na) *anat* kidney

nýrnabaun *n fem* (-ar, -ir, -a) kidney bean

nýrnakáss|a *n fem* (-u, -ur, -a) kidney stew

nýrnastein|n *n masc* (-s, -ar, -a) *med* kidney stone

Nýsjálending|ur *n masc* (-s, -ar, -a) New Zealander *(person)*

nýsjálensk|ur *adj* (-, -t) New Zealander

nýsköp|un *n fem* (-ar) innovation

nýsköpunarfyrirtæk|i *n neu* (-is, ~, -a) innovation company

nýstárleg|ur *adj* (-, -t) novel

---

nýt|a *v* (-i, -ti, -t) use; exploit
næð|i *n neu* (-s) privacy
nægilega *adv* adequately
nægileg|ur *adj* (-, -t) adequate,
  sufficient
nægjusam|ur *adj* (-söm, -t) content,
  does not ask for much
næg|ur *adj* (-, -t) ample
næl|a *n fem* (-u, -ur, -na) pin
nælon *n neu* (-s) nylon
nælonsokkabux|ur *n fem pl* (-na)
  pantyhose
nælonsokk|ur *n neu* (-ar) nylon
  socks
næm|ur *adj* (-, -t) perceptive
næp|a *n fem* (-u, -ur, -na) turnip
nær|a *v* (-i, -ði, -t) nourish
nærbux|ur *n fem pl* (-na) underpants,
  briefs
nærfataversl|un *n fem* (-unar, -anir,
  -ana) lingerie shop
nærfatnað|ur *n masc* (-ar) underwear
nærföt *n neu pl* (-fata) underwear
næring *n fem* (-ar) nourishment,
  nutrition

næringarefni *n neu* (-s) nutrient
næringarrík|ur *adj* (-, -t) nutritious
næringarskort|ur *n masc* (-s) lack
  of nutrients
nærri *adv* almost: **hann var ~ dáinn**
  he almost died
nærsýni *n fem* (-) near-sightedness
nærsýn|n *adj* (-, -t) near-sighted
nærver|a *n fem* (-u) presence
næs *adj slang* nice
næst *adv* next
næstbest|ur *adj superl* (-, -) second-
  best
næstum því *adv* almost, nearly
næst|ur *adj* (-, -) next, nearest
næturklúbb|ur *n masc* (-s, -ar, -a)
  night club
næturvörð|ur *n masc* (-varðar,
  -verðir, -varða) night porter
nögl *n fem* (naglar, neglur, nagla)
  (finger)nail
nörd *n masc* (-s, -ar, -a) *slang* nerd

O

o.s.frv. (= og svo framvegis) *abbrev*
etc. (= etcetera)
oddhvass *adj* (-hvöss, -t) pointed
oddmjó|r *adj* (-, -tt) pointed
odd|ur *n masc* (-s, -ar, -a) point, peak
of *adv* too
ofan 1 *adv* down; **2** *prep* + *gen* above
ofbeldi *n neu* (-s) violence
ofbeldisfull|ur *adj* (-, -t) violent
ofeldað|ur *adj* (-elduð, -) overcooked
offit|a *n fem* (-u) obesity
ofgnótt *n fem* (-ar) affluence
ofhita *v* (~, -ði, -ð) overheat
ofhlað|a *v* (-hleð, -hlóð, -hlóðum,
-hlaðið) overload
oflæti *n neu* (-s) arrogance
ofn *n masc* (-s, -ar, -a) oven; heater,
radiator
ofnæmi *n neu* (-s) allergy
ofnbakað|ur *adj* (-bökuð, -) oven-
baked
ofnklukk|a *n fem* (-u, -ur, -na) timer
(on a stove)
ofsækj|a *v* (-sæki, -sótti, -sótt) haunt;
persecute
ofsalega *adv* tremendously
ofsaleg|ur *adj* (-, -t) tremendous
ofs|i *n masc* (-a, -ar, -a) rage
ofsókn|ir *n fem pl* (-a) persecution
ofstækismað|ur *n masc* (-manns,
-menn, -manna) extremist
oft *adv* frequently
og svo framvegis (= **o.s.frv.**) *phr*
etcetera (= etc.)
okkar *pron* us; our
okra *v* (~, -aði, -að) overcharge
okrari *n masc* (-a, -ar, -a) profiteer
október *n masc* (~) October
olí|a *n fem* (-u, -ur, ~) oil
olíumæl|ir *n masc* (-is, -ar, -a) oil
gauge

olíumálverk *n neu* (-s, -, -a) oil
painting
olíusí|a *n fem* (-u, -ur, ~) oil filter
olnbog|i *n masc* (-a, -ar, -a) *anat* elbow
op *n neu* (-s, -, -a) gap
opið. See **opinn**
opinber *adj* (-, -t) official
opinbera *v* (~, -ði, -ð) reveal
opinberlega *adv* publicly, officially
opinber|un *n fem* (-nar, -anir, -ana)
revelation
opin|n *adj* (-, opið) open, outgoing;
opni háskólinn Open University
opinská|r *adj* (-, -tt) frank
opna *v* (~, -ði, -ð) open, unlock
opnunartím|i *n masc* (-a, -ar, -a)
opening hours
orð *n neu* (-s, -, -a) word
orð|a 1 *n fem* (-u, -ur, ~) decoration,
medal; **2** *v* (~, ða, -ð) put into words,
say
orðabók *n fem* (-ar, -bækur, -bóka)
dictionary
orðaforð|i *n masc* (-a) vocabulary
orðaleik|ur *n masc* (-s, -ir, -ja) pun,
word play
orðalist|i *n masc* (-a, -ar, -a) glossary
orðaröð *n fem* (-raðar, -raðir, -raða)
word order
orðasafn *n neu* (-s, -söfn, -a)
vocabulary list
orðasamband *n neu* (-s, -bönd, -a)
ling phrase
orðaskipt|i *n neu pl* (-a) exchange of
words, dialogue
orðatiltæk|i *n neu* (-is, ~, -ja) *ling*
expression
orðflokk|ur *n masc* (-s, -ar, -a) *ling*
part of speech
orðlaus *adj* (-, -t) speechless

orðræðuögn *n fem* (-agnar, -agnir,
-agna) *ling* discourse particle
orðróm|ur *n masc* (-s, -ar, -a) rumor
orðstír *n masc* (-s) reputation,
renown
orðtak *n neu* (-s, -tök, -a) *ling* idiom
org *n neu* (-s, -, -a) scream
ork|a *n fem* (-u) energy, power
orkuver *n neu* (-s, -, -a) energy plant
orm|ur *n masc* (-s, -ar, -a) *zool*
worm; snake
orsaka *v* (~, -ði, -ð) cause
orsök *n fem* (-sakar, -sakir, -saka)
cause

ostafondú *n neu* (-s) cheese fondue
ostakak|a *n fem* (-köku, -kökur,
-kakna) cheesecake
ostakex *n neu* (-, -, -a) cheese
crackers
ostasós|a *n fem* (-u, -ur, ~) cheese
sauce
ostborgar|i *n masc* (-a, -ar, -a)
cheeseburger
ostr|a *n fem* (-u, -ur, ~) oyster
ost|ur *n masc* (-s, -ar, -a) cheese
Ottawa *N fem* Ottawa
otur *n masc* (-s, otrar, otra) *zool* otter

Ó

óaðgengileg|ur *adj* (-, -t) inaccessible
óáfeng|ur *adj* (-, -t) non-alcoholic
óásættanleg|ur *adj* (-, -t) unacceptable
óbein|n *adj* (-, -t) indirect
óbeit *n fem* (-ar) repulsion
óblandað|ur *adj* (-blönduð, -) pure, unmixed; solid, straight
óbó *n neu* (-s, -, -a) *mus* oboe
óborganleg|ur *adj* (-, -t) hilarious
óbrjótandi *adj* unbreakable
óbyggð|ir *n fem pl* (-a) wasteland
ódáinsveig *n fem* (-ar, -ar, -a) nectar
ódýr *adj* (-, -t) cheap, inexpensive
óð|ur 1 *adj* (-, ótt) angry, mad, crazy; 2 *n masc* (-s/ar) ode
óformleg|ur *adj* (-, -t) informal
ófríð|ur *adj* (-, ófrítt) ugly
óeirð|ir *n fem pl* (-a) riot
óeldað|ur *adj* (óelduð, -) uncooked
ófær *adj* (-, -t) unable; **Það er ófært í dag** the road is closed today
ófrísk|ur *adj* (-, -t) pregnant
ófrjó|r *adj* (-, ófrjótt) sterile
ófrjósam|ur *adj* (-söm, -t) sterile
ógagnsæ|r *adj* (-, -sætt) opaque
ógeð *n neu* (-s, -, -a) disgust; creep
ógeðsleg|ur *adj* (-, -t) disgusting, nasty, obnoxious, repugnant, repulsive, revolting, sickening
ógift|ur *adj* (-, -) unmarried
ógilda *v* (~, -ði, -ð) reverse, repeal, revoke
ógilding *n fem* (-ar, -ar, -a) revocation
óglað|ur *adj* (óglöð, óglatt) *med* nauseous: **mér er óglatt** I'm feeling nauseous
ógleði *n fem* (-) *med* nausea
ógnandi *adj* threatening
ógnvænleg|ur *adj* (-, -t) scary, alarming
óhamingj|a *n fem* (-u) unhappiness

óhamingjusam|ur *adj* (-söm, -t) unhappy
óhefðbundin|n *adj* (-, -bundið) alternative: **óhefðbundin læknismeðferð** alternative treatment, **óhefðbundnar lækningar** alternative medicine
óheflað|ur *adj* (óhefluð, -) rustic
óheiðarleg|ur *adj* (-, -t) dishonest, fraudulent
óheiðarleik|i *n masc* (-a) dishonesty
óheilbrigð|ur *adj* (-, óheilbrigt) unhealthy
óheillavænleg|ur *adj* (-, -t) ominous
óheppileg|ur *adj* (-, -t) unfortunate
óheppin|n *adj* (-, óheppið) unlucky, unfortunate
óheppni *n fem* (-) bad luck, mishap
óhjákvæmilega *adv* inevitably
óhjákvæmileg|ur *adj* (-, -t) inevitable
óhófleg|ur *adj* (-, -t) extravagant
óholl|ur *adj* (-, -t) unhealthy
óhreinsað|ur *adj* (óhreinsuð, -) unrefined
ójafn *adj* (-, -t) uneven
ójafnrétti *n neu* (-s) inequality
ókei *interj* okay
ókeypis *adj* free of charge: ~ **aðgangur** free admission
ókomin|n *adj* not arrived; **ókomnar kynslóðir** posterity, generations to come
ókost|ur *n masc* (-ar, -ir, -a) disadvantage, drawback
ókunnug|ur *adj* (-, -t) unfamiliar
ókunn|ur *adj* (-) unknown
ókurteis *adj* (-, -t) impolite, rude
ókyrrð *n fem* (-ar, -ir, -a) turbulence
ólétt|a *n fem* (-u) pregnancy
óléttupróf *n neu* (-s, -, -a) pregnancy test

óléttur adj (-, -) pregnant
óljós adj (-, -t) obscure; unclear
ólíf|a n fem (-u, -ur, ~) olive
ólífuolí|a n fem (-u, -ur, ~) olive oil
ólíkleg|ur adj (-, -t) unlikely
ólík|ur adj (-, -t) unlike
Ólympíuleik|ar N masc pl (-anna) Olympic Games
ólæs adj (-, -t) illiterate
ólæsi n neu (-s) illiteracy
ólæsileg|ur adj (-, -t) illegible
ólöglega adv illegally
ólögleg|ur adj (-, -t) illegal
Óman N neu (-/s) Oman
ómengað|ur adj (ómenguð, -) pure, unpolluted
ómerk|ur adj (-, -t) insignificant
ómetanleg|ur adj (-, -t) priceless
ómettað|ur adj (ómettuð, -) unsaturated
ómikilvæg|ur adj (-, -t) unimportant
ómsjá n fem (-r, -r, -a) sonar
ómskoð|un n fem (-unar, -anir, -ana) ultrasound
ómöguleg|ur adj (-, -t) impossible
ónauðsynleg|ur adj (-, -t) unnecessary
ónóg|ur adj (-, -t) insufficient
ónotaleg|ur adj (-, -t) unfriendly
ónæmi n neu (-s) immunity
ónæmiskerfi n neu (-s) med immune system
ónæm|ur adj (-, -t) immune
óp n neu (-s, -, -a) scream; cry
ópal|l n masc (-s, -ar, -a) geol opal
óper|a n fem (-u, -ur, ~) opera
óperuhús n neu (-s, -, -a) opera house
ópíum n neu (-s) opium
óráð n neu (-s) med disorientation
óraunhæf|ur adj (-, -t) unrealistic
óreganó n neu (-s) oregano
óregluleg|ur adj (-, -t) irregular, uneven
óreið|a n fem (-u) muddle; chaos
ósamkomulag n neu (-s) disagreement
ósammála adv in disagreement: **ég er** ~ I disagree
ósanngjarn adj (-gjörn, -t) unfair

óseyr|i n fem (-ar, -ar, -a) delta
ósigur n masc (-s, ósigrar, ósigra) defeat, loss
ósjálfstæði n neu (-s) dependence
ósjálfstæð|ur adj (-, -stætt) dependent
óska v (~, -ði, -ð) wish
óskilamun|ur n masc (-ar, -ir, -a) lost and found
óskilgetin|n adj (-, -getið) illegitimate
óskiljanleg|ur adj (-, -t) incomprehensible
óskynsamleg|ur adj (-, -t) unreasonable
óskynsam|ur adj (-söm, -t) stupid, insensible
óskýr adj (-, -t) unclear, out of focus
Ósló N fem (-ar) Oslo
ósnyrtileg|ur adj (-, -t) untidy
ósoðin|n adj (-, -soðið) uncooked
óson n neu (-s) ozone
ósonlag n neu (-s) ozone layer
óspennandi adj unexciting
óstöðug|ur adj (-, -t) unstable, rocky, unsteady
ósvífin|n adj (-, ósvífið) shameless
ósætt|ir n fem pl (-sátta) disagreement
ótakmarkað|ur adj (-mörkuð, -) unlimited
óteljandi adj uncountable
ótt|i n masc (-a) fear
ótímabær adj (-, -t) premature
ótrúleg|ur adj (-, -t) incredible, amazing
ótrú|r adj (-, -tt) unfaithful
ótta|st v refl (~, -ðist, ~) fear
óundirbúin|n adj (-, -búið) unprepared
óvarkár adj (-, -t) careless
óvarlega adv carelessly
óvart adv by accident
óveður n neu (-s, -, óveðra) storm
óvenjulega adv unusually
óvenjuleg|ur adj (-, -t) unusual, extraordinary
óvild n fem (-ar) hostility
óvingjarnleg|ur adj (-, -t) unkind, unfriendly
óvin|ur n masc (-ar, -ir, -a) enemy, adversary

óvirkur *adj* (-, -t) disable; ~ **alki** non-drinking alcoholic
óviss *adj* (-, -t) uncertain
óviss|a *n fem* (-u) uncertainty
óvænt *adv* unexpectedly
óvænt|ur *adj* (-, -) unexpected, surprising
óþægileg|ur *adj* (-, -t) uncomfortable, unpleasant, awkward
óþarf|i *n masc* (-a, -ar, -a) redundance, redundancy
óþarf|ur *adj* (óþörf, -t) redundant

óþef|ur *n masc* (-s/jar) stink
óþekktarorm|ur *n masc* (-s, -ar, -a) rascal
óþekkt|ur *adj* (-, -) unknown
óþekk|ur *adj* (-, -t) naughty
óþolandi *adj* unbearable
óþolinmóð|ur *adj* (-, -mótt) impatient
óþreyj|a *n fem* (-u) impatience
óþroskað|ur *adj* (óþroskuð, -) unripe
óörugg|ur *adj* (-, -t) unsafe

P

pabb|i *n masc* (-a, -ar, -a) dad
Pakistan *N neu* (-/s) Pakistan
pakistansk|ur *adj* (pakistönsk, -t)
Pakistani
pakka *v* (~, -ði, -ð) pack, box
pakk|i *n masc* (-a, -ar, -a) parcel
pakkning *n fem* (-ar, -ar, -a) packaging
pallbíl|l *n masc* (-s, -ar, -a) pickup
truck
pallborðsumræð|ur *n fem pl* (-na)
panel discussions
pall|ur *n masc* (-s, -ar, -a) patio,
terrace; loading platform
Panama *N neu* (-) Panama
Panamamað|ur *n masc* (-manns,
-menn, -manna) Panamanian
(person)
panil|l *n masc* (-s, -ar, -a) panel
pann|a *n fem* (pönnu, pönnur, ~)
skillet, frying pan
panta *v* (~, -ði, -ð) order
pantað|ur *adj* (pöntuð, -) ordered,
booked
papajaávöxt|ur *n masc* (-vaxtar,
-vextir, -vaxta) papaya
papp|i *n masc* (-a, -ar, -a) cardboard
pappír *n masc* (-s, -ar, -a) paper
paprik|a *n fem* (-u, -ur, ~) bell pepper
Papúa Nýja-Gínea *N fem* (Nýju-
Gíneu) Papua New Guinea
par *n neu* (-s, pör, -a) couple, pair
para *v* (~, -ði, -ð) make pairs; ~
saman make pairs; ~ **sig** mate
paradís *n fem* (-ar, -ir, -a) paradise
Paragvæ *N neu* (-) Paraguay
Paragvæ|i *n masc* (-ja, -jar, -ja)
Paraguayan *(person)*
paragvæsk|ur *adj* (-, -t) Paraguayan
pardusdýr *n masc* (-s, -, -a) *zool*
panther
París *N fem* (-ar) Paris

parmesanost|ur *n masc* (-s, -ar, -a)
parmesan cheese
partí *n neu* (-s, -, -a) party
part|ur *n masc* (-s, -ar, -a) section,
part, segment
passa *v* (~, -ði, -ð) fit; look after
pasta *n neu* (-) pasta
pastellit|ur *n masc* (-ar, -ir, -a) pastel
color
pastinakk|a *n fem* (-nökku, -nökkur,
~) parsnip
pattstað|a *n fem* (-stöðu, -stöður, ~)
stalemate
páfagauk|ur *n masc* (-s, -ar, -a) *zool*
parrot
Páfastól|l *N masc* (-s) Holy See
(Vatican City)
páf|i *n masc* (-a, -ar, -a) pope
páfugl *n masc* (-s, -ar, -a) *zool*
peacock
pák|a *n fem* (-u, -ur, -a) *mus* timpani
pálmaolí|a *n fem* (-u) palm oil
pálmasunnudag|ur *n masc* (-s, -ar,
-a) Palm Sunday
pálmatré *n neu* (-s, -, -trjáa) *flora*
palm tree
pás|a *n fem* (-u, -ur, -a) pause
páskaegg *n neu* (-s, -, -ja) Easter egg
páskafrí *n neu* (-s, -, -a) Easter
holiday
páskalilj|a *n fem* (-u, -ur, ~) *flora*
narcissus
pásk|ar *n masc pl* (-a) Easter
PC-tölv|a *n fem* (-u, -ur, ~) personal
computer
pedal|i *n masc* (-a, -ar, -a) pedal
pekanhnet|a *n fem* (-u, -ur, ~) pecan
Peking *N fem* (-) Beijing
Pekingönd *n fem* (-andar, -endur,
-anda) Peking duck
pels *n masc* (-, -ar, -a) fur coat

pendúll|l *n masc* (-s, -ar, -a) pendulum
peningakass|i *n masc* (-a, -ar, -a) cashier machine
peningaseðil|l *n masc* (-s, -seðlar, -seðla) banknote
pening|ur *n masc* (-s, -ar, -a) money
penn|i *n masc* (-a, -ar, -a) pen
pensla *v* (~, -ði, -ð) brush
pepperónípyls|a *n fem* (-u, -ur, -na) pepperoni
per|a *n fem* (-u, -ur, ~) pear
perl|a *n fem* (-u, -ur, ~) pearl
perluhænsn *n neu pl* (-a) *zool* guinea fowl
permanent *n neu* (-s) *(for hair)* permanent
perr|i *n masc* (-a, -ar, -a) *slang* pervert
persnersk|ur *adj* (-, -t) Persian
persón|a *n fem* (-u, -ur, ~) person
persónugerving *n fem* (-ar) personification
persónulega *adv* personally
persónuleg|ur *adj* (-, -t) personal
persónuleik|i *n masc* (-a, -ar, -a) character, personality
persónuskilrík|i *n neu pl* (-ja) identification (ID) card
persónuvottorð *n neu* (-s, -, -a) identity document
Perú *N neu* (-) Peru
Perúmað|ur *n masc* (-manns, -menn, -manna) Peruvian *(person)*
perúsk|ur *adj* (-, -t) Peruvian
peys|a *n fem* (-u, -ur, ~) jumper, pullover, sweater
pikka *v* (~, -ði, -ð) type
pikkolóflaut|a *n fem* (-u, -ur, -na) *mus* piccolo
pill|a *n fem* (-u, -ur, ~) pill
pils *n neu* (-, -, -a) skirt
pilsner *n masc* (-s, -ar, -a) beer with low alcohol content
pilt|ur *n masc* (-s, -ar, -a) boy
pinn|i *n masc* (-a, -ar, -a) peg
pintobaun *n fem* (-ar, -ir, -a) pinto bean
pipar *n masc* (-s) pepper

piparkak|a *n fem* (-köku, -kökur, -kakna) gingerbread
piparkerling *n fem* (-ar, -ar, -a) spinster
piparmey *n fem* (-jar, -ar, -ja) bachelorette
piparmint|a *n fem* (-u, -ur, ~) mint, peppermint *(herb)*
piparmintute *n neu* (-s, -, -a) peppermint tea
piparrót *n fem* (-ar, -rætur, -a) horseradish
piparsteik *n fem* (-ur, -ur, -a) pepper steak
piparsvein|n *n masc* (-s, -ar, -a) bachelor
piparsós|a *n fem* (-u, -ur, ~) pepper sauce
pirra *v* (~, -ði, -ð) irritate; annoy; aggravate
pirrað|ur *adj* (pirruð, -) irritated, annoyed
pirrandi *adj* irritating, annoying
pistasíuhnet|a *n fem* (-u, -ur, ~) pistachios
pits|a *n fem* (-u, -ur, ~) pizza
pitsustað|ur *n masc* (-ar, -ir, -a) pizza parlor
píanó *n neu* (-s, -, -a) piano
pík|a *n fem* (-u, -ur, -na) pussy
pílagrím|i *n masc* (-s, -ar, -a) pilgrim
pílagrímsferð *n fem* (-ar, -ir, -a) pilgrimage
Pílates *n neu* (-) Pilates
pílukast *n neu* (-s) game of darts
pín|a *v* (-i, -di, -t) agonize
pínu *adv* a bit
pínulítil|l *adj* (-, -lítið) tiny
píp|a *n fem* (-u, -ur, -na) pipe, tube
píp|a *v* (-i, -ti, -t) peep
pípulagningamað|ur *n masc* (-manns, -menn, -manna) plumber
píramíð|i *n masc* (-a, -ar, -a) pyramid
píslarvott|ur *n masc* (-s, -ar, -a) martyr
pítubrauð *n neu* (-s, -, -a) pita bread
plakat *n neu* (-s, plaköt, -a) poster

plank|i *n masc* (-a, -ar, -a) plank
plant|a *n fem* (plöntu, plöntur, -na) plant
plantekr|a *n fem* (-u, -ur, ~) plantation
plast *n neu* (-s, plöst, -a) plastic
plastdós *n fem* (-ar, -ir, -a) plastic container
plastfilm|a *n fem* (-u, -ur, ~) plastic wrap
plastpok|i *n masc* (-a, -ar, -a) plastic bag
plat *n neu* (-s) bluff
plat|a *n fem* (plötu, plötur, -na) album; plate; tablet; **2 plata** *v* (~, -ði, -ð) bluff, fool, trick
platína *n fem* platinum
platónsk|ur *adj* (-, -t) platonic
plág|a *n fem* (-u, -ur, ~) pest, plague, nuisance
plánet|a *n fem* (-u, -ur, ~) planet
pláss *n neu* (-, -, -a) space, room
plástur *n masc* (-s, plástrar, plástra) bandage
plokka *v* (~, -ði, -ð) pluck
plóg|ur *n masc* (-s, -ar, -a) plow
plóm|a *n fem* (-u, -ur, -na) plum
plús *n masc* (-s, -ar, -a) plus
plæg|ja *v* (-i, -ði, -t) plow
plötuumslag *n neu* (-s, -slög, -a) vinyl sleeve
pok|i *n masc* (-a, -ar, -a) pouch, bag: **plastpoki** plastic bag
poll|ur *n masc* (-s, -ar, -a) puddle
poppa *v* (~, -ði, -ð) pop; make popcorn
popphljómsveit *n fem* (-ar, -ir, -a) pop band
poppkorn *n neu* (-s) popcorn
popptónleik|ar *n masc pl* (-a) pop concert
popptónlist *n fem* (-ar) pop music
portrett *n neu* (-s, -, -a) portrait
portrettamálar|i *n masc* (-a, -ar, -a) portrait artist
Portúgal *N neu* (-/s) Portugal
Portúgal|i *n masc* (-a, -ar, -a) Portuguese *(person)*

portúgalsk|a *n fem* (-gölsku) the Portuguese language
postulín *n neu* (-s) china, porcelain
pota *v* (~, -ði, -ð) poke
pottalepp|ur *n masc pl* (-s, -ar, -a) oven mitt
pottrétt|ur *n masc* (-ar, -ir, -a) casserole
pott|ur *n masc* (-s, -ar, -a) pot
póker *n masc* (-s) poker
pólitík *n fem* (-ur) *colloq* politics
pólitíkus *n masc* (-s, -ar, -a) *colloq* politician
pólitískt *adv* politically
pólitísk|ur *adj* (-, -t) political: **pólitískt hæli** political asylum
Pólland *N neu* (-s) Poland
póló *n neu* (-s) *sports* polo
pólsk|a *n fem* (-u) Polish language
pólsk|ur *adj* (-, -t) polish
Pólverj|i *n masc* (-a, -ar, -a) Pole (a person from Poland)
póstafgreiðsl|a *n fem* (-u, -ur, -na) post office
póstávís|un *n fem* (-unar, -anir, -ana) money order
póstburðarmað|ur *n masc* (-manns, -menn, -manna) postman
póstfang *n neu* (-s, -föng, -a) mail address
pósthólf *n neu* (-s, -, -a) postbox
póstkass|i *n masc* (-a, -ar, -a) mailbox, letter box
póstkort *n neu* (-s, -, -a) postcard
póstleggja *v* (-legg, -lagði, -lagt) post, mail, put in the mail
póstnúmer *n neu* (-s, -, -a) postal code
póst|ur *n masc* (-s, -ar, -a) mail
Prag *N fem* (-) Prague
pragmatík *n fem* (-ur) pragmatism
pragmatísk|ur *adj* (-, -t) pragmatic
prakkarastrik *n neu* (-s, -, -a) prank
prakkar|i *n masc* (-a, -ar, -a) prankster
predika *v* (~, -ði, -ð) preach
predikar|i *n masc* (-a, -ar, -a) preacher
prenta *v* (~, -ði, -ð) print

prentar|i *n masc* (-a, -ar, -a) printer
prent|un *n fem* (-unar, -anir, -ana)
  printing
press|a 1 *n fem* (-u) pressure;
  squeezer: **sítrónupressa** lemon
  squeezer; **2 pressa** *v* (~, -ði, -ð)
  press, squeeze
pressukann|a *n fem* (-könnu, -könnur,
  ~) coffee press
prest|ur *n masc* (-s, -ar, -a) parson,
  priest
prik *n neu* (-s, -, -a) stick
prins *n masc* (-, -ar, -a) prince
prinsess|a *n fem* (-u, -ur, ~) princess
Pristín|a *N fem* (-u) Pristina (capital
  of Kosovo)
prjóna *v* (~, -ði, -ð) knit
prjónahúf|a *n fem* (-u, -ur, ~) knit cap
prjón|n *n masc* (-s, -ar, -a) needle;
  needle for knitting; chopstick
próf *n neu* (-s, -, -a) test, exam
prófa *v* (~, -ði, -ð) test, try
prófessor *n masc* (-s, -ar, -a) professor
próf|un *n fem* (-unar, -anir, -ana) test
prósent|a *n fem* (-u, -ur, ~) percentage
prós|i *n masc* (-a, -ar, -a) *lit* prose
prótín *n neu* (-s, -, -a) *bio* protein
prútta *v* (~, -ði, -ð) bargain
pump|a 1 *n fem* (-u, -ur, ~) pump; **2**
  pumpa *v* (~, -ði, -ð) pump
pund *n neu* (-s, -, -a) pound
pung|ur *n masc* (-s, -ar, -a) balls;
  anat scrotum
punkt|ur *n masc* (-s, -ar, -a) dot; full
  stop; *ling* period

puttaferðalang|ur *n masc* (-s, -ar,
  -a) hitchhiker
púð|i *n masc* (-a, -ar, -a) pillow
púður *n neu* (-s) powder
púðursykur *n masc* (-s) brown sugar
púls *n masc* (-, -ar, -a) *med* pulse
púm|a *n fem* (-u, -ur, ~) *zool* puma
púrr|a *n fem* (-u, -ur, ~) leek
púrrulauk|ur *n masc* (-s, -ar, -a)
  leek
púsl *n neu* (-s, -, -a) puzzle
púsluspil *n neu* (-s, -, -a) jigsaw
  puzzle
pússa *v* (~, -ði, -ð) polish
púströr *n neu* (-s, -, -a) exhaust pipe
pyls|a *n fem* (-u, -ur, -na) sausage,
  hotdog: ~ **í brauði** hotdog in a bun
pylsuvagn *n masc* (-s, -ar, -a) hotdog
  stand
pynta *v* (~, -ði, -ð) torture
pýtonslang|a *n fem* (-slöngu, -slöngur,
  -na) *zool* python
pækil|l *n masc* (-s, pæklar, pækla)
  (method of preservation) pickle
pækilsaltað|ur *adj* (-söltuð, -)
  pickled
pöbb *n masc* (-s, -ar, -a) pub
pönkar|i *n masc* (-a, -ar, -a) punk
pönktónlist *n fem* (-ar) punk music
pönnukak|a *n fem* (-köku, -kökur,
  -na) pancake, crepe
pönnusteikt|ur *adj* (-, -) pan-fried
pönt|un *n fem* (-unar, -anir, -ana)
  order; reservation

R

rabarbar|i *n masc* (-a, -ar, -a)
rhubarb
rabbín|i *n masc* (-a, -ar, -a) rabbi
radís|a *n fem* (-u, -ur, ~) radish
radíus *n masc* (-s, -ar, -a) *math* radius
raða *v* (~, -ði, -ð) arrange
raðbundin|n *adj* (-, bundið)
sequential
raðtal|a *n fem* (-tölu, -tölur, -na)
math ordinal number
rafal|l *n masc* (-s, -ar, -a) *mech*
generator
rafbók *n fem* (-ar, -bækur, -a) e-book
rafeind *n fem* (-ar, -ir, -a) *chem*
electron
rafeindatækn|i *n fem* (-) *(technology)*
electronics
rafeindatæk|i *n neu* (-s, -i, -ja)
electronic devices
rafhlað|a *n fem* (-hlöðu, -hlöður, -na)
battery
rafmagn *n neu* (-s) electricity
rafmagnsbass|i *n masc* (-a, -ar, -a)
electric base
rafmagnshljóðfær|i *n neu* (-is, ~, -a)
mus electronic instrument
rafmagnsleysi *n neu* (-s) power outage
rafmagnsrof|i *n masc* (-a, -ar, -a)
power button
rafmagnssnúr|a *n fem* (-u, -ur, ~)
electric cable
rafmagnstafl|a *n fem* (-töflu, -töflur,
-na) fuse box
raforkuver *n neu* (-s, -, -a) power
station
rafrás *n fem* (-ar, -ir, -a) circuit
rafstuð *n neu* (-s, -, -a) electric shock
raftækjaversl|un *n fem* (-unar, -anir,
-ana) electronics shop
ragú *n neu* (-s) ragout
raka *v* (~, -ði, -ð) shave

rakakrem *n neu* (-s, -, -a) moisturizing cream
rakar|i *n masc* (-a, -ar, -a) barber
rakburst|i *n masc* (-a, -ar, -a) shaving
brush
rakett|a *n fem* (-u, -ur, ~) firecracker
rakhníf|ur *n masc* (-s, -ar, -a) razor
rak|i *n masc* (-a) humidity
raksáp|a *n fem* (-u, -ur, ~) shaving
cream
rakspír|i *n masc* (-a, -ar, -a) aftershave
rak|ur *adj* (rök, -t) damp
rakvél *n fem* (-ar, -ar, -a) shaver
rall *n neu* (-s, röll, -a) rally; partying
ramm|i *n masc* (-a, -ar, -a) frame
ramm|ur *adj* (römm, -t) pungent
ramp|ur *n masc* (-s, -ar, -a) ramp
rang|a *n fem* (röngu) reverse side
rangeygð|ur *adj* (-, -t) cross-eyed
ranghugmynd *n fem* (-ar, -ir, -a)
delusion
ranglega *adv* wrongly
rangstæð|ur *adj* (-, -stætt) *sports*
offside
rang|ur *adj* (röng, -t) incorrect,
wrong
ran|i *n masc* (-a, -ar, -a) elephant
trunk
rannsaka *v* (~, -ði, -ð) research,
study, investigate, explore
rannsókn *n fem* (-ar, -ir, -a) research,
study, investigation
rannsóknarlögreglumað|ur *n masc*
(-manns, -menn, -manna) detective
rannsóknastof|a *n fem* (-u, -ur, ~)
laboratory
raska *v* (~, -ði, -ð) upset
rasp *n neu* (-s) breading
rasskinn *n fem* (-ar, -ar, -a) buttock
ratsjárstöð *n fem* (-var, -var, -va)
tracking station

Rauðahaf *N neu* (-s) Red Sea
rauðbrún|n *adj* (-, -t) *color* walnut
rauðgul|ur *adj* (-, -t) *color* orange
rauðhærð|ur *adj* (-, hært) redhaired
Rauði hálfmáninn *N* Red Crescent
Rauði krossinn *N* Red Cross
rauðkál *n neu* (-s) red cabbage
rauðróf|a *n fem* (-u, -ur, -na) beet, beetroot
rauðrófusúp|a *n fem* (-u, -ur, -na) borsch
rauðsprett|a *n fem* (-u, -ur, ~) plaice
rauð|ur *adj* (-, rautt) *color* red: **rauði dregillinn** the red carpet, **rauð blóðkorn** red blood cells
rauðvín *n neu* (-s, -, -a) red wine
raunsæi *n neu* (-s) realism
raunsæismað|ur *n masc* (-manns, -menn, -manna) realist
raunsæisstefn|a *n fem* (-u) realism
raunsæ|r *adj* (-, -tt) realistic
raunverulega *adv* really
raunveruleg|ur *adj* (-, -t) real, actual; substantial; positive
raunveruleik|i *n masc* (-a, -ar, -a) reality
raunvísind|i *n neu pl* (-a) natural sciences
ráð *n neu* (-s, -, -a) advice
ráð|a *v* (ræð, réð, réðum, ráðið) employ, be in charge; ~ **ríkjum** reign; solve: ~ **gátu** solve a riddle
ráðabrugg *n neu* (-s) plot
ráðandi *adj* ruling, dominant
ráð|ast *v* (ræðst, réðst, réðumst, ráðist) ~ **á** attack, ambush
ráðgát|a *n fem* (-u, -ur, -na) mystery
ráðgjaf|i *n masc* (-a, -ar, -a) adviser, consultant, counselor
ráðgjöf *n fem* (-gjafar) consultation
ráðherra *n masc* (-, -r, -) minister
ráðhús *n neu* (-s, -, -a) town hall
ráðlegg|ja *v* (-legg, -lagði, -lagt) advise
ráðning *n fem* (-ar, -ar, -a) hiring
ráðstefn|a *n fem* (-u, -ur, ~) conference, convention

ráðstefnusal|ur *n masc* (-ar, -ir, -a) convention hall
ráðuneyt|i *n neu* (-is, ~, -a) ministry
ráðvillt|ur *adj* (-, -) confused
ráfa *v* (~, -ði, -ð) wander, ramble
rán *n neu* (-s, -, -a) robbery
rándýr *n neu* (-s, -, -a) predator
rás *n fem* (-ar, -ir, -a) track; radio station
realism|i *n masc* (-a) realism
refsa *v* (~, -ði, -ð) punish
refsing *n fem* (-ar, -ar, -a) penalty, punishment
ref|ur *n masc* (-s, -ir, -a) *zool* fox: **íslenski refurinn** the arctic fox
regl|a *n fem* (-u, -ur, -na) rule
reglulega *adv* regularly
regluleg|ur *adj* (-, -t) regular
reglustik|a *n fem* (-u, -ur, ~) ruler
regn *n neu* (-s) rain
regnhatt|ur *n masc* (-s, -ar, -a) rain hat
regnheld|ur *adj* (-, -helt) rainproof
regnhlíf *n fem* (-ar, -ar, -a) umbrella
regnjakk|i *n masc* (-a, -ar, -a) raincoat
regnkáp|a *n fem* (-u, -ur, ~) raincoat
regnskúr *n fem* (-ar, -ir, -a) rain shower
regnstakk|ur *n masc* (-s, -ar, -a) raincoat
regnþétt|ur *adj* (-, -) rainproof
reiði *n fem* (-) anger, outrage
reiðilega *adv* angrily
reiðmað|ur *n masc* (-manns, -menn, -manna) rider
reiðskól|i *n masc* (-a, -ar, -a) horse-riding school
reiðtyg|i *n neu pl* (-ja) riding equipment
reiðubúin|n *adj* (-, -búið) ready and willing
reiðufé *n neu* (-fjár) cash
reið|ur *adj* (-, reitt) angry
reika *v* (~, -ði, -ð) wander
reikistjarn|a *n fem* (-stjörnu, -stjörnur, ~) planet
reikna *v* (~, -ði, -ð) calculate, sum, reckon

reikning|ur *n masc* (-s, -ar, -a) account, bill

reim *n fem* (-ar, -ar, -a) (shoe)string

reis|a *v* (-i, -ti, -t) erect

reit|a *v* (-i, -ti, -t) ~ **til reiði** anger

reit|ur *n masc* (-s/-ar, -ir, -a) square; lot

rek|a *v* (-, rak, rákum, rekið) fire, sack, expell; ~ **út** kick out

rek|ast *v refl* (-st, rakst, rákumst, rekist) driven forward; ~ **á** crash into

rekavið|ur *n masc* (-ar, -ir, -a) driftwood

rekj|a *v* (rek, rak, rákum, rekið) trace

rekstur *n masc* (-s, rekstrar, rekstra) operation; running a business

rengj|a *v* (rengi, rengdi, rengt) dispute

renn|a *v* (-i, -di, -t) slide, slip, zip, roll; ~ **niður** unzip; ~ **sér á skíðum** ski; ~ **sér** slide; ~ **út** expire; ~ **yfir** scan, read fast

rennibraut *n fem* (-ar, -ir, -a) slide in a playground

rennilás *n masc* (-s, -ar, -a) zipper

rennsl|i *n neu* (-is, ~, -a) flow

repjuolí|a *n fem* (-u) rapeseed oil

resept *n neu* (-s, -, -a) *med* prescription

reykháf|ur *n masc* (-s, -ar, -a) chimney

reykingamað|ur *n masc* (-manns, -menn, -manna) smoker

reyking|ar *n fem pl* (-a) smoking

reykj|a *v* (reyki, reykti, reykt) smoke

Reykjavík *N fem* (-ur) Reykjavik (capital of Iceland)

reyklaus *adj* (-, -t) non-smoking

reykskynjar|i *n masc* (-a, -ar, -a) smoke detector

reykt|ur *adj* (-, -) smoked: ~ **silungur** smoked trout

reyk|ur *n masc* (-kjar/s, -ir, -kja) smoke; smog

reyn|a *v* (-i, -di, -t) try, test, attempt, experience

reyn|ir *n masc* (-is) *flora* rowan

reynsl|a *n fem* (-u) experience; trial

reynslulausn *n fem* (-ar, -ir, -a) parole, probation

reynslumikil|l *adj* (-, -mikið) experienced

reynslutím|i *n masc* (-a) probation

reyrsykur *n masc* (-s) sugarcane

reyt|a *v* (-i, -ti, -t) pluck

rétt *adv* correctly, accurately

rétt hjá *phr* near, close to: **rétt hjá hótelinu** close to the hotel

rétt|a *v* (-i, -i, -t) hand over

rétthyrning|ur *n masc* (-s, -ar, -a) *math* rectangle

réttilega *adv* rightly

rétt|ir *n fem pl* (-a) *(sheepfarming)* roundup: **fara í** ~ go to the round-ups

réttlátlega *adv* righteously

réttlát|ur *adj* (-, -t) just, righteous

réttlæt|a *v* (-i, -ti, -t) justify, rationalize

réttlætanleg|ur *adj* (-, -t) justified

réttlæti *n neu* (-s) justice

rétt|ur *adj* (-, -) correct, right; rights; court of law; *(food)* course, ~ **dagsins** today's special

riðstraumsrafal|l *n masc* (-s, -ar, -a) *mech* alternator

rif *n neu* (-s, ~, -ja) *anat* ribs

rif|a *n fem* (-u, -ur, ~) tear, rip; grate

rifbein *n neu* (-s, -, -a) rib

riffil|l *n masc* (-s, rifflar, riffla) rifle

rifin|n *adj* (-, rifið) grated; torn

rifja *v* (~, -ði, -ð) ~ **upp** review, remind someone of past events

rifjárn *n neu* (-s, -, -a) grater

rifrild|i *n neu* (-is, ~, -a) argument

rifsber *n neu* (-s, -, -ja) red currant

rign|a *v* (-i, -di, -t) rain

rigning *n fem* (-ar) rain

rigningardag|ur *n masc* (-s, -ar, -a) rainy day

rimlagirðing *n fem* (-ar, -ar, -a) railing

ringlað|ur *adj* (ringluð, -) confused

ringulreið *n fem* (-ar) confusion

ris *n neu* (-s, -, -a) climax; top floor under a leaning roof

risarækj|a *n fem* (-u, -ur, ~) large prawn; scampi

ris|i *n masc* (-a, -ar, -a) giant

risottó *n neu* (-) risotto

risp|a 1 *n fem* (-u, -ur, ~) scratch; **2 rispa** *v* (~, -ði, -ð) scratch

rissa *v* (~, -ði, -ð) sketch

rist *n fem* (-ar, -ir, -a) grate

rista *v* (~, -ði, -ð) roast; broil, toast; slash

ristað|ur *adj* (ristuð, -) roasted; toasted: **ristað brauð** toast

ritað|ur *adj* (rituð, -) written

ritar|i *n masc* (-a, -ar, -a) secretary

ritdóm|ur *n masc* (-s, -ar, -a) review; book review

ritföng *n neu* (-fanga) stationery

ritgerð *n fem* (-ar, -ir, -a) essay, paper

rithátt|ur *n masc* (-ar, -hættir, -hátta) notation

rithöfund|ur *n masc* (-ar, -ar, -a) author, writer

ritskoð|un *n fem* (-unar, -anir, -ana) censorship

ritstjór|i *n masc* (-a, -ar, -a) editor

ritstýr|a *v* (-i, -ði, -t) edit

ritverk *n neu* (-s, -, -a) writing, written work

ritvinnsl|a *n fem comp* (-u, -ur, ~) *comp* word processing

ríð|a *v* (-, reið, riðum, riðið) ride; *slang* have sex, fuck

ríf|a *v* (-, reif, rifum, rifið) tear

ríf|ast *v refl* (-st, reifst, rifumst, rifist) argue, fight, quarrel

Ríga *N fem* (-) Riga (capital of Latvia)

ríki *n neu* (-is, ~, -ja) state

ríkidæm|i *n neu* (-is, -, -a) wealth

ríkisborgar|i *n masc* (-a, -ar, -a) citizen; **ríkisborgarar utan Evrópusambandsins** non-EU citizens

ríkisborgararétt|ur *n masc* (-ar) citizenship

ríkisskuldabréf *n neu* (-s, -, -a) *econ* state bonds

ríkisstarfsmað|ur *n masc* (-manns, -menn, -manna) public servant

ríkisstjórn *n fem* (-ar, -ir, -a) government

ríkj|a *v* (ríki, ríkti, ríkt) predominate, prevail

ríkjandi *adj* dominant

ríkjasamband *n neu* (-s, -bönd, -a) federation

ríkulega *adv* generously

rík|ur *adj* (-, -t) rich, wealthy, affluent

rím *n neu* (-s, -, -a) rhyme

rís|a *v* (-, reis, risum, risið) arise

rjómaboll|a *n fem* (-u, -ur, ~) cream puff

rjómaost|ur *n masc* (-s, -ar, -a) cream cheese

rjómatert|a *n fem* (-u, -ur, -na) cream cake

rjóm|i *n masc* (-a) cream

rjúp|a *n fem* (-u, -ur, -na) *zool* grouse, ptarmigan

roð|i *n masc* (-a, -ar, -a) blush

roðna *v* (~, -ði, -ð) blush

rof|i *n masc* (-a, -ar, -a) switch

rok *n neu* (-s) gale

rokka *v* (~, -ði, -ð) rock

rokk|ur *n masc* (-s, -ar, -a) spinning wheel

romm *n neu* (-s) rum

rosalega *adv* extremely

roskin|n *adj* (-, roskið) old, elderly

rostung|ur *n masc* (-s, -ar, -a) *zool* walrus

rotvarnarefn|i *n neu* (-is, ~, -a) food preservatives

rotin|n *adj* (-, rotið) rotten, decayed

rotna *v* (~, -ði, -ð) rot, decay

rotnun *n fem* (-ar) decay

rott|a *n fem* (-u, -ur, ~) *zool* rat

ró *n fem* (-ar, rær, -a) tranquility, calmness, repose

róa *v* **1** (~, -ði, -ð) calm down; **2** (ræ, réri, rérum, róið) paddle, row

róandi *adj med* sedative; ~ **lyf** *med* tranquilizer

róð|ur *n masc* (róðrar/s, -róðrar, róðra) rowing, paddling

róf *n neu* (-s, -, -a) spectrum

róf|a *n fem* (-u, -ur, -na) rutabaga,
beet; tail

rókókóstíl|l *n masc* (-s) Rococo style

ról|a 1 *n fem* (-u, -ur, ~) swing; **2**
róla *v* (~, -ði, -ð) swing

rólega *adv* calmly, slowly; calm,
quiet

Róm *N fem* (-ar) Rome

Rómafólk *n neu* (-s) Roma people

rómantík *n fem* (-ur) romance;
Romanticism

rómantísk|ur *adj* (-, -t) romantic

rós *n fem* (-ar, -ir, -a) *flora* rose

rósakál *n neu* (-s) Brussels sprouts

rósavatn *n neu* (-s) rose water

rósavín *n neu* (-s, -, -a) rosé wine

rósmarín *n neu* (-s) rosemary

rót *n fem* (-ar, rætur, -a) root

róteind *n fem* (-ar, -ir, -a) *chem*
proton

rótgróin|n *adj* (-, -gróið) rooted

róttækling|ur *n masc* (-s, -ar, -a)
extremist

róttæk|ur *adj* (-, -t) radical

ruddaleg|ur *adj* (-, -t) obscene

ruddaskap|ur *n masc* (-ar) obscenity

ruðning|ur *n masc* (-s) *sports* rugby

rugga *v* (~, -ði, -ð) rock

rugl *n neu* (-s) nonsense

rugla *v* (~, -ði, -ð) confuse, muddle,
perplex

rugling|ur *n masc* (-s) confusion

rukka *v* (~, -ði, -ð) charge

run|a *n fem* (-u, -ur, ~) sequence

runn|i *n masc* (-a, -ar, -a) *flora* shrub

rusl *n neu* (-s) garbage, junk, litter,
rubbish, waste, trash

ruslabíl|l *n masc* (-s, -ar, -a) garbage
truck

ruslafat|a *n fem* (-fötu, -fötur, ~)
garbage bin

ruslahaug|ur *n masc* (-s, -ar, -a)
landfill

ruslapok|i *n masc* (-a, -ar, -a) garbage
bag

ruslatunn|a *n fem* (-u, -ur, ~) garbage
can

ruslfæði *n neu* (-s) junk food

ruslpóst|ur *n masc* (-s) junk mail

Rúanda *N neu* (-) Rwanda

Rúandamað|ur *n masc* (-manns,
-menn, -manna) Rwandan *(person)*

rúandsk|ur *adj* (rúöndsk, -t) Rwandan

rúbín *n masc* (-s, -ar, -a) *geol* ruby

rúð|a *n fem* (-u, -ur, -na) window pane

rúðuþurrk|a *n fem* (-u, -ur, -na)
windshield wiper

rúgbrauð *n neu* (-s, -, -a) rye bread

rúg|ur *n masc* (-s) rye

rúll|a *n fem* (-u, -ur, ~) roll

rúllukragapeys|a *n fem* (-u, -ur, ~)
turtleneck shirt

rúllustig|i *n masc* (-a, -ar, -a) escalator

rúm *n neu* (-s, -, -a) bed

Rúmen|i *n masc* (-a, -ar, -a) Romanian
(person)

Rúmení|a *N fem* (-u) Romania

rúmensk|a *n fem* (-u) Romanian
language

rúmensk|ur *adj* (-, -t) Romanian

rúmföt *n neu pl* (-fata) bedding,
sheets

rúmgóð|ur *adj* (-, -gott) spacious

rúmmál *n neu* (-s, -, -a) *math* volume

rúm|ur *adj* (-, -t) spacious

rúnnstykk|i *n neu* (-is, ~, -ja) bun,
roll

rúnta *v* (~, -ði, -ð) cruise

rúnt|ur *n masc* (-s) cruising; **fara á**
rúntinn cruising around

rúsín|a *n fem* (-u, -ur, ~) raisin

Rúss|i *n masc* (-a, -ar, -a) Russian
(person)

Rússland *N neu* (-s) Russia

rússnesk|a *n fem* (-u) Russian
language

rússnesk|ur *adj* (-, -t) Russian

rúst *n fem* (-ar, -ir, -a) ruins

rút|a *n fem* (-u, -ur, ~) shuttle bus

rútubílstjór|i *n masc* (-a, -ar, -a)
busdriver

ryð *n neu* (-s) rust

ryðfrí|r *adj* (-, -tt) does not rust:
ryðfrítt stál stainless steel

ryðga *v* (~, -ði, -ð) rust
ryðgað|ur *adj* (ryðguð, -) rusty
ryk *n neu* (-s) dust
rykfrakk|i *n masc* (-a, -ar, -a) trench coat
ryksug|a *n fem* (-u, -ur, -na) vaccum cleaner
rýja *v* (~, -ði, -ð) shear
rým|a *v* (-i, -di, -t) vacate
rým|i *n neu* (-is, ~, -a) space
rýming *n fem* (-ar) evacuation
rýmingarsal|a *n fem* (-sölu, -sölur, -na) clearance sale
rýr *adj* (-, -t) meager
ræð|a 1 *n fem* (-u, -ur, -na) speech, oration; 2 *v* (-i, ræddi, rætt) discuss
ræðismannsskrifstof|a *n fem* (-u, -ur, ~) consulate
ræðumað|ur *n masc* (-manns, -menn, -manna) speaker, orator
ræðustól|l *n masc* (-s, -ar, -a) pulpit, rostrum
ræfil|l *n masc* (-s, ræflar, ræfla) loser
rækilega *adv* thoroughly
rækj|a *n fem* (-u, -ur, rækna) shrimp
ræktað|ur *adj* (ræktuð, -) cultivated
ræn|a *v* (-i, -di, -t) rob, plunder

rænd|ur *adj* (-, rænt) robbed
ræning|i *n masc* (-ja, -jar, -ja) robber
rödd *n fem* (raddar, raddir, radda) voice
röð *n fem* (raðar, raðir, raða) row, queue; order, array, sequence
rökfast|ur *adj* (-föst, -) *(in debates)* consistent
rökfræði *n fem* (-) *phil* logic
rökrétt|ur *adj* (-, -t) logical
rökræð|a *v* (-i, -ræddi, -rætt) debate
rökræn|n *adj* (-, -t) logical
rökstuðning|ur *n masc* (-s) rationale
rökstyðj|a *v* (-styð, -studdi, -stutt) rationalize
rökvilla *n fem* (-u, -ur, -na) fallacy
rölt|a *v* (-i, -i, -t) stroll
rönd *n fem* (randar, rendur/randir, randa) stripe
röndótt|ur *adj* (-, -) striped
röntgengeisl|i *n masc* (-a, -ar, -a) *med* x-ray
röntgenmyndataka *n fem* (-töku, -tökur, ~) *med* x-ray examination
rör *n neu* (-s, -, -a) straw; pipe, tube
rösk|ur *adj* (-, -t) agile

S

sabbatsdag|ur *n masc* (-s, -ar, -a)
Sabbath
sadd|ur *adj* (södd, satt) full
saffran *n neu* (-s) saffron
saf|i *n masc* (-a, -ar, -a) juice
safír *n masc* (-s, -ar, -a) *geol* sapphire
safn *n neu* (-s, söfn, -a) museum;
collection
safna *v* (~, -ði, -ð) collect, accumulate, save; ~ **saman** gather
safnar|i *n masc* (-a, -ar, -a) collector
sag|a 1 *n fem* (sögu, sögur, sagna)
history; story, tale; **2 saga** *v* (~, -ði,
-ð) saw
sagnaminni *n neu* (-s, -, -a) *lit* motif
sagnfræðileg|ur *adj* (-, -t) historical
sagnfræðing|ur *n masc* (-s, -ar, -a)
historian
sagnorð *n neu* (-s, -, -a) *ling* verb
Sagreb *N fem* (-) Zagreb (capital of
Croatia)
sakaruppgjöf *n fem* (-gjafar, -gjafir,
-gjafa) amnesty
sakaskrá *n fem* (-r, -r, -a) *leg* criminal record
sakkarín *n neu* (-s) saccharin
saklaus *adj* (-, -t) innocent
sakna *v* (~, -ði, -ð) miss
sakir *prep* + *gen* because of: ~
heilsubrests because of health
problems
sakrament *n neu* (-s) sacrament
saksóknar|i *n masc* (-a, -ar, -a) *leg*
prosecutor
sal|a *n fem* (sölu, sölur, -na) sale
salat *n neu* (-s, salöt, -a) salad
salatbland|a *n fem* (-blöndu, -blöndur,
-blandna) mixed salad
salatblöð *n neu* (-blaða) greens
salathöfuð *n neu* (-s, -, -höfða)
lettuce

salatsós|a *n fem* (-u, -ur, ~) salad
dressing
salerni *n neu* (-s, -, -a) toilet
salernispappír *n masc* (-s, -ar, -a)
toilet paper
salsa *n neu* (-) salsa
salt *n neu* (-s, sölt, -a) salt
salta *v* (~, -ði, -ð) salt
saltað|ur *adj* (söltuð, -) salted
saltkex *n neu* (-, -, -a) salt crackers
saltkjöt *n neu* (-) cured meat
saltstauk|ur *n masc* (-s, -ar, -a) salt
container
salt|ur *adj* (sölt, -) salty
sal|ur *n masc* (-ar, -ir, -a) hall,
auditorium
Salvador|i *n masc* (-a, -ar, -a)
Salvadoran *(person)*
salvadorsk|ur *adj* (-, -t) Salvadoran
salví|a *n fem* (-u) *flora (herb)* sage
saman *adv* together, jointly
samanburð|ur *n masc* (-ar)
comparison
samansafn *n neu* (-s) collection of
something
samantekt *n fem* (-ar, -ir, -a)
recapitulation
samband *n neu* (-s, -bönd, -a) relationship, contact; union; plug
Sambí|a *N fem* (-u) Zambia
sambland *n neu* (-s) combination of
something
samdrátt|ur *n masc* (-ar, -drættir,
-drátta) decrease, recession; *med*
contraction
sameiginlega *adv* jointly
sameiginleg|ur *adj* (-, -t) joint, com-
mon, mutual
sameina *v* (~, -ði, -ð) join, unite
sameinað|ur *adj* (sameinuð, -) united
sameina|st *v refl* (~, -ðist, ~) unite

sameind *n fem* (-ar, -ir, -a) *chem* molecule

Sameinuðu arabísku furstadæmin *N neu* (-dæmanna) United Arab Emirates

Sameinuðu þjóðirnar *N neu* (-anna) United Nations

samfesting|ur *n masc* (-s, -ar, -a) jumpsuit

samfélag *n neu* (-s, -félög, -a) society, community

samfélagsleg|ur *adj* (-, -t) social

samgöngukerf|i *n neu* (-is, ~, -a) transit system

samgöng|ur *n fem pl* (-gangna) transportation

samhengi *n neu* (-s) context

samhljóð|i *n masc* (-a, -ar, -a) *ling* consonant

samhljóm|ur *n masc* (-s, -ar, -a) harmony, accord

samhryggj|ast *v refl* (-hryggist, -hryggðist, -hryggst) **ég samhryggist þér** my condolences

sami *pron* same

samkennd *n fem* (-ar) empathy

samkeppni *n fem* (-) competition, contest, rivalry

samkeppnisaðil|i *n masc* (-a, -ar, -a) competitor

samkomulag *n neu* (-s) agreement

samkomustað|ur *n masc* (-ar, -ir, -a) gathering place

samkvæmt *adv* according to

samkynhneigð|ur *adj* (-, -t) homosexual

samlagning *n fem* (-ar) *math* addition

samliggjandi *adj* adjacent, adjoining

samlok|a *n fem* (-u, -ur, ~) sandwich; *zool* clam

sammála *adv* in agreement: **ertu ~ mér?** do you agree with me?

samningarétt|ur *n masc* (-ar) *leg* contract law

samningaviðræð|ur *n fem pl* (-na) negotiation

samning|ur *n masc* (-s, -ar, -a) contract, agreement

Samóa *N neu* (-) Samoa

Samóamað|ur *n masc* (-manns, -menn, -manna) Samoan *(person)*

samósk|ur *adj* (-, -t) Samoan

samrun|i *n masc* (-a, -ar, -a) fusion

samræm|a *v* (-i, -di, -t) coordinate, integrate

samræm|ast *v* (-i, -di, -t) be in accordance to

samræmi *n neu* (-s) accordance, symmetry

samsett|ur *adj* (-, -t) compound: **samsett orð** compound words

samsíða *adv* parallel

samskiptastaðal|l *n masc* (-s, -staðlar, -staðla) *comp* communication protocol

samskipt|i *n neu pl* (-a) interaction

samstarfsfélag|i *n masc* (-a, -ar, -a) colleague

samstarfshóp|ur *n masc* (-s, -ar, -a) collaborative team

samstarfsmað|ur *n masc* (-manns, -menn, -manna) colleague, associate

samsteyp|a *n fem* (-u, -ur, -na) *econ* concern

samstæð|a *n fem* (-u, -ur, -na) set, matching pair

samsvarandi *adj* corresponding

samt 1 *adv* anyway: **hann vill ekki fara en fer ~** he doesn't want to go but goes anyway; **2** *conj* yet, still: **~ fer hann á hverju ári** still he goes every year

samt sem áður *adv* nevertheless, however, anyway

samtal *n neu* (-s, -töl, -a) dialogue, talk

samtal|a *n fem* (-tölu, -tölur, -talna) sum

samtals *adv* in total: **þetta eru ~ þúsund krónur** this is one thousand kronas in total

samtenging *n fem* (-ar, -ar, ~) *ling* conjunction

samtímabókmennt|ir *n fem pl* (-a) contemporary literature

samtímalist *n fem* (-ar) contemporary art

samtímis *adv* simultaneously

samtök *n neu pl* (-taka) union; society

samúð *n fem* (-ar) sympathy

samúðarkveðj|ur *n fem pl* (-a) condolences

samvinn|a *n fem* (-u) cooperation

samþykki *n neu* (-s) approval

samþykkj|a *v* (-þykki, -þykkti, -þykkt) accept, approve

samþætt|a *v* (-i, -i, -) integrate

sandal|i *n masc* (-a, -ar, -a) sandal

sandhverf|a *n fem* (-u, -ur, ~) *zool* turbot

sandreyð|ur *n fem* (-ar, -ir, -a) *zool* sei whale

sand|ur *n masc* (-s, -ar, -a) sand

sanna *v* (~, -ði, -ð) prove

sannarlega *adv* certainly

sannfær|a *v* (-i, -ði, -t) assure, convince, persuade

sannfærð|ur *adj* certain, sure

sannfæring *n fem* (-ar) persuasion

sanngirni *n fem* (-) fairness

sanngjarn *adj* fair, reasonable

sannleik|ur *n masc* (-s) truth

sann|ur *adj* (sönn, satt) real, true

Santíagó *N fem* (-) Santiago (capital of Chile)

Sarajevó *N fem* (-) Sarajevo (capital of Bosnia and Herzegovina)

sardín|a *n fem* (-u, -ur, ~) sardine

Satan *N masc* (-s) Satan

satín *n neu* (-s) satin

satír|a *n fem* (-u, -ur, ~) satire

sauðburð|ur *n masc* (-ar, -ir, -a) *period of time during which sheep give birth*

sauð|ur *n masc* (-ar/s, -ir, -a) *zool* sheep

sauma *v* (~, -ði, -ð) sew

saumakon|a *n fem* (-u, -ur, -kvenna) seamstress

saumaskap|ur *n masc* (-ar) sewing

saumavél *n fem* (-ar, -ar, -a) sewing machine

saum|ur *n masc* (-s, -ar, -a) stitch

sautján *num* seventeen

sautjándi *ord* (-a, -a) seventeenth

saxa *v* (~, -ði, -ð) chop

saxað|ur *adj* (söxuð, -) chopped

saxófón|n *n masc* (-s, -ar, -a) *mus* saxophone

sá *pron* (sú, það) the one: ~ **hlær best sem síðast hlær** the one who laughs last laughs the most

Sádi Arabí|a *N fem* (-u) Saudi Arabia

sál *n fem* (-ar, -ir, -a) soul; psyche

sálarlaus *adj* (-, -t) soulless

sálfræði *n fem* (-) psychology

sálfræðileg|ur *adj* (-, -t) psychological

sálfræðimeðferð *n fem* (-ar, -ir, -a) psychotherapy

sálfræðing|ur *n masc* (-s, -ar, -a) psychologist

sálm|ur *n masc* (-s, -ar, -a) psalm, hymn

Salómonseyj|ar *N fem pl* (-a) Solomon Islands

sálræn|n *adj* (-, -t) psychic

sáluhjálp *n fem* (-ar) salvation

sán|a *n fem* (-u, -ur, ~) sauna

sáning *n fem* (-ar, -ar, -a) sowing

sáp|a *n fem* (-u, -ur, -a) soap

sápuóper|a *n fem* (-u, -ur, ~) soap opera

sár 1 *adj* (-, -t) wounded, hurt; **2** *n neu* (-s, -, -a) wound, sore, cut

sárasótt *n fem* (-ar) *med* syphilis

sáraumbúð|ir *n fem pl* (-a) bandage

sáravatn *n neu* (-s) sterilizing solution

sárbæn|a *v* (-i, -di, -t) beg

sársaukafull|ur *adj* (-, -t) painful

sársauk|i *n masc* (-a) pain; sting

sátt *n fem* (-ar, sættir, -a) atonement

sáttasemjar|i *n masc* (-a, -ar, -a) mediator

sebrahest|ur *n masc* (-s, -ar, -a) *zool* zebra

seðjandi *adj* filling, rich

sefa *v* (~, -ði, -ð) soothe

sefandi *adj* soothing

segj|a *v* (segi, sagði, sagt) say, tell, remark: ~ **upp** resign

segj|ast v refl (segist, sagðist, sagst) say about oneself: **hann segist vera frá Íslandi** he says he is from Iceland

segl n neu (-s, -, -a) sail

seglbát|ur n masc (-s, -ar, -a) sailing boat

seglbrett|i n neu (-is, ~, -a) windsurfing board

segulbandstæk|i n neu (-is, ~, -ja) tape recorder

segulljós n neu (-s, -, -a) polar light

segulrönd n fem (-randar, -rendur/ -randir, -randa) magnetic strip

segulstál n neu (-s, -, -a) magnet

seig|ur adj (-, t) tough, chewy

seinast|ur adj superl (seinust, -) latest

seinka v (~, -ði, -ð) delay

seink|un n fem (-unar, -anir, -ana) delay

sein|n adj (-, -t) late, delayed

seinn|i adj compar (~, -a) latter

sekk|ur n masc (-jar/s, -ir, -ja) sack

sekt n fem (-ar, -ir, -a) fine

sektarkennd n fem (-ar) guilt

sekúnd|a n fem (-u, -ur, -na) (time) second

sek|ur adj (-, -t) guilty

seld|ur adj (-, selt) sold

selj|a v (sel, seldi, selt) sell

selj|ast v refl (selst, seldist, selst) sell: **húsið seldist strax** the house was sold right away

seljand|i n masc (-a, -endur, -enda) seller

sellerí n neu (-s) celery

selló n neu (-s, -, -a) mus cello

selsíus n mas celsius: **tvær gráður á ~** two degrees celsius

sel|ur n masc (-s, -ir, -a) zool seal

sem betur fer phr fortunately

sem fyrst adv as soon as possible

sement n neu (-s) cement

semíkomm|a n fem (-u, -ur, ~) ling semicolon

semj|a v (sem, samdi, samið) negotiate; compose

send|a v (-i, -i, -t) send, remit; **~ frá sér** publish, release; **~ út** transmit

send|ast v refl (-ist, -ist, -st) run errands; go very fast: **~ með pakka** deliver a package

sendand|i n masc (-a, -endur, -enda) sender

sendiboð|i n masc (-a, -ar, -a) messenger

sendiferðabíl|l n masc (-s, -ar, -a) van

sendiherra n masc (-, -r, -) ambassador

sendil|l n masc (-s, sendlar, sendla) deliverer

sending n fem (-ar, -ar, -a) delivery

sendingakostnað|ur n masc (-ar) delivery cost

sendin|n adj (-, sendið) sandy

send|ir n masc (-is, -ar, -a) transmittor

sendiráð n neu (-s, -, -a) embassy: **~ Norður-Ameríku í Reykjavík** The American Embassy in Reykjavik

sendlafyrirtæk|i n neu (-is, ~, -ja) carrier

Senegal N neu (-/s) Senegal

senegalsk|ur adj (senegölsk, -t) Senegalese

sennilega adv presumably, probably

sennileg|ur adj (-, -t) probable

sent n neu (-s, -, -a) econ cent

sentímetr|i n masc (-a, -ar, -a) centimeter

Seoul N fem (-) Seoul (capital of South Korea)

september n masc (-) September

Serbi n masc (-a, -ar, -a) Serbian (person)

Serbí|a N fem (-u) Serbia

serbnesk|a n fem (-u) Serbian language

serbnesk|ur adj (-, -t) Serbian

serbókróatísk|a n fem (-u) Serbo-Croatia

serí|a n fem (-u, -ur, ~) series

servíett|a n fem (-u, -ur, -na) napkin

sesamfræ n neu (-s, -, -ja) sesame seeds

setj|a v (set, setti, sett) put, place, set; **~ á svið** stage; **~ fram** formulate

setj|ast *v refl* (sest, settist, sest) sit down; ~ **að** settle down

setning *n fem* (-ar, -ar, -a) *ling* clause

setningafræði *n fem* (-) *ling* syntax

sett *n neu* (-s, -, -a) set

settaugarbólg|a *n fem* (-u) *med* sciatica

setustof|a *n fem* (-u, -ur, ~) sitting room, lounge, parlor

sex *num* six

sextán *num* sixteen

sextándi *ord* (-a, -a) sixteenth

sextíu *num* sixty

sextugast|i *ord* (-a, -a) sixtieth

sextug|ur *adj* (-, -t) sixty years old

Seychelles-eyj|ar *N fem pl* (-a) Seychelles

séð|ur *adj* (-, -) calculating

sér 1 *pron refl dat* himself, herself, themselves, oneself; **kaupa ~ kaffi** buy oneself a cup of coffee; **2** *excl* **hugsa ~!** just imagine!

sérfræðing|ur *n masc* (-s, -ar, -a) expert, specialist

sérfæð|i *masc neu* (-is) special diet

sérgrein *n fem* (-ar, -ar, -a) specialty

sérhver *pron* (-, -t) each: **sérhvert andartak** each moment

sérhljóð|i *n masc* (-a, -ar, -a) *ling* vowel

sérhæf|a *v* (-i, -ði, -t) specialize: ~ **sig** get specialized

sérhæfð|ur *adj* (-, -hæft) specialized

sérkenni *n neu* (-s, -, -a) distinction

sérkennileg|ur *adj* (-, -t) singular; quaint; outlandish

sérrí *n neu* (-s) sherry

sérstaklega *adv* specifically, specially, particularly, particularly

sérstak|ur *adj* (-stök, -t) distinctive, separate, specific, unique

sérþarf|ir *n fem pl* (-þarfa) special needs

sértrúarsöfnuð|ur *n masc* (-safnaðar, -ir, -a) sect

siðaregl|ur *n fem pl* (-na) protocol

siðaskipti *n neu pl* (-a) reformation

siðblinding|i *n masc* (-ja, -jar, -ja) psychopath

siðferð|i *n neu* (-s) ethics

siðferðileg|ur *adj* (-, -t) ethical, moral

siðferðislega *adv* morally

siðfræði *n fem* (~) ethics

siðlaus *adj* (-, -t) immoral

siðleys|i *n neu* (-s) immorality; perversion

sig *pron refl acc* (*dat* sér; *gen* sín) herself, himself, themselves, oneself: **hann meiddi ~** he hurt himself

sigketil|l *n masc* (-s, -katlar, -katla) *geol* caldera

sigl|a *v* (-i, -di, -t) sail, navigate, cruise

sigling *n fem* (-ar, -ar, -a) sailing; cruise

siglingafræðing|ur *n masc* (-s, -ar, -a) navigator

sigra *v* (~, -ði, -ð) win, triumph, prevail

sigta *v* (~, -ði, -ð) sieve, sift

sigt|i *n neu* (-is, ~, -a) sieve

sigur *n masc* (-s, sigrar, sigra) victory, triumph

sigursæl|l *adj* (-, -t) victorious

sigurvegar|i *n masc* (-a, -ar, -a) winner

Sikiley *N fem* (-jar) Sicily

silfur *n neu* (-s) *geol* silver

silfurhúð *n fem* (-ar, -ir, -a) silver plate

silfursmið|ur *n masc* (-s, -ir, -a) silversmith

silki *n neu* (-s) silk

silung|ur *n masc* (-s, -ar, -a) trout

sinfóní|a *n fem* (-u, -ur, ~) *mus* symphony

sinfóníuhljómsveit *n fem* (-ar, -ir, -a) symphony orchestra

sin|n *pron* (sín, sitt) his, her, their: **hún talaði við manninn ~** she talked to her husband

sinnep *n neu* (-s) mustard

sinnepskál *n neu* (-s) mustard greens

sinnuleysi *n neu* (-s) lethargy

sirka *adv* circa, about

sirkus *n masc* (-s, -ar, -a) circus

sitj|a *v* (sit, sat, sátum, setið) sit; ~ **fyrir** model, pose for the camera; ~ **yfir** invigilate

sí|a *n fem* (-u, -ur, ~) filter

síað|ur *adj* (síuð, -) filtered

síder *n masc* (-s, -ar, -a) *colloq* cider

síð|a *n fem* (-u, -ur, -na) side, flank

síðan 1 *adv* since: ~ **fimm** since five; ago: **fyrir tólf árum** ~ twelve years ago; **2** *conj* then: ~ **fór ég í búðina** then I went to the store

síðast|ur *adj* (síðust, -) final, last; **síðasti söludagur** expiration date

síðdegis *adv* in the afternoon

síðdegissýning *n fem* (-ar, -ar, -a) matinée

síðkjól|l *n masc* (-s, -ar, -a) evening gown

síðufót|ur *n masc* (-ar, -fætur, -fóta) *comp* footer

síð|ur *adj* (-, sítt) long; **síðar nærbuxur** long johns; **sítt hár** long hair

Síerra Leóne *N neu* (-s) Sierra Leone

Síerra Leóne-maðl|ur *n masc* (-manns, -menn, -manna) Sierra Leonean *(person)*

síerralónsk|ur *adj* (-, -t) Sierra Leonean

sífelld|ur *adj* (-, sífellt) continous

sífellt *adv* continuously, non-stop

sígarett|a *n fem* (-u, -ur, ~) cigarette

sígild|ur *adj* (-, sígilt) classical

sík|i *n neu* (-is, ~, -ja) trench

síld *n fem* (-ar, -ir, -a) herring

Síle *N neu* (-) Chile

Sílemað|ur *N masc* (-manns, -menn, -manna) Chilean *(person)*

sílesk|ur *adj* (-, -t) Chilean

sílófón|n *n masc* (-s, -ar, -a) *mus* xylophone

símakort *n neu* (-s, -, -a) phone card

símanúmer *n neu* (-s, -, -a) telephone number

símaskrá *n fem* (-r, -r, -a) phone book, telephone directory

sím|i *n masc* (-a, -ar, -a) telephone

símklef|i *n masc* (-a, -ar, -a) phone booth

símreikning|ur *n masc* (-s, -ar, -a) telephone bill

símskeyt|i *n neu* (-is, ~, -a) telegram

símtal *n neu* (-s, -töl, -a) phone call

sín *pron refl gen* himself, herself, oneself, themself; **þeir skammast** ~ they are ashamed (of themselves)

síren|a *n fem* (-u, -ur, ~) siren

síróp *n neu* (-s) syrup, molasses

sítrón|a *n fem* (-u, -ur, ~) lemon

sítrónubörk|ur *n masc* (-barkar, -berkir, -barka) zest

sítrónusaf|i *n masc* (-a, -ar, -a) lemon juice

sítrusávöxt|ur *n masc* (-ávaxtar, -ávextir, ávaxta) citrus

sjaldan *adv* rarely

sjaldgæf|ur *adj* (-, -t) rare

sjampó *n neu* (-s, -, -a) shampoo

sjarma *v colloq* (~, -ði, -ð) charm

sjá *v* (sé, sá, sáum, séð) see; ~ **eftir** regret

sjáaldur *n neu* (-s, -öldur, -aldra) *anat* pupil

sjáand|i *n masc* (-a, -endur, -enda) clairvoyant

sjálfbær *adj* (-, -t) sustainable: ~ **þróun** sustainable development

sjálfboðaliðl|i *n masc* (-a, -ar, -a) volunteer

sjálfsafgreiðsl|a *n fem* (-u, -ur, -na) self-service

sjálfsagt *adv* goes without saying

sjálfselsk|a *n fem* (-u) egotism, narcissism

sjálfskipting *n fem* (-ar, -ar, -a) *mech* automatic transmission

sjálfskoðun *n fem* (-ar) introspection

sjálfsmorð *n neu* (-s, -, -a) suicide: **fremja** ~ commit suicide

sjálfstjórn *n fem* (-ar) self control; autonomy

sjálfsvörn *n fem* (-varnar) self-defense
sjálfstæði *n neu* (-s) independence
sjálfstæð|ur *adj* (-, -stætt) independent
sjálf|ur *pron* (-, -t) self; **sjálfum sér nógur** self-sufficient
sjálfvirkt *adv* automatically
sjálfvirk|ur *adj* (-, -t) automatic
sjá|st *v* (sést, sást, sáumst, sést) to be visible: **hún sást í gær** she was seen (visible) yesterday; show: **það sést ekki** it doesn't show
sjávarbakk|i *n masc* (-a, -ar, -a) sea front
sjávarbotn *n masc* (-s) sea bed; **á sjávarbotni** at the bottom of the sea
sjávardýr *n neu* (-s, -, -a) sea animal
sjávarfall *n neu* (-s, -föll, -a) tide
sjávarloft *n neu* (-s) sea air
sjávarmál *n neu* (-s) sea level
sjávarrétt|ur *n masc* (-ar, -ir, -a) seafood
sjávarsnigil|l *n masc* (-s, -sniglar, snigla) sea snail
sjopp|a *n fem* (-u, -ur, ~) *colloq* convenience store
sjóð|a *v* (sýð, sauð, suðum, soðið) boil; ~ **niður** preserve
sjóðandi *adj* scalding; ~ **heitt** scalding hot
sjóð|ur *n masc* (-s, -ir, -a) fund
sjófugl *n masc* (-s, -ar, -a) sea bird
sjóher *n masc* (-s, -ir, -a) navy
sjómað|ur *n masc* (-manns, -menn, -manna) seaman, sailor
sjómennsk|a *n fem* (-u) sailing
sjón *n fem* (-ar, -ir, -a) sight, vision
sjónarhól|l *n masc* (-s, -ar, -a) perspective
sjónarhorn *n neu* (-s, -, -a) perspective, viewpoint
sjónarmið *n neu* (-s, -, -a) aspect
sjónauk|i *n masc* (-a, -ar, -a) binoculars
sjóndeildarhring|ur *n masc* (-s) skyline
sjónglerjafræðing|ur *n masc* (-s, -ar, -a) *med* optometrist

sjónhimn|a *n fem* (-u, -ur, ~) *anat* retina
sjónmæling *n fem* (-ar, -ar, -a) vision examination
sjónmál *n neu* (-i) view; **úr sjónmáli** out of sight
sjónpróf *n neu* (-s, -, -a) *med* vision examination
sjóntækjasmið|ur *n masc* (-s, -ir, -a) optician
sjónvarp *n neu* (-s, -vörp, -a) television
sjónvarpa *v* (~, -ði, -ð) broadcast on television
sjónvarpsleik|ur *n masc* (-s, -ir/ar, -ja/a) game show
sjónvarpsþátt|ur *n masc* (-ar, -þættir, -þátta) television series
sjó|r *n masc* (-s/sjávar, -ir, -a) sea
sjóræning|i *n masc* (-ja, -jar, -ja) pirate
sjórán *n neu* (-s, -, -a) piracy
sjósund *n neu* (-s, -, -a) swimming in the sea
sjóvarnargarð|ur *n masc* (-s, -ar, -a) sea wall
sjóveik|ur *adj* (-, -t) seasick
sjúg|a *v* (sýg, saug, sugum, sogið) suck
sjúkdómseinkenn|i *n neu pl* (-is, ~, -a) *med* symptoms
sjúkdómsgrein|a *v med* (-i, -di, -t) diagnose
sjúkdómsgreining *n fem* (-ar, -ar, -a) *med* diagnosis
sjúkdómsmynd *n fem* (-ar, -ir, -a) *med* syndrome
sjúkdóm|ur *n masc* (-s, -ar, -a) disease, illness, sickness, ailment
sjúkleg|ur *adj* (-, -t) morbid
sjúkleik|i *n masc* (-a, -ar, -a) malady
sjúkling|ur *n masc* (-s, -ar, -a) *med* patient
sjúkrabíl|l *n masc* (-s, -ar, -a) ambulance
sjúkrabæt|ur *n fem pl* (-bóta) sickness benefit

sjúkrabör|ur *n fem pl* (-bara) stretcher
sjúkrahús *n neu* (-s, -, -a) hospital
sjúkrakass|i *n masc* (-a, -ar, -a) first-aid kit
sjúkrapening|ur *n masc* (-s, -ar, -a) sick pay
sjúkrastof|a *n fem* (-u, -ur, ~) *med* patient room
sjúkratrygging *n fem* (-ar, -ar, -a) health insurance
sjö *num* seven
sjötíu *num* seventy
sjött|i *ord* (-a, -a) sixth
sjötugast|i *ord* (-a, -a) seventieth
sjötug|ur *adj* (-, -t) seventy years old
sjöund|i *ord* (-a, -a) seventh
skaða *v* (~, -ði, -ð) afflict, harm
skaðabæt|ur *n fem pl* (-bóta) compensation
skaðabótakraf|a *n fem* (-kröfu, -kröfur, -krafna) insurance claim
skaðabótarétt|ur *n masc* (-ar) *leg* law in civil liability for damages
skaðbrenn|a *v* (-, -di, -t) scald: ~ **sig** scald oneself
skað|i *n masc* (-a, -ar, ~) damage, harm
skaðlaus *adj* (-, -t) harmless
skafrenning|ur *n masc* (-s) snow drift
skag|i *n masc* (-a, -ar, -a) peninsula
skakk|ur *adj* (skökk, -t) skewed; wrong
skalottulauk|ur *n masc* (-s, -ar, -a) shallot
skamma *v* (~, -ði, -ð) scold, rebuke
skammarleg|ur *adj* (-, -t) shameful, embarrassed
skammbyss|a *n fem* (-u, -ur, ~) pistol
skamm|ir *n fem pl* (-a) scolding
skammstöf|un *n fem* (-unar, -stafnir, -stafana) abbreviation
skammsýn|i *n fem* (-) myopia
skammtímabílastæð|i *n neu* (-is, -, -a) short-term parking
skammt|ur *n masc* (-s, -ar, -a) dose, portion, ration
skandal|l *n masc* (-s, -ar, -a) scandal

Skandinaví|a *N fem* (-u) Scandinavia
skandinavísk|ur *adj* (-, -t) Scandinavian; **skandinavísk tungumál** Scandinavian languages
skank|i *n masc* (-a, -ar, -a) shank
skanna *v* (~, -ði, -ð) scan
skann|i *n masc* (-a, -ar, -a) scanner
skap *n neu* (-s) mood
skapa *v* (~, -ði, -ð) create
skapandi *adj* creative
skapmikil|l *adj* (-, -mikið) moody
skaprauna *v* (~, -ði, -ð) irritate
skapvond|ur *adj* (-, -vont) bad-tempered
skarkol|i *n masc* (-a, -ar, -a) *zool* plaice
skarpskyggni *n fem* (-) sagacity
skarpskyggn *adj* (-, -t) sagacious
skarp|ur *adj* (skörp, -t) acute; clever
skartgripabúð *n fem* (-ar, -ir, -a) jewelry shop
skartgripasal|i *n masc* (-a, -ar, -a) jeweler
skartgripaskrín *n neu* (-s, -, -a) jewelbox
skartgrip|ur *n masc* (-s, -ir, -a) jewelry
skat|a *n fem* (skötu, skötur, ~) *zool* skate; **kæst** ~ fermented skate *(an Icelandic specialty)*
skattgreiðand|i *n masc* (-a, -endur, -enda) taxpayer
skattlagning *n fem* (-ar, -ar, -a) taxation
skattleggj|a *v* (-legg, -lagði, -lagt) tax
skatt|ur *n masc* (-s, -ar, -a) tax
skaut *n neu* (-s, -, -a) *geol* pole
skauta *v* (~, -ði, -ð) skate
skautahlaup *n neu* (-s) *sports* speed skating
skaut|i *n masc* (-a, -ar, -a) *sports* skate
skáp|ur *n masc* (-s, -ar, -a) closet, cupboard
skák *n fem* (-ar, -ir, -a) chess
skál 1 *n fem* (-ar, -ir, -a) bowl; **2** *interj* Cheers!

skála *v* (~, -ði, -ð) make a toast
skáldsag|a *n fem* (-sögu, -sögur, -sagna) *lit* novel
skáldsagnahöfund|ur *n masc* (-ar, -ar, -a) *lit* novelist
skáldskaparform *n neu* (-s, -, -a) literary genre
skál|i *n masc* (-a, -ar, -a) pavilion; cottage
skát|i *n masc* (-a, -ar, -a) scout
skegg *n neu* (-s, -, -ja) beard
skeið 1 *n fem* (-ar, -ir, -a) spoon; **2** *n neu* (-s, -, -a) period, age
skeif|a *n fem* (-u, -ur, -na) horseshoe
skel *n fem* (-jar, -jar, -ja) seashell
skeldýr *n neu* (-i, -, -a) shellfish
skelf|a *v* (-i, -di, -t) frighten
skelfileg|ur *adj* (-, -t) frightening, alarming
skelfisk|ur *n masc* (-s, -ar, -a) shellfish
skelflett|a *v* (-i, -i, -) shell
skelkað|ur *adj* (skelkuð, -) afraid
skellinaðr|a *n fem* (-nöðru, -nöðrur, -naðra) moped
skemm|a *v* (-i, -di, -t) spoil, sabotage
skemm|ast *v refl* (-ist, -dist, -st) get spoiled, go bad: **mjólkin skemmist** the milk goes bad
skemmdarverk *n neu* (-s, -, -a) sabotage
skemmd|ur *adj* (-, skemmt) damaged, spoiled
skemmt|a *v* (-i, -i, -t) entertain, amuse
skemmtanalíf *n neu* (-s) nightlife
skemmtiferð *n fem* (-ar, -ir, -a) outing
skemmtiferðasigling *n fem* (-ar, -ar, -a) cruise
skemmtiferðaskip *n neu* (-s, -, -a) cruiseliner
skemmtigarð|ur *n masc* (-s, -ar, -a) amusement park
skemmtikraft|ur *n masc* (-s, -ar, -a) performer
skemmtileg|ur *adj* (-, -t) amusing, fun
skemmt|un *n fem* (-unar, -anir, -ana) amusement, fun, entertainment, show

sker *n neu* (-s, -, -ja) skerry
sker|a *v* (-, skar, skárum, skorið) cut: ~ **niður** cut down; downsize; retrench
skerð|a *v* (-i, skerti, skert) decrease, cut down, limit
skerð|ast *v* (~, -tist, skerst) decrease, cut down: **launin** ~ the salary is decreased
skerðing *n fem* (-ar, -ar, -a) reduction
skerjagarð|ur *n masc* (-s, -ar, -a) archipelago
skerm|ur *n masc* (-s, -ar, -a) screen; shade
skessuketil|l *n masc* (-s, -katlar, -katla) pothole
skikkj|a *n fem* (-u, -ur, skikkna) robe
skil *n neu pl* (-a) return
skila *v* (~, -ði, -ð) return
skilaboð *n neu pl* (-a) message
skiladag|ur *n masc* (-s, -ar, -a) due date
skilafrest|ur *n masc* (-s, -ir, -a) deadline
skilgrein|a *v* (-i, -di, -t) define
skilgreining *n fem* (-ar, -ar, -a) definition
skilin|n *adj* (-, skilið) divorced; separated
skilj|a *v* (skil, skildi, skilið) understand: **ég skil** I understand, I see; divorce; separate; ~ **við** separate from
skilmáli *n masc* (-a, -ar, -a) terms
skilnað|ur *n masc* (-ar, -ir, -a) divorce; separation
skilningarvit *n neu* (-s, -, -a) sense
skilningsrík|ur *adj* (-, -t) sympathetic
skilning|ur *n masc* (-s) understanding, comprehension, insight; sense
skilt|i *n neu* (-is, ~, -a) sign
skilurðu *interj* do you understand?, you see?, y'know?
skilvirkni *n fem* (-) effectiveness
skilyrð|i *n neu* (-is, ~, -a) prerequisite, requirement, condition
skilyrt|ur *adj* (-, -) conditional
skima *v* (~, -ði, -ð) scan

skink|a *n fem* (-u, -ur, ~) ham

skinkuálegg *n neu* (-s) sliced ham

skinkusamlok|a *n fem* (-u, -ur, ~) ham sandwich

skinn *n neu* (-s, -, -a) skin

skip *n neu* (-s, -, -a) ship

skipa *v* (~, -ði, -ð) appoint; command

skipahöfn *n fem* (-hafnar, -hafnir, -hafna) harbor

skipaleg|a *n fem* (-u, -ur, -na) anchorage

skipalæg|i *n neu* (-is, ~, -ja) anchorage

skipaskurð|ur *n masc* (-ar, -ir, -a) ship canal

skipasmíðastöð *n fem* (-var, -var, -va) shipyard

skipt|a *v* (-i, -i, -) exchange, trade; split; ~ **máli** matter

skipt|ast *v refl* (-ist, -ist, skipst) split: ~ **í miðju** split in the middle; exchange: ~ **á bréfum** exchange letters; ~ **á** take turns

skiptimið|i *n masc* (-a, -ar, -a) transfer ticket

skiptimynt *n fem* (-ar) small change

skipstjór|i *n masc* (-a, -ar, -a) captain

skipulag *n neu* (-s) planning

skipulagð|ur *adj* (-lögð, -lagt) organized

skipulagning *n fem* (-ar) organization

skipulagsleg|ur *adj* (-, -legt) organizational

skipuleggj|a *v* (-legg, -lagði, -lagt) plan, organize

skip|un *n fem* (-unar, -anir, -ana) directive; appointment

skiss|a *n fem* (-u, -ur, ~) sketch

skíða *v* (~, -ði, -ð) *sports* ski

skíðagöngubraut *n fem* (-ar, -ir, -a) *sports* cross-country ski trail

skíðaíþrótt *n fem* (-ar, -ir, -a) *sports* skiing

skíðakloss|i *n masc* (-a, -ar, -a) ski boot

skíðalyft|a *n fem* (-u, -ur, ~) ski lift

skíðamað|ur *n masc* (-manns, -menn, -manna) skier

skíðaskál|i *n masc* (-a, -ar, -a) skiers' lodge

skíðastað|ur *n masc* (-ar, -ir, -a) ski resort

skíðastaf|ur *n masc* (-s, -ir, -a) ski stick

skíðastökk *n neu* (-s, -, -a) ski jump

skíðasvæð|i *n neu* (-is, ~, -a) ski resort

skíð|i *n neu* (-is, ~, -a) *sports* ski

skíf|a *n fem* (-u, -ur, ~) disk

skífuberg *n neu* (-s) *geol* slate

skín|a *v* (-, skein, skinum, skinið) shine

skínandi *adj* luminous

skír|a *v* (-i, -ði, -t) baptize

skírdag|ur *n masc* (-s) Maundy Thursday, Holy Thursday, Sheer Thursday

skírn *n fem* (-ar, -ir, -a) christening, baptism

skírnarfont|ur *n masc* (-s, -ar, -a) baptismal font

skírnarnafn *n neu* (-s, -nöfn, -a) Christian name

skírskot|un *n fem* (-unar, -anir, -ana) allusion

skíthæl|l *n masc* (-s, -ar, -a) *vul slang* scumbag, asshole

skítug|ur *adj* (-, -t) filthy, dirty

skít|ur *n masc* (-s) filth, dirt

skjal *n neu* (-s, skjöl, -a) document

skjalasafn *n neu* (-s, -söfn, -a) archives

skjaldbak|a *n fem* (-böku, -bökur, ~) tortoise, turtle

skjaldkirtil|l *n masc* (-s, -kirtlar, -kirtla) *anat* thyroid

skjall *n neu* (-s, skjöll, -a) flattery

skjalla *v* (~, -ði, -ð) flatter

skjálf|a *v* (skelf, skalf, skulfum, skolfið) shake, quiver, quake, shudder

skjálfandi *adj* shaky

skjálftamiðj|a *n fem* (-u, -ur, ~) *geol* epicenter

skjálft|i *n masc* (-a, -ar, -a) shivers

skjá|r *n masc* (-s, -ir, -a) *comp* screen, monitor

skjávarp|i *n masc* (-a, -ar, -a) projector

skjól *n neu* (-s, -, -a) cover, refuge, shelter

skjó|r *n masc* (-s, -ir, -a) *zool* magpie

skjót|a *v* (skýt, skaut, skutum, skotið) shoot

skjót|ast *v refl* (skýst, skaust, skutumst, skotist) go for a short trip, run: ~ **í búðina** run to the store

skjöld|ur *n masc* (skjaldar, skildir, skjalda) shield

sko *interj* you see, look, y'know

skoða *v* (~, -ði, -ð) look at, inspect

skoð|un *n fem* (-unar, -anir, -ana) opinion; inspection

skoðunarferð *n fem* (-ar, -ir, -a) sightseeing tour

skokk *n neu* (-s) jogging

skokka *v* (~, -ði, -ð) jog

skola *v* (~, -ði, -ð) rinse

skolhærð|ur *adj* (-, hært) ash blonde

skons|a *n fem* (-u, -ur, ~) scone

Skopje *N fem* (-) Skopje (capital of Macedonia)

skopskyn *n neu* (-s) sense of humor

skopstæling *n fem* (-ar, -ar, -a) parody

skopteikning *n fem* (-ar, -ar, -a) caricature

skora *v* (~, -ði, -ð) *sports* score: ~ **mark** score a goal; ~ **á** challenge

skordýr *n neu* (-s, -, -a) insect, bug

skordýrabit *n neu* (-s, -, -a) insect bite

skordýraeitur *n neu* (-s) pesticide, insect repellant

skorp|a *n fem* (-u, -ur, -na) crust; rind

skort|a *v* (-i, -i, -) lack

skort|ur *n masc* (-s) lack, shortage, deficiency

skosk|a *n fem* (-u) Scottish language

skosk|ur *adj* (-, -t) Scottish; **skoskt viskí** scotch whiskey

skot *n neu* (-s, -, -a) alcove; discharge; shot from a gun

skotheld|ur *adj* (-, -helt) bullet-proof

Skot|i *n masc* (-a, -ar, -a) Scot

Skotland *N neu* (-s) Scotland

skotmark *n neu* (-s, -mörk, -a) target

skott *n neu* (-s, -, -a) car trunk, tail

skottulækn|ir *n masc* (-is, -ar, -a) quack *(fake doctor)*

skóbúð *n fem* (-ar, -ir, -a) shoe store

skófl|a *n fem* (-u, -ur, -na) shovel

skógarbjörn *n masc* (-bjarnar, -birnir, -bjarna) *zool* bear

skógarrjóður *n neu* (-s, -, -rjóðra) opening in the woods

skógrækt *n fem* (-ar) afforestation; forestry

skógræktarsvæð|i *n neu* (-is, ~, -a) plantation

skóg|ur *n masc* (-ar, -ar, -a) forest, woods

skóhorn *n neu* (-s, -, -a) shoehorn

skólabók *n fem* (-ar, -bækur, -a) textbook

skólabúning|ur *n masc* (-s, -ar, -a) school uniform

skólafélag|i *n masc* (-a, -ar, -a) classmate, friend from school

skólastjór|i *n masc* (-a, -ar, -a) school principal

skólastof|a *n fem* (-u, -ur, ~) classroom

skólatask|a *n fem* (-tösku, -töskur, ~) school bag

skó|r *n masc* (-s, ~, -a) shoe

skóreim *n fem* (-ar, -ar, -a) shoestring

skósmið|ur *n masc* (-s, -ir, -a) shoe shop

skrapa *v* (~, -ði, -ð) scrape

skraut *n neu* (-s, -, -a) ornament

skrauthlið *n neu* (-s, -, -a) portal

skrautskrift *n fem* (-ar, -ir, -a) calligraphy

skrá 1 *n fem* (-r, -r, -a) file: **tölvuskrá** computer file; record, schedule, register: **afbrotaskrá** crime register; catalog: **símaskrá** telephone catalog; **2** *v* (-i, -ði, -ð) file, record, register, schedule, list

skráarsnið *n neu* (-s, -, -a) *comp* file format

skráarþjón|n *n masc* (-s, -ar, -a) *comp* file server

skrám|a *n fem* (-u, -ur, -na) scrape, scratch

skráning *n fem* (-ar, -ar, -a) registration

skráningarspjald *n neu* (-s, -spjöld, -a) index card

skráningarstof|a *n fem* (-u, -ur, ~) registry office
skrásetj|a *v* (-set, setti, sett) record
skrásetjar|i *n masc* (-a, -ar, -a) recorder
skref *n neu* (-s, -, -a) step
skreið *n fem* (-ar) stock fish
skrepp|a *v* (-, skrapp, skruppum, skroppið) go somewhere for a short while: ~ **í búðina** pop into the store
skreyt|a *v* (-i, -ti, -t) decorate, garnish
skreyting *n fem* (-ar, -ar, -a) decoration, garnish
skriðdrek|i *n masc* (-a, -ar, -a) tank
skriðdýr *n neu* (-s, -, -a) reptile
skriðufall *n neu* (-s, -föll, -a) mudslide
skrifa *v* (~, -ði, -ð) write
skrifað|ur *adj* (skrifuð, -) written
skrifblokk *n fem* (-ar, -ir, -a) writing pad
skrifborð *n neu* (-s, -, -a) desk
skriffinnsk|a *n fem* (-u) bureaucracy
skriffinn|ur *n masc* (-s, -ar, -a) bureaucrat
skrifstof|a *n fem* (-u, -ur, ~) office, study; agency
skrifstofuhúsnæð|i *n neu* (-is) office building
skrifstofumað|ur *n masc* (-manns, -menn, -manna) office worker
skrifstofustarf *n neu* (-s, -störf, -a) office work
skríð|a *v* (-, skreið, skriðum, skriðið) crawl
skrípamynd *n fem* (-ar, -ir, -a) caricature
skrolla *v comp* (~, -ði, -ð) scroll
skruna *v comp* (~, -ði, -ð) scroll
skrúðgang|a *n fem* (-göngu, -göngur, -gangna) parade, procession
skrúðgarð|ur *n masc* (-s, -ar, -a) park
skrúf|a 1 *n fem* (-u, -ur, na) peg, pin, screw; **2 skrúfa** *v* (~, -ði, -ð) screw: ~ **af** unscrew
skrúfjárn *n neu* (-s, -, -a) screwdriver
skrýtin|n *adj* (-, skrýtið) strange, weird, peculiar

skrölt|a *v* (-i, -i, -t) rattle
skröltorm|ur *n masc* (-s, -ar, -a) rattlesnake
skugg|i *n masc* (-a, -ar, -a) shade; shadow
skuld *n fem* (-ar, -ir, -a) debt
skulda *v* (~, -ði, -ð) owe
skuldabréf *n neu* (-s, -, -a) *econ* bond
skuldar|i *n masc* (-a, -ar, -a) debtor
skuldbind|a *v* (-, -batt, -bundum, -bundið) oblige
skuldbinding *n fem* (-ar, -ar, -a) commitment
skulu *v* (skal *only in present tense*) *(promising)* will: **ég skal gera þetta** I will do this; *(threatening)* shall: **ég skal hefna mín!** I shall seek revenge!
skurðaðgerð *n fem* (-ar, -ir, -a) *med* surgery
skurðhníf|ur *n masc* (-s, -ar, -a) *med* scalpel
skurðlækning|ar *n fem pl* (-a) *med* surgery
skurðlækn|ir *n masc* (-is, -ar, -a) surgeon
skurðstof|a *n fem* (-u, -ur, ~) *med* surgery, theater
skurð|ur *n masc* (-ar, -ir, -a) cut, slash; trench
skurn *n fem* (-ar, -ir, -a) shell
skúff|a *n fem* (-u, -ur, ~) drawer
skúf|ur *n masc* (-s, -ar, -a) tassle
skúr 1 *n fem* (-ar, -ir, -a) rain shower; **2** *n masc* (-s, -ar, -a) shed
skvaldur *n neu* (-s) mumble, murmur
skvamp *n neu* (-s) plop
skvett|a *v* (-i, -i, -) dash
skyggni *n neu* (-s) view: **hvernig er skyggnið í dag?** how is the view today?
skyld|a *n fem* (-u, -ur, -na) obligation
skyldleik|i *n masc* (-a, -ar, -a) kinship
skyldug|ur *adj* (-, skyldugt) obliged, obligatory
skyld|ur *adj* (-, skylt) related to
skylming|ar *n fem pl* (-a) *sport* fencing

skyndibitastað|ur *n masc* (-ar, -ir,
-a) fast-food restaurant
skyndibit|i *n masc* (-a, -ar, -a) fast food
skyndihjálp *n fem* (-ar) first aid
skyndilega *adv* abruptly, suddenly
skyndileg|ur *adj* (-, -t) abrupt, sudden
skyndimat|ur *n masc* (-ar) fast food
skyndipróf *n neu* (-s, -, -a) quiz
skynja *v* (~, -ði, -ð) perceive
skynjanleg|ur *adj* (-, -t) perceptible
skynj|un *n fem* (-unar, -anir, -ana)
perception
skynsamlega *adv* reasonably, sensibly, rationally
skynsamleg|ur *adj* (-, -t) reasonable,
sensible, rational, sound
skynsam|ur *adj* (-söm, -t) reasonable,
sensible
skynsemi *n fem* (-) rationality
skyr *n neu* (-s) skyr *(an Icelandic
dairy product)*
skyrbjúg|ur *n masc* (-s) *med* scurvy
skyrt|a *n fem* (-u, -ur, -na) shirt
skyss|a *n fem* (-u, -ur, ~) mistake
skytt|a *n fem* (-u, -ur, -na) musketeer
ský *n neu* (-s, -, -ja) cloud
skýjað|ur *adj* (skýjuð, -) cloudy,
overcast
skýjakljúf|ur *n masc* (-s, -ar, -a)
skyscraper
skýl|a *v* (-i, -di, -t) shelter, shield
skýl|i *n neu* (~s, ~, -a) shelter
skýr *adj* (-, -t) clear, sharp, smart
skýr|a *v* (-i, -ði, -t) clarify
skýring *n fem* (-ar, -ar, -a) explantion
skýringarmynd *n fem* (-ar, -ir, -a)
diagram
skýrsl|a *n fem* (-u, -ur, -na) report
skýstrók|ur *n masc* (-s, -ar, -a) tornado
skær|i *n neu pl* (-a) scissors
sköflung|ur *n masc* (-s, -ar, -a) *anat*
tibia
sköllótt|ur *adj* (-, -) bald
skömm *n fem* (skammar, skammir,
skamma) shame
skömmu síðar *adv* a little bit later
skömmustuleg|ur *adj* (-, -t) ashamed

sköp *n neu* (skapa) *anat* genitals
sköp|un *n fem* (-unar, skapanir,
skapana) creation
sköpunargáf|a *n fem* (-u) creativity
skötusel|ur *n masc* (-s, -ir, -a) *zool*
monkfish, angler fish
slabb *n neu* (-s) slush
slagæð *n fem* (-ar, -ir, -a) *anat* artery
slagsmál *n neu pl* (-s, -, -a) fighting
slaka *v* (~, -ði, -ð) slack; ~ á relax
slak|ur *adj* (slök, -t) relaxed
slang|a *n fem* (slöngu, slöngur, -na)
hose; inner tube
slangur *n neu* (-s) *ling* slang; ~ af
fólki a bunch of people
slappa *v* (~, -ði, -ð) ~ af relax
slapp|ur *adj* (slöpp, -t) unwell, weak
slasa *v* (~, -ði, -ð) hurt
slasað|ur *adj* (slösuð, -) hurt in an
accident
slasa|st *v refl* (~, -ðist, ~) get hurt in
an accident
slauf|a *n fem* (-u, -ur, -a) bowtie
slá *v* (slæ, sló, slógum, slegið) beat,
punch, strike
slá|st *v* (slæst, slóst, slógumst, slegist)
fight
slátra *v* (~, -ði, -ð) slaughter
slátrar|i *n masc* (-a, -ar, -a) butcher
slátt|ur *n masc* (-ar, slættir, -a) mowing
slátur *n neu* (-s) blood sausage
(Icelandic specialty)
sleif *n fem* (-ar, -ar, -a) ladle
sleikibrjóstsykur *n masc* (-s, -sykrar,
-sykra) lollipop
sleikjó *n masc* (-s, -ar, -a) lollipop
slepp|a *v* (-i, -ti, -t) omit, release
slétt|a *n fem* (-u, -ur, -a) prairie
slétt|a *v* (-i, -i, -) level
slétt|ur *adj* (-, -) even, smooth; plane
slipp|ur *n masc* (-s, -ir, -a) shipyard
slitur *n neu* (-s, -, slitra) shreds,
fragments
slíkur *pron* such
slím *n neu* (-s, -, -a) mucus; slime
slít|a *v* (-, sleit, slitum, slitið) tear
apart

sljó|r *adj* (-, -tt) obtuse, slow to understand

slopp|ur *n masc* (-s, -ar, -a) robe

slóð *n fem* (-ar, -ir, -a) track, trail

slóð|i *n masc* (-a, -ar, -a) laggard

slóra *v* (~, -ði, -ð) lag

slóttug|ur *adj* (-, -t) sly

Slóvak|i *N masc* (-a, -ar, -a) Slovak *(person from Slovakia)*

Slóvakí|a *N fem* (-u) Slovakia

slóvakísk|a *n fem* (-u) Slovak language

slóvakísk|ur *adj* (-, -t) Slovak

Slóven|i *n masc* (-a, -ar, -a) Slovene, *(person from Slovenia)*

Slóvení|a *N fem* (-u) Slovenia

slóvensk|a *n fem* (-u) Sovene language

slóvensk|ur *adj* (-, -t) Slovene *(person from Slovenia)*

slydd|a *n fem* (-u, -ur, ~) sleet

slys *n neu* (-s, -, -a) accident

slæm|ur *adj* (-, -t) bad

slæp|ast *v* (-ist, -tist, -st) do nothing

slökkva *v* (slekk, slökkti, slökkt) turn off; ~ **eld** put out fire

slökkvar|i *n masc* (-a, -ar, -a) switch

slökkvilið *n neu* (-s, -, -a) fire department

slökkviliðsmað|ur *n masc* (-manns, -menn, -manna) firefighter

slökkvistöð *n fem* (-var, -var, -va) fire station

slökkvitæk|i *n neu* (-is, ~, -ja) fire extinguisher

slök|un *n fem* (-unar, slakanir, slakana) relaxation

smakka *v* (~, -ði, -ð) taste

smaragð|ur *n masc* (-s, -ar, -a) *geol* emerald

smá *adv* bit: ég tala ~ íslensku I speak a little bit of Icelandic

smáatrið|i *n neu* (-is, ~, -a) detail

smáauglýsing *n fem* (-ar, -ar, -a) classified advertisement

smábarn *n neu* (-s, -börn, -a) baby, infant, toddler

smáborgaraleg|ur *adj* (-, -t) petty bourgeois

smáfisk|ur *n masc* (-s, -ar, -a) *zool* whitebait

smáhest|ur *n masc* (-s, -ar, -a) *zool* pony

smákaka *n fem* (-köku, -kökur, -kakna) cookie

smákaupmað|ur *n masc* (-manns, -menn, -manna) retailer

smám saman *adv* gradually

smámunasam|ur *adj* (-söm, -t) pedantic

smámunasemi *n fem* (-) pedantry

smár|i *n masc* (-a, -ar, -a) clover

smárút|a *n fem* (-u, -ur, ~) minibus

smásag|a *n fem* (-sögu, -sögur, -sagna) *lit* short story

smásal|a *n fem* (-sölu) retail

smástein|n *n masc* (-s, -ar, -a) pebble

smástelp|a *n fem* (-u, -ur, -na) young girl

smástirn|i *n neu* (-is, ~, -a) asteroid; a minor celebrity

smásöluverð *n neu* (-s) retail price

smávægileg|ur *adj* (-, -t) slight

smáþarm|ar *n masc pl* (-a) *anat* small intestine

smekklaus *adj* (-, -t) tasteless, tacky

smekkmað|ur *n masc* (-manns, -menn, -manna) a man with good taste

smekk|ur *n masc* (-s, -ir, -a/ja) bib; taste

smell|a 1 *n fem* (-u, -ur, ~) button; **2** *v* (-i, -ti, -t) click

smell|ur *n masc* (-s, -ir, -a) click, pop

smið|ur *n masc* (-s, -ir, -a) carpenter

smita *v* (~, -ði, -ð) infect

smitandi *adj* contagious

smitber|i *n masc* (-a, -ar, -a) *med* carrier of a virus

smíða *v* (~, ði, -ð) build

smjör *n neu* (-s) butter

smjörbaun *n fem* (-ar, -ir, -a) lima bean

smjördeig *n neu* (-s) puff pastry

smjördeigshorn *n neu* (-s, -, -a) croissant

smjörhníf|ur *n masc* (-s, -ar, -a) butter knife

smjörlík|i *n neu* (-is, ~, -ja) margarine

smokkfisk|ur *n masc* (-s, -ar, -a) calamari, squid

smokk|ur *n masc* (-s, -ar, -a) condom

smurálegg *n neu* (-s, -, -ja) spread

smurning *n fem* (-ar, -ar, -a) lubrication

smurolí|a *n fem* (-u, -ur, ~) lubricant

smurost|ur *n masc* (-s, -ar, -a) spread cheese

smyrja *v* (smyr, smurði, smurt) spread (butter etc); lubricate

smyrsl *n neu* (-s, -, -a) ointment

smækka *v* (~, -ði, -ð) minimize

smætta *v* (~, -ði, -ð) reduce

smöl|un *n fem* (-unar, smalanir, smalana) roundup

snarbremsa *v* (~, -ði, -ð) brake quickly

snarl *n neu* (-s) snack

snarlbar *n masc* (-s, -ir, -a) snack bar

snartúlkun *n fem* (-ar) simultaneous interpretation

snák|ur *n masc* (-s, -ar, -a) snake

sneið *n fem* (-ar, -ar, -a) slice

sneið|a *v* (-i, sneiddi, sneitt) slice

snekkj|a *n fem* (-u, -ur, ~) yacht

snemma *adv* early

snert|a *v* (-i, -i, -) touch

snert|ast *v refl* (-ist, -ist, snerst) touch each other

snerting *n fem* (-ar, -ar, -a) touch

snertiskjá|r *n masc* (-s, -ir, -a) touch screen

snið *n neu* (-s, -, -a) format; cut of clothing

sniðug|ur *adj* (-, -t) funny, witty

snigil|l *n masc* (-s, sniglar, snigla) gastropod, snail

snilld *n fem* (-ar, -ir, -a) cleverness; something very positive: **þetta er algjör ~!** This is fantastic!

snilling|ur *n masc* (-s, -ar, -a) genius

snitsel *n neu* (-s) schnitzel

sníð|a *v* (-, sneið, sniðið) format; cut for clothing

sníkjudýr *n neu* (-s, -, -a) parasite

snjall *adj* (snjöll, -t) clever

snobb *n neu* (-s) snob

snobbað|ur *adj* (snobbuð, -) snobbish

snotur *adj* (-, -t) pretty

snjóa *v* (~, -ði, -ð) snow

snjóbrett|i *n neu* (-is, ~, -a) snowboard

snjóflóð *n neu* (-s, -, -a) avalanche

snjógall|i *n masc* (-a, -ar, -a) snowsuit

snjóhús *n neu* (-s, -, -a) igloo

snjóhvít|ur *adj* (-, -tt) snow white

snjókarl *n masc* (-s, -ar, -a) snow man

snjókom|a *n fem* (-u) snow fall

snjókorn *n neu* (-s, -, -a) snowflake

snjóplóg|ur *n masc* (-s, -ar, -a) snow plow

snjór *n masc* (-s) snow

snjósleð|i *n masc* (-a, -ar, -a) snowmobile

snóker *n neu* (-s) snooker

snú|a *v* (sný, sneri, snúið) turn, flip, convert; **~ aftur** come back, return

snú|ast *v refl* (snýst, snerist, snúist) turn, spin; convert

snúð|ur *n masc* (-s/ar, -ar, -a) bun

snúning|ur *n masc* (-s, -ar, -a) turn, rotation, twist

snúr|a *n fem* (-u, -ur, ~) cord

snyrt|a *v* (-i, -i, -) trim

snyrtilega *adv* neatly

snyrtileg|ur *adj* (-, -t) orderly, neat, tidy

snyrting *n fem* (-ar, -ar, -a) bathroom, restroom, washroom

snyrtistof|a *n fem* (-u, -ur, ~) beauty salon

snyrtivör|ur *n fem pl* (-vara) cosmetics, toiletry

snyrtivöruversl|un *n fem* (-unar, -anir, -ana) perfume shop

snýt|a *v* (-i, -ti, -t) blow a nose; **~ sér** blow one's nose

snæld|a *n fem* (-u, -ur, ~) cassette

snær|i *n neu* (-is, ~, -a) string

snögglega *adv* quickly, rapidly

snöggsteikt|ur *adj* (-, -) sautéed

snögg|ur *adj* (-, -t) quick, prompt, rapid

soð *n neu* (-s) gravy, broth
soðin|n *adj* (-, soðið) boiled
sof|a *v* (sef, svaf, sváfum, sofið) sleep; *colloq* ~ **hjá** have sex
sofandi *adj* asleep
soga *v* (~, -ði, -ð) suck
soja *n neu* (-) soya
sojabaun *n fem* (-ar, -ir, -a) soybean
sojamjólk *n fem* (-ur) soymilk
sojaolí|a *n fem* (-u, -ur, ~) soya oil
sojasós|a *n fem* (-u, -ur, ~) soya sauce
sokkabux|ur *n fem pl* (-na) tights
sokk|ur *n masc* (-s, -ar, -a) sock
soltin|n *adj* (-, soltið) starving
son|ur *n masc* (-ar, synir, -a) son
sonardótt|ir *n fem* (-ur, -dætur, -dætra) granddaughter *(daughter of a son)*
sonarson|ur *n masc* (-ar, -synir, -a) grandson *(son of a son)*
sop|i *n masc* (-a, -ar, -a) sip
sorg *n fem* (-ar, -ir, -a) sorrow, grief, mourning
sorgleg|ur *adj* (-, -t) sad, something that makes others sad: **sorgleg mynd** a sad movie
sorgmædd|ur *adj* (-, -mætt) sad: **ekki vera ~!** don't be sad!
sorp *n neu* (-s) garbage, trash
sorpbíl|l *n masc* (-s, -ar, -a) garbage/trash truck
sorppok|i *n masc* (-a, -ar, -a) garbage/trash bag
sorptunn|a *n fem* (-u, -ur, ~) garbage/trash can
sort *n fem* (-ar, -ir, -a) sort, type
sortera *v* (~, -ði, -ð) sort
sóa *v* (~, -ði, -ð) waste
sódavatn *n neu* (-s) mineral water
sóða *v* (~, -ði, -ð) mess
sóðaleg|ur *adj* (-, -t) messy, dirty, untidy
sóðaskap|ur *n masc* (-ar) mess
sóð|i *n masc* (-a, -ar, -a) slob
Sófía *N fem* (-u) Sofia *(capital of Bulgaria)*
sókn *n fem* (-ar, -ir, -a) parish: **sóknarbörn** people in the parish;

sports strike: **sóknarmaður** forward, striker
sól *n fem* (-ar, -ir, -a) sun
sóla *v* (~, -ði, -ð) retread
sólarlag *n neu* (-s, -lög, -a) sunset
sólarljós *n neu* (-s, -, -a) sunlight
sólarork|a *n fem* (-u) solar energy
sólarupprás *n fem* (-ar, -ir, -a) sunrise
sólarvörn *n fem* (-varnar, -varnir, -varna) sunscreen lotion
sólbað *n neu* (-s, -böð, -a) sunbath
sólbaðstof|a *n fem* (-u, -ur, ~) solarium
sólber *n neu* (-s, -, -ja) black currant
sólblóm *n neu* (-s, -, -a) *flora* sunflower
sólblómafræ *n neu* (-s, -, -ja) sunflower seed
sólblómaolí|a *n fem* (-u, -ur, ~) sunflower oil
sólbrun|i *n masc* (-a) sunburn
sólbrúnk|a *n fem* (-u) tan
sólgleraugu *n neu pl* (-augna) sunglasses
sólhlíf *n fem* (-ar, -ir, -a) parasol, sunshade
sólkerf|i *n neu* (-is, ~, -a) solar system
sólkol|i *n masc* (-a, -ar, -a) lemon sole
sólmyrkv|i *n masc* (-a, -ar, -a) eclipse of the sun
sóló *n neu* (-s, -, -a) solo
sólóflug *n neu* (-s, -, -a) solo flight
sólpall|ur *n masc* (-s, -ar, -a) sun deck
sólpanel|l *n masc* (-s, -ar, -a) sun panel
sólrík|ur *adj* (-, -t) sunny
sólskin *n neu* (-s) sunshine
sólsting|ur *n masc* (-s, -ir, -a) sunstroke
sólstöð|ur *n fem* (-staða) solstice
sólþurrkað|ur *adj* (-þurrkuð, -) sun-dried
Sómal|i *n masc* (-a, -ar, -a) Somali *(person from Somalia)*
Sómalí|a *N fem* (-u) Somalia
sómalísk|a *n fem* (-u) Somali language
sómalísk|ur *adj* (-, -t) Somali
són|n *n masc* (-s, -ar, -a) dial tone
sópa *v* (~, -ði, -ð) sweep
sópran *n masc* (-s, -ar, -a) soprano

sóp|ur *n masc* (-s, -ar, -a) duster, sweeper

sós|a *n fem* (-u, -ur, ~) sauce

sósíaldemókrat|i *n masc* (-a, -ar, -a) social democrat

sósíalist|i *n masc* (-s, -ar, -a) socialist

sósuskál *n fem* (-ar, -ir, -a) saucepan

sótthreinsa *v* (~, -ði, -ð) disinfect

sótthreinsandi *adj* antiseptic

sótthreins|ir *n masc* (-is) germicide

sótthreinsivökv|i *n masc* (-a, -ar, -a) antiseptic liquid

sóttkví *n fem* (-ar) quarantine

spað|i *n masc* (-a, -ar, -a) spade; spatula; *sports* racket

spagetti *n neu* (-s) spaghetti

spakmæli *n neu* (-s, -, -a) words of wisdom

spara *v* (~, -ði, -ð) save

spari *adv* for special occasions: **ég nota þetta ~** I use this for special occasions

spariföt *n neu* (-fata) dress clothing

spariskó|r *n masc* (-s, ~, a) dress shoes

spark *n neu* (-s, spörk, -a) kick

sparka *v* (~, -ði, -ð) kick

sparnað|ur *n masc* (-ar) savings

sparsam|ur *adj* (-söm, -t) frugal

spastísk|ur *adj* (-, -t) spastic

spá 1 *n fem* (-r, -r, -a) forecast, projection, prophecy, prediction; **2** *v* (-i, -ði, ð) forecast, project, predict

spádóm|ur *n masc* (-s, -ar, -a) prediction, prophecy

spákon|a *n fem* (-u, -ur, -kvenna) prophetess

spámað|ur *n masc* (-manns, -menn, -manna) prophet

Spán|n *N masc* (-ar) Spain

Spánverj|i *n masc* (-a, -ar, -a) Spaniard *(person from Spain)*

spássera *v* (~, -ði, -ð) stroll

spássí|a *n fem* (-u, -ur, ~) margin

spegilflöt|ur *n masc* (-flatar, -fletir, -flata) reflector

spegil|l *n masc* (-s, speglar, spegla) mirror

spegl|un *n fem* (-unar, -anir, -ana) reflection

spelti *n neu* (-s) spelt flour

spendýr *n neu* (-s, -, -a) *bio* mammal

spenn|a 1 *n fem* (-u, -ur, -a) tension; voltage; stress; thrill; **2** *v* (-i, -ti, -t) stretch

spennandi *adj* exciting, thrilling

spennt|ur *adj* (-, -) excited, thrilled

spennumynd *n fem* (-ar, -ir, -a) action movie

spergilkál *n neu* (-s, -, -a) broccoli

spergill *n masc* (-s, sperglar, spergla) asparagus

sperra 1 *n fem* (-u, -ur, -a) beam; **2** *v* (-i, -ti, -t) **~ eyrun** listen carefully

spil *n neu* (-s, -, -a) card

spila *v* (~, -ði, -ð) play: **~ á spil** play cards; **~ undir** accompany

spilaborð *n neu* (-s, -, -a) game board

spilakass|i *n masc* (-a, -ar, -a) arcade game

spilastokk|ur *n masc* (-s, -ar, -a) deck of cards

spilavél *n fem* (-ar, -ar, -a) gambling machine

spilavít|i *n neu* (-is, ~, -a) casino

spill|a *v* (-i, -ti, -t) corrupt

spilling *n fem* (-ar) corruption

spillt|ur *adj* (-, -) corrupt

spínat *n neu* (-s) spinach

spír|a *n fem* (-u, -ur, ~) sprout

spír|i *n masc* (-a, -ar, -a) liquor

spítal|i *n masc* (-a, -ar, -a) hospital

spjaldtölv|a *n fem* (-u, -ur, ~) e-tablet

spjall *n neu* (-s, spjöll, -a) talk, chat, small talk

spjalla *v* (~, -ði, -ð) chat, talk

spjallrás *n fem* (-ar, -ir, -a) *comp* chat room

spjót *n neu* (-s, -, -a) spear, lance

spjöll *n neu pl* (spjalla) destruction

spjör *n fem* (spjarar, spjarir, spjara) clothing

spor *n neu* (-s, -, -a) track

sporðdrek|i *n masc* (-a, -ar, -a) *zool* scorpion

Sporðdrek|inn *n masc pl* (-ans) *astro* Scorpio

sporð|ur *n masc* (-s, -ar, -a) tail

sportbíl|l *n masc* (-s, -ar, -a) sportscar

sporvagn *n masc* (-s, -ar, -a) streetcar

sporöskjulagað|ur *adj* (-löguð, -) oval

spól|a *n fem* (-u, -ur, ~) cassette, reel, tape

spóla *v* (~, -ði, -ð) ~ **til baka** rewind; ~ **áfram** fast forward

spraut|a 1 *n fem* (-u, -ur, ~) *med* shot, injection; syringe; **2 sprauta** *v* (~, -ði, -ð) inject

sprek *n neu* (-s, -, -a) stick

sprengidag|ur *n masc* (-s) Mardi Gras, Fat Tuesday

sprengigos *n neu* (-s, -, -a) *geol* explosive volcano

sprenging *n fem* (-ar, -ar, -a) boom, explosion

sprengj|a *n fem* (-u, -ur, sprengna) bomb

sprengjuárás *n fem* (-ar, -ir, -a) bombardment

sprengjuhót|un *n fem* (-unar, -anir, -ana) bomb threat

sprett|ur *n masc* (-s, -ir, -a) run

sprey *n neu* (-s, -, -ja) spray

spreyja *v* (~, -ði, -ð) spray

spring|a *v* (-, sprakk, sprungum, sprungið) explode, burst; ~ **út** bloom

sprotafyrirtæk|i *n neu* (-is, ~, -ja) startup company

sprung|a *n fem* (-u, -ur, -na) crack, rift

sprungin|n *adj* (-, sprungið) cracked

spurning *n fem* (-ar, -ar, -a) question

spurningakeppn|i *n fem* (-i, -ir, -a) quiz show

spurningalist|i *n masc* (-a, -ar, -a) questionnaire

spún|n *n masc* (-s, -ar, -a) spinner

spyrj|a *v* (spyr, spurði, spurt) ask

spyrj|ast *v* (spyrst, spurðist, spurst) ~ **fyrir** ask around; ~ **út** the news gets out

spægipyls|a *n fem* (-u, -ur, ~) salami

spænsk|a *n fem* (-u) Spanish language

spænsk|ur *adj* (-, -t) Spanish

spörfugl *n masc* (-s, -ar, -a) *zool* sparrow

Srí Lanka *N neu* (-s) Sri Lanka

Srí Lanka-mað|ur *N masc* (-manns, -menn, -manna) Sri Lankan *(person)*

srílansk|ur *adj* (srílönsk, -t) Sri Lankan

stað|a *n fem* (stöðu, stöður, -na) position, rank, status, situation

staðal|l *n masc* (-s, staðlar, staðla) standard

staðbundin|n *adj* (-, -bundið) regional

staðfest|a *v* (-i, -i, -) confirm, affirm, validate

staðfesting *n fem* (-ar, -ar, -a) confirmation, affirmation

staðfugl *n masc* (-s, -ar, -a) local bird

staðgengil|l *n masc* (-s, -genglar, -gengla) substitute

staðhæf|a *v* (-i, -ði, -t) claim

staðhæfing *n fem* (-ar, -ar, -a) claim, statement

staðlað|ur *adj* (stöðluð, -) standard, standardized

staðnað|ur *adj* (stöðnuð, -) stale; not developing, makes no progress

staðreynd *n fem* (-ar, -ir, -a) fact

staðsetj|a *v* (-set, -setti, -sett) locate

staðsetning *n fem* (-ar, -ar, -a) location

staðsett|ur *adj* (-, -) located

stað|ur *n masc* (-ar, -ir, -a) place, site

stafa *v* (~, -ði, -ð) spell

stafróf *n neu* (-s, -, -a) alphabet

stafræn|n *adj* (-, -t) digital: **stafræn myndavél** digital camera; ~ **tökuvél** digital camcorder

stafsetj|a *v* (-set, -setti, -sett) spell

stafsetning *n fem* (-ar) spelling

stafsetningarvill|a *n fem* (-u, -ur, -na) spelling mistake

staf|ur *n masc* (-s, -ir, -a) letter; staff, rod

stag *n neu* (-s, stög, -a) guy rope

stakk|ur *n masc* (-s, -ar, -a) light jacket

stak|ur *adj* (stök, -t) single
stand|a *v* (stend, stóð, stóðum, staðið) stand
stand|ast *v refl* (stenst, stóðst, stóðumst, staðist) stand off, resist
stans 1 *n neu* (-) stop; **2** *interj* stop!
stansa *v* (~, -ði, -ð) stop
stapp *n neu* (-s, stöpp, -a) stamp
stappa *v* (~, -ði, -ð) stamp, tramp, mash
stappað|ur *adj* (stöppuð, -) mashed: **stappaðar kartöflur** mashed potatoes
star|a *v* (-i, -ði, -að) stare
starf *n neu* (-s, störf, -a) work, job, occupation
starfa *v* (~, -ði, -ð) work
starfandi *adj* working
starfsferil|l *n masc* (-s) career
starfsfólk *n neu* (-s) personnel, staff, employees
starfslið *n neu* (-s) workforce
starfslýsing *n fem* job description
starfsmað|ur *n masc* (-manns, -menn, -manna) employee, worker
starfsreynsl|a *n fem* (-u) job experience
starr|i *n masc* (-a, -ar, -a) starling
start *n neu* (-s, stört, -a) *mech* ignition
starta *v* (~, -ði, -ð) start; start a car
startkapal|l *n masc* (-as, -kaplar, -kapla) *mech* jumper cables
stauk|ur *n masc* (-s, -ar, -a) shaker for salt or pepper
staup *n neu* (-s, -, -a) goblet
staur *n masc* (-s, -ar, -a) stake, pole
stál *n neu* (-s) steel
stefn|a 1 *n fem* (-u, -ur, ~) aim; **2** *v* (-i, -di, -t) aim, set a direction; **~ á** head towards
stefnand|i *n masc* (-a, -endur, -enda) *leg* plaintiff
stefnulaus *adj* (-, -t) aimless
stefnumót *n neu* (-s, -, -a) date, rendezvous
stefnuskrá *n fem* (-r, -r, -a) platform: **~ flokksins** platform of the party
stefnuyfirlýsing *n fem* (-ar, -ar, -a) manifesto

steik *n fem* (-ur, -ur, -a) roast; steak
steik|ja *v* (steiki, steikti, steikt) fry; roast
steikt|ur *adj* (-, -) fried: **steiktar kartöflur** potato fries
steinbít|ur *n masc* (-s, -ar, -a) *zool* rock salmon, wolffish
steind|ur *adj* (-, steint) **~ gluggi** stained-glass window
steinefn|i *n neu* (-is, ~, -a) minerals
Steingeit|in *n fem def* (-urinnar) *astro* Capricorn
steingerving|ur *n masc* (-s, -ar, -a) fossil
steinlaus *adj* (-, -t) pitted, seedless
stein|n *n masc* (-s, -ar, -a) stone, rock; kernel; seed
steinolí|a *n fem* (-u) paraffin
steinselj|a *n fem* (-u) parsley
steinsteyp|a *n fem* (-u) cement
steinsug|a *n fem* (-u, -ur, a) *zool* lamprey eel
stel|a *v* (-, stal, stálum, stolið) steal
stel|ast *v* (-st, stalst, stálumst, stolist) sneak, do something secretly
stelling *n fem* (-ar, -ar, -a) position, pose, posture
stelp|a *n fem* (-u, -ur, -na) girl
sterkj|a *n fem* (-u) starch
sterklega *adv* strongly
sterk|ur *adj* (-, -t) strong: **~ drykkur** strong drink; spicy; **sterk sósa** hot sauce
stert|ur *n masc* (-s, -ar, -a) tail
steyp|a 1 *n fem* (-u) concrete; **2** *v* (-i, -ti, -t) to build with concrete: **~ tröppur** make concrete stairs; **3** *v* **~ sér** plunge
steypireyð|ur *n fem* (-ar, -ir, -a) *zool* blue whale
steypujárn *n neu* (-s, -, -a) cast iron
stél *n neu* (-s, -, -a) tail
stétt *n fem* (-ar, -ir, -a) class; pavement
stig *n neu* (-s, -, -a) score; stage, phase
stigagang|ur *n masc* (-s, -ar, -a) stairwell
stig|i *n masc* (-a, -ar, -a) stairs; ladder

stigmagna|st *v* (~, -ðist, ~) escalate
stigvaxandi *adj* escalating
stilk|ur *n masc* (-s, -ar, -a) stem of a flower
still|a *v* (-i, -ti, -t) align, adjust; *mus* tune
stilling *n fem* (-ar, -ar, -a) alignment, adjustment; poise
still|ir *n masc* (-is, -ar, -a) regulator
stimpilklukk|a *n fem* (-u, -ur, -na) time clock
stimpil|l *n masc* (-s, stimplar, stimpla) stamp
stimpla *v* (~, -ði, -ð) stamp
sting|a *v* (-, stakk, stungum, stungið) sting; prick
sting|ur *n masc* (-s, -ir, -ja) sting
stinn|ur *adj* (-, -t) firm
stirnd|ur *adj* (-, stirnt) starry
stífkramp|i *n masc* (-a) *med* tetanus
stífl|a *n fem* (-u, -ur, -na) blockage; dam
stíflað|ur *adj* (stífluð, -) blocked, clogged
stíf|ur *adj* (-, -t) stiff, rigid
stíg|a *v* (-, steig, stigum, stigið) step
stíg|ur *n masc* (-s, -ar, -a) path, track
stígvél *n neu* (-s, -, -a) boot
stíla *v* (~, -ði, -ð) address
stílabók *n fem* (-ar, -bækur, -a) notebook
stílist|i *n masc* (-a, -ar, -a) stylist
stíl|l *n masc* (-s, -ar, -a) style; *med* suppository
stílræn|n *adj* (-, -t) stylistic
stjarf|ur *adj* (-stjörf, -t) rigid
stjarn|a *n fem* (stjörnu, stjörnur, ~) star, asterisk
stjórn *n fem* (-ar, -ir, -a) administration, board, council, management, board of trustees, regime, control
stjórna *v* (~, -ði, -ð) control, steer; regulate; *mus* conduct: ~ **hljómsveit** conduct an orchestra
stjórnand|i *n masc* (-a, -endur, -enda) manager, operator; *mus* conductor
stjórnarandstað|a *n fem* (-stöðu, -stöður, ~) opposition

stjórnarandstæðing|ur *n masc* (-s, -ar, -a) member of the opposition
stjórnarerindrek|i *n masc* (-a, -ar, -a) diplomat
stjórnarfund|ur *n masc* (-ar, -ir, -a) council meeting; board meeting
stjórnarskrá *n fem* (-r, -r, -a) *leg* constitution
stjórnarstefn|a *n fem* (-u, -ur, ~) government policy
stjórnborð|i *n masc* (-a) starboard
stjórnleysing|i *n masc* (-ja, -jar, -ja) anarchist
stjórnmál *n neu pl* (-a) politics
stjórnmálaflokk|ur *n masc* (-s, -ar, -a) political party
stjórnmálaleg|ur *adj* (-, -t) political
stjórnmálamað|ur *n masc* (-manns, -menn, -manna) politician
stjórnsam|ur *adj* (-söm, -t) possessive
stjórnskipunarrétt|ur *n masc* (-ar) *leg* constitutional law
stjórnun *n fem* (-ar) leadership, lead, supervision; regulation; **stjórnunarkostnaður** administrative cost; **stjórnunarsvæði** administrative district
stjúpbarn *n neu* (-s, -börn, -a) stepchild
stjúpbróð|ir *n masc* (-ur, -bræður, -bræðra) stepbrother
stjúpdótt|ir *n masc* (-ur, -dætur, dætra) stepdaughter
stjúpfað|ir *n masc* (-föður, -feður, -feðra) stepfather
stjúpmóð|ir *n masc* (-ur, -mæður, -mæðra) stepmother
stjúpsyst|ir *n fem* (-ur, -ur, -ra) stepsister
stjúpson|ur *n masc* (-ar, -synir, -sona) stepson
stjörnuathugunarstöð *n fem* (-var, -var, -va) astronomical observatory
stjörnubjart|ur *adj* (-björt, -) starlit
stjörnufisk|ur *n masc* (-s, -ar, -a) *zool* starfish
stjörnufræði *n fem* (-) astrology
stjörnuhrap *n neu* (-s, -hröp, -a) meteor

stjörnukík|ir *n masc* (-is, -jar, -ja)
telescope
stjörnulaga *adj* star-shaped
stjörnumerk|i *n neu* (-is, ~, -ja)
astro zodiac
stoð *n fem* (-ar, -ir, -a) support
stof|a *n fem* (-u, -ur, ~) living room
stofn *n masc* (-s, -ar, -a) stem
stofna *v* (~, -ði, -ð) establish, start,
open up, found
stofnand|i *n masc* (-a, -endur, -enda)
founder
stofnsáttmál|i *n masc* (-a, -ar, -a)
charter
stofn|un *n fem* (-unar, -anir, -ana)
institute
Stokkhólm|ur *N masc* (-s) Stockholm
(capital of Sweden)
stolin|n *adj* (-, stolið) stolen
stolt *n neu* (-s) pride
stolt|ur *adj* (-, -) proud
stopp 1 *n neu* (-s, -, -a) stop; **2** *interj*
halt!
stoppa *v* (~, -ði, -ð) stop
storkandi *adj* provocative
storknað|ur *adj* (storknuð, -) congealed
stork|ur *n masc* (-s, -ar, -a) stork
stormasam|ur *adj* (-söm, -t) stormy
storm|ur *n masc* (-s, -ar, -a) blizzard
stormviðvör|un *n fem* (-unar, -anir,
-ana) storm warning
stóðhest|ur *n masc* (-s, -ar, -a) *zool*
stallion, stud
stóla *v colloq* (~, -ði, -ð) ~ **á** rely on
stól|l *n masc* (-s, -ar, -a) chair
stólp|i *n masc* (-a, -ar, -a) stake, pole
stór *adj* (-, -t) large, big
stóra bóla *n fem med* smallpox
Stóra-Bretland *N neu* (-s) Great
Britain
stórborg *n fem* (-ar, -ir, -a) big city,
metropolis
stórhríð *n fem* (-ar, -ir, -a) snowstorm
stórhýs|i *n neu* (-is, ~, -a) mansion
stórkostleg|ur *adj* (-, -t) fantastic,
terrific, awsome
stórlúð|a *n fem* (-u, -ur, -a) halibut

stórmarkað|ur *n masc* (-ar/s, -ir, -a)
supermarket
straff *n neu* (-s, ströff, -a) punishment
straffa *v* (~, -ði, -ð) punish, penalize
strandvörð|ur *n masc* (-varðar, -verðir,
-varða) beach guard, lifeguard
stranglega *adv* strictly
strangtrúað|ur *adj* (-trúuð, -)
orthodox
strang|ur *adj* (ströng, -t) strict, severe,
austere, rigorous
strauja *v* (~, -ði, -ð) iron (clothing)
straujárn *n neu* (-s, -, -a) iron
straumbreyt|ir *n masc* (-is, -ar, -a)
transformer, adapter
straum|ur *n masc* (-s, -ar, -a) stream,
current
strax *adv* right now, right away
strák|ur *n masc* (-s, -ar, -a) boy
strásykur *n masc* (-s) granulated
sugar
strá 1 *n neu* (-s, -, -a) straw; **2** *v* (-i,
-ði, -ð) scatter, sprinkle
streit|a *n fem* (-u) stress
streituvaldandi *adj* stressful, causes
stress
strekkt|ur *adj* (-, -) tense, tight
strengjabaun *n fem* (-ar, -ir, -a)
green beans
strengjahljóðfær|i *n neu* (-is, ~, -a)
mus string instrument
strengjakvartett *n masc* (-s, -ar, -a)
mus string quartet
strengjasveit *n fem* (-ar, -ir, -a) *mus*
string orchestra
streng|ur *n masc* (-s, -ir, -ja) string
stress *n neu* (-) stress
stressað|ur *adj* (stressuð, -) stressed
stressandi *adj* stressful
streym|a *v* (-i, -di, -t) stream
strig|i *n masc* (-a, -ar, -a) canvas
strik *n neu* (-s, -, -a) line
strimil|l *n masc* (-s, strimlar, strimla)
slip
strita *v* (~, -ði, -ð) struggle
stríð *n neu* (-s, -, -a) war
stríð|a *v* (-i, stríddi, strítt) tease

strjúk|a v (strýk, strauk, strukum, strokið) stroke; run away, escape

stroka v (~, -ði, -ð) ~ **út** erase

strokleður n neu (-s, -, -leðra) eraser

stromp|ur n masc (-s, -ar, -a) chimney

strút|ur n masc (-s, -ar, -a) zool ostrich

stræt|i n neu (-is, ~, -a) street

strætó n masc (-s, -ar, -a) colloq bus

strætóbílstjór|i n masc (-a, -ar, -a) busdriver

strætóstopp n neu (-s, -, -a) bus stop

strætóstöð n fem (-var, -var, -va) bus terminal

strönd n fem (strandar, strandir, stranda) beach, seashore

stuðar|i n masc (-a, -ar, -a) bumper, fender

stuðla v (~, -ði, -ð) contribute; ~ **að** stimulate, encourage, cause

stuðlaberg n neu (-s) geol basalt column, columnar basalt

stuðningsmað|ur n masc (-manns, -menn, -manna) supporter

stuðning|ur n masc (-s) support

stund n fem (-ar, -ir, -a) hour; time; while

stunda v (~, -ði, -ð) pursue, practice on a regular basis

stundatafl|a n fem (-töflu, töflur, -taflna) timetable

stundum adv sometimes

stundvís adj (-, -t) punctual

stundvísi n fem (-) punctuality

stung|a n fem (-u, -ur, -na) prick; sting

sturt|a n fem (-u, -ur, ~) shower; ~ **niður** flush

stuttbux|ur n fem pl (-na) shorts

stuttermabol|ur n masc (-s, -ir, -a) t-shirt

stutt|ur adj (-, -) short

stúdent n masc (-s, -ar, -a) university student; graduate from high school

stúdentagarð|ur n masc (-s, -ar, -a) student house, dormitory

stúdíó n neu (-s, -, -a) studio

stúlk|a n fem (-u, -ur, -na) girl

styðja v (styð, studdi, stutt) support, aid

styðjast v refl (styðst, studdist, stuðst) ~ **við** be based on, make reference to

stygg|ur adj (-, -t) skittish

stykk|i n neu (-is, ~, -ja) piece

styrj|a n fem (-u, -ur, ~) beluga, sturgeon

styrjuhrogn n neu pl (-a) beluga caviar

styrjöld n fem (-aldar, -aldir, -alda) war

styrking n fem (-ar, -ar, -a) reinforcement

styrkj|a v (styrki, styrkti, styrkt) reinforce; sponsor

styrktaraðil|i n masc (-a, -ar, -a) sponsor

styrkt|ur adj (-, -) fortified

styrk|ur n masc (-s, -ir, -ja) strength, potency

stytt|a n fem (-u, -ur, -na) statue

stýr|a v (-i, -ði, -t) control, direct

stýr|i n neu (-is, ~, -a) steering wheel

stýripinn|i n masc (-a, -ar, -a) comp joystick

stækka v (~, -ði, -ð) enlarge

stærð n fem (-ar, -ir, -a) size

stærðfræði n fem (-) mathematics

stærr|i adj compar (-i, -a) larger, bigger

stöð n fem (-var, -var, -va) station

stöðl|un n fem (staðlanir) standardization

stöðn|un n fem (-unar) stagnation

stöðnunarverðbólg|a n fem (-u) econ stagflation

stöðugleik|i n masc (-a) stability

stöðug|ur adj (-, -t) stable, constant, steady

stöðuhækk|un n fem (-unar, -anir, -ana) promotion

stöðumælasekt n fem (-ar, -ir, -a) parking ticket

stöðumæl|ir n masc (-is, -ar, -a) parking meter

stöðuvatn *n neu* (-s, -vötn, -a) lake

stöðva *v* (~, -ði, -ð) stop

stöðvunarskilt|i *n neu* (-is, ~, -a) stop sign

stökk *n neu* (-s, -, -a) jump, leap

stökkbrett|i *n neu* (-is, ~, -a) diving board

stökkbreyting *n fem* (-ar, -ar, -a) *bio* mutation

stökk|ur (-, -t) *adj* crunchy

stökk|va *v* (stekk, stökk, stukkum, stokkið) jump, leap

stöng *n fem* (stangar, stangir, stanga) stick, staff, rod

suð|a *n fem* (-u, -ur, ~) boil *(in cooking)*

suðaustur *adv* southeast

Suðausturland *n neu* (-s) southeast Iceland

suðræn|n *adj* (-, -t) southern: **suðræn lönd** southern countries

suður *adv* south

Suður-Afríka *N fem* (-u) South Africa

Suður-Afríkan|i *n masc* (-a, -ar, -a) South African *(person)*

suður-afrísk|ur *adj* (-, -t) South African

Suður-Ameríkan|i *n masc* (-a, -ar, -a) South American *(person)*

suður-ameríkansk|ur *adj* (-ameríkönsk, -t) South American

Suður-Kóre|a *N fem* (-u) South Korea

Suðurland *N neu* (-s) south Iceland

Suður-Súdan *N neu* (-/s) South Sudan

suðutæk|i *n neu* (-is, ~, -ja) cooker

sukk *n neu* (-s) revelry

sukkar|i *n masc* (-a, -ar, -a) reveler

sult|a *n fem* (-u, -ur, ~) jam, preserves

sult|ur *n masc* (-ar/s) starvation, hunger

sumar *n neu* (-s, sumur, sumra) summer

sumaráætl|un *n fem* (-unar, -anir, -ana) summer schedule

sumarfrí *n neu* (-s, -, -a) summer holiday

sumarjafndægur *n neu pl* (-s, -, -dægra) summer solstice

summ|a *n fem* (-u, -ur, ~) sum

sum|ir *pron* (-ar, -) some, some people: ~ **nenna ekki að vakna snemma** some people don't want to wake up early

sund *n neu* (-s, -, -a) swim; *geog* channel

sundföt *n neu pl* (-fata) swimsuit

sundla *v* (~, -ði, -ð) feel dizzy

sundlaug *n fem* (-ar, -ar, -a) swimming pool

sundlaugarvörð|ur *n masc* (-varðar, -verðir, -varða) lifeguard at a swimming pool

sundskýl|a *n fem* (-u, -ur, ~) swim trunks

sundurliða *v* (~, -ði, -ð) itemize

sundurliðað|ur *adj* (-liðuð, -) itemized: ~ **reikningur** itemized bill

sunnan 1 *adv* south: **að ~** from the south, **fyrir ~** in the south; **2** *prep* south of: ~ **fjalls** on the south side of the mountain

sunnlensk|ur *adj* (-, -t) southern

sunnudag|ur *n masc* (-s, -ar, -a) Sunday

sushi *n neu* (-s) sushi

sú. *See* **sá**

Súdan *N neu* (-) Sudan

Súdan|i *N masc* (-a, -ar/ir, -a) Sudanese *(person)*

súdansk|ur *adj* (súdönsk, -t) Sudanese

súkkulað|i *n neu* (-is, ~, -a) chocolate

súkkulaðikak|a *n fem* (-köku, -kökur, -kakna) chocolate cake; brownie

súkkulaðisós|a *n fem* (-u, -ur, ~) chocolate syrup

súkkulaðistykk|i *n neu* (-is, ~, -ja) chocolate bar

súkkulaðitruffl|a *n fem* (-u, -ur, -na) chocolate truffles

súl|a *n fem* (-u, -ur, -na) pole, pillar; *zool* gannet

súltan rúsín|a *n fem* (-u, -ur, ~) sultana, raisin

súp|a dagsins *phr* soup of the day

súp|a *n fem* (-u, -ur, -na) soup

súpudisk|ur *n masc* (-s, -ar, -a) soup bowl

súputening|ur *n masc* (-s, -ar, -a) bouillon cube

súr *adj* (-, -t) sour, acidy

súrdeigsbrauð *n neu* (-s, -, -a) sourdough bread

súrefni *n neu* (-s) oxygen

súrefnisgrím|a *n fem* (-u, -ur, -na) oxygen mask

súrhey *n neu* (-s) silage

Súrínam *N neu* (-) Surinam

súrkál *n neu* (-s) sauerkraut

súrmjólk *n fem* (-ur) buttermilk

súrna *v* (~, -ði, -ð) turn sour; smart

súrsa *v* (~, -ði, -ð) pickle

svahílí *n neu* (-) Swahili

svakalega *adv* terribly

svaladrykk|ur *n masc* (-jar, -ir, -ja) refreshment

sval|ir *n fem pl* (-a) balcony

svall *n neu* (-s, svöll, -a) revelry

sval|ur *adj* (svöl, -t) cool

svampbotn *n masc* (-s, -ar, -a) bottom for a sponge cake

svamp|ur *n masc* (-s, -ar, -a) sponge

svang|ur *adj* (svöng, -t) hungry

svan|ur *n masc* (-s, -ir, -a) *zool* swan

svar *n neu* (-s, svör, -a) answer, reply, response

svara *v* (~, -ði, -ð) answer, reply, respond

Svartahaf *N neu* (-s) Black Sea

svartbaun *n fem* (-ar, -ir, -a) black bean

Svartfjallaland *N neu* (-s) Montenegro

svartsýni *n fem* (-) pessimism

svartsýnismað|ur *n masc* (-manns, -menn, -manna) pessimist

svartsýn|n *adj* (-, -t) pessimistic

Svasíland *N neu* (-s) Swaziland

svefn *n masc* (-s) sleep

svefnherberg|i *n neu* (~s, ~, -ja) bedroom

svefnleysi *n neu* (-s) insomnia

svefnpok|i *n masc* (-a, -ar, -a) sleeping bag

svefnsýki *n fem* (~) sleeping sickness

svefntöfl|ur *n fem pl* (-taflna) sleeping pills

sveifl|a *n fem* (-u, -ur, -na) swing

sveifla *v* (~, -ði, -ð) swing

sveigjanleg|ur *adj* (-, -t) flexible

sveigjanleik|i *n masc* (-a) flexibility

sveit *n fem* (-ar, -ir, -a) country side: **búa í ~** live in the country side; rural area; *mus* band

sveitabæ|r *n masc* (-jar, -ir, -ja) farm

sveitarfélag *n neu* (-s, -félög, -a) municipality

sveitatónlist *n fem* (-ar) *mus* country music

svelt|a *v* (svelt, svalt, sultum, soltið) starve

svengd *n fem* (-ar) hunger; starvation

sveppasós|a *n fem* (-u, -ur, ~) mushroom sauce

svepp|ur *n masc* (-s, -ir, -a) fungus, mushroom

sverð *n neu* (-s, -, -a) sword

sverðfisk|ur *n masc* (-s, -ar, -a) swordfish

sverj|a *v* (sver, sór, sórum, svarið) swear

sveskj|a *n fem* (-u, -ur, sveskna) prune

svið *n neu* (-s, -, -a) **1** domain, scope, stage; **2** charred lamb heads *(Icelandic specialty)*

sviðna *v* (~, -ði, -ð) singe

sviðsmynd *n fem* (-ar, -ir, -a) *(film, theater)* scene

sviðsstjór|i *n masc* (-a, -ar, -a) stage manager

svifdrek|i *n masc* (-a, -ar, -a) hang glider

svifflug|a *n fem* (-u, -ur, -na) glider

svig *n neu* (-s) *sports* slalom

svig|i *n masc* (-a, -ar, -a) parenthesis

svigrúm *n neu* (-s) space, elbow-room

svigskíði *n neu pl* downhill skiing

svik *n neu pl* (-a) betrayal
svikahrapp|ur *n masc* (-s, -ar, -a) betrayer, impostor
svim|i *n masc* (-a) faint, dizziness
svindl *n neu* (-s) fraud
svindla *v* (~, -ði, -ð) cheat
svindlar|i *n masc* (-a, -ar, -a) cheater, swindler
svip|a *n fem* (-u, -ur, ~) whip
svipað|ur *adj* (svipuð, -) alike, similar
svip|ur *n masc* (-s, -ir, -a) likeness, similarity, resemblance; phantom
Sviss *N neu* (~) Switzerland
svissnesk|ur *adj* (-, -t) Swiss
svitahol|a *n fem* (-u, -ur, ~) *anat* pore
svitalyktareyð|ir *n masc* (-is, -ar, -a) deodorant
svit|i *n masc* (-a) sweat, perspiration
svitna *v* (~, -ði, -ð) sweat, perspire
svíð|a *v* (-, sveið, sviðum, sviðið) char, sear; smart
Sví|i *N masc* (-a, -ar, -a) Swede *(person from Sweden)*
svíkj|a *v* (svík, sveik, svikum, svikið) betray
svín *n neu* (-s, -, -a) *zool* pig
svínafeiti *n fem* (-) lard
svínakjöt *n neu* (-s) pork
svínakótilett|a *n fem* (-u, -ur, ~) pork chop
svínalær|i *n neu* (-is, ~, -a) pork loin
svínapyls|a *n fem* (-u, -ur, ~) pork sausage
svínasteik *n fem* (-ur, -ur, -a) pork roast
svínastí|a *n fem* (-u, -ur, ~) pigsty
svínavöðv|i *n masc* (-a, -ar, -a) pork fillet
svít|a *n fem* (-u, -ur, ~) suite
Svíþjóð *N fem* (-ar) Sweden
svívirðileg|ur *adj* (-, -t) outrageous
svo *adv* so: **það var ~ gaman** it was so much fun; then: **~ fórum við í sund** then we went to the pool
svolítið *adv* slightly
svona *adv* like that
svunt|a *n fem* (-u, -ur, ~) apron

svæðaskipting *n fem* (-ar, -ar, -a) zoning
svæð|i *n neu* (-is, ~, -a) area, district, part, region, territory, zone
svæðisbundin|n *adj* (-, -bundið) regional
svæðisnúmer *n neu* (-s, -, -a) area code (phone)
svæfing *n fem* (-ar, -ar, ~) *med* narcosis
syfjað|ur *adj* (syfjuð, -) sleepy
sykr|a *n fem* (-u, -ur, ~) carbohydrate
sykrað|ur *adj* (sykruð, -) candied
sykur *n masc* (-s) sugar
sykurlaus *adj* (-, -t) sugar-free; **sykurlaust gos** diet soda
sykurpúð|i *n masc* (-a, -ar, -a) marshmallow
sykursjúkling|ur *n masc* (-s, -ar, -a) *med* diabetic
sykursýki *n fem* (-) *med* diabetes
syll|a *n fem* (-u, -ur, -na) ledge, shelf
symbólism|i *n masc* (-a) *lit* symbolism
synagóg|a *n fem* (-u, -ur, ~) synagogue
synd *n fem* (-ar, -ir, -a) sin
synd|a *v* (-i, synti, synt) swim
syndga *v* (~, -ði, -ð) sin
syngj|a *v* (syng, söng, sungum, sungið) sing
synja *v* (~, -ði, -ð) refuse, rebuff
synj|un *n fem* (-unar, -anir, -ana) refusal, rebuff
syrgj|a *v* (syrgi, syrgði, syrgt) mourn, lament
syrgjand|i *n masc* (-a, -endur, -enda) mourner
syst|ir *n fem* (-ur, -ur, -ra) sister
systkin|i *n neu* (-is, ~, -a) siblings
systurdótt|ir *n fem* (-ur, -dætur, -dætra) niece *(daughter of a sister)*
systurson|ur *n masc* (-ar, -synir, -sona) nephew *(son of a sister)*
sýfilis *n neu* (-/s) *med* syphilis
sýkil|l *n masc* (-s, sýklar, sýkla) germ
sýking *n fem* (-ar, -ar, -a) *med* sepsis, infection, inflammation
sýklalyf *n neu* (-s, -, -ja) *med* antibiotics

sýkna *v* (~, -ði, -ð) *leg* acquit

sýkn|un *n fem* (-unar, -anir, -ana) *leg* acquittal

sýkt|ur *adj* (-, -) *med* infected

sýn *n fem* (-ar, -ir, -a) view, vision

sýn|a *v* (-i, -di, -t) show, exhibit, present, screen

sýndarmennsk|a *n fem* (-u) show-off

sýnileg|ur *adj* (-, -t) visible

sýning *n fem* (-ar, -ar, -a) exhibition, show

sýningarmun|ur *n masc* (-ar, -ir, -a) exhibit

sýningarstjór|i *n masc* (-a, -ar, -a) curator

sýnisbók *n fem* (-ar, -bækur, -a) anthology

sýnishorn *n neu* (-s, -, -a) sample

sýr|a *n fem* (-u, -ur, ~) acid

sýrð|ur *adj* (-, sýrt) sour: ~ **rjómi** sour cream

Sýrland *N neu* (-s) Syria

sýrlensk|ur *adj* (-, -t) Syrian

sýrustig *n neu* (-s, -, -a) *chem* pH

sýsl|a *n fem* (-u, -ur, -na) *administrative unit in Iceland*

sýslumað|ur *n masc* (-manns, -menn, -manna) sheriff

sæð|i *n neu* (-is, ~, -a) semen, sperm

sækj|a *v* (sæki, sótti, sótt) fetch; ~ **um** apply

sækj|ast *v refl* (sækist, sóttist, sóst) progress; **ferðin sóttist vel** the travel went well; ~ **eftir** pursue

sælgæti *n neu* (-is) sweets

sæljón *n neu* (-s, -, -a) *zool* sea lion

sælker|i *n masc* (-a, -ar, -a) gourmand

sæl|l 1 *adj* (-, -t) happy; **2** *excl* hi!

sæluvím|a *n fem* (-u) rapture

sæmd *n fem* (-ar, -ir, -a) honor

sæmilega *adv* all right, okay

sæmileg|ur *adj* (-, -t) okay: **maturinn var** ~ the food was okay

sæng *n fem* (-ur, -ur, ~) duvet

sængurver *n neu* (-s, -, -a) duvet cover

sænsk|a *n fem* (-u) Swedish language

sænsk|ur *adj* (-, -t) Swedish

sær|a *v* (-i, -ði, -t) wound; *(hair)* trim

særandi *adj* hurting

særð|ur *adj* (-, sært) wounded

sæt|i *n neu* (-is, ~, -a) seat

sætt|a *v* (-i, -i, -t) reconcile

sætti|r *n masc* (-s) reconciliation

sætuefn|i *n neu* (-is, ~, -a) sweetener

sæt|ur *adj* (-, -t) sweet, pretty

söfnuð|ur *n masc* (safnaðar, -ir, safnaða) parish

sög *n fem* (sagar, sagir, saga) saw

sögn *n fem* (sagnar, sagnir, sagna) *ling* verb

söguhetj|a *n fem* (-hetju, -hetjur, ~) *lit* protagonist

söguleg|ur *adj* (-, -t) historic: **söguleg bygging** historic building, ~ **staður** historic site

sögumað|ur *n masc* (-manns, -menn, -manna) *lit* narrator

sögusvið *n neu* (-s, -, -a) *lit* scene, setting, stage

söguþráð|ur *n masc* (-ar, -þræðir, -þráða) *lit* plot

sökk|va *v* (sekk, sökk, sukkum, sokkið) sink

sökum *prep + gen* because of, due to: ~ **aldurs** due to old age

söl *n neu pl* (-va) *bio* red dulse *(an edible red alga)*

söltun *n fem* (-ar) curing

söluaðil|i *n masc* (-a, -ar, -a) dealer, vendor

sölulaun *n neu pl* (-a) sales commission

sölumað|ur *n masc* (-manns, -menn, -manna) salesman, merchant

söluskatt|ur *n masc* (-s, -ar, -a) sales tax

sölutorg *n neu* (-s, -, -a) market square

söluvar|a *n fem* (-vöru, -vörur, ~) merchandise

söluvarning|ur *n masc* (-s) merchandise

söngleik|ur *n masc* (-s, -ir, -ja) musical

söngnám *n neu* (-s) singing lessons

söngtext|i *n masc* (-a, -ar, -a) *mus*
  lyrics
söng|ur *n masc* (-s, -var, -va) singing
söngvar|i *n masc* (-a, -ar, -a) singer
sönn|un *n fem* (-unar, sannanir,
  sannana) proof

sönnunarbyrð|i *n fem* (-i/-ar) *leg*
  burden of proof
sönnunargagn *n neu* (-s, -gögn, -a)
  leg proof; exhibit

T

tabasco sós|a *n fem* (-u, -ur, -a) tabasco sauce

tabú *n neu* (-s, ~, -a) taboo

tað *n neu* (-s) pressed manure used as fuel

Tadsíkistan *N neu* (-) Tajikistan

tadsíksk|ur *adj* (-, -t) Tajikistan

tafarlaus *adj* (-, -t) immediate

tafarlaust *adv* promptly, immediately

tafl|a *n fem* (töflu, töflur, -na) table, chart, board; *med* tablet, pill

taflborð *n neu* (-s, -, -a) chessboard

taflsett *n neu* (-s, -, -a) chess set

tagl *n neu* (-s, tögl, -a) tail

taílensk|ur *adj* (-, -t) Taiwanese

Taívan *N neu* (-) Taiwan

tak *n neu* (-s, tök, -a) hold

tak|a *v* (tek, tók, tókum, tekið) take; ~ **þátt** participate; ~ **upp** record; ~ **út** withdraw; ~ **við** receive

takk *interj* thanks!; ~ **fyrir** thanks

takk|i *n masc* (-a, -ar, -a) button

takmark *n neu* (-s, -mörk, -a) aim, objective; limit

takmarka *v* (~, -ði, -ð) limit, restrict

takmarkað|ur *adj* (-mörkuð, -) limited, restricted

takmörk *n neu pl* limits

takmörk|un *n fem* (-unar, -markanir, -markana) limitation, restriction

taktfast|ur *adj* (-föst, -) rhythmic

takt|ur *n masc* (-s, -ar, -a) *mus* beat, rhythm

tal *n neu* (-s) talk

tal|a 1 *n fem* (tölu, tölur, -na) number; **2 tala** *v* (~, -ði, -ð) talk, speak

talað|ur *adj* (töluð, -) spoken

talin|n *adj* (-, talið) presumed

Tallinn *n fem* (-) Tallinn *(capital of Estonia)*

talning *n fem* (-ar, -ar, -a) count

talsetj|a *v* (-set, -setti, -sett) dub

talsett|ur *adj* (-, -) dubbed: **talsett teiknimynd** dubbed cartoon

talsmað|ur *n masc* (-manns, -menn, -manna) spokesperson

talstöð *n fem* (-var, -var, -va) radio, walkie-talkie

talsverð|ur *adj* (-, -vert) substantial

talþjálfun *n fem* (-ar) speech therapy

tangó *n masc* (-s, -ar, -a) tango

tank|ur *n masc* (-s, -ar, -a) tank

tannburst|i *n masc* (-a, -ar, -a) toothbrush

tannfræðing|ur *n masc* (-s, -ar, -a) dental hygienist

tannheils|a *n fem* (-u) dental care

tannkrem *n neu* (-s, -, -a) toothpaste

tannlækn|ir *n masc* (-is, -ar, -a) dentist

tannpín|a *n fem* (-u) toothache

tannskemmd *n fem* (-ar, -ir, -a) cavity, dental decay

tannstöngul|l *n masc* (-s, -stönglar, -stöngla) toothpick

tanntak|a *n fem* (-töku, -tökur, ~) teething

tannþráð|ur *n masc* (-ar, -þræðir, -þráða) dental floss

Tansan|i *n masc* (-a, -ar/ir, -a) Tanzanian *(person)*

Tansaní|a *N fem* (-u) Tanzania

tansanísk|ur *adj* (-, -t) Tanzanian

tap *n neu* (-s, töp, -a) loss, defeat, deficit

tapa *v* (~, -ði, -ð) lose, defeat

tapíókamjöl *n neu* (-s) tapioca

taplið *n neu* (-s, -, -a) losing team

tappatogar|i *n masc* (-a, -ar, -a) corkscrew

tapp|i *n masc* (-a, -ar, -a) plug, top, stopper

taró *n neu* (-s) taro

tartarasós|a *n fem* (-u, -ur, ~) tartar sauce

task|a *n fem* (tösku, töskur, ~) bag, purse

tattú *n neu* (-s, -, -a) tattoo

taug *n fem* (-ar, -ar, -a) nerve

taugaáfall *n neu* (-s, -föll, -a) *med* nervous breakdown

taugafræði *n fem* (-) *med* neurology

taugafrum|a *n fem* (-u, -ur, ~) *bio* neutron

taugafræðing|ur *n masc* (-s, -ar, -a) *med* neurologist

taugakerf|i *n neu* (-is, ~, -a) *anat* nervous system

taugaóstyrk|ur *adj* (-, -t) nervous, tense

taugaspenn|a *n fem* (-u) tension

taugaveiklað|ur *adj* (-veikluð, -) nervous

taugaveiklun *n fem* (-ar) nervousness

tauta *v* (~, -ði, -ð) mutter

tá *n fem* (-r, tær, -a) toe

tákn *n neu* (-s, -, -a) sign, signal, symbol, token

tákna *v* (~, -ði, -ð) mean, symbolize

táknmál *n neu* (-s, -, -a) sign language

táknræn|n *adj* (-, -t) *lit* symbolic

táknsæisstefn|a *n fem* (-u) *lit* symbolism

tálga *v* (~, -ði, -ð) carve

táning|ur *n masc* (-s, -ar, -a) teenager

tár *n neu* (-s, -, -a) tear

te *n neu* (-s, -, -a) tea

tefj|a *v* (tef, tafði, tafið) delay, hold up

tegund *n fem* (-ar, -ir, -a) kind, sort, type; breed, species

teikna *v* (~, -ði, -ð) draw, depict

teiknaður *adj* (teiknuð, -) animated

teiknimynd *n fem* (-ar, -ir, -a) cartoon

teiknimyndablað *n neu* (-s, -blöð, -a) comic paper

teikning *n fem* (-ar, -ar, -a) drawing

tein|n *n masc* (-s, -ar, -a) rail, skewer

tekj|ur *n fem pl* (tekna) earnings, income

tekjuskatt|ur *n masc* (-s, -ar, -a) *econ* income tax

telj|a *v* (tel, taldi, talið) count; presume; reckon, think: **ég tel að þetta sé rétt** I think that this is right

teljanleg|ur *adj* (-, -t) countable

teljar|i *n masc* (-a, -ar, -a) *math* numerator

tengdadótt|ir *n fem* (-ur, -dætur, -dætra) daughter-in-law

tengdafað|ir *n masc* (-föður, -feður, -feðra) father-in-law

tengdamamm|a *n fem* (-mömmu, -mömmur, -mamma) **1** *colloq* mother-in-law; **2** staple remover

tengdamóð|ir *n fem* (-ur, -mæður, -mæðra) mother-in-law

tengdapabb|i *n masc* (-a, -ar, -a) *colloq* father-in-law

tengdason|ur *n masc* (-ar, -synir, -sona) son-in-law

tengd|ur *adj* (-, tengt) *comp* connected, online

tengikví *n fem* (-ar, -ar, -a) *comp* docking cradle

tengil|l *n masc* (-s, tenglar, tengla) *comp* hyperlink

tenging *n fem* (-ar, -ar, -a) connection

tengivagn *n masc* (-s, -ar, -a) trailer

tengj|a *v* (tengi, tengdi, tengt) link, connect, relate

tengj|ast *v refl* (tengist, tengdist, tengst) associate, bond, relate

tengsl *n neu pl* (-a) affiliation, relation

tengslanet *n neu* (-s, -, -a) network

tening|ur *n masc* (-s, -ar, -a) dice; cube

tennis *n neu* (-) tennis

tennisolnbog|i *n masc* (-a, -ar, -a) *med* tennis elbow

tennisvöll|ur *n masc* (-vallar, -vellir, -valla) tennis court

tenór *n masc* (-s, -ar, -a) *mus* tenor

tepp|i *n neu* (-is, ~, -a) blanket; carpet

tert|a *n fem* (-u, -ur, -na) cake, torte

teskeið *n fem* (-ar, -ir, -a) teaspoon

testof|a *n fem* (-u, -ur, ~) tearoom

textafræði *n fem* (-) philology
textafræðileg|ur *adj* (-, -t) philological
textafræðing|ur *n masc* (-s, -ar, -a) philologist
text|i *n masc* (-a, -ar, -a) text
teygj|a *v* (teygi, teygði, teygt) stretch; rubber band
teygjanleg|ur *adj* (-, -t) elastic
teygjubind|i *n neu* (-is, ~, -a) elastic support bandage
teygjustökk *n neu* (-s, -, -a) bungee-jumping
Tékk|i *n masc* (-a, -ar, -a) Czech
Tékkland *N neu* (-s) Czech Republic
tékknesk|a *n fem* (-u) Czech language
tékknesk|ur *adj* (-, -t) Czech
tif *n neu* (-s, -, -a) tick
til *prep* + *gen* to: *(traveling)* fljúga ~ **Íslands** fly to Iceland, keyra ~ **Reykjavíkur** drive to Reykjavik; *(gifts etc)* to: ~ **mömmu** to mom; ~ **dæmis** for example; ~ **hliðar** aside, sideways
tilboð *n neu* (-s, -, -a) offer, special offer
tilbrigð|i *n neu* (-is, ~, -a) variation
tilbúin|n *adj* (-, tilbúið) ready
tilbúning|ur *n masc* (-s) fabrication
tilefn|i *n neu* (-is, ~, -a) occasion
tileinka *v* (~, -ði, -ð) dedicate; ~ **sér** get into the habit of something
tileink|un *n fem* (-unar, -anir, -ana) dedication
tilfallandi *adj* odd: ~ **verkefni** odd jobs
tilfell|i *n neu* (-is, ~, -a) case, instance
tilfinning *n fem* (-ar, -ar, -a) emotion, feeling
tilfinningalaus *adj* (-, -t) soulless
tilfinningalega *adv* emotionally
tilfinningalíf *n neu* (-s) emotional life
tilfinningasam|ur *adj* (-söm, -t) emotional
tilgangslaus *adj* (-, -t) senseless
tilgang|ur *n masc* (-s) aim, purpose, reason
tilgát|a *n fem* (-u, -ur, -na) hypothesis

tilgerð *n fem* (-ar) affectation, pretext
tilgerðarleg|ur *adj* (-, -t) pretentious
tilgrein|a *v* (-i, -di, -t) specify
tilhlökkun *n fem* (-ar) excitement for something
tilhneiging *n fem* (-ar, -ar, -a) trend, tendency
tilkomumikil|l *adj* (-, -mikið) grand
tilkynn|a *v* (-i, -ti, -t) notify, announce
tilkynning *n fem* (-ar, -ar, -a) notice, announcement, notification
tilkynningartafl|a *n fem* (-töflu, -töflur, -na) message board
tillag|a *n fem* (-lögu, -lögur, -na) proposal, proposition, suggestion
tillit *n neu* (-s) consideration
tilnefnd|ur *adj* (-, -nefnt) nominated
tilnefning *n fem* (-ar, -ar, -a) nomination
tilraun *n fem* (-ar, -ir, -a) experiment, attempt
tilraunadýr *n neu* (-s, -, -a) guinea pig
tilskipun *n fem* (-ar, -ir, -a) order, decree
tilsögn *n fem* (-sagnar) guidance
tiltekin|n *adj* (-, -tekið) specific
tiltekt *n fem* (-ar, -ir, -a) cleaning
tilver|a *n fem* (-u) existence
tilvilj|un *n fem* (-unar, -anir, -ana) coincidence, chance
tilvitn|un *n fem* (-unar, -anir, -ana) reference, quote: **bein** ~ direct quote
timburmenn *n masc pl* (-manna) hangover
tind|ur *n masc* (-s, -ar, -a) peak, top
tipp|i *n neu* (-is, ~, -a) *anat* penis
titil|l *n masc* (-s, titlar, titla) title
titla *v* (~, -ði, -ð) address as; give a title to someone
titra *v* (~, -ði, -ð) quake
tíð *n fem* (-ar, -ir, -a) *ling* tense
tíðarhvörf *n neu pl* (-hvarfa) *med* menopause
tíðarverk|ir *n masc pl* (-ja) *med* menstrational cramps

tíðatapp|i *n masc* (-a, -ar, -a) tampon
tíð|ir *n fem pl* (-a) menstruation, period
tíðn|i *n fem* (-i, -ir, -a) frequency
tíð|ur *adj* (-, -tt) frequent
tígul|l *n masc* (-s, tíglar, tígla) *(cards)* diamond
tímaáætl|un *n fem* (-unar, -anir, -ana) timetable
tímabil *n neu* (-s, -, -a) period, term, range
tímabundin|n *adj* (-, -bundið) temporary
tímamót *n neu pl* (-a) milestone
tímarit *n neu* (-s, -, -a) journal, magazine, periodical
tím|i *n masc* (-a, -ar, -a) time
tímían *n neu* (-s) thyme
tín|a *v* (-i, -di, -t) pick up, collect
Tírana *N fem* (-) Tirana *(capital of Albania)*
tísk|a *n fem* (-ur, ~) fashion, trend
tískuvöruversl|un *n fem* (-unar, -anir, -ana) fashion store
títuprjón|n *n masc* (-s, -ar, -a) pin
tíu *num* ten
tíundi *ord* (-a, -a) tenth
tívolí *n neu* (-s, -, -a) amusement park
tjald *n neu* (-s, tjöld, -a) tent; screen
tjalda *v* (~, -ði, -ð) camp
tjaldbúð|ir *n fem pl* (-a) camp
tjaldbú|i *n masc* (-a, -ar, -a) camper
tjaldhæl|l *n masc* (-s, -ar, -a) tent peg
tjaldstæð|i *n neu* (-is, ~, -a) campground
tjaldsúl|a *n fem* (-u, -ur, -na) tent pole
tjald|ur *n masc* (-s, -ar, -a) oystercatcher
tjaldútbúnað|ur *n masc* (-ar) camping equipment
tjaldvagn *n masc* (-s, -ar, -a) trailer tent
tjá *v* (-i, -ði, -ð) express, convey
tjáning *n fem* (-ar) expression
tjón *n neu* (-s) damage
tjörn *n fem* (tjarnar, tjarnir, tjarna) pond

tog *n neu* (-s) pull
togar|i *n masc* (-a, -ar, -a) trawler
togna *v* (~, -ði, -ð) *med* sprain
tognað|ur *adj* (tognuð, -) *med* sprained
togn|un *n fem* (-unar, -anir, -ana) *med* sprain; ~ á ökkla sprained ankle
tollfrjáls *adj* (-, -t) duty-free
tollhús *n neu* (-s, -, -a) customs house
tollskoð|un *n fem* (-unar, -anir, -ana) customs control
tollskýrsl|a *n fem* (-u, -ur, -na) customs declaration
toll|ur *n masc* (-s, -ar, -a) customs; toll
tomból|a *n fem* (-u, -ur, ~) raffle
Tonga *N neu* (-) Tonga
tonn *n neu* (-s, -, -a) ton
topp|ur *n masc* (-s, -ar, -a) top, peak
torf *n neu* (-s, -, -a) sod
torfæruhjól *n neu* (-s, -, -a) off-road motorcycle
torfbæ|r *n masc* (-jar, -ir, -ja) sod house *(traditional Icelandic building style)*
torg *n neu* (-s, -, -a) square
tortill|a *n fem* (-u, -ur, ~) tortilla
tortryggileg|ur *adj* (-, -t) suspicious
tóbak *n neu* (-s) tobacco
tóbaksbúð *n fem* (-ar, -ir, -a) tobacco shop
tóbaksplant|a *n fem* (-plöntu, -plöntur, -na) tobacco plant
tófú *n neu* (-) tofu
Tógó *N neu* (-) Togo
Tókíó *N fem* (-) Tokyo *(capital of Japan)*
tól *n neu* (-s, -, -a) tool
tólf *num* twelve
tólfti *ord* (-a, -a) twelfth
tólg *n fem* (-ar) tallow
tómatpúrr|a *n fem* (-u) tomato paste
tómatsós|a *n fem* (-u, -ur, -a) ketchup
tómat|ur *n masc* (-s, -ar, -a) tomato
tómhent|ur *adj* (-, -) empty-handed
tómhyggj|a *n fem* (-u) *phil* nihilism
tómstundagaman *n neu* (-s) hobby

tómstund|ir *n fem pl* (-a) pastime
tóm|ur *adj* (-, -t) empty, vacant
tónik *n neu* (-s) tonic water
tónleik|ar *n masc pl* (-a) concert, recital, gig
tónleikastað|ur *n masc* (-ar, -ir, -a) venue for a concert
tónlist *n fem* (-ar) music
tónlistarhátíð *n fem* (-ar, -ir, -a) pop festival
tónlistarmað|ur *n masc* (-manns, -menn, -manna) musician
tónlistarversl|un *n fem* (-unar, -anir, -ana) music store
tón|n *n masc* (-s, -ar, -a) *mus* tone
tónskáld *n neu* (-s, -, -a) composer
tónsmíð *n fem* (-ar, -ir, -a) musical composition
tónsvið *n neu* (-s, -, -a) *mus* musical register
tónverk *n neu* (-s, -, -a) *mus* musical composition
traktor *n masc* (-s, -ar, -a) tractor
tramp *n neu* (-s) stamp
trampa *v* (~, -ði, -ð) stamp
trampólín *n neu* (-s, -, -a) trampoline
trapp|a *n fem* (tröppu, tröppur, ~) stair
trassa *v* (~, -ði, -ð) neglect
trassaskap|ur *n masc* (-ar) negligence
traust *n neu* (-s) confidence, trust
traust|ur *adj* (-, -) reliable, solid, safe
trefil|l *n masc* (-s, -treflar, -trefla) scarf
tregða *n fem* (-u, -ur, ~) reluctance
treglega *adv* unwillingly
treg|ur *adj* (-, -t) reluctant, unwilling; slow
trekk|ur *n masc* (-s) drag
treyj|a *n fem* (-u, -ur, ~) sweater
treyst|a *v* (-i, -i, -) trust; ~ á rely on
tré *n neu* (-s, -, -trjáa) tree; wood
tréblásturshljóðfær|i *n neu pl* (-is, ~, -a) *mus* woodwind
trilljón *n fem* (-ar, -ir, -a) trillion
trill|a *n fem* (-u, -ur, ~) trolley; small fishing boat

trillukarl *n masc* (-s, -ar, -a) fisherman who has his own boat
Trínidad og Tóbagó *N neu* (-) Trinidad and Tobago
Trínidad|i *n masc* (-a, -ar, -a) Trinidadian *(person)*
trínidadísk|ur *adj* (-, -t) Trinidadian
tríó *n neu* (-s, -, -a) trio
Trípólí *N fem* (-) Tripoli *(capital of Libya)*
trítla *v* (~, -ði, -ð) trot
trjónukrabb|i *n masc* (-a, -ar, -a) spider crab
troð|a *v* (treð, tróð, tróðum, troðið) force something somewhere: **hann troð sér inn í bílinn** he forced himself into the car
troðin|n *adj* (-, troðið) trodden
troðning|ur *n masc* (-s, -ar, -a) pressure because of too many people; path in the woods
tromm|a *n fem* (-u, -ur, ~) *mus* drums
tromma *v* (~, -ði, -ð) drum
trommar|i *n masc* (-a, -ar, -a) drummer
trommusett *n neu* (-s, -, -a) *mus* drumset
trompet *n neu* (-s, -, -a) *mus* trumpet
trópísk|ur *adj* (-, -t) tropical
trufla *v* (~, -ði, -ð) bother, disturb, interrupt
truflandi *adj* disturbing
trufl|un *n fem* (-unar, -anir, -ana) interference, interruption
trú *n fem* (-ar) belief; religion
trú|a *v* (-i, -ði, -að) believe
trúað|ur *adj* (trúuð, -) religious
trúarbrögð *n neu pl* (-bragða) religion
trúbadúr *n masc* (-s, -ar, -a) troubadour
trúboð|i *n masc* (-a, -ar, -a) missionary
trúð|ur *n masc* (-s, -ar, -a) clown
trúleysing|i *n masc* (-ja, -jar, -ja) atheist
trúlof|un *n fem* (-unar, -anir, -ana) engagement
trúnaðarupplýsing|ar *n fem pl* (-a) confidential information

trúnað|ur *n masc* (-ar) confidence, trust

trú|r *adj* (-, -tt) devoted

tryggð *n fem* (-ar, -ir, -a) devotion

trygging *n fem* (-ar, -ar, -a) insurance

tryggingafélag *n neu* (-s, -félög, -a) insurance company

tryggingarskírtein|i *n neu* (-is, ~, -a) insurance card

tryggj|a *v* (tryggi, tryggði, tryggt) secure; get insurance

trygg|ur *adj* (-, -t) secure

tryllingslega *adv* wildly

trýni *n neu* (-s, -, -a) muzzle

tröll *n neu* (-s, -, -a) troll, giant

trönuber *n neu* (-ja, -, -ja) cranberry

tung|a *n fem* (-u, -ur, -na) tongue, language

tungl *n neu* (-s, -, -a) moon

tunglmyrkv|i *n masc* (-a, -ar, -a) eclipse of the moon

tungumál *n neu* (-s, -, -a) language

tungumálanámskeið *n neu* (-s, -, -a) language course

tunn|a *n fem* (-u, -ur, ~) barrel

turn *n masc* (-s, -ar, -a) tower

tusk|a *n fem* (-u, -ur, -na) rag

tuttugasti *ord* (-a, -a) twentieth

túb|a *n fem* (-u, -ur, ~) *mus* tuba

túlipan|i *n masc* (-a, -ar, -a) tulip

túlka *v* (~, -ði, -ð) interpret

túlk|un *n fem* (-unar, -anir, -ana) interpretation

túlk|ur *n masc* (-s, -ar, -a) interpreter

túnfífil|l *n masc* (-s, -fíflar, -fífla) *flora* dandelion

túnfisk|ur *n masc* (-s, -ar, -a) tuna

Túnis *N neu* (~) Tunisia; Tunis

túnisk|ur *adj* (-, -t) Tunisian

túnsúr|a *n fem* (-u, -ur, ~) *flora* sorrel

túp|a *n fem* (-u, -ur, ~) tube

túr *n masc* (-s, -ar, -a) menustration, period; *slang* tour

túrism|i *n masc* (-a) tourism

túrist|i *n masc* (-a, -ar, -a) tourist

Túrkmen|i *n masc* (-a, -ar, -a) Turkmen

Túrkmenistan *N neu* (-/s) Turkmenistan

túrkmensk|ur *adj* (-, -t) Turkmen

túrmerik *n neu* (-s) turmeric

túrtapp|i *n masc* (-a, -ar, -a) *colloq* tampon

túrverk|ir *n masc pl* (-ja) *colloq* menstrual cramps

Túvalú *N neu* (-) Tuvalu

tvenn|ir *adj pl* (-ar, -) *(for plural words)* two: **tvennar buxur** two pairs of trousers; *(things that come in a pair)* a pair: ~ **sokkar** two pairs of socks, **tvenn hjón** two couples

tveir *num masc* (tvo, tveimur, tveggja) two: ~ **miðar** two tickets

tvinn|i *n masc* (-a, -ar, -a) thread

tvist *n neu* (-s) twist

tvist|ur *n masc* (-s, -ar, -a) number two

tvisvar *adv* twice

tvíbak|a *n fem* (-böku, -bökur, ~) rusk

Tvíbur|arnir *n masc pl def* (-anna) *astro* Gemini

tvíbur|i *n masc* (-a, -ar, -a) twin

tvímælalaust *adv* undoubtedly

tvípunkt|ur *n masc* (-s, -ar, -a) *ling* colon; umlaut

tvíræðni *n fem* (-) ambiguity

tvíræð|ur *adj* (-, -rætt) ambiguous

tvístra *v* (~, -ði, -ð) scatter

tvístrað|ur *adj* (tvístruð, -) scattered

tvítug|ur *adj* (-, -t) twenty years old

tvítyngd|ur *adj* (-, -tyngt) bilingual

tvær *num fem* (tvær, tveimur, tveggja) two

tvö *num neu* (tvö, tveimur, tveggja) two

tvöfalda *v* (~, -ði, -ð) double

tvöfald|ur *adj* (-föld, -falt) double

tyggigúmmí *n neu* (-s, -, -a) chewing gum

tyggitafl|a *n fem* (-töflu, -töflur, -na) chewable tablet

tyggj|a *v* (tygg, tuggði, tuggið) chew

tyggjó *n neu* (-s, -, -a) *colloq* chewing gum

tylft *n fem* (-ar, -ir, -a) dozen
Tyrk|i *n masc* (-ja, -ir, -ja) Turk
Tyrkland *N neu* (-s) Turkey
tyrknesk|a *n fem* (-u) Turkish
  language
tyrknesk|ur *adj* (-, -t) Turkish
týn|a *v* (-i, -di, -t) lose; ~ **lífi** perish
týn|ast *v* (-ist, -dist, -st) get lost
týnd|ur *adj* (-, týnt) lost, missing
tæk|i *n neu* (-is, ~, -ja) device
tækifær|i *n neu* (-is, ~, -a) occasion,
  opportunity
tækifærismennsk|a *n fem* (-u)
  opportunism
tækla *v* (~, -ði, -ð) tackle
tækni *n fem* (-) technique; technology
tæknileg|ur *adj* (-, -t) technical
tæknimað|ur *n masc* (-manns, -menn,
  -manna) technician
Tæland *N neu* (-s) Thailand
tælensk|ur *adj* (-, -t) Thai
tæm|a *v* (-i, -di, -t) empty, vacate
tæt|a *v* (-i, -ti, -t) shred
tætar|i *n masc* (-a, -ar, -a) shredder
töflureikn|ir *n masc* (-is) *comp*
  spreadsheet
töfralækn|ir *n masc* (-is, -ar, -a)
  shaman
töframað|ur *n masc* (-manns, -menn,
  -manna) magician

töfr|ar *n masc pl* (-a) magic
töfrasprot|i *n masc* (-a, -ar, -a)
  magic wand
tölfræði *n fem* (-) statistics
tölfræðileg|ur *adj* (-, -t) statistical
tölublað *n neu* (-s, -blöð, -a) *(of a
  publication)* issue
tölustaf|ur *n masc* (-s, -ir, -a) digit,
  number
töluverð|ur *adj* (-, -vert) consider-
  able, substantial
tölv|a *n fem* (-u, -ur, -a) computer
tölvugrafík *n fem* (-ur) computer
  graphics
tölvuleikjasal|ur *n masc* (-ar, -ir, -a)
  games arcade
tölvuleik|ur *n masc* (-s, -ir/ar, -ja/a)
  computer game
tölvumús *n fem* (-ar, -mýs, -a) *comp*
  mouse
tölvunet *n neu* (-s, -, -a) *comp* network
tölvupóst|ur *n masc* (-s, -ar, -a)
  comp e-mail
tölvuskjá|r *n masc* (-s, -ir, -a)
  computer screen
tölvuvírus *n masc* (-s, -ar, -a)
  computer virus
tönn *n fem* (tannar, tennur, tanna)
  tooth

U

ufs|i *n masc* (-a, -ar, -a) *zool* coalfish, pollock, saithe
uggandi *adj* alarmed
ugl|a *n fem* (-u, -ur, ~) owl
ull *n fem* (-ar) wool
ullarvör|ur *n fem pl* (-vara) woolens
um *prep* (+ *acc*) about: **saga ~ konu** a story about a woman
um borð *adv* on board
um það bil *adv* approximately
umboðsmað|ur *n masc* (-manns, -menn, -manna) agent, ombudsman
umboðsskrifstof|a *n fem* (-u, -ur, ~) agency
umbót *n fem* (-ar, -bætur, -a) reform
umbótasinn|i *n masc* (-a, -ar, -a) reformer
umbreyt|a *v* (-i, -ti, -t) change, transform
umbreyt|ast *v* (-ist, -tist, -breyst) transform
umbúð|ir *n fem pl* (-a) packaging; *med* bandage
umbun *n fem* (-ar) reward
umburðarlyndi *n neu* (-s) tolerance
umdeilanleg|ur *adj* (-, -t) controversial
umfang *n neu* (-s) extent, scope
umfangsmikil|l *adj* (-, -mikið) extensive
umferð *n fem* (-ar, -ir, -a) traffic
umferðarljós *n neu* (-s, -, -a) traffic light
umferðarmiðstöð *n fem* (-var, -var, -va) traffic terminal
umferðaróhapp *n neu* (-s, -óhöpp, -a) traffic accident
umferðarslys *n neu* (-s, -, -a) traffic accident
umferðaröngþveit|i *n neu* (-is, ~, -a) traffic jam
umferðaröryggi *n neu* (-s) traffic safety

umfjöllunarefn|i *n neu* (-is, ~, -a) subject matter, theme, topic
umfram *prep* + *acc* in addition to
umgjörð *n fem* (-gjarðar, -gjarðir, -gjarða) frame
umhverfi *n neu* (-s) surroundings, environment, setting
umhverfis *prep* + *acc* around: ~ jörðina around Earth
umhverfisvæn|n *adj* (-, -t) environmentally friendly
umhverfisverndarsinn|i *n masc* (-a, -ar, -a) environmentalist
umhyggjusam|ur *adj* (-söm, -t) caring
umkringj|a *v* (-kringi, -kringdi, -kringt) surround
ummæl|i *n neu pl* (-a) comment, remark
ummerk|i *n neu* (-ja) trace
umorða *v* (~, -ði, -ð) rephrase
umrita *v* (~, -ði, -ð) transcribe
umrædd|ur *adj* (-, -rætt) the one that is being talked about
umræð|a *n fem* (-u, -ur, -na) discourse
umræðuefn|i *n neu* (-is, ~, -a) topic of discussion
umræðuvettvang|ur *n masc* (-s) forum
umsjón *n fem* (-ar) supervision
umskipt|i *n neu* (-a) transformation, shift
umslag *n neu* (-s, -slög, -a) envelope
umsókn *n fem* (-ar, -ir, -a) application
umsvif *n neu pl* (-a) activity
umvandar|i *n masc* (-a, -ar, -a) moralist
umönnun *n fem* (-ar) care
undan *prep* + *dat* from underneath: ~ borðinu from underneath the table; **kvarta ~ þjónustunni** complain about the service; **koma ~** decend from
undanfar|i *n masc* (-a, -ar, -a) precursor

undanlátssam|ur *adj* (-söm, -t)
lenient

undanrenn|a *n fem* (-u, -ur, ~) skim
milk

undantekning *n fem* (-ar, -ar, -a)
exception

undantekningarlaus *adj* (-, -t)
without exception

undanþág|a *n fem* (-u, -ur, ~)
exception

undanþegin|n *adj* (-, -þegið) exempt

undarlega *adv* oddly

undarleg|ur *adj* (-, -t) strange, odd,
peculiar

undir *prep* + *acc (location)* under:
~ **borðinu** under the table; below:
~ **fjallinu** below the mountain;
(amount) under, less than: ~ **hundrað krónum** less than a hundred
kronas; + *acc (movement)* under:
barnið skreið ~ borðið the child
crawled under the table; *(storage
space)* for: **geymsla ~ dót** a storage room for stuff; *(time)* close to:
hún kom heim ~ kvöld she came
home close to the evening

undirbú|a *v* (-bý, -bjó, -bjuggum,
-búið) prepare

undirbúin|n *adj* (-, -búið) prepared

undirbúning|ur *n masc* (-s)
preparation

undirkafl|i *n masc* (-a, -ar, -a) section
of a chapter

undirliggjandi *adj* underlying

undiroka *v* (~, ði, -ð) oppress

undirok|un *n fem* (-nar) repression

undirrita *v* (~, -ði, -ð) sign

undirskál *n fem* (-ar, -ar, -a) saucer

undirskrift *n fem* (-ar, -ir, -a) signature

undirskriftasöfn|un *n fem* (unar,
-safnanir, -safnana) petition

undirstað|a *n fem* (-stöðu, -stöður,
-na) foundation

undirstrika *v* (~, -ði, -ð) highlight,
emphasize

undirstöðuatrið|i *n neu* (-is, ~, -a)
basics

undirtext|i *n masc* (-a, -ar, -a) *(on
television)* subtitles

undirtitil|l *n masc* (-s, -titlar, -titla)
subtitle

undrandi *adj* surprised

undra|st *v* (~, -ðist, ~) wonder

undraverð|ur *adj* (-, -vert) phenomenal

undrun *n fem* (-ar) astonishment,
surprise

undursamlegur adorable

ungbarn *n neu* (-s, -börn, -a) infant,
baby

ungbarnamjólk *n fem* (-ur) infant
formula

ungfrú *n fem* (-ar, -r, -a) Miss

unglingaból|ur *n fem pl* (-a) acne

ungling|ur *n masc* (-s, -ar, -a) teenager

ungnaut *n neu* (-s, -, -a) *zool* steer

ung|ur *adj* (-, -t) young

Ungverjaland *N neu* (-s) Hungary

Ungverj|i *N masc* (-a, -ar, -a) Hun-
garian *(person)*

ungversk|a *n fem* (-u) Hungarian
language

ungversk|ur *adj* (-, -t) Hungarian

unnust|a *n fem* (-u, -ur, ~) fiancée

unnust|i *n masc* (-a, -ar, -a) fiancé

upp *adv* up, upwards

uppáhald *n neu* (-s) favorite

uppáklædd|ur *adj* (-, -klætt) dressed up

uppástung|a *n fem* (-u, -ur, -na) sug-
gestion, proposal, proposition

uppboð *n neu* (-s, -, -a) auction

uppbókað|ur *adj* (-bókuð, -) fully
booked

uppbyggileg|ur *adj* (-, -t) contructive

uppdópað|ur *adj* (-dópuð, -) intoxi-
cated by drugs

uppfinning *n fem* (-ar, -ar, -a)
invention

uppfletting *n fem* (-ar, -ar, -a) *comp*
pageview, hit

uppfyll|a *v* (-i, -ti, -t) satisfy

uppfylling *n fem* (-ar, -ar, -a)
satisfaction

uppfærð|ur *adj* (-, -fært) updated

uppgerð *n fem* (-ar, -ir, -a) pretense

uppgerð|ur *adj* (-, -gert) restored
uppgjör *n neu* (-s, -, -a) settlement;
econ final accounts: **ársuppgjör**
annual accounts
uppgötva *v* (~, -ði, -ð) discover
uppgötvað|ur *adj* (-götvuð, -)
discovered
uppgötv|un *n fem* (-unar, -anir, -ana)
discovery
upphaf *n neu* (-s) start; opening;
outbreak
upphaflega *adv* initially, originally
upphafleg|ur *adj* (-, -t) initial,
original
upphafsmað|ur *n masc* (-manns,
-menn, -manna) originator
upphafsstaf|ur *n masc* (-s, -ir, -a)
(letter) initial
upphátt *adv* aloud
upphitað|ur *adj* (-hituð, -) warmed up,
heated, re-heated
upphitun *n fem* (-ar) heating
upphróp|un *n fem* (-unar, -anir, -ana)
ling interjection, exclamation
upphrópunarmerk|i *n neu* (-is, ~,
-a) *ling* exclamation mark
upphæð *n fem* (-ar, -ir, -a) amount
uppi *adv* up; upstairs
uppistandar|i *n masc* (-a, -ar, -a)
standup comedian
uppkast *n neu* (-s, -köst, -a) draft
upplausn *n fem* (-ar, -ir, -a) breakdown; *comp* solution
uppleysandi *adj* solvent
upplif|a *v* (-i, -ði, -að) experience,
live through
uppljóstr|un *n fem* (-unar, -anir,
-ana) disclosure
upplýs|a *v* (-i, -ti, -t) communicate,
inform, illuminate
upplýsingaborð *n neu* (-s, -, -a)
information desk
upplýsing|ar *n fem pl* (-a) information
upplýsingaskrifstof|a *n fem* (-u, -ur,
~) information office; tourist office
upplýsingatafl|a *n fem* (-töflu, -töflur,
-taflna) bulletin board

uppnám *n neu* (-s) uneasiness, agita-
tion, turmoil
uppræt|a *v* (-i, -ti, -t) destroy
uppreisn *n fem* (-ar, -ir, -a) rebellion,
mutiny
uppreisnargjarn *adj* (-gjörn, -t)
rebellious
uppreisnarmað|ur *n masc* (-manns,
-menn, -manna) rebel
upprétt|ur *adj* (-, -) erect
upprifj|un *n fem* (-unar, -anir, -ana)
review
upprunaleg|ur *adj* (-, -t) original,
authentic; **upprunaleg útgáfa**
original version
uppprun|i *n masc* (-a, -ar, -a) origin
upppröð|un *n fem* (-unar, -raðanir,
-raðana) arrangement
uppseld|ur *adj* (-, -selt) sold out
uppsker|a *n fem* (-u) harvest, reap
uppskrift *n fem* (-ar, -ir, -a) recipe
uppskriftabók *n fem* (-ar, -bækur, -a)
cookbook
uppskurð|ur *n masc* (-ar, -ir, -a)
surgery
uppsláttarrit *n neu* (-s, -, -a) reference book
uppsprett|a *n fem* (-u, -ur, ~) source,
well, spring
uppspun|i *n masc* (-a) fiction
uppstúf *n neu* (-s) white sauce
uppsöfnun *n fem* (-ar) accumulation
uppsögn *n fem* (-sagnar, -sagnir,
-sagna) resignation
upptak|a *n fem* (-töku, -tökur, ~)
recording
upptakar|i *n masc* (-a, -ar, -a) bottle
opener
upptalning *n fem* (-ar, -ar, -a) recitation
upptekin|n *adj* (-, tekið) busy,
occupied
uppþembd|ur *adj* (-, -þembt) bloated
uppþot *n neu* (-s, -, -a) riot
uppþvottavél *n fem* (-ar, -ar, -a)
dishwasher
uppþvott|ur *n masc* (-a, -ar/s, -a)
dirty dishes; washing-up

upptökustúdíó *n neu* (-s, -, -a)
recording studio
upptökutæk|i *n neu* (-is, ~, -a)
recorder
urrið|i *n masc* (-a, -ar, -a) *zool*
brown trout
USB-tengil|l *n masc* (-s, -tenglar,
-tengla) *comp* USB port
uss *interj* shush
ussa *v* (~, -ði, -ð) shush
utan *prep* + *gen* outside of: ~ **vinnu-
tíma** outside of work hours; off:
~ **vega** off road
utanaðkomandi *adj* external

utangarðsmað|ur *n masc* (-manns,
-menn, -manna) outsider
utanríkisráðherra *n masc* (-, -r, -)
Minister of Foreign Affairs
utanríkisráðuneyt|i *n neu* (-is, ~,
-a) Ministry for Foreign Affairs;
Utanríkisráðuneyti Íslands The
Icelandic Ministry for Foreign
Affairs
uxahalasúp|a *n fem* (-u, -ur, -na)
oxtail soup
uxahal|i *n masc* (-a, -ar, -a) oxtail

Ú

úða *v* (~, -ði, -ð) spray, sprinkle
úðarigning *n fem* (-ar) drizzle
úð|i *n masc* (-a, -ar, -a) spray
Úganda *N neu* (-) Uganda
Úgandamað|ur *N masc* (-manns, -menn, -manna) Ugandan *(person)*
úgansk|ur *adj* (úgönsk, -t) Ugandan
Úkraín|a *N fem* (-u) Ukraine
úkraínsk|a *n fem* (-u) Ukrainian language
úkraínsk|ur *adj* (-, -t) Ukrainian
Úkraínumað|ur *N masc* (-manns, -menn, -manna) Ukrainian *(person)*
úlfabaun *n fem* (-ar, -ir, -a) lupin bean
úlf|ur *n masc* (-a, -ar, -a) *zool* wolf
úlnlið|ur *n masc* (-ar/r, -ir, -a) wrist
úns|a *n fem* (-u, -ur , ~) ounce
úlp|a *n fem* (-u, -ur, -na) parka, winter jacket
úr 1 *n neu* (-s, -, -a) watch; **2** *prep + dat* from: **ég er ~ sveit** I´m from the countryside; out of: **peysan er ~ ull** the sweater is made out of wool
úr því að *adv* since; because
úrdrátt|ur *n masc* (-ar, -drættir, -drátta) understatement
úreld|ur *adj* (-, úrelt) archaic, obsolete, outdated
úrfellingarmerk|i *n neu* (-is, ~, -ja) apostrophe
úrgang|ur *n masc* (-s) trash, waste
úrlausn *n fem* (-ar, -ir, -a) solution
úrræð|i *n neu* (-is, ~, -a) remedy; resource
úrskurða *v* (~, -ði, -ð) pronounce; rule
úrskurð|ur *n masc* (-ar, -ir, -a) verdict
úrslit *n neu pl* (-a) outcome; *sports* final score
úrsmið|ur *n masc* (-s, -ir, -a) watch-maker

Úrúgvæ *N neu* (-) Uruguay
úrval *n neu* (-s) selection
úrvinda *adj* exhausted
úrvinnsl|a *n fem* (-u) processing: ~ **gagna** processing data
Úsbekistan *N neu* (-) Uzbekistan
úsbeksk|ur *adj* (-, -t) Uzbek
út *adv* out: **fara ~** go out
útblástur *n masc* (-s) emission
útbreidd|ur *adj* (-, -breitt) widespread
útbreiðsl|a *n fem* (-u) prevalence
útbrot *n neu* (-s, -, -a) rash
útbúnað|ur *n masc* (-ar) outfit
útdrátt|ur *n masc* (-ar, -drættir, -drátta) summary, recapitulation
útfararstjór|i *n masc* (-a, -ar, -a) undertaker
útferð *n fem* (-ar) *med* discharge
útflutningsvar|a *n fem* (-vöru, -vörur, ~) export goods
útflutning|ur *n masc* (-s) export
útför *n fem* (-farar, -farir, -fara) funeral
útgáf|a *n fem* (-u, -ur, -na) publication, edition, version
útgáfufyrirtæk|i *n neu* (-is, ~, -ja) publishing house, press; record label
útgáfuhóf *n neu* (-s, -, -a) book launch; record launch
útgáfurétt|ur *n masc* (-ar) publishing rights
útgáfustarfsemi *n fem* (-) publishing
útgang|ur *n masc* (-s, -ar, -a) exit
útgefand|i *n masc* (-a, -endur, -enda) publisher
útgeislun *n fem* (-ar) radiation
útgjöld *n neu pl* (-gjalda) expenditure
útgöngubann *n neu* (-s) curfew
úthaf *n neu* (-s, -höf, -a) ocean
úthald *n neu* (-s) persistence

úthluta *v* (~, -ði, -ð) allocate

úthlut|un *n fem* (-unar, -anir, -ana) allocation

úthverf|i *n neu* (-is, ~, -a) suburb

úthverf|ur *adj* (-, -t) inside out

úti *adv* out, outside, outdoors: **vera** ~ be outside

útibú *n neu* (-s, -, -a) branch

útigangsmað|ur *n masc* (-manns, -menn, -manna) homeless person

útihurð *n fem* (-ar, -ir, -a) entrance door

útihús *n neu* (-s, -, -a) outbuilding

útilaug *n fem* (-ar, -ar, -a) open-air pool, outdoor pool

útiloka *v* (~, -ði, -ð) exclude

útilok|un *n fem* (-unar, -anir, -ana) exclusion

útisundlaug *n fem* (-ar, -ar, -a) open-air pool, outdoor pool

útivistarbúnað|ur *n masc* (-ar) outdoor equipment

útivistarföt *n neu pl* (-fata) outdoor clothing

útjaðar *n masc* (-s, -jaðrar, -jaðra) outskirts

útkeyrsl|a *n fem* (-u, -ur, -na) *(for cars)* exit

útkljá *v* (-i, -ði, -ð) settle

útkom|a *n fem* (-u, -ur, ~) outcome

útlag|i *n masc* (-a, -ar, -a) outlaw

útlendingaótt|i *n masc* (-a) xeno-phobia

útlending|ur *n masc* (-s, -ar, -a) foreigner

útlensk|ur *adj* (-, -t) foreign

útlista *v* (~, -ði, -ð) explain, elaborate

útlit *n neu* (-s) appearance, looks

útprent|un *n fem* (-unar, -anir, -ana) printout

útreiðartúr *n masc* (-s, -ar, -a) horseback tour

útreikning|ur *n masc* (-s, -ar, -a) calculation

útrunnin|n *adj* (-, -runnið) out-of-date

útrýmingarhætt|a *n fem* (-u, -ur, ~) endangered

útrýmingarherferð *n fem* (-ar, -ir, -a) holocaust

útsaum|ur *n masc* (-s, -ar, -a) embroidery

útsending *n fem* (-ar, -ar, -a) broad-cast, transmission

útskrifa *v* (~, -ði, -ð) discharge

útskrifað|ur *adj* (-skrifuð, -) dis-charged; graduated

útskrifa|st *v refl* (~, ðist, ~) graduate

útskrift *n fem* (-ar, -ir, -a) graduation

útskurð|ur *n masc* (-ar, -ir, -a) carving

útskúfað|ur *adj* (útskúfuð, -) ostracize

útskýr|a *v* (-i, -ði, -t) explain, clarify

útskýring *n fem* (-ar, -ar, -a) explanation

útsmogin|n *adj* (-, -smogið) cunning

útstilling *n fem* (-ar, -ar, -a) display

útstöð *n fem* (-var, -var, -va) *comp* terminal

útsýni *n neu* (-s) view

úttekt *n fem* (-ar, -ir, -a) assessment, appraisal

úttektarmið|i *n masc* (-a, -ar, -a) voucher

útúrsnúning|ur *n masc* (-s, -ar, -a) quibble

útvarp *n neu* (-s, -vörp, -a) radio

útvarpa *v* (~, -ði, -ð) broadcast on radio

útvega *v* (~, -ði, -ð) supply, provide, procure

útþensl|a *n fem* (-u) expansion

útöndun *n fem* (-ar) exhale

V

vað|a *v* (veð, óð, óðum, vaðið) wade
vaðfugl *n masc* (-s, -ar, -a) *zool*
  shorebird, wader
vafalaust *adv* surely, doubtless
vafasam|ur *adj* (-söm, -t) questionable
vaffl|a *n fem* (vöfflu, vöfflur, ~)
  waffle
vafra *v comp* (~, -ði, -ð) browse
vafr|i *n masc* (-a, -ar, -a) *comp*
  browser
vagg|a *n fem* (vöggu, vöggur, ~)
  cot, crib
vagn *n masc* (-s, -ar, -a) carriage,
  wagon
vakandi *adj* awake
vakna *v* (~, -ði, -ð) rouse, wake up
vakning *n fem* (-ar) wake-up call
vakt *n fem* (-ar, -ir, -a) work shift
vakta *v* (~, -ði, -ð) guard, patrol
val *n neu* (-s) choice, option, selection,
  alternative
vald *n neu* (-s, völd, -a) authority,
  power
valda *v* (veld, olli, valdið) cause,
  generate
valdamikil|l *adj* (-, -mikið) powerful
valdatíð *n fem* (-ar, -ir, -a) reign
valfrjáls *adj* (-, -t) optional, elective
valhnet|a *n fem* (-u, -ur, ~) walnut
valin|n *adj* (-, valið) selected, select
valkost|ur *n masc* (-ar, -ir, -a)
  alternative
vallhumal|l *n masc* (-s, -humlar,
  -humla) *flora* yarrow
valmú|i *n masc* (-a, -ar, -a) *flora*
  poppy
vandað|ur *adj* (vönduð, -) elaborate,
  carefully crafted
vandamál *n neu* (-s, -, -a) problem
vandasam|ur *adj* (-söm, -t)
  problematic

vandlát|ur *adj* (-, -t) particular,
  picky
vandlega *adv* carefully
vandræðaleg|ur *adj* (-, -t) embarrassed
vandræði *neu pl* problem: **lenda í
  vandræðum** have problems
vandvirk|ur *adj* (-, -t) careful, thor-
  ough while working
vangasvip|ur *n masc* (-s, -ir, -a)
  profile
vanget|a *n fem* (-u) inability
vanhelga *v* (~, -ði, -ð) profane
vanhæf|ur *adj* (-, -t) incompetent
van|i *n masc* (-a, -ar, -a) custom,
  practice
vanill|a *n fem* (-u) vanilla
vanilludrop|ar *n masc pl* (-ar)
  vanilla essence
vanillusós|a *n fem* (-u) custard
vannæring *n fem* (-ar) malnutrition
vanrækj|a *v* (-ræki, -rækti, -rækt)
  neglect
vanræksl|a *n fem* (-u) misconduct,
  neglect
vanþekking *n fem* (-ar) ignorance
vanþróað|ur *adj* (-þróuð, -) backward,
  underdeveloped: **vanþróuð ríki**
  underdeveloped countries
Vanúatú *N neu* (-s) Vanuatu
van|ur *adj* (vön, -t) experienced
vara- *prefix* spare: **~dekk** spare tire
var|a 1 *n fem* (vöru, vörur, ~) goods,
  commodity, product, article; **2** *v*
  (~, -ði, -ð) ~ **við** warn
varadekk *n neu* (-s, -, -ja) spare tire
varahlut|ur *n masc* (-ar, -ir, -a) spare
  part
varalit|ur *n masc* (-ar, -ir, -a) lipstick
varanleg|ur *adj* (-, -t) permanent
varða *v* (~, -ði, -ð) concern
varðandi *adj* concerning

varðhald *n neu* (-s) custody
varðveisl|a *n fem* (-u) preservation, retention
varðveit|a *v* (-i, -ti, -t) preserve, conserve, store, retain
varkár *adj* (-, -t) careful
varla *adv* hardly
varlega *adv* carefully, safely
varmafræði *n fem* (-) *phys* thermodynamics
varnarleysi *n neu* (-s) vulnerability
varnarvegg|ur *n masc* (-jar/s, -ir, -ja) rampart
varpa *v* (~, -ði, -ð) project
Varsjá *N fem* (-r) Warsaw
vart|a *n fem* (vörtu, vörtur, ~) *med* wart
vartar|i *n masc* (-a, -ar, -a) sea bass
varúð *n fem* (-ar) caution
varúðarráðstöf|un *n fem* (-unar, -anir, -ana) precaution
vasaklút|ur *n masc* (-s, -ar, -a) handkerchief
vasaljós *n neu* (-s, -, -a) *(electric)* torch
vasapening|ur *n masc* (-s, -ar, -a) allowance
vasareikn|ir *n masc* (-is, -ar, -a) calculator
vas|i *n masc* (-a, -ar, -a) pocket; vase: **blómavasi** flower vase
vaskahús *n neu* (-s, -, -a) *colloq* laundry room
vask|ur *n masc* (-s, -ar, -a) sink, basin
Vatíkanborgrík|ið *N neu def* (-isins) Vatican City
vatn *n neu* (-s, vötn, -a) water; lake
vatnakarf|i *n masc* (-a, -ar, -a) *zool* carp; minnow
vatnakrabb|i *n masc* (-a, -ar, -a) *zool* crayfish
vatnasleð|i *n masc* (-a, -ar, -a) jet-ski
vatnsafl *n neu* (-s, -öfl, -a) *phys* hydroelectric power
vatnsaflsvirkj|un *n fem* (-unar, -anir, -ana) hydroelectric power station
Vatnsber|inn *n masc* (-ans) *astro* Aquarius

vatnsflask|a *n fem* (-flösku, -flöskur, -na) water bottle
vatnsgeym|ir *n masc* (-is, -ar, -a) reservoir
vatnshnet|a *n fem* (-u, -ur, ~) water chestnut
vatnskann|a *n fem* (-könnu, -könnur, ~) pitcher of water
vatnskran|i *n masc* (-a, -ar, -a) water faucet
vatnslit|ur *n masc* (-ar, -ir, -a) watercolor
vatnsmelón|a *n fem* (-u, -ur, ~) watermelon
vatnsrennibraut *n fem* (-ar, -ir, ~) water slide
vatnstank|ur *n masc* (-s, -ar, -a) water tank, reservoir
vatnsþétt|ur *adj* (-, -) waterproof
vatt *n neu* (-s, vött, -a) *phys* watt
vax|a *v* (vex, ók, uxum, vaxið) grow
vaxbaun *n fem* (-ar, -ir, -a) wax bean
vátryggingarskírtein|i *n neu* (-is, ~, -a) insurance policy
veð *n neu* (-s, ~, -a) *econ* mortgage
veðhlaup *n neu* (-s, -, -a) horse racing
veðja *v* (~, -ði, -ð) bet, gamble
veðmál *n neu* (-s, -, -a) bet
veðsetja *v* (-, -ti, -sett) mortgage
veður *n neu* (-s, -, veðra) weather
veðurfrétt|ir *n fem pl* (-a) weather report
veðurfræði *n fem* (-) meteorology
veðurfræðing|ur *n masc* (-s, -ar, -a) meteorologist
veðurspá *n fem* (-r, -r, -a) weather forecast
veðurteppt|ur *adj* (-, -) snowbound
veffang *n neu* (-s, -föng, -a) *comp* URL
vefgátt *n fem* (-ar, -ir, -a) *comp* web portal
vefj|a 1 *n fem* (-u, -ur, -a) wrap: **kjúklinga~** chicken wrap; **2** *v* (vef, vafði, vafið) wrap: **vefjasýnitak|a** *n fem* (-töku, -tökur, ~) *med* biopsy
vefmyndavél *n fem* (-ar, -ar, -a) *comp* webcam

vefnaðarvara

vefnaðarvar|a *n fem* (-vöru, -vörur, ~) textiles

vefsíð|a *n fem* (-u, -ur, ~) website

vef|ur *n masc* (-jar/s, -ir, -ja) web

vefþjón|n *n masc* (-s, -ar, -a) *comp* webserver

veg|a *v* (veg, vó, vógum, vegið) weigh, scale; *arch* slay

vegabréf *n neu* (-s, -, -a) passport

vegabréfaskoð|un *n fem* (-unar, -anir, -ana) passport control

vegabréfsárit|un *n fem* (-unar, -anir, -ana) visa

vegabréfsnúmer *n neu* (-s, -, -a) passport number

vegahótel *n neu* (-s, -, -a) motel

vegamót *n neu pl* (-a) highway interchange, junction

vegan *adj* vegan: **ég er ~** I'm vegan

veganfólk *n neu* (-s) vegans

veggjakrot *n neu* (-s, -, -a) graffiti

veggmynd *n fem* (-ar, -ir, -a) mural

veggspjald *n neu* (-s, -spjöld, -a) poster

veggtennis *n neu* (-s) racquetball

veggtjald *n neu* (-s, -tjöld, -a) tapestry

vegg|ur *n masc* (-jar/s, -ir, -ja) wall

vegna *prep + gen* because of: **~ verkfalls** because of strike

vegna þess að *conj* because

veg|ur *n masc* (-ar/s, -ir, -a) way, street, road

vegvís|ir *n masc* (-is, -ar, -a) signpost

veið|a *v* (-i, veiddi, veitt) hunt

veið|ar *n fem pl* (-a) hunting

veið|i *n fem* (-i) fishing

veiðigall|i *n masc* (-a, -ar, -a) fishing wear

veiðileyf|i *n neu* (-is, ~, -a) fishing license

veiðimað|ur *n masc* (-manns, -menn, -manna) fisherman; hunter

veiðimennsk|a *n fem* (-u) fishing; hunting

veiðistöng *n fem* (-stangar, -stangir, -stanga) fishing rod

veifa *v* (~, -ði, -ð) wave

veigalítil|l *adj* (-, lítið) flimsy

veikburða *adj* weak

veikindafrí *n neu* (-s, -, -a) sick leave

veikind|i *n neu pl* (-a) sickness, illness

veik|ur *adj* (-, -t) sick, ill, ailing

veina *v* (~, -ði, -ð) scream

veisl|a *n fem* (-u, -ur, -na) party, feast

veit|a *v* (-i, -ti, -t) give, render; **~ verðlaun** award; **~ athygli** notice, pay attention; **~ stuðning** support

veiting|ar *n fem pl* (-a) food and drink

veitingastað|ur *n masc* (-ar, -ir, -a) restaurant, diner

vekj|a *v* (vek, vakti, vakið) wake

vekjaraklukk|a *n fem* (-u, -ur, -na) alarm clock

vel *adv* well

velferð *n fem* (-ar) welfare

velferðarrík|i *n neu* (-is, ~, -ja) welfare state

velgengni *n fem* (-) success

velgjörðarmað|ur *n masc* (-manns, -menn, -manna) patron

velj|a *v* (vel, valdi, valið) choose, pick, select

velkomin|n **1** *adj* (-, velkomið) welcome; **2** *interj* (-, velkomið) welcome!

vellíðan *n fem* (-líðunar) well-being, wellness

velling|ur *n masc* (-s) gruel

velmeg|un *n fem* (-unar, -anir, -ana) prosperity

velsk|a *n fem* (-u) Welsh language

velsk|ur *adj* (-, -t) Welsh

velsæmi *n neu* (-s) propriety

velt|a *n fem* (-u, -ur, ~) turnover

velt|a *v* (-i, -i, -) roll

velt|ast *v refl* (-ist, -ist, velst) roll: **~ um af hlátri** roll around in laughter

veltureikning|ur *n masc* (-s, -ar, -a) user account

velverðarkerf|i *n neu* (-is, ~, -a) welfare system

velvild *n fem* (-ar) benevolence

Venesúela *N neu* (-) Venezuela

Venesúelamað|ur *n masc* (-manns, -menn, -manna) Venezuelan *(person)*

venesúelsk|ur *adj* (-, -t) Venezuelan

venj|a *n fem* (-u, -ur, ~) custom, tradition

venjulega *adv* normally, typically, usually

venjuleg|ur *adj* (-, -t) usual, ordinary, regular, plain, mainstream

ver|a 1 *n fem* (-u, -ur, ~) creature; **2** *v* (er, var, vorum, verið) be; ~ **til** exist

veraldarvef|ur *n masc* (-jar/s) World Wide Web

veraldleg|ur *adj* (-, -t) secular

verð *n neu* (-s, -, -a) price

verð|a *v* (-, varð, urðum, orðið) become: **ég ætla að ~ kennari** I'm going to become a teacher; must, have to: **þú verður að prófa** you have to try

verðbólg|a *n fem* (-u) *econ* inflation

verðbréfamarkað|ur *n masc* (-ar/s, -ir, -a) *econ* stock exchange

verðbréfasal|i *n masc* (-a, -ar, -a) *econ* trader

verðgildi *n neu* (-s, -, -a) value

verði þér að góðu *phr* bon appetit

verðlaun *n neu pl* (-a) award, prize, premium

verðlauna *v* (~, -ði, -ð) award

verðlaunahaf|i *n masc* (-a, -ar, -a) laureate

verðlaunapening|ur *n masc* (-s, -ar, -a) medal

verðleggj|a *v* (-legg, -lagði, -lögðum, -lagt) appraise, assess the price

verðmat *n neu* (-s) valuation

verðmet|a *v* (-, -mat, -mátum, -metið) appraise, assess the price

verðmið|i *n masc* (-a, -ar, -a) price tag

verðmætamat *n neu* (-s) appraisal

verðmæti *n neu* (-s, -, -a) valuables

verðmæt|ur *adj* (-, -t) valuable

verðtilboð *n neu* (-s, -, -a) quotation, offer for a price

verðug|ur *adj* (-, -t) worthy

verj|a *v* (ver, varði, varið) defend

verka *v* (~, -ði, -ð) work, have an effect

verkalýðsdagurinn *n masc* (-dagsins) Labor Day

verkamað|ur *n masc* (-manns, -menn, -manna) blue-collar worker

verkefn|i *n neu* (-s, ~, -a) project, task

verkfall *n neu* (-s, -föll, -a) strike

verkfræði *n fem* (-) engineering

verkfræðing|ur *n masc* (-s, -ar, -a) engineer

verkfærastik|a *n fem* (-u, -ur, ~) *comp* toolbar

verkfær|i *n neu* (-is, ~, -a) tool

verkjastill|ir *n masc* (-is, -ar, -a) painkiller

verkjatafl|a *n fem* (-töflu, -töflur, -na) painkiller

verknað|ur *n masc* (-ar, -ir, -a) deed

verksmiðj|a *n fem* (-u, -ur, ~) factory

verksmiðjusal|a *n fem* (-sölu, -sölur, -na) factory outlet

verkstjór|i *n masc* (-a, -ar, -a) foreman

verkstæð|i *n neu* (-is, ~, -a) repair shop, workshop

verktak|i *n masc* (-a, -ar, -a) contractor

verk|ur *n masc* (-jar, -ir, -ja) ache, cramp

vernd *n fem* (-ar) conservation, protection

vernda *v* (~, -ði, -ð) protect, guard, shield

verndað|ur *adj* (vernduð, -) preserved

verndargrip|ur *n masc* (-s, -ir, -a) amulet

verndar|i *n masc* (-a, -ar, -a) patron

verndarsvæð|i *n neu* (-is, ~, -a) preserve

verndarvæng|ur *n masc* (-s/jar, -ir, -ja) patronage

vernd|un *n fem* (-unar, -anir, -ana) protection, prevention

verr|i *adj comparative* (-i, -a) worse

vers *n masc* (~, ~, -a) verse

versla *v* (~, -ði, -ð) shop

versl|un *n fem* (-unar, -anir, -ana) store, shop, trade

verslunareigand|i *n masc* (-a, -endur, -enda) shopkeeper

verslunarétt|ur *n masc* (-ar) *leg* commercial law

verslunargat|a *n fem* (-götu, götur, -gatna) shopping street

verslunarmiðstöð *n fem* (-var, -var, -va) shopping mall, shopping center

versna *v* (~, -ði, -ð) aggrevate, get worse

verst|ur *adj superl* (-, -) worst

veruleg|ur *adj* (-, -t) considerable, substantial: ~ **hagnaður** substantial profit

veruleik|i *n masc* (-a) reality

veröld *n fem* (-aldar, -aldir, -alda) world

verönd *n fem* (-andar, -andir, -anda) terrace

vesen *n neu* (-s) *colloq* bother, hassle

vesk|i *n neu* (-is, -, -ja) wallet

vesp|a *n fem* (-u, -ur, ~) wasp; scooter

vestan *prep + gen* on the west side of, west of: ~ **Reykjavíkur** west of Reykjavik

vest|i *n neu* (-is, ~, -a) vest, waistcoat

vestr|i *n masc* (-a, -ar, -a) *(film)* western

vestræn|n *adj* (-, -t) western

vestur 1 *n neu* (-s) west; **2** *adv* west; **fara ~ á firði** go to the West Fjords

Vestur-Indí|ur *N fem pl* (-a) West Indies

Vestur-Kongó *N neu* (-) Republic of the Congo

vesturlensk|ur *adj* (-, -t) western

vetni *n neu* (-s) *chem* hydrogen

vetrarbraut *n fem* (-ar, -ir, -a) galaxy

vetrarsólstöð|ur *n fem pl* (-staða) winter solstice

vettling|ur *n masc* (-s, -ar, -a) mitten

vettvangsferð *n fem* (-ar, -ir, -a) field trip

vettvangsvinn|a *n fem* (-u) field work

vettvang|ur *n masc* (-s) scene, site; realm

vetur *n masc* (vetrar, ~, vetra) winter

véfrétt *n fem* (-ar, -ir, -a) oracle

vél *n fem* (-ar, -ar, -a) machine

vélbát|ur *n masc* (-s, -ar, -a) motor boat

vélbúnað|ur *n masc* (-ar) machinery

vélhjól *n neu* (-s, -, -a) motorcycle

vélmenni *n neu* (-s, -, -a) robot

vélrita *v* (~, -ði, -ð) type

vélsleð|i *n masc* (-a, -ar, -a) snowmobile

vélvirk|i *n masc* (-ja, -jar, -ja) mechanic

við 1 *pron* (*acc/dat* okkur; *gen* okkar) we; **2** *prep + dat (reaction)* against, to: **lyf ~ astma** drugs against asthma; **hver eru viðbrögð hans ~ þessu?** what were his reactions to this?; *+ acc (approximate location)* at, by: ~ **húsið** by the house; *(circumstances)* **hann situr ~ skriftir** he is writing; *(cooperation/relation)* to, with: **samskipti ~ kennara** communication with teachers; *(a point in time)* at: ~ **áramót** at New Year's, ~ **mánaðarmót** at the beginning of a month, ~ **sólarupprás** at sunrise

við hliðina á *prep (+ dat)* beside, next to

við og við *adv* once in a while

viðar- *prep* wooden

viðbjóðsleg|ur *adj* (-, -t) disgusting, loathsome, revolting

viðbjóð|ur *n masc* (-s, -ir, -a) horror, something disgusting

viðbót *n fem* (-ar, -bætur, -a) supplement, addition

viðbragð *n neu* (-s, -brögð, -a) reaction, reflex; feedback

viðburð|ur *n masc* (-ar, -ir, -a) event, happening

viðbygging *n fem* (-ar, -ar, -a) building extension

viðeigandi *adj* appropriate

viðfangsefn|i *n neu* (-is, ~, -a) topic, subject matter

viðgerð *n fem* (-ar, -ar, -a) repair, renovation

viðhafnarkjól|l *n masc* (-s, -ar, -a) formal dress

viðhafnarklæðnað|ur *n masc* (-ar) formal wear

viðhafnarmikil|l *adj* (-, -mikið) pompous

viðhafnarsal|ur *n masc* (-ar, -ir, -a) stateroom

viðhald *n neu* (-s) maintenance; mistress, lover

viðhald|a *v* (-held, -hélt, -héldum, -haldið) maintain

viðhorf *n neu* (-s, -, -a) attitude

viðhöfn *n fem* (-hafnar) pageantry, pomp

viðkomandi *adj* relevant; the person in question

viðkunnanleg|ur *adj* (-, -t) friendly, sympathetic, amiable

viðkvæmni *n fem* (-) sensitivity, delicacy

viðkvæm|ur *adj* (-, -t) sensitive, tender, touchy

viðlag *n neu* (-s, -lög, -a) chorus

viðmið|un *n fem* (-unar, -anir, -ana) criterion; comparison

viðræð|ur *n fem pl* (-na) discussions, talk

viðskeyt|i *n neu* (-is, ~, -a) *ling* suffix

viðskiptafélag|i *n masc* (-a, -ar, -a) business partner

viðskiptavin|ur *n masc* (-ar, -ir, -a) customer, client

viðskipt|i *n neu pl* (-a) business, trade, transaction, dealings; affair

viðsnúning|ur *n masc* (-s, -ar, -a) reversal

viðstadd|ur *adj* (-stödd, -statt) present

viðtakand|i *n masc* (-a, -endur, -enda) addressee, recipient, receiver

viðtal *n neu* (-s, -töl, -a) interview

viðtalstím|i *n masc* (-a, -ar, -a) office hours; reception hours

viðtengingarhátt|ur *n masc* (-ar, -hættir, -hátta) *ling* subjunctive

viðundur *n neu* (-s, -, -undra) freak

við|ur *n masc* (-ar, ir, -a) wood

viðurkenn|a *v* (-i, -di, -t) acknowledge, recognize; admit, confess

viðurkenning *n fem* (-ar, -ar, -a) recognition; confession

viðvaning|ur *n masc* (-s, -ar, -a) amateur

viðvíkjandi *adj* regarding

viðvör|un *n fem* (-unar, -anir, -ana) warning

viðvörunarbjall|a *n fem* (-bjöllu, -bjöllur, -na) alarm

viðvörunarljós *n neu* (-s, -, -a) red light

vift|a *n fem* (-u, -ur, ~) fan

viftureim *n fem* (-ar, -ar, -a) fan belt

vigt *n fem* (-ar, -ir, -a) scale

vigta *v* (~, -ði, -ð) weigh

vik|a *n fem* (-u, -ur, -na) week

vikudag|ur *n masc* (-s, -ar, -a) weekday

vikulega *adv* weekly

vikuleg|ur *adj* (-, -t) weekly

vikur *n neu* (-s) *geol* pumice

vildarsal|ur *n masc* (-ar, -ir, -a) VIP lounge

Viliníus *N fem* (-ar) Vilnius *(capital of Lithuania)*

vilj|a *v* (vil, vildi, viljað) want

viljalaus *adj* (-, -t) passive

viljandi *adv* deliberately, on purpose

viljastyrk|ur *n masc* (-s, -ir, -ja) resolution, strength of will

vilj|i *n masc* (-a) will, willingness

viljug|ur *adj* (-, -t) willing

vill|a *n fem* (-u, -ur, -na) error

villandi *adj* misleading

vill|ast *v* (-ist, -tist, -st) lose one's way

villibráð *n fem* (-ar, -ir, -a) game

villidýr *n neu* wild animal

villikött|ur *n masc* (-kattar, -kettir, -katta) *zool* wildcat

villiönd *n fem* (-andar, -endur, -anda) *zool* wild duck

villt|ur *adj* (-, -) lost, astray; wild, savage

vin *n fem* (-ar, ir, -a) oasis

vinaigrette sós|a *n fem* (-u) vinaigrette

vinátt|a *n fem* (-u) friendship
vindasam|ur *adj* (-söm, -t) windy
vindátt *n fem* (-ar, -ir, -a) wind direction
vindhrað|i *n masc* (-a) wind speed
vindil|l *n masc* (-s, vindlar, vindla) cigar
vindjakk|i *n masc* (-a, -ar, -a) windbreaker
vindmyll|a *n fem* (-u, -ur, -a) windmill
vindork|a *n fem* (-u) wind energy
vindstyrk|ur *n masc* (-s) wind force
vindsæng *n fem* air mattress
vindubrú *n fem* (-ar, -brýr, -a) drawbridge
vind|ur *n masc* (-s, -ar, -a) wind
vingjarnleg|ur *adj* (-, -t) friendly, kind
vinka *v* (~, -ði, -ð) wave
vinn|a *n fem* (-u, -ur, ~) work, labor, effort; win, triumph
vinnandi *adj* working
vinnubók *n fem* (-ar, -bækur, -a) workbook
vinnufélag|i *n masc* (-a, -ar, -a) colleague
vinnupall|ur *n masc* (-s, -ar, -a) scaffold
vinnustof|a *n fem* (-u, -ur, ~) studio
vinnuveitand|i *n masc* (-a, -endur, -enda) employer
vinsamlegast *adv* kindly
vinstrimað|ur *n masc* (-manns, -menn, -manna) leftist
vinstrisinnað|ur *adj* (-sinnuð, -) left-wing
vinsæld|ir *n fem pl* (-a) popularity
vinsæl|l *adj* (-, -t) popular
vin|ur *n masc* (-ar, -ir, -a) friend
vinveitt|ur *adj* (-, -) allied
virð|a *v* (-i, virti, virt) respect; ~ fyrir sér look at, observe
virð|ast *v* (-ist, virtist, virst) seem
virð|i *n neu* (-is) value
virðing *n fem* (-ar) prestige, respect, status
virðingarfull|ur *adj* (-, -t) reverential
virðingarfyllst *adv* sincerely

virðisaukaskatt|ur *n masc* (-s, -ar, -a) value-added tax
virka *v* (~, -ði, -ð) function, work
virk|i *n neu* (-is, ~, -a) fortress
virkilega *adv* really
virkja *v* (~, -ði, -ð) activate
virkj|un *n fem* (-unar, -anir, -ana) power station
virk|ur *adj* (-, -t) active
virt|ur *adj* (-, -) prestigious
visk|a *n fem* (-u) wisdom
viskastykk|i *n neu* (-is, ~, -ja) dish towel
viskí *n neu* (-s, -, -a) whiskey
viss *adj* (-, -t) certain, sure, positive
vissulega *adv* indeed
vistfræði *n fem* (-) ecology
vistkerf|i *n neu* (-is, ~, -a) ecosystem
vit *n neu* (-s) sense
vit|a *v* (veit, vissi, vitað) know
vit|i *n masc* (-a, -ar, -a) lighthouse
vitlaus *adj* (-, -t) senseless, stupid, dumb; wrong
vitn|i *n neu* (-is, ~, -a) witness
vitnisburð|ur *n masc* (-ar, -ir, -a) testimony
vídd *n fem* (-ar, -ir, -a) width
víða *adv* widely
víðáttumikil|l *adj* (-, -mikið) vast
víð|ir *n masc* (-is) willow
víðmynd *n fem* (-ar, -ir, -a) panorama
víðtæk|ur *adj* (-, -t) vast
víð|ur *adj* (-, vítt) wide; loose
Víetnam *N neu* (-/-s) Vietnam
Víetnam|i *n masc* (-a, -ar, -a) Vietnamese *(person)*
víetnamsk|a *n fem* (-nömsku) Vietnamese language
víetnamsk|ur *adj* (víetnömsk, -t) Vietnamese
vík *n fem* (-ur, -ur, -a) bay
víkingaskip *n neu* (-s, -, -a) Viking ship
víkingaöld *n fem* (-aldar, -aldir, -alda) Viking age
víking|ur *n masc* (-s, -ar, -a) Viking
víkj|a *v* (vík, vék, véku, vikið) yield

vím|a *n fem* (-u, -ur, -na) intoxication

vín *n neu* (-s, -, -a) wine: ~ **hússins** house wine; alcohol

vínandi *n masc* alcohol

Vínarborg *N fem* (-ar) Vienna *(capital of Austria)*

vínarbrauð *n neu* (-s, -, -a) Danish pastry

vínber *n neu* (-s, -, -ja) grape

vínberjasaf|i *n masc* (-a, -ar, -a) grape juice

vínbúð *n fem* (ar, -ir, -a) wine store

vínekr|a *n fem* (-u, -ur, ~) vineyard

vínglas *n neu* (-s, -glös, -a) wine glass

vínkjallar|i *n masc* (-a, -ar, -a) wine cellar

vínlist|i *n masc* (-a, -ar, -a) wine list

vínuppsker|a *n fem* (-u) vintage

vínvið|ur *n masc* (-ar, -ir, -a) vine

vjól|a *n fem* (-u, -ur, ~) *mus* viola

vír *n masc* (-s, -ar, -a) wire

vírus *n masc* (-s, -ar, -a) *med* virus

vís|a *n fem* (-u, -ur, -na) *lit* stanza

vísa *v* (~, -ði, -ð) point, direct; ~ **í** refer to; ~ **til** refer to

vísakort *n neu* (-s, -, -a) visa card

vísbending *n fem* (-ar, -ar, -a) hint, indication

vísifing|ur *n masc* (-s, ~, -ra) *anat* forefinger

vísindaleg|ur *adj* (-, -t) scientific, clinical

vísindamað|ur *n masc* (-manns, -menn, -manna) scientist

vísind|i *n neu pl* (-a) science

víst *adv* certainly, for sure

vís|un *n fem* (-unar, -anir, -ana) allusion, reference

vítahring|ur *n masc* (-s) vicious circle

vítamín *n neu* (-s, -, -a) vitamin

vítamínspraut|a *n fem* (-u) boost

vodk|i *n masc* (-a) vodka

vof|a *n fem* (-u, -ur, ~) ghost; vapor

vog *n fem* (-ar, -ir, -a) scale

voga *v* (~, -ði, -ð) dare

Vog|in *n fem def* (-arinnar) *astro* Libra

volg|ur *adj* (-, -t) lukewarm

von *n fem* (-ar, -ir, -a) hope

vonbrigð|i *n neu pl* (-a) disappointment

vond|ur *adj* (-, vont) bad, evil

vongóð|ur *adj* (-, -gott) hopeful

vonsvikin|n *adj* (-, -svikið) disappointed

vopn *n neu* (-s, -, -a) weapon, arms

vopnabúr *n neu* (-s, -, -a) armory, arsenal

vopnað|ur *adj* (vopnuð, -) armed

vopnaleit *n fem* (-ar, -ir, -a) airport security; security check

vopna|st *v refl* (~, -ðist, ~) arm

vor 1 *n neu* (-s, -, -a) spring; 2 *pron* (-, -t) *arch* our

vorlauk|ur *n masc* (-s, -ar, -a) spring onion

vottorð *n neu* (-s, -, -a) certificate

vot|ur *adj* (-, -t) wet

vægðarlaus *adj* (-, -t) relentless

væg|ur *adj* (-, -t) slight

vænd|i *n neu* (-s) prostitution

vændiskon|a *n fem* (-u, -ur, -kvenna) prostitute

vængjasvepp|ur *n masc* (-s, -ir, -a) chanterelle

væng|ur *n masc* (-s/jar, -ir, -ja) wing

væntanleg|ur *adj* (-, -t) expected, prospective

vænting *n fem* (-ar, -ar, -a) expectation

væntumþykj|a *n fem* (-u) affection

væt|a *v* (-i, -ti, -t) moisten

vætukars|i *n masc* (-a, -ar, -a) watercress

vöðvaþraut|ir *n fem pl* (-a) *med* myalgia

vöðvaverk|ur *n masc* (-jar, -ir, -ja) *med* myalgia

vöðv|i *n masc* (-a, -ar, -a) muscle

vöfflujárn *n neu* (-s, -, -a) waffle iron

vögguvís|a *n fem* (-u, -ur, ~) lullaby

vökv|i *n masc* (-a, -ar, -a) fluid, liquid

völl|ur *n masc* (vallar, vellir, valla) field

völundarhús *n neu* (-s, -, -a) maze, labyrinth

---

vömb *n fem* (vambar, vambir, vamba)
tripe

vör *n fem* (varar, varir, vara) lip

vörð|ur *n masc* (varðar, verðir,
varða) guard

vörn *n fem* (varnar, varnir, varna)
defense, protection, prevention

vörubíl|l *n masc* (-s, -ar, -a) lorry

vörugeymsl|a *n fem* (-u, -ur, -na)
warehouse

vöruhús *n neu* (-s, -, -a) department
store

vörulist|i *n masc* (-a, -ar, -a) sales
catalog

vörumerk|i *n neu* (-is, ~, -ja) brand,
trademark

vörur. *See* **vara**

Vötnin miklu *N neu pl* (Vatnanna
miklu) Great Lakes

vöxt|ur *n masc* (vaxtar) growth

Y

yddar|i *n masc* (-a, -ar, -a) pencil sharpener

yfir *prep* + *dat (location)* over, above: **hanga ~ borðinu** hang over the table; *(reason)* over: **gleðjast ~ fréttunum** be happy over the news; *(lead)* in charge: **hún er ~ öllum skólanum** she is in charge of the whole school; + *acc) (movement)* over, across: **keyra ~ brúna** drive over the bridge; *(time)* during, through: **~ daginn** during the day, **hvað borgarðu ~ árið?** what do you pay through the year?; *(quantity)* over, more than: **miðinn kostar ~ fimm þúsund** the ticket costs over five thousand

yfirbjóð|a *v* (-býð, -bauð, -buðum, -boðið) outbid

yfirborð *n neu* (-s, -, -a) coating, surface

yfirborðskennd|ur *adj* (-, -kennt) shallow, superficial

yfirburð|ir *n masc pl* (-a) preeminence

yfirdrátt|ur *n masc* (-ar) overdraft

yfirfar|a *v* (-fer, -fór, -fórum, -farið) inspect, check

yfirfær|a *v* (-i, -ði, -t) transfer

yfirgef|a *v* (-gef, -gaf, -gáfum, -gefið) abandon, desert, leave, forsake

yfirgefin|n *adj* (-, -gefið) abandoned, deserted

yfirgengileg|ur *adj* (-, -t) extreme

yfirgnæf|a *v* (-i, -ði, -t) be louder than; **tónlistin yfirgnæfði hann** I couldn't hear him because of the music

yfirhershöfðing|i *n masc* (-ja, -jar, -ja) marshal

yfirheyr|a *v* (-i, -ði, -t) question, interrogate

yfirheyrsl|a *n fem* (-u, -ur, ~) cross-examination, interrogation

yfirhöfn *n fem* (-hafnar, -hafnir, -hafna) overcoat

yfirlið *n neu* (s, -, -a) faint

yfirlit *n neu* (-s, -, -a) index; overview, summary

yfirlýsing *n fem* (-ar, -ar, -a) statement

yfirmað|ur *n masc* (-manns, -menn, -manna) chief, head, boss

yfirnáttúruleg|ur *adj* (-, -t) supernatural; psychic

yfirráð *n neu pl* (-a) dominance, reign

yfirráðasvæð|i *n neu* (-is, ~, -a) territory under governance

yfirset|a *n fem* (-u, -ur, ~) invigilation

yfirsetumað|ur *n masc* (-manns, -menn, -manna) invigilator

yfirskin *n neu* (-s) pretence, pretext

yfirstandandi *adj* ongoing

yfirtak|a *n fem* (-töku, -tökur, ~) takeover

yfirvaraskegg *n neu* (-s, -, -ja) moustache

yfirvega *v* (~, -ði, -ð) consider, premeditate

yfirvigt *n fem* (-ar, -ir, -a) *(luggage)* overweight: **þú ert með tíu kíló í ~** your luggage is 10 kilos over the limit

yfirvinn|a *n fem* (-u) overtime

yfirþjón|n *n masc* (-s, -ar, -a) head waiter

yndisleg|ur *adj* (-, -t) wonderful

ynging *n fem* (-ar) rejuvenation

yngj|ast *v* (yngist, yngdist, yngst) rejuvenate, get younger

yngr|i *adj compar* (-i, -a) younger

yngst|ur *adj superl* (-, -) youngest

yrkisefn|i *n neu* (-is, ~, -a) subject matter in a poem

ysting|ur *n masc* (-s) curds

ytr|i *adj compar* (-i, -a) outer

Ý

ýkj|a 1 *n fem* (-u, -ur, -a) exaggerations;
   2 *v* (ýki, ýkti, ýkt) exaggerate
ýkt|ur *adj* (-, -) extreme, exaggerated
ýmis *pron* (-, -t) of various kind,
   several: **ýmsir menn** several men
ýmist ... eða *conj* either ... or **það
   er ýmist rigning eða rok** it's
   either rainy or windy; **ýmist í
   ökkla eða eyra** either too much or
   too little

ýmsir *pron* various: **ýmsir
   möguleikar** various options
ýs|a *n fem* (-u, -ur, ~) haddock
ýsuflak *n neu* (-s, -flök, -a) a fillet of
   a haddock
ýt|a *v* (-i, -ti, -t) push, press

Z

zip-drif *n neu* (-s, -, -a) *comp* zip
   drive

þ

það *pron* it

þaðan *adv* from there: **ég er** ~ I'm from there

þagga *v* (~, -ði, -ð) suppress

þak *n neu* (-s, þök, -a) roof

þakglugg|i *n masc* (-a, -ar, -a) sky light; sunroof

þakin|n *adj* (-, þakið) coated

þakka *v* (~, -ði, -ð) thank; ~ **þér fyrir** thanks!

þakkir. *See* **þökk**

þakklát|ur *adj* (-, -t) grateful

þang *n neu* (-s) seaweed

þangað *adv* to there: **ég ætla** ~ I'm going there

þangað til *adv* until

þankahríð *n fem* (-ar, -ir, -a) brainstorming

þankastrik *n neu* (-s, -, -a) hyphen

þannig *adv* so; in that way

þar *adv* there; ~ **á eftir** after that

þar af leiðandi *conj* therefore, consequently

þar fyrir utan *conj* in addition

þar sem *conj* whereas

þarfna|st *v refl* (~, -ðist, ~) require, need

þar|i *n masc* (-a, -ar, -a) seaweed

þarm|ur *n masc* (-s, -ar, -a) *anat* gut, bowel

þarna *adv* over there

þau *pron neu* they, them

þá *adv* then

þátttak|a *n fem* (-töku) participation, involvement

þátttakand|i *n masc* (-a, -endur, -enda) participant

þátt|ur *n masc* (-þáttar, -þættir, -þátta) program; factor, part; *lit* act

þef|ur *n masc* (-s/jar) smell

þegar *pron* when

þegiðu *excl* shut up!, keep quiet!

þegj|a *v* (þegi, þagði, þagað) keep silent, refrain from talking

þeim *pron dat* them

þeir *pron masc nom* they

þeirra *pron gen* their, them; theirs

þekj|a *v* (þek, þakti, þakið) cover

þekj|ast *v refl* (þekst, þaktist, þakist) be covered

þekking *n fem* (-ar) knowledge

þekkj|a *v* (þekki, þekkti, þekkt) identify, recognize, know: **ég þekki hann** I know him

þekkj|ast *v refl* (þekkist, þekktist, þekkst) know each other; accept: ~ **boðið** accept the offer

þem|a *n neu* (-a, -u, -a) theme

þenj|a *v* (þen, þandi, þanið) expand, stretch

þenj|ast *v refl* (þenst, þandist, þanist) ~ **út** expand

þess *pron gen* its

þess konar *adj* that kind of

þess vegna *conj* therfore, thus, hence

þessi *pron* (þessi, þetta) this: ~ **maður** this man, ~ **kona** this woman

þetta *pron neu* that, this: **hvað er** ~? what is this?, ~ **barn** this child

þeyting|ur *n masc* (-s) smoothie

þeytirjóm|i *n masc* (-a) whipping cream

þeytt|ur *adj* (-, -) whipped

þéttbyggð|ur *adj* (-, -byggt) populous

þéttbýliskjarn|i *n masc* (-a, -ar, -a) township

þéttleik|i *n masc* (-a) density

þéttskipað|ur *adj* (-skipuð, -) crowded

þétt|ur *adj* (-, -) compact

þind *n fem* (-ar, -ir, -a) *anat* diaphragm

þing *n neu* (-s, þing, -a) congress; parliament

þinghús *n neu* (-s, -, -a) state house

þingkon|a *n fem* (-u, -ur, -kvenna)
congresswoman

þingmað|ur *n masc* (-manns, -menn,
-manna) congressman

þin|n *pron* (þín, þitt) your: **bíllinn** ~
your car

þin|ur *n masc* (-s, -ir, -a) *flora* fir

þistilhjart|a *n neu* (-a, -hjörtu,
-hjartna) artichoke

þitt *pron neu* your: **barnið** ~ your
child

þín *pron fem* your: **tölvan** ~ your
computer

þjá *v* (þjái, þjáði, þjáð) afflict

þjálfa *v* (~, -ði, -ð) coach

þjálfa|st *v refl* (~, -ðist, ~) get trained,
get routinized

þjálfað|ur *adj* (þjálfuð, -) trained

þjálfar|i *n masc* (-a, -ar, -a) coach,
trainer

þjálfun *n fem* (-ar) training; therapy:
sjúkraþjálfun physiotherapy

þjáning *n fem* (-ar, -ar, -a) suffering,
affliction

þjá|st *v refl* (-ist, -ðist, -ðst) suffer

þjóð *n fem* (-ar, -ir, -a) nation; folk

þjóðaratkvæðagreiðsl|a *n fem* (-u,
-ur, -na) national referendum

þjóðarmorð *n neu* (-s, -, -a) genocide

þjóðdans *n masc* (-, -ar, -a) folk
dance

þjóðern|i *n neu* (-is, ~, -a) nationality

þjóðernishyggj|a *n fem* (-u)
nationalism

þjóðfélag *n neu* (-s, -félög, -a) society

þjóðgarð|ur *n masc* (-s, -ar, -a)
national park

þjóðhöfðing|i *n masc* (-ja, -jar, -ja)
head of state

þjóðlag *n neu* (-s, -lög, -a) folk music

þjóðlagatónlist *n fem* (-ar) folk music

þjóðleg|ur *adj* (-, -t) national

þjóðlistasafn *n neu* (-s, -söfn, -a)
national gallery

þjóðminjasafn *n neu* (-s, -söfn, -a)
national museum

þjóðnýt|a *v* (-i, -ti, -t) nationalize

þjóðnýting *n fem* (-ar) nationalization

þjóðrækin|n *adj* (-, -rækið) patriotic

þjóðsag|a *n fem* (-sögu, -sögur, -sagna)
legend

Þjóðskrá *n fem* (-r) Icelandic registry office

þjóðsöng|ur *n masc* (-s, -var, -va)
national anthem

þjóðtung|a *n fem* (-u, -ur, -na)
vernacular

þjóðveg|ur *n masc* (-ar/s, -ir, -a)
main road

Þjóðverj|i *n masc* (-a, -ar, -a) Ger-
man *(person)*

þjófavörn *n fem* (-varnar, -varnir,
-varna) alarm

þjófnað|ur *n masc* (-ar, -ir, -a) theft,
stealing

þjóf|ur *n masc* (-s, -ar, -a) thief

þjóna *v* (~, -ði, -ð) serve

þjón|n *n masc* (-s, -ar, -a) waiter,
servant; *comp* server: **vef**~ server

þjónust|a *n fem* (-u, -ur, ~) service

þjónustugjald *n neu* (-s, -gjöld, -a)
service fee

þjónustustúlk|a *n fem* (-u, -ur, -na)
waitress

þjórfé *n neu* (-fjár) gratuity, tip

þjót|a *v* (þýt, þaut, þutum, þotið) rush

þjótak *n neu* (-s, -tök, -a) *med* sciatica

þjöl *n fem* (þjalar, þjalir, þjala) file

þok|a *n fem* (-u) fog

þokkalega *adv* fairly

þokk|i *n masc* (-a) charm

þokuljós *n neu* (-s, -, -a) foglight

þolfimi *n fem* (-) *sports* aerobics

þolinmæði *n fem* (-) patience

þolinmóð|ur *adj* (-, -mótt) patient

þor *n neu* (-s) courage

þor|a *v* (-i, -ði, -að) dare

þorp *n neu* (-s, -, -a) village; township

þorr|i *n masc* (-a) *the first month
of the year on the old Icelandic
calender*

þorrablót *n neu* (-s, -, -a) Icelandic
midwinter feast

þorsk|ur *n masc* (-s, -ar, -a) cod

þorst|i *n masc* (-a) thirst

þot|a *n fem* (-u, -ur, ~) jet plane

þotuþreyt|a *n fem* (-u) jet lag

þó *conj* though, although

þókna|st *v* (~, -ðist, ~) please, satisfy

þókn|un *n fem* (-unar, -anir, -ana) compensation

þótt að *conj* though, although

þramma *v* (~, -ði, -ð) plod

þraut *n fem* (-ar, -ir, -a) problem, riddle; pain

þrautseigj|a *n fem* (-u) perseverance

þrá *v* (-i, -ði, -ð) desire, lust

þráa|st *v* (~, -ðist, ~) insist: ~ **við** not to give up

þráðlaus *adj* (-, -t) wireless; **þráðlaust net** wireless Internet

þráð|ur *n masc* (-ar, þræðir, -a) thread, fiber

þráhyggj|a *n fem* (-u) obsession

þrálát|ur *adj* (-, -t) chronic

þrátt fyrir *prep* despite

þrekvirki *n neu* (-s, -, -ja) big achievement

þrengsl|i *n neu* (-a) lack of space

þrenn|ir *adj pl* (-ar, -) *(for plural nouns)* three: **þrennar buxur** three pairs of trousers; *(for things that come in couples)* three pairs: ~ **vettlingar** three pairs of mittens

þrep *n neu* (-s, -, -a) step

þrettán *num* thirteen

þrettánd|i *ord* (-a, -a) thirteenth

þreyt|a 1 *n fem* (-u) fatigue, exhaustion; **2** *v* (-i, -ti, -t) make tired, exhaust

þreytandi *adj* tiring, wearing

þreytt|ur *adj* (-, -) tired, drowsy

þriðji *ord* (-a, -a) third

þriðjudag|ur *n masc* (-s, -ar, -a) Tuesday

þrifaleg|ur *adj* (-, -t) tidy

þrist|ur *n masc* (-s, -ir, -a) number three

þrisvar *adv* three times

þrífót|ur *n masc* (-ar, -fætur, -a) tripod

þríhyrning|ur *n masc* (-s, -ar, -a) *math* triangle

þríleik|ur *n masc* (-s, -ir, -ja) trilogy

þrír *num masc* (þrjá, þremur, þriggja) three

þrítugasti *ord* (-a, -a) thirtieth

þrítug|ur *adj* (-, -t) thirty years old

þrjár *num fem* (þrjár, þremur, þriggja) three

þrjátíu *num* thirty

þrjósk|a *n fem* (-u) stubbornness, obstinacy

þrjóska|st *v* (~, -ðist, ~) persist

þrjósk|ur *adj* (-, -t) stubborn, obstinate, persistent

þrjót|ur *n masc* (-s, -ar, -a) rascal

þrjú *num neu* (þrjú, þremur, þriggja) three

þroskað|ur *adj* (þroskuð, -) mature, aged, ripe: **þroskaðir tómatar** ripe tomatoes

þroskahöml|un *n fem* (-unar, -anir, -ana) retardation

þroska|st *v* (~, -ðist, ~) age, mature

þrosk|i *n masc* (-a) maturity

þróa *v* (~, -ði, -ð) develop

þróa|st *v refl* (~, -ðist, ~) develop, emerge

þróttleysi *n neu* (-s) fatigue

þró|un *n fem* (-unar, -anir, -ana) development

þróunarfræðileg|ur *adj* (-, -t) evolutionary

þrum|a *n fem* (-u, -ur, -a) thunder

þrumuveður *n neu* (-s, -, -veðra) thunderstorm

þrúgugúrk|a *n fem* (-u, -ur, -na) gherkins

þrútin|n *adj* (-, þrútið) swollen

þrýsting|ur *n masc* (-s) pressure: **loft~** air pressure

þrældóm|ur *n masc* (-s) slavery

þrælkun *n fem* (-ar) slavery

þræl|l *n masc* (-s, -ar, -a) slave

þræta *v* (-i, -ti, -t) argue

þröngsýni *n fem* (-) narrowmindedness, tunnel vision

þröng|ur *adj* (-, -t) narrow

þröngva *v* (~, -ði, -ð) impose

þröst|ur *n masc* (þrastar, þrestir, þrasta) *zool* thrush

þul|a *n fem* (-u, -ur, -na) rhyme; announcer on television or radio

þumalfingur *n masc* (-s, ~, -fingra) thumb

þumal|l *n masc* (-s, þumlar, þumla) thumb

þumlung|ur *n masc* (-s, -ar, -a) inch

þungað|ur *adj* (þunguð, -) pregnant

þungamiðj|a *n fem* (-u) pivot

þungarokkar|i *n masc* (-a, -ar, -a) metal head

þunglyndi *n neu* (-s) depression, melancholia

þunglynd|ur *adj* (-, -t) depressed, melancholy

þung|un *n fem* (-unar, -anir, -ana) pregnancy

þungunarpróf *n neu* (-s, -, -a) pregnancy test

þung|ur *adj* (-, -t) heavy

þunn|ur *adj* (-, -t) **1** thin, watery: **þunnt kaffi** watery coffee; **2** *slang* hung over

þurfa *v* (þarf, þurfti, þurft) need, require

þurr *adj* (-, -t) dry

þurrhreinsun *n fem* (-ar) dry cleaning

þurrka *v* (~, -ði, -ð) dry; ~ **af** dust; ~ **út** wipe out

þurrkað|ur *adj* (þurrkuð, -) dried

þurrkar|i *n masc* (-a, -ar, -a) clothes dryer

þurrk|ur *n masc* (-s, -ar, -a) drought

þú *pron* you

þú veist *interj* y'know

þúf|a *n fem* (-u, -ur, -na) tussock

þúsund *n neu* (-s, -, -a) thousand

þúsundast|i *ord* (-a, -a) thousandth

þúsundfætl|a *n fem* (-u, -ur, -na) centipede

þvaður *n neu* (-s) *slang* rubbish, bullshit

þvætting|ur *n masc* (-s) rubbish

þvag *n neu* (-s) urine

þvagfærasýking *n fem* (-u, -ar, -a) *med* urinary tract infection

þvegil|l *n masc* (-s, þveglar, þvegla) mop

þvera *v* (~, -ði, -ð) cross

þverflaut|a *n fem* (-u, -ur, ~) *mus* flute

þvermál *n neu* (-s, -, -a) diameter

þversögn *n fem* (-sagnar, -sagnir, -sagna) paradox

þvert yfir 1 *adv* across; **2** *prep* (+ acc) across

því ... þeim mun ... *conj* the ... the ...: **því fleiri því betra** the more the merrier

því miður *adv* unfortunately, sadly

því síður *adv* even less

því 1 *pron neu dat* it: **gleymdu ~** forget it; **2** *conj* because: **~ ég þarf að fara** because I have to go

þvílíkur *pron* (-, -t) such: **~ léttir** such a relief

þvo *v* (þvæ, þvoði, þvoðum, þvegið) wash

þvottaaðstað|a *n fem* (-stöðu) laundry facilities

þvottaduft *n neu* (-s) washing powder

þvottaefn|i *n neu* (-s, -, -a) washing powder, detergent

þvottahús *n neu* (-s, -, -a) launderette, laundromat, laundry room

þvottasnúr|a *n fem* (-u, -ur, ~) washing line

þvottaþjónust|a *n fem* (-u, -ur, ~) laundry service

þvottavél *n fem* (-ar, -ar, -a) washing machine

þvottheld|ur *adj* (-, -helt) washable

þvott|ur *n masc* (-ar/s, -ar, -a) laundry

þybbin|n *adj* (-, þybbið) chubby

þyk|ja *v* (-i, þótti, þótt) find, consider: **hann þykir fyndinn** he is considered to be funny; + *dat subj* **mér þykir það leitt** I'm sorry

þykj|ast *v* (þykist, þóttist, þóst) pretend

þykkni *n neu* (-s) concentrate
þykkt *n fem* (-ar, -ir, -a) thickness
þykk|ur *adj* (-, -t) thick
þyngd *n fem* (-ar, -ir, -a) weight, gravity
þynn|a *v* (-i, -ti, -t) dilute
þynnk|a *n fem* (-u, -ur, ~) *slang* hangover
þynnt|ur *adj* (-, -) thinned
þyrl|a *n fem* (-u, -ur, -na) helicopter
þyrp|ast *v* (-ist, -tist, -st) cluster
þyrping *n fem* (-ar, -ar, -a) cluster
þyrst|ur *adj* (-, -) thirsty
þýð|a *v* (-i, -ddi, -tt) mean; translate
þýðand|i *n masc* (-a, -endur, -enda) translator
þýðing *n fem* (-ar, -ar, -a) translation; relevance, significance
þýðingarmikil|l *adj* (-, -mikið) significant, momentous

þýsk|a *n fem* (-u) the German language
Þýskaland *N neu* (-s) Germany
þýsk|ur *adj* (-, -t) German
þægilega *adv* comfortably, pleasantly
þægileg|ur *adj* (-, -t) comfortable, pleasant; convenient
þægind|i *n neu* (-a) comfort, amenities
þær *pron fem* they, them
þögn *n fem* (þagnar, þagnir, þagna) silence
þögul|l *adj* (-, -t) quiet, silent, mute
þökk *n fem* (þakkar, þakkir, þakka) thank; **kærar þakkir** thanks!
þörf *n fem* (þarfar, þarfir, þarfa) requirement
þörung|ur *n masc* (-s, -ar, -a) *flora* algae, seaweed

Æ

æ 1 *adv* **æ fleiri** more and more; **sí
og æ** all the time; **æ ofan í æ** over
and over again; **2** *interj* ouch!

æð *n fem* (-ar, -ar, -a) vein

æð|a *v* (-i, æddi, ætt) rush

æðahnút|ur *n masc* (-s, -ar, -a) *med*
vericose veins; hemorrhoids

æðardún|n *n masc* (-s) eiderdown,
down feathers from the eider duck

æðarfugl *n masc* (-s, -ar, -a) *flora*
eider

æði *n neu* (-s, -, -a) hype, mania

æðisleg|ur *adj* (-, -t) terrific, fantastic,
great

æðr|i *adj compar* (-i, -a) superior,
higher: ~ **máttarvöld** higher power

æðst|ur *adj superl* (-, -) paramount,
supreme: **Óðinn var ~ goða** Odin
was supreme to all gods

æð|ur *n fem* (-ar, -ar, -a) eider

æf|a *v* (-i, -ði, -t) exercise, practice,
rehearse

æfing *n fem* (-ar, -ar, -a) exercise,
practice, rehearsal, study, training

æfingagall|i *n masc* (-a, -ar, -a)
training suit

æi *interj* oh, ouch

æl|a *n fem* (-u, -ur, ~) vomit, throw up

ælupest *n fem* (-ar, -ir, -a) *med*
stomach flu, gastroenteritis

æp|a *v* (-i, -ti, -t) scream, shout

æs|a *v* (-i, -ti, -t) excite, make excited

æsing|ur *n masc* (-s) thrill

æsk|a *n fem* (-u) youth, childhood

ætíð *adv form* always

ætisvepp|ur *n masc* (-s, -ir, -a)
mushroom

ætiþistil|l *n masc* (-s, -þistlar, -þistla)
artichoke

ætla *v* (~, -ði, -ð) going to do; intend; plan: **ég ~ í bíó** I'm going to
the movies; **ég ~ að fá …** I would
like to have …

ætl|un *n fem* (-unar, -anir, -ana)
intention

ætt *n fem* (-ar, -ir, -a) family, stock

ættarerj|ur *n fem pl* (-a) feud

ættarnafn *n neu* (-s, -nöfn, -a)
surname

ættartal|a *n fem* (-tölu, -tölur, -na)
pedigree

ættartengsl *n neu pl* (-a) kinship

ættartré *n neu* (-s, -, -trjáa) family
tree

ættaveld|i *n neu* (-is, ~, -a) dynasty

ættern|i *n neu* (-is) family background,
origin

ættflokk|ur *n masc* (-s, -ar, -a) tribe

ætti. *See* **eiga**

ætting|i *n masc* (-ja, -jar, -ja) relative

ættjarðarást *n fem* (-ar, -ir, -a)
patriotism

ættleið|a *v* (-i, -leiddi, -leitt) adopt

ættmenn|i *n neu* (-is, ~, -a) relative

æt|ur *adj* (-, -t) edible

æviminning|ar *n fem pl* (-a) memoirs

ævintýr|i *n neu* (-is, ~, -a) adventure;
lit fairy tale, folk tale

ævisag|a *n fem* (-sögu, -sögur, -sag-
na) *lit* biography, memoir

æxla|st *v* (~, -ðist, ~) *bio* reproduce,
propagate; develop

æxl|i *n neu* (-is, ~, -a) *med* tumor

æxlun *n fem* (-ar) *bio* reproduction,
propagation

æxlunarfær|i *n neu pl* (-a) *anat*
reproductive organs

Ö

öðla|st *v* (~, -ðist, ~) obtain, get; ~ **frægð** become famous

öðruvísi *adv* different

öfgafull|ur *adj* (-, -t) extreme

öfgamað|ur *n masc* (-manns, -menn, -manna) extremist

öfg|ar *n fem pl* (-a) extremes

öfugsnúin|n *adj* (-, -snúið) perverse

öfuguggahátt|ur *n masc* (-ar, -hættir, -hátta) perversion

öfugugg|i *n masc* (-a, -ar, -a) pervert

öfund *n fem* (-ar) jealousy

öfundsjúk|ur *adj* (-, -t) jealous

ögn *n fem* (agnar, agnir, agna) a little bit; *ling* particle

ögra *v* (~, -ði, -ð) provoke

ögrandi *adj* (-, -) provocative

ögr|un *n fem* (-ar, -anir, -ana) provocation

ökkl|i *n masc* (-a, -ar, -a) *anat* ankle

ökuskírtein|i *n neu* (-is, ~, -a) driver's license

öl *n neu* (-s) beer, ale

öld *n fem* (aldar, aldir, alda) century

öldungadeildarþingmað|ur *n masc* (-manns, -menn, -manna) senator

öldungaráð *n neu* (-s, -, -a) senate

ölmus|a *n fem* (-u, -ur, ~) alms

ölvað|ur *adj* (ölvuð, -) intoxicated, drunk

ölvun *n fem* (-ar) drunkenness

ölvunarakstur *n masc* (-s) drunk driving

önd *n fem* (andar, endur, anda) *zool* duck

öndun *n fem* (-ar) breathing

öndunarkerf|i *n neu* (-is, ~, -a) *anat* respiratory system

öndunarpíp|a *n fem* (-u, -ur, -na) snorkel

öndunartæk|i *n neu* (-is, ~, -ja) *med* aspirator

öndunarveg|ur *n masc* (-ar, -ir, -a) *anat* respiratory tract

öndvegissetur *n neu* (-s, -, -setra) center of excellence

önn *n fem* (annar, annir, anna) term: **vorönn** spring term

önnur. *See* **annar**

ör 1 *adj* (-, -t) quick, fast; ~ **hjarts-láttur** palpitations; **2** *n fem* (-var, -var, -va) arrow; **3** *n neu* (-s, -, -a) scar

örbylgjuofn *n masc* (-s, -ar, -a) microwave

örk *n fem* (arkar, arkir, arka) ark

örlög *n neu pl* (-laga) fate

örn *n masc* (arnar, ernir, arna) *zool* eagle

örugglega *adv* definitely, surely

örugg|ur *adj* (-, -t) secure, safe; confident

örva *v* (~, -ði, -ð) stimulate

örvæntingarfullt *adv* desperately

örvæntingarfull|ur *adj* (-, -t) desperate

öryggi *n neu* (-s) security, safety

öryggisbelt|i *n neu* (-is, ~, -a) safety belt

öryggisgeymsl|a *n fem* (-u, -ur, -na) vault

öryggishjálm|ur *n masc* (-s, -ar, -a) crash helmet

öryggisnæl|a *n fem* (-u, -ur, -na) safety pin

öryggisskoð|un *n fem* (-unar, -anir, -ana) security check

öryggisvest|i *n neu* (-is, ~, -a) safety jacket

ös *n fem* (asar) rush

öskra *v* (~, -ði, -ð) yell, scream, shout, roar

öskubakk|i *n masc* (-a, -ar, -a) ashtray

öskudag|ur *n masc* (-s) Ash Wednes-
day
öskur *n neu* (-s, -, öskra) scream,
shout, roar
ösp *n fem* (aspar, aspir, aspa) *flora*
aspen; populus

öxi *n fem* (axar, axir, axa) axe
öxl *n fem* (axlar, axlir, axla) *anat*
shoulder
öxul|l *n masc* (-s, öxlar, öxla) axis;
axle

ENGLISH-ICELANDIC DICTIONARY

A

a *indef art* [*not used in Icelandic*]: ~
house hús
A.D. *abbrev* e. Kr.
a.m. *abbrev* fyrir hádegi
abalone *n* sæeyra
abandon *v* yfirgefa
abandoned *adj* yfirgefinn
abbey *n* klaustur
abbreviation *n* skammstöfun
abdomen *n anat* kviður: **lower ~**
neðra kviðarhol
abduction *n* mannrán
ability *n* hæfileiki, kunnátta:
according to one's ~ miðað við
getu; **have the ~ to do sth** geta
gert eitthvað; **lack the ~ to do
sth** kunna ekki að gera eitthvað;
(*capacity*) geta: **have the ~ to take
on more tasks** geta tekið að sér
fleiri verkefni
able *adj* geta gert: **I'm ~ to do it** ég
get gert það; **I'm not ~ to go** ég
get ekki farið
aboard *adv/prep* um borð: **~ the
plane** um borð í vélinni
aboriginal *adj* upprunalegur; **~
people** frumbyggjar
abort *v* hætta við; (*miscarry*) missa
fóstur; (*terminate*) eyða fóstri
abortion *n* fóstureyðing
about 1 *adv* um það bil: **at ~ two
o'clock** um tvöleitið; **~ as big as
this house** um það bil eins stórt
og þetta hús; (*location*) einhvers
staðar: **~ here** einhvers staðar hér;
2 *prep* um: **a book ~ Iceland** bók
um Ísland; **what ~** hvað með: **what
~ dinner?** hvað með hádegismat?
above 1 *prep* fyrir ofan: **~ the sofa**
fyrir ofan sófann; **~ average** yfir
meðallagi; **~ all** fyrst og fremst;

2 *adv* fyrir ofan: **the apartment ~**
íbúðin fyrir ofan; **from ~** að ofan
abroad *adv* í útlöndum, erlendis:
from ~ frá útlöndum, að utan; **go ~**
fara til útlanda, fara út
abrupt *adj* skyndilegur
abruptly *adv* skyndilega, snögglega,
allt í einu
abscess *n med* kýli
absence *n (due to traveling)* fjarvera:
after an ~ of two weeks eftir
tveggja vikna fjarveru; (*from work
or school*) fjarvist: **~ from work**
fjarvist frá vinnu; **leave of ~**
tímabundið leyfi
absent *adj* fjarverandi, ekki mættur
absinthe *n* absint
absolute *adj* algjör
absolutely *adv* algjörlega, gjörsamlega
absorb *v* drekka í sig
abstract 1 *adj* hugrænn, óáþreifanlegur;
(*painting*) abstrakt; **2** *n* ágrip
absurd *adj* fáránlegur
abuse 1 *n* misnokun; **2** *v* misnota
academic 1 *adj* akademískur; **2** *n*
háskólamaður, menntafólk
academy *n* akademía
accelerator *n mech* bensíngjöf
accent *n ling (emphasis)* áhersla;
(*pronunciation*) framburður; (*foreign*) hreimur: **she speaks with an
American ~** hún talar með amerísk-
um hreim
accept *v* samþykkja
acceptable *adj* ásættanlegur
access 1 *n* aðgangur, aðgengi; **2** *v*
hafa aðgang að: **~ computer file**
hafa aðgang að tölvuskrá, **gain ~
to** fá aðgang að
accident *n* slys: **have a car ~** lenda
í bílslysi; (*fatal*) banaslys; (*bad*

luck) óheppni: **this was just an ~**
þetta var bara óheppni; *(good luck)*
af tilviljun: **it is no ~ that** það er
engin tilviljun að
accidentally *adv* fyrir tilviljun, óvart
accommodation *n (adjustment)*
aðlögun
accommodations *n* gisting
accompany *v* fylgja, koma með; *mus*
spila undir
accomplish *v* gera, koma í verk, afreka
accomplished *adj* fær
accomplishment *n* afrek
accord *n mus* hljómur; *(agree-*
ment) samkomulag: **enter an ~** ná
samkomulagi
accordance *n* samræmi: **in ~ with** í
samræmi við
according to *prep* samkvæmt
account 1 *n* reikningur: **bank ~**
bankareikningur, **checking ~**
veltureikningur, **joint ~** sameiginlegur reikningur, **open an ~** stofna
reikning, **close an ~** loka reikningi,
pay money into an ~ greiða inn á
reikning, **take money out of one's**
~ taka peninga út af reikningi;
(bill) reikningur; *(story)* frásögn,
lýsing; **2** *v* gera grein fyrir, útskýra
accountant *n* bókhaldari: **certified ~**
löggiltur bókhaldari
accumulate *v* safna
accumulation *n* safn, uppsöfnun
accurate *adj* nákvæmur
accurately *adv* nákvæmt, rétt
accusative case *n ling* þolfall
accuse *v* ásaka: **~d of** ásakaður um
ache 1 *n* verkur; **2** *v* vera með verk,
vera illt: **my legs ~** ég er með verk
í fótunum, mér er illt í fótunum
achieve *v (goal)* ná takmarki: **~**
one's aim ná takmarki sínu, **~ a**
victory sigra; *(result)* ná árangri,
sýna árangur: **girls ~d better re-**
sults than boys stúlkur náðu betri
árangri en drengir
achievement *n* árangur: **great ~**
mjög góður árangur

acid 1 *adj* súr; **2** *n* sýra: **stomach ~**
magasýra
acid precipitation *n* súrt regn
acid rain *n* súrt regn
acknowledge *v* viðurkenna
acne *n med* unglingabólur
acorn *n* akarn
acquaintance *n* kunningi: **meet an ~**
hitta kunningja
acquaint *v* kynna; **become ~ed**
kynnast; **I'm ~ed with him** ég
kannast við hann
acquire *v* fá, eignast
acquisition *n* eign
acquit *v leg* sýkna
acquittal *n leg* sýknun
acre *n* ekra
across *adv/prep* yfir, þvert yfir: **~**
and over þvers og kruss; **walk ~**
the street ganga yfir götuna
acrylic *adj* akrýl-: **~ paint** akrýllitur
act 1 *n* verknaður, athöfn: **~ of vio-**
lence ofbeldisverk; **an ~ of justice**
réttlætisverk; *(in theater)* þáttur;
(entertainment) atriði; **2** *v (behave)*
hegða sér, haga sér, láta: **~ silly**
haga sér bjánalega; *(theater)* leika;
(work) starfa
acting 1 *adj* settur: **~ superintendent**
settur skólastjóri; **2** *n (theater)*
leiklist
action *n* atburður; atburðarrás: **the ~**
takes place in Iceland atburðirnir
gerast á Íslandi; **take ~** grípa til
aðgerða; **is there any ~ tonight?**
er eitthvað um að vera í kvöld?;
take legal ~ kæra
action movie *n* spennumynd,
hasarmynd
activate *v* virkja: **~ the credit card**
virkja kreditkortið
active *adj* virkur: **Hekla is an ~**
volcano Hekla er virkt eldfjall
activist *n* aðgerðasinni
activity *n* starfsemi; **outdoor activi-**
ties útivist; *med* **bodily ~** líkams-
starfsemi

actor *n* leikari

actress *n* leikkona

actual *adj* raunverulegur, eiginlegur

actually *adv* í rauninni, eiginlega

acupuncture *n* nálarstunga

acute *adj (intense)* hastarlegur, alvarlegur; ~ **pain** sársaukafullur verkur; *(sudden)* bráður, bráða-; *(sharp)* beittur, skarpur; *math* ~ **angle** hvasst horn

ad *n* auglýsing

adapt *v* aðlaga; *(oneself)* aðlagast; *(a play)* skrifa leikgerð; **ability to** ~ aðlögunarhæfni

adapter *n* straumbreytir

add *v math* leggja saman: ~ **2 plus 2** leggja saman tvo og tvo; *(in writing, speaking)* bæta við: **I would like to** ~ **that** ég vil bæta því við að; *(increase)* auka: **this ~s flavor** þetta eykur bragðið

addicted *adj* háður: ~ **to drugs** háður fíkniefnum

addiction *n* fíkn, misnotkun

addition *n math* samlagning; *(in writing, speaking)* athugasemd; *(increase)* aukning; **in** ~ auk þess, þar fyrir utan: **in** ~ **to the host there were three people at the party** fyrir utan húsráðanda voru þrír gestir í veislunni

additional *adj* auka: **could you bring** ~ **chairs?** gætir þú komið með auka stóla?

address 1 *n* heimilisfang: **home** ~ heimilisfang, **permanent** ~ fast heimilisfang; **mailing** ~ póstfang; **e-mail** ~ netfang; *(talk)* ávarp; *(terms of address)* ávarp; **2** *v (~ a letter)* árita, skrifa utan á; *(in writing)* stíla á; *(talk to)* ávarpa; *(by title)* titla

addressee *n* viðtakandi

adept *adj* fær, flinkur

adequate *adj* fullnægjandi

adequately *adv* nægilega

ADHD *n med* athyglisbrestur

adhere *v* festast við; *(follow)* fylgja

adhesive tape *n* heftiplástur

adjacent *adj* samliggjandi

adjective *n ling* lýsingarorð

adjoining *adj* samliggjandi

adjust *v (adapt)* laga að; aðlaga: ~ **expenses to income** laga útgjöld að tekjum; *(adapt oneself)* aðlagast; *(clothes)* laga; *(instrument, tools)* stilla

adjustment *n* aðlögun, stilling; **flavor** ~ bæta bragðið

administration *n* stjórn, framkvæmdastjórn

administrative *adj* stjórnunar-: ~ **expenses** stjórnunarkostnaður; ~ **district** stjórnunarsvæði

admiration *n* aðdáun

admire *v* dá, dýrka

admirer *n* aðdáandi

admission *n* innritun: ~ **to university** innritun í háskóla, ~ **fee** innritunargjald, ~ **to the hospital** innritun á sjúkrahús; *(show, concert)* aðgangur: ~ **fee** aðgangseyrir, **free** ~ ókeypis aðgangur; *(confession)* játning

admit *v (into university)* innrita; *(allow to enter)* hleypa inn; *(confess)* viðurkenna, játa

admittance *n* aðgangur: **no** ~ aðgangur bannaður

adopt *v (a child)* ættleiða; *(an opinion, attitude)* tileinka sér

adorable *adj* aðdáunarverður, undursamlegur

adore *v* dýrka, dá

adult *adj* fullorðinn: ~ **education** fullorðinsfræðsla; **2** *n* fullorðinn: **children and ~s** börn og fullorðnir

advance 1 *adj* fyrirfram-: ~ **payment** fyrirframgreiðsla; ~ **booking** bókanir, pantanir; ~ **sale** forsala; **2** *n (progress)* framfarir; *(increase)* aukning; *(money)* fyrirframgreiðsla; **3** *v (positive progress)* taka framförum; *(negative progress)* ágerast: **her disease ~d** veikindi hennar ágerðust

advanced *adj (science, medicine)*
nýjasti: ~ **technology** nýjasta
tækni; *(education)* framhalds-: ~
Icelandic framhaldsnámskeið í
íslensku
advantage *n* kostur, forréttindi
adventure *n* ævintýri
adverb *n ling* atviksorð
adversary *n* óvinur
adversity *n* erfiðleikar: **in times of** ~
þegar erfiðleikar steðja að
advertise *v* auglýsa
advertisement *n (on television)*
auglýsing; *(personal)* smáauglýsing
advertising *n* auglýsingamarkaðurinn:
she works in ~ hún vinnur á
auglýsingamarkaðinum; ~ **agency**
auglýsingastofa; ~ **executive**
auglýsingastjóri
advice *n* ráð: **ask for** ~ biðja um ráð
advise *v* ráðleggja
adviser/advisor *n* ráðgjafi
advocate 1 *n* málflutningsmaður,
lögmaður; *(spokesperson)*
talsmaður; **2** *v* verja, tala fyrir
aerial *adj* loft-
aerobics *n* þolfimi
aesthetic *adj lit* fagurfræðilegur; ~
value fagurfræðilegt gildi
affair *n (business)* viðskipti; *(sexual)*
ástarsamband
affect 1 *n* áhrif; **2** *v* hafa áhrif á
affectation *n* gera sér upp, tilgerð:
an ~ **of interest** gera sér upp áhuga
affection *n* væntumþykja, ást,
kærleikur
affidavit *n* skrifleg yfirlýsing
affiliation *n* tengsl
affinity *n* skyldleiki
affirm *v* staðfesta
affirmation *n* staðfesting
afflict *v* skaða, þjá
affliction *n* þjáning
affluence *n* gnægð, ofgnótt
affluent *adj* ríkur, auðugur, vel stæður
afford *v* hafa efni á
afforestation *n* skógrækt

Afghan 1 *adj* afganskur; ~ **art**
afgönsk list; **2** *n* Afgani: **he is an** ~
hann er Afgani
Afghanistan *n* Afganistan
afraid *adj* hræddur
Africa *n* Afríka; **I'm from** ~ ég er
frá Afríku
African 1 *adj* afrískur; ~ **languages**
afrísk tungumál; **2** *n* Afríkani
after 1 *conj* eftir að; **2** *prep* eftir;
(behind) á eftir, fyrir aftan; *(time)*
yfir: **ten** ~ **ten** tíu mínútur yfir tíu;
~ **all** þegar öllu er á botninn hvolft;
~ **a while** skömmu síðar; ~ **this**
eftir þetta
afternoon *n* síðdegi, eftir hádegi;
this ~ eftir hádegi; **in the early**
~ fljótlega eftir hádegi; **Friday** ~
föstudagssíðdegi
aftershave *n* rakspíri
afterwards *adv* á eftir
afterword *n* eftirmáli
again *adv* aftur
against *prep* á móti
age 1 *n* aldur: **at her** ~ á hennar al-
dri; **legal** ~ sjálfræðisaldur; **under**
~ ósjálfráða; **what** ~ **are you?**
hvað ertu gamall?; **at the** ~ **of five**
þegar hann var fimm ára; **be of** ~
vera sjálfráða; *(epoch)* tímabil: **art
of that** ~ list þess tíma; **what** ~ **are
we living in?** á hvaða tímum lifum
við?; **the dark** ~s myrkar miðaldir;
2 *v (become/make older)* eldast;
(cheese, wine) þroska, geyma
aged *adj* gamall, aldraður; *(mature)*
þroskaður: **the cheese is** ~ osturinn
er þroskaður
agency *n* umboðsskrifstofa
agenda *n* dagskrá
agent *n* fulltrúi; *(for an artist)*
umboðsmaður
aggravate *v* ágerast, versna; *(annoy)*
ergja, pirra
aggression *n* árásargirni
aggressive *adj* árásargjarn
agile *adj* röskur

agitate v hvetja til
ago adv síðan: **long time** ~ langt síðan;
  three years ~ fyrir þremur árum
agonize v kvelja, pína
agony n angist, kvöl
agrarian adj landbúnaðar-
agree v *(same opinion)* vera sammála:
  ~ **with sby** vera sammála einhverjum; *(say yes)* samþykkja: ~ **to do**
  sth samþykkja að gera eitthvað;
  (correspond) í samræmi við; **as** ~**d**
  eins og samþykkt hefur verið
agreement n samkomulag; *(contract)* samningur; samræmi: **in** ~
  with í samræmi við
agricultural adj landbúnaðar-
agriculture n landbúnaður
agronomy n búfræði, búvísindi
ahead adv á undan: **be** ~ **of schedule**
  vera á undan áætlun, **be** ~ **of one's**
  time vera á undan sinni samtíð;
  fyrir framan: **the car** ~ bíllinn fyrir
  framan; framundan: **think** ~ hugsa
  fram í tímann; **plan** ~ skipuleggja
  fram í tímann; með forskot: ~ **of**
  all the others með forskot á alla
  hina
ahead of prep á undan, fyrir framan
aid 1 n hjálp, aðstoð; *(assisting*
  device) hjálpartæki; **hearing** ~
  heyrnartæki; **2** v hjálpa, aðstoða,
  styðja, veita stuðning
AIDS n med eyðni, alnæmi
ailing adj veikur, lasinn
ailment n med veikindi, sjúkdómur
aim 1 n tilgangur, markmið, stefna;
  2 v miða, stefna að: ~ **at the bird**
  miða á fuglinn, ~ **at a target**
  stefna að markmiði
aimless adj stefnulaus
air n loft, andrúmsloft; **go by** ~
  fljúga; **in the open** ~ undir berum
  himni; *(radio/television)* **on the** ~
  í loftinu
air bag n loftpúði
air conditioning n loftræstikerfi,
  loftræsting

air mattress n vindsæng
air-conditioned adj loftræstur
aircraft n flugfarartæki
airline n flugfélag
airmail n flugpóstur; **by** ~ með
  flugpósti
airplane n flugvél
airport n flugvöllur: **Keflavik** ~
  Keflavíkurflugvöllur; ~ **terminal**
  flugvallarálma; ~ **tax** flugvallar-
  skattur; ~ **security** vopnaleit
aisle n gangur: **would you like an**
  ~ **or window seat?** viltu sitja við
  ganginn eða gluggann?
alarm 1 n bjalla, viðvörunarbjalla,
  (fire ~*)* brunabjalla, *(burglary* ~*)*
  þjófavörn; ~ **clock** vekjaraklukka;
  2 v *(warn)* vara við; *(frighten)*
  hræða, vekja óróa
alarmed adj uggandi, áhyggjufullur
alarming adj skelfilegur, ógnvænlegur
Albania n Albanía
Albanian adj albanskur
Albanian n *(nationality)* Albani:
  the ~ **people** Albanar; *(language)*
  albanska: **do you speak** ~**?** talarðu
  albönsku?
albatross n albatrosi
albeit conj þó, þótt að
album n *(photos)* albúm; *(vinyl)* plata;
  (CD) geisladiskur
alchemy n gullgerðarlist
alcohol n áfengi, vín; colloq alkóhól;
  chem vínandi; **hard** ~ sterkt áfengi
alcoholic 1 adj áfengur; **2** n
  áfengissjúklingur, drykkjumaður;
  colloq alkóhólisti
alcoholic beverage/drink n áfengur
  drykkur
alcoholism n áfengissýki; colloq
  alkóhólismi
alcove n skot, krókur
ale n bjór, öl
alfalfa sprouts n alfaalfa-spírur
algae n þörungur
algebra n algebra
Algeria n Alsír

Algerian 1 *adj* alsírskur; **2** *n* Alsíringur:
he is ~ hann er Alsíringur
Algiers (capital of Algeria) *n*
Algeirsborg (höfuðborg Alsírs)
alias *n* leyninafn
alibi *n* fjarvistarsönnun
alien 1 *adj (from another country)*
erlendur, útlenskur; *(strange)*
framandi; **2** *n (from another country)*
útlendingur; *(extraterrestrial)*
geimvera
align *v* stilla, laga
alignment *n* stilling; **margin** ~ stilling
spássíu; **tire** ~ hjólbarðastilling
alimony *n* framfærslustuðningur
alive *adj* lifandi, á lífi: **be** ~ vera á lífi
all *pron* allur, öll: ~ **the men** allir
mennirnir, ~ **the women** allar ko-
nurnar, ~ **the children** öll börnin,
~ **of us** við öll; ~ **of it** allt; ~ **day**
allan daginn; ~ **night** alla nóttina;
~ **day long** allan liðlangan daginn;
best of ~ best af öllu; ~ **too nice**
allt of almennilegur; **above** ~ fyrst
og fremst; **after** ~ þegar öllu er á
botninn hvolft; **not at** ~ alls ekki;
~ **the same** skiptir ekki máli; ~
the better þeim mun betra; **for** ~ **I**
know eftir því sem ég best veit; ~
in ~ þegar allt kemur til alls; **not** ~
there ekki með öllum mjalla
all over *adv* alls staðar
all right *interj* allt í lagi: **it's** ~ þetta
er allt í lagi
allegation *n* ásökun
allergic *adj* vera með ofnæmi: **I'm** ~
to ... ég er með ofnæmi fyrir ...
allergy *n* ofnæmi: **food** ~ fæðuofnæmi,
medicine ~ lyfjaofnæmi
alleviation *n* léttir
alley *n* stígur, lítil gata
allied *adj* vinveittur
allocate *v* úthluta
allocation *n* úthlutun
allow *v* leyfa
allowance *n* vasapeningur
allowed *adj* leyfilegur: **be** ~ **to** mega;

not ~ bannaður; **smoking not** ~
reykingar bannaðar
all-purpose flour *n* hveiti
allspice *n* allrahanda
all-terrain bicycle *n* fjallahjól
all-terrain vehicle *n* jeppi
allure *v (tempt by sth desirable)*
lokka; *(charm)* heilla, laða að sér;
colloq sjarmera
allusion *n* skírskotun, vísun
ally 1 *n* bandamaður; **2** *v* vera í
bandalagi
almond *n* mandla; ~ **butter**
möndlusmjör; ~ **oil** möndluolía
almost *adv* næstum því, nærri
alms *n* ölmusa
aloe *n* biturblöðungur, aloe
alone *adj* einn; *(lonely)* einmana;
leave me ~ láttu mig í friði
along *prep* meðfram, með; **come/**
bring ~ koma með; **get** ~ **with** líka
vel við
alongside *prep* meðfram
aloud *adv* upphátt: **read** ~ lesa upphátt
alphabet *n* stafróf
alphabetical *adj* í stafrófsröð
alphabetically *adv* í stafrófsröð
Alps, the *N* Alparnir
already *adv* nú þegar
also *adv* líka, einnig
altar *n* altari; ~ **piece** altaristafla
alter *v* breyta
alteration *n* breyting
alternate 1 *adj* annar: ~ **route** önnur
leið, ~ **lines** önnur hver lína; **2** *v*
skiptast á, víxla á milli
alternative 1 *adj* óhefðbundinn,
öðruvísi, jaðar-; ~ **lifestyle**
óvenjulegur lífstíll; ~ **music**
jaðartónlist; ~ **medicine** óhefðbundnar lækningar; ~ **treatment**
óhefðbundin læknismeðferð; **2** *n*
val, valkostur, kostur
alternatively *adv* að öðrum kosti,
annars
alternator *n mech* riðstraumsrafall;
colloq alternator

although *subj* þó, þótt að
altimeter *n* hæðarmælir
altitude *n* hæð
altogether *adv* samtals
aluminum *n* ál
aluminum foil *n* álpappír
always *adv* alltaf, ávallt, ætíð
amateur 1 *adj* áhugamanna-: ~
  theater áhugamannaleikhús; ~
  orchestra áhugamannasveit; **2** *n*
  áhugamaður, viðvaningur; *colloq*
  amatör; **act like an** ~ haga sér eins
  og viðvaningur
amaze *v* koma einhverjum á óvart
amazed *adj* hissa
amazing *adj* frábær, ótrúlegur:
  this is an ~ band þetta er frábær
  hljómsveit
ambassador *n* sendiherra: ~ **of
  the United States** Sendiherra
  Bandaríkjanna, **the American** ~
  ameríski sendiherrann
ambiguity *n* tvíræðni
ambiguous *adj* tvíræður
ambition *n* metnaður, metnaðargirni,
  framagirni, stórhugur; *(goal)*
  markmið: **my ~ is to finish school**
  markmið mitt er að klára skólann
ambitious *adj* metnaðargjarn,
  framagjarn
amble *v* slæpast
ambulance *n* sjúkrabíll, neyðarbíll
ambush *v* ráðast á
amenable *adj* meðfærilegur
amenities *n* þægindi; **hotel** ~
  hótelþjónusta
America *N* Ameríka; **North America**
  Norður-Ameríka
American 1 *n* Ameríkani, Bandaríkjamaður; **2** *adj* amerískur,
  bandarískur
amiable *adj* viðkunnanlegur,
  félagslyndur
amicable *adj* almennilegur
amino acids *n chem* amínósýrur
amity *n* vinátta, friðsamleg samskipti
Amman (capital of Jordan) *N*

  Amman (höfuðborg Jórdaníu)
amnesia *n med* minnistap
amnesty *n* sakaruppgjöf, náðun;
  grant ~ to sby veita einhverjum
  sakaruppgjöf
among *prep* meðal
amount *n* upphæð
ample *adj* nægur
amplifier *n* magnari
amplify *v* magna
ampoule *n* lyfjabiða, ampúla
Amsterdam (capital of Netherlands)
  N Amsterdam (höfuðborg Hollands)
amulet *n* verndargripur
amuse *v* skemmta
amusement *n* skemmtun
amusement park *n* skemmtigarður,
  tívolí
amusing *adj* skemmtilegur
an *indef art* [not used in Icelandic]
anemia *n med* blóðleysi
analysis *n* greining
analyst *n* greinandi
analyze *v* greina
anarchist *n* stjórnleysingi; *colloq*
  anarkisti
anatomy *n* líffærafræði; *colloq*
  anatómía
ancestor *n (female)* formóðir, *(male)*
  forfaðir
anchor *n* akkeri
anchorage *n* bátalægi, skipalægi,
  skipalega: **no ~** bannað að leggja að
anchovy *n* ansjósa
ancient *adj* forn: ~ **relics** fornar minjar
and *conj* og: **mom ~ dad** mamma og
  pabbi, ~ **so on** og svo framvegis
Andorra *N* Andorra
anemia *n med* blóðleysi
anesthesia *n med* deyfing
anesthetic *adj med* deyfandi
angel *n* engill
angelica *n* hvönn
anger 1 *n* reiði; **2** *v* reita til reiði,
  ergja: **this ~s me** þetta ergir mig
angina *n med* hjartakveisa, hjartaöng
angle *n* horn: **acute ~** hvasst horn;

what's your ~ ? hvað færð þú út úr þessu?

angler fish *n zool* skötuselur

Angola *N* Angóla

angrily *adv* reiðilega

angry *adj* reiður

animal *n* dýr; *(domestic)* húsdýr; *(wild)* villidýr; *(pet)* gæludýr; **~ feed** dýrafóður; **~ rights** réttindi dýra

animated *adj* teiknaður; **~ film** teiknimynd

animation *n* hreyfimynd

animosity *n* ófriður

anise *n* anís

aniseed *n* anísfræ

Ankara (capital of Turkey) *N* Ankara (höfuðborg Tyrklands)

ankle *n anat* ökkli

annihilate *v* gjöreyða, gjöreyðileggja, þurrka út

annihilation *n* gjöreyðing, útrýming

anniversary *n* afmæli: **wedding ~** brúðkaupsafmæli; **death ~** dánardægur; **happy ~!** *phr* til hamingju með daginn!

announce *v* tilkynna

announcement *n* tilkynning; *(warning)* viðvörun

announcer *n* kynnir; *(on television and radio)* þula

annoy *v* pirra, angra

annoyed *adj* pirraður

annoying *adj* pirrandi

annual *adj* árlegur: **~ celebration** árleg hátíðarhöld; **~ balance sheet** ársreikningur; **~ meeting** aðalfundur; **~ report** ársskýrsla

annually *adv* árlega

anonymity *n* nafnleysi

anonymous *adj* nafnlaus

anorak *n* anórakkur

anorexia *n med* lystarstol, *colloq* anórexía

another *adj* annar

answer 1 *n* svar; **2** *v* svara: **~ a letter** svara bréfi, **~ an e-mail** svara tölvupósti, **~ the door** fara til dyra

ant *n* maur

antelope *n zool* antílópa

anthem *n* söngur, sálmur; **national ~** þjóðsöngur

anthology *n* sýnisbók, safnrit

anthropologist *n* mannfræðingur

anthropology *n* mannfræði

anti- *prefix* and-

antibiotics *n med* sýklalyf, fúkalyf: **prescribe ~** skrifa lyfseðil fyrir sýklalyfjum, skrifa út sýklalyf

antibody *n med* mótefni

anticipate *v* gera ráð fyrir, eiga von á, búast við: **I ~ the trip will take four hours** ég geri ráð fyrir að ferðin taki fjóra tíma; *(foresee)* sjá fyrir: **~ the sequence of events** sjá atburðina fyrir

antidote *n med* móteitur

antifreeze *n* frostlögur

anti-government *adj* stjórnarandstæðingur

anti-nuclear *adj* kjarnorkuandstæðingur

antipathy *n* andúð

antique *n* fornmunir, fornminjar, forngripur; **~ store** forngripaverslun

antiseptic 1 *adj* sótthreinsandi; **2** *n* sótthreinsivökvi

antler *n* horn

anxiety *n* áhyggjur, angist

anxious *adj* áhyggjufullur, angistarfullur

any *pron (with questions)* einhver, eitthvað: **do you have ~ milk?** áttu einhverja mjólk?; *(with negation)* enginn, ekki nokkur: **I don't have ~ time** ég hef engan tíma; *(all)* allir: **~ one would do it** allir myndu gera það; **~ time** hvenær sem er; **~ one** hver sem er

anybody *pron (with questions)* einhver: **does ~ speak English?** talar einhver ensku?; *(with negation)* enginn, ekki neinn: **I**

haven't seen ~ ég hef ekki séð neinn; *(everybody)* allir
anyhow *adv* einhvern veginn; *(in any case)* allavega; *(still)* samt
anyone *pron (with questions)* einhver; *(with negation)* enginn, ekki neinn: **I haven't seen** ~ ég hef ekki séð neinn; *(everybody)* allir
anything *pron (with questions)* eitthvað: **did you see** ~? sástu eitthvað?, **would you like to have** ~? má bjóða þér eitthvað?; *(whatever)* hvað sem er: **you can have** ~ **you want** þú getur fengið hvað sem er
anyway *adv (still)* samt sem áður; *(in any case)* hvað um það, allavega
anywhere *adv* nokkurs staðar, neins staðar, hvergi
apart *adv* aðskilinn
apart from *prep* fyrir utan
apartment *n* íbúð; ~ **building** blokk
aperitif *n* fordrykkur m
apiary *n* býflugnabú
apologize *v* afsaka sig, biðjast afsökunar: **I** ~ ég biðst afsökunar
apology *n* afsökun: **ask for an** ~ biðjast afsökunar, **own an** ~ þurfa að biðjast afsökunar
apostrophe *n ling* úrfellingarmerki
apparent *adj* augljós
apparently *adv* augljóslega
appeal 1 *n* aðdráttarafl; *leg* áfrýjun; **2** *v* höfða til; *leg* áfrýja
appear *v* koma fram, birtast
appearance *n (look)* útlit; **make one's** ~ sýna sig; *(in a film)* vera í, koma fyrir í
appendicitis *n med* botnlangakast
appendix *n anat* botnlangi; *lit* viðauki
appetite *n* matarlyst
appetizer *n* forréttur; *(drink)* fordrykkur
appetizing *adj* lystaukandi

apple *n* epli; ~ **juice** eplasafi; ~ **tart** eplakaka
applesauce *n* eplamauk
application *n* umsókn
apply *v* sækja um
appoint *v* skipa
appointment *n* tilnefning, *(employment)* ráðning; *(meeting)* viðtalstími: **make an** ~ panta viðtalstíma, **have an** ~ eiga viðtalstíma
appraisal *n* úttekt, verðmætamat
appraise *v* gera úttekt, verðmeta
appreciate *v* kunna að meta
apprentice *n* lærlingur
approach 1 *n* nálgun; **2** *v* nálgast, koma að
appropriate *adj* viðeigandi
approval *n* samþykki
approve (of) *v* samþykkja
approximate 1 *adj* nálægur, lauslegur: **the** ~ **time is 1 o'clock** klukkan er um það bil eitt; **2** *v* nálgast
approximately *adv* um það bil, hér um bil, sirka
apricot *n* apríkósa; ~ **jam** apríkósumauk; ~ **preserves** niðursoðnar apríkósur
April *n* apríl
April Fool *n* aprílgabb; ~**'s Day** fyrsti apríl
apron *n* svunta
aquarium *n* fiskabúr
Aquarius *n astro* Vatnsberinn
aquavit *n* ákavíti
Arab *n* Arabi
Arabian *adj* arabískur
Arabic 1 *adj* arabískur: ~ **numbers** arabískir tölustafir; **2** *n* arabíska: **speak** ~ tala arabísku
arcade game *n* spilakassi
arch 1 *n* bogi; **2** *v* beygja
archaic *adj* gamaldags: ~ **word** gamalt orð
archbishop *n* erkibiskup
archeology *n* fornleifafræði
archipelago *n* skerjagarður
architect *n* arkitekt

architecture *n* byggingarlist, *colloq* arkitektúr

archives *n* skjalasafn

Arctic 1 *n* norðurskauts-; **2** *N* Norðurskaut, Norðurpóll

Arctic Circle *N* heimskautsbaugur

Arctic Ocean *N* Norðuríshaf

area *n* svæði; *(neighborhood)* nágrenni: **he lives in the ~** hann býr í nágrenninu; *(stretch of land)* svæði: **New York covers a big ~** New York nær yfir stórt svæði, **surrounding ~** svæðið í kring; *(field, subject)* grein: **be knowledgable in several ~s** vera vel að sér í mörgum greinum

area code *n* svæðisnúmer

Argentina *N* Argentína

Argentine 1 *adj* argentínskur; **2** *n* Argentínumaður

argue *v* rífast, þræta

argument *n* rifrildi

Aries *n astro* Hrúturinn

arise *v* rísa, koma upp; **a problem arose** það kom upp vandamál

aristocracy *n* aðalsstétt; *(government)* aðalsveldi

aristocrat *n* aðalsmaður, hefðarmaður

ark *n* örk

arm 1 *n anat* handleggur; *(on a body, chair, clock)* armur; **2** *v* vopna; **to ~ oneself** vopnast

armed *adj* vopnaður

Armenia *N* Armenía

Armenian 1 *adj* armenskur; **2** *n (nationality)* Armeni; *(language)* armenska

armor *n* brynja

armory *n* vopnabúr

armpit *n* handakriki

arms *n* vopn

army *n* her

aroma *n* ilmur

aromatic *adj* ilmsterkur, angandi

around *prep* í kringum, í kring, um, í hringi; **~ the neck** um hálsinn; **~ two o'clock** um tvöleytið; **spin ~** snúast í hringi; **walk ~ the house** ganga í

kringum húsið; **sleep ~** vera lauslátur

arrange *v* raða

arrangement *n* uppröðun

array *n* samsafn, fjöldi, röð

arrest 1 *n* handtaka; **2** *v* handtaka

arrested *adj* handtekinn

arrival *n* koma

arrive *v* koma: **~ by plane** koma með flugvél, **~ by bus** koma með strætó, **~ by car** koma með bíl

arrow *n* ör; *comp* **mouse ~** músarbendill

arrowroot *n flora* örvarrót

arsenal *n* vopnabúr

arsenic *n chem* arsenik

arson *n* íkveikja

art *n* list, listgrein; **~ gallery** lista-gallerí; **~ museum** listasafn

artery *n anat* slagæð

arthritis *n med* gigt: **have ~** vera með gigt

artichoke *n* ætiþistill; **~ heart** þistilhjarta

article *n* grein; *leg* grein; *ling* greinir

artificial *adj* gervi-; **~ sweetener** gervisykur;

artificial coloring *n* litarefni

artificial flavor *n* bragðefni

artisan *n* handverksmaður

artist *n* listamaður, listakona

artistic *adj* listrænn

artwork *n* listaverk

arugula *n* klettasalat

as *conj (time)* þegar, um leið og: **I saw him ~ I stepped on the bus** ég sá hann um leið og ég steig upp í strætó; **~ soon as we arrive** um leið og við erum komin; *(reason)* þar sem: **~ I have never been here before** þar sem ég hef aldrei verið hér áður; *(like)* eins og: **~ you know ...** eins og þú veist ...; **~ from** frá og með; **~ good ~** svo gott sem; **such ~** til dæmis

ASAP *abbrev* eins fljótt og hægt er, sem fyrst; **let me know ~** láttu mig vita sem fyrst

ash *n* aska; **volcanic ~** eldfjallaaska

ashamed *adj* skömmustulegur
ashtray *n* öskubakki
Asia *N* Asía
Asian 1 *adj* asískur; **2** *n* Asíumaður, Asíubúi
aside *adv* til hliðar, afsíðis; **I took him** ~ ég fór með hann afsíðis; ~ **from** fyrir utan
ask *v* spyrja: ~ **a question** spyrja, ~ **about** spyrja um, ~ **for** spyrja eftir
asleep *adj* sofandi
asparagus *n* spergill, aspas; ~ **soup** spergilsúpa, aspassúpa
aspartame *n* aspartam
aspect *n* sjónarmið; *ling* horf
aspen *n* ösp
aspirator *n* *med* öndunartæki
aspirin *n* *med* verkjatafla, magnyl
assassin *n* morðingi, leyniskytta
assassinate *v* drepa, myrða
assassination *n* morð úr launsátri
assault *n* árás
assess *v* meta, dæma, verðleggja
assessment *n* mat; *(in education)* einkunnagjöf
asset *n* eign
assist *v* aðstoða
assistance *n* aðstoð
assistant *n* aðstoðarmaður
associate 1 *n* samstarfsmaður; **2** *v* tengja; ~**d with** tengist
association *n* félagsskapur, félag
assorted *adj* blandaður; ~ **cheeses** blandaðir ostar; ~ **vegetables** blandað grænmeti
assume *v* gera ráð fyrir
assumption *n* ályktun
assure *v* sannfæra
asterisk *n* stjarna
asteroid *n* smástirni
asthma *n* *med* asmi, astmi; **have** ~ vera með asma
astonish *v* koma á óvart
astonishment *n* undrun
astray *adv* villtur; **go** ~ villast
astrology *n* stjörnufræði
astronaut *n* geimfari

astronomer *n* geimvísindamaður
astronomical observatory *n* stjörnuathugunarstöð
astronomy *n* geimvísindi
asylum *n* griðarstaður
at *prep* við, hjá: ~ **the lake** við vatnið, ~ **my parent's place** hjá foreldrum mínum; ~ **first** í fyrstu; ~ **last** loksins; ~ **least** að minnsta kosti
atheist *n* trúleysingi
Athens (capital of Greece) *N* Aþena (höfuðborg Grikklands)
athletics *n* íþróttir
Atlantic Ocean *N* Atlantshaf; **in the** ~ í Atlantshafi
ATM *abbrev* hraðbanki
atmosphere *n* andrúmsloft
atom *n* frumeind, atóm
atomic *adj* atóm-
atonement *n* friðþæging
attach *v* festa
attached *adj* áfastur, bundinn við
attack 1 *v* ráðast á; **2** *n* árás; **heart** ~ *med* hjartaáfall
attempt 1 *n* tilraun; **2** *v* reyna
attend *v* mæta
attention *n* athygli, eftirtekt
attitude *n* viðhorf
attorney *n* lögfræðingur
attract *v* draga að sér
attraction *n* aðdráttarafl
attractive *adj* myndarlegur
attribute 1 *n* einkenni, *ling* einkunn; **2** *v* kenna um, tengja við
aubergine *n* eggaldin
auction 1 *n* uppboð; **2** *v* bjóða upp
audience *n* áhorfandi
audio-guide *n* leiðsögn á hljóðbandi
audit 1 *n* endurskoðun; *(buildings)* eftirlit; **2** *v* endurskoða; ~ **a building** skoða byggingu; ~ **a class** sitja í tímum
auditor *n* endurskoðandi
August *n* ágúst
aunt *n* frænka, *(on mother's side)* móðursystir, *(on father's side)* föðursystir

aurora *n* segulljós
aurora borealis *n* norðurljós
austere *adj* strangur, nægjusamur
Australia *N* Ástralía
Australian 1 *adj* Ástralskur; **2** *n*
  Ástrali
Austria *N* Austurríki
Austrian 1 *adj* austurrískur; **2** *n*
  Austurríkismaður
authentic *adj* upprunalegur, alvöru
author *n* rithöfundur, höfundur
authority *n* vald, húsbóndavald
authorize *v* leyfa
authorized *adj* leyfður; *leg* löggiltur
autocracy *n* einræði, einræðisvald
autocrat *n* einvaldur
automatic *adj* sjálfvirkur
automatic transmission *n mech*
  sjálfskipting
automatically *adv* sjálfvirkt
automobile *n* bifreið, bíll; ~ **insurance card** vátryggingaskírteini
autumn *n* haust
auxiliary *adj* hjálpar-, aðstoðar-; *ling*
  ~ **verb** hjálparsögn
availability *n* framboð
available *adj* fáanlegur
avalanche *n* snjóflóð
avenue *n* breiðgata
average 1 *adj* meðal-: ~ **person**
  meðalmaður, meðaljón, venjuleg
  manneskja; **2** *n* meðaltal

aviation *n* flug
avocado *n* avakadó, lárpera
avoid *v* forðast
awake *adj* vakandi
award 1 *n* verðlaun; **2** *v* verðlauna,
  veita verðlaun
aware *adj* meðvitaður
awareness *n* meðvitund; **to raise** ~
  vekja athygli á
away *adv* í burtu: **far** ~ langt í burtu;
  excl **go** ~! farðu!
awe *n* hrifning
awful *adj* hræðilegur
awfully *adv* hræðilega
awkward *adj* bjánalegur, asnalegur,
  óþægilegur: **an** ~ **moment** óþægilegt
  augnablik
awkwardly *adv* óþægilega, asnalega,
  bjánalega
axe *n* öxi, exi
axis *n* öxull
axle *n* öxull m
Azerbaijan *n* Aserbaísjan
Azerbaijani 1 *adj* aserskur; **2** *n*
  (nationality) Aseri; *(language)*
  aserska

B

babble *v* bulla
bamboo shoot *n* bambussproti
baby *n* ungbarn, smábarn
baby back ribs *n* smárefjar
baby clothes *n* barnaföt
baby food *n* barnamatur
baby stroller *n* barnakerra
baby wipes *n* blautþurrka
babychair *n* barnastóll
babysitter *n* barnapía
babywear *n* barnaföt
bachelor *n* piparsveinn; ~ **party**
  steggjapartí
bachelorette *n* piparmey; ~ **party**
  gæsapartí
back 1 *adj* aftur-, bak-: ~ **door** *(house)*
  bakdyr, *(car)* afturhurð, ~ **wheel**
  afturhjól; *(previous)* gamall: ~
  issues gamlar útgáfur, ~ **bills**
  gamlir reikningar; **2** *n (anat)* bak:
  ~ **pain** bakverkur; *(of two sides)*
  bakhlið; *(in a car, train etc)* aftari
  hluti: **sit in the** ~ sitja aftur í; **3**
  v (go backwards) bakka: ~ **a car**
  bakka bíl; *(support)* styðja; **4** *adv*
  aftur, aftur á bak; *(return)* til baka:
  come ~ komdu til baka
backache *n* bakverkur
backdoor *n (house)* bakdyr, *(car)*
  afturhurð
background *n* bakgrunnur
backhand *n* bakhönd
backpack *n* bakpoki
backseat *n* aftursæti
backspace *n comp* ~ **key** bakktakki
backup *n comp* afrit; *(support)*
  stuðningur
backward 1 *adj* sem fer aftur á bak;
  (mentally) seinþroska; *(under-*
  developed) vanþróaður; *(hesitating)*
  óframfærinn; **2** *adv* aftur á bak:

drive ~ keyra aftur á bak; ~ **and**
  forward fram og til baka
bacon *n* beikon: ~ **and eggs** beikon
  og egg, ~ **strips** beikonstrimlar
bacteria *n* baktería
bacterial *adj med* bakteríu-
bad *adj* vondur, illur; *(food)* skemmdur
badly *adv* illilega
badminton *n sports* badminton
bad-tempered *adj* skapvondur
bag *n* poki, taska: **plastic** ~ plastpoki,
  paper ~ pappírspoki, **tote** ~ taska
bagel *n* beygla
baggage *n* farangur
baggage cart *n* farangurskerra
baggage check-in counter *n*
  farangursinnritun
baggage claim area *n*
  farangursmóttaka
Baghdad (capital of Iraq) *N*
  Bagdad (höfuðborg Íraks)
Bahamas, The *N* Bahamaeyjar
bail bond *n leg* lausnargjald: **he was**
  released on ~ honum var sleppt
  fyrir lausnargjald
bake *v* baka
baked *adj* bakaður
baked potato *n* bökuð kartafla
baker *n* bakari
bakery *n* bakarí
baking pan *n* bökunarform
baking powder *n* bökunarduft
baking sheet *n* bökunarpappír
baking soda *n* matarsódi, natron
Baku (capital of Azerbaijan) *N*
  Bakú (höfuðborg Aserbaídsjan)
balaclava *n* lambhúshetta
balance 1 *n* jafnvægi: **put somebody**
  out of ~ koma einhverjum úr
  jafnvægi; *(financial)* jöfnuður; **2** *v*
  halda jafnvægi; *(account)* gera upp

balance sheet *n econ* efnahagsreikningur
balcony *n* svalir
bald *adj* sköllóttur
ballet *n* ballett
balloon *n (birthday)* blaðra; *(hot air)* loftbelgur
ballot *n (voting slip)* kjörseðill; *(voting)* kosningar; ~ **box** kjörkassi; **secret** ~ leynilegar kosningar
balm *n* salvi, áburður, smyrsl; **lip** ~ varasalvi
balsamic vinegar *n* balsamedik
Baltic Sea *N* Eystrasalt
bamboo *n* bambus; ~ **shoots** bambussprotar
ban 1 *n* bann; **2** *v* banna
banana *n* banani; ~ **leaf** bananalauf; ~ **bread** bananabrauð
banana republic *n* bananalýðveldi
band *n (music)* hljómsveit, grúppa, sveit; *(wedding ring)* giftingahringur
bandage *n* sáraumbúðir, umbúðir
band-aid *n* plástur
bandit *n* glæpamaður
Bangkok (capital of Thailand) *N* Bankok (höfuðborg Tælands)
bank *n* banki; ~ **card** bankakort; ~ **charges** þjónustugjöld
bank account *n* bankareikningur
banker *n* bankastarfsmaður
banknote *n* peningaseðill
bankrupt 1 *adj* gjaldþrota; **2** *v* gera gjaldþrota; **go** ~ fara á hausinn
bankruptcy *n* gjaldþrot
baptism *n* skírn
baptismal font *n* skírnarfontur
bar 1 *n* bar, pöbb, krá, knæpa; **wine** ~ vínbar; ~ **service** opinn bar; *(rod)* stöng; *(prison)* fangelsi: **behind ~s** á bak við lás og slá; *(road door)* hlið; ~ **of chocolate** súkkulaðistykki; ~ **of soap** sápustykki; **2** *v* sperra, setja upp hlið
barbecue 1 *n* grill, glóðarsteiking; ~ **sauce** grillsósa; ~ **flavor** grillbragð; **2** *v* grilla, glóðarsteikja

barber *n* rakari
bargain 1 *n* kostaboð; **2** *v* prútta
bark *n* gelt, hundgá
barley *n* bygg
barn *n* hlaða
barometer *n* loftþrýstivog
Baroque style *n* barokkstíll
barrel *n* tunna
bartender *n* barþjónn
basalt *n geol* basalt: **columnar** ~ stuðlaberg
base 1 *n* grunnur; ~ **sauce** grunnsósa; **2** *v* byggja á; **~d on** byggt á
baseball *n sports* hafnabolti
basement *n* kjallari
basic *adj* grunn-
basically *adv* eiginlega, í rauninni
basil *n* basilika
basin *n* vaskur
basis *n* grunnur; ~ **of** grunnurinn að
basket *n* karfa
basketball *n sports* körfubolti
basmati rice *n* basmatíhrísgrjón
bass 1 *adj mus* bassa-: ~ **guitar** bassagítar; **2** *n mus* bassi; **electric** ~ rafmagnsbassi; **double string** ~ kontrabassi; **3** *n zool* laxaborri
bassoon *n* fagott
bastard *n (illegitimate)* óskilgetið barn; *obs* skepna, ógeð, asni; *excl* **you ~**! skepnan þín!, ógeðið þitt!
bat *n zool* leðurblaka
bath *n* bað
bath towel *n* baðhandklæði
bathe *v* baða
bathing suit *n* sundföt
bathroom *n* baðherbergi, klósett, snyrting
bathtub *n* baðkar, baðker
batter *n* deig: **pancake** ~ pönnukökudeig, **pastry** ~ smákökudeig
battery *n* rafhlaða, batterí
battle *n* barátta, bardagi: **historic** ~ sögulegur bardagi
bay *n* flói, vík, fjörður; **to keep at** ~ halda í skefjum
bay leaf *n* lárviðarlauf

be *v* vera; ~ **sick** vera veikur; **have you been there?** hefurðu komið þangað?; **for the time ~ing** eins og er
beach *n* strönd
beak *n* goggur
beam *n (wood)* bjálki; *(light)* geisli
bean *n* baun; ~ **sprouts** baunaspírur; ~ **bag** baunapoki
bear **1** *n zool* björn: **polar** ~ ísbjörn, **grizzly** ~ skógarbjörn; **2** *v* bera; ~ **in mind** hafa í huga
beard *n* skegg; **full** ~ alskegg
beat **1** *n mus* sláttur, taktur; **2** *v (hit)* slá; *(win)* vinna
beautiful *adj* fallegur
beautifully *adv* fallega
beauty *n* fegurð
because *conj* vegna þess að, úr því að
become *v* verða: ~ **a teacher** verða kennari, ~ **famous** verða frægur; *(look good on)* klæða, fara vel: **this ~s you** þetta fer þér vel
bed *n* rúm
bed and breakfast *n* gistiheimili
bed linen/sheet *n* sængurföt
bedding *n* rúmföt
bedroom *n* svefnherbergi; **master** ~ hjónaherbergi
bee *n (insect)* býfluga
beech *n flora* beyki, beykitré
beef *n* nautakjöt; ~ **tongue** nautatunga; ~ **meatballs** kjötbollur; ~ **burger** nautahamborgari
beef jerky *n* þurrkað nautakjöt
beehive *n* býkúpa; býflugnabú
beer *n* bjór: **canned** ~ bjór í dós, **bottled** ~ bjór í flösku, ~ **on tap** bjór á krana, kranabjór
beet *n* rófa
beetle *n* bjalla
beetroot *n* rauðrófa
before **1** *prep* á undan: ~ **me** á undan mér; **2** *conj* áður en; **3** *adv* áður
beforehand *adv* fyrirfram
beggar *n* betlari
begin *v* byrja

beginner *n* byrjandi
beginning *n* byrjun
behalf *n* **on** ~ **of sby** fyrir hönd einhvers; **on my** ~ fyrir mína hönd
behave *v* hegða sér
behavior *n* hegðun, atferli
behind **1** *prep* á bak við: ~ **the car** á bak við bílinn; **2** *adv* á eftir, eftir: **the suitcase was left** ~ ferðataskan var skilin eftir
beige *n* drapplitaður
Beijing (capital of China) *N* Peking (höfuðborg Kína)
Beirut (capital of Lebanon) *N* Beirút (höfuðborg Líbanons)
Belarus *N* Hvíta-Rússland
Belarusian *n* Hvít-Rússi
Belgian **1** *adj* belgískur; **2** *n* Belgi
Belgium *N* Belgía
Belgrade (capital of Serbia) *N* Belgrad (höfuðborg Serbíu)
belief *n* trú
believe *v* trúa
bell *n* bjalla
bell pepper *n* papríka: **red/yellow/green** ~ rauð/gul/græn papríka
belly *n* magi
belong *v* vera eign einhvers; **this book ~s to me** *phr* ég á þessa bók
below **1** *adv* undir; *(downstairs)* niðri: **my brother lives** ~ bróðir minn býr niðri; **2** *prep* undir: ~ **the surface** undir yfirborðinu
belt *n* belti; **below the** ~ neðan beltis; **Bible** ~ biblíubeltið
beluga *n zool* styrja
beluga caviar *n* styrjuhrogn
beluga whale *n zool* mjaldur
bench *n* bekkur
bend **1** *n* beygja; **2** *v* beygja
beneath **1** *prep* fyrir neðan, undir: ~ **the surface** undir yfirborðinu; **2** *adv* fyrir neðan
beneficial *adj* gagnlegur
beneficiary *n* arfþegi
benefit **1** *n* kostur, gróði; **2** *v* græða
benevolence *n* velvild

benevolent *adj* góðviljaður

benign *adj med* góðkynja; ~ **tumor** góðkynja krabbamein

bent *adj* beyglaður

Berlin (capital of Germany) *N* Berlín (höfuðborg Þýskalands)

Bern (capital of Switzerland) *N* Bern (höfuðborg Sviss)

berry *n* ber

beside *prep* við hliðina á

best **1** *adj* bestur; *excl* ~ **wishes!** bestu óskir, ~ **greetings!** bestu kveðjur!; **2** *adv* best

bet **1** *v* veðja; **2** *n* veðmál

better *adj compar* betri

between *prep/adv* á milli

beverage *n* drykkur; **alcoholic** ~ áfengur drykkur

beware *v* hafa varann á; ~ **of dog** varið ykkur á hundinum; *excl* **beware!** varúð!;

beyond **1** *adv* fyrir handan; **2** *prep* hinum megin við, handan; *(longer than)* fram yfir: ~ **midnight** fram yfir miðnætti; ~ **belief** ótrúlegur; ~ **understanding** óskiljanlegt

bias *n* fordómar

bib *n* smekkur

Bible *n* biblía

bicycle *n* hjól

bicycle lane *n* hjólabraut

bicyclist *n* hjólreiðarmaður

bid **1** *n* boð, tilboð; **2** *v* bjóða í

big *adj* stór

bigger *adj compar* stærri

biking path *n* hjólastígur

bikini *n* bikiní

bilberry *n* aðalbláber

bilingual *adj* tvítyngdur

bill *n (amount owed)* reikningur: **the** ~ **please** gæti ég fengið reikninginn; *(paper money)* seðill: **dollar** ~**s** dollaraseðlar

billiards *n* biljarður

billion *n num* milljarður

bin *n* ruslafata

bind *v* binda

binoculars *n* kíkir, sjónauki

biodegradable *adj* ~ **waste** lífrænt sorp

biodiversity *n* líffræðilegur fjölbreytileiki

biography *n* ævisaga

biological *adj* líffræðilegur

biology *n* líffræði

biopsy *n med* vefjasýnitaka

biotechnology *n* líftækni

birch *n flora* birki

bird *n* fugl

birth *n* fæðing

birth certificate *n* fæðingarvottorð

birthday *n* afmæli

birthday party *n* afmælisveisla

biscuit *n* kex

bishop *n* biskup: ~ **of Iceland** biskup Íslands

bison *n zool* bíson-naut

bit *n* smá, pínu; **in a** ~ eftir smá stund; **a little** ~ smá, pínu

bite **1** *n (small piece)* biti; *(by insect, animal)* bit: **insect** ~ skordýrabit; **2** *v* bíta

bite-size *adj* munnbiti

bitter *adj* bitur

bitterly *adv* biturlega

bizarre *adj* fáránlegur

black *adj* svartur; ~ **coffee** svart kaffi; ~ **and white** svarthvítur; ~ **pepper** svartur pipar

black currant *n* sólber

black rice *n* svört hrísgrjón

Black Sea *N* Svartahaf

blackbean *n* svartbaun

black-eyed peas *n* augnbaunir

blackmail **1** *n* fjárkúgun; **2** *v* kúga út fé

bladder *n anat* blaðra

blade *n* blað

blame **1** *n* sök; **he got the** ~ honum var kennt um; **I got the** ~ mér var kennt um; **2** *v* kenna um, álasa

bland *adj* daufur, bragðdaufur

blank **1** *adj* auður, tómur; **2** *v* eyða: **fill in the** ~ fylltu í eyðurnar

blanket *n* teppi

blaze *n* bál
bleach 1 *n* klór; **2** *v* setja í klór
bleed *v* blæða
blend *v* blanda; **~ed** blandaður
blender *n* blandari: **hand ~** töfrasproti
bless *v* blessa; **God ~ you!** Guð blessi þig!
blind *adj* blindur
blink *v* depla
blister *n* blaðra
blizzard *n* stórhríð, stormur; **~ warning** stormviðvörun
bloated *adj* uppþembdur
block *n* blokk; drumbur; **~ of ice** klakadrumbur; stykki
blockage *n* stífla
blocked *adj* stíflaður: **the sink is ~** vaskurinn er stíflaður; lokaður: **the road is ~** gatan er lokuð
blonde 1 *adj* ljóshærður; **2** *n* ljóska
blood *n* blóð: **~ type** blóðflokkur, **~ test** blóðprufa
blood orange *n* blóðappelsína
blood pressure *n med* blóðþrýstingur; **~ monitor** blóðþrýstingsmælir
blouse *n* blússa
blow 1 *n* högg: **get a ~ on the head** fá höfuðhögg, **take the ~** taka á sig höggið, **with one ~** í einu höggi; **2** *v* blása; *(nose)* snýta sér; *(spend)* eyða; *(a tire/balloon)* blása upp; **~ a kiss** senda fingurkoss
blow up *v* sprengja
blow-dry 1 *n* hárblástur; **2** *v* blása hárið
blowfish *n zool* kúlufiskur
blue *adj (color)* blár; *(sad)* leiður, sorgmæddur; **out of the ~** *expr* eins og þruma úr heiðskíru lofti; **once in a ~ moon** *expr* mjög sjaldan
blue mussel *n zool* kræklingur
blue whale *n zool* steypireyður
blueberry *n* bláber
bluff 1 *n* plat; **2** *v* plata
blush 1 *n* roði; *(wine)* rósavín; **2** *v* roðna

board 1 *n (writing)* tafla; *(committee)* stjórn, nefnd: **~ of directors** stjórn, **~ of education** menntamálanefnd; *(floor)* planki, *(food)* fæði; **ironing ~** strauborð; **cutting ~** skurðbretti; **2** *v* fara um borð: **~ a train** fara um borð í lest, **~ a ship** fara um borð í bát, **~ a plane** fara um borð í flugvél
board game *n* borðspil
boarding pass *n* brottfararspjald
boat *n* bátur
body *n* líkami, kroppur; **~ of literary work** rithöfundarverk
bodybuilder *n masc* líkamsræktarmaður, *(fem)* líkamsræktarkona
Bogota (capital of Columbia) *N* Bógóta (höfuðborg Kólumbíu)
boil 1 *n* suða; **bring water to a ~** sjóðið vatnið; **2** *v* sjóða
boiled *adj* soðinn
boiler *n* ketill; **~ room** ketilherbergi
Bolivia *N* Bólivía
Bolivian 1 *adj* bólivískur; **2** *n* Bólivíumaður
bomb 1 *n* sprengja; **~ threat** sprengjuhótun; **2** *v* sprengja
bombard *v* gera sprengjuárás
bombardment *n* sprengjuárás
bon appetit! *phr* verði þér/ykkur að góðu!
bon voyage! *phr* góða ferð!
bonbon *n* brjóstsykur
bond *n* **1** *(attachment)* tengsl; *econ* skuldabréf: **government ~s** ríkisskuldabréf; **2** *v* tengjast
bone *n* bein
boneless *adj* beinlaus: **~ fish** beinlaus fiskur
bonus *n* bónus
book 1 *n* bók; **audio ~** hljóðbók; *econ* bókfærsla: **keep ~s** bókfæra; **go by the ~** fylgja reglunum til hins ýtrasta; **2** *v* bóka: **I ~ed a flight to Reykjavík** ég bókaði flug til Reykjavíkur; *econ* bókfæra
booking *n* bókun

booklet *n* bæklingur
bookmark 1 *n* bókamerki; 2 *v* merkja
við: ~ **website** setja bókamerki við
vefsíðu
bookstore *n* bókabúð
boom 1 *n* sprengja; **tourist** ~ ferða-
mannasprengja; 2 *v* springa út,
ganga vel: **business has been ~ing**
viðskiptin hafa gengið vel
boost 1 *n* vítamínsprauta: **a** ~ **for
the economy** vítamínsprauta fyrir
atvinnulífið; 2 *v* gefa orku
boot *n* stígvél
border 1 *n* landamæri; 2 *v* vera nálægt,
nálgast
border guard *n* landamæravörður
border state *n* nágrannaríki
borderline case *n* jaðartilfelli
bore *v* valda leiðindum
bored *adj* leiðist: **I'm** ~ mér leiðist
boring *adj* leiðinlegur
born *adj* fæddur
borrow *v* fá lánað
borrower *n* lántakandi
borsch *n* rauðrófusúpa
Bosnia and Herzegovina *N* Bosnía
og Hersegóvína
Bosnian 1 *adj* bosnískur; 2 *n*
Bosníumaður
bosom *n* barmur, brjóst
boss *n* yfirmaður
botanical *adj* bótanískur
botanical garden *n* grasagarður
both *adj* báðir
both ... and ... *conj* bæði ... og ...:
he is interested in ~ **math** ~
literature hann hefur áhuga bæði
á stærðfræði og bókmenntum
bother 1 *n* vandamál: **be a** ~ **to sby**
vera vandamál fyrir einhvern; 2
v skapa vandamál, trufla: ~ **sby
about sth** trufla einhvern út af
einhverju
bottle 1 *n* flaska; 2 *v* setja á flösku
bottle opener *n* tappatogari
bottled *adj* á flösku, í gleri: ~ **water**
vatn á flösku

bottlenose whale *n zool* andanefja
bottom *n* botn
bouillion *n* kjötsoð; ~ **cube**
súputeningur
bound *adj (books)* innbundinn; *(tied)*
bundinn; ~ **to fail** dæmdur til að
mistakast; ~ **for** á leið til
boundary *n* takmörk
bourgeois *adj* borgaralegur,
smáborgaralegur
bowel *n anat* þarmur
bowel movements *n* hægðir; **to have
regular** ~ að vera með reglulegar
hægðir
bowl *n* skál
bowling *n* keila; **to go** ~ að fara í
keilu; ~ **shoes** keiluskór; ~ **ball**
keilukúla
box 1 *n* box, kassi; *(metal or plastic)*
dós; *(safe-deposit)* öryggishólf;
post ~ pósthólf; 2 *v (put into
boxes)* pakka, setja í kassa; *sports*
boxa
box office *n (theater)* miðasala
boxing *n sports* hnefaleikar, box; ~
ring hnefaleikahringur
boy *n* strákur, drengur, piltur; *slang*
gæi, gaur
boycott *v* sneiða hjá
boyfriend *n* kærasti
bra *n* brjóstahaldari
bracelet *n* armband
braces *n* axlabönd; *(dental)* spangir
bracket *n* hornklofi
braille *n* blindraletur; ~ **alphabet**
blindrastafróf
brain *n* heili; **he got the** ~**s** hann er
klár; **pick sby's** ~**s** *expr* nota þekk-
ingu einhvers; ~ **concussion** *med*
heilahristingur
brain damage *n* heilaskaði
brainstorming *n* þankahríð
brainwashing *n* heilaþvottur
brake *n/v* bremsa: **apply the** ~**s**
bremsa; ~ **light** bremsuljós
bran *n* klíð
branch *n (tree)* grein; *(bank)* útibú

brand n vörumerki
brand-new adj glænýr
Brasilia (capital of Brazil) N
Brasilía (höfuðborg Brasilíu)
brass n látún
brassiere n veitingastaður
Bratislava (capital of Slovakia) N
Bratislava (höfuðborg Slóvakíu)
brave adj hugaður, djarfur
Brazil N Brasilía
Brazilian 1 adj brasilískur; **2** n
Brasilíumaður
breach 1 n slit, brot; leg ~ **of contract** samningsslit, ~ **of promise**
svik, ~ **of law** lögbrot; **2** v slíta,
brjóta; ~ **a promise** brjóta loforð;
leg ~ **a contract** svíkja samning
bread n brauð: **naan** ~ nanbrauð,
white ~ franskbrauð, **crisp** ~
hrökkbrauð, **loaf of** ~ brauðhleifur,
rye ~ rúgbrauð, **sourdough** ~
súrdeigsbrauð, **multi-grain** ~
fjölkornabrauð; slang **earn one's** ~
vinna sér salt í grautinn
bread soup n brauðsúpa
bread stick n brauðstöng
breadcrumbs n brauðmolar
breaded adj í raspi: ~ **fish** fiskur í
raspi
breading n rasp
breadknife n brauðhnífur
breadline n matarúthlutunarröð
breadwinner n fyrirvinna
break 1 n (fracture) brot; (breach)
brot: ~ **of the rules** brot á reglum;
(breaking up) skilnaður; (time off)
frí; (pause) hlé, pása; (chance)
tækifæri; **2** v brjóta, skemma; (~
a code) leysa; (money) skipta; ~
away slít sig lausan; ~ **down** bila;
~ **in** brjótast inn; ~ **off** hætta
breakdown n niðurbrot; med **nervous**
~ taugaáfall
breakfast n morgunmatur, morgunverður: **English** ~ enskur morgunverður, heitur morgunverður;
continental ~ kaldur morgunverður; ~ **cereal** morgunkorn; ~
bar morgunverðarhlaðborð
breast n brjóst
breath n andardráttur
breathe v anda
breathing n öndun
breed 1 n tegund; **2** v rækta
breeze n gola
brewery n brugghús, bjórgerð
bribe 1 v múta; **2** n fem pl mútur
brick n múrsteinn
bridal adj brúðar-: ~ **gift** brúðargjöf
bride n brúður;
bridegroom n brúðgumi
bridesmaid n brúðarmær
bridge 1 n brú; **2** v brúa
brief 1 adj stuttur, skammur, hnit-
miðaður; **2** v kynna stöðuna, segja
frá stöðu mála
briefly adv í stuttu máli
briefs n nærbuxur
bright adj (light) bjartur; (smart) klár
brilliant adj frábær
bring v koma með, færa; fig veita; ~
happiness veita gleði
Britain N Bretland
British adj breskur: ~ **food** breskur
matur
broad adj breiður, víður; (general)
almennur
broad bean n hestabaun
broadband n breiðband; ~ **connection** breiðbandstenging; ~ **Internet**
internet í gegnum breiðbandið
broadcast 1 n útsending; **2** v (radio)
útvarpa; (television) sjónvarpa
broadly adv almennt
broccoli n spergilkál, brokkólí; ~ **soup**
brokkólísúpa
brochure n bæklingur
broil v rista, grilla
broken adj brotinn, bilaður, ónýtur;
~ **bone** beinbrot
broker n econ miðlari: **stock**~ verð-
bréfamiðlari
bronchitis n med berkjubólga,
bronkítís

bronze *n* brons
broth *n* soð: **chicken** ~ kjúklingasoð,
 fish ~ fiskisoð
brother *n* bróðir: **half** ~ hálfbróðir;
 blood ~ blóðbróðir; **foster** ~
 fóstbróðir
brotherhood *n* fóstbræðralag
brown *adj (color)* brúnn
brown rice *n* brún hrísgrjón
browned *adj* brúnaður
browned butter *n* brúnað smjör
brownie *n* súkkulaðikaka, klessukaka
browse *v comp* vafra; ~ **the Internet**
 vafra á netinu
browser (Internet ~) *n comp* vafri
bruise 1 *n* mar; 2 *v* merja, fá marblett
brunch *n* dögurður, *colloq* bröns
brunette *adj* dökkhærður
brush 1 *n* bursti; 2 *v (hair)* bursta;
 (food) pensla; ~ **against** strjúkast
 við
brushwood *n* kjarr
Brussels (capital of Belgium) *N*
 Brussel (höfuðborg Belgíu)
Brussels sprouts *n* rósakál
bubble *n* bóla, loftbóla
Bucharest (capital of Romania) *N*
 Búkarest (höfuðborg Rúmeníu)
bucket *n* fata
buckwheat *n* bókhveiti
Budapest (capital of Hun-
 gary) *N* Búdapest (höfuðborg
 Ungverjalands)
budget *n* fjárhagsáætlun
Buenos Aires (capital of Argentina)
 N Buenos Aires (höfuðborg
 Argentínu)
buffalo wings *n* kjúklingavængir
bug 1 *n (insect)* skordýr; *(computer)*
 tölvuvírus; *(listening device)*
 hlerunarbúnaður; 2 *v (bother)*
 trufla, pirra, *colloq* bögga; *(spy)* hlera
buggy *n* innkaupakerra, kerra
build 1 *n* líkamsbygging; 2 *v* byggja
builder *n* verkamaður í byggingar-
 vinnu
building *n* bygging

built *adj* byggður
Bulgaria *N* Búlgaría
Bulgarian 1 *adj* búlgarskur; 2 *N*
 (nationality) Búlgari; *(language)*
 búlgarska
bull *n zool* naut, nautgripur; **take the**
 ~ **by the horn** takast á við vandann
bullet *n* byssukúla
bulletin board *n* upplýsingatafla
bullet-proof *adj* skotheldur
bumblebee *n* hunangsfluga
bumper *n* stuðari
bun *n (bread)* bolla, brauðbolla,
 rúnstykki: **sesame seed** ~
 rúnstykki með sesamfræjum;
 (hair) hnútur
bunch *n* knippi: ~ **of carrots**
 gulrótarknippi; klasi: ~ **of grapes**
 vínberjaklasi; hópur: ~ **of people**
 hópur af fólki
bungee-jumping *n* teygjustökk
burden 1 *n* byrði; 2 *v* íþyngja
burden of proof *n leg* sönnunarbyrði
bureaucracy *n* skriffinnska
bureaucrat *n* skriffinnur, *colloq*
 bjúrókrati, kontóristi
burger *n* (ham)borgari; **veggie**
 ~ grænmetisborgari; **cheese** ~
 ostaborgari
burn 1 *n* bruni; 2 *v* brenna
burned *adj* brunninn; **sun**~ sólbrunninn
burnt *adj* brenndur; ~ **toast** brennt
 ristabrauð
burrito *n* burrító; **bean and cheese**
 ~ burrító með baunum og osti
burst *v* springa
bury *v* grafa
bus *n (city)* strætó, strætisvagn; **tour**
 ~ rúta; ~ **lane** strætisvagnaakrein
bus driver *n (city bus)* strætóbíl-
 stjóri; *(coach)* rútubílstjóri
bus terminal *n* strætóstöð; *(traffic
 center)* umferðarmiðstöð
bush *n* runni
business *n* viðskipti; ~ **class** fyrsta
 farrými; ~ **hours** afgreiðslutími;
 ~ **card** nafnspjald

busy *adj* upptekinn, frátekinn
but 1 *conj* en; **2** *prep* nema: **nobody ~ me** enginn nema ég
butane gas *n* bútangas
butcher *n* slátrari
butte *n* stapi
butter *n* smjör; **cocoa ~** kókóssmjör; **peanut ~** hnetusmjör
butterfly *n* fiðrildi
buttermilk *n* súrmjólk
buttock *n* rasskinn
button *n* *(electronic)* takki; *(clothing)* hnappur, smella
buy *v* kaupa; **to ~** að kaupa
buyer *n* kaupandi

by 1 *prep (next to)* við: **I live ~ the lake** ég bý við vatnið; *(made by)* eftir: **a book ~ Laxness** bók eftir Laxness; **~ accident** fyrir slysni; **~ all means** endilega; **2** *adv* **to get ~** að komast af
bye! *phr* bless!, bless bless!; *(to men)* vertu blessaður, vertu sæll; *(to women)* vertu blessuð, vertu sæl; *colloq* bæ
bypass *n* hjáleið; **heart ~** *med* hjáveituaðgerð
by-product *n* afleiddar vörur

C

cab *n* leigubíll, *colloq* taxi
cabaret *n* kabarett
cabbage *n* kál: **green** ~ kál, **white**
~ hvítkál, **red** ~ rauðkál, **savoy** ~
blöðrukál; ~ **soup** kálsúpa
cabin *n* kofi; *(on a boat)* káeta; *(on a train)* klefi
cabinet *n* skápur; *(administrative)*
ráðuneyti: **a** ~ **meeting**
ríkisstjórnarfundur
cable *n* *(rope)* kaðall; *(electric)*
rafmagnssnúra
cable television/TV *n* kapalsjónvarp
cactus *n* kaktus
café *n* kaffihús
cafeteria *n* kaffitería
caffeine *n* koffín
caffeine-free *adj* koffínlaus
cage *n* búr
cage-free *adj* frjáls; ~ **chicken** frjálsir
kjúklingar; ~ **hen** frjálsir hænur;
~ **eggs** hamingjusöm egg; ~ **beef**
nautgripir sem ganga úti
Cairo (capital of Egypt) *N* Kairó
(höfuðborg Egyptalands)
cake *n* kaka, terta: **cup~** bollakaka;
sponge ~ svampbotn; **wedding** ~
brúðkaupsterta
calamari *n* smokkfiskur
calamity *n* hörmungar
calcium *n* kalsíum
calculate *v* reikna út
calculating *adj* séður, útsmoginn
calculation *n* útreikningur
calculator *n* vasareiknir; **scientific** ~
fullkominn vasareiknir
caldera *n* sigketill
calendar *n* dagatal
calf *n* *zool* kálfur
call *n* *(phone)* símtal; **2** *v* kalla;
(phone) hringja: ~ **for** hringja í,

~ **collect** hringja kollekt
calligraphy *n* skrautskrift
calm 1 *adj* rólegur, afslappaður; **2** *n*
(no wind) logn; **3** *v* róa
calmly *adv* rólega
calorie *n* kalóría
Cambodia *N* Kambódía
camera *n* myndavél; ~ **case** mynda-
vélataska; ~ **shop** ljósmyndaverslun
Cameroon *N* Kamerún
camomile *n* kamilla
camp 1 *n* búðir; tjaldbúðir; ~ **site**
tjaldstæði; **2** *v* tjalda
campaign *n* *(political)* kosninga-
barátta; *(advertisement)* auglýsingaherferð
camper *n* *(person)* tjaldbúi; *(vehicle)*
húsbíll
campground *n* tjaldstæði
camping equipment *n* tjaldútbúnaður,
útivistarbúnaður
can 1 *n* dós: **~ned food** dósamatur;
~ **opener** dósaopnari; **2** *v* *(skills)*
kunna: **I** ~ **swim** ég kann að synda;
(able) geta: ~ **you help me?**
geturðu hjálpað mér?
Canada *N* Kanada
Canadian 1 *adj* kanadískur; **2** *n*
Kanadamaður, Kanadabúi
canal *n* skurður, skipaskurður
Canberra (capital of Australia) *N*
Canberra (höfuðborg Ástralíu)
cancel *v* afboða, afpanta
canceled *adj* afboðaður, afturkallaður
cancer *n* *med* krabbamein
Cancer *n* *astro* Krabbinn
candidate *n* *(political)* frambjóðandi;
(potential) efni: **a** ~ **for** efni í
candied *adj* sykraður: ~ **fruit**
sykraður ávöxtur
candle *n* kerti

candlestick *n* kerti
candy *n* sælgæti, *colloq* nammi; **hard** ~ brjóstsykur; **gummy** ~ hlaup
candy cane *n* brjóstsykursstafur
cane syrup *n* sykursíróp
canoe *n* kanó: ~ **rental** kanóaleiga
cantaloupe *n* kantalúpmelóna
canvas *n* strigi
cap *n* lok
capability *n* geta
capacity *n* geta
Cape Town *N* Höfðaborg
Cape Verde *N* Grænhöfðaeyjar
capers *n* kapers
capital *n* höfuðborg
capricious *adj* dyntóttur: ~ **boss** dyntóttur yfirmaður
Capricorn *n astro* Steingeitin
caps lock key *n comp* hástafalás
capsule *n* hylki
captain *n (military)* kafteinn; *(ship)* skipstjóri
captive *n* fangi
captivity *n* fangelsun
car *n* bíl; **by** ~ á bíl; **rental** ~ bílaleigubíll
car dealer *n* bílasala
car wash *n (washing)* bílaþvottur; *(station)* bílaþvottastöð
carafe *n* karafla; **wine** ~ vínkarafla; **water** ~ vatnskanna
caramel *n* karamella: ~ **sauce** karamellusósa; ~ **cream** karamellukrem; **dark** ~ dökk karamella
caramelized *adj* brúnaður: ~ **onion** brúnaður laukur
caravan *n* hjólhýsi
caraway *n* kúmen
caraway seeds *n* kúmenfræ
carbohydrate *n* sykra: **complex** ~ flóknar sykrur; **simple** ~ einfaldar sykrur
carbon *n* kolefni
carbonated *adj* kolsýrður; ~ **water** kolsýrt vatn
carburetor *n* blöndungur

card *n (greeting ~)* kort; *(playing ~)* spil; **to play ~s** að spila á spil
card number *n* kortanúmer
cardamom *n* kardimomma
cardboard *n* pappi
care 1 *n* umönnun; 2 *v* vera umhugað um; **take ~ of** hugsa um; **don't ~ for** vera sama um
career *n* starfsferill
careful *adj* varkár
carefully *adv* varlega
careless *adj* óvarkár
carelessly *adv* óvarlega, glannalega
Caribbean Sea *N* Karíbahaf
Caribbean Islands *N* Antillaeyjar
caricature *n* skrípamynd; skopstæling
caring *adj* umhyggjusamur
carnival *n* kjötkveðjuhátíð
carp *n zool* vatnakarfi
carpet *n* teppi
carrier *n (mail)* sendlafyrirtæki; *(of a disease)* smitberi
carrier bag *n* handfarangur
carrot *n* gulrót; ~ **cake** gulrótarkaka
carry *v* halda á: ~ **books** halda á bókum; *(~ money)* vera með á sér: **I never ~ a lot of cash** ég er aldrei með mikinn pening á mér; *(transport)* flytja; *(stock)* selja: **this store carries books** þessi búð selur bækur; *(about appearance)* bera sig; ~ **a risk** felur í sér áhættu; ~ **on** halda áfram; ~ **a child** ganga með barn; ~ **out** framkvæma; ~ **over** færa á milli
carry-on luggage *n* handfarangur
cart *n* vagn; kerra; **grocery** ~ innkaupakerra
carton *n* ferna: **milk** ~ mjólkurferna
cartoon *n* teiknimynd; **animated** ~ hreyfimynd
carve *v* skera út, tálga; *(meat)* skera
carving 1 *n* útskurður; ~ **knife** útskurðarhnífur
case *n* tilfelli: **in ~ of an emergency** í neyðartilvikum; **that is not the ~** það er ekki tilfellið; **in any ~**

allavega; **in that** ~ þá; **in** ~ ef;
leg dómsmál; *ling* fall; **pillow**~
koddaver; *(box)* kassi
cash 1 *n* reiðufé: **withdraw** ~ taka
út reiðufé; **pay in** ~ greiða með
reiðufé; **2** *v* leysa út: ~ **a check**
leysa út ávísun
cash dispenser *n* hraðbanki
cash register *n* peningakassi,
búðarkassi
cashew *n* kasjúhneta
cashier *n* afgreiðslumaður á kassa
casino *n* spilavíti
cassava *n* kassavarót
casserole *n* pottréttur
cassette *n* kassetta, spóla, snælda
cast 1 *n* afsteypa; **2** *v* steypa
cast iron *n* steypujárn; ~ **stove**
steypujárnseldavél
castle *n* kastali, höll
casual *adj* hversdagslegur
cat *n* köttur, *colloq* kisi, kisa
Catalan *n* katalónska
catalog *n* vörulisti
catch *v (a ball)* grípa; *(an animal)*
veiða
category *n* flokkur
cater *v* selja mat
catering *n* matvælaþjónusta; ~ **service**
matvælaþjónusta
caterpillar *n* lirfa
cathedral *n* dómkirkja
Catholic *adj* kaþólskur, katólskur
catnip *n* kattarminta
cattle *n* nautgripur
cauliflower *n* blómkál
cause 1 *n* ástæða, orsök; *(support)*
málefni: **worthy** ~ verðugt málefni;
2 *v* valda, orsaka
caution *n* varúð
cave *n* hellir
caviar *n* kavíar
cavity *n* tannskemmd
cayenne pepper *n* cayenne pipar
CD *n* geisladiskur; ~ **burner** geisladiskabrennari; ~ **player** geislaspilari
cease *v* hætta

ceiling *n* loft: **in the** ~ í loftinu
celebrate *v* fagna
celebration *n* fagnaður, hátíðarhöld
celery *n* blaðselja, sellerí; ~ **root**
sellerírót; ~ **stick** sellerístöngull
cell *n (prison)* klefi; *(biology)* fruma
cello *n mus* selló, knéfiðla
cellphone *n* farsími
cellulose *n* appelsínuhúð
celsius *n* selsíus
cement *n* steinsteypa, sement
cemetery *n* kirkjugarður, grafreitur
censorship *n* ritskoðun
census *n* manntal
cent *n econ* sent
centenary *n* aldarafmæli
center *n* miðstöð; **shopping** ~
verslunarmiðstöð; ~ **of excellence**
öndvegissetur
center of town *n* miðbær: ~ **of**
Reykjavík miðbær Reykjavíkur
centimeter *n* sentimetri
centipede *n* þúsundfætla
central *adj* mið-
Central African Republic *N* Mið-
Afríkuríki
Central America *N* Mið-Amería
Central American *adj* frá Mið-
Ameríku; ~ **food** matur frá Mið-
Ameríku
central heating *n* hitaveita
century *n* öld
ceramic *adj* keramík-
ceramics *n* keramík
cereal *n* morgunkorn: **whole grain**
~ morgunkorn úr grófu korni,
sweet ~ sykrað morgunkorn, **oat** ~
morgunkorn úr höfrum
ceremony *n* athöfn; **wedding** ~
brúðkaup; **graduation** ~ útskrift
certain *adj* viss, sérstakur
certainly *adv* vissulega, sannarlega
certificate *n* vottorð: **birth** ~
fæðingarvottorð; ~ **of deposit**
kvittun fyrir greiðslu
Caesar salad *n* sesar salat
chain 1 *n* keðja; **2** *v* binda

chair *n (furniture)* stóll; *(of a meeting)*
fundarstjóri; **wheel~** hjólastóll
chairman *n (meeting)* fundarstjóri;
(committee) formaður
challenge 1 *n* áskorun; **2** *v* skora á
chamber *n* herbergi, svefnherbergi;
judge's ~ dómaraherbergi
champagne *n* kampavín
champignon *n* ætisveppur
championship *n* sigur
chance *n (possibility)* möguleiki: **have
no ~** eiga enga möguleika; *(coincidence)* tilviljun: **by ~** fyrir tilviljun
chancellor *n* kanslari
change 1 *n* breyting; **2** *v* skipta: **~
buses** skipta um strætó, **~ a diaper**
skipta um bleyju
changing room *n (sports facility)*
búningsklefi; *(in a store)*
mátunarklefi
channel *n (sea)* sund: **the English
~** Ermarsund; *(television)* stöð:
change the ~ skipta um stöð
chanterelle *n* vængjasveppur,
kantarella
chapel *n* kapella
chapter *n* kafli
char *v* svíða
char fish *n zool* bleikja
character *n* persónuleiki, karakter
characteristic 1 *adj* einkennandi; **2**
n einkenni, lyndiseinkunn
charcoal *n* grillkol; **~-grilled** grillað
með kolum
chard *n* blaðbeðja
charge 1 *n* miðaverð; **2** *v (money)*
rukka; *(attack)* ráðast á; *leg* kæra:
bring ~s against kæra
charity *n* góðgerðamál
charm 1 *n (attraction)* þokki;
(mascot) heillagripur, lukkudýr; **2**
v heilla, *colloq* sjarma
charming *adj* heillandi
chart *n* tafla, kort, yfirlit; *mus:* **on top
of the ~s** efst á vinsældarlistum
charter *n* stofnsáttmáli
charter flight *n* leiguflug

chase *v* elta
chat 1 *n* spjall; **2** *v* spjalla
chat room *n comp* spjallrás
chauffeur *n* bílstjóri
cheap *adj* ódýr
cheaper *adj compar* ódýrari
cheapest *adj superl* ódýrastur
cheaply *adv* ódýrt
cheat 1 *n* svindl; **2** *v* svindla
check 1 *n (bank)* ávísun, tékki;
(search) athugun, skoðun; **2** *v*
athuga; *(chess)* skáka; **~ in** tékka
sig inn, innrita sig; **~ out** tékka út;
coat ~ fatahengi
checkbook *n* ávísanahefti
checkout *n* afgreiðslukassi
checkpoint *n* eftirlitsstöð
cheek *n* kinn
cheer *v* hvetja áfram
cheerful *adj* glaðlegur
cheerfully *adv* glaðlega
cheers! *excl* skál!
cheese *n* ostur: **goat ~** geitaostur;
blue ~ mygluostur
cheese fondue *n* ostafondú
cheese sauce *n* ostasósa
cheesecake *n* ostakaka
chef *n* kokkur
chemical 1 *adj* efnafræðilegur,
efnafræði-; **2** *n* efni
chemist *n* efnafræðingur
chemistry *n* efnafræði
cherry *n* kirsuber; **~ pie** kirsuberja-
baka; **~ liqueur** kirsuberjalíkjör;
~ sauce kirsuberjasósa
cherry tomato *n* kirsuberjatómatur
chervil *n* kerfill
chess *n* skák
chess set *n* taflsett
chessboard *n* taflborð
chest *n anat* brjóstkassi; **~ of draw-
ers** kommóða
chestnut *n* kastaníuhneta
chew *v* tyggja
chewable *adj* **~ tablet** tyggitafla;
~ supplement tyggjanlegt
fjölvítamín

chewing gum *n* tyggigúmmí, *colloq* tyggjó
chicken *n* kjúklingur; ~ **breast** kjúklingabringa; ~ **soup** kjúklingasúpa; ~ **wings** kjúklingavængir
chickpea *n* kjúklingabaun
chicory *n flora* kaffifífill
chief 1 *adj* aðal-; **2** *n* yfirmaður; *(tribal)* höfðingi
child *n* barn; ~'s **seat** barnastóll; ~'s **bed** barnarúm; **children's discount** barnaafsláttur; **children's menu** barnamatseðill; **children's pool** barnalaug; **children's portion** barnaskammtur
childcare *n* barnagæsla
childhood *n* æska
childproof cap *n* lok með barnaöryggi
children. *See* **child**
childrenswear *n* barnaföt
Chile *N* Síle
Chilean 1 *adj* síleskur; **2** *N* Sílemaður
chili *n* chilli: ~ **pepper** chillipipar; ~ **powder** chilliduft; ~ **sauce** chillisósa
chill 1 *n* kuldi; **2** *v (cool)* kæla; *(relax)* slappa af
chilled *adj* kældur, kaldur
chills *n* hrollur, kuldatilfinning; **I have** ~ ég er með hroll
chilly *adj* kalt, kuldalegt
chimney *n* strompur, reykháfur
chin *n* haka
china *n* postulín
China *N* Kína
Chinese 1 *adj* kínverskur: ~ **food** kínverskur matur; **2** *N* Kínverji
chip *n (wood)* flís; *(food)* flaga: **potato** ~ kartöfluflögur, **tortilla** ~ maísflögur
chiropractor *n med* kírópraktor, hnykklæknir
chives *n pl* graslaukur
chlorine *n chem* klór
chocolate *n* súkkulaði; **box of** ~**s** súkkulaðiaskja; ~ **filling** súkkulaðifylling

chocolate bar *n* súkkulaðistykki
chocolate syrup *n* súkkulaðisósa
choice *n* val
choir *n* kór: **men's** ~ karlakór; **women's** ~ kvennakór
choke *v* kafna
choose *v* velja
chop 1 *n* kótiletta: **lamb** ~**s** lambakótilettur; **2** *v* skera niður; *(~ finely)* saxa, hakka; *(~ wood)* höggva
chopped *adj* niðurskorinn, hakkaður, saxaður
chopstick *n* prjónn m
chord *n mus* hljómur
choreographer *n* danshöfundur
choreography *n* danshreyfingar
chorizo *n* chorizopylsa
chorus *n* viðlag
Christ *N* Kristur
christen *v* skíra
christening *n* skírn
Christian *adj* kristinn
Christian name *n* skírnarnafn
Christmas *n* jól; **Merry** ~! Gleðileg jól!; ~ **card** jólakort; ~ **Day** jóladagur; ~ **decoration** jólaskraut; ~ **Eve** aðfangadagur; ~ **gift** jólagjöf; ~ **holiday** jólafrí; ~ **party** jólaboð; ~ **tree** jólatré
chromosome *n bio* litningur
chronic *adj* þrálátur, varanlegur, *colloq* króvískur
chunky *adj* grófur; ~ **pieces** grófir bitar
church *n* kirkja; ~ **service** guðsþjónusta
chutney *n* mauk: **pineapple** ~ ananasmauk, **apple** ~ eplamauk
cider *n* síder: **apple** ~ eplasíder
cigar *n* vindill
cigarette *n* sígaretta; ~ **paper** sígarettupappír; **electric** ~ rafretta
cilantro *n* kóríaner
cinema *n (theater)* kvikmyndahús, bíó; *(artform)* kvikmynagerðarlist
cinnamon *n* kanill: ~ **roll** kanilsnúður, ~ **stick** kanilstöng, ~ **powder** kanelduft

circa (*abbrev* **ca**) *adv* um það bil
(*abbrev* u.þ.b.), hér um bil, *colloq*
sirka
circle 1 *n* hringur: **go in a** ~ fara í
hring; **a vicious** ~ vítahringur; ~ **of
friends** vinahópur; **2** *v* fara
í hringi
circuit *n* rafrás; **short** ~ skammhlaup
circuit breaker *n* rofi
circulation *n* hringrás
circumstance *n* aðstæður
circus *n* fjölleikahús, sirkus
citizen *n* ríkisborgari; **senior** ~
eldriborgari; ~ **of the world**
heimsborgari
citizenship *n* ríkisborgararéttur
citrus *n* sítrus: ~ **flavor** með sítrus-
bragði; ~ **fruit** sítrusávöxtur; ~
juice sítrussafi
city *n* borg: ~ **wall** borgarmúr; ~ **limits**
borgarmörk; ~ **center** miðbær
civil *adj* borgaralegur: ~ **ceremony**
borgaraleg gifting, ~ **rights**
borgararéttindi
civilian *n* almennur borgari
claim 1 *n* (*assertion*) staðhæfing;
(*demand*) krafa; **2** *v* (*assert*) staðhæfa,
halda fram; (*demand*) krefja
claim check *n* farangurskvittun
clam *n* samloka, skeldýr; ~ **bisque**
frönsk skeldýrasúpa; ~ **chowder**
skeldýrapottréttur
clamor *n* gól, org, öskur
clap 1 *n* klapp; **2** *v* klappa
clapping *n* klapp
clarify *v* útskýra
clarinet *n* *mus* klarinetta
class *n* (*category*) flokkur; (*social*)
stétt; (*school*) bekkur; (*lesson*)
kennslustund; (*graduating*)
árgangur; (*travel, quality*) farrými:
travel first ~ ferðast á fyrsta
farrými
classic 1 *adj* klassískur, sígildur; **2** *n*
sígilt verk, klassík
classical *adj* klassískt, sígilt

classical music *n* klassísk tónlist,
sígild tónlist
Classicism *n* klassík, *colloq* klassisismi
classics *n* *lit* sígildar bókmenntir,
heimsbókmenntir
classification *n* flokkun
classified ad *n* smáauglýsing
classify *v* flokka
classroom *n* kennslustofa, skólastofa
classy *adj* glæsilegur, fínn
clause *n* *ling* setning: **main** ~
aðalsetning, **subordinate** ~
aukasetning; *leg* grein
clay *n* leir
clean 1 *adj* hreinn; **2** *v* hreinsa, þvo;
to ~ **up** að laga til
cleaning *n* tiltekt, hreinsun; **dry** ~
þurrhreinsun
clear *v* hreinsa; ~ **the table** taka af
borðinu; ~ **through customs** fara í
gegnum tollinn
clearance sale *n* rýmingarsala
clearly *adv* greinilega
clementine *n* klementína
clerk *n* afgreiðslumaður
clever *adj* gáfaður, klár
click 1 *n* smellur; **2** *v* smella: *comp* ~
with mouse smella með mús
client *n* viðskiptavinur
cliff *n* klettur
climate *n* loftslag
climax *n* *lit* ris, hápunktur: **the** ~ **of
the film** hápunktur myndarinnar
climb 1 *n* klifur; **2** *v* klifra
climbing *n* klifur
clinic *n* heilsugæslustöð; (*at hospital*)
deild
clinical *adj* klínískur, vísindalegur
cloakroom *n* fatahengi
clock *n* klukka; **alarm** ~ vekjaraklukka
clog *n* (*shoes*) klossi: **wear** ~**s** ganga
í klossum; (*in drain*) stífla
clogged *adj* stíflaður; ~ **drain** stíflað
niðurfall
clone *v* klóna
cloning *n* klónun
close 1 *adj* nálægur: ~ **to** nálægt;

náinn: **a ~ friend** náinn vinur,
to be ~ to sby að vera náinn
einhverjum; *(thorough)* ítarlegur:
a ~ examination ítarleg rannsókn;
2 *v (shut)* loka: **~ the door** loka
hurðinni; **~ the curtains** draga
fyrir; **~ off** loka, sperra af; *(finish)* ljúka, klára; **~ down** hætta
starfsemi
close-knit *adj* samrýmdur
closely *adv* með athygli, vandlega,
ítarlega; **watch ~** fylgjast vel með;
to read ~ lesa ítarlega
closet *n* skápur, fataskápur; **come
out of the ~** koma út úr skápnum
clot 1 *n* kökkur; **blood ~** blóðtappi; **2**
v kekkjast
cloth *n* efni
clothes *n* föt, fatnaður, klæðnaður,
spjör: **put ~ on** klæða sig, **take ~
off** fara úr fötum
clothes dryer *n* þurrkari
clothes hanger *n* herðatré
clothing *n* föt, fatnaður, klæðnaður;
~ store fataverslun, fatabúð
clotted *adj* kekkjóttur: **~ cream**
kekkjóttur rjómi, **~ sauce** kekkjótt
sósa
cloud *n* ský
cloudberry *n* múltuber
cloudy *adj* skýjaður
clove *n* geiri: **garlic ~** hvítlauksgeiri
clover *n flora* smári
clown *n* trúður
club *n (group)* félagsskapur, félag,
klúbbur: **golf ~** golfklúbbur; *(in
cards)* lauf; *(stick)* lurkur
clubhouse *n* félagsheimili
cluster 1 *n* klasi, þyrping; **2** *v* þyrpast
clutch *n mech* kúpling: **~ pedal**
kúpling, pedali fyrir kúplingu
coach 1 *n (bus)* rúta; *(carriage)* vagn;
(trainer) þjálfari; **2** *v* þjálfa
coal *n* kol
coalfish *n zool* svartþorskur, ufsi,
drungi
coarse *adj* grófur

coast *n* strönd, fjara; **~ guard** land-
helgisgæslan; **~line** strandlína
coat 1 *n* jakki, *(women)* kápa; *(fur)*
pels; *(paint)* umferð; **2** *v* hjúpa;
(prevent from rusting) ryðverja
coat hanger *n* herðatré
coated *adj* þakinn, húðaður; **sugar-~**
sykurhúðaður; **glaze ~** með gljáa
coating *n* yfirborð, húð
cocaine *n* kókaín
cockroach *n* kakkalakki
cocktail *n* kokteill, hanastél
cocoa *n* kakó
coconut *n* kókoshneta: **~ cream**
kókoshneturjómi, **~ milk** kókoshnetumjólk
cod *n* þorskur
code *n* kóði, lykilnúmer; **area ~**
svæðisnúmer
coffee *n* kaffi; **~ cup** kaffibolli;
~maker kaffivél; **~ mug** kaffikrús;
~ pot kaffikanna; **~ press** pressu-
kanna; **~ shop** kaffihús
coin *n* mynt: **~ collection** myntsafn
coincide *v* vera á sama tíma
coke *n (drink)* kók: **one ~, please**
gæti ég fengið eina kók
cold *adj* kaldur: **feel ~** vera kalt, **~
drink** svaladrykkur; *n med* **have a
~** vera með kvef
cold cuts *n* kjötálegg
coldly *adv* kuldalega
coleslaw *n* hrásalat
collapse 1 *n* hrun; **2** *v* hrynja, brotna
saman
collards *n* grænkál
colleague *n* samstarfsfélagi, vinnufélagi
collect *v* safna
collect call *n* samtal greitt af viðtakanda
collection *n* safn
collector *n* safnari
college *n* háskóli, iðnskóli
Colombia *N* Kólumbía
Colombian 1 *adj* kólumbískur; **2** *n*
Kólumbíumaður
colon *n gram* tvípunktur; *anat* ristil\|l
color 1 *n* litur: **~ film** kvikmynd í lit,

bíómynd í lit; **2** *v* lita
colored *adj* litaður; **multi~** marglitaður
coloring *n* litun; **food ~** matarlitur
coloring book *n* litabók
column *n (building)* súla; *(on paper)* dálkur
columnar basalt *n geol* stuðlaberg
coma *n med* dauðadá
comb *n/v* greiða
combination *n* sambland, blanda
combine *v* blanda saman
come *v* koma
come back *v* snúa aftur
comedy *n* grín, grínmynd, gaman-mynd; *(theater)* gamanleikrit
comfort 1 *n* þægindi; **2** *v* hugga
comfortable *adj* þægilegur
comfortably *adv* þægilega
comic 1 *adj* fyndinn, hlægilegur; **2** *n* grínisti; **stand up ~** uppistandari; **~ book** teiknimyndablað
comical *adj* fyndinn, hlægilegur
comics *n* (skop)teikning
comma *n ling* komma; **inverted ~s** gæsalappir
command 1 *n* skipun; *(leadership)* stjórnun, forysta; **have a ~ of Icelandic** geta talað íslensku; **2** *v* skipa: **~ sby to do sth** skipa einhverjum að gera eitthvað; **~ respect** njóta virðingar
commemoration *n* minningarathöfn
comment 1 *n* athugasemd; **2** *v* gera athugasemd við, tjá sig um
commentary *n* athugasemd
commercial 1 *adj* viðskiptalegur: **~ television** einkastöð; **2** *n* auglýsing
commercial law *n* verslunaréttur
commission *n (committee)* nefnd; *(salary)* sölulaun
commit *v (to bind or obligate)* standa við: **~ oneself to a promise** standa við loforð; *(crime)* fremja: **~ a suicide** fremja sjálfsmorð; **~ murder** myrða
commitment *n* skuldbinding
committee *n* nefnd

commodity *n econ* vara, söluvara
common *adj (usual)* venjulegur, algengur, einfaldur; *(mutual)* sameiginlegur: **~ friend** sameiginlegur vinur, **to have sth in ~** að eiga eitthvað sameiginlegt
common sense *n* brjóstvit
commonly *adv* almennt
communicate *v* eiga í samskiptum; *(inform)* upplýsa
communication *n* samskipti; *(message)* tilkynning, skilaboð; *(convey)* samgöngur: **means of ~** samgöngumáti; **~ protocol** *n comp* samskiptastaðall
communion *n* altarisganga
communism *n* kommúnismi
communist *adj* kommúnisti
community *n* samfélag
commute *v* ferðast til vinnu
compact *adj* þéttur
compact disc (CD) *n* geisladiskur; **~ burner** geisladiskabrennari; **~ cover** geisladiskahulstur
companion *n* félagi
company *n* fyrirtæki; *(companion-ship)* félagsskapur: **keep sby ~** vera einhverjum félagsskapur
comparative *adj* samanburðar-; **~ literature** almenn bókmenntafræði
compare *v* bera saman
comparison *n* samanburður
compass *n* áttaviti
compensate *v* bæta
compensation *n* bætur, skaðabætur, uppbót; **receive ~ for sth** fá skaðabætur fyrir eitthvað; *(salary)* þóknun
compete *v* keppa
competition *n* samkeppni
competitive *adj* samkeppnis-
competitor *n* samkeppnisaðili
complain *v* kvarta
complainant *n* kvörtunaraðili; *leg* málsækjandi
complaint *n* kvörtun: **file a ~** leggja fram kvörtun
complete 1 *adj* algjör, heill: **~ meal**

heil máltíð; **2** *v* klára, ljúka við; ~ **a form** fylla í eyðublað
completely *adv* algjörlega
complex *adj* flókinn, margbrotinn, margþættur: ~ **personality** margbrotinn persónuleiki
complexion *n* litarhaft
complicate *v* flækja: **~d matters** flókin mál, erfið mál
complicated *adj* flókinn
comply with *v* fara eftir
component *n* hluti, þáttur
compose *v* semja: ~ **music** semja tónlist, ~ **a poem** semja ljóð
composed *adj* samsettur: **be ~ of** vera samsettur úr
composer *n* tónskáld
composition *n* *mus* tónverk, tónsmíð; *art* myndbygging; *lit* form
compost *n* lífrænt sorp
compote *n* mauk, grautur: **fruit ~** ávaxtamauk, ávaxtagrautur, **apple ~** eplamauk, eplagrautur
compound *adj* samsettur: *ling* ~ **word** samsett orð; *econ* ~ **interest** vaxtavextir
comprehension *n* skilningur
comprise *v* fela í sér; **be ~d of** samsett úr
compromise 1 *n* málamiðlun, millivegur; **2** *v* komast að samkomulagi, fara milliveginn
compute *v* reikna út
computer *n* tölva: ~ **game** tölvuleikur, ~ **mouse** tölvumús, ~ **programmer** forritari, ~ **screen** tölvuskjár, ~ **virus** tölvuvírus
conceive *v (a baby)* verða ólétt, verða ófrísk; *(an idea)* móta; *(imagine)* ímynda sér
concentrate 1 *n* þykkni: **juice ~** safaþykkni, **fruit ~** ávaxtaþykkni; **2** *v* einbeita sér
concentration *n* einbeiting
concept *n* hugmynd
conception *n (pregnancy)* ólétta, þungun; *(of an idea)* skilningur, hugmynd

concern 1 *n (company)* samsteypa; *(consideration)* áhyggjur; **2** *v* koma við: **it doesn't ~ you** þetta kemur þér ekki við
concerned *adj* áhyggjufullur; **as far as I am ~** hvað mig varðar
concerning *prep* varðandi, viðvíkjandi
concert *n* tónleikar; ~ **hall** tónleikahöll; **live ~** tónleikar
concerto *n* *mus* konsert, hljómsveitarverk fyrir einleikshljóðfæri: ~ **for violin and piano** konsert fyrir fiðlu og píanó
conclude *v* draga ályktun
conclusion *n* niðurstaða; **draw a ~** draga ályktun; **jump to a ~** draga fljótfærnislega ályktun; **come to a ~** komast að niðurstöðu
concrete 1 *adj* áþreifanlegur: ~ **solution** áþreifanleg lausn; **2** *n* steypa
concussion *n* *med* heilahristingur: **he has a ~** hann er með heilahristing
condensed milk *n* niðursoðin mjólk
condiments *n* krydd, bragðefni
condition *n* skilyrði: **under the ~ that** með því skilyrði að, **stipulate ~s** setja skilyrði; *(physical)* ástand: **not in a ~ to drive** ekki í ástandi til að keyra; *(health, shape)* form: **be in good ~** vera í góðu formi; *(for driving etc)* færð: **how are the driving ~s?** hvernig er færðin?; *(for skiing)* færi: **good skiing ~s** gott skíðafæri
conditional *adj* skilyrtur
conditioner *n* hárnæring
condolence *n* samúðarkveðjur
condom *n* smokkur
conduct 1 *n* hegðun; **2** *v (lead)* leiða, stjórna, stýra; *mus* stjórna
conductor *n (of bus, train)* miðasali; *mus* stjórnandi
cone *n* köngull
confectioners' sugar *n* flórsykur
conference *n* ráðstefna
conference call *n* hópsímtal
conference room *n* fundarherbergi

confess *v* viðurkenna
confession *n* viðurkenning, játning
confidence *n* traust: **have full ~ in sby** bera fullt traust til einhvers; **put ~ in** treysta; **self~** sjálfstraust, sjálfsöryggi; *(privacy)* trúnaður: **in complete ~** í algjörum trúnaði
confident *adj* öruggur
confidential *adj* trúnaðar-: **~ data** trúnaðarupplýsingar
confidently *adv* í trúnaði
confine *v (limit)* takmarka; *(in prison)* loka inni
confined *adj* innilokaður; **~ to bed** rúmliggjandi
confirm *v* staðfesta
conflict *n* deila, rifrildi, óeining
confront *v* horfast í augu við
confuse *v* rugla, brengla
confused *adj* ráðvilltur, ringlaður, brenglaður
confusing *adj* villandi
confusion *n* ringulreið
congealed *adj* storknaður: **~ fat** storknuð fita
Congo, Democratic Republic of the *N* Austur-Kongó, Lýðræðislega lýðveldið Kongó
Congo, Republic of the *N* Vestur-Kongó
Congolese *N* Kongóbúi
congratulate *v* óska til hamingju
congratulations *n* hamingjuóskir; *interj* til hamingju!
congress *n* þing: **the US ~** Bandaríska þingið; **member of ~** þingmaður
congressman *n* þingmaður
congresswoman *n* þingkona
conjunction *n ling* samtenging
connect *v* tengja; *(on the phone)* gefa samband: **can you ~ me?** geturðu gefið mér samband?
connected *adj* tengdur
connection *n* tenging, tengsl: **have good ~s** vera með góð tengsl, **in ~ with/to** í tengslum við; *(electric)* samband; *(Internet)* tenging

conscious *adj* meðvitaður
consciousness *n* meðvitund: **to gain ~** að komast til meðvitundar
consequence *n* afleiðing
consequently *adv* þar af leiðandi
conservation *n* verndun, vernd; **~ of environment/nature** náttúruvernd
conservation area *n* náttúruverndarsvæði
conservative 1 *adj* íhaldssamur; **2** *n* íhaldsmaður
conserve *v* varðveita, geyma
consider *v* íhuga, hafa í huga
considerable *adj* töluverður: **~ odds** töluverðar líkur
considerably *adv* töluvert
consideration *n* tillit
consist of *v* samanstanda af
consistent *adj* rökfastur
consistently *adv* undantekningarlaust
consonant *n ling* samhljóði
constant *adj* stöðugur
constantly *adv* stöðugt
constipated *adj med* með harðlífi
constipation *n med* harðlífi
constitute *v* mynda, gera; *leg* lögskipa
constitution *n* stjórnarskrá
constitutional *adj leg* stjórnarskrár-: **~ law** stjórnskipunarréttur
constraint *n* hömlur
construct *v* byggja
construction *n* bygging; **under ~** í vinnslu
consulate *n* ræðisskrifstofa, *colloq* konsúlat
consult *v* leita ráða
consultant *n* ráðgjafi
consultation *n* ráðgjöf; **~ room** læknastofa
consumer *n* neytandi
consumption *n* neysla
contact 1 *n* samband: **be in ~ with** vera í sambandi við; **2** *v* hafa samband
contact lens *n* (augn)linsa: **eye drops for ~** augndropar fyrir linsur
contagious *adj* smitandi

contain

corn 215

contain *v* innihalda
container *n* gámur
container ship *n* gámaskip
contemporary *adj* samtíma-: ~ **art** samtímalist
content *n* innihald: **dietary** ~ næringarinnihald; **protein** ~ próteinmagn; **fat** ~ fitumagn
contest *n* samkeppni
context *n* samhengi
continent *n* heimsálfa
continental *adj* frá meginlandinu
continental breakfast *n* kaldur morgunverður
continue *v* halda áfram
continuous *adj* sífelldur, stöðugur, áframhaldandi
continuously *adv* stöðugt, sífellt
contraception *n* getnaðarvörn
contraceptive *n* getnaðarvörn: ~ **pill** getnaðarvarnarpilla
contract *n* samningur
contract law *n* samingaréttur
contraction *n med* samdráttir: **have** ~**s** vera með samdrætti
contractor *n* verktaki
contrast 1 *n* andstæða; 2 *v* *(comparison)* bera saman; *(in opposition to)* stangast á við
contribute *v* stuðla að
contribution *n* framlag
control 1 *n* stjórn: **out of** ~ stjórnlaus, **have** ~ **over sth** hafa stjórn á einhverju; **self-**~ sjálfstjórn; 2 *v* stjórna, stýra: ~ **oneself** stjórna sjálfum/ sjálfri sér
convenience *adj* þægindi
convenience food *n* tilbúinn matur
convenience store *n* kjörbúð, sjoppa
convenient *adj* þægilegur
convent *n* klaustur, nunnuklaustur
convention *n (tradition)* siður; *(conference)* ráðstefna: ~ **hall** ráðstefnusalur
conventional *adj* hefðbundinn
conversation *n* samtal
convert *v* snúast: ~ **to Christianity**

snúast til kristinnar trúar
convey *v* tjá: ~ **a feeling** tjá tilfinningu
convince *v* sannfæra
cook 1 *n* kokkur, matreiðslumaður; 2 *v* elda, búa til mat
cookbook *n* matreiðslubók, uppskriftabók
cooker *n* suðutæki
cookie *n* kex, smákaka: **baked** ~ smákökur; **Internet** ~**s** (vef)kökur
cooking *n* eldamennska: ~ **facilities** eldunaraðstaða; ~ **instructions** eldunarleiðbeiningar
cool 1 *adj (cold)* kaldur, kuldalegur, svalur: ~ **temperature** kuldi; *(currently in)* flottur, svalur: ~ **music** flott tónlist; *slang* kúl; *(calm)* rólegur; 2 *v* kæla: ~ **off** kæla sig; ~ **down** slappa af, róa sig
cooperation *n* samvinna
cooperative *adj* samvinnu-
coordinate 1 *n math* hnit; 2 *v* samræma
co-owner *n* meðeigandi
cop *n* lögregla, lögreglumaður, *colloq* lögga
cope with *v* geta tekist á við: **I can't** ~ **this now** ég get ekki tekist á við þetta núna
Copenhagen (capital of Denmark) *N* Kaupmannahöfn (höfuðborg Danmerkur)
copper *n* kopar
copy 1 *n* afrit, ljósrit: **make a** ~ taka afrit, ljósrita; 2 *v* taka afrit; *(imitate)* herma eftir
copy machine *n* ljósritunarvél
copyright *n leg* höfundarréttur; ~ **law** lög um höfundarrétt
cord *n* snúra
core *n* kjarni: **apple** ~ eplakjarni; **the** ~ **of the matter** kjarni málsins; **he is conservative to the** ~ hann er íhaldsmaður fram í fingurgóma
coriander *n* kóríander
cork *n* korkur
corkscrew *n* tappatogari
corn *n* maís: **ear of** ~ maískólfur,

~ **flour/meal** maísmjöl, ~ **oil**
maísolía, ~ **syrup** maíssíróp
cornbread *n* maísbrauð
corner *n* horn
cornerstone *n* hornsteinn
cornflakes *n* kornflex, maísflögur,
cornstarch *n* maíssterkja,
maizenamjöl
corporation *n* hlutafélag
correct 1 *adj* rétt: **that's ~!** það er
rétt!; **2** *v* rétta, leiðrétta
correctly *adv* rétt
correlation *n* fylgni
correspond *v* ~ **to** samsvara; ~
with jafngilda; *(exchange letters)*
skrifast á
corresponding *adj* samsvarandi
corrupt 1 *adj* spilling; **2** *v* spilla
corrupted *adj* spilltur
corruption *n* spilling
cosmetics *n* snyrtivörur: ~ **department** snyrtivörudeild
cosmos *n* alheimur
cost *n* kostnaður
costume *n* búningur
cot *n* vagga
Cote d'Ivoire *n* Fílabeinsströndin
cottage *n* kofi
cottage cheese *n* kotasæla
cotton *n* bómull, baðmull; ~ **plant**
baðmullarplanta
cotton grass *n flora* fífa
cough *v* hósta; ~ **medicine** hóstasaft;
~ **syrup** hóstasaft
could. *See* can
council *n* ráð, nefnd, stjórn: **student
~** nemendaráð, **local ~** bæjarstjórn;
~ **meeting** nefndarfundur,
stjórnarfundur
counsel 1 *n (advice)* ráðgjöf;
leg lögfræðingur: **legal ~**
lögfræðiráðgjöf; **2** *v* veita ráðgjöf
counselor *n* ráðgjafi
count 1 *n* talning: **head ~** hausatalning;
(title) greifi: **C~ Dracula** Drakúla
greifi; **2** *v* telja: ~ **to ten** telja upp
að tíu; *(included)* teljast með, telja:

that doesn't ~ þetta telst ekki með
countable *adj* teljanlegur
counter 1 *n* borð; **store ~** afgreiðsluborð; **kitchen ~** eldhúsbekkur;
over the ~ án lyfseðils; **2** *adv*
andstætt: ~ **to** andstætt; **3** *v* veita
viðnám
country 1 *adj* sveita-: ~ **inn** sveitakrá,
~ **music** sveitatónlist, kántrítónlist;
2 *n* land; ~ **code** landsnúmer
countryside *n* dreifbýli, sveit
county *n* hérað
couple *n* par
courage *n* áræðni, dirfska, þor
course *n (meal)* réttur; *(school)*
námskeið; *(route)* átt; *(progress)*
gangur: **run its ~** hafa sinn gang;
in the ~ of time eftir því sem
tíminn líður; **of ~** *phr* að sjálfsögðu
court *n leg* réttur, dómstóll; *(royal)*
hirð: **a ~ fool** hirðfífl
courtesy *n* kurteisi
courthouse *n* dómshús
courtyard *n* hlað; **rear ~** bakgarður
couscous *n* kúskús
cousin *n* frændsystkin
cover 1 *n (on pots)* lok; *(on books)*
kápa; **read from ~ to ~** lesa
spjaldanna á milli; *(shelter)* skjól,
þak: **seek ~** leita að skjóli; **2** *v (an
object)* þekja; *(expenses)* greiða;
(insurance) tryggja, bæta: **are you
fully ~ed?** ertu tryggður að fullu?
cover charge *n* aðgöngumiði
cow *n zool* kýr
coward *n* aumingi, hræðslupúki,
ræfill
cowshed *n* fjós
crab *n* krabbi
crack 1 *n* sprunga; **2** *v* bresta, brjóta
cracked *adj* sprunginn
crackers *n* ostakex; **salted ~** saltkex
craft *n* handverk; ~**s** handverksvörur;
~ **store** *n* handverksbúð
cramp *n* verkur, krampi
cranberry *n* trönuber: ~ **juice** trönu-
berjasafi, ~ **sauce** trönuberjasósa

crash *n (noise)* skellur, dynkur;
  (car) árekstur; *(airplane)* flugslys;
  (economic) hrun
crash helmet *n* öryggishjálmur
crater *n geol* gígur
crayfish *n* vatnakrabbi
crazy *adj* brjálaður, klikkaður,
  geðveikur
cream *n* rjómi: ~ **sauce** rjómalögð
  sósa, ~ **soup** rjómalögð súpa
cream cheese *n* smurostur
cream puff *n* rjómabolla
create *v* skapa, búa til
creation *n* sköpun, sköpunarverk
creative *adj* skapandi
creativity *n* sköpunargáfa
creature *n* vera
credit *n* kredit
credit card *n* greiðslukort; ~ **num-**
  ber greiðslukortanúmer
creditor *n* kröfuhafi, lánardrottinn,
  skuldareigandi
creep 1 *n* gerpi, lúsablesi, mannræfill,
  ógeð; **he gives me the ~s** mér hryllir
  við honum; **2** *v (crawl)* krjúpa, skríða;
  (slowly and secretly) læðast, laumast
crepe *n* pönnukaka: **French** ~ frönsk
  pönnukaka, **fruit** ~ pönnukaka
  með ávöxtum
crevasse *n geol* jökulsprunga
crew *n* mannskapur; *(on a plane/*
  boat) áhöfn
crib *n* vagga
crime *n* glæpur, afbrot
criminal 1 *adj* glæpa-: ~ **investigation**
  glæparannsókn; **2** *n* glæpamaður,
  afbrotamaður
crisis *n* kreppa, *colloq* krísa
crisp *adj (food)* ferskur; *(weather)*
  fráskandi; *(appearance)* snyrtilegur
crisp bread *n* hrökkbrauð
criterion *n* viðmiðun
critic *n* gagnrýnandi: **film** ~ kvik-
  myndagagnrýnandi, **literary** ~
  bókmenntagagnrýnandi
critical *adj* gagnrýninn, *colloq*
  krítískur

criticism *n* gagnrýni
criticize *v* gagnrýna
critique *n* gagnrýni
Croatia *N* Króatía
Croatian 1 *adj* króatískur; **2** *n*
  (nationality) Króati; *(language)*
  króatíska
croissant *n* smjördeigshorn
cross 1 *adj* þver-, rang-: ~**-eyed**
  rangeygður; **2** *n* kross; **3** *v* þvera,
  fara þvert yfir
cross-country *adj* ~ **skiing** gönguskíði;
  ~ **ski trail** skíðagöngubraut
cross-examination *n leg* yfirheyrsla
crossing *n* gangbraut
crossing guard *n* gangbrautarvörður
crouton *n* brauðteningur
crow *n* kráka
crowd *n* mannfjöldi, mannmergð
crowded *adj* troðinn, mannmargur,
  þéttskipaður
crown 1 *n* kóróna; **2** *v* krýna
crucial *adj* afgerandi
cruel *adj* grimmur
cruelty *n* grimmd
cruise 1 *n (boat)* skemmtiferðasigling;
  2 *v (on a boat)* sigla; *(in a car)*
  rúnta
cruiseliner *n* skemmtiferðaskip
crumb *n* mylsna: **bread** ~ brauð-
  mylsna
crumble *v* molna, molna niður
crunch *v* bryðja
crunchy *adj* stökkur
crush 1 *n* hrifning: **to have a ~ on**
  sby að vera skotinn í einhverjum;
  2 *v* brjóta: ~ **a glass** brjóta glas, ~
  a rebellion brjóta uppreisn á bak
  aftur; ~ **sby's heart** brjóta hjarta
  einhvers; *(fruit)* kreista, pressa
crushed *adj* brotinn, ~ **ice** ísmylsna;
  ~ **almonds** mönduspænir
crust *n (bread)* skorpa; *(snow)* hjarn;
  pie ~ botn fyrir böku
crutch *n* hækja: **use ~es** ganga með
  hækjur
cry 1 *n* hróp, öskur; **a far ~ from**

langt frá; **2** *v* gráta; *(scream)* öskra; *(call)* kalla
crystal *n* kristall
crystallized *adj* kristallaður
Cuba *N* Kúba
Cuban 1 *adj* kúbverskur; **2** *n* Kúbverji
cube *n* teningur
cucumber *n* gúrka, agúrka: ~ **soup** agúrkusúpa
cuisine *n* eldhús, matarmenning: **French** ~ franskt eldhús, frönsk matarmenning
cultivate *v* rækta
cultivated *adj* ræktaður: ~ **land** ræktað land
cultural *adj* menningarlegur
culture *n* menning
cumin *n* krosskúmen: ~ **powder** kúmenduft; ~ **seeds** kúmenfræ
cunning *adj* lævís, slóttugur, lymskur
cup 1 *n* bolli: ~ **and saucer** bolli og undirskál; **not my** ~ **of tea** *expr* þetta er ekki fyrir mig; *sports* bikar
cupboard *n* skápur
cupcake *n* bollakaka
curator *n* sýningarstjóri
curb *v* gangstéttarbrún
curds *n* ystingur
cure 1 *n med* lækning; **2** *v med* lækna; *(food)* salta, sjóða niður
cured *adj (people)* læknaður; *(food)* saltaður: ~ **meat** saltkjöt *(Icelandic specialty)*
curfew *n* útgöngubann
curing *v (food)* söltun: ~ **of meat** söltun á kjöti
curious *adj* forvitinn
curl *n/v* krulla
curling *n sports* krulla
curly *adj* krullaður
currants *n (red)* rifsber; *(black)* sólber
currency *n econ* gjaldmiðill: ~ **exchange** gjaldeyrisafgreiðsla

current 1 *adj* núverandi; ~ **affairs** atburðir líðandi stundar; **2** *n* straumur
currently *adv* eins og er, eins og staðan er núna
curry *n* karrí: **Indian** ~ indverskt karrí, **chicken** ~ kjúklingur í karrí; ~ **powder** karríduft
cursor *n comp* bendill
curtain *n* window ~s gardínur, gluggatjöld; **theater** ~s leiktjöld
custard *n* vanillusósa
custody *n (foreldrar)* forræði; *(imprisonment)* varðhald: **be in** ~ sitja í varðhaldi
custom *n* vani, siður
customer *n* viðskiptavinur; ~ **parking** bílastæði fyrir viðskiptavini
customer service *n* afgreiðsla
customs *n* tollur: ~ **forms** tollaeyðublöð, ~ **declaration** tollskýrsla, ~ **official** tollafgreiðslumaður, ~ **control** tollskoðun; ~ **house** tollhús
cut 1 *n (of clothing)* snið; *(hair)* klipping; *(meat)* sneið; *(profit share)* hluti; **cold** ~s kjötálegg; **2** *v* skera
cutlery *n* hnífapör
cutlet *n* kótiletta, *(minced)* buff: **lamb** ~ lambakótiletta, *(minced)* lambabuff
cuttlefish *n zool* kolkrabbi
cycle *n (goes round)* hringrás; *(bicycle)* hjól: ~ **lock** hjólalás; *lit* flokkur, ritröð
cycling *n* hjólreiðar; ~ **helmet** hjólahjálmur; ~ **path** hjólastígur
Cyprus *N* Kýpur
cyst *n med* blaðra
Czech 1 *adv* tékkneskur; **2** *n (nationality)* Tékki; *(language)* tékkneska
Czech Republic *N* Tékkland

D

dad *n* pabbi
daily 1 *adj* daglegur; **2** *adv* daglega
dairy *n* mjólkur-: **non-~** mjólkur-laus; *(farm)* mjólkurbú: **~ products** mjólkurvörur
dam *n* stífla
damage *n* skaði
damaged *adj* skaddaður, skemmdur
Damascus (capital of Syria) *N* Damaskus (höfuðborg Sýrlands)
damp *adj* rakur
dance 1 *n* dans; **2** *v* dansa
dancer *n* dansari
dancing *n* dans: **go ~** fara að dansa
dandelion *n flora* (tún)fífill: **~ greens/leaves** fíflablöð
danger *n* hætta, vá
dangerous *adj* hættulegur
Danish 1 *adj* danskur; **~ pastry** vínarbrauð; **2** *n (nationality)* Dani; *(language)* danska
dare *v* þora, voga
dark 1 *adj* dökkur, dimmur; **grow ~** dimma; **2** *n* dimma
darker *adj compar* dekkra, dimmara
darts (game of ~) *n* pílukast
dash 1 *v* skvetta; **2** *n* örlítið: **~ of salt** örlítið af salti; **~ of pepper** örlítið af pipar
data *n* gögn
database *n comp* gagnagrunnur: **computer ~** tölvugagnagrunnur
date 1 *n* dagsetning; **~ of birth** fæðingardagur; **to ~** fram að þessu; *(social)* stefnumót; **2** *v (time)* tímasetja; *(social)* fara á stefnumót
dative case *n ling* þágufall
daughter *n* dóttir
daughter-in-law *n* tengdadóttir
dawn *n* dagrenning
day *n* dagur: **during the ~** á daginn,

in three ~s eftir þrjá daga, **in the middle of the ~** um miðjan dag; **~ trip** dagsferð; **~ pass** dagskort; **the ~ after tomorrow** ekki á morgun heldur hinn
daycare *n* leikskóli, barnaheimili
daytime *n* dagtími, á daginn
dead *adj (people)* dáinn, látinn; *(animals)* dauður; **~ battery** ónýt rafhlaða
dead end *n (road)* botnlangi
Dead Sea *N* Dauðahaf
deadline *n* skilafrestur
deaf *adj* heyrnarlaus
deal 1 *n (business)* viðskipti; *(issue)* mál; **a good ~ of money** mikill peningur; **2** *v (do business)* skipta við; *(about)* fjalla um: **the article ~s with global warming** greinin fjallar um hlýnun jarðar; *(cards)* gefa
dealer *n* söluaðili; **drug ~** eiturlyfjasali; **car ~** bílasali
dealings *n* viðskipti
dear 1 *adj* kær: **~ Anna** kæra Anna, **~ John** kæri John; *(expensive)* dýr, dýrmætur; **2** *interj* **oh ~!** almáttugur!
death *n* dauði, andlát, dauðsfall; **a cause of ~** banamein; **life after ~** líf eftir dauðann; **be bored to ~** drepast úr leiðindum
death notice *n* andlátstilkynning, dánarfregnir
death sentence *n* dauðadómur
debate 1 *n* umræða, kappræður; **2** *v* rökræða, ræða
debit card *n econ* debetkort
debt *n* skuld
debtor *n* skuldari, skuldunautur
debut *n* frumraun
decade *n* áratugur
decaffeinated *adj* koffínlaus

decay 1 *n* hnignun, hrörnun, eyðing, rotna; **fall into** ~ liggja undir skemmdum; **tooth** ~ tannskemmd; **2** *v* hnigna, hrörna, eyðast, rotna
December *n* desember
decide *v* ákveða
decision *n* ákvörðun: ~ **making** ákvörðunartaka
deck *n (porch)* sólpallur; *(on a ship)* dekk; *(on a bus)* hæð; ~ **of cards** spilastokkur
declare *v* lýsa yfir
declension *n ling* fallbeyging
decline 1 *n* hnignun: **the** ~ **of the Roman Empire** hnignun Rómaveldis; lækkun: ~ **in prices** verðlækkun; **2** *v (say no)* afþakka: **I must** ~ **your offer** ég verð að afþakka boðið; *(grow smaller)* minnka, draga úr: **strength** ~**s with age** það dregur úr kröftum með aldrinum; *ling* fallbeygja
decorate *v* skreyta
decoration *n* skreyting
decorative *adj* skraut-
decrease 1 *n* minnkun, samdráttur, skerðing; **2** *v* minnka, hjaðna, dragast saman, skerðast
decree *n* tilskipun
dedicate *v* tileinka
dedicated *adj* einarður, einlægur: **a** ~ **supporter** einarður stuðningsmaður, **a** ~ **fan** einlægur aðdáandi
dedication *n* tileinkun
deduct *v* draga frá
deep 1 *adj* djúpur: ~ **end of pool** djúpa laugin, ~**fried** djúpsteiktur; **2** *adv* djúpt
deer *n zool* hjörtur
defeat 1 *n* ósigur, tap; **2** *v* tapa
defend *v* verja
defendant *n leg* ákærði
defense *n* vörn
deficiency *n (shortage)* skortur; *(fault, defect)* galli
deficit *n* tap
define *v* skilgreina

definite *adj* ákveðinn: *ling* ~ **article** ákveðinn greinir
definitely *adv* örugglega
definition *n* skilgreining
defrost *v* afþýða
degree *n* gráða, stig
deity *n* guðdómur
delay 1 *n* frestun, seinkun; **2** *v* fresta, seinka
delayed *adj* seinn
delegate 1 *n* fulltrúi; **2** *v* deila út verkefnum
delete *v* eyða: *comp* ~ **a file** eyða skjali; *comp* ~ **key** bakktakki,
deli *n* matsölustaður
deliberate *adj* viljandi
deliberately *adv* viljandi, að yfirlögðu ráði, af ásetu ráði
delicacy *n (food)* góðgæti, hnossgæti; *(subtlety, nuance)* viðkvæmni
delicate *adj* fínlegur; *(beautiful, subtle)* viðkvæmur; *(health)* lélegur; *(problematic)* viðkvæmur: **a** ~ **situation** viðkvæmt mál
delicatessen (deli) *n* matsölustaður
delicious *adj* góður, bragðgóður
delight *n* gleði
delighted *adj* glaður
delirious *adj med* með óráði
deliver *v* færa, afhenda
delivery *n* sending: **upon** ~ við afhendingu, **express** ~ hraðsending; *(birth)* fæðing: ~ **room** fæðingarstofa
delta *n* óseyri
delusion *n* ranghugmynd
demand 1 *n* krafa; **2** *v* krefja, krefjast *refl*
democracy *n* lýðveldi
demonstrate *v* mótmæla
demonstration *n* mótmæli, kröfuganga
denim *n* gallabuxnaefni
Denmark *N* Danmörk
density *n* þéttleiki
dental *adj* tann-: ~ **care** tannheilsa, ~ **decay** tannskemmd, ~ **floss** tannþráður

dentist *n* tannlæknir
deny *v* neita
deodorant *n* svitalyktareyðir
depart *v* fara, yfirgefa
department *n* *(at university, in store)*
deild; *(in government)* ráðuneyti
department head *n* deildarstjóri
department store *n* vöruhús
departure *n* brottför: **time of** ~ brott-
farartími; ~ **lounge** brottfararsalur
depend *v* fara eftir: **it ~s on the
weather** það fer eftir veðri; *(rely
on)* treysta á, stóla á: **I** ~ **on you** ég
treysti á þig
dependence *n* ósjálfstæði
dependent 1 *adj* ósjálfstæður; **2** *n*
they have two ~s þau eru með tvö
börn á framfæri
depending on *adj* fer eftir: ~ **weather**
fer eftir veðri
depict *v* *(verbally)* lýsa; *(visually)*
teikna, mála
depopulation *n* mannfækkun
deportation *n* brottvísun
deposit *n* *(in a bank)* innborgun: ~
money greiða inn á; *(wine)* botnfall
depot *n* birgðageymsla
depreciation *n* verðfall; *econ*
afskráning
depress *v* hefta
depressed *adj* þunglyndur
depressing *adj* veldur þunglyndi
depression *n* þunglyndi; *econ* kreppa
depth *n* dýpt
describe *v* lýsa
description *n* lýsing
desert 1 *n* eyðimörk; **2** *v* yfirgefa
deserted *adj* yfirgefinn
deserve *v* eiga skilið
design 1 *n* hönnun; **2** *v* hanna
designed *adj* hannaður
designer *n* hönnuður
desire 1 *n* girnd, þrá, löngun; **2** *v*
girnast, þrá, langa í
desk *n* borð, skrifborð
desperate *adj* örvæntingarfullur
desperately *adv* örvæntingarfullt

despicable *adj* fyrirlitlegur
despite *prep* þrátt fyrir
dessert *n* eftirréttur, *colloq* desert
dessert wine *n* eftirréttavín
destination *n* áfangastaður
destroy *v* eyðileggja
destroyed *adj* eyðilagður
destruction *n* eyðilegging
detach *v* losa frá
detail *n* smáatriði: **in** ~ í smáatriðum;
go into ~s fara í smáatriði
detailed *adj* nákvæmur, ítarlegur
detect *v* taka eftir, finna
detective *n* rannsóknarlögreglumaður;
~ **stories** glæpasögur, *colloq*
krimmar
detergent *n* þvottaefni
determination *n* ákveðni
determine *v* ákveða
determined *adj* ákveðinn
detour *n* krókaleið, krókur: **take a** ~
fara krókaleið
develop *v* þróa; þroskast, þróast
refl; *(a photo)* framkalla: ~ **film**
framkalla filmu
development *n* *(progress)* framfarir,
þróun; *(biological, psychological)*
þroski; *(of film)* framköllun
device *n* tæki
devil *n* djöfull
devote *v* helga, helga sig *refl*
devoted *adj* einlægur, einarður
devour *v* gleypa
dew *n* dögg
diabetes *n med* sykursýki
diabetic *adj med* sykursýkis-; **2** *n*
med sykursjúklingur
diagnose *v med* sjúkdómsgreina
diagnosis *n med* sjúkdómsgreining
diagram *n* skýringarmynd
dial *v* velja númer
dialect *n ling* mállýska
dialing tone *n* sónn
dialogue *n* samtal
diameter *n math* þvermál
diamond *n* demantur; *(cards)* tígull
diaper *n* bleyja: ~ **rash** bleyjuútbrot,

change a ~ skipta á bleyju, **reusable** ~ taubleyja, **disposable** ~ einnota bleyja

diaphragm *n anat* þind; *(contraceptive)* hetta

diarrhea *n med* niðurgangur: **have** ~ vera með niðurgang

diary *n* dagbók: **keep a** ~ halda dagbók

dice *n* teningar: **roll the** ~ kasta teningunum

dictionary *n* orðabók

die *v* deyja

diesel *n* dísill: ~ **motor** dísilvél

diet *n (eating habits)* mataræði: **a healthy** ~ heilsusamlegt mataræði; *(to lose weight)* megrun: **be on a** ~ vera í megrun

diet soda *n* sykurlaust gos

dietary *adj* mataræðis-; ~ **fiber** trefjar í mat; ~ **supplements** fæðubótarefni; ~ **restrictions** sérþarfir varðandi mataræði

differ *v* vera öðruvísi; *(disagree)* vera ósammála

difference *n* munur, mismunur

different *adj* öðruvísi

differently *adv* öðruvísi

difficult *adj* erfiður, þungur, flókinn

difficulty *n* erfiðleikar

dig *v* grafa

digest *v* melta

digestive system *n* meltingarfæri

digital *adj* stafrænn: ~ **camcorder** stafræn tökuvél, ~ **camera** stafræn myndavél

dill *n* dill

dilute *v* þynna; ~**d** þynntur

dimension *n* hlutföll

dine *v* borða kvöldmat; ~ **out** fara út að borða

diner *n* veitingastaður

dining *n* borða kvöldmat: ~ **room** borðstofa

dinner *n* kvöldmatur

dip 1 *n* ídýfa; **2** *v* dýfa

diplomat *n* stjórnarerindreki, diplómat

direct 1 *adj* beinn: ~ **flight** beint flug; **2** *v* beina, stjórna: ~ **traffic** stjórna umferð; leikstýra: ~ **a movie** leikstýra kvikmynd

direction *n* átt; **in the** ~ **of** í átt að

directive *n* skipun, leiðbeiningar

directly *adv* beint

director *n* stjórnandi, forstjóri; ~ **of a company** stjórnandi fyrirtækis; *(film)* leikstjóri

directory *n* skrá: **telephone** ~ símaskrá

dirt *n* skítur, drulla

dirty *adj* skítugur

disability *n* fötlun, hreyfihömlun

disable *v* gera óvirkan

disabled *adj (alarm, bomb)* óvirkur; *(person)* fatlaður, hreyfihamlaður

disabled person *n* fatlaður einstaklingur

disadvantage *n* ókostur

disagree *v* vera ósammála

disagreement *n* ósamkomulag, ósættir

disappear *v* hverfa

disappearance *n* hvarf

disappoint *v* valda vonbrigðum

disappointed *adj* vonsvikinn

disappointing *adj* vera leiðinlegt: **it's** ~ það er leiðinlegt

disappointment *n* vonbrigði

disapprove *v* vera ósammála, samþykkja ekki, vera á móti: **I** ~ ég er á móti þessu

disaster *n* stórslys, hamfarir

disc *n* diskur m

discharge 1 *n (shot)* skot; *(from work)* uppsögn; *(from hospital)* útskrift; *med* útferð; **2** *v (a gun)* skjóta; *(from work)* reka; *(from hospital)* útskrifa; *(from custody)* láta lausan; *(a ship)* afferma

discharged *adj (from hospital)* útskrifaður; *(from work)* rekinn; *(from custody)* sleppt úr haldi

discipline *n (field)* (fræði)grein; *(behavior)* agi

disclose *v* afhjúpa, segja frá

disclosure *n* afhjúpun, uppgötvun

discotheque *n* diskó(tek)
discount *n* afsláttur: children's ~
barnaafsláttur, senior ~ afsláttur
fyrir eldri borgara
discount store *n* útsölubúð
discourse *n* umræða
discover *v* uppgötva
discovered *adj* uppgötvaður
discovery *n* uppgötvun
discriminate *v* mismuna
discrimination *n* mismunun
discuss *v* ræða
discussion *n* umræða
disease *n* sjúkdómur, veikindi
disgust 1 *n* ógeð, viðbjóður; 2 *v*
vekja viðbjóð, this ~s me mér
býður við þessu
disgusted *adj* I'm ~ mér býður við
þessu
disgusting *adj* ógeðslegur,
viðbjóðslegur
dish *n* diskur, *(big plate)* fat; *(food)*
réttur
dish towel *n* viskastykki
dishes *n* uppþvottur: do the ~ þvo upp
dishonest *adj* óheiðarlegur
dishonestly *adv* óheiðarlega
dishwasher *n* uppþvottavél: ~ proof
má setja í uppþvottavél
disinfect *v* sótthreinsa
disk *n* skífa, diskur
dislike *v* mislíka
dislocated *adj med* úr lið
dismiss *v (from a job)* reka; *(from a*
room) hleypa út; *(thoughts)* bægja
frá sér; *leg* vísa frá
dismissal *n leg* frávísun
disorder *n* ringulreið, óspektir, uppþot
display 1 *n (exhibit)* sýning; *(store)*
útstilling: ~ window útstillingar-
gluggi; *comp* skjár; 2 *v* sýna, láta
í ljós
disposable *adj* einnota: ~ camera
einnota myndavél, ~ diapers
einnota bleyjur
disposal *n* umráð: at my ~ mér til
umráða

dispute 1 *n (discussion)* umræða,
rökræða; *(argument)* ágreiningur,
deila; 2 *v (argue)* deila; *(oppose)*
rengja, mótmæla
dissolve *v* leysa upp: ~ in water
leysið upp í vatni
distance *n* fjarlægð: keep your ~
haltu þér í fjarlægð
distant *adj* fjarlægur
distill *v* eima
distilled *adj* eimaður: ~ water eimað
vatn, ~ vinegar eimað edik
distinct *adj* greinilegur, skýr: ~ difference greinilegur munur
distinction *n* mismunur, sérkenni;
(honor) sæmd: with ~ með sæmd
distinctive *adj* auðkennandi, sérstakur
distinguish *v* þekkja í sundur
distribute *v* dreifa
distribution *n* dreifing
distributor *n* dreifingaraðili
district *n* svæði
disturb *v* trufla: do not ~ truflið ekki,
~ the peace trufla friðinn
disturbing *adj* truflandi, óþægilegur:
~ images óþægilegar myndir
dive 1 *n* dýfa; 2 *v* dýfa sér *refl*, stinga
sér *refl*
divide *v* deila, skipta
dividend *n econ* arður
diving *n (into water)* dýfingar;
no ~ bannað að stinga sér;
(scuba ~) köfun: ~ equipment
köfunarbúnaður
diving board *n* stökkbretti
division *n* skipting; *(department)*
deild: second ~ önnur deild
divorce 1 *n* skilnaður; 2 *v* skilja
divorced *adj* (frá)skilinn
dizzy *adj (feel ~)* svima: I'm ~ mig
svimar
DNA *abbrev bio* DNA, erfðaefni
do *v* gera: what ~ you ~ for living?
við hvað starfarðu?; *(fix, take care*
of) laga, sjá um: ~ hair laga hárið;
(feeling) vegna; ~ing well vegna
vel; *(be enough)* duga: that will

have to ~ þetta verður að duga;
(emphatic) endilega, virkilega: **I**
~ **want to go** mig langar virkilega
að fara
dock 1 *n* bryggja, hafnarbakki; **2** *v*
leggja að
docket *n leg* málaskrá
docking cradle *n comp* tengikví
doctor *n* læknir
doctor's office *n* læknastofa
document *n* skjal
documentary *n* heimildarmynd
dog *n zool* hundur
dogfish *n zool* háfur
doll *n* dúkka, *form* brúða
dollar *n econ* dollari, *form* dalur: **20**
~**s** tuttugu dollarar
dolphin *n zool* höfrungur
domain *n* svið; *comp* ~ **name**
lénsheiti
dome *n* hvelfing
domestic *adj* heimilis-: ~ **appliances**
heimilistæki, ~ **violence** heimilis-
ofbeldi; ~ **animal** húsdýr
dominant *adj* ríkjandi, ráðandi
dominate *v* drottna, ráða ríkjum
Dominican Republic *n* Dóminíkanska
lýðveldið
donate *v* gefa, láta af hendi rakna: ~
blood gefa blóð, ~ **bone marrow**
gefa beinmerg; ~**d by** gefandi
donation *n* framlag, gjöf
donkey *n zool* asni
donor *n* gefandi; *med* gjafi: **blood** ~
blóðgjafi
door *n* hurð, dyr
doorway *n* dyr, dyragætt: **stand in
the** ~ standa í dyrunum
dormitory *n (school)* heimavist;
(university) stúdentagarður
dosage *n med* (lyfja)skammtur
dose *n med* (lyfja)skammtur: **recom-
mended** ~ ráðlagður skammtur
dot 1 *n* punktur; **on the** ~ á slaginu;
2 *v* setja punkt
dot-com *n* punktur com
double 1 *adj* tvöfaldur: ~ **bed**

tvíbreitt rúm; ~ **room** herbergi
fyrir tvo; *mus* ~ **bass** kontrabassi;
2 *v* tvöfalda
doubt 1 *n* efasemdir, efi; **2** *v* efa,
efast *refl*
dough *n* deig: **cookie** ~ smákökudeig
doughnut *n* kleinuhringur: **glazed** ~
kleinuhringur með glassúr; **chocolate** ~ súkkulaðikleinuhringur
dove *n* dúfa
down *adv (location)* niðri: **I'm** ~ **in
the basement** ég er niðri í kjallara;
(movement to) niður: **go** ~ **to the
basement** farðu niður í kjallara;
(movement from) neðan úr: **I came**
~ **from the basement** ég kom
neðan úr kjallara
downhill skiing *n* svigskíði
download *v comp* hala niður: **free** ~
frítt niðurhal, ~ **file** hala niður skjal
downstairs 1 *adj* sem er á neðri hæð:
~ **bathroom** baðherbergið á neðri
hæðinni; **2** *n* neðri hæð; **3** *adv
(movement)* niður: **go** ~ fara niður;
(location) niðri, á neðri hæð
downtown 1 *adj* sem er í miðbænum:
~ **apartment** íbúð í miðbænum; **2**
n miðbær: **I'm** ~ ég er í miðbænum
downward *adj* niður á við
dowry *n* heimanmundur
doze *v* blundur
dozen *n* tylft; ~**s of times** oft og
margsinnis, margoft
draft 1 *adj* ~ **beer** bjór á krana; **2**
n (text) uppkast; *(bank)* víxill; **3**
v (compose text, idea) gera uppkast
drag 1 *n (of air)* trekkur; *(dressed)*
in ~ í dragi; **2** *v* draga, drösla; *(air)*
trekkir
drag queen *n* dragdrottning
dragon *n* dreki
drain 1 *n (canal)* skurður; *(opening)*
niðurfall, frárennsli; **2** *v (land)*
þurrka upp; *(strain)* sigta
drama *n* drama, leiklist: ~ **class**
leiklistartími, ~ **teacher** leiklist-
arkennari

dramatic *adj* dramatískur, örlagaríkur, átakamikill
dramatically *adv* mjög mikið: **my life changed ~ when I had a baby** líf mitt breyttist mjög mikið þegar ég eignaðist barn
draw *v (art)* teikna; *(a prize, a conclusion)* draga: **~ the line at** draga mörkin við; *(attract)* laða að: **~ a crowd** laða að fólk; *(a bow)* spenna, strekkja; **~ on an experience** byggja á reynslu
drawback *n* ókostur
drawbridge *n* vindubrú
drawer *n* skúffa; **chest of ~s** kommóða
drawing *n (art)* teikning; *(lottery)* dráttur
dream 1 *n* draumur; **2** *v* dreyma
dreamer *n* draumóramaður
dress 1 *n* kjóll: **evening ~** síðkjóll; **full ~** hátíðarbúningur, hátíðarklæðnaður; **~ code** kröfur um klæðaburð; **2** *v (in clothes)* klæða sig; *(a wound)* búa um; *(decorate)* skreyta
dress rehearsal *n* generalprufa
dressed *adj* klæddur: **be all ~ up** vera uppáklæddur
dresser *n (furniture)* kommóða
dressing *n* salatsósa, dressing: **Italian ~** ítölsk salatsósa, **French ~** frönsk salatsósa, **honey mustard ~** salatsósa með hunangi og sinnepi
dressing room *n sports* búningsklefi; *(store)* mátunarklefi
dried *adj* þurrkaður: **~ sausage** þurrkuð pylsa, **~ fruit** þurrkaðir ávextir, **~ meat** þurrkað kjöt
driftwood *n* rekaviður
drink 1 *n* drykkur; **can I get you a ~?** má ég bjóða þér í glas?; **2** *v* drekka; **~ to sby's health** skála fyrir einhverjum; **be on a ~ing spree** vera á fylleríi
drinkable *adj* drekkandi
drinkable water *n* drykkjarhæft vatn, drykkjarvatn

drinking *n* drykkja
drinking problem *n* áfengissýki, áfengisvandamál
drip 1 *n* dropi; **2** *v* leka
drive 1 *n (driving)* keyrsla, bíltúr, bílferð: **go for a ~** fara í bíltúr; **2** *v* keyra
driven *adj (car)* keyrður; *(energetic)* framtakssamur
driver *n* bílstjóri m
driver's license *n* ökuskírteini
driving *n* akstur; **off road ~** akstur utan vega
drizzle 1 *n* úði; **2** *v* úða, rigna
drone *n* dróni
drop 1 *n* dropi: **~ in the bucket** dropi í hafið; *(fall)* fall; *(candy)* moli; **2** *v (let go)* missa: **~ on the floor** missa í gólfið; *(prices, temperature)* lækka; *(quit, close)* hætta: **~ school** hætta í skóla; **~ sby off** skutla einhverjum
drop-down menu *n comp* felligluggi
drought *n* þurrkur
drown *v (self)* drukkna; *(someone)* drekkja; **~ing in work** drukkna í vinnu
drowsy *adj* þreyttur
drug *n (medical)* lyf, meðal; *(recreational)* fíkniefni, dóp
drug dealer *n* fíkniefnasali, dópsali
drugstore *n* apótek, lyfjaverslun
drum 1 *n mus* tromma: **play the ~s** spila á trommur; **2** *v mus* tromma
drummer *n mus* trommari
drum set *n mus* trommusett
drunk 1 *adj* fullur: **get ~** drekka sig fullan, **be ~** vera fullur; **dead ~** dauðadrukkinn; **2** *n* drykkjumaður, *colloq* fyllibytta
drunk driving *n* ölvunarakstur
dry 1 *adj* þurr; **2** *v* þurrka; **~ out** þorna
dry cleaner *n* fatahreinsun
dry cleaning *n* fatahreinsun
dryer *n* þurrkari
dub *v* talsetja
dubbed *adj* talsettur: **~ movie** talsett mynd

Dublin (capital of Ireland) *N* Dublin, Dyflinni (höfuðborg Írlands)
duck *n zool* önd: **wild** ~ villiönd
duckling *n zool* andarungi
due *adj* skyldugur; **the amount** ~ upphæð; *(books)* kominn framyfir skiladag; *(invoice)* gjaldfallinn; *(pregnancy)* komin á tíma: **she is** ~ **in January** hún á von á sér í janúar; *(because of)* vegna: ~ **to weather** vegna veðurs; **in** ~ **course** með tímanum
due date *n* skiladagur, skilafrestur; *(invoice)* gjalddagi; *(pregnancy)* settur dagur
duet *n mus* dúett
duke *n* hertogi
dull *adj (uninspired)* óspennandi; *(boring)* leiðinlegur; *(knife)* bitlaus
dulse *n (seaweed)* söl
dumb *adj* vitlaus, heimskur; *(mute)* mállaus
dump 1 *n* ruslahaugur; **2** *v* henda, fleygja
dune *n* sandalda
duo *n mus* dúett
duration *n* endingartími, varanleiki

during *prep* í: ~ **lunch** í hádeginu, ~ **the war** í stríðinu, ~ **class** í tímanum
dust 1 *n* ryk; **2** *v* þurrka ryk
dustcloth *n* afþurrkunarklútur
duster *n* sópur
dustpan *n* fægiskófla
Dutch 1 *adj* hollenskur; **2** *n (nationality)* Hollendingur; *(language)* hollenska
duty *n* skylda: **do one's** ~ gera skyldu sína; **be on** ~ vera á vakt, **be off** ~ vera ekki á vakt; *(tax)* tollur
duty-free *adj* tollfrjáls: ~ **goods** tollfrjálsar vörur, ~ **shop** fríhöfn, tollfrjáls verslun
duvet *n* sæng; ~ **cover** sængurver
DVD *n* DVD-diskur
DVD player *n* DVD-spilari
dye 1 *n* litur, litarefni; **2** *v* lita
dying *adj* að deyja
dynamic *adj* athafnasamur, framtakssamur, aðsópsmikill, drífandi, dugandi
dynamite *n* dýnamít
dynasty *n* ættarveldi

E

e.g. (for example) *abbr* til dæmis
(= t.d.)
each 1 *pron (out of two)* hvor, hvor
um sig; *(out of many)* hver, hver
um sig: ~ **of us** hvert okkar, ~
and every day hvern einasta dag,
~ **one** hver og einn; **2** *adv* hver,
á mann, stykki: **they cost 1000
kronas** ~ þetta kostar þúsund
krónur stykkið
each other *pron* hver annan
eagle *n* örn
ear *n* eyra; *mus* **play by** ~ spila af
fingrum fram
ear drops *n* eyrnadropar
ear infection *n med* eyrnabólga
ear plugs *n* eyrnatappar
earache *n med* eyrnaverkur
earl *n* jarl
earlier *adv compar* fyrr
early *adv* snemma
earmuff *n* eyrnaskjól
earn *v* græða, vinna sér inn; *(deserve)*
hafa unnið sér inn, eiga skilið
earnings *n econ* tekjur
earphones *n* heyrnatól
earring *n* eyrnalokkur
earth *n* jörð; **the** ~ jörðin; **what on**
~? *excl* hvað í ósköpunum?
earthquake *n* jarðskjálfti
earthworm *n* ánamaðkur
ease 1 *n* léttir; **2** *v* létta, draga úr,
lina, milda
easily *adv* auðveldlega, án vandræða
east 1 *adj* austur-; **2** *n* austur: **in
the** ~ í austri; **3** *adv (movement)*
austur, í austur: **we are driving**
~ við keyrum í austur; *(location)*
fyrir austan: **I live in the** ~ ég bý
fyrir austan
East fjords *n* Austfirðir

East Iceland *n* Austurland
East Timor *N* Austur-Tímor
Easter *n* páskar: **on** ~ um páskana,
~ **Sunday** páskadagur, **Happy** ~!
Gleðilega páska!, ~ **egg** páskaegg,
~ **holiday** páskafrí
eastern *adj* austur-
eastward *adv* í austurátt
easy *adj* auðvelt, létt, einfald; **take it**
~ taktu því rólega, slappaðu af
easygoing *adj* afslappaður
eat *v (about people)* borða; *(about
animals)* éta
eatery *n* matsölustaður
ebb *v* fjara
e-book *n* rafbók
e-business *n* netviðskipti
echo 1 *n* bergmál; **2** *v* bergmála,
endurtaka
eclipse *n* myrkvi: **solar** ~ sólmyrkvi
ecology *n* vistfræði
e-commerce *n* netverslun
economical *adj* hagsýnn, aðhaldssamur
economics *n* hagfræði
economist *n* hagfræðingur
economy *n* hagkerfi
ecosystem *n* vistkerfið
Ecuador *N* Ekvador
edge *n* brún, kantur
edible *adj* ætur; **non-~** óætur
edit *v* ritstýra
edition *n* útgáfa
editor *n* ritstjóri
editorial *n* leiðari
educate *v* mennta, fræða
educated *adj* menntaður, mennta-
education *n* menntun
eel *n zool* áll: **smoked** ~ reyktur áll
effect *n* áhrif
effective *adj* áhrifamikill
effectively *adv* áhrifamikið, skilvirkt

effectiveness *n* skilvirkni, áhrifageta
efficiency *n* skilvirkni, áhrifageta
efficient *adj* áhrifamikill
effort *n* vinna, framlag: **my ~s are bearing fruit** vinnan mín er farin að bera ávöxt, **make an ~** leggja sig fram
effusive volcano *n geol* hraungos
egg *n* egg: **~ white** eggjahvíta, **~ yolk** eggjarauða, **~ shell** eggjaskurn, **~ slicer** eggjaskeri
eggplant *n* eggaldin
ego *n* egó, sjálf
egotism *n* sjálfselska
Egypt *N* Egyptaland
Egyptian *adj* Egypti
eider *n* æður, æðarfugl
eiderdown *n* æðardúnn
eight *num* átta
eighteen *num* átján
eighteenth *ord* átjándi
eighth *ord* áttundi
eightieth *ord* átjándi
eighty *num* áttatíu
either **1** *pron* annar hvor, hvor um sig, hvor sem er; *(negation)* hvorugur; **2** *adv (negation)* heldur: **I don't like this place ~** mér líkar ekki heldur við þennan stað
either ... or *conj* annað hvort ... eða: **either today or tomorrow** annað hvort í dag eða á morgun
El Salvador *N* El Salvador
elaborate **1** *adj* vandaður, margbrotinn, flókinn, vel útfærður; **2** *v* útlista nánar, útfæra
elastic *adj* teygjanlegur
elbow *n* olnbogi
elderly *adj* aldraður, roskinn, gamall: **~ couple** eldri hjón, öldruð hjón
elect *v* kjósa, velja
election *n* kosningar
elective *adj* kjör-, valfrjáls
electorate *n* kjósendur
electric *adj* rafmagns-
electric toothbrush *n* rafmagnstannbursti

electric razor *n* rakvél
electrical *adj* rafmagns-
electrical outlet *n* innstunga
electricity *n* rafmagn
electron *n* rafeind
electronic *adj* rafeinda-; **~ instruments** rafmagnshljóðfæri
electronics *n (science)* rafeindatækni; *(appliances)* raftæki
electronics shop *n* raftækjaverslun
elegance *n* glæsileiki
elegant *adj* glæsilegur
element *n chem* frumefni; *(essential parts)* frumatriði; **the ~s** náttúruöflin
elevator *n* lyfta
eleven *num* ellefu
eleventh *ord* ellefti
elf *n* álfur
eliminate *v* útiloka
elimination *n* útilokun
elixir *n* elixír, heilsudrykkur
elk *n zool* elgur
eloquence *n* mælska
eloquent *adj* mælskur
else annað, annars: **who ~?** hver annar?, **nothing ~** ekkert annað, **where ~ could he be?** hvar annars staðar getur hann verið?
elsewhere *adv (location)* annars staðar; *(movement)* annað
e-mail **1** *n* tölvupóstur; **2** *v* senda tölvupóst
e-mail address *n* netfang: **what is your ~?** hvað er netfangið þitt?
emancipate *v* frelsa, leysa úr ánauð
emancipation *n* frelsun, lausn úr ánauð
embarrass *v* gera vandræðalegan
embarrassed *adj* vandræðalegur
embarrassing *adj* vandræðalegt
embarrassment *n* vandræði, óþægindi, vandræðamál
embassy *n* sendiráð
embrace **1** *n* faðmlag; **2** *v* faðma, taka utan um
embroidery *n* útsaumur
embryo *n* fóstur
emerald *n* smaragður

emerge *v* koma fram, koma í ljós,
birtast
emergency 1 *adj* neyðar-; 2 *n* neyð;
(hospital) bráðadeild: ~ **medical
service** bráðaþjónusta
emergency brake *n* neyðarbremsa
emergency exit *n* neyðarútgangur
emergency room *n* bráðamóttaka
emigrate *v* flytjast úr landi, flytjast
af landi brott
emigration *n* flutningur úr landi
emissary *n* sendiboði
emission *n* útblástur
emotion *n* tilfinning, geðshræring
emotional *adj* tilfinningasamur;
(sensitive) viðkvæmur; ~ **life**
tilfinningalíf
emotionally *adv* tilfinningalega
emphasis *n* áhersla: **put** ~ **on sth**
leggja áherslu á eitthvað, **main** ~
aðaláhersla
emphasize *v* leggja áherslu á; *(highlight)* undirstrika
empire *n* keisaradæmi, heimsveldi:
The Roman ~ rómverska keis-
aradæmið, rómverska heimsveldið
employ *v* ráða
employee *n* starfsmaður: **part-time**
~ starfsmaður í hlutastarfi
employer *n* vinnuveitandi
employment *n* vinna, ráðning, starf
employment office *n* atvinnumiðlun
empress *n* keisarynja
empty 1 *adj (box etc.)* tómur; *(space)*
auður; *(words, etc)* innantómur,
merkingarsnauður; 2 *v* tæma
empty-handed *adj* tómhentur, með
tvær hendur tómar
empty-headed *adj* vitlaus, óskynsamur,
tómur í kollinum
enable *v* gera kleift að: ~ **sby to do
sth** gera einhverjum kleift að gera
eitthvað
enamel *n* med glerungur
encounter *n (meeting)* fundur, mót;
(fight) bardagi; 2 *v* hitta, mæta,
rekast á

encourage *v* hvetja: ~ **sby to do sth**
hvetja einhvern til að gera eitthvað
encouragement *n* hvatning
end 1 *n* endir, lok: **at the** ~ að lokum;
2 *v* ljúka, hætta, enda
endangered species *n* dýr í
útrýmingarhættu; ~ **list** listi yfir
dýr í útrýmingarhættu
ending *n* endir, lok: **the** ~ **of sth** lok
einhvers; *ling* beygingarending
enemy *n* óvinur
energy *n* orka, afl, kraftur: **thermal**
~ varmaorka; *(physical strength)*
þrek
engage *v (hire)* ráða; *(book a room)*
panta, bóka; *(participate)* taka þátt:
~ **in politics** taka þátt í stjórn-
málastarfi
engaged *adj* pantaður, frátekinn;
(phone) upptekinn; *(to marry)*
trúlofaður
engagement *n* trúlofun
engine *n mech* vél
engineer *n* verkfræðingur; **electrical**
~ rafmagnsverkfræðingur
engineering *n* verkfræði
England *N* England
English 1 *adj* enskur; 2 *n (nationality)* Englendingur; *(language)* enska,
ensk tunga
English-speaking *adj* enskumælandi
engraving *n* útskurður, myndskurður
engulf *v* gleypa
enhance *v* auka, draga fram
enjoy *v* njóta, líka við, finnast gaman
að: **I** ~ **singing** mér finnst gaman að
syngja; ~ **oneself** skemmta sér vel;
~ **your meal!** *phr* verði þér/ykkur
að góðu
enjoyable *adj* skemmtilegur; *(food)*
góður: **the food was** ~ maturinn
var góður
enjoyment *n* skemmtun
enlarge *v* stækka
enmity *n* fjandskapur
enormous *adj* gífurlegur, risastór,
heljarmikill

enough *adj* nógur, nægilegur: **is this ~?** er þetta nóg?; **2** *adv* nóg, nægilega: **did you sleep ~?** svafstu nóg?

ensure *v* tryggja

enter *v* koma inn, færa inn

enter key *n comp* færsluhnappur

enterprise *n (company)* fyrirtæki; *(achievement)* framtakssemi

entertain *v* skemmta

entertainer *n* skemmtikraftur

entertaining *adj* skemmtilegur

entertainment *n* skemmtun

enthusiasm *n* ákafi, hrifning

enthusiastic *adj* ákafur

entice *v* lokka

enticing *adj* lokkandi

entire *adj* allur: **the ~ world** allur heimurinn

entirely *adv* alveg, algjörlega

entitle *v (name)* nefna; *(rights)* veita réttindi: **be ~d to do sth** eiga rétt á að gera eitthvað

entrance *n* inngangur

entrapment *n* gildra

entrée *n* aðalréttur

entry *n* innkoma

entry visa *n* landvistarleyfi

envelope *n* umslag

environment *n* umhverfi

environmental *adj* umhverfisvænn

environmentalist *n* umhverfisverndarsinni

environmentally friendly *adj* umhverfisvænn

environs *n* umhverfi

envy *n* öfund

enzymes *n* ensími

epicenter *n geol* skjálftamiðja

epicure *n* sælkeri

epidemic *n* farsóttar-

epileptic 1 *adj med* flogaveikur; **2** *n med* flogaveikisjúklingur

epilogue *n* eftirmáli

episode *n* þáttur

epoch *n* tímabil

equal 1 *adj* jafn: **~ rights** jafnrétti; **2** *n* jafningi; **3** *v* vera jafn

equality *n* jafnræði

equally *adv* jafn

equation *n* jafna

equator *n* miðbaugur

equilibrium *n* jafnvægi

equipment *n* útbúnaður

equity *n* sanngirni; *econ* almenn hlutabréf

equivalent 1 *adj* jafngildur; **2** *n* jafngildi

era *n* tímabil, öld

eradicate *v* uppræta

eraser *n* strokleður

erect 1 *adj* uppréttur; **2** *v* reisa

erotic *adj* erótískur

error *n* villa

escalate *v* stigmagnast

escalator *n* rúllustigi

escape *n* flótti

escape *v* flýja; **~ abroad** flótti úr landi; **the thought ~d me** mér datt þetta ekki í hug; **nothing ~s her eyes** hún tekur eftir öllu

especially *adv* sérstaklega

espresso *n* espresso: **~ coffee maker** espressókanna

essay *n* ritgerð

essence *n* dropar: **almond ~** möndludropar; **vanilla ~** vanilludropar

essential 1 *adj* nauðsynlegur; *(basic)* undirstöðu-, grundvallar-; **2** *n* grundvallaratriði

essentially *adv* í grundvallaratriðum

establish *v* stofna, koma á fót; *(~ one's self)* koma sér fyrir

establishment *n* stofun

estate *n* landareign

estimate 1 *n* mat; **2** *v* meta, áætla

Estonia *N* Eistland

Estonian 1 *adj (nationality)* Eisti; **2** *n (language)* eistneska

estuary *n* ármynni

et al. (and others) *abbrev* með fleirum (= m.fl.)

etc. (etcetera) *abbrev* og svo framvegis (= o.s.frv)

ethical *adj* siðferðilegur

ethics *n (science)* siðfræði; *(moral)* siðferði
Ethiopia *N* Eþíópía
Ethiopian 1 *adj* eþíópískur; 2 *n* Eþíópumaður
ethnic *adj* þjóðlegur
etiquette *n* mannasiðir; *(at work)* starfsreglur
EU (European Union) *abbrev* ESB (Evrópusambandið)
Eurasian Plate *n geol* Evrasíufleki
euro *n* evra
Europe *N* Evrópa
European *adj* evrópskur
European Union (EU) *n* Evrópusambandið (ESB): ~ country Evrópusambandsland, ~ citizen íbúar Evrópusambandsins
evacuate *v* rýma
evacuation *n* rýming
evaluate *v* meta, áætla
evaluation *n* mat
evaporated milk *n* dósamjólk
even *adj* sléttur, jafn: ~ numbers jafnar tölur; 2 *adv* jafnvel, meira að segja: ~ I didn't know meira að segja ég vissi ekkert, ~ if jafnvel þótt; ~ so samt
evening *n* kvöld: good ~ gott kvöld, this ~ í kvöld
evening service *n* aftansöngur
event *n* atburður
eventually *adv* að lokum
ever *adv* einhvern tímann, nokkurn tímann: have you ~ been there? hefurðu einhvern tímann komið þangað?; for ~ að eilífu
evergreen *n flora* sígræn planta
everlasting *adj* eilífur, endalaus
every *adj* hver: ~ day á hverjum degi, ~ week í hverri viku; fresti: ~ hour á klukkutíma fresti; ~ ten minutes á tíu mínútna fresti
everyday *adj* hversdagslegur
everyone *pron* allir
everything *pron* allt
everywhere *adv* alls staðar

evict *v* bera út
eviction *n* útburður
evidence *n* sönnunargagn; *(signs)* ummerki
evident *adj* augljós
evil *adj* illur, illgjarn, vondur
evolution *n* þróun
evolutionary *adj* þróunarfræðilegur
evolve *v* þróa, þróast *refl*
ex- *prefix* fyrrverandi; ~husband fyrrverandi eiginmaður, my ~ minn fyrrverandi
exact *adj* nákvæmur: ~ amount nákvæm upphæð
exact change *n* nákvæm upphæð
exactly *adv* nákvæmlega
exaggerate *v* ýkja
exaggerated *adj* ýktur
exaggeration *n* ýkjur
exam *n* próf
examination *n (school, university)* próf; *(medical)* rannsókn
examine *v* rannsaka, skoða
example *n* dæmi: for ~ til dæmis
exceed *v* fara fram úr, vera meira en
excellent *adj* frábær, mjög góður
except *prep* nema, fyrir utan
exception *n* undantekning
excess *n* ofgnótt; ~ baggage yfirvigt
excessive *adj* of mikill
exchange *v* skipta: ~ a purchase skipta vöru
exchange office *n econ* gjaldeyrisskiptistöð
exchange rate *n econ* gengi
excite *v* gera spenntan, æsa
excited *adj* spenntur
excitement *n* spenna, æsingur, tilhlökkun
exciting *adj* spennandi
exclamation *n* upphrópun; *ling* ~ point upphrópunarmerki
exclude *v* útiloka
excluding *prep* fyrir utan
exclusion *n* útilokun
exclusive *adj (private)* einka-: ~ rights einkaréttur; *(fine)* fínn,

úrvals-: ~ **school** úrvalsskóli; **mutually** ~ sem útiloka hvor annan
exclusively *adv* eingöngu
excursion *n* ferð
excuse 1 *n* afsökun; **2** *v* afsaka
excuse me *phr* afsakið
execution *n* framkvæmd; *(capital punishment)* aftaka
executive 1 *adj* framkvæmda-; **2** *n* framkvæmdastjórn, framkvæmdastjóri
exempt *v* undanþeginn
exemption *n* undanþága
exercise 1 *n* æfing; **2** *v* æfa
exhaust *v* þreyta
exhaust pipe *n* púströr
exhausted *adj* úrvinda: **I'm totally ~!** ég er algjörlega úrvinda!
exhibit 1 *n* sýningarmunur; *leg* sönnunargagn; **2** *v* sýna
exhibition *n* sýning
exist *v* vera til
existence *n* tilvera
exit *n* útgangur; *(on the road)* útkeyrsla
exotic *adj* framandi
expand *v* stækka, þenjast út
expansion *n* aukning, stækkun
expect *v* eiga von á: ~ **a baby** eiga von á barni, ~ **guests** eiga von á gestum
expectation *n* vænting, von
expected *adj* væntanlegur, sem von er á
expenditure *n* útgjöld, eyðsla
expense *n* kostnaður
expensive *adj* dýr: **this is too** ~ þetta er of dýrt
experience 1 *n* reynsla; *(work)* starfsreynsla; **2** *v* reyna, upplifa
experienced *adj* reynslumikill, reyndur: ~ **driver** reyndur bílstjóri
experiment 1 *n* tilraun; **2** *v* gera tilraun
experimental *adj* tilrauna-; ~ **music** framúrstefnutónlist
expert 1 *adj* mjög fær, snjall; **2** *n* sérfræðingur

expertise *n* kunnátta, þekking
expiration *n* lok; *(breathing)* útöndun
expiration date *n* síðasti söludagur
expire *v* renna út, falla úr gildi
expiry date *n* gildistími
explain *v* útskýra
explanation *n* útskýring
explode *v* springa
exploit 1 *v* (hag)nýta; *(negative)* arðræna; **2** *n* þrekvirki
exploitation *n* (hag)nýting; *(negative)* arðrán
exploration *n* könnun, athugun
explore *v* rannsaka, kanna, athuga
explosion *n* sprenging
explosive volcano *n geol* sprengigos
export 1 *n econ* útflutningur, útflutningsvara; **2** *v* flytja út: **Iceland ~s fish to ...** Ísland flytur út fisk til ...
expose *v (show)* sýna; *(secrets)* afhjúpa, fletta ofan af; *(children)* bera út
exposure *n* varnarleysi; *(of secrets)* afhjúpun, uppljóstrun; *(photography)* lýsing
express 1 *adj (fast)* hrað-: ~ **bus** hraðferð, ~ **mail** hraðpóstur; *(clear up)* skýr; **2** *v* tjá sig, segja frá: ~ **worries** segja frá áhyggjum; *(squeeze)* pressa; *(mail)* senda í hraðpósti
expression *n (communication)* tjáning; *(phrase)* orðatiltæki; *(facial)* svipur: **look at his** ~ sjáðu svipinn á honum
extend *v (reach)* ná; *(make longer)* lengja; *(stretch)* rétta, teygja úr
extension *n* aukning, framlenging: *(for a deadline)* framlenging á skilafrest; *(building)* viðbygging; *(phone line)* innanhússími
extension cord *n* framlengingarsnúra
extensive *adj* víðáttumikill, umfangsmikill: ~ **damages** umfangsmiklar skemmdir
extent *n* umfang; **to some** ~ að sumu

leyti; **to a certain** ~ að vissu leyti
external *adj* ytri, utanaðkomandi
extra 1 *adj* auka-; **2** *n* aukahlutur,
aukabúnaður; **3** *adv* sérstaklega,
óvenjulega
extract 1 *n* þykkni: **fruit** ~ ávaxtaþykkni, **orange** ~ appelsínuþykkni,
vanilla ~ vanilludropar; **2** *v* draga út
extraordinary *adj* óvenjulegur,
furðulegur
extraterrestrial *n* geimvera
extravagant *adj* eyðslusamur,
óhóflegur
extreme 1 *adj* öfgafullur, róttækur;
2 *n* öfgar

extremely *adv* ákaflega, gífurlega,
svakalega, rosalega
extremist *n* öfgamaður, róttæklingur,
ofstækismaður
eye *n* auga: *med* ~ **test** sjónpróf,
sjónmælingar
eyeball *n* augnknöttur
eyebrow *n* augabrún
eyeglasses *n* gleraugu
eyelash *n* augnhár
eyeshadow *n* augnskuggi
eyewash *n* augnskolun

F

fabric *n* efni
fabricate *v* búa til, falsa; *(make)* framleiða
fabrication *n* tilbúningur, uppspuni; *(made)* framleiðsla
face 1 *n* andlit; 2 *v* horfast í augu við
facial *n* andlits-; ~ **treatment** andlitsmeðferð; ~ **features** andlitsdrættir
facilities *n* aðstaða
facility *n* leikni, færni
fact *n* staðreynd, veruleiki
factor *n* þáttur
factory *n* verksmiðja
Fahrenheit *n* Fahrenheit-, á Fahrenheitkvarða
fail *v* mistakast; *(test)* falla; *(crops)* bregðast; *(body)* gefa sig: **the heart ~ed** hjartað gaf sig
failure *n* mistök; **heart** ~ hjartabilun; **bank** ~ gjaldþrot
faint 1 *adj (smell, hope etc)* daufur, óljós; *(body)* veikur, máttfarinn, **I feel ~** mig svimar; 2 *v* missa meðvitund, falla í yfirlið
fair *adj* sanngjarn; *(good)* góður, allgóður, sæmilegur; *(sky)* léttskýjaður; *(blonde)* ljóshærður: ~ **skin** ljóst hörund
fairground *n (exhibit)* sýningarsvæði; *(amusement)* skemmtisvæði
fairly *adv* réttlátlega; *(all right)* sæmilega, þokkalega
fairy *n* álfur
fairy tale *n* ævintýri
faith *n* trú; *(honesty)* tryggð, trúnaður: **in good** ~ í góðri trú, einlæglega
faithful *adj* trúr, tryggur; *(exact)* nákvæmur
faithfully *adv* einlæglega: **yours** ~ þinn einlægur
falafel *n* falafel

falcon *n zool* fálki
fall 1 *n* fall; *(temperature, price)* lækkun; *(rocks)* hrun; *(season)* haust: **last** ~ síðastliðið haust; 2 *v* falla, detta; *(in war)* falla; *(on floor)* halla; ~ **apart** detta í sundur; ~ **behind** dragast aftur úr; ~ **for** verða hrifinn af; ~ **over** detta; ~ **through** detta upp fyrir
fallacy *n* röng ályktun, rökvilla: **this is a** ~ þetta er rangt
fallopian tube *n anat* eggjaleiðari
false *adj* rangur; *(dishonest character)* falskur, ótrúr; *(forged)* falsaður
fame *n* frægð: **world** ~ heimsfrægð
familiar *adj (familiar with)* kunnugur; *(familiar to)* kunnulegur, venjulegur; *(informal)* óformlegur
family *n* fjölskylda; *(distant ~)* ætt, skyldmenni
family tree *n* ættartré
famine *n* hungursneyð
famous *adj* frægur
fan *n (device)* vifta: ~ **belt** viftureim; *(admirer)* aðdáandi; *(interested in)* áhugamaður
fancy 1 *adj* áberandi; 2 *n* ímyndun, ímyndunarafl, hugarflug; 3 *v (imagine)* ímynda sér; *(want)* langa í
fantastic *adj* frábær, stórkostlegur
fantasy *n* ímyndun, ímyndunarafl, hugarflug, *lit* furðusaga, fantasía
far 1 *adj (location)* fjarlægur, langt í burtu; *(away)* langur: **a** ~ **journey** löng ferð; 2 *adv* langt, fjarri: **how** ~**?** hve langt?; *(much)* miklu: ~ **better** miklu betra
faraway *adj* fjarlægur
fare *n* fargjald
farewell *interj* bless bless!; *(to a*

man) vertu sæll!; *(to a woman)* vertu sæl!

farm *n* bóndabær, sveitabær, bær

farm-fresh *adj* beint af býli

farmer *n* bóndi

farmhouse *n* bóndabær

farming *n* búskapur

Faroe Islands *N* Færeyjar

Faroese 1 *adj* færeyskur; **2** *n (nationality)* Færeyingur; *(language)* færeyska

far-sighted *adj* fjarsýnn

farther *adj compar* lengra

farthest *adj superl* lengst

fascinate *v* hrífa, heilla

fascinated *adj* hrifinn, heillaður

fascinating *adj* heillandi

fashion *n* tíska

fashionable *adj* sem er í tísku, vinsæll

fast 1 *adj* fljótur, hraður; *(cannot move)* fastur; **2** *adv* hratt, skjótt

fast food *n* skyndimatur, skyndibiti: **~ restaurant** skyndibitastaður

fasten *v* festa, festast *refl*

fat 1 *adj* feitur: **a ~ person** feit manneskja; **non-~** fitusnauður; **2** *n* fita: **~ content** fituinnihald, **percent body ~** fituhlutfall líkamans; *(for cooking)* feiti: **cook in ~** elda í feiti

fatalism *n* forlagatrú

fatally *adv* lífshættulega

fate *n* örlög, forlög

fat-free *adj* fitusnauður

father *n* faðir

father-in-law *n* tengdafaðir

fatigue *n* þreyta

fatten *v* fita; *(oneself)* fitna

fatty *adj* feitur

faucet *n* krani

fault *n* galli; *(to blame)* sök; *phr* **it's not my ~** þetta er ekki mér að kenna

faulty *adj* gallaður

fava beans *n* bóndabaunir

favor *n* greiði: **can you do me a ~?** geturðu gert mér greiða?

favorite 1 *adj* uppáhalds-: **my ~**

band uppáhaldshljómsveitin mín; **2** *n* uppáhald

fax 1 *n* fax, bréfasími: **~ machine** faxtæki; **2** *v* faxa, senda fax

FBI (US Federal Bureau of Investigation) *abbrev* Alríkislögregla Bandaríkjanna

fear 1 *n* hræðsla, ótti; **2** *v* hræðast, óttast

feasible *adj* framkvæmanlegur, mögulegur

feast *n* veisla, hátíð

feather *n* fjöður

feature 1 *n* andlitsdrættir, einkenni; *(film)* kvikmynd í fullri lengd; **2** *v* einkenna, móta; *(film)* hafa í aðalhlutverki

February *n* febrúar, febrúarmánuður; **in ~** í febrúar

federal *adj* sambands-, bandalags-

federation *n* ríkjasamband

fee *n* greiðsla, gjald: **entrance ~** aðgangseyrir

feed 1 *n* fóður: **chicken ~** kjúklingafóður, **pig ~** svínafóður; **2** *v (~ children)* mata, gefa að borða; *(~ animal)* fóðra

feedback *n* viðbrögð, endurgjöf

feel *v (touch)* snerta, koma við; *(sense)* finna fyrir, skynja; **I ~ hot/cold** mér er heitt/kalt; **I ~ sick** mér líður illa

feeling *n* tilfinning

feet *n* fætur

fellow *n* félagi, náungi; **teaching ~** lausráðinn kennari; **~ student** skólafélagi

felony *n* glæpsamlegt athæfi

female 1 *adj* kvenkyns-, kvenna-; **2** *n (human)* kvenmaður; *(animal)* kvendýr

feminine *adj* kvenlegur

feminism *n* femínismi, kvenréttindastefna

feminist *n* femínisti, kvenfrelsissinni

fence *n* grindverk, girðing

fencing *n* girðingar; *sport* skylmingar

fender *n* stuðari

fennel *n* fenníka
fenugreek *n* grikkjasmári
ferment *v* gerja
ferry *n* ferja, bílaferja
fertile *adj* frjósamur
fertilizer *n* áburður
fervent *adj* ákafur, innilegur
fervor *n* ákafi, hrifning
festival *n* hátíð: **music** ~ tónlistarhátíð
fetch *v* sækja, ná í
feud *n* (ættar)erjur
feudal *adj* lénsskipulag
fever *n med* hiti, hitasótt: **he has (a high)** ~ hann er með (háan) hita
feverish *adj med* með sótthita
few *pron* fáir, fáeinir
fiancé *n* kærasti, unnusti
fiancée *n* kærasta, unnusta
fiasco *n* skandall, fíaskó
fiber *n* þráður
fiction *n* uppspuni
fictional *adj* skáldskapar-
fiduciary *n leg* fjárvörsluaðili
field *n (farming)* akur; *(sports)* völlur: **soccer** ~ fótboltavöllur, **hockey** ~ íshokkívöllur; *(horses)* skeiðvöllur; *(science)* grein; ~ **work** vettvangsvinna; ~ **trip** vettvangsferð, skoðunarferð
field hockey *n* grashokkí
fiery *adj* logandi, brennandi
fifteen *num* fimmtán
fifteenth *ord* fimmtándi
fifth *ord* fimmti
fiftieth *ord* fimmtugasti
fifty *num* fimmtíu
fig *n* fíkja
fight 1 *n* slagsmál, bardagi, áflog; *(orally)* rifrildi; **2** *v* berjast, slást; *(orally)* rífast
fighting *n* slagsmál, bardagi, áflog; *(orally)* rifrildi
figment *n* tilbúningur
figurative *adj* myndrænn: ~ **speech** myndmál
figure 1 *n* tala, tölustafur; *(visual)* skýringarmynd; *(statue)* fígúra;

(body shape) líkamsbygging; *(person)* persóna; **2** *v* álíta, telja, halda
Fiji *N* Fídjí
Fijian *adj* fidjískur
file 1 *n (documents)* (spjald)skrá; *(computer)* skjal; *(rasp)* þjöl; **2** *v (organize)* skrá
file format *n comp* skráarsnið
file server *n comp* skráarþjónn
Filipino *adj* filippseyskur
fill *v* fylla; ~ **a role** gegna hlutverki; ~ **a vacancy** ráða í stöðu
fillet *n (meat)* (kjöt)sneið; *(fish)* (fisk) flak; **chicken** ~ kjúklingabringa; **haddock** ~ ýsuflak
filling *n* fylling: **fruit** ~ ávaxtafylling, **meat** ~ kjötfylling
film *n (for camera)* filma; *(movie)* (bíó)mynd, kvikmynd: **watch a** ~ horfa á bíómynd
filo dough *n* blaðdeig
filter 1 *n* sía, filter; **coffee** ~ kaffipoki; **without** ~ filterslaus; **2** *v* sía
filtered *adj* síaður: ~ **water** síað vatn, hreinsað vatn
filth *n* skítur
filthy *adj* skítugur
fin whale *n zool* langreyður
final *adj* síðastur; *(in sports)* úrslita-: **the** ~ **game** úrslitaleikur
finality *n* endanleiki
finally *adv* loksins
finance 1 *n* fjármál, efnahagsmál; *(science)* fjármálavísindi; *(status of a country)* fjárhagur, efnahagur; **2** *v* fjármagna
financial *adj* fjárhagslegur
find *v* finna; *(opinion)* finnast *refl*, þykja: **I** ~ **it okay** mér finnst þetta allt í lagi; ~ **out** komast að
finding *n* niðurstaða
fine 1 *adj (beautiful)* fínn; *(powder etc.)* fínlegur; **2** *n* sekt
fine arts *n* fagrar listir
finely *adv* fínlega
finger *n anat* fingur

fingernail *n* nögl
fingertip *n* fingurgómur
finish *v* ljúka, klára, hætta
finished *adj* búinn, hættur: **I'm ~
eating** ég er búin(n) að borða
Finland *N* Finnland
Finn *n (nationality)* Finni
Finnish 1 *adj* finnskur; **2** *n (language)*
finnska
fiord *n* fjörður
fir *n flora* þinur
fire 1 *n* eldur: **~ pit** eldstæði; **2** *v*
segja upp, reka
fire alarm *n* brunabjalla
fire department *n* slökkvilið
fire escape *n* brunastigi
fire extinguisher *n* slökkvitæki
fire station *n* slökkvistöð
fire truck *n* brunabíll
firecrackers *n* flugeldar, rakettur
firefighter *n* slökkviliðsmaður
fireplace *n* arinn
firewall *n* nettálmi
firewood *n* eldiviður
fireworks *n* flugeldar, rakettur
firm 1 *adj* stinnur, þéttur, fastur fyrir;
2 *n* fyrirtæki; **3** *v* festa; **4** *adv* fast
firmly *adv* eindregið
first 1 *ord* fyrstur: **on the ~ floor**
á fyrstu hæð, **the ~ course** fyrsti
rétturinn; **2** *adv* fyrst, í fyrsta lagi
first aid *n* skyndihjálp
first class *n* fyrsti klassi
first course *n* forréttur
first lady *n* forsetafrú
first place *n* fyrsta sæti
first-aid kit *n* sjúkrakassi
first-rate *adj* fyrsta flokks
firth *n* fjörður
fish *n* fiskur: **~ sauce** fiskisósa, **~ allergy** fiskiofnæmi, **~ stall** fiskborð,
~ jelly fiskihlaup, **~ stock** fiskisoð,
~ store fiskbúð
fishballs *n* fiskibollur
fisherman *n* veiðimaður, sjómaður
fishing *n* veiði: **~ license** veiðileyfi,
~ net fiskinet, **~ rod** veiðistöng, **~**

wear veiðigalli, **~ permitted** má
veiða, **no ~** bannað að veiða
fist *n* hnefi
fit 1 *adj (suitable)* við hæfi; *(in good
shape)* hraustur, vel á sig kominn;
2 *v (clothes)* passa; *(behavior)*
hæfa; *(put)* koma fyrir
fitness *n* hreysti, *colloq* fitness
fitting *n* mátun; **~ room** mátunarklefi
five *num* fimm
fix *v (repair)* laga; *(find for sby)*
útvega: **~ a job** útvega vinnu
fixed *adj* fastur: **~ price** fast verð
flag *n* fáni
flagship *n* flaggskip
flakes *n* flögur; **corn~** maísflögur,
kornflex
flambé *n* flambering
flame 1 *n* logi, eldur; **2** *v* loga
flammable *adj* eldfimur
flan *n* baka
flank *n* síða
flare *v* blossa upp
flash 1 *n* leiftur; **2** *v* glampa
flash photography *n* flassmyndataka
flashlight *n* flass, flassljós
flat 1 *adj* flatur, sléttur; *(tire)* sprunginn;
(beer) flatur: **the beer is ~** bjórinn er
flatur; *(battery)* tómur; **2** *n*
(apartment) íbúð
flat bread *n* flatbrauð
flat rate *n* fast gjald
flat tire *n* sprungið dekk
flatfish *n* flatfiskur
flatter *v* skjalla
flattery *n* skjall
flavor *n* bragðtegund: **what ~s do
you have?** hvaða bragðtegundir
eruð þið með?
flavored *v* bragðbættur: **~ water**
bragðbætt vatn, **chocolate ~** með
súkkulaðibragði, **vanilla ~** með
vanillubragði
flavoring *n* bragðefni
flax *n* hör: **~ seed** hörfræ
flea *n* fló
flea market *n* flóamarkaður

238 flesh

flesh *n* hold
flexibility *n* sveigjanleiki
flexible *adj* sveigjanlegur
flicker *n* leiftur
flight *n* flug: ~ **attendant** flugþjónn, ~ **information** flugupplýsingar, ~ **number** flugnúmer; **in** ~ **service** þjónusta um borð
flimsy *adj* þunnur, veigalítill
flip *v (turnover)* snúa; *(~ pages)* fletta: ~ **through a book** fletta í gegnum bók
flip-flops *n* ilskór
float *v* fljóta
flood 1 *n* flóð; **2** *v* flæða
floor *n* gólf; **sea** ~ sjávarbotn
florist *n* blómasali, blómabúð
flounder *n* flyðra
flour *n* hveiti
flourish *v* blómstra, ganga vel
flow 1 *n* rennsli, straumur, flóð; **2** *v* renna, streyma
flower 1 *n* blóm; **2** *v* blómstra
flu *n* flensa
fluency *n* færni
fluent *adj* altalandi: ~ **in Icelandic** altalandi á íslensku, talar íslensku reiprennandi
fluid 1 *adj* fljótandi; **2** *n* vökvi: **brake** ~ bremsuvökvi
flush *v (with water)* spúla, skola; *(toilet)* sturta niður; *(become red)* roðna
flute *n mus* (þver)flauta
fly 1 *n* fluga; **2** *v* fljúga
flying *adj* fljúgandi; ~ **field** lítill flugvöllur
foal *n zool* folald
focus 1 *n* fókus, miðpunktur, brennidepill: **in** ~ í fókus, í brennidepli; **2** *v* beina athyglinni að: ~ **on driving** beina athyglinni að akstrinum; *(~ a camera)* fókusera
fog *n* þoka; ~ **light** þokuljós
foggy *adj* hulinn þoku
fold *v* brjóta saman
folk 1 *adj* þjóð-, alþýðu-: ~ **art**

alþýðulist, ~ **dance** þjóðdans, ~ **music** þjóðlagatónlist; **2** *n* fólk: **my** ~**s** fjölskyldan mín; *(nation)* þjóð, alþýða
follow *v* fylgja, elta: ~ **on Twitter** fylgja á Twitter, **the police** ~ **the car** lögreglan elti bílinn
followers *n* fylgjendur
following 1 *adj* eftirfarandi; **2** *n* fylgjendur
font *n* letur: **large** ~ stórt letur, **small** ~ smátt letur
food *n* matur
food additives *n* aukaefni
food coloring *n* matarlitur
food festival *n* matarhátíð
food poisoning matareitrun
food preservatives *n* rotvarnarefni
food pyramid *n* fæðupíramídi
fool 1 *n* asni, bjáni; **2** *v* plata, gabba
foosball *n* fótboltaspil
foot *n* fótur
football *n (American)* amerískur fótbolti; *(soccer)* fótbolti
footbridge *n* göngubrú
footer *n* (síðu)fótur: **add a** ~ **to a document** setja síðufót í skjal
footpath *n* göngustígur
for *prep* fyrir: **I work** ~ **them** ég vinn fyrir þá; *(recipient)* handa, til: **gift** ~ **you** gjöf handa þér, gjöf til þín; *(destination)* til: **leaving** ~ **London** fara til London; *(aim)* til: ~ **pleasure** til ánægju; *(preparation)* fyrir, til, undir: **studying** ~ **an exam** læra fyrir/undir próf; *(reason)* fyrir, vegna, af: ~ **this reason** af þessum sökum; *(time)* í: ~ **a year** í ár, ~ **a week** í viku; *(price)* fyrir: **I bought it** ~ **1000 krónas** ég keypti það fyrir þúsund krónur; *(taking sides)* með: **vote** ~ **or against** að kjósa með eða á móti; ~ **example** til dæmis; ~ **good** til frambúðar; ~ **instance** til dæmis; ~ **now** í bili; ~ **rent** til leigu; ~ **the sake of** fyrir

forbidden adj bannaður

force 1 n kraftur; **2** v neyða

forceful adj kröftugur, kraftmikill

forcemeat n (kjöt)hakk

forearm n anat framhandleggur

forecast 1 n spá; **2** v spá fyrir um

forefinger n anat vísifingur

forehead n anat enni

foreign adj erlendur, útlenskur: ~ **currency** erlend mynt, erlendur gjaldmiðill, ~ **languages** erlend tungumál

foreigner n útlendingur; (man) erlendur maður, útlenskur maður; (woman) erlend kona, útlensk kona

foreleg n anat framfótur

foreman n verkstjóri

foremost adj fremstur: **first and** ~ fyrst og fremst

forerunner n fyrirrennari, forveri; (signs) fyrirboði

foresight n fyrirhyggja

forest n skógur

forestry n skógrækt

forever adv að eilífu

foreword n formáli

forge v falsa

forged adj falsaður; ~ **money** falsaðir peningar

forgery n fölsun

forget v gleyma: **don't** ~ **to ...** ekki gleyma að ...; ~ **it!** gleymdu því!

forgetful adj gleyminn

forget-me-not n flora gleymmérei

forgive v fyrirgefa

fork n gaffall; (tool) kvísl, forkur

form 1 n (shapes, molds) form; (to fill in) eyðublað; ling (beygingar) mynd; **2** v mynda, myndast refl, móta, mótast refl

formal adj formlegur, hátíðar-

formal dress n viðhafnarkjóll, galakjóll

formal wear n viðhafnarklæðnaður

formally adv formlega

format 1 n (book) útlit; comp snið; **2** v comp sníða: ~ **document** sníða skjal

formation n mótun, myndun

former adj fyrrverandi

formerly adv fyrrum

formula n (in words) fast orðalag; math formúla

formulate v setja fram

forsake v yfirgefa

fortieth ord fertugasti

fortified adj styrktur

fortnight n hálfur mánuður: **every** ~ á hálfsmánaðar fresti

fortress n virki, borg

fortunately adv sem betur fer

fortune n örlög; (wealth) auður

fortuneteller n miðill; (woman) spákona; (man) spámaður

forty num fjörutíu

forum n umræðuvettvangur

forward 1 adj fram-; (character) framhleypinn; **2** v senda áfram; **3** adv áfram, fram á við

fossil n geol steingervingur; ~ **fuel** eldsneyti unnið úr jarðefnum

foster 1 adj fóstur-: ~ **brother** fósturbróðir, ~ **parents** fósturforeldrar, ~ **sister** fóstursystir; **2** v ala, hlúa að

foul 1 adj ógeðslegur, viðbjóðslegur, fúll; **2** n sports brot; **3** v sports brjóta á

found v stofna, koma á fót

foundation n grunnur

founder n stofnandi

fountain n brunnur, gosbrunnur

four num fjórir

four-door car n fjögurradyra bíll

fourteen num fjórtán

fourteenth ord fjórtándi

fourth ord fjórði

four-wheel drive n mech fjórhjóladrif

fowl 1 n alifugl; **2** v skjóta fugl

fox n zool refur; **arctic** ~ heimskautarefur, fjallarefur

foyer n anddyri

fraction n math brot

fracture n brot, brestur, sprunga: **bone** ~ beinbrot

fragment *n* brot, slitur
fragrant *n* ilmandi
frame 1 *n (structure)* grind; *(on a wall)* rammi; *(glasses)* umgjörð; **2** *v* setja upp, móta; *(a picture)* ramma inn; *(glasses)* setja í umgjörð; *(a crime)* koma sökinni á
framework *n* grind, innviðir
France *N* Frakkland: **from** ~ frá Frakklandi
franchise *n* einkaumboð; **the** ~ kosningaréttur
Francophone *adj* frönskumælandi
frank *adj* hreinskilinn
frantic *adj* frávita
fraud *n* (fjár)svik
fraudulent *n* óheiðarlegur
freak *n* viðundur, frík
free 1 *adj (not tied)* frjáls, laus; *(not tied to rules)* frjálslegur: ~ **translation** lausleg þýðing; *(no cost)* ókeypis: ~ **admission** ókeypis inn, ~ **food** ókeypis veitingar, ~ **of charge** ókeypis, ~ **ride** ókeypis far; ~ **gift** gjöf; ~ **ticket** frímiði; ~ **time** frítími, tómstundir; **2** *v* frelsa, láta lausan
freedom *n* frelsi: ~ **of speech** málfrelsi
freely *adv* frjálslega, opinskátt
freeze *v* frysta
freeze-dried *adj* frostþurrkaður
freezer *n* frystir: **in the** ~ í frystinum
freezing *adj* frosinn
French 1 *adj* franskur: ~ **food** franskur matur; **2** *n (language)* franska: **speak** ~ tala frönsku
french fries *n* franskar kartöflur
French horn *n* horn
French toast *n* franskt eggjabrauð
frequency *n* tíðni
frequent *adj* tíður: **a** ~ **guest** tíður gestur
frequently *adv* oft
fresco *n* freska
fresh *adj* ferskur, nýr: ~ **fish** ferskur fiskur, ~ **fruit** ferskir ávextir, ~ **produce** fersk matvæli, ~ **water** ferskvatn

freshly *adv* ný-: ~ **made bread** nýbakað brauð
Friday *n* föstudagur: **last** ~ síðastliðinn föstudag, **next** ~ föstudag í næstu viku, **every** ~ á hverjum föstudegi
fridge *n* ísskápur
fried *adj* steiktur: ~ **calamari** steiktur smokkfiskur
friend *n* vinur
friendly *adj* vingjarnlegur
friendship *n* vinátta
fries *n* franskar kartöflur
frighten *v* hræða, skelfa
frightened *adj* hræddur, skelkaður
frightening *adj* vekur ótta
frigid *adj* jökulkaldur, kuldalegur
frog *n* froskur: ~**'s legs** froskalappir
front 1 *adj* fram-; **2** *n* framhlið; **in** ~ **of** fyrir framan
front desk *n* afgreiðsla
front door *n* aðaldyr
front light *n* framljós
front seat *n* framsæti: **sit in the** ~ sitja fram í
front wheel *n* framdekk
frost 1 *n* frost; **2** *v* hríma
frosted *adj* hrímaður
frosting *n* kökukrem
frozen *adj* frosinn: ~ **food** frosinn matur, ~ **vegetables** frosið grænmeti
frozen ice *n* klaki
fructose *n* ávaxtasykur, frúktósi
frugal *adj* sparsamur
fruit *n* ávöxtur: ~ **juice** ávaxtasafi, ~ **salad** ávaxtasalat, ~ **syrup** ávaxtaþykkni
fry *v* steikja
frying pan *n* (steikar)panna
fuck *vul slang* **1** *v* ríða *obs*; **2** *n* uppáferð *obs*; **3** *interj* andskotans! *obs*, djöfulsins! *obs*, fokk! *slang*
fucking *adj* *vul slang* andskotans *obs*, djöfulsins *obs*
fudge *n* karamella
fuel *n* eldsneyti

fuel gauge *n* eldsneytismælir, bensínmælir

fuel tank *n* eldsneytistankur, bensíntankur

full *adj (filled up)* fullur; *(whole)* allur, heill: ~ **amount** öll upphæðin; **in** ~ að fullu; *(after eating)* saddur: **I'm** ~ ég er saddur; *(thorough)* ítarlegur: **a** ~ **account** ítarleg lýsing; *(voice)* hljómmikill; ~ **board** með fullu fæði; ~ **moon** fullt tungl; ~ **stop** punktur

full-time work *n* full vinna

fully *adv* fullkomlega, fyllilega; ~ **booked** uppbókaður

fulmar *n zool* fýll

fumarole *n geol* gufuhver

fumble *v* fálma

fun 1 *adj* skemmtilegur; **2** *n* gaman, skemmtun: **for** ~ til gamans, **have** ~ skemmta sér

function 1 *n* hlutverk, starf: **have a** ~ gegna hlutverki; **2** *v* gegna hlutverki; *(machine)* virka, ganga

function key *n comp* aðgerðahnappur

functional *adj* hagnýtur

fund 1 *n* sjóður; **2** *v* fjármagna

fundamental *adj* undirstöðu-, grundvallar-

funding *n* fjármögnun

fundraiser *n* fjáröflun

funeral *n* jarðarför, útför

fungus *n* sveppur

funny *adj* fyndinn, sniðugur; *(to laugh at)* hlægilegur

fur *n* feldur, skinn: ~ **coat** loðfeldur, pels

furnace *n* miðstöðvarketill

furnish *v* búa húsgögnum

furnished *adj* með húsgögnum

furniture *n* húsgögn

further 1 *adj* fjarlægari, lengra í burtu; *(additional)* nánari: ~ **information** nánari upplýsingar; **2** *v* styrkja, efla; **3** *adv* enn fremur, auk þess

furthermore *adv* enn fremur, auk þess

furthest *adj* lengst í burtu

fuse *n* kveikiþráður

fuse box *n* rafmagnstafla

fusion *n* samruni

fusion cuisine *n* blandað eldhús

fuss *n* læti, vesen: **make a** ~ vera með vesen

future 1 *adj* framtíðar-; **2** *n* framtíð

G

Gabon *N* Gabon
gain 1 *n (money)* hagnaður, gróði;
(growth) vöxtur; *(progress)* framför; **2** *v* fá, ná, öðlast
galaxy *n* vetrarbraut
gale *n* hvass vindur, hvassviðri, rok:
~ **warning** stormviðvörun
gall bladder *n anat* gallblaðra
gallery *n (art exhibit)* sýningarsalur;
(art for sale) gallerí; *(theater)* svalir
gallon *n* gallon
gamble 1 *n* áhætta; **2** *v* spila fjárhættuspil, veðja
gambling *n* fjárhættuspil: ~ **machine**
spilavél
Gambia, the *N* Gambía
game *n (wild animals)* villibráð;
(play, sports) leikur: ~ **board**
spilaborð, ~ **room** leikjasalur, ~
show sjónvarpsleikur, **~s arcade**
tölvuleikjasalur
gannet *n zool* súla
gap *n* op, gat
garage *n (private)* bílskúr, *(municipal)*
bílageymsla
garbage *n* rusl, sorp: ~ **bag** ruslapoki,
sorppoki, ~ **can** ruslatunna,
sorptunna, ~ **truck** ruslabíll, sorpbíll
garden 1 *n* garður: ~ **apartment** íbúð
með garði, ~ **center** garðyrkjusala,
garðyrkjuverslun; **2** *v* vinna í
garðinum
gardening *n* garðyrkja
garlic *n* hvítlaukur: ~ **mayonnaise**
hvítlauksmajónes, ~ **powder**
hvítlauksduft, ~ **sauce** hvítlaukssósa
garnet *n geol* granat
garnish 1 *n* skreyting; **2** *v* skreyta
gas *n (gasoline)* bensín: ~ **pump**
bensíndæla, ~ **station** bensínstöð,
~ **tank** bensíntankur; *(air)* gas:

~ **bottle** gaskútur, ~ **cylinder**
gaskútur, ~ **gauge** gasmælir
gasoline *n* bensín. *See* **gas**
gastritis *n med* magabólga
gastroenteritis *n med* ælupest
gastronomy *n* matargerðarlist
gastropod *n* snigill
gate *n* hlið
gather *v* safna saman, safnast saman
refl
gathering place *v* samkomustaður
gay 1 *adj (happy)* glaður, kátur,
glaðlegur; *(homosexual)* samkynhneigður, hýr: ~ **club** homma-
staður, hommabar; **2** *n (male)*
hommi; *(female)* lesbía
GDP (Gross Domestic Product)
abbrev verg landsframleiðsla
gear 1 *n mech* gír; *(equipment)*
útbúnaður; **2** *v* aðlaga
gearbox *n mech* gírkassi
gearshift lever *n mech* gírstöng
gel *n* hlaup
gelatin *n* gelatín
gem *n geol* gimsteinn, eðalsteinn
Gemini *n astro* Tvíburarnir
gemstone *n geol* gimsteinn, eðalsteinn
gender *n* kyn
gene *n bio* erfðavísir
general *adj* almennur: ~ **elections**
almennar kosningar, ~ **knowledge**
almenn þekking, ~ **strike**
allsherjarverkfall
general practitioner *n med*
heimilislæknir
general store *n* krambúð
generally *n* almennt
generate *v* búa til, kalla fram, valda
generation *n* kynslóð; *(time)*
mannsaldur
generator *n* rafall, dínamór

generosity *n* gjafmildi
generous *n* gjafmildur
generously *adv* ríkulega
genetic *adj* erfðafræðilegur
genetically *adj* erfðafræðilega: ~
modified food erfðabreyttur matur
genetics *n* erfðafræði
genitals *n anat* kynfæri
genitive *n ling* eignarfall
genius *n* snilli; *(a person)* snillingur
genocide *n* þjóðarmorð
genre *n* skáldskaparform
gentle *n* blíður, ljúfur, mildur
gentleman 1 *n* herramaður, maður; 2
interj herrar mínir!: **ladies and ~!**
herrar mínir og frúr!
gently *n* blíðlega, mjúklega
genuine *adv* ekta; *(honest)* einlægur
genuinely *adv* í einlægni, sannarlega
geographer *n* landfræðingur
geography *n* landafræði
geological *adj* jarðfræðilegur
geologist *n* jarðfræðingur
geology *n* jarðfræði
geophysics *n* jarðeðlisfræði
Georgia *N* Georgía
Georgian *adj* georgískur
geothermal *adj* jarðhita-, jarðvarma-;
~ **area** jarðhitasvæði, háhitasvæði
germ *n bio* sýkill
German 1 *adj* þýskur; 2 *n (nationality)* Þjóðverji; *(language)* þýska
Germany *N* Þýskaland: **in ~** í Þýskalandi, **from ~** frá Þýskalandi
germicide *n* sótthreinsir, sótthreinsi-
lögur
gerund *n ling* sagnarnafnorð
gesture *n* bending; *(symbol)* merki
get *v (acquire)* fá, hljóta: ~ **a present**
fá gjöf; *(become)* verða: ~ **tired**
verða þreyttur; *(reach)* koma: ~
home koma heim; *(have done)*
láta: ~ **a haircut** láta klippa sig;
(understand) skilja: **I don't ~**
it ég skil ekki; ~ **back** fá aftur,
endurheimta; ~ **lost** farðu!; ~ **off**
fara úr: **can you tell me where to**

~**?** geturðu sagt mér hvar ég á að
fara úr?; ~ **rid of** losna við
geyser *n geol* goshver
Ghana *n* Gana
Ghanaian 1 *adj* ganverskur; 2 *n*
(nationality) Ganverji
gherkins *n* þrúgugúrka
ghost *n* draugur, vofa
giant 1 *adj* risa-, risastór; 2 *n* risi,
tröll, jötunn
gift *n (talent)* gáfa; *(present)* gjöf: ~
shop gjafavöruverslun
gig *n* tónleikar; gigg *slang*
gin *n* gin: ~ **and tonic** gin og tónik
ginger *n* engifer: ~ **ale** engiferöl,
~ **beer** engiferbjór, ~ **powder**
engiferduft
gingerbread *n* piparkaka
giraffe *n zool* gíraffi
girl *n* stelpa, stúlka: **little ~** smástelpa
girlfriend *n* kærasta
give *v* gefa: ~ **a gift** gefa gjöf; *(sell)*
láta fá: **please ~ me ...** gætirðu
látið mig fá ...; *(hand over)* rétta:
~ **the salt** rétta saltið; *(execute)*
halda: ~ **a party** halda partí, ~ **a**
talk halda fyrirlestur;
give birth (to) *v* fæða
give up *v* hætta: ~ **smoking** hætta
að reykja
give way *n* biðskylda
glacier *n geol* jökull: ~ **burst** jökulhlaup, ~ **river** jökulá
glad *adj* glaður; *(looks)* gladðlegur
gladly *adv* með glöðu geði
glamor *n* glans
gland *n bio* kirtill
glass *n* gler: **magnifying ~** stækkunargler, ~ **recycling** endurvinnsla
glers
glasses (eyeglasses) *n* gleraugu:
wear ~ vera með gleraugu, nota
gleraugu
glassware *n* glervörur
glaze *n* gljái
glider *n (plane* sviffluga; *(pilot)*
svifflugmaður

glimpse *n* leiftur: **get a ~** sjá bregða fyrir
global *adj* hnattrænn
global warming *n* hlýnun jarðar
globalization *n* hnattvæðing
glory *n* dýrð
gloss 1 *n (shine)* glans, gljái; *(comment)* glósa, skýring; **2** *v (words)* skrifa athugasemd, útskýra, þýða
glossary *n* orðalisti, orðasafn, textaskýringar
glove *n* hanski
glucose *n bio* blóðsykur, glúkósi
glue 1 *n* lím; **2** *v* líma
gluten *n* glúten: **~ allergy** glútenofnæmi, **~-free** glútenlaus
glycerin *n* glýseról
go *v* fara: **~ to the store** fara í búðina, **~ out for a meal** fara út að borða, **~ shopping** fara í búðina, **~ skiing** fara á skíði, **~ for a walk** fara í göngutúr, **~ wrong** fara úrskeiðis; *(lead to)* liggja að: **this road ~es to a waterfall** þessi vegur liggur að fossi; *(progressing)* ganga: **how are your studies ~ing?** hvernig gengur námið?, **how is it ~ing?** hvernig gengur?; *(happening)* gerast: **what's ~ing on?** hvað er að gerast; *(become)* verða: **~ bad** skemmast, **~ sour** súrna; *(be)* vera **~ hungry** vera svangur; *(sell for)* fara á: **the house ~es for twenty million** húsið fer á tuttugu milljónir; *(intention)* ætla að: **going to ~** ætla að fara; **let's ~!** drífum okkur!, komum!
go away! *excl* farðu burtu!
goal *n* markmið; *sports* mark
goalkeeper *n sports* markvörður
goat *n* geit: **kid ~** kiðlingur, **~ cheese** geitaostur, **~ meat** geitakjöt
goblet *n* staup, bikar
god *n* guð; *(heathen)* goð
goggle *n* hlífðargleraugu
going-out-of-business sale *n* rýmingarsala

gold 1 *adj geol* gull-; *(color)* gulllitur, gylltur; **2** *n geol* gull
gold medal *n* gullverðlaun
gold mine *n* gullnáma
gold plate *n* gullhúð
golden *adj* gylltur
goldsmith *n* gullsmiður
golf *n* golf
golf cart *n* golfbíll
golf club *n (equipment)* golfkylfa; *(organization)* golfkúbbur
golf course *n* golfvöllur
gondola *n* kláfur, togvagn
gone *adj* farinn
gonorrhea *n med* lekandi
good *adj* góður: **~ food** góður matur, **very ~** mjög góður, **not very ~** ekki svo góður; *(much)* dágóður, vænn; *(more than)* rúmur: **a ~ kilometer** rúmur kílómeter
good afternoon *phr* góðan daginn
good evening *phr* góða kvöldið, gott kvöld
Good Friday *n* föstudagurinn langi
good luck! *excl* gangi þér vel!
good morning *phr* góðan daginn
good night *phr* góða nótt
goodbye *interj* bless bless, vertu sæl(l)
goods *n* vörur
goose *n zool* gæs: **~ liver** gæsalifur
goose bumps *n* gæsahúð
gorge *n* gljúfur, gil
gorgeous *adj* dýrlegur
gorgonzola cheese *n* gorgonzola ostur
Gothic style *n* gotneskur stíll
gouda cheese *n* gouda ostur
goulash *n* gúllas: **Hungarian ~** ungverskt gúllas, **~ soup** gúllassúpa
gourmand *n* sælkeri
gourmet 1 *adj* sælkera-; **2** *n* sælkeri
govern *v* stjórna; *ling* stýra: **~ a case** stýra falli
government *n* ríkisstjórn: **the Icelandic ~** ríkisstjórn Íslands
governor *n (of USA state)* fylkisstjóri; *(of company, university)* stjórnarnefndarmaður

governor-general *n (in Canada)* landstjóri

grab *v* grípa, hrifsa

grade 1 *n* þrep; *(in school)* bekkur; *(on a test)* einkunn; **2** *v* flokka; *(rate schoolwork)* gefa einkunn

gradually *adv* smám saman

graduate 1 *n* útskrifaður nemandi; *(from high school)* stúdent; **2** *v* útskrifast

grain *n* korn

gram *n* gramm: **hundred ~s of ...** hundrað grömm af ...

grammar *n* málfræði

grammatical *adj* málfræði-; *(correct)* málfræðilega rétt

grand *adj* tilkomumikill, stórlátur

Grand Canyon *n* Miklagljúfur

grand piano *n* flygill

grandchild *n* barnabarn

granddaughter *n (woman's)* dótturdóttir; *(man's)* sonardóttir

grandfather *n* afi

grandmother *n* amma

grandnephew *n* frændi

grandniece *n* frænka

grandparent *n (maternal)* móðurforeldrar; *(paternal)* föðurforeldrar

grandson *n (daughter's son)* dóttursonur; *(son's son)* sonardóttir

granduncle *n* frændi

granny *n* amma

granola *n* granóla; **~ bar** granólastöng, **~ cereal** granólakorn

grant 1 *n* námsstyrkur; **2** *v (accept)* verða við; *(admit)* viðurkenna; *(scholarship)* veita námsstyrk

granulated *adj* kornóttur

granulated sugar *n* strásykur

grape *n* vínber: **~ juice** vínberjasafi

grapefruit *n* greip

graph *n* graf, línurit

graphic *adj* myndrænn, grafískur

graphic art *n* grafisk list

graphic design *n* grafísk hönnun

graphics *n* grafík: **computer ~** tölvugrafík; **~ card** *comp* myndkort

grass *n* gras

grate 1 *n* rist; **2** *v* rífa

grated *adj* rifinn: **~ cheese** rifinn ostur

grateful *adj* þakklátur

grater *adj* rifjárn

gratuity *n* þjórfé, tips

grave 1 *adj* alvarlegur; **2** *n* gröf, leiði

gravestone *n* legsteinn

gravity *adj (weight)* þyngd; *(seriousness)* alvara; *geol* aðdráttarafl

gravy *n* sósa: **beef ~** nautasoð, sósa með nautasoði,

gray *adj (color)* grár

gray-haired *adj* gráhærður

graze *v* vera á beit

grease *n* feiti: **cooking ~** matarfeiti

greasy *adj* fitugur: **~ hair** fitugt hár

great *adj* mikill: **Cathrine the Great** Katrín mikla, **the ~ Lakes** Vötnin miklu; *(fantastic)* frábær, stórkostlegur; *excl* frábært!

Great Britain *N* Stóra-Bretland

greatly *adv* mikið, mjög

Greece *N* Grikkland

Greek 1 *adj* grískur; **2** *n (nationality)* Grikki; *(language)* gríska

green *adj* grænn: **~ banana** grænn banani, **~ peas** grænar ertur, **~ pepper** græn paprika, **~ tea** grænt te

green beans *n* strengjabaunir

greengrocer *n* grænmetissali

greenhouse *n* gróðurhús: **~ effect** gróðurhúsaáhrif

Greenland *N* Grænland

Greenland Sea *N* Grænlandshaf

Greenlander *n* Grænlendingur

greens *n* salatblöð: **mixed ~** blandað salat

greet *v* heilsa

greeting *n* kveðja

Grenada *n* Grenada

Grenadian *adj* grenadískur

grey *adj (color)* grár

grief *n* sorg

grievance *n* kvörtunarefni

grill 1 *n* grill, glóðarsteiking; **2** *v* grilla, glóðarsteikja

grilled *adj* grillaður: ~ **cheese
sandwich** grilluð ostasamloka,
~ **fish** grillaður fiskur; ~ **sausage**
grillaðar pylsur
grilling oil *n* grillolía
grillstones *n* grillsteinar
grind *v* mala: ~ **pepper** mala pipar
grocer *n* kaupmaður
grocery *n* matarinnkaup
grocery store *n* kjörbúð
groin *n* anat nári
ground 1 *adj* malaður: ~ **coffee**
malað kaffi, ~ **pepper** malaður
pipar; **2** *v* mala; **3** *n* jörð, yfirborð
jarðar: ~ **floor** jarðhæð;
group 1 *n* hópur, flokkur; **2** *v* setja í
hópa, flokka
grouse *n* zool rjúpa
grow *v* rækta; ~ **up** stækka, vaxa
growth *n* vöxtur
gruel *n* vellingur, hafraseyði
guacamole *n* gvakamól
guarantee 1 *n* ábyrgð; **2** *v* ábyrgjast
guard 1 *n* vörður; **2** *v* verja, vernda
guardian *n* fjárhaldsmaður
guardianship *n* fjárhald
Guatemala *N* Gvatemala
Guatemalan *adj* Gvatemalskur
guess 1 *n* ágiskun; **2** *v* giska á, geta
sér til um
guest *n* gestur: **dinner** ~ matargestur
guesthouse *n* gistiheimili
guidance *n* leiðsögn, tilsögn
guide 1 *n* leiðsögumaður, fararstjóri;
2 *v* veita leiðsögn
guidebook *n* ferðahandbók
guided tour *n* skoðunarferð (með
leiðsögumanni)

guidedog *n* blindrahundur
guidelines *n* leiðbeiningar
guilt *n* sekt, sektarkennd
guilty *adj* sekur
Guinea *N* Gínea
guinea fowl *n* zool perluhænsn
guinea pig *n* zool naggrís; *slang (for
testing)* tilraunadýr
Guinea-Bissau *N* Gínea-Bissaú
guitar *n* gítar: **acoustic** ~ klassískur
gítar, **electric** ~ rafmagnsgítar
guitarist *n* gítarleikari
gulf *n* flói, fjörður
Gulf of Mexico *N* Mexikóflói
gum *n* anat gómur; *(from trees)*
trjákvoða; **chewing** ~ tyggigúmmí
gumdrop *n* hlaup
gun *n* byssa
gunshot *n* byssuskot
gust *n* gustur, hviða
gut *n* **1** þarmur, meltingarvegur; **2** *v*
slægja: ~ **fish** slægja fisk
guy *n* maður, strákur
Guyana *N* Gvæjana
Guyananese *adj* gvæjanskur
gym *n* líkamsræktarstöð: **go to the** ~
fara í líkamsrækt
gymnasium *n* íþróttasalur, íþróttahús
gymnast *n* fimleikamaður,
fimleikakona
gymnastics *n* fimleikar
gynecologist *n* med kvensjúkdóma-
læknir
gynecology *n* med kvensjúkdómafræði
Gypsy *n* Rómafólk

H

habit *n* ávani: **a bad** ~ slæmur ávani,
  out of ~ af gömlum vana; **get in
  the** ~ **of doing sth** venja sig á
  eitthvað
habitat *n* búsvæði, kjörbýli, náttúrulegt
  umhverfi
haddock *n zool* ýsa
Hague, the *n* Haag
hail *n* haglél
hair *n* hár
hair conditioner *n* hárnæring
hair dryer *n* hárblásari, hárþurrka
hair mousse *n* hárfroða, froða
hairbrush *n* hárbursti
haircut *n* klipping: **have a** ~ fara í
  klippingu
hairdo *n* hárgreiðsla
hairdresser *n (male)* hárgreiðslumaður;
  (female) hárgreiðslukona; klippari
  colloq
hairdresser salon *n* hárgreiðslustofa
hairspray *n* hársprey, hárúði
hairy *n* loðinn
Haiti *N* Haítí
Haiti *n* haítískur
Haitian *n* haítíbúi
half 1 *adj* hálf-: **the plane is** ~ **empty**
  flugvélin er hálftóm, ~ **bottle** hálf
  flaska, ~ **price** á hálfvirði, ~ **past
  (two)** hálf (þrjú); ~ **board** hálft
  fæði; hálfur: ~ **a cheese** hálfur
  ostur; **2** *n* helmingur
halibut *n zool* lúða, stórlúða
hall *n* salur; *(hallway)* forstofa,
  gangur: **residence** ~ stúdentagarðar;
  city ~ ráðhús
halt! *interj* stopp!, stans!
halva *n* halva
ham *n* skinka; ~ **sandwich**
  skinkusamloka
hamburger *n* hamborgari: ~ **bun**

hamborgarabrauð, ~ **steak**
  hamborgarakjöt
hammer *n* hamar
hammock *n* hengirúm
hamster *n* hamstur
hand 1 *n anat* hönd: **be in good** ~s
  vera í góðum höndum, **fall into
  the wrong** ~s komast í rangar
  hendur, **made by** ~ handunninn,
  handgerður, **shake** ~s **with sby**
  taka í höndina á einhverjum, **write
  by** ~ handskrifa; *expr* **on the
  one** ~ annars vegar; *expr* **on the
  other** ~ hins vegar; *expr* **out of** ~
  stjórnlaus; *expr* **change** ~s skipta
  um eigendur; *expr* **keep your** ~s
  off! láttu vera!; **lend a** ~ hjálpa;
  (clock) vísir; **2** *v* rétta: ~ **over** rétta
hand luggage *n* handfarangur
hand washable *adj* þvegið í
  höndunum
handbag *n* handtaska, veski
handball *n* handbolti
handbrake *n* handbremsa; handhemill
handcuff *n* handjárn
handicap *n* fötlun; hreyfihömlun
handicapped *adj* hreyfihamlaður,
  fatlaður
handicrafts *n* handavinna
handkerchief *n* vasaklútur
handle 1 *n* handfang; **2** *v* handfjatla,
  fara með; *(control)* stjórna, sjá um;
  (sell) versla með
handlebars *n* handföng
handmade *adj* handgerður, gerður í
  höndunum, handunninn,
handsewn *adj* handsaumaður,
  saumaður í höndunum
handsome *adj* myndarlegur
hang *v* hanga
hangglider *n* svifdreki

hangover *n* þynnka, timburmenn
happen *v* gerast *refl*: **what ~ed?** hvað gerist?; eiga sér stað
happily *adv* með ánægju
happiness *n* hamingja
happy *adj* glaður, hamingjusamur
happy birthday! *phr* til hamingju með afmælið!
Happy Easter! *phr* Gleðilega páska!
Happy New Year! *phr* Gleðilegt ár!
harass *v* áreita
harassment *n* áreiti
harbor *n* höfn, skipahöfn
harbor area *n* hafnarsvæði
hard 1 *adj (not soft)* harður: *comp* ~ **disc** harður diskur; *(difficult)* erfiður: ~ **task** erfitt verkefni; *(alcohol)* sterkur: ~ **liquor** sterkt áfengi; **2** *adv* stíft, mikið: **work ~** vinna mikið
hard cash *n* reiðufé
hard copy *n* pappírseintak
hardboiled egg *n* harðsoðið egg
hardly *adv* varla
hardware *n comp* vélbúnaður; *(tools)* málmvörur, *(weapons)* vopn
hardware store *n* byggingavöru-verslun;
hare *n zool* héri
harm 1 *n* skaði; **it won't do him any** ~ hann mun ekki saka; **2** *v* skaða; **do** ~ meiða, skaða; **be ~ed** skaðast
harmful *adj* hættulegur
harmless *adj* ekki hættulegur, skaðlaus
harmony *n* samhljómur; *(teamwork)* samhljómur; *(peace)* friður: **live in** ~ **with sby** búa í friði með einhverjum
harness *n* aktygi, reiðtygi
harp *n mus* harpa
harvest *n (gathering of crops)* uppskera; *(period)* uppskerutími
hash *v* skera í litla bita
hashish *n* hass
hat *n* hattur; *(for winter)* húfa
hatchet *n* exi, öxi

hate 1 *n* hatur; **2** *v* hata
hatred *n* hatur
haunt *v* elta, ofsækja; **the memories** ~ **her** minningarnar sækja á hana; **this house is ~ed** það er reimt í þessu húsi
Hawaiian *adj* Hawaiibúi
have *v (family)* eiga: ~ **a son** eiga son; *(emphasize ownership)* eiga: **I** ~ **a big house** ég á stór hús; *(have around)* vera með: **I** ~ **a television at home** ég er með sjónvarp heima; *(abstract)* hafa: ~ **time** hafa tíma; *(must)* verða, þurfa: **I** ~ **to go** ég verð að fara, ég þarf að fara
hawk *n zool* haukur
hay *n* hey
hay fever *n med* heymæði
hazard *n* hætta
hazelnut *n* heslihneta
he *pron* hann
head 1 *adj* yfir-; **2** *n anat* höfuð; haus *colloq*; **shake one's** ~ hrista hausinn; *(leader)* stjórnandi, yfirmaður, leiðtogi: ~ **of state** þjóðarleiðtogi; *(counting people)* maður, haus: **3 dollars per** ~ þrír dollarar á mann; **from** ~ **to toe** *expr* frá toppi til táar; **off the top of my** ~ *expr* án umhugsunar; **3** *v* stefna
head waiter *n* yfirþjónn m
headache *n* höfuðverkur, hausverkur, illt í hausnum: **I have a** ~ ég er með höfuðverk, mér er illt í hausnum
heading *n* fyrirsögn
headlight *n* framljós
headphones *n* heyrnatól
headroom *n* gólfhæð
headset kit *n* handfrjáls búnaður
headstrong *adj* ákveðinn, þrjóskur
heal *v* gróa
health *n* heilsa: ~ **center** heilsugæsla, heilsugæslustöð
health food *n* heilsufæði: ~ **store** heilsubúð
health insurance *n* sjúkratrygging

healthy *adj* heilbrigður, hraustur, hress

hear *v* heyra: ~ **about** heyra um

hearing *n* heyrn: ~ **aid** heyrnartæki, ~ **test** heyrnarmæling

hearsay *n* kjaftasaga

heart *n anat* hjarta: ~ **attack** *med* hjartaáfall, ~ **condition** *med* hjartveiki

heartbeat *n* hjartsláttur

heat **1** *n* hiti; **2** *v* hita: **pre-~** hita, ~ **oven** hita ofninn

heater *n* ofn

heating *n* upphitun, kynding; **central** ~ hitaveita

heaven *n* himinn

heavy *adj* þungur; *(strong)* sterkur, kröftugur: ~ **smell** sterk lykt

Hebrew *n* hebreska

heel *n* hæll

heifer *n* kvíga

height *n* hæð: ~ **above sea level** hæð fyrir ofan sjávarmál

helicopter *n* þyrla

hell *n* helvíti

hello *interj* halló

helmet *n* hjálmur

help **1** *n* hjálp, aðstoð: **I need** ~ ég þarf hjálp; **2** *v* hjálpa: **can you** ~ **me?** geturðu hjálpað mér?;

helpful *adj* hjálplegur

Helsinki (capital of Finland) *N* Helsinki, Helsingfors (höfuðborg Finnlands)

hemorrhoids *n* æðahnútur

hen *n* hæna; **~ house** hænsnakofi

hence *adv* þess vegna, þar af leiðandi

herb *n* kryddjurt

herbal *adj* kryddjurta-

herbal tea *n* jurtate, grasate

herbivore *n* grasæta

here *adv (of place)* hér, hérna: **they live** ~ þau eiga heima hérna; *(towards)* hingað: **come** ~ komdu hingað; *(away)* héðan: **I'm from** ~ ég er héðan; *(handing over)* ~ **you are** gjörðu svo vel

heritage *n* arfur

hernia *n med* kviðslit

hero *n* hetja

heroin *n* kvenhetja

herring *n* síld: **pickled** ~ niðursoðin síld

hers *pron* hennar

herself *pron* sig *acc*; sér *dat*: **she enjoyed** ~ hún skemmti sér; *(on her own)* sjálf(ur): **she can do it** ~ hún getur gert þetta sjálf

hesitate *v* hika

heterosexual *adj* gagnkynhneigður

hey *interj* hei!: ~ **there** hei þú!

heyday *n* blómaskeið

hi *interj (to a man)* sæll, blessaður; *(to a woman)* sæl, blessuð; hæ *colloq*

hibernate *v* fara í híði

hibernation *n* liggja í híði

hiccup *n* hiksti

hidden people *n* huldufólk

hide *v* fela, fela sig *refl*

high **1** *adj* hár; **2** *adv* hátt uppi

high quality *adj* gæða-

high school *n* menntaskóli

high voltage line *n* háspennulína

high-beam lights *n* háljós

highland *n* hálendi

highlight **1** *n* hápunktur: ~ **of the trip** hápunktur ferðarinnar; *(hair)* ~**s** strípur; **2** *v* leggja áherslu á

highly *adv* mjög

high-rise *n* háhýsi

high-tech *adj* hátækni-

highway *n* hraðbraut: ~ **exit** útkeyrsla af hraðbraut, ~ **interchange** vegamót við hraðbraut

hike *v* fjallganga, ganga í óbyggðum

hiking boots *n* gönguskór

hiking gear fjallgöngubúnaður

hiking routes *n* gönguleið

hilarious *adj* fyndinn

hill *n* hæð, hóll, ás

hilly *adj* hæðóttur, hólóttur

him *pron* hann *acc*; honum *dat*

himself *pron* sig *acc*; sér *dat*: **he**

enjoyed ~ hann skemmti sér; *(on his own)* sjálfur: **he can do it** ~ hann getur gert þetta sjálfur
hint 1 *n* vísbending; **2** *v* gefa í skyn, gefa vísbendingu
hip *n* mjöðm
hire 1 *n* leiga: **for** ~ til leigu; **2** *v (employee)* ráða
his *pron* hans *gen*
historian *n* sagnfræðingur
historic *adj* sögulegur: ~ **building** söguleg bygging, ~ **site** sögulegur staður
historical *adj* sögulegur, sagnfræðilegur
history *n* saga, mannkynssaga
hit 1 *n (slap)* högg; *(song)* vinsælt lag; *(Internet)* fletting: **website** ~**s** flettingar á síðu; **2** *v (slap)* slá; *(score)* hitta, fara í: **the ball** ~ **the wall** boltinn fór í vegginn; **let's** ~ **the road** *expr* leggjum af stað
hitchhike *v* fara á puttanum
hither *adv* hingað
HIV *abbrev med* HIV
HIV-positive *adj med* HIV-jákvæður
hobby *n* áhugamál
hockey *n* íshokkí
hold 1 *n* tak: **get a** ~ **of sth** ná tökum á einhverju; **get** ~ **of sby by phone** ná í einhvern í síma; **2** *v* halda: ~ **sby's hand** halda í höndina á einhverjum, ~ **a meeting** halda fund, ~ **back** halda aftur að; ~ **to** halda í; ~ **sth against sby** nota eitthvað gegn einhverjum
hold on *v* bíða
hold up *v* tefja
holder *n* eigandi, -hafi: **a** ~ **of a license** leyfishafi
hole *n* hola, gat
holiday *n* frí, leyfi: ~ **discount** hátíðarafsláttur, ~ **resort** ferðamannastaður, ~ **schedule** opnunartími yfir hátíðirnar
hollow *adj* holur
holocaust *n* útrýmingarherferð

holy *adj* heilagur
Holy See (Vatican City) *N* páfastóll
home *n* heimili; *adv (location)* heima: **at** ~ heima; *(movement towards)* heim: **go** ~ farðu heim; *(movement from)* heiman: **from** ~ að heiman
home furnishings *n* húsbúnaður
homeland *n* fósturjörð, föðurland
homeless *adj* heimilislaus, útigangs-
homeless person *n* heimilislaus, útigangsmaður
homemade *adj* heimagerður; ~ **meal** heimilismatur
homeopathy *n* grasalækningar
homepage *n comp* heimasíða
home-style cooking *n* heimilismatur
homework *n* heimavinna
homicide *n* manndráp
homosexual 1 *adj* samkynhneigður; **2** *n (male)* hommi; *(female)* lesbía
Honduras *N* Hondúras
honest *adj* heiðarlegur
honestly *adv* í sannleika sagt
honey *n* hunang
honey mustard *n* hungssinnep
honeybee *n* hungangsfluga
honeymoon *n* brúðkaupsferð: **on a** ~ í brúðkaupsferð
honk *v* flauta
honor 1 *n* heiður; **2** *v* heiðra
hood *n* hetta
hook 1 *n* krókur; **2** *v* krókur, krækja
hooray *excl* húrra, vei, jibbí
hope 1 *n* von; **2** *v* vona, vonast til
hopeful *adj* vongóður
horizontal *adj* láréttur
horn *n* horn
horrible *adj* hræðilegur
horror *n* hryllingur
horror film *n* hryllingsmynd
horse *n zool* hestur: ~ **racing** veðhlaup, ~ **rental** hestaleiga
horseback riding *n* fara á hestbak, hestamennska
horseradish *n* piparrót
horse-riding school *n* reiðskóli

horseshoe *n* skeifa
hospital *n* sjúkrahús, spítali
hospitality *n* gestrisni
host 1 *n* gestgjafi; **2** *v* vera gestgjafi
hostage *n* gísl
hostel *n* farfuglaheimili
hostile *adj* fjandsamlegur, illúðlegur
hot *adj (temperature)* heitur: ~ **tea**
   heitt te; *(spicy)* kryddaður
hot chocolate *n* kakó, heitt súkkulaði
hot dog *n* pylsa í brauði; ~ **stand**
   pylsuvagn
hot sauce *n* sterk sósa
hot spring *n* hver *geol*
hotel *n* hótel
hour *n* klukkutími, tími, klukkustund
house *n* hús: ~ **for rent** hús til leigu,
   ~ **salad** salat hússins, ~ **wine** vín
   hússins
household 1 *adj* heimilis-, hús-;
   ~ **goods** húsmunir; **2** *n* heimilisfólk
housekeeping *n* heimilishald
housewife *n* húsmóðir, heimavinnandi húsmóðir
housework *n* heimilisstörf
housing *n* búseta
how *adv* hvernig: ~ **are you?** hvað
   segirðu gott?; ~ **long?** hversu
   lengi?; ~ **are things?** hvað segirðu
   gott?, hvað er að frétta?, hvernig
   hefurðu það?
however *adv* samt sem áður
hubcap *n* hjólkoppur
hug 1 *n* faðmlag: **give a** ~ faðma; **2**
   v faðma
huge *adj* stór, mikill, risastór
human 1 *adj* mannlegur, mann-; **2** *n*
   manneskja, mannvera
human rights *n* mannréttindi
humble *adj* auðmjúkur
humidity *n* raki
humiliate *v* niðurlægja
humiliation *n* niðurlæging
humility *n* auðmýkt

hummus *n* húmmus
humorous *adj* fyndinn
humpback whale *n zool* hnúfubakur
hundred *num* hundrað
hundredth *ord* hundraðastur
Hungarian 1 *adj* ungverskur; **2** *n*
   (nationality) Ungverji; *(language)*
   ungverska
Hungary *N* Ungverjaland
hunger *n* hungur, sultur
hungry *adj* svangur, hungraður,
   soltinn
hunt *v* veiða
hunter *n* veiðimaður
hunting *n* veiðar
hurry 1 *n* flýtir; **2** *v* flýta sér: ~ **up!**
   flýttu þér!, **be in a** ~ vera að flýta
   sér
hurt 1 *adj* meiddur, sár: **be** ~ vera
   meiddur; **where does it** ~? hvar
   finnurðu til?; **2** *v* meiða, særa
husband *n* eiginmaður, maður: **my** ~
   maðurinn minn
husk *n* hismi
hut *n* kofi
hybrid *n* blanda, af blönduðu kyni
hydroelectric power *n* vatnsafl; ~
   station vatnsaflsvirkjun
hydrogen *n* vetni
hydropower *n phys* vatnsafl
hyena *n zool* hýena
hygienic *adv* hreinlátur
hygienist *n* tannfræðingur
hymn *n mus* sálmur
hype *n* æði, bóla; hæp *colloq*
hyperlink *n* tengill
hyphen *n* þankastrik
hypnotism *n* dáleiðsla
hypnotize *v* dáleiða
hypothesis *n* tilgáta
hysteria *n* móðursýki
hysterical *adj* móðursjúkur

I

I *pron* ég
ice 1 *adj* ís-; **2** *n* ís, klaki; *(in cubes)* ísmoli: **with** ~ með klaka, **without** ~ án klaka, **no** ~ engan klaka; **3** *v* frysta, setja á ís
ice cream *n* ís, rjómaís: **light** ~ léttís, **non-fat** ~ fitusnauður ís, ~ **cake** ísterta, ~ **cone** ísbrauð, ~ **parlor** ísbúð
ice hockey *n sports* íshokkí
ice pops *n* frostpinni
ice skate *v sports* fara á skauta, renna sér á skautum
iceberg *n* ísjaki
iceberg lettuce *n* jöklasalat, ísbergssalat
ice-breaker *n* ísbrjótur
iced *adj* hrímaður
iced tea *n* íste
Iceland *N* Ísland
Icelander *n* Íslendingur
Icelandic 1 *adj* íslenskur; **2** *(language)* íslenska: **I'm studying** ~ ég er að læra íslensku, **I speak a little** ~ ég tala smá íslensku
icing *n* kökukrem: **flavored** ~ bragðbætt kökukrem, **chocolate** ~ súkkulaðikrem
icy *adj* ís-
ID card *n* (persónu)skilríki
idea *n* hugmynd
ideal 1 *adj* ákjósanlegur; **2** *n* hugsjón, fyrirmynd,
idealism *n* hugsjónamennska, hughyggja
idealist *n* hugsjónamaður
idealistic *adj* hugsjóna-
identical *adj* eins: **they are** ~ þau eru eins; *(about twins)* eineggja: ~ **twins** eineggja tvíburar
identification *n* auðkenning, skilríki

identify *v* þekkja, auðkenna
identity *n (separates from others)* auðkenni; *(sense of self)* sjálfsmynd
identity card (ID) *n* (persónu)skilríki
identity document *n* persónuvottorð
ideological *adj* hugsjóna-
idiom *n ling* orðtak
idle *adj* aðgerðalaus; *(lazy)* latur
if *conj* ef
igloo *n* snjóhús
ignite *v* kveikja á, starta
ignition *n* start: ~ **key** bíllykill, startlykill
ignorance *n* vanþekking, heimska
ignorant *adj* heimskur
ignore *v* leiða hjá sér
ill 1 *adj* veikur; **2** *n* illska, grimmd
illegal *adj* ólöglegur: ~ **entry** fara ólöglega inn í landið, **it is** ~ **to** það er ólöglegt að, **is it** ~? er þetta ólöglegt?
illegally *adv* ólöglega
illegible *adj* ólæsilegur
illegitimate *adj* óskilgetinn
illiteracy *n* ólæsi
illiterate *adj* ólæs
illness *n* sjúkdómur, veikindi
illuminate *v* upplýsa
illumination *n* lýsing: ~**s in medieval manuscripts** lýsingar í handritum frá miðöldum
illustrate *v* myndskreyta
illustration *n* myndskreyting
image *n (picture)* mynd; *fig* ímynd: **the** ~ **of a company** ímynd fyrirtækisins
imagery *n lit* myndmál
imaginary *adj* ímyndaður
imagination *n* ímyndun
imaginative *adj* hugmyndaríkur
imagine *v* ímynda sér

imitate *v* herma eftir
imitation *n* eftirlíking
immediate *adj* tafarlaus
immediately *adv* samstundis, tafarlaust
immigrant *n* innflytjandi, nýbúi
immigration *n* aðflutningur
immoral *adj* siðlaus
immune *adj med* ónæmur
immune system *n* ónæmiskerfi
immunity *n* ónæmi
immunization *n* bólusetning
impact *n* högg; áhrif *fig*
impatient *adj* óþolinmóður
impatiently *adv* óþolinmótt, með óþolinmæði, með óþreyju
imperative 1 *adj* nauðsynlegur; **2** *n* nauðsyn; *ling* boðháttur
impersonate *v* herma eftir
impersonation *n* eftirhermun
implement *v* hrinda í framkvæmd
implementation *n* framkvæmd
implication *n* það sem er gefið í skyn
imply *v* gefa í skyn, gefa vísbendingu
impolite *adj* ókurteis, dónalegur
import 1 *n* innflutningur; **2** *v* flytja inn; *comp* ~ **files** hlaða niður skjölum
importance *n* mikilvægi
important *adj* mikilvægur: **this is (not)** ~ þetta er (ekki) mikilvægt
impose *v* þröngva
impossible *adj* ómögulegur
impostor *n* svikari, svindlari, loddari
imposture *n* svik, svindl
impress *v* hrífa, heilla, hafa áhrif á
impressed *adj* hrifinn
impression *n* áhrif
impressive *adj* hrífandi
improve *v* batna, taka framförum, lagast
improved *adv* endurbættur
improvement *n* framfarir
in 1 *prep (location)* í, á: ~ **school** í skólanum, ~ **USA** í Bandaríkjunum, ~ **Iceland** á Íslandi, ~ **the library** á bókasafninu; *(time)* í, eftir: ~ **January** í janúar, ~ **a**

moment eftir smá stund, ~ **one year** eftir eitt ár, ~ **a hurry** í flýti, með hraði; ~ **case of emergency** í neyðartilfellum; ~ **charge of** með umsjón yfir; ~ **detail** í smáatriðum; ~ **exchange (for)** í skiptum fyrir; ~ **front (of)** fyrir framan; ~ **honor of** til heiðurs; ~ **memory of** til minningar um; ~ **order to** til þess að; ~ **public** opinberlega; ~ **return** í staðinn; ~ **the end** að lokum; **2** *adv* inn: **go** ~! farðu inn!
in addition *adv* auk
in advance *adv* fyrirfram
in case (of) *prep* ef
in common *adv* sameiginlegur
in favor (of) *expr* fyrir
in general *expr* almennt séð
inability *n* vangeta
inaccessible *adj* óaðgengilegur
incarceration *n leg* fangelsun
incentive *n* hvati
inch 1 *n* þumlungur; **2** *v* feta sig áfram
incidence *n* fjöldi atvika
incident *n* atvik
incise *v* skera í
incline *n* hneigð
include *v* telja með
including *prep* þar með talið
inclusive *adj* innifalið: **all** ~ allt innifalið
income *n* laun, tekjur
income tax *n* tekjuskattur
incompetent *adj* vanhæfur
incomprehensible *adj* óskiljanlegur
incorrect *adj* rangur, vitlaus
increase 1 *n* aukning; **2** *v* auka
increasingly *adv* meira og meira
incredible *adj* ótrúlegur
incriminate *v* ásaka um glæp
indeed *adv* vissulega, víst
independence *n* sjálfstæði
independent *adj* sjálfstæður
independently *adv* sjálfstætt
index *n* yfirlit, efnisyfirlit
index card *n* skráningarspjald
India *N* Indland

Indian 1 *adj* indverskur: ~ **food**
indverskur matur, ~ **tea** indverskt
te, ~ **seasoning** indverskt krydd;
2 *n (nationality)* Indverji
Indian Ocean *N* Indlandshaf
indicate *v* gefa í skyn, benda til
indication *n* vísbending
indigestion *n* meltingartruflanir
indirect *adj* óbeinn
indirectly *adv* óbeint
individual 1 *adj* einstaka, stakur:
~ **tickets** stakir miðar; **2** *n*
einstaklingur
Indonesia *N* Indónesía
Indonesian *adj* indónesískur
indoor *adj* inni, innanhúss: ~ **soccer**
innanhússfótbolti, ~ **pool** innilaug
indoors *adv* inni
induce *v* kalla fram
induction *n phil* aðleiðsla
industrial *adj* iðnaðar-
industrial district *n* iðnaðarhverfi
industry *n* iðnaður: **music** ~ tónlistar-
iðnaður, **energy** ~ orkuiðnaður,
tourist ~ ferðamannaiðnaður
inequality *n* ójafnrétti
inevitable *adj* óhjákvæmilegur
inevitably *adv* óhjákvæmilega
inexpensive *adj* ódýr; billegur *colloq*
infant *n* ungbarn
infant formula *n* ungbarnamjólk
infantry *n* frumbernska
infect *v* smita
infected *adj* sýktur
infection *n med* sýking
infectious *adj* smitandi
infinitive *n ling* nafnháttur
inflammation *n* sýking
inflation *n* verðbólga
influence 1 *n* áhrif; **2** *v* hafa áhrif
influenza *n med* inflúensa, flensa
inform *v* upplýsa
informal *adj* óformlegur, frjálslegur
information *n* upplýsingar
information desk *n* upplýsingaborð:
where is the ~? hvar er
upplýsingaborðið?

infrastructure *n* innviðir
ingredient *n* innihald
initial 1 *adj* upphaflegur; **2** *n*
upphafsstafur
initially *adv* upphaflega
initiative *n* frumkvæði
inject *v* sprauta
injection *n* sprauta
injure *v* meiða, slasa
injured *adj* meiddur, slasaður
injury *n* meiðsl
ink *n* blek
inn *n* krá, knæpa, vertshús
innate *adj* meðfæddur
inner *adj* innri: **in the ~ circle** í innsta
hring
inner tube *n* slanga
innocent *adj* saklaus
innovate *v* koma með nýjung
innovation *n* nýjung
inoculation *n med* bólusetning
input 1 *n* innlögn; **2** *v* leggja inn
inquiry *n* fyrirspurn
insect *n* skordýr: ~ **bite** skordýrabit,
~ **repellant** skordýraeitur
insert *v* setja inn
inside 1 *prep* inni í: ~ **the house** inni
í húsinu; **2** *adv (location)* inni: **be**
~ vera inni; *(coming from)* innan,
innan úr, úr: **from the** ~ að innan;
(towards) inn: **go** ~ fara inn, ~ **and**
out út og inn
inside out *adj* úthverfur
insight *n* skilningur, innsýn
insist on *v* halda fast við
insistence *n* fastheldni
insomnia *n* andvaka, svefnleysi
inspect *v* skoða, rannsaka, yfirfara
inspection *n* rannsókn, skoðun
inspiration *n* innblástur
inspire *v* hreyfa við, vera innblástur,
hrífa
install *v* setja upp: *comp* ~ **a program**
setja upp forrit
installation *n* innsetning; *comp*
uppsetning
instance *n* tilfelli

instant *adj* skyndi-: ~ **coffee**
  skyndikaffi
instead *adv* í staðinn: ~ **of** í staðinn
  fyrir
instigate *v* hefja
instinct *n* eðlisávísun, hvöt
institute 1 *n* stofnun; 2 *v* hefja, stofna,
  koma á fót
institution *n* stofnun
institutional *adj* stofnana-
instruction *n* leiðbeiningar
instructor *n* leiðbeinandi, kennari
instrument *n mus* hljóðfæri; *(tool)*
  verkfæri
instrumental *adj* hljóðfæra-
insufficient *adj* ónógur
insulin *n med* insúlín
insult 1 *v* móðga, særa; 2 *n* móðgun
insulting *adj* móðgandi, særandi
insurance *n* trygging: ~ **card**
  tryggingarskírteini, ~ **claim**
  skaðabótakrafa, ~ **company**
  tryggingafélag
integrate *v* samþætta, samræma,
  aðlaga
integrated *adj* samþættur, aðlagaður
integration *n* samþættun, aðlögun
intellectual 1 *adj* gáfaður, klár; 2 *n*
  gáfumenni, menntamaður
intellectual property *n* hugverk
intelligence *n* gáfur
intelligent *adj* gáfaður, klár
intend *v* ætla
intense *adj* ákafur
intension *n* ásetningur
intensity *n* ákafi, styrkur
intensive *adj* ákafur, öflugur
intensive care *n* gjörgæsla: ~ **unit**
  gjörgæsludeild
intention *n* ætlun: **it was not my** ~
  það var ekki ætlun mín
interact *v* fléttast saman
interaction *n* samskipti
interactive *adj* gagnvirkur: *comp* ~
  program gagnvirkt forrit
interest *n* áhugi m
interested *adj* áhugasamur: ~ **in**

  áhugasamur um
interesting *adj* áhugaverður
interference *n* truflun
interim *adj* bráðabirgða-
interior 1 *adj* innanríkis-, innri:
  ~ **design** innanhússhönnun, ~
  designer innanhússhönnuður; 2 *n*
  the ~ **of Iceland** hálendið
intermediate *adj* milli-
intermission *n* hlé
internal *adj* innri; *med* innvortis
international *adj* alþjóðlegur:
  ~ **student card** alþjóðlegt
  námsmannaskírteini
international call *n* millilandasímtal
Internet *n comp* internetið: ~ **café**
  netkaffihús, ~ **service provider**
  netþjónusta, ~ **user** netnotandi
interpret *v* túlka
interpretation *n* túlkun
interpreter *n* túlkur
interrupt *v* trufla, grípa fram í
interruption *n* truflun, frammígrip
intersection *n* gatnamót
interval *n* hlé: **in** ~**s** með hléum
intervene *v* skipta sér af
intervention *n* afskipti
interview 1 *n* viðtal; 2 *v* taka viðtal
intimacy *n* nánd
intimate *adj* náinn
into *prep* inn í
intrinsic *adj* innri
introduce *v* kynna: **may I** ~ **John?**
  má ég kynna John?, ~ **oneself**
  kynna sig
introduction *n* kynning
introspect *v* horfa inn á við
introspection *n* sjálfskoðun
intrude *v* ráðast inn á
intruder *n* innrásarmaður
intrusion *n* innrás
Inuktitut *n* grænlenska
inward *adv* inn á við
invent *v* finna upp, búa til
invention *n* uppfinning
invest *v* fjárfesta
investigate *v* rannsaka

investigation *n* rannsókn
investment *n* fjárfesting
investor *n* fjárfestir
invigilate *v* sitja yfir
invigilation *n* yfirseta
invigilator *n* yfirsetumaður
invitation *n* boð
invite *v* bjóða
involved in *adj* í, innblandaður: **he's ~ politics** hann er í pólitík
involvement *n* þátttaka
iodine *n* joð
ion *n* *chem* jón, fareind
Iran *N* Íran
Iranian *adj* íranskur
Iraq *N* Írak
Iraqi *adj* Íraki
Ireland *N* Írland
Ireland, Northern *N* Norður-Írland
Irish 1 *adj* írskur; **2** *n (nationality)* Íri; *(language)* írska
iron 1 *n* járn; *(for clothes)* straujárn: **steam ~** gufustraujárn; **2** *v* strauja
ironic *adj* háðskur
irony *n lit* háð, írónía
irregular *adj* óreglulegur
irrigation *n* áveita
irritate *v* pirra, skaprauna, trufla
irritated *adj* pirraður
irritating *adj* pirrandi
Islamabad (capital of Pakistan) *N* Íslamabad (höfuðborg Pakístan)

Islamic *adj* íslamskur
island *n* eyja
isolate *v* einangra
isolated *adj* einangraður
isolation *n* einangrun: **~ room** einangrunarherbergi
Israel *N* Ísrael
Israeli 1 *adj* ísraelskur; **2** *n* Ísraelsmaður
issue 1 *n (matter)* mál: **the main ~** aðal málið; **what is the ~ ?** hvað er að?; *(book, edition)* útgáfa; *(journal)* tölublað; **2** *v* gefa út
it *pron* það
Italian 1 *adj* ítalskur; **2** *n (nationality)* Ítali; *(language)* ítalska
Italy *N* Ítalía
itch *v* klæja
item *n (product)* hlutur; *(on agenda)* (dagskrár)liður
itemize *v* sundurliða
itemized *adj* sundurliðaður: **~ bill** sundurliðaður reikningur
itinerary *n* ferðaáætlun
its *pron* þess *gen*
itself *pron* sig *acc*; sér *dat*; *(on its own)* sjálfur
Ivory Coast *N* Fílabeinsströndin

J

jacket *n* jakki, úlpa, stakkur
jail *n* fangelsi
jalapeno *n* jalapenjó: **~ peppers**
jalapenjó-pipar
jam *n* sulta, mauk: **fruit ~** ávaxtamauk
Jamaica *n* Jamaíka
January *n* janúar
Japan *N* Japan
Japanese 1 *adj* japanskur: **~ tea**
japanskt te; **2** *n (nationality)* Japani;
(language) japanska
jar *n* krukka
jasmine *n* jasmín: **~ tea** jasmínute,
~ flower jasmínublóm
jaw *n anat* kjálki
jazz *n* djass, djasstónlist
jazzband *n* djasssveit, djassband
jealous *adj* öfundsjúkur
jeans *n* gallabuxur
jeep *n* jeppi
jello *n* hlaup
jelly *n* hlaup
jellyfish *n* marglytta
jerk 1 *n* kippur; *slang (person)*
skíthæll, durgur; **2** *v* kippa; **~ off**
runka sér *obs*
Jerusalem (capital of Israel) *N*
Jerúsalem (höfuðborg Ísraels)
jet **(~ plane)** *n* þota
jet lag *n* þotuþreyta: **suffer from ~**
vera með þotuþreytu
jet-ski *n* vatnasleði
Jew *n* gyðingur
jewel *n* gimsteinn
jeweler *n* skartgripasali
jewelry *n* skartgripur; **~ shop** skartgripabúð
Jewish *adj* gyðinga-: **~ area** gyðinga-
hverfi, **~ festival** gyðingahátíð
jigsaw puzzle *n* púsluspil
job *n* vinna, starf, verkefni; **what's**

your ~? hvað gerirðu?, við hvað
starfarðu?
job advertisement *n* atvinnuauglýsing
job center *n* atvinnumiðlun
job description *n* starfslýsing
jockey *n* knapi
jogging *n* skokk, hlaup
join *v (connect, link)* tengja,
sameina; *(enter, enroll)* skrá sig
í, ganga í: **~ a party** ganga í stjórn-
málaflokk, **~ the EU** ganga í ESB
joint 1 *adj* sameiginlegur: **a ~ effort**
sameiginlegt átak, **~ passport**
sameiginlegt vegabréf; **2** *n anat*
liður
jointly *adv* sameiginlega, saman
joke 1 *n* brandari, grín; **2** *v* grínast:
are you joking? ertu að grínast?
Jordan *N* Jórdan
Jordanian 1 *adj* jórdanskur; **2** *n*
Jórdani
journal *n* tímarit
journalism *n* fréttamennska
journalist *n* fréttamaður
journey *n* ferð, ferðalag
joy *n* gleði
joystick *n* stýripinni
judge 1 *n* dómari; **2** *v* dæma, skera úr
judgement *n* dómur: **pronounce**
~ fella dóm; *(evaluation)* mat,
umsögn, álit: **I leave it to your ~**
ég læt þig skera úr um það
Judgement Day *n* dómsdagur
judiciary *n leg* dómstóla-, lög-
judo *n* júdó
jug *n* kanna
juice *n* safi, djús
July *n* júlí
jump 1 *n* stökk, hopp; **2** *v* stökkva,
hoppa
jumper *n* peysa, treyja

jumper cables *n* startkapall
jumpsuit *n* samfestingur
junction *n (intersection)* vegamót;
  (connection) tenging
June *n* júní
jungle *n* frumskógur
junior *adj* yngri, ungmenna-:
  ~ **league** ungmennahreyfing,
  ungmennadeild, ~ **high school**
  gagnfræðaskóli
juniper berries *n* einiber
junk *n* rusl: ~ **food** ruslfæði,
  skyndibiti, ~ **mail** ruslpóstur

junkyard *n* bílapartasala
jurisdiction *n* dómssvæði
jury *n* kviðdómur
just 1 *adj* réttlátur, just; **2** *adv (exactly)* nákvæmlega, einmitt, akkúrat:
  ~ **now** akkúrat núna; *(only)* bara: ~
  kidding bara að grínast; *(absolutely)* algjörlega, bara: **it's** ~ **fantastic**
  þetta er algjörlega frábært
justice *n* réttlæti
justified *adj* réttlætanlegt
justify *v* réttlæta

K

Kabul (capital of Afghanistan) *N*
Kabúl (höfuðborg Afganistan)
kale *n* grænkál
karate *n* karate
Kazakhstan *N* Kasakstan
Kazakhstani *n* Kasakstani
kebab *n* kebab: **lamb** ~ lambakebab,
chicken ~ kjúklingakebab
keen *adj* áhugasamur
keep *v* geyma, halda: ~ **out** halda sér
frá einhverju; ~ **the change** *expr*
þú mátt eiga afganginn
kefir *n* kefír, súrmjólk: **strawberry**
~ jarðaberjasúrmjólk, **vanilla** ~
vanillusúrmjólk
kennel *n* hundakofi
Kenya *N* Kenía
Kenyan 1 *adj* kenískur; **2** *n* Keníamaður
kernel *n* kjarni
ketchup *n* tómatsósa
kettle *n* nautgripur
key 1 *adj* aðal-: ~ **figure** aðalpersóna;
2 *n* lykill: ~ **cutting** lyklasmiði,
~ **ring** lyklakippuhringur
keyboard *n comp* lyklaborð
keyword *n comp* lykilorð
kick 1 *n* spark; **2** *v* sparka
kick-off *n* byrjun, upphaf
kid *n* krakki
kiddie pool *n* barnalaug, buslulaug
kidnap *v* ræna manneskju
kidnapper *n* mannræningi
kidney *n anat* nýra
kidney bean *n* nýrnabaun
kidney stew *n* nýrnakássa
kidney stone *n med* nýrnasteinn
kill *v* drepa
killer whale *n zool* háhyrningur
killing *n* dráp, morð
kilobyte *n comp* kílóbæti: **file size in**
~**s** stærð skjals í kílóbætum
kilogram *n* kíló, kílógramm

kilometer *n* kílómetri
kind 1 *adj* góður, vingjarnlegur; **2** *n*
tegund; **what** ~ **of** hverskonar
kindergarten *n* leikskóli
kindly *adv* vinsamlegast
kindness *n* góðmennska
king *n* konungur, kóngur
kinship *n* ættartengsl
kiss 1 *v* kyssa; kyssast *recip*; **2** *n* koss
kit *n* kettlingur
kitchen *n* eldhús: ~ **counter** eldhúsbekkur, ~ **utensils** eldhúsverkfæri
kitchenette *n* eldhúskrókur
kitten *n zool* kettlingur
kiwi *n* kíví
knapsack *n* bakpoki
knead *v* hnoða
knee *n anat* hné
knife *n* hnífur
knit *v* prjóna: ~ **cap** prjónahúfa
knock 1 *n* bank; **2** *v* banka
knot *n* hnútur
know *v (facts)* vita: ~ **something**
vita eitthvað; *(people)* þekkja: ~
someone þekkja einhvern
knowledge *n* þekking
kohlrabi *n* hnúðkál
Korea, North *N* Norður-Kórea
Korea, South *N* Suður-Kórea
Korean 1 *adj* kóreskur; **2** *n (nationality)* Kóreumaður; *(language)*
kóreska
kosher *adj* kósher: **non-**~ ekki kósher,
~ **meal** kósher máltíð
Kosovo *N* Kósóvó
Kuwait *N* Kúveit
Kuwaiti *adj* Kúveitbúi
Kyiv (capital of Ukraine) *N* Kiev
(höfuðborg Úkraínu)
Kyrgyzstan *N* Kírgistan
Kyrgyzstani *adj* kírgistanskur

L

label 1 *n* merki, merkimiði; *(music)*
    útgáfufyrirtæki; **2** *v* merkja
labor 1 *n (work)* vinna; *(giving birth)*
    fæðing: **in** ~ í fæðingu, ~ **pain**
    fæðingarhríðir; **2** *v* vinna, streða
Labor Day *n* verkalýðsdagur
laboratory *n* rannsóknarstofa
lace *n* blúnda
lack *n* skortur; **2** *v* skorta: **I** ~ **time**
    mig skortir tíma
lacquer 1 *n* lakk; **2** *v* lakka
lactose *n* mjólkursykur, laktósi:
    I am ~ **intolerant** ég er með
    mjólkursykursóþol
lad *n* strákur, drengur, piltur
ladder *n* stigi
ladies restroom *n* kvennaklósett,
    kvennasnyrting
ladieswear *n* kvenföt
ladle *n* sleif
lady *n* kona, dama; **Ladies and**
    Gentlemen *expr* dömur mínar og
    herrar!; **first** ~ forsetafrú
lag *v* slóra, hangsa; ~ **behind** dragast
    aftur úr
laggard *n* slóði
lagoon *n* lón: **The Blue** ~ Bláa lónið
lake *n* vatn, stöðuvatn
lamb *n* lamb; **loin of** ~ lambalæri
lame *adj (crippled)* fatlaður; *slang*
    slappur, hallærislegur
lament *v* syrgja, harma
lamentation *n* kveinstafir
lamp *n* lampi: **bedside** ~ náttborðs-
    lampi
lamprey *n* heimskautasuga
lance *n* spjót
land 1 *n (country)* land; *(field)* jörð,
    land; **2** *v (aircraft)* lenda; *(boat)*
    landa, koma að *(bryggju)*; ~ **a job**
    fá vinnu

landlord *n* leigusali, húseigandi
landmark *n* kennileiti
landscape *n* landslag
lane *n* akrein
language *n* tungumál, tunga, mál:
    the Icelandic ~ íslensk tunga,
    native ~ móðurmál, **in what** ~?
    á hvaða tungumáli?, ~ **course**
    tungumálanámskeið; *(speech)*
    orðfæri; **colloquial** ~ hversdagslegt
    mál; *(dialect)* mállýska
languish *v* þjást *refl*
Laos *N* Laós
lapse *n (failure)* glappaskot; *(in time)*
    framvinda
laptop *n comp* fartölva
larch *n flora* lerki
lard *n* svínafeiti
large *adj* stór; *expr* **be at** ~ vera laus;
    expr **by and** ~ almennt séð
largely *adv* aðallega
larger *adj* stærri
lark *n zool* lævirki; *(fun)* gaman, stuð
laryngitis *n med* barkabólga
lasagna *n* lasagna
laser *n* leysir: ~ **beam** leysigeisli; ~
    printer laserprentari
last 1 *adj* síðastur: ~ **call** síðasta
    tilkynning, ~ **month** í síðasta
    mánuði, ~ **stop** síðasta stopp, ~
    week í síðustu viku; **at** ~ loksins;
    2 *adv* síðast; **3** *v* endast
last name *n* eftirnafn
last night *n* gærkvöld
last year *n* í fyrra, síðastliðið ár
late *adj* seinn; *(dead)* heitinn: **my** ~
    grandfather afi minn heitinn
later 1 *adj compar* seinni; **2** *adv*
    compar seinna
latest *adj superl* seinastur: **my** ~ **trip**
    seinasta ferð mín

latitude *n* breiddargráða
latter *adj* seinni
Latvia *N* Lettland
Latvian 1 *adj* lettneskur; 2 *n (language)* lettneska
laudable *adj* lofsamlegur
laugh 1 *n* hlátur; 2 *v* hlæja
laughter *n* hlátur
launch 1 *n (for a book)* útgáfuhóf; *(for a boat)* sjósetning; 2 *v* hleypa af stokkunum; *(an attack)* hefja, byrja
launderette *n* þvottahús með sjálfsafgreiðslu
laundromat *n* þvottahús með sjálfsafgreiðslu
laundry *n* þvottur: ~ **facilities** þvottaaðstaða, ~ **room** þvottahús, vaskahús, ~ **service** þvottaþjónusta
laureate *n* verðlaunahafi, orðuhafi
laurel *n* lárviður: ~ **leaves** lárviðarlauf
lava *n* hraun: ~ **field** hraunbreiða
lavatory *n* klósett, baðherbergi, snyrting
lavender *n* lofnarblóm, lavender
law *n* lög
lawsuit *n* málssókn, mál
lawyer *n* lögfræðingur
laxative *n* hægðalyf
lay *v* leggja
lay person *n* leikmaður
layer *n* lag; ~ed í lögum; ~s lög
layover *n* stopp
lazy *adj* latur
lead 1 *n* stjórnun; 2 *v* leiða, stjórna
leaded *adj* með blýi: ~ **gasoline** bensín með blýi
leader *n* leiðtogi
leadership *n* stjórnun
lead-free *adj* blýlaus: ~ **gas** blýlaust bensín
leading *adj* leiðandi
leaf *n* laufblað
league *n* deild
leak 1 *n* leki; 2 *v* leka
lean 1 *adj* magur: ~ **meat** magurt kjöt; 2 *v* halla

leap 1 *n* stökk, hopp; 2 *v* stökkva, hoppa
learn *v* læra, fá að vita
lease 1 *n* leiga, leigusamningur; 2 *v* leigja, taka á leigu
least *adv* minnst, síst: ~ **off of all** allra síst, **not** ~ ekki síst; **to say the** ~ *expr* svo ekki sé meira sagt
leather *n* leður: ~ **goods** leðurvörur, ~ **jacket** leðurjakki
leave *v* fara; ~ **in peace** láta í friði; ~ **me alone** láttu mig í friði; ~ **out** skilja útundan
Lebanese *adj* líbanskur
Lebanon *n* Líbanon
lecture 1 *n* fyrirlestur; 2 *v* halda fyrirlestur
lecturer *n* fyrirlesari; *(university)* lektor
ledge *n* sylla
leech *n* igla, blóðsuga
leek *n* púrra, púrrulaukur: ~ **soup** púrrulaukssúpa
left *adj* vinstri: **on the** ~ vinstra megin, á vinstri hönd
leftist *n* vinstrimaður
leftover *adj* afgangur
left-wing *adj* vinstrisinnaður
leg *n anat* fótur, fótleggur; *(table)* borðfótur
legal *adj* löglegur: **is it** ~? er þetta löglegt?
legalization *n* lögleiðing
legally *adv* löglega
legend *n lit* þjóðsaga; *(on a map)* skýringartexti
leggings *n* leggings
legislation *n* löggjöf
legislator *n* löggjafi
legislature *n* löggjafi
legumes *n* belgjurt
leguminous seeds *n* belgjurtafræ
leisure *n* frítími, tómstund
lemon *n* sítróna; ~ **extract** sítrónusafi
lemonade *n* límonaði
lemongrass *n* sítrónugras
lend *v* lána; **could you** ~ **me X?**

gætirðu lánað mér x?; ~ **a hand**
expr hjálpa
lender *n* lánardrottinn
length *n* lengd
leniency *n* linkind
lenient *adj* undanlátssamur
lens *n* linsa; *(eye)* augasteinn; ~ **cap**
linsulok
Lent *n* fasta
lentil *n* linsubaun: ~ **soup** linsubauna-
súpa, **black** ~**s** svartar linsubaunir,
green ~**s** grænar linsubaunir
Leo *n astro* Ljónið
leopard *n zool* blettatígur
lesbian 1 *adj* lesbískur; **2** *n* lesbía
less 1 *adj compar* minni; **2** *adv compar* minna: **drink** ~ drekktu minna,
no ~ hvorki meira né minna; **none
the** ~ *expr* samt sem áður
lesson *n* kennslustund
let *v* láta: ~ **me know** láttu mig vita;
~ **me take your coat** ég skal taka
jakkann þinn
lethargy *n* sinnuleysi
letter *n (note)* bréf; *(alphabetical)*
stafur
letter box *n* póstkassi
lettuce *n* salathöfuð: **leaf** ~ græn-
salat, **iceberg** ~ jöklasalat, **butter**
~ salathöfuð
level 1 *adj* láréttur, sléttur; **2** *v* slétta,
jafna
levy *n* álagning, skattur
liability *n leg* ábyrgð
liable *adj leg* ábyrgur
liar *n* lygari
libel *n leg* meiðyrði
liberal *adj* frjálslyndur
liberal arts *n* frjálsar menntir
Liberia *n* Líbería
Libra *n astro* Vogin
librarian *n* bókasafnsfræðingur
library *n* bókasafn
Libya *N* Líbía
Libyian *adj* líbískur
lice *n pl* lýs
license *n* leyfi

license plate *n* bílnúmeraplata
license plate number *n* bílnúmer
licorice *n* lakkrís: **red** ~ rauður lakkrís,
black ~ svartur lakkrís
lid *n* lok
lie 1 *n* lygi; **2** *v (tell untruth)* ljúga;
(lie down) leggjast *refl*
Liechtenstein *N* Lichtenstein
Liechtensteiner *adj* Lichtensteinbúi
lieutenant *n* liðsforingi
life *n* líf
life jacket *n* björgunarvesti
lifeboat *n* björgunarbátur
lifeguard *n* lífvörður; *(beach)* strand-
vörður; *(pool)* sundlaugarvörður
lift 1 *n* lyfta: ~ **pass** lyftupassi; **2** *v*
lyfta
light 1 *adj* léttur: ~ **beer** léttbjór, ~
meal léttur málsverður; **2** *n* ljós; **3**
v kveikja
lightbulb *n* ljósapera
lighter *n* kveikjari
lighthouse *n* viti
lighting *n* lýsing
lightly *adv* léttilega: ~ **salted** létt-
saltaður
lightning *n* elding
like 1 *adj* líkur, svipaður; **2** *v* geðjast
að, líka: **do you** ~ **him?** líkar þér
vel við hann?; *(like taste)* finnast
góður: **do you** ~ **fish?** finnst þér
fiskur góður?; *(want)* langa í, vilja:
I would ~ **a beer** mig langar í bjór;
(ordering) **I would** ~ **to have a ...**
gæti ég fengið ...; *(Facebook)* líka
við; læka *colloq*; **3** *prep* eins og:
you talk ~ **a teacher** þú talar eins
og kennari; ~ **that** svona: **don't
talk** ~ ekki segja svona
likely 1 *adj* líklegur; **2** *adv* líklega
lilac 1 *adj* lillablár; **2** *n flora* dísar-
runni, síréna
lily *n flora* lilja
Lima (capital of Peru) *N* Líma
(höfuðborg Perú)
lima bean *n* smjörbaun
lime *n* límóna: ~ **juice** límónusafi,

~ **extract** límónuþykkni
limestone *n geol* kalksteinn
limit 1 *n* takmark; **2** *v* takmarka
limitation *n* takmörkun
limited *adj* takmarkaður
limousine *n* límósína
linden tree *n flora* linditré
line *n* lína, strik; *(rope for laundry)* snúra
linear *adj* línulegur
linen *n* hör, lín
lingerie *n* nærfatnaður; ~ **shop** nærfataverslun
linguist *n* málvísindamaður
linguistics *n* málvísindi
link 1 *n* hlekkur; **website** ~ krækja; **2** *v* tengja
lion *n zool* ljón
lip *n* vör
lipstick *n* varalitur
liqueur *n* líkjör
liquid 1 *adj* fljótandi; ~ **soap** fljótandi sápa; **2** *n* vökvi
liquor *n* sterkt áfengi, spíri; ~ **store** áfengisverslun, vínbúð
Lisbon (capital of Portugal) *N* Lissabon (höfuðborg Portúgals)
list 1 *n* listi; **2** *v* skrá, setja á skrá
listed building *n* friðuð bygging
listen *v* hlusta
listener *n* hlustandi
liter *n* lítri
literal *adj* bókstaflegur
literary *adj* bókmennta-
literature *n* bókmenntir
Lithuania *N* Litháen
Lithuanian 1 *adj* litháskur; **2** *n (nationality)* Lithái; *(language)* lithávska
litter *n* rusl; **no ~ing** fleygið ekki rusli, ekki henda rusli
little 1 *adj* lítill; **2** *adv* lítið: **I slept** ~ ég svaf lítið; *(a little)* smá, pínu, aðeins: **I speak a ~ Icelandic** ég tala smá íslensku
live 1 *adj* lifandi: ~ **music** lifandi tónlist; **2** *v* lifa; ~ **together** búa saman

livelihood *n* lifibrauð
lively *adj* hress, glaðlegur
liver *n* lifur
liverwurst *n* lifrapylsa
living *adj* lifandi: ~ **standard** lífstíll; **do for a** ~ starfa við
living room *n* stofa
lizard *n zool* eðla
Ljubljana (capital of Slovenia) *N* Ljúblana (höfuðborg Slóveníu)
llama *n zool* lamadýr
load 1 *n* hlass, farmur; **2** *v* hlaða
loaf *n* hleifur: ~ **of bread** brauðhleifur
loan *n* lán
loath *adj* tregur
loathsome *adj* fyrirlitlegur, viðbjóðslegur
lobby *n* móttaka
lobster *n* humar: ~ **bisque** humarsúpa
local 1 *adj* staðar-; ~ **pub** hverfis-pöbb; ~ **food** matur úr sveitinni; ~ **speciality** sérréttur svæðisins, þjóðarréttur; **2** *n* heimamaður
locally *adv* á staðnum, á svæðinu
locate *v* finna, staðsetja
located *adj* staðsettur
location *n* staðsetning, staður
lock 1 *n* lás; **2** *v* læsa; ~ **out** læsa úti
locker *n* læstur skápur; ~ **for baggage** farangursgeymsla
locust *n* engispretta
lodestar *n* leiðarstjarna
log in/on *v comp* skrá sig inn
log out/off *v comp* skrá sig út
logic *n* rökfræði
logical *adj* rökrænn
login ID *n comp* notendanafn
loin *n* lend
lollipop *n* sleikibrjóstsykur; sleikjó *colloq*
London (capital of United Kingdom) *N* London, Lundúnir (höfuðborg Bretlands)
lonely *adj* einmana
lonesome *adj* einmana
long *adj* langur
long-distance *adj* lang-, langferða:

~ **call** langlínusímtal
long johns *n* síðar nærbuxur
long-distance bus *n* rúta
long-grain rice *n* löng hrísgrjón
longer *adj* lengri
longevity *n* langlífi
longitude *n* lengdargráða
longship *n arch* langskip
long-sighted *n* fjarsýnn
long-term *adj* langtíma-: ~ **parking** langtíma bílastæði
look 1 *n* útlit: **great** ~ flott útlit; **2** *v* horfa; ~ **after** sjá um, passa, gæta; ~ **around** skoða sig um; ~ **for** leita að; ~ **forward to** hlakka til; ~ **like** líkjast; **I'm just** ~**ing** ég er bara að skoða
loose *adj* víður
loose-fitting *adj* víður
loosely *adv* lauslega
lord *n* herra; *(God)* drottinn; *(title)* lávarður: **L~ Byron** Byron lávarður
lorry *n* vörubíll
lose *v* týna, glata, missa: ~ **blood** missa blóð, ~ **one's way** villast, týnast
loser *n* taplið, sá sem tapar: **he is a bad** ~ hann er tapsár
loss *n (financial)* tap, tjón; *(in a game)* tap
lost *adj* týndur: **be** ~ vera týndur, **get** ~ týnast, villast
lost and found office *n* óskilamunir, tapað-fundið
lot 1 *n (for building)* lóð; *(destiny)* hlutskipti; **2** *adv* mikið: **a** ~ **of people** mikið af fólki, ~**s of time** mikill tími
lotion *n* krem
lottery *n* lotterí, happadrætti
loud 1 *adj* hávær; **2** *adv* hátt
louder *adv compar* hærra
loudly *adv* hátt
loudness *n* hljóðstyrkur
lounge *n* setustofa

louse *n* lús
love 1 *n* ást; **2** *v* elska: **I** ~ **you** ég elska þig
lovely *adj* indæll
lover *n* elskhugi
low 1 *adj* lágur; **2** *adv* lágt; **lie** ~ hafa hægt um sig
low-alcohol beer *n* pilsner
low-beam *n* lágu ljósin
low-calorie *adj* hitaeiningasnauður
lower *v* lækka
low-fat *adj* fitusnauður
lowland *n* láglendi
loyal *adj* trúr, tryggur
lubricant *n* smurolía
lubricate *v* smyrja
lubrication *n* smurning
luck *n* heppni: **good** ~! *excl* gangi þér vel!
lucky *adj* heppinn
lucrative *adj* ábatasamur
luggage *n* farangur: **piece of** ~ ferðataska, ~ **cart** farangurskerra, ~ **locker** farangurgeymsla, ~ **allowance** leyfður farangur
lukewarm *adj* volgur
lullaby *n* vögguvísa
luminous *adj* lýsandi, skínandi
lump *n* kökkur
lunatic *n* brjálæðingur
lunch *n* hádegismatur, hádegisverður
lunchbox *n* nestisbox
lunchmeat *n* kjötálegg
lunchtime *n* hádegi
lung *n* lunga
lupin *n zool* lúpína
lupin bean *n* úlfabaun
lush *adj* blómlegur
lust *n* girnd, losti, þrá
Luxembourg *n* Lúxemborg
luxury *n* lúxus: ~ **goods** lúxusvara
lychee *n flora* litkatré
lyric 1 *adj* ljóðrænn; **2** *n* söngtexti

M

macaroni *n* makkaróna: ~ **salad**
 makkarónusalat, ~ **and cheese**
 ostur og makkarónur
macaroon *n* makkarónukaka
macaw *n zool* arnpáfi
Macedonia *N* Makedónía
Macedonian *adj* makedónskur
machine *n* vél
machine-washable *adj* má setja í
 þvott
machinery *n* vélbúnaður
mackerel *n zool* makríll
mad *adj* reiður, brjálaður
Madagascar *N* Madagaskar
madam *n* frú: ~ **president** frú forseti
Madrid (capital of Spain) *N* Madríd
 (höfuðborg Spánar)
magazine *n* tímarit
magic 1 *adj* töfra-, galdra-; **2** *n* töfrar,
 galdur
magician *n* töframaður, galdramaður
magma *n geol* kvika: ~ **chamber**
 kvikuhólf
magnesium *n* magnesíum
magnet *n* segulstál
magnetic *adj* segul-: ~ **strip** segulrönd
magnificent *adj* frábær, dásamlegur,
 dýrlegur
magnifying glass *n* stækkunargler
magnitude *n* magn
magpie *n* skjór
maid *n* mær: **brides**~ brúðarmær
maiden name *n* ættarnafn kvenna
 fyrir giftingu: **my** ~ **was Smith** ég
 hét Smith áður en ég gifti mig
mail 1 *n* póstur; **2** *v* senda í pósti
mailbox *n* póstkassi
main *adj* aðal-: ~ **building** aðalbygging,
 ~ **course** aðalréttur, ~ **entrance**
 aðalinngangur, ~ **square** aðaltorg,
 ~ **street** aðalgata

mainly *adv* aðallega
mainstream 1 *n* meginstraumur; **2**
 adj venjulegur
maintain *v* viðhalda
maintenance *n* viðhald
maize *n* maís
major 1 *adj* stærri, meiriháttar; **2**
 n mus dúr; *(university)* aðalfag:
 a history ~ háskólanemi með
 sagnfræði sem aðalfag
majority *n* meirihluti
make 1 *v* búa til; *(food)* elda; *(build)*
 smíða; ~ **a phone call** hringja;
 ~ **friends (with)** kynnast; ~ **fun**
 of gera grín að; ~ **sth up** búa til,
 bulla; ~ **sure** tryggja, fullvissa
 sig um
maker *n* framleiðandi
make-up *n* farði
malady *n med* sjúkleiki
malaria *n med* malaría
Malawi *N* Malaví
Malaysia *N* Malasía
Malaysian *adj* malasískur
Maldives *N* Maldívur
male 1 *adj* karlkyns: ~ **teacher**
 karlkyns kennari; **2** *n* karlmaður
Mali *N* Malí
malice *n* illgirni, illvilji
malicious *adj* illur, vondur, illgjarn
malignant *adj* illkynjaður
mall *n* verslunarmiðstöð
mallet *n* kylfa
malnutrition *n* næringarskortur,
 vannæring
malpractice *n* afglöp
malt *n* malt
Malta *N* Malta
mammal *n* spendýr
mammoth *n* mammútur; loðfíll
man *n* maður

manage v *(control)* stjórna; *(cope with)* ráða við
management n stjórn
manager n stjórnandi
managerial adj stjórnanda-
mandarin orange n mandarína
mandatory adj skyldu-
mango n mangó: ~ **jam** mangósulta, ~ **chutney** mangómauk
mania n oflæti; *(interest)* della, æði
manicure n naglasnyrting
manifesto n stefnuyfirlýsing
Manila (capital of Philippines) N Manila (höfuðborg Filippseyja)
mannequin n gína
manner n *(style)* háttur; *(behavior)* framkoma, hegðun
manners n *(politeness)* mannasiðir
mansion n stórhýsi
manslaughter n manndráp
manual 1 adj handa-; **2** n leiðarvísir, leiðbeiningabæklingur
manual transmission n mech beinskipting
manufacture 1 n framleiðsla; **2** v framleiða, búa til
manufacturing n framleiðsla
manure n áburður, tað
manuscript n handrit: ~ **studies** handritafræði
many pron margir: ~ **people** margir, ~ **times** mörgum sinnum, ~ **years ago** fyrir mörgum árum
map n (landa)kort
maple n hlynur: ~ **syrup** hlynsíróp
marathon n maraþon
marble n geol marmari; *(glass ball)* glerkúla
March n mars, marsmánuður
march 1 n mars; *(demonstration)* kröfuganga; **2** v marsera
margarine n smjörlíki
margin n brún; *(in writing)* spássía; *(time)* svigrúm
marijuana n maríúana
marinade n marínering
marinated adj maríneraður

marine adj sjó-, sjávar-; *(navy)* flota-, sjóliðs-
marionberry n brómber
marital status n hjúskaparstaða
marjoram n majóran
mark 1 n merki; **2** v merkja
marked adj merktur
marker n merkipenni
market n markaður
market price n markaðsverð
marketing n markaðssetning
marketplace n markaður, sölutorg
marmalade n marmelaði
marriage n hjúskapur, hjónaband
married adj giftur
marrow n mergur
marry v gifta, giftast recip
Mars n Mars
marsh n mýri, fen
marshal n yfirhershöfðingi
marshmallow n sykurpúði: **hot choclate with ~s** heitt kakó með sykurpúðum
martyr n píslarvottur
marvellous adj frábær, dásamlegur, dýrlegur
marzipan n marsipan
mascara n maskari
mascot n lukkudýr
masculine adj karlmannlegur
mashed adj stappaður: ~ **potatoes** kartöflustappa
mask 1 n gríma: **diving ~** köfunargríma; **2** v hylja með grímu
mass n *(collection, pile)* hrúga; *(many)* fjöldi; *(church service)* messa
massacre n fjöldamorð
massage n nudd
masseur n nuddari
massive adj *(solid)* gegnheill; *(large)* (gríðar)stór: **a ~ building** gríðarstór bygging
master n húsbóndi
master bedroom n hjónaherbergi
Master of Arts n meistari í hugvísindum
Master of Science n meistari í raunvísindum

masterpiece *n* meistaraverk
master's degree *n* meistaragráða
masturbate *v* fróa sér
masturbation *n* sjálfsfróun
mat *n* motta
match 1 *n (for fire)* eldspýta; 2 *v*
   jafnast á við, passa við
matches *n* eldspýtur
mate 1 *n* félagi; 2 *v* para sig
material 1 *adj* efnislegur; 2 *n* efni
mathematics *n* stærðfræði
matinée *n* síðdegissýning
matron *n* forstöðukona
matter 1 *n* efni; 2 *v* skipta máli: it
   doesn't ~ það skiptir ekki máli;
   what's the ~ hvað er að?
mattress *n* dýna
mature *v* þroskast *refl*
maturity *n* þroski
Mauritania *n* Máritanía
Mauritius *n* Máritíus
mausoleum *n* grafhýsi
maxim *n* spakmæli
maximize *v* hámarka
maximum 1 *adj* hámarks-: ~ speed
   hámarks hraði; 2 *n* hámark
may *v* geta, mega
May *n (month)* maí, maímánuður
May Day *n* frídagur verkamanna,
   fyrsti maí
maybe *adv* kannski
mayonnaise *n* majónes, majónessósa
mayor *n* borgarstjóri, bæjarstjóri
maze *n* völundarhús
me *pron* mig *acc*; mér *dat*; mín *gen*
mead *n* mjöður
meadow *n* engi
meager *adj* rýr
meal *n* máltíð
mean 1 *adj* illgjarn; 2 *v (content)*
   þýða, tákna: what does this ~?
   hvað þýðir þetta?; *(intend to say)*
   meina: he ~s well hann meinar vel,
   hann vill vel
meaning *n* merking
means *n* leið, aðferð; by all ~ fyrir
   alla muni

meanwhile *adv* á meðan
measles *n med* mislingar
measure 1 *n* mæling; 2 *v* mæla
measurement *n* mál, mæling
measuring cup *n* mál
meat *n* kjöt; ~ stock kjötsoð
meatballs *n* kjötbollur
meatless dishes *n* kjötlausir réttir
meatloaf *n* kjöthleifur
mechanic *n* vélvirki
mechanical *n* vél-
mechanics *adj* aflfræði
mechanism *n* vélbúnaður
medal *n (sports)* verðlaunapeningur;
   (honor) orða
media *n* fjölmiðlar: in the mass ~ í
   fjölmiðlum
mediate *v* miðla málum
mediation *n* málamiðlun
mediator *n* milligöngumaður,
   sáttasemjari
medic *n* læknir; *(before medical
   license)* læknakandídat
medical *adj* lækna-; *n* læknisskoðun
medication *n* lyfjameðferð
medicine *n* lyf
medieval *n* miðalda-: ~ history
   miðaldasaga, ~ literature miðalda-
   bókmenntir
mediocre *adj* miðlungs
mediocrity *n* meðalmennska
meditation *n* hugleiðsla
Mediterranean *adj* Miðjarðarhafs-:
   ~ food matur frá Miðjarðarhafinu
Mediterranean Sea *N* Miðjarðarhaf
medium 1 *adj* meðal-; 2 *n (in
   between)* meðalvegur; *(way of
   presenting)* miðill
meet *v* hitta; pleased to ~ you *expr*
   gaman að kynnast þér
meeting *n* fundur: ~ place fundar-
   staður, ~ room fundarherbergi
megabyte *n comp* megabæti: file size
   in ~s skráarstærð í megabætum
melancholia *n med* þunglyndi
melancholy *adj (person)* þunglyndur;
   (story, film) sorglegur, sorgmæddur

melody *n* laglína, melódía
melon *n* melóna
melt *v* bráðna
member *v* meðlimur
membership *n* félagsaðild
membrane *n* himna
memo *n* minnisblað
memoir *n* ævisaga, æviminningar
memorial *n (statue)* minnisvarði;
  (ceremony) minningarathöfn;
  (fund) minningarsjóður
memory *n* minni
menace *n* hótun; plága
meningitis *n med* heilahimnubólga
menopause *n med* tíðarhvörf
mens' restroom *n* karlaklósett,
  karlasnyrting; **where is the ~?**
  hvar er karlaklósettið?
menstruation *n* tíðir, túr *colloq*
menswear *n* karlmannsföt,
  karlmannsfatnaður
mental *adj* andlegur, huglægur; *(of*
  illness) geðbilaður, klikkaður: **a ~**
  institute geðhæli
mentally *adv* andlega
menthol *n* mentól
mention *v* minnast á: **don't ~ it** ekki
  minnast á það
menu *n* matseðill: **~ of the day**
  matseðill dagsins
merchandise *n* söluvarningur
merchant *n* sölumaður
mercury *n chem* kvikasilfur
mere *adj* ekkert annað
merely *adv* bara, aðeins, einungis
merge *v* steypa saman
meridian *n geog* lengdarbaugur
meringue *n* marens: **lemon ~**
  sítrónumarens, **~ pie** marenskaka
merry *adj* glaður, gleðilegur; *phr*
  ~ Christmas gleðileg jól!
mess 1 *n* sóðaskapur, drasl, rusl:
  what a ~! þvílíkur sóðaskapur!;
  (unorganized) óreiða; **2** *v* sóða út;
  ~ around fíflast: **I'm just ~ing**
  around ég er bara að fíflast
message *n* skilaboð

message board *n* tilkynningatafla
messenger *n* sendiboði: **don't shoot**
  the ~ *expr* ekki skjóta sendiboðann
metabolic *adj* efnaskipta-
metabolism *n* efnaskipti
metal 1 *adj* málm-; **2** *n* málmur
metaphor *n* myndlíking
meteor *n* stjörnuhrap
meteorologist *n* veðurfræðingur
meteorology veðurfræði
meter *n (tool to measure)* mælir;
  (unit) metri
method *n* aðferð
metro *n* metró, neðanjarðarlest
metro station *n* metróstöð, lestarstöð
  fyrir neðanjarðarlest
metropolis *n* stórborg
metropolitan *adj* stórborgar-
Mexican *n* Mexíkói
Mexico *N* Mexíkó
Mexico City (capital of Mexico) *N*
  Mexíkóborg (höfuðborg Mexíkó)
Micronesia, Federated States of *N*
  Míkrónesía
microphone *n* hljóðnemi
microwave 1 *n* örbylgja: **~ oven**
  örbylgjuofn, **~ dinner** örbylgju-
  réttur; **2** *v* setja í örbylgjuofn
midday *n* hádegi
middle *n* miðja
Middle East *N* Austurlönd nær
Middle Eastern *adj* frá Austurlöndum
  nær: **~ food** matur frá Austurlöndum nær
midnight *n* miðnætti
Midsummer *n* hásumar; *(June 24th)*
  Jónsmessa
midwife *n* ljósmóðir: **I need a ~** ég
  þarf að tala við ljósmóður
might. *See* **may**
migraine *n med* mígreni
mild *adj* mildur, daufur
mile *n* míla
mileage *n* vegalengd í mílum
milestone *n* tímamót: **this is a big**
  ~ for us þetta eru mikil tímamót
  fyrir okkur

military *adj* her-, hernaðar-: ~ **service**
  herþjónusta
milk *n* mjólk: **low-fat** ~ léttmjólk,
  skim ~ undanrenna, ~ **substitute**
  jurtamjólk, ~ **bar** mjólkurbar
milkshake *n* mjólkurhristingur;
  sjeik *colloq*: **strawberry** ~
  jarðaberjahristingur, **chocolate**
  ~ súkkulaðihristingur, **vanilla** ~
  vanilluhristingur
millet *n* hirsi
milligram *n* milligramm
millimeter *n* millímetri
million *num* milljón
millionaire *n* milljónamæringur
mime *n* látbragðsleikur
mince 1 *n* hakk; 2 *v* hakka, brytja,
  saxa
minced meat *n* (kjöt)hakk
mind 1 *n* hugur; 2 *v* gæta, passa;
  do you ~? er þér sama?; **never** ~
  skiptir ekki máli
mine 1 *pron* minn; **that's** ~ ég á
  þetta; 2 *n* náma
mineral 1 *adj* steinefna-; 2 *n* steinefni
mineral water *n* sódavatn
miniature *n* smámynd
minibar *n* míníbar
minibus *n* smárúta
minimize *v* smækka: *comp* ~ **screen**
  smækka gluggann
minimum 1 *adj* lágmarks-: ~ **charge**
  lágmarksverð; 2 *n* lágmark
minister *n* ráðherra
ministry *n* ráðuneyti
mink *n* minkur
minnow *n zool* vatnakarfi
minor 1 *adj (small)* minni háttar:
  ~ **accident** minni háttar slys; 2 *n*
  (young person) barn; *mus* moll
minority *n* minnihluti
Minsk (capital of Belarus) *N* Minsk
  (höfuðborg Hvíta-Rússlands)
mint 1 *adj* piparmintu-: ~ **tea** piparmintute; 2 *n (herb)* minta; **breath**
  ~ minttöflur
minuscule *adj* agnarsmár

minute *n* mínúta; **just a** ~ augnablik,
  andartak, **one** ~ augnablik, andartak
mirror 1 *n* spegill; 2 *v* endurspegla
miscalculate *v* misreikna
miscarriage *n (pregnancy)* fósturlát
mischief *n (damage)* mein; *(prank)*
  prakkarastrik
mischievous *adj (hurtful)* illkvittnislegur; *(teasing)* stríðnislegur
misconception *n* misskilningur
misconduct *n* vanræksla
misdemeanor *n* slæm hegðun
mishap *n* óheppni, slys
miss 1 *n* ungfrú, fröken *arch*; 2 *v*
  (too late) missa af; *(miss a target)*
  hitta ekki; *(long for someone)* sakna
missile *n* flugskeyti
missing *adj* týndur
missionary *n* trúboði
mistake *n* mistök
mistaken *adj* skjátlast: **if I'm not** ~
  ef mér skjátlast ekki
mistress *n (woman of the house)*
  húsfreyja; *(teacher)* kennslukona;
  (lover) hjákona
mistrial *n* ómerk réttarhöld
misunderstanding *n* misskilningur:
  there's been a ~ þetta er einhver
  misskilningur
mitten *n* lúffa, vettlingur
mix 1 *n* blanda; 2 *v* blanda, hræra
mixed *adj* blandaður: ~ **herbs**
  kryddjurtablanda, ~ **nuts** blandaðar
  hnetur, ~ **salad** salatblanda
mixer *n* hrærivél; **hand** ~ handþeytari
mixture *n* blanda
mobile 1 *adj* hreyfanlegur; 2 *n*
  (phone) farsími; *(decoration)* órói
mobile phone *n* farsími: ~ **operator**
  farsímafyrirtæki
mobility *n* hreyfanleiki
mockery *n* háð, spott
modal *n linq* háttar-; ~ **auxiliaries**
  hjálparsagnir
mode *n* háttur
model 1 *n (small copy)* líkan; *(good
  example)* fyrirmynd; *(fashion)*

fyrirsæta; *(type)* gerð; **2** *v (fashion)*
sitja fyrir
modem *n comp Internet* mótald,
módem
modern *adj* nútímalegur
modest *adj* hógvær, lítillátur
modification *n* breytingar
modify *v* breyta, aðlaga
moisten *v* væta
moisturizing cream *n* rakakrem
molar *n* jaxl
molasses *n* síróp
mold 1 *n bio* mygla; **2** *v* mygla
Moldova *N* Moldavía
moldy *adj* myglaður
mole *n (birthmark)* fæðingarblettur;
(animal) moldvarpa
molecular *adj* sameindar-
molecule *n* sameind
molest *v* áreita
molestation *n* áreiti; *(sexual)*
kynferðislegt áreiti
molten *adj* bráðinn
mom *n* mamma
moment *n* augnablik, andartak: **at
the ~** í augnablikinu
momentary *n* augnabliks-
momentous *adj* þýðingarmikill
Monaco *N* Mónakó
monarch *n* konungborinn þjóðhöfðingi
monarchy *n* konungsveldi
monastery *n* klaustur
Monday *n* mánudagur: **I arrive
on ~** ég kem á mánudag, **on ~s** á
mánudögum, **next ~** á mánudag,
last ~ síðastliðinn mánudag
monetary *adj* peninga-
money *n* peningur
money order *n* póstávísun
Mongolia *N* Mongólía
Mongolian 1 *adj* mongólskur; **2** *n
(nationality)* Mongóli; *(language)*
mongólska
monitor 1 *n (screen)* skjár; **computer ~** tölvuskjár; **2** *v* fylgjast með
monkey *n zool* api
monkfish *n zool* skötuselur

monogamy *n* einkvæni
monologue *n* einræða
mononucleosis *n med* einkirningasótt,
eitlasótt
monopoly *n* einokun
Monrovia (capital of Liberia) *N*
Monróvía (höfuðborg Líberíu)
Montenegro *N* Svartfjallaland
month *n* mánuður: **this ~** í þessum
mánuði, **every ~** í hverjum mánuði
monthly 1 *adj* mánaðarlegur; **2** *adv*
mánaðarlega
monument *n* minnisvarði, minnis-
merki
mood *n* skap: **I'm in a good ~** ég
er í góðu skapi; *ling* háttur: **the
imperative ~** boðháttur
moody *adj* skapmikill
moon *n* tungl
moor *n* mýri
moose *n zool* elgur
moot *adj* umdeilanlegur
mop 1 *n* moppa, þvegill; **2** *v* moppa:
~ the floor moppa gólfið
mope *v* vera leiður
moped *n* skellinaðra
moral *adj* siðferðislegur, uppbyggi-
legur
moralist *n* umvandari
morally *adv* siðferðislega
morbid *adj* sjúklegur
more *pron* meira: **some ~** aðeins meira
moreover *adv* auk þess
morning *n* morgunn: **in the ~** um
morguninn, **this ~** í morgun; *expr*
good ~! góðan daginn!
morning-after pill *n med* neyðar-
getnaðarvörn, neyðarpillan
Moroccan 1 *adj* marokkóskur; **2** *n
(nationality)* Marokkómaður
Morocco *N* Marokkó
morphia *n* morfín
morphine *n* morfín
morsel *n* matarbiti
mortadella *n* mortadella-pylsa
mortal *adj* dauðlegur
mortality *n (number of deaths)*

dánartíðni: **infant ~ in Iceland**
ungbarnadauði á Íslandi; *(ability
to die)* dauðleiki; *(causality)*
manntjón
mortar *n* mortél
mortgage 1 *n* veð; **2** *v* veðsetja
mortify *v* niðurlægja
mosaic *n* mósaík
Moscow (capital of Russia) *N*
Moskva (höfuðborg Rússlands)
mosque *n* moska
mosquito *n* moskítófluga: **~ bite**
moskítóbit, **~ net** flugunet
moss *n* mosi
most *adv* flestir
mostly *adv* aðallega
motel *n* vegahótel
moth *n* mölfluga
mother *n* móðir
mother tongue *n* móðurmál
motherhood *n* móðurhlutverk
mother-in-law *n* tengdamóðir,
tengdamamma
motif *n* sagnaminni
motion *n* hreyfing
motion sickness *n med* bílveiki
motivate *v* hvetja
motivation *n* hvatning
motive *n* ástæða
motor *n* mótor
motor scooter *n* vespa
motorbike *n* mótorhjól, vélhjól
motorboat *n* mótorbátur m, vélbátur
motorcycle *n* mótorhjól, vélhjól
motorway *n* hraðbraut
motto *n* mottó
mound *n* haugur
mount 1 *n* fjall-; **2** *v (a horse)* fara á
bak, *(mountain)* klifra
mountain *n* fjall: **~ bike** fjallahjól;
~ climbing fjallaklifur; **~ range**
fjallgarður
mountaineer *n* fjallgöngumaður
mountaineering *n* fjallaklifur
mountainous *adj* fjöllóttur
mourn *v* syrgja
mourner *n* syrgjandi

mournful *adj* sorglegur
mourning *n* sorg
mouse *n comp* mús, (tölvu)mús; *zool*
hagamús
mousse *n* frauðbúðingur; mús *colloq*: **chocolate ~** súkkulaðimús
moustache *n* yfirvaraskegg
mouth *n anat* munnur; *(on animals)*
kjaftur; *(of lion, wolf)* gin
mouth ulcer *n med* munnangur
mouthful *adj* munnfylli
movable *adj* færanlegur
move *v (to a new home)* flytja;
(furniture) færa, flytja; *(touch,
affect)* snerta
movement *n* hreyfing; *(organization)* samtök, hreyfing, félag;
(music) kafli: **third ~** þriðji kafli
mover *n* flutningsmaður
movie *n* bíómynd, kvikmynd
movie theater *n* bíó, kvikmyndahús
movies *n* bíó: **would you like to go
to the ~?** viltu koma í bíó?
mozzarella *n* mozzarella-ostur:
~sticks mozzarellastangir
Mr. *abbrev* herra
Mrs. *abbrev* frú
Ms. *abbrev* ungfrú, fröken
much 1 *pron* mikill; **2** *adv* mikið
mucus *n* slím
mud *n* leðja, drulla, aur
muddle 1 *n* óreiða; **2** *v* rugla
mudflow *n* aurskriða
muesli *n* múslí
muffin *n* múffa: **blueberry ~** bláberja-
múffur
muffle *v* vefja
muffler *n* trefill
mug *n* kanna, krús, kolla: **coffee
~** kaffikanna, **beer ~** bjórkolla,
bjórkanna
muggy *adj* mollulegur
mulberry *n* mórber
mule *n zool* múldýr, múlasni
mulled wine *n* glögg
mullion *n* póstur
multimedia *n* margmiðlun

multinational *adj* fjölþjóðlegur
multiple *adj* margfaldur
multiplication *n* margföldun
multiplicity *n* fjölbreytileiki
multiply *v* margfalda
multi-tiered cake *n* lagkaka
multitude *n* fjöldi
mumble *v* muldra
mummy *n (Egyptian)* múmía
mumps *n* hettusótt
munch *v* maula
mundane *adj* hversdagslegur
mung beans *n* mungbaun
municipal *adj* bæjar-, borgar-
municipality *n* sveitarfélag
munificent *adj* gjafmildur
mural *n* veggmynd, veggskreyting
murder 1 *n* morð: **commit** ~ fremja
  morð; **2** *v* myrða
murderer *n* morðingi
murmur *v (from people)* muldur;
  (from traffic, nature) niður
muscle *n* vöðvi
muscular *adj* vöðva-
muse *n* andagift
museum *n* safn
mush *n* mauk
mushroom *n* sveppur: ~ **sauce**
  sveppasósa
music *n* tónlist: ~ **stand** nótnastatíf,
  ~ **store** tónlistarverslun
musical 1 *adj* tón(listar)-: ~ **genius**
  tónlistarsnillingur; *(has a talent for*
  music) músíkalskur; **2** *n* söngleikur
musical instrument *n* hljóðfæri
musician *n (male)* tónlistarmaður,
  (female) tónlistarkona
musketeer *n* skytta
Muslim *adj* múslimi

mussels *n* kræklingur, bláskel
must 1 *n* er nauðsynlegt: **this is a** ~
  þetta er alveg nauðsynlegt; **2 must**
  v verða
mustard *n* sinnep
mustard greens *n* sinnepskál
muster *v* safna saman
musty *adj* myglaður
mutation *n* stökkbreyting
mute *adj* þögull
mutilate *v* lemstra
mutilation *n* limlesting
mutiny *n* uppreisn
mutter *v* tauta
mutton *n* kindakjöt
mutual *adj* sameiginlegur
muzzle *n* trýni
my *pron* minn
myalgia *n med* vöðvaverkur,
  vöðvaþrautir
Myanmar (Burma) *N* Mjanmar
myopia *n med* nærsýni; *(characteristic)*
  þröngsýni, skammsýni
myrrh *n* mirra
myself *pron* mig *acc*; mér *dat*: **I hurt**
  ~ ég meiddi mig; *(on my own)*
  sjálf(ur): **I'll do it** ~ ég geri þetta
  sjálf(ur); *(alone)* ein(n): **I went by**
  ~ ég fór ein(n)
mysterious *adj* dularfullur
mystery *n* ráðgáta
mystic *adj* dulrænn
mysticism *n* dulspeki
mystify *v* gera undrandi
myth *n* goðsögn
mythical *adj* goðsögulegur
mythology *n* goðafræði: **Norse** ~
  norræn goðafræði

N

nachos *n* nachos
nail 1 *n (on finger)* nögl; *(metal tool)* nagli; **2** *v* negla
naive *adj* barnalegur, hrekklaus
naked *adj* nakinn, ber
name 1 *n* nafn: **first ~** skírnarnafn; *phr* **what's your ~?** hvað heitirðu?; *phr* **my ~ is** ég heiti; **2** *v* nefna, kalla
Namibia *N* Namibía
nape *n* hnakki
napkin *n* servíetta, munnþurrka
narcissism *n* sjálfselska
narcissus *n flora* hátíðalilja, páskalilja
narcosis *n* svæfing, lyfjadá
narcotic *n (drug)* deyfilyf; *(illegal drugs)* eiturlyf; *(drug abuser)* eiturlyfjafíkill, dópisti
narrative 1 *adj* frásagnar-; **2** *n* frásögn
narrator *n* sögumaður
narrow *adj* þröngur
narwhal *n zool* náhvalur
nasty *adj (disgusting)* ógeðslegur; *(evil)* illkvittnislegur; *(difficult)* slæmur
nation *n* þjóð
national *adj* þjóðlegur: **~ gallery** þjóðlistasafn, **~ museum** þjóðminjasafn
national holiday *n* almennur frídagur
nationalism *n* þjóðernishyggja
nationality *n* þjóðerni
nationalization *n econ* þjóðnýting
nationalize *v econ* þjóðnýta
native 1 *adj* innfæddur: **~ country** föðurland; **2** *n* innfæddur maður, frumbyggi
natural *adj* náttúrulegur: **~ flavors** náttúrulegt bragð, **~ ingredients** náttúruleg efni, **~ sciences** náttúruvísindi; *(normal)* eðlilegur
natural arch *n geog* klettabogi

naturalize *v* veita ríkisborgararétt; aðlagast
naturally *adv* auðvitað, sjálfsagt, náttúrulega
nature *n* náttúra: **~ reserve** náttúruverndarsvæði, **~ trail** náttúrustígur
naughty *adj* óþekkur
nausea *n med* ógleði
nauseous *adj med* óglatt: **I'm ~** mér er óglatt
naval *adj (military)* sjó-
navel *n anat* nafli
navigate *v* sigla, stýra
navigation *n* stjórn
navigator *n* siglingafræðingur
navy *n (military)* sjóher
near 1 *adj* nálægur, náinn; **2** *adv* nálægt, nærri; **3** *prep* nálægt, rétt hjá: **the bar is ~ the hotel** barinn er rétt hjá hótelinu
nearby *adj* nálægur
nearest *adj superl* næstur: **~ drugstore is across the street** næsta apótek er hinum megin við götuna
nearly *adv* næstum því
near-sighted *adj* nærsýnn
neat *adj (clean)* snyrtilegur, snotur; *(clever)* sniðugur
neatly *adv (clean)* snyrtilega; *(clever)* flott
necessarily *adv* nauðsynlega
necessary *adj* nauðsynlegur
neck *n* hnakki
necklace *n* hálsmen
nectar *n* ódáinsveig
nectarine *n* nektarína
need 1 *n* nauðsyn, þörf; **2** *v (necessary action)* **~ to** þurfa, verða; *(lack)* vanta: **I ~ information** mig vantar upplýsingar
needle *n* nál

negative *adj* neikvæður
neglect 1 *n* vanræksla; **2** *v (family/ job)* vanrækja; *(tasks)* trassa; *(garden, house)* vanhirða
negligence *n* trassaskapur, hirðuleysi
negotiate *v* semja
negotiations *n pl* samningaviðræður
neighbor *n* nágranni
neighborhood *n* nágrenni
neither *pron* hvorugur
neither ... nor *conj* hvorki ... né
Nepal *N* Nepal
Nepali 1 *adj* nepalskur; **2** *N* Nepali
nephew *n* frændi, *(son of a brother)* bróðursonur, *(son of a sister)* systursonur
nepotism *n* frændhygli
Neptune *n* Neptúnus
nerve *n* taug: **this gets on my ~s** þetta fer í taugarnar á mér
nerveless *adj* rólegur, öruggur
nervous *adj* taugaóstyrkur, taugaveiklaður
nervous system *n anat* taugakerfi
nest 1 *n* hreiður; **2** *v* búa til hreiður; *(people)* hreiðra um sig
net *n* net
Netherlands, The *N* Holland
nettle *n* brenninetla
network *n* net, tengslanet: **computer ~** tölvunet
neurologist *n med* taugafræðingur
neurology *n med* taugafræði
neurosis *n* taugaveiklun, geðflækja
neuter *n ling* hvorugkyn
neutral *adj* hlutlaus
neutralize *v* gera hlutlausan, gera skaðlausan
neutron *n bio* taugafruma
never *adv* aldrei
never mind *conj* skiptir ekki máli
nevertheless *adv* samt sem áður
new *adj* nýr: **~ potatoes** nýjar kartöflur, **~ release** nýútgefið efni
New Delhi (capital of India) *N* Nýja Delhi (höfuðborg Indlands)
New Year *n* nýjár: **~'s Day** nýjárs-

dagur, **~'s Eve** gamlárskvöld
New Zealand *N* Nýja Sjáland
New Zealander 1 *adj* nýsjálenskur; **2** *n (nationality)* Nýsjálendingur
Newfoundland *N* Nýfundnaland
newly *adv* nýlega
news *n* fréttir
newspaper *n* dagblað
next 1 *adj* næstur: **~ stop!** næsta stopp!; **2** *adv* næst
next to *prep* við hliðina á: **~ the hotel** við hliðina á hótelinu
nib *n* pennaoddur
nibble 1 *n* nart; **2** *v* narta
Nicaragua *N* Níkaragva
Nicaraguan 1 *adj* níkaragskur; **2** *n* Níkaragvamaður
nice *adj (characteristic)* indæll, fínn; *(looks)* fallegur, laglegur
nicely *adv* fallega: **ask ~** biddu fallega; *(well)* vel, ágætlega: **this fits ~** þetta passar vel
nickname *n* gælunafn
nicotine *n* nikótín
niece *n* frænka, *(daugher of a brother)* bróðursystir, *(daughter of a sister)* systurdóttir
Niger *N* Níger
Nigeria *N* Nígería
Nigerian 1 *adj* nígerískur; **2** *n* Nígeríumaður
night *n* nótt: **at ~** á nóttunni, **good ~** góða nótt, **spend the ~** eyða nóttunni, **~ after ~** nótt eftir nótt; **one-~ stand** einnar nætur gaman; **~ porter** næturvörður
nightclub *n* næturklúbbur
nightlife *n* skemmtanalíf; *colloq* djammið
nightmare *n* martröð
nihilism *n* tómhyggja, níhílismi
nimble *n* fimur
nimbus *n* geislabaugur
nine *num* níu
nineteen *num* nítján
nineteenth *ord* nítjándi
ninetieth *ord* nítugasti

ninety *num* níutíu

ninth *ord* níundi

nipple *n* geirvarta

nitrogen *n* köfnunarefni

no 1 *adj* enginn: **I have ~ time** ég hef engan tíma; *excl* **~ way!** kemur ekki til greina!; **2** *adv* nei: **yes or ~?** já eða nei?

nobility *n* aðall

noble *adj* göfugur, göfuglyndur

nobleman *n* aðalsmaður

nobody *pron* enginn

node *n* hnútur

noise *n* hávaði

nomination *n* tilnefning

nominative case *n ling* nefnifall

nominee *n* sá sem er tilnefndur

non-alcoholic *adj* óáfengur: **~ beverage** óáfengur drykkur, **~ beer** óáfengur bjór

nonchalance *n* kærulaus framkoma

nonchalant *adj* kæruleysislegur

none *pron* enginn

nonfiction *n* fræðirit

nonlinear *adj* ólínulegur

nonreturnable *adj* má ekki skila

nonsense *n* bull, þvaður

non-smoker *n (male)* reyklaus maður; *(female)* reyklaus kona

non-smoking *adj* reyklaus

nonstop *adv* sífellt, stöðugt

noodle *n* núðla

noon *n* hádegi: **at ~** á hádegi

nor *conj* né: **neither you ~ me** hvorki ég né þú; ekki heldur: **I can't go, ~ can you** ég get ekki farið og ekki þú heldur

nordic *adj* norrænn

Nordic Council *N* Norðurlandaráð

Nordic Council of Ministers, the *N* Norræna ráðherranefndin

Nordic studies *n* norræn fræði

norm *n* norm, venja

normal *adj* venjulegur: **~ skin** venjuleg húð

normalize *v* samræma

normally *adv* venjulega

Norse languages *n* norrænar tungur

Norse mythology *n* norræn goðafræði

Norse paganism *n* Ásatrú

Norsemen *n* norrænir menn

north 1 *adj* norður-: **~ Iceland** Norðurland; **2** *n* norður; **3** *adv* norður, í norður, í norðurátt: **drive ~** keyra norður

North America *n* Norður-Ameríka

North American *n/adj* Ameríkani, Bandaríkjamaður: **~ food** amerískur matur, **~ culture** amerísk menning

North American Plate *n geog* Norður-Ameríkufleki

North Sea *N* Norðursjór

northeast *adj* norðaustur-

northern *adj* norður-: **~ Iceland** Norðurland, **~ Europe** Norður-Evrópa

northwest *adj* norðvestur

Norway *N* Noregur

Norwegian 1 *adj* norskur; **2** *n (nationality)* Norðmaður; *(language)* norska

nose *n* nef

nostalgia *n* fortíðarþrá

nosy *adj* forvitinn

not *adv* ekki: **~ at all** alls ekki, **~ bad** ekki slæmt

notable *adj* áberandi

notably *adv* greinilega

notation *n* rithéttur

note 1 *n* minnispunktur; *(in school)* glósur; **2** *v* skrifa hjá sér; *(in school)* glósa

notebook *n* stílabók, glósubók

noteworthy *adj* eftirtektarverður

nothing *pron* ekkert: **~ else** ekkert fleira

notice 1 *n* tilkynning; **2** *v* taka eftir, veita athygli

noticeable *adj* eftirtektarverður

noticeboard *n* tilkynningartafla

notification *n* tilkynning

notify *v* tilkynna

notion *n (idea)* hugmynd; *(opinion)* skoðun

notorious *adj* alræmdur
nougat *n* núggat
noun *n ling* nafnorð
nourish *v* næra
nourishment *n* næring
novel 1 *adj* nýstárlegur, frumlegur; 2 *n* skáldsaga
novelist *n* skáldsagnahöfundur
novelty *n* nýbreytni
November *n* nóvember
now *adv* nú, núna: ~ I'm leaving nú fer ég, I'm leaving ~ ég fer núna
nowadays *adv* nú á dögum
nowhere *adv* hvergi
nuclear *adj* kjarnorka: ~ bomb kjarnorkusprengja, ~ energy kjarnorka, ~ power station kjarnorkustöð, ~ testing kjarnorkutilraunir, ~ tests kjarnorkutilraunir, ~ weapons kjarnorkuvopn
nucleus *n* kjarni
nudist beach *n* nektarströnd
nuisance *n* plága
number *n* númer, tala: ~ plate númeraplata, bílnúmer

numerator *n math* teljari
numerous *adj (many)* margir, fjölmargir; *(many in a group)* fjölmennur, stór: ~ groups fjölmennur hópur, stór hópur
nun *n* nunna
nunnery *n* nunnuklaustur
nurse *n* hjúkrunarfræðingur
nursery *n (baby's room)* barnaherbergi; *(daycare)* leikskóli, dagheimili
nursing home *n* hjúkrunarheimili
nut *n (food)* hneta; *(crazy person)* brjálæðingur
nutmeg *n* múskat
nutrient *n* næringarefni
nutrition *n* næring
nutritious *adj* næringarríkur
nuts *adj (crazy)* brjálæður, klikkaður, geggjaður: I'm ~ about choclate ég er brjálaður í súkkulaði
nutty *adj* hnetu-; *(crazy)* brjálaður, klikkaður, geggjaður
nylon *adj* nælon

O

o'clock *adv* klukkan: **breakfast
starts at six** ~ morgunmatur byrjar
klukkan átta
oak *n* eik
oasis *n* vin
oath *n* eiður
oatmeal *n* haframjöl
oats *n* hafrar
obese *adj* feitur
obesity *n* offita
obey *v* hlýða
obituary *n* minningargrein
object 1 *n (thing)* hlutur; *(purpose)*
tilgangur, markmið; *ling* andlag; **2**
v andmæla, mótmæla
objection *n* andmæli, mótmæli
objectionable *adj* andstyggilegur
objective 1 *adj (to do with facts)*
hlutlægur; *(unbiased)* hlutlaus;
ling (~ case) andlags-; **2** *n* takmark, markmið
oblation *n* fórn
obligation *n* skylda
obligatory *adj* skyldu-
oblige *v* skuldbinda, skylda
oblique *adj* ská-; *(indirect)* óbeinn
obliterate *v* eyða, þurrka út
obliteration *n* eyðing
oblivion *n* gleymska
oblivious *adj* gleyminn
obnoxious *adj* andstyggilegur,
ógeðslegur, viðbjóðslegur
oboe *n mus* óbó
obscene *adj* ruddalegur
obscenity *n* ruddaskapur
obscure 1 *adj (unclear)* óljós, óskýr;
(unknown) óþekktur, lítt þekktur; **2**
v hylja, skyggja á
observation *n* athugun
observatory *n* stjörnuathugunarstöð
observe *v* fylgjast með

observer *n* sá sem fylgist með
obsess *v* heltaka: **he is ~ed** hann er
heltekinn, hann er með þráhyggju
obsession *n* þráhyggja
obsolete *adj* úreltur
obstacle *n* hindrun
obstinacy *n* þrjóska
obstinate *adj* þrjóskur; *(disease)*
þrálátur
obstruct *v* loka, hindra
obstruction *n* hindrun, fyrirstaða
obstructive *adj* hindrandi
obtain *v* fá, öðlast
obtuse *adj* sljór
obvious *adj* augljós
obviously *adv* augljóslega
occasion *n* tækifæri, tilefni
occupancy *n* umráð
occupant *n* íbúi
occupation *n* (at)vinna, starf; *(of
a house)* búseta; *(by an army)*
hernám
occupied *adj* frátekinn: **is this chair
~?** er þessi stóll frátekinn?
occupy *v (live in)* búa í; *(use time)*
vera upptekinn við: **I'm occupied
with reading** ég er upptekinn við
lestur
occur *v* gerast *refl*, eiga sér stað
occurrence *n* atvik
ocean *n* úthaf
octagon *n math* átthyrningur
October *n* október
octopus *n zool* kolkrabbi
ocular *adj* augn-
oculist *n* augnlæknir
odd *adj (not even)* stakur; *(strange)*
skrýtinn: **how ~!** en skrýtið!
odd jobs *n* tilfallandi störf
odd number *n* oddatala
oddly *adv* undarlega, furðulega:

~ enough þótt undarlega megi virðast

odds *n* líkur

ode *n* óður: **~ to joy** óður gleðinnar

odious *adj* andstyggilegur

odium *n* óvild

odometer *n* aksturmælir

odor *n* lykt

odorous *adj* lyktar-

of *prep* um, frá

of course *adv* auðvitað, að sjálfsögðu

off 1 *adv (away)* af: **this fell ~** þetta datt af; *(distance)* í burtu; *(electronics, lights)* slökkt, ekki í gangi: **lights are ~** það er slökkt á ljósunum; *(on vacation)* í fríi: **she's ~** hún er í fríi; **~ and on** annað slagið; **2** *prep (leaving, taking away)* af, úr: **get ~ the horse** fara af hestinum, **get ~ the bus** fara úr strætó; *(location)*: til hliðar við, nálægt, af, frá: **~ Broadway** nálægt Broadway; *(quit)* hættur: **he's ~ drugs** hann er hættur að nota eiturlyf; *(discount)* afsláttur: **20 percent ~** tuttugu prósenta afsláttur

offal *n* innmatur

offend *v (crime)* brjóta af sér; *(insult)* móðga

offense *n* afbrot

offensive *adj (behavior)* móðgandi; *(smell)* óþægilegur

offer 1 *n* tilboð; **2** *v* bjóða

offering *n* boð, tilboð

offhand *adj* óundirbúinn

office *n* skrifstofa: **~ building** skrifstofuhúsnæði, **~ hours** afgreiðslutími, **~ work** skrifstofustarf, **~ worker** skrifstofumaður

officer *n (police)* lögreglumaður, lögregluþjónn; *(governmental)* embættismaður; *(army)* liðsforingi

official 1 *adj* opinber; **2** *n* opinber starfsmaður

officially *adv* opinberlega

officious *adj* framhleypinn

offline *adj comp* frátengdur; **I'm ~** ég er ekki nettengd(ur); **webpage is ~** vefsíðan liggur niðri

off-peak electricity *n* næturrafmagn

off-road motorcycle *n* torfæruhjól

offset *v* vega á móti

offside *adj* rangstæður

offspring *n (child)* afkomandi; *(result)* afsprengi

often *adv* oft; **every so ~** við og við

ogle *v* gjóa augum

oh *interj (receiving unexpected information)* nú!; *(I understand)* já, ég skil; *(sudden realization)* æi!: **~ I forgot to tell you** æi, ég gleymdi að segja þér

oil *n* olía: **sesame ~** sesamolía, **olive ~** ólífuolía, **canola ~** repjuolía, **~ filter** olíusía, **~ gauge** olíumælir

oil painting *n* olíumálverk

oily *adj* olíu-, fitugur; **~ skin** feit húð

ointment *n* smyrsl

okay *adj* (allt) í lagi: **I'm ~** ég er í lagi

okra *n* okrabaun

old *adj* gamall: **how ~ are you?** hvað ertu gamall/gömul?, **in the ~ days** í gamla daga

Old Icelandic *n* forníslenska

Old Norse *n* norræna, fornnorræna

old town *n* gamli bærinn

old-fashioned *adj* gamaldags

oleo *n* smjörlíki

oligarchy *n* fámennisstjórn

olive *n* ólífa: **black ~** svört ólífa, **green ~** græn ólífa, **pitted ~** steinlaus ólífa

olive oil *n* ólífuolía

Olympic Games *n* Ólympíuleikar

Oman *n* Óman

omelet *n* eggjakaka

omen *n* fyrirboði

ominous *adj* óheillavænlegur

omit *v* sleppa

omnipotence *n* almætti

omnipotent *adj* almáttugur

omnipresent *adj* alltumlykjandi

omnivore *n* alæta

on 1 *adv* áfram: **go ~** haltu áfram,
keep ~ haltu áfram; **hold ~** bíddu
aðeins; **2** *prep (location)* á, í: **~
the table** á borðinu, **~ the plane**
~ í flugvélinni; *(movement to a
location)* á, í: **put it ~ the table**
settu þetta á borðið; *(close to)* við:
~ the beach við ströndina; *(time)*
á: **~ Monday** á mánudag; **~ board**
um borð; **~ purpose** viljandi; **~ tap**
á krana: **what do you have ~ tap?**
hvað ertu með á krana?; *expr* **~ the
house** í boði hússins; *expr* **~ the
rocks** með klaka
once *adv* einu sinni
one *num* einn
one another *pron* hver annan
onerous *adj* þungbær
one-way *adj* einstefna: **~ street**
einstefnugata, **~ traffic** einstefnuakstur
one-way ticket *n* miði aðra leið
onion *n* laukur: **red ~** rauðlaukur,
yellow ~ laukur, **spring ~** vorlaukur, **green ~** vorlaukur, **~ rings**
laukhringir, **~ soup** lauksúpa
online *adj* tengdur, vera á netinu: **to
go ~** fara á netið, **search ~** leita á
netinu
online game *n* netleikur
only *adv* bara, aðeins, einungis,
einvörðungu
onto *prep* á, upp á: **get ~ a horse**
fara á bak
opal *n* ópall
opaque *adj* ógagnsær
open 1 *adj* opinn: **~ here** opið; **~
university** opni háskólinn; **2** *v* opna
open-air *adj* undir berum himni
open-air pool *n* útilaug
opening *n* op; *(beginning)* upphaf;
(opportunity) tækifæri; *(first show)*
frumsýning; *(vacant job)* laus staða;
~ hours opnunartími
openly *adv* hreinskilningslega,
opinberlega
opera *n* ópera: **~ house** óperuhús

operate *v (work)* ganga; *(surgery)*
skera upp; *(~ a machine, car)*
stýra, stjórna
operation *n (surgery)* uppskurður,
aðgerð; *(business)* rekstur
operational *adj* rekstrar-
operating room *n med* aðgerðadeild
operator *n (machine)* stjórnandi;
(telephone) símavörður
opinion *n* skoðun
opium *n* ópíum
opponent *n* andstæðingur
opportunism *n* tækifærismennska
opportunity *n* tækifæri
oppose *v* andmæla
opposite 1 *adj* gagnstæður, andstæður;
2 *n* andstæða; **3** *prep* á móti, gegnt,
andspænis
opposition *n* andstaða; *(parliament)*
stjórnarandstaða
oppress *v* undiroka, kúga
oppression *n* kúgun
oppressor *n* kúgari
opthalmologist *n* augnskurðlæknir
optical *adj* augn-, sjón-
optical illusion *n* skynvilla
optical scanner *n* myndlesari
optician *n* sjóntækjasmiður; *(store)*
gleraugnaverslun
optimism *n* bjartsýni
optimist *n* bjartsýnismaður
optimistic *adj* bjartsýnn
optimum *adj* ákjósanlegastur
option *n* val; *(business)* forkaupsréttur
optional *adj* valfrjáls
optometrist *n med* sjónglerjafræðingur
or *conj* eða
oracle *n* véfrétt
oracular *n* véfréttar-
oral *adj* munnlegur
orally *adv* munnlega
orange 1 *adj (color)* appelsínugulur,
rauðgulur; **2** *n (fruit)* appelsína:
blood ~ blóðappelsína, **~ juice**
appelsínusafi, appelsínudjús, **~
peel** appelsínubörkur
oration *n* ræða

orator *n* ræðumaður
oratory *n* mælskulist
orbit 1 *n* braut; **2** *v* fara í kringum
orchard *n* aldingarður
orchestra *n* hljómsveit
orchestral *adj* hljómsveitar-
order 1 *n (alphabetical etc)* röð: **numerical** ~ í númeraröð; *(in working condition)* **in** ~ í lagi; **out of** ~ bilaður; *(a command)* skipun: **this is an** ~! þetta er skipun!; *(rule)* regla; **2** *v* panta: ~ **food** panta mat, **we are ready to** ~ við erum tilbúin að panta
orderly *adj (tidy)* snyrtilegur; *(precise)* nákvæmur
ordinal number *n* raðtala
ordinary *adj* venjulegur
ore *n geol* málmgrýti
oregano *n* óreganó
organ *n bio* líffæri; *mus* orgel
organic *adj* lífrænn: ~ **milk** lífræn mjólk, ~ **chicken** lífrænn kjúklingur, ~ **produce** lífræn ræktun
organism *n bio* lífvera
organization *n (putting in order)* skipulagning; *(institution)* stofnun; *(group of people)* félag
organizational *adj* skipulagslegur
organize *v* skipuleggja
organized walk *n* skipulögð ganga
orgasm *n* fullnæging
oriental *adj* austurlenskur
origin *n* uppruni
original 1 *adj* upprunalegur: ~ **version** upprunaleg útgáfa; **2** *n (image, picture)* frummynd
originally *adv* upphaflega, í fyrstu
originator *n* upphafsmaður
ornament *n* skraut
orphan *n* munaðarleysingi
orphanage *n* munaðarleysingjahæli
orthodox *adj* bókstafstrúar, strangtrúaður
Oslo (capital of Norway) *N* Ósló (höfuðborg Noregs)
ostracize *v* útskúfaður

ostrich *n zool* strútur
other 1 *pron* hinn: **the** ~ **woman** hin konan, ~ **side** hinum megin; *(someone else)* annar: **she is brighter than any** ~ **person I know** hún er gáfaðri en nokkur annar sem ég þekki; **one after the** ~ hver á eftir öðrum; **the** ~ **day** um daginn
otherwise *adv* annars
Ottawa (capital of Canada) *N* Ottawa (höfuðborg Kanada)
otter *n zool* otur
ought *v* ætti: **you** ~ **to go** þú ættir að fara, **there** ~ **to be more taxis here** það ættu að vera fleiri leigubílar hér
ounce *n (measurement)* únsa; *(little)* ögn
our *pron* okkar: ~ **home** heimili okkar
ours *pron* okkar; **this is** ~ við eigum þetta
ourselves *pron* okkur; sjálf: **we should do it** ~ við ættum að gera þetta sjálf
out *adv* út: **I'm going** ~ ég er að fara út, **way** ~ útgangur, **eat** ~ borða úti
out of *prep* út úr: ~ **the house** út úr húsinu; *(part of)* af: **in one case** ~ **five** einn af hverjum fimm; *(material)* úr: **is the sweater made** ~ **wool?** er peysan úr ull?; *(finished)* -laus: **I'm** ~ **gas** ég er bensínlaus
outbid *v* yfirbjóða
outbreak *n* upphaf; *(riot)* uppreisn; ~ **of flu** inflúensufaraldur; **after the** ~ **of war** eftir að stríðið skall á
outbuilding *n* útihús
outcome *n* útkoma, niðurstaða; *sports* úrslit
outcry *n* óp, hróp
outdated *adj* úreltur
outdo *v* gera betur en
outdoor *adj* úti-; ~ **swimming pool** útisundlaug
outdoors *adv* úti, undir beru lofti; **eating** ~ borða úti
outer *n* ytri; ~ **door** útihurð

outfit *adj* föt: **nice ~ !** flott föt!;
(camping equipment etc) útbúnaður:
hiking ~ útivistarföt
outgoing *n* opinn, félagslyndur: **she
is very ~** hún er mjög félagslynd
outing *adj* skemmtiferð, gönguferð
outlandish *n* sérkennilegur
outlaw 1 *n* útlagi; **2** *v* leg banna *(með
lögum)*
outlet *n* útsölumarkaður; **factory ~**
verksmiðjusala
outlive *v* lifa lengur en; *(survive)*
lifa af
outlook *n (view)* útsýni; *(attitude)*
viðhorf; *(expected outcome)* horfur:
the ~ is not good horfurnar eru
ekki góðar
outnumber *v* vera fleiri en
out-of-date *adj* útrunninn
out-patient department *n* med
göngudeild
output *n* afrakstur
outrage *n* reiði
outrageous *adj* svívirðilegur
outside 1 *adj* úthliðar-; **2** *n* úthlið;
3 *adv (location)* úti: **the children
are ~** börnin eru úti; *(movement)*
út: **the children want to go ~**
börnin vilja fara út; **4** *prep (location)* fyrir utan, utan við: **~ the
house** fyrir utan húsið; *(except)*
nema, fyrir utan: **nobody knows ~
him** enginn veit nema hann
outsider *n* utangarðsmaður
outskirts *n* útjaðar
outspoken *adj* hreinskilinn
outstanding *adj (very good)* framúrskarandi; *(obvious)* áberandi;
(unsettled) útistandandi
oval *adj* sporöskjulagaður
ovary *n* anat eggjastokkur
ovulation *n* med egglos
oven *n* ofn: **~-roasted** steiktur í ofni;
~ mitts pottaleppar
oven-baked *adj* ofnbakaður
over 1 *adv* yfir; *(repeatedly)* aftur:
I read it ~ and ~ ég las það aftur

og aftur; **2** *prep (location)* yfir: **~
the table** yfir borðinu; *(movement)*
~ the table yfir borðið; *(amount)*
meira en: **~ one thousand dollars**
meira en þúsund dollarar
over here *adv* hérna
over there *adv* þarna
overall *adv* samtals; á heildina litið
overcast *adj* skýjað
overcharge *v* setja of hátt verð
overcoat *n* yfirhöfn
overcome *v* komast yfir
overdone *adj* ofeldaður
overdose 1 *n* of stór skammtur; **2** *v*
taka of stóran skammt
overdraft *n* yfirdráttur
overdraw *v* fara yfir á reikningi
overdue *adj* gjaldfallinn: **~ bills**
gjaldfallnir reikningar
overheat *v* ofhita
overlap *v* skarast
overload *v* ofhlaða, yfirfylla
overlook *v* sjást yfir
overnight *adv* yfir nótt; **stay ~** gista
overseas 1 *adj* utanríkis-; **2** *adv*
erlendis
oversight *n* yfirsjón
overtake *v* taka yfir
overtime *n (work)* yfirvinna; *(sports)*
framlenging
overweight *adj* yfirvigt
owe *v* skulda: **how much do I ~?**
hvað skulda ég mikið?
owl *n zool* ugla
own 1 *adj* eiginn: **my ~ car** minn
eiginn bíll, **I saw it with my ~
eyes** ég sá það með eigin augum;
(accomplish by oneself) sjálfur:
I did it on my ~ ég gerði það
sjálf(ur); *(alone)* einn, aleinn: **I
was on my ~** ég var alein(n); **2**
v eiga
owner *n* eigandi
ownership *n* eign: **private ~** í
einkaeigu
oxtail *n* uxahali: **~ soup** *n* uxahalasúpa
oxygen *n* súrefni

oxygen mask *n* súrefnisgríma
oyster *n* ostra: ~ **soup** ostrusúpa, ~
   shell ostruskel
oystercatcher *n zool* tjaldur
ozone *n* óson: ~ **layer** ósonlag

P

pace n *(speed)* hraði; *(step)* skref; *(horse)* skeið
pacemaker n *med* gangráður
pacific adj *(calm)* friðsæll, *(peaceful)* friðsamur
Pacific Ocean N Kyrrahaf
pacifier n snuð; snudda
pacify v friða, róa
pack 1 n pakki; *(animals)* flokkur, hjörð; ~ **of cards** spilastokkur; **a six** ~ kippa; ~ **of cigarettes** sígarettupakki; 2 v pakka: ~ **a suitcase** pakka í ferðatösku
package n pakki: **a holiday** ~ pakkaferð
packed adj pakkaður: **I'm all** ~ ég er búin(n) að pakka; ~ **lunch** nesti
packet n smápakki
pad n púði; *(for writing)* skrifblokk, minnismiðar; *(for ink)* stimpilpúði
paddle 1 n ár: **canoe** ~**s** kanóárar; 2 v róa: ~ **a kayak** róa kajaka
padlock n hengilás
page 1 n blaðsíða; 2 v kalla upp: **could you** ~ **Mr. Smith?** gætir þú kallað upp Mr. Smith?
pageant n sýning; **beauty** ~ fegurðarsamkeppni
pageantry n viðhöfn
pageview n uppfletting; **website** ~**s** heimsóknir á vefsíðu
paid adj greiddur
pail n fata
pain n sársauki; **be in** ~ vera kvalinn; **I have** ~ mér er illt, ég er með verki
painful adj sársaukafullur
painkiller n verkjatafla: **do you have** ~**s?** ertu með verkjatöflur?
painstaking adj vandvirkur, nákvæmur
paint 1 n málning; 2 v mála

painter n *(houses)* (húsa)málari; *(art)* listmálari
painting n málun; *(the art of)* málaralist; *(artwork)* málverk
pair 1 n par; 2 v para
pajamas n náttföt
Pakistan N Pakistan
Pakistani adj pakistanskur
palace n höll
palatable adj bragðgóður
pale adj fölur
palette n litaspjald
palm n *(hand)* lófi; *(tree)* pálmatré
palm oil n pálmaolía
Palm Sunday n pálmasunnudagur
palmist n lófalesari
palmistry n lófalestur
palpable adj áþreifanlegur
palpitate v *(heart)* slá hratt; *(tremble)* titra
palpitations n ör hjartsláttur
palsy n *med* lömun
pamper v dekra
pamphlet n bæklingur
pan n panna
pan-fried adj steiktur á pönnu, pönnusteiktur
Panama N Panama
Panamanian adj Panamamaður
pancake n pönnukaka
pane n rúða
panel n panill, þil; *(discussions)* pallborðsumræður; *(cars)* mælaborð
panorama n víðmynd
pant v mása
panther n *zool* pardusdýr, hlébarði
pantomime n látbragðsleikur
pantry n matarbúr
pants n buxur; *(underwear)* nærbuxur
pantyhose n nælonsokkabuxur
pap smear n *med* legstrok

papaya *n* papajaávöxtur
paper *n* pappír: ~ **recycling**
 endurvinnsla pappírs; **a sheet of** ~
 blað; *(an essay)* ritgerð; *(article)*
 grein; *(identification)* skilríki
paper punch *n* gatari
paperback *n* kilja
paprika *n* paprika
Papua New Guinea *N* Papúa Nýja-
 Gínea
parable *n lit* dæmisaga
parachute **1** *n* fallhlíf; **2** *v* stökkva í
 fallhlíf, fara í fallhlífarstökk
parade *n* skrúðganga; *(soldiers)*
 hersýning
paradise *n* paradís
paradox *n* þversögn
paraffin *n* steinolía
paragon *n* fyrirmynd
paragraph *n ling* efnisgrein
Paraguay *N* Paragvæ
Paraguayan **1** *adj* paragvæskur; **2** *n*
 Paragvæi
parallel *adj* samsíða
paralysis *n* lömun
paralyze *v* lama
parameter *n* breyta
paramount *adj* æðstur
parasite *n bio* sníkjudýr
parasol *n* sólhlíf
parcel *n* pakki
parchment paper *n* bókfell
pardon *v* afsaka, fyrirgefa: ~ **me?**
 afsakið?: *leg* náða
parent *n* foreldri; ~**s** foreldrar
parenthesis *n* svigi
Paris (capital of France) *N* París
 (höfuðborg Frakklands)
parish *n* söfnuður, sókn
park **1** *n* (almennings)garður;
 (amusement) skemmtigarður;
 (botanical) skrúðgarður; **national**
 ~ þjóðgarður; **2** *v* leggja (bíl)
parking *n* bílastæði: ~ **area** bílastæði,
 ~ **garage** bílakjallari, ~ **lot**
 bílastæði, ~ **space** laust bílastæði
parking meter *n* stöðumælir

parking ticket *n* stöðumælasekt
parliament *n* þing: ~ **building**
 þinghús
parlor *n* setustofa
Parmesan cheese *n* parmesanostur
parody *n lit* skopstæling
parole *n leg* reynslulausn
parrot **1** *n* páfagaukur; **2** *v* herma
 eftir (eins og páfagaukur)
parsley *n* steinselja: ~ **flakes** þurrkuð
 steinselja
parsnip *n* nípa, pastinakka
parson *n* prestur, klerkur
part **1** *n* hluti, partur; *(area)* svæði;
 (drama) hlutverk: **play a** ~ leika
 hlutverk; *(participation)* þáttur:
 take ~ **in** taka þátt í; **2** *v (into two
 pieces)* slíta; *(separate)* aðskilja;
 (leave) fara frá, skilja við; *(split in
 two)* greinast *refl*
part of speech *n ling* orðflokkur
partial eclipse *n* deildarmyrkvi
partially *adv* að hluta til
participant *n* þátttakandi
participate *v* taka þátt
participle *n ling* lýsingarháttur:
 present ~ lýsingarháttur nútíðar,
 past ~ lýsingarháttur þátíðar
particle *n* ögn; *ling* orðræðuögn;
 phys eind
particular *adj (specific)* ákveðinn,
 tiltekinn; *(picky)* vandlátur; *(exact)*
 nákvæmur
particularly *adv* sérstaklega
partisan *n* fylgismaður
partly *adv* að hluta til
partner *n (friend)* félagi; *(business)*
 viðskiptafélagi; *(spouse)* maki
partnership *n* félag
partridge *n zool* akurhæna
part-time *adj* hluta-: ~ **job** hlutastarf
party *n* hópur, flokkur; *(political)*
 stjórnmálaflokkur; *(celebration)*
 veisla, partí, boð; *(individual)*
 aðili, þátttakandi
pass *v (go through)* fara í gegn:
 ~ **through** fara í gegnum; *(let*

through) hleypa í gegn; ~ **me the salt please** gætirðu rétt mér saltið; *leg* ~ **a law** samþykkja lög; *sports* ~ **a ball** gefa bolta; *(school)* ~ **an exam** ná prófi; *med* ~ **out** líða yfir
passage *n* leið
passenger *n* farþegi: ~ **terminal** farþegabygging
passion *n* ástríða
passion fruit *n* ástríðuávöxtur
passionate *adj* ástríðufullur
passive *adj* óvirkur, viljalaus
Passover *n* stórhátíð gyðinga
passport *n* vegabréf: ~ **control** vegabréfaskoðun, ~ **number** vegabréfanúmer
password *n* aðgangsorð; **login with** ~ skrá sig inn með aðgangsorði
past **1** *adj* liðinn, fyrri: ~ **generations** fyrri kynslóðir; *(used to be)* fyrrverandi: ~ **president** fyrr-verandi forseti; **2** *n* fortíð: **delve in the** ~ dveljast í fortíðinni; **3** *adv* framhjá; **4** *prep* yfir, framyfir; *(further than)* framhjá: **walk ~ the church** farðu framhjá kirkjunni; *(time)* **half ~ eleven** hálf tólf
pasta *n* pasta
paste **1** *n* smjördeig; **2** *v* lím: **copy and** ~ klippa og líma
pastel **1** *adj* pastel-; **2** *n* pastellitur
pasteurized *adj* gerilsneyddur: **non-** ~ **milk** ógerilsneydd mjólk
pastime *n* tómstundagaman, áhugamál
pastry *n* hveitideig: **low-carb** ~ lágkolvetnadeig; **non-sugar** ~ sykurlaust deig
pasture *n* beitiland
pat **1** *n* klapp, bank; **2** *v* klappa
patch **1** *n* bót; **2** *v* bæta
paté *n* kæfa
patent *n* leg einkaleyfi
path *n* stígur
pathetic *adj* aumkunarverður
patience *n* þolinmæði: **have ~!** vertu þolinmóð(ur)!
patient **1** *adj* þolinmóður: **be ~!**

vertu þolinmóð(ur); **2** *n* med sjúklingur: **doctor's** ~ sjúklingur hjá lækni, **~'s room** sjúkrastofa
patisserie *n* bakarí
patriot *n* föðurlandsvinur
patriotic *n* þjóðrækinn
patriotism *n* ættjarðarást
patrol *v* vakta
patron *n* velgjörðarmaður, verndari
patronage *n* verndarvængur, stuðningur
pattern *n* munstur; *(sewing)* snið; *(model)* fyrirmynd
pauper *n* fátæklingur
pause **1** *n* hlé; **2** *v* taka hlé
pavement *n* gangstétt
pavilion *n* garðskáli, hljómskáli, skáli
paving stone *n* hella
paw *n* loppa; *(large animals)* hrammur
pay **1** *n* *(salary)* laun, kaup: ~ **slip** launaseðill; **2** *v* borga, greiða; ~ **attention** veita athygli; ~ **a visit** heimsækja
pay phone *n* gjaldsími, almenningssími
payable *adj* greiðanlegur: ~ **to bearer** greiðist handhafa; *(due)* gjaldfallinn
payment *n* greiðsla
payroll *n* launaskrá
pea *n* baun: ~ **soup** baunasúpa
peace *n* *(not war)* friður; *(calmness)* ró
peaceful *adj* friðsamur, rólegur
peach *n* ferskja
peacock *n zool* páfugl
peak *n* toppur, oddur; *(mountain)* (fjalls)tindur, toppur
peanut *n* jarðhneta: ~ **butter** jarð-hnetusmjör, ~ **oil** jarðhnetuolía
pear *n* pera
pearl *n* perla
peas *n* baunir: **green** ~ grænar baunir, **sugar snap** ~ sykurbaunir
pebble *n* smásteinn
pecan *n* pekanhneta: ~ **pie** pekanbaka
peculiar *adj* *(specific to)* einkennandi; *(strange)* skrýtinn, undarlegur, furðulegur; *(different)* sérstakur
pedagogy *n* kennslufræði

pedal *n* pedali, fótstig
pedant *n* smámunasamur maður
pedantic *adj* smámunasamur
pedantry *n* smámunasemi
pedestal *n* stallur: **put sby on a** ~ hefja einhvern á stall
pedestrian *n* gangandi vegfarandi: ~ **crossing** gangbraut, ~ **zone** göngugata
pediatrician *n med* barnalæknir
pedigree *n (family tree)* ættartala; *(origin)* ætterni
peel **1** *n* flus, hýði; **orange** ~ appelsínubörkur; **2** *v* flysja, taka utan af
peep *v (sound)* pípa; *(look)* kíkja
peer *n* jafningi
peg *n (wooden piece)* pinni; *(tent)* hæll; *(violin)* skrúfa; *(laundry)* klemma; *(degree)* stig, þrep
Peking duck *n* Pekingönd
pen *n* penni: **ball point** ~ kúlupenni
penalize *v* straffa
penalty *n* refsing
pencil *n* blýantur
pencil sharpener *n* yddari
pendulum *n* pendúll
penetrate *v* fara inn í, síast inn
penetration *n (enter)* það að smjúga inn; *(insight, understanding)* skarpskyggni, innsæi
penguin *n zool* mörgæs
peninsula *n* skagi, nes
penis *n anat* tippi, (getnaðar)limur
pension *n* (elli)lífeyrir, eftirlaun
pensioner *n* lífeyrisþegi
pentagon *n math* fimmhyrningur
people *n* fólk
pepper *n* pipar: **green** ~ græn papríka, **red** ~ rauð papríka, ~ **sauce** piparsósa, ~ **steak** piparsteik
peppermint *n* piparminta
pepperoni *n* pepperónípylsa
per *prep* á, fyrir: ~ **hour** á tímann, ~ **night** fyrir nóttina, ~ **week** fyrir vikuna
perceive *v* finna, skynja

percent *n* prósenta
percentage *n* prósenta
perceptible *adj* skynjanlegur
perception *n* skynjun, skilningur
perceptive *adj* næmur
perch *n* fuglaprik
perfect *adj* fullkominn
perfection *n* fullkomnun
perfectly *adv* fullkomlega
perfidy *n* svik
perform *v* framkvæma; *(art)* koma fram, flytja: ~ **a play** setja á svið
performance *n* frammistaða, framkvæmd; *mus* flutningur
performer *n* skemmtikraftur; *(theater)* leikari; *(music)* tónlistarmaður
perfume *n* ilmvatn
perfume shop *n* snyrtivöruverslun
perhaps *adv* kannski
peril *n* hætta
perilous *adj* hættulegur
period *n (era)* tímabil; *(menstruation)* tíðir, túr *colloq*; ~ **cramps** tíðaverkir, túrverkir *colloq*
periodic *adj* reglubundinn: ~ **pain** reglubundnir verkir
periodical *n lit* tímarit
periodically *adv* reglulega
perish *v* farast, týna lífi, deyja
perishable *adj* vara sem getur skemmst
perjury *n leg* meinsæri
perm *n* permanent
permanent *adj* varanlegur; ~ **collection** gripir í eigu safnsins
permanently *adv* til frambúðar
permission *n* leyfi
permit **1** *n* leyfi; **driver's** ~ ökuskírteini; ~ **required** krefst ökuskírteinis; **~holders only** aðeins fyrir handhafa ökuskírteinis; **2** *v* leyfa
permitted *adj* leyfilegur
perpetual *adj* eilífur, varanlegur
perpetuate *v* varðveita
perplex *v* rugla í ríminu: **this ~ed me** þetta ruglaði mig í ríminu
perplexity *n* fát

persecute *v* ofsækja, áreita
persecution *n* ofsóknir
perseverance *n* þrautseigja
persevere *v* gefast ekki upp
Persian *adj* persnerskur
persimmon *n* döðluplóma
persist *v* þrjóskast
persistence *n (stability)* stöðugleiki; *(stubborness)* þrjóska; *(not giving up)* úthald
persistent *adj* þrjóskur; *(longlasting)* varanlegur
person *n* persóna, manneskja
personage *n (female)* háttsett kona, *(male)* háttsettur maður
personal *adj* persónulegur
personal computer (PC *abbrev***)** *n* einkatölva, PC tölva
personality *n* persónuleiki
personally *adv* persónulega
personification *n lit* persónugerving
personnel *n* starfsfólk
perspective *n (large picture)* heildarsýn; *(angle)* sjónarhóll: **from this ~** frá þessum sjónarhóli séð
perspiration *n* sviti
perspire *v* svitna
persuade *v* sannfæra
persuasion *n* fortölur; *(certainty)* sannfæring
pertain *v* snerta, varða
Peru *N* Perú
Peruvian 1 *adj* perúskur; **2** *n* Perúmaður
pervade *v* gegnsýra
perverse *adj* öfugsnúinn; *(unethical)* siðlaus
perversion *n* siðleysi, öfuggugaháttur
pervert *n* öfuguggi, *colloq* perri
pessimism *n* svartsýni, bölsýni
pessimist *n* svartsýnismaður, bölsýnismaður
pessimistic *adj* svartsýnn, bölsýnn
pest *n* plága
pesticide *n* skordýraeitur
pestilence *n med* drepsótt
pet *n* gæludýr
pet shop *n* gæludýraverslun

petal *n flora* krónublað
petition *n* undirskriftasöfnun, bænaskrá
petrol *n* bensín
petticoat *n* millipils
petulance *n* fýla
pH *n chem* sýrustig
Ph.D. *abbrev* dr.; doktor í hugvísindum
phantom *n* draugur, svipur
pharmacy *n* apótek, lyfjaverslun, lyfjabúð
phase *n* stig, fasi
pheasant *n zool* fasani
phenomenal *adj* undraverður
phenomenon *n* fyrirbæri
philanthropic *adj* mannúðar-
philanthropist *n* mannvinur
philanthropy *n* mannkærleikur
Philippines *N* Filippseyjar
philological *adj* fílólógískur, textafræðilegur
philologist *n* fílólóg, textafræðingur
philology *n* fílólógía, textafræði
philosopher *n* heimspekingur
philosophy *n* heimspeki
phone *n* sími: **~ book** símaskrá, **~ booth** símklefi, **~ call** símtal, **~ card** símakort, **~ number** símanúmer; **make a ~ call** hringja
phonetics *n* hljóðfræði
phosphorous *n* fosfór
photo *n* ljósmynd: **take a ~** taka (ljós)mynd, **~ booth** ljósmyndasjálfsali
photocopier *n* ljósritunarvél
photocopy 1 *n* ljósrit; **2** *v* ljósrita
photograph 1 *n* (ljós)mynd: **take a ~** taka ljósmynd; **2** *v* taka mynd
photographer *n* ljósmyndari
photography *n* ljósmyndun
phrase *n ling* orðasamband, frasi
physical 1 *adj (material)* áþreifanlegur; *(to do with physics)* eðlisfræðilegur, eðlis-: **~ science** eðlisvísindi; *(body)* líkamlegur: **~ injuries** líkamleg meiðsl; **2** *n med* læknisskoðun

physically *adv (body)* líkamlega; *(physics)* eðlisfræðilega
physician *n* læknir
physicist *n* eðlisfræðingur
physics *n* eðlisfræði
piano *n mus* píanó
piccolo *n mus* pikkolóflauta
pick *v (gather)* tína: ~ **blueberries** tína bláber; *(choose)* velja, kjósa: ~ **a seat** veldu sæti; *(teeth)* stinga, pikka; ~ **sby up** ná í einhvern; ~ **sth up** taka eitthvað upp
pickle *v* pækill; *(cucumber)* súr gúrka; **2** *v* súrsa
pickled *adj* saltaður, niðursoðinn: ~ **herring** niðursoðin síld
pickup truck *n* pallbíll
picnic *n* lautarferð
picnic area *n* áningarstaður
picture **1** *n* mynd; *(cinema)* (bíó)mynd; **2** *v* ímynda sér
picturesque *adj* fallegur
pie *n* baka: **apple** ~ eplabaka, **blueberry** ~ bláberjabaka
piece *n (part)* hlutur, partur; *(painting, music)* stykki; ~ **of furniture** húsgagn, ~ **of land** landsvæði, landspilda
pier *n* bryggja
pig *n zool* svín; *(figuratively)* sóði: **you** ~! sóðinn þinn!
pigeon *n zool* dúfa
pigsty *n* svínastía
pike *n zool* gedda
Pilates *n* Pílates
pile **1** *n* hrúga, haugur; **2** *v* hrúgast upp
pilfer *v* hnupla
pilgrim *n* pílagrími
pilgrimage *n* pílagrímsferð
pill *n* tafla, pilla; **the** ~ pillan
pillar *n* súla
pillow *n* koddi, púði
pillowcase *n* koddaver
pilot *n* flugmaður
pilot light *n* kveikilogi
pilot whale *n zool* grindhvalur
pimple *n* bóla

pin **1** *n* títuprjónn; *(tent)* hæll; *(violin)* skrúfa; **2** *v* næla
pinch **1** *n* klípa; ~ **of salt** salt á hnífsoddi; **2** *v* klípa
pine *n* fura, furutré
pine seed *n* furuhnetur
pineapple *n* ananas
ping-pong *n* borðtennis
pink *adj (color)* bleikur
pinnacle *n* hátindur
pint *n* hálfur pottur; ~ **of beer** stór bjór
pinto bean *n* pintobaun
pioneer *n (explorer)* landnemi; *(first)* frumkvöðull
pious *adj* guðhræddur
pipe *n* pípa, rör: **smoking** ~ pípa
pipe dream *n* draumórar
piquant *adj* bragðsterkur
piracy *n (on the sea)* sjórán; *(of artwork)* hugverkaþjófnaður
pirate *n* sjóræningi
Pisces *n astro* Fiskarnir
pistachios *n* pistasíuhnetur
pistol *n* skammbyssa
pita *n* píta: ~ **bread** pítubrauð
pitch **1** *n (throw)* kast; *(voice)* tónhæð; **2** *v* kasta
pitcher *n (water)* vatnskanna; *(other drinks)* kanna; *(baseball)* kastari
piteous *adj* aumkunarverður
pitfall *n* gildra
pitiable *adj* aumkunarverður
pitiful *adj* aumkunarverður
pitiless *adj* harðbrjósta
pitted *adj* steinlaus: ~ **olives** steinlausar ólífur, ~ **dates** steinlausar döðlur
pity *n* meðaumkun, samúð
pivot *n* þungamiðja
pizza *n* pitsa: **cheese** ~ pitsa með osti, **vegetable** ~ grænmetispitsa, **meat** ~ pitsa með kjöti/kjötáleggi
pizza parlor *n* pitsustaður
pizzeria *n* pitsustaður
placard *n* plakat
place **1** *n* staður: ~ **of birth** fæðingarstaður; *(work)* staða; *(in a*

theater, e.g.) pláss; *(results in competition)* sæti: **first** ~ fyrsta sæti; *(home)* bústaður; **2** *v* setja, láta

placebo *n* lyfleysa

placid *adj* kyrrlátur

plague *n* plága

plaice *n zool* rauðspretta, skarkoli

plain *adj (clear)* greinilegur; *(everyday)* hversdagslegur; *(normal)* venjulegur: ~ **milk** venjuleg mjólk; ~ **yogurt** hrein jógúrt

plaintiff *n* stefnandi

plan 1 *n* áætlun: **do you have any ~s for tonight?** ertu að gera eitthvað í kvöld?; **2** *v* skipuleggja: ~ **a trip** skipuleggja ferð

plane 1 *adj* sléttur, flatur; **2** *n (airplane)* flugvél

planet *n* pláneta, reikistjarna

plank *n* planki

planning *n* skipulag: **city ~** borgarskipulag

plant 1 *n flora* planta, jurt; *(factory)* verksmiðja: **power ~** orkuver; **2** *v* gróðursetja, planta

plantain *n* mjölbanani

plantation *n* plantekra; *(forest)* skógræktarsvæði

plasma *n med* blóðvökvi

plaster *n (for wounds)* plástur; *(for broken bones)* gifs

plastic 1 *adj* plast-: ~ **bag** plastpoki, ~ **wrap** plastfilma; **2** *n* plast

plate *n* diskur, *(large)* fat; *(metal)* plata; *expr* **have a lot on one's ~** vera með of mikið á sinni könnu

plate tectonics *n geol (theory)* flekakenning; *(movements)* jarðskorpuhreyfingar

plateau *n* háslétta

platform *n (for giving a speech)* (ræðu)pallur, svið; *(political)* stefnuskrá

platform shoes *n* þykkbotna skór

platinum *n chem* platína; ~ **(credit) card** platínukort

platonic *adj* platónskur

platoon *n* flokkur

platter *n* diskur, fat, bakki: **meat ~** kjötbakki, **seafood ~** sjávarréttabakki, **appetizer ~** forréttabakki

play 1 *n (theater)* leikrit; *(game)* leikur; **2** *v (theater)* leika: ~ **Hamlet** leika Hamlet; *(game)* leika sér; *(instrument)* spila á: ~ **the violin** spila á fiðlu; *(sports)* spila, leika: **I ~ soccer** ég spila fótbolta, ~ **cards** spila á spil

player *n* leikmaður

playground *n* leikvöllur, leiksvæði

playing cards *n* spil

playing field *n sports* íþróttavöllur

playschool *n* leikskóli

plea *n* beiðni

plead *v* biðja

pleasant *adj* þægilegur, notalegur, ánægjulegur: ~ **surprise** óvænt ánægja

pleasantly *adv* þægilega, notalega

pleasantry *n* grín, gamansemi

please 1 *v* þóknast, gera til geðs; **2** *interj (asking others to do sth)* gerðu svo vel (að): ~ **have a seat** gerðu svo vel að fá þér sæti; *phr* **could I have coffee, ~?** gæti ég fengið kaffi?

pleasing *adj* ánægjulegur

pleasure *n* ánægja

plebiscite *n* þjóðaratkvæðagreiðsla

pledge 1 *n* pantur; *(promise)* loforð; **2** *v* veðsetja

plenty 1 *adj* nægur, kappnógur; **2** *n* allsnægtir; **3** *adv* alveg: **this is ~ good enough** þetta er alveg nógu gott

plight *n* slæmar aðstæður

plod *v (walk)* þramma; *(work hard)* erfiða

plop *n* skvamp

plot 1 *n (garden)* reitur; *(building)* lóð; *(betrayal)* ráðabrugg; *(story)* söguþráður; **2** *v (plan)* skipuleggja; *(story)* semja söguþráð

plow 1 *n* plógur; **2** *v* plægja
pluck *v* reyta, plokka
plug 1 *n* tappi: **pull the** ~ taka tappann úr; **electric** ~ innstunga; **2** *v*
setja tappa í: ~ **in** setja í samband
plum *n* plóma: ~ **pudding** plómu-
búðingur, ~ **jam** plómusulta
plumber *n* pípulagningamaður
plunder *v* ræna
plunge *v* steypa sér, steypast: ~ **into
the pool** steypa sér út í laugina
plural 1 *adj ling* fleirtölu-; **2** *n ling*
fleirtala
plus 1 *adj* plús-; **2** *n* plús; **3** *conj* auk
þess: ~ **I never wanted to go** auk
þess vildi ég aldrei fara
PM *abbrev* eftir hádegi
pneumonia *n med* lugnabólga
pocket *n* vasi
poem *n* ljóð, kvæði
poet *n* ljóðskáld
poetic *adj* ljóð-; ~ **justice** makleg
málagjöld
poetics *n* ljóðlist, ljóðagerð
poetry *n* ljóðlist, ljóðagerð
poignant *adj (grief)* sár, beiskur;
(touching) áhrifamikill; *(obvious)*
augljós; *(important)* áríðandi;
(smell) sterkur: **a** ~ **smell** sterk lykt
point 1 *n (knife, pen)* oddur; *(agenda)*
liður; *(argument)* **good** ~ góður
punktur, **what is your** ~ **?** hvað
ertu að reyna að segja?; *(geography)* nes, tangi, oddi; *(drawing)*
punktur; *(time)* stund: **at this** ~ á
þessari stundu; **when it comes to
the** ~ þegar á reynir; *(place)* ~ **of
interest** áhugaverður staður; **2** *v*
benda (á): ~ **with a mouse** benda
með músinni
pointed *adj* oddmjór, oddhvass
poise *n* stilling
poison 1 *n* eitur; **2** *v* eitra
poisonous *adj* eitraður
poke *v* pota
poker *n (card game)* póker; *(for fire)*
skörungur

Poland *N* Pólland
polar *adj* heimskauts-, heimskauta-:
~ **circle** heimskautsbaugur
polar bear *n zool* ísbjörn
pole *n geog* skaut, póll: **North P**~
Norðurpóllinn, **South P**~ Suður-
póllinn
police *n* lögregla: ~ **report** lögreglu-
skýrsla, ~ **car** lögreglubíll, ~ **station**
lögreglustöð
policeman *n* lögreglumaður,
lögregluþjónn
policy *n* stjórnarstefna, stefnumál:
foreign ~ utanríkisstefna, **insurance** ~ vátryggingaskírteini
Polish 1 *adj* pólskur: ~ **food** pólskur
matur, ~ **store** pólsk búð; **2** *n
(nationality)* Pólverji; *(language)*
pólska: **do you speak** ~**?** talaðu
pólsku?
polish 1 *n* gljái; **2** *v* pússa: ~ **shoes**
pússa skó
polite *adj* kurteis, háttvís: *expr* **be** ~ **!**
vertu kurteis!
politely *adv* kurteisislega
political *adj* pólitískur, stjórnmálalegur:
~ **asylum** pólitískt hæli
politically *adv* pólitískt, stjórnmálalega
politician *n* stjórnmálamaður,
pólitíkus *colloq*
politics *n* stjórnmál, pólitík *colloq*
poll booth *n* kjörklefi: ~ **station**
kjörstaður
pollen *n* frjókorn: ~ **allergy**
frjókornaofnæmi, ~ **count**
frjókornamæling
pollock *n* ufsi
polls *n* kosningar
pollute *v* menga, spilla
pollution *n* mengun: **air** ~ loftmengun,
land ~ jarðvegsmengun, **water** ~
vatnsmengun
polo *n sports* póló; *(shirt)*
rúllukragapeysa
polyester *adj* pólýester-
polygamous *adj* fjölkvænis-
polygamy *n* fjölkvæni

polyglot *n* fjöltyngdur
pomegranate *n* granatepli
pomp *n* viðhöfn
pompous *adj (person)* merkilegur með sig; *(ceremony)* viðhafnarmikill
pond *n* tjörn
ponder *v* íhuga, hugleiða
pony *n zool* smáhestur
pool *n* sundlaug: **swimming ~** sundlaug
poor *adj* fátækur
pop 1 *n (soda)* gos: **a bottle of ~** gosflaska; **2** *v* **~ popcorn** poppa, búa til poppkorn; **~ a balloon** sprengja blöðru; **~ by the store** koma við í búðinni; **~ up** skjótast upp
pop band *n* popp(hljóm)sveit
pop concert *n* popptónleikar
pop festival *n* tónlistarhátíð
pop music *n* popptónlist
popcorn *n* poppkorn
pope *n* páfi: **P~ Francis** Francis páfi
poppy *n flora* valmúi; **arctic ~** melasól; **Iceland ~** garðasól
poppy seed *n* birkifræ
popsicle *n* íspinni
popular *adj* vinsæll
popularity *n* vinsældir
population *n* íbúar; *(number of inhabitants)* íbúafjöldi
populous *adj* þéttbyggður
porcelain *n* postulín
porch *n* yfirbyggður pallur
pore *n anat* svitahola
pork *n* svínakjöt: **~ chop** svínakóteletta, **~ fillet** svínavöðvi, **~ loin** svínalæri, **~ roast** svínasteik, **~ sausage** svínapylsa
porpoise *n zool* hnísa
porridge *n* grautur
port *n* höfn: **tax-free ~** fríhöfn
portable *adj* ferða-, far-: **~ crib** ferðavagga
portage *n* flutningur
portal *n* skrauthlið; **webb ~** vefgátt
portend *v* boða
porter *n* burðarmaður

portfolio *n* mappa
portion *n* hluti; *(food)* skammtur
portrait *n (in painting, photo)* portrett: **~ artist** portrettamálari; *(in words)* mannlýsing
portray *v (paint)* mála; *(describe)* lýsa
Portugal *n* Portúgal
Portuguese 1 *adj* portúgalska; **2** *n (nationality)* Portúgali; *(language)* portúgalska
pose 1 *n* stelling; **2** *v* stilla sér upp: **~ for the camera** stilla sér upp fyrir myndatöku; bera fram: **~ a question** bera fram spurningu
position *n (at work)* staða; *(of body)* stelling; *(view)* afstaða: **what is your ~ on this?** hver er þín afstaða í þessu máli?
positive *adj (characteristic)* jákvæður; *(certain)* viss; *(real)* raunverulegur; *(result)* jákvæður
possess *v* eiga
possession *n* eign
possessive 1 *adj* stjórnsamur, drottnunargjarn; **2** *n ling* eignarfall: **in the ~ case** í eignarfalli
possibility *n* möguleiki
possible *adj* mögulegur, hugsanlegur; **as soon as ~** eins fljótt og hægt er
possibly *adv* mögulega, hugsanlega
post 1 *n* póstur; **2** *v* setja í póst
post office *n* póstafgreiðsla, póstur
postage *n* burðargjald: **~ paid** burðargjald greitt
postal code *n* póstnúmer
postbox *n* pósthólf
postcard *n* póstkort
poster *n* plakat, veggspjald
posterity *n* ókomnar kynslóðir
postgraduate 1 *adj* framhaldsstigs-; **2** *n* nemi í framhaldsnámi
postman *n* póstburðarmaður
postpone *v* fresta
postponement *n* frestur
postscript *n* eftirmáli
posture *n* líkamsstaða, stelling

pot *n (cooking)* pottur; *(flower)*
krukka, blómapottur; *(money)*
pottur; *(drugs)* marijúana
potato *n* kartafla: **baked** ~ bökuð
kartafla, **roasted** ~ steiktar
kartöflur, **red** ~ rauðar kartöflur,
~ **chips** kartöfluflögur, **salted** ~
kartöfluflögur með salti, ~ **soup**
kartöflusúpa, **~es au gratin**
kartöflugratín
potency *n* styrkur, kraftur
potential **1** *adj* mögulegur, hugsanlegur; **2** *n* möguleiki
pothole *n* hola; skessuketill *geol*
potter *n* leirkerasmiður
pottery *n (art)* leirkeragerð; *(product)*
leirmunur; *(workshop)* leirkera-
vinnustofa
pouch *n* poki
poultry *n* alifuglar
pound **1** *n* pund: **one hundred ~s**
hundrað pund; **2** *v* hamra
pour *v* hella
poverty *n* fátækt
powder *n* duft, púður; *(cosmetic)*
púður
powdered *adj* í duftformi
powdered sugar *n* flórsykur
power **1** *n (energy)* kraftur; *(electric)*
orka; *phys* afl; *(government)* vald:
be in ~ vera við völd; ~ **of God**
máttur Guðs
power button *n* rafmagnsrofi
power outage *n* rafmagnsleysi
power outlet *n* innstunga
power station *n* virkjun, raforkuver
powerful *adj (strong)* sterkur; *(authority)* valdamikill; *(influential)*
áhrifamikill
practical *adj* hagnýtur, gagnlegur
practically *adv* nánast, eiginlega:
they are ~ married þau eru nánast
gift
practice **1** *n (exercise)* æfing; *(way
to do something)* framkvæmd;
(habit) vani; *(custom)* hefð; *(doctor's/lawyer's office)* starfsemi; **2**

v (exercise) æfa; *(do regularly)*
temja sér; *(do)* framkvæma, gera;
(law, medicine) starfa sem: **I** ~ **law**
ég starfa sem lögfræðingur
practitioner *n* sérfræðingur
pragmatic *adj* raunsær, jarðbundinn;
phil pragmatískur
pragmatism *n phil* pragmatík
Prague (capital of Czech Republic)
N Prag (höfuðborg Tékklands)
prairie *n* slétta
prairie dog *n zool* sléttuúlfur
praise **1** *n* hrós; **2** *v* hrósa; *excl* ~ **the
Lord!** Guði sé dýrð
praiseworthy *adj* lofsverður
prank *n* hrekkur
prattle *n* hjal, babl
prawn *n zool* djúphafsrækja
pray biðja
prayer *n* bæn
preach *v* predika
preacher *n* predikari
preamble *n* formáli
precaution *n* varúðarráðstöfun
precautionary *adj* til varnaðar
precede *v* koma á undan
precedence *n* forgangur
precedent *n* fordæmi
precept *n* lífsregla
precious *adj* dýrmætur
precise *adj* nákvæmur, akkúrat
precisely *adv* nákvæmlega, akkúrat,
einmitt
precision *adj* nákvæmni
precook *v* forsjóða
precursor *n* undanfari, forveri
precussion instruments *n mus*
ásláttarhljóðfæri
predator *n* rándýr
predecessor *n* forveri
predestination *n* forlagatrú
predetermine *v* ákveða fyrirfram
predicament *n* vandræði
predict *v* spá, segja fyrir um
prediction *n* spá, spádómur
predominant *adj* ríkjandi
predominate *v* ríkja, yfirgnæfa,

preeminence *n* yfirburðir
preeminent *adj* yfirburða-
preface *n* formáli
prefer *v* taka fram yfir
preference: what are your ~s? hvað
vilt þú helst?
prefix *n ling* forskeyti
pregnancy *n* þungun, ólétta; **~ test**
þungunarpróf, ólétttupróf
pregnant *adj* þungaður, óléttur,
ófrískur, með barni
prehistoric *adj* forsögulegur: **~ art**
list frá forsögulegum tímum
prejudice *n* fordómar
prelate *n* biskup, hefðarklerkur
preliminary *adj* undirbúnings-,
bráðabirgða-
prelude *n* forleikur
premature *adj* ótímabær
premeditate *v* yfirvega, undirbúa
premeditation *n* ásetningur
premier *n* æðstur, fremstur
premiere *n* frumsýning
premises *n* forsenda
premium *n (insurance)* iðgjald;
(award) verðlaun; *(bonus)*
aukagjald
premonition *n* hugboð
preoccupy *v* gagntaka
preparation *n* undirbúningur
prepare *v* undirbúa
prepared *adj* undirbúinn; **~ dish**
tilbúinn réttur
preposition *n ling* forsetning
prerequisite *n* forsenda, skilyrði
prerogative *n* forréttindi
prescribe *v* fyrirskipa; *(advice)*
ráðleggja; **~ medicine** skrifa
lyfseðil
prescription *n* fyrirskipun; *med*
lyfseðill, resept
presence *n* nærvera
present 1 *adj (current)* núverandi;
(here) viðstaddur; *(topic)* umræddur:
the ~ author umræddur rithöfundur; *ling* nútíðar-; **2** *n (gift)* gjöf;
(time) líðandi stund, nútíminn;

at ~ núna; **3** *v (introduce)* kynna;
(show) sýna; *(theater)* sýna; *(give)*
afhenda
present participle *n ling* lýsingarháttur nútíðar
present perfect *n ling* núliðin tíð
present tense *n ling* nútíð
presentation *n (introduction)* kynning; *(of awards etc)* afhending;
(social) framsetning
preservatives *n* rotvarnarefni
preserve 1 *n (jam)* sulta; *(fruits)*
niðursoðnir ávextir; *(nature)*
verndarsvæði; **2** *v* varðveita,
geyma; *(jam)* sulta; *(fruits)* sjóða
niður; *(nature)* friða
preserved *adj* verndaður
president *n (head of state)* forseti:
~ of Iceland forseti Íslands; *(of a
company)* forstjóri
press 1 *n (newspaper)* pressa, blöð:
the ~ pressan, **~ conference** blaða-
mannafundur, **~ photographer**
blaðaljósmyndari; *(book publisher)*
útgáfufyrirtæki, bókaforlag; *(by
crowd)* troðningur; *(by stress)* álag;
(machine) pressa: **paper ~** blaða-
pressa; **2** *v* ýta, þrýsta: **~ the button** ýttu á hnappinn; *(with an iron)*
pressa: **~ pants** pressa buxurnar
pressing *adv* áríðandi
pressure *n* þrýstingur
prestige *n* virðing
prestigious *adj* virtur: **~ awards**
virt verðlaun, **~ university** virtur
háskóli
presumably *adv* sennilega, líklega
presume *v (consider)* álíta, telja;
(dare) dirfast, voga
presumed *adj* álitinn, talinn: **~ dead**
talin(n) af
presumption *n (view)* álit; *(arrogance)* hroki
presuppose *v* ganga út frá, gera ráð
fyrir
presupposition *n* forsenda
pretence *n (pretending)* uppgerð;

(false reason) yfirskin: **on false ~s** á fölskum forsendum

pretend *v* þykjast

pretension *n (right)* tilkall; *(show off)* sýndarmennska

pretentious *adj* tilgerðarlegur

pretext *n (false reason)* yfirskin; *(reason to avoid)* fyrirsláttur

pretty 1 *adj* fallegur, laglegur, sætur; **2** *adv* ansi, frekar, býsna, heldur: **this is ~ expensive** þetta er ansi dýrt

prevail *v* sigra, hafa betur; *(spread)* ríkja, vera útbreiddur

prevalence *n* útbreiðsla

prevalent *adj* algengur, tíður

prevent *v* koma í veg fyrir, afstýra, hindra: **~ an accident** koma í veg fyrir slys

prevention *n* verndun, varnir, hindrun

preventive *adj* fyrirbyggjandi: **~ measures** fyrirbyggjandi aðgerðir

previous *adj* fyrri

previously *adv* áður, fyrr

prey 1 *n* bráð; **2** *v* lifa á, veiða sér til matar

price *n* verð: **low ~s** lágt verð; **~ per liter** verða á lítra; *phr* **what is the ~ of this?** hvað kostar þetta?

priceless *adj (very precious)* ómetanlegur; *(amusing)* óborganlegur

prick 1 *n* stunga; **2** *v* stinga, pikka

pride *n* stolt: **take ~ in** vera stolt(ur) af

priest *n* prestur

prima facie *phr leg* við fyrstu sýn

primarily *adv* aðallega, fyrst og fremst

primary 1 *adj* frum-, grunn-: **~ school** grunnskóli; **2** *n (elections)* forkosningar

prime *n* frum-, megin-, aðal-, grundvallar; **~ time** besti tíminn; **~ cost** framleiðslukostnaður

prime minister *n* forsætisráðherra

prime number *n* grunntala

primer *n* grundvallarrit, byrjendabók

primeval *adj* fornsögulegur

primitive *adj* frumstæður

prince *n* prins

princess *n* prinsessa

principal 1 *adj* aðal, megin; **2** *n (in school)* skólastjóri

principally *adv* aðallega, helst

principle *n* meginregla, lögmál; **of ~** af prinsipástæðum

print 1 *v* prenta, þrykkja; **2** *n* prent; *(publication)* prentun, útgáfa: **1st ~** fyrsta útgáfa, **out of ~** uppseld; *(mark)* far: **finger~** fingrafar

print out *n* útprentun

printer *n* prentari

printing *n* prentun

prior *adj* fyrri

prior to *prep* á undan

priority *n* forgangur

prison *n* fangelsi

prisoner *n* fangi

Pristina (capital of Kosovo) *N* Pristína (höfuðborg Kósovo)

privacy *n* næði, einkalíf: **I need some ~** ég þarf að fá smá næði; *(secrecy)* leynd

private *adj* einka-, persónulegur: **a ~ message** einkaskilaboð, **~ account** einkareikningur, **~ hospital** einkasjúkrahús, **~ property** einkaeign, **~ school** einkaskóli; *(secret)* leynilegur

privately *adv* einslega

privatization *n* einkavæðing

privilege *n* forréttindi

prize *n* verðlaun; *(lottery)* vinningur

pro *adv* meðfylgjandi

probability *n* líkindi

probable *adj* líklegur, sennilegur: **~ cause** *leg* sennileg ástæða

probably *adv* líklega, sennilega

probation *n* reynslutími; *leg (from prison)* reynslulausn

problem *n* vandamál

problematic *adj* vandasamur

procedure *n* aðferð

proceed *v* halda áfram; **~ to the gate** farið að hliðinu

proceeding *n* framvinda; *leg* málarekstur

proceeds *n* ágóði

process 1 *n (method)* ferli; *(food etc)* úrvinnslu; *leg* málaferli; 2 *v* vinna, meðhöndla: to ~ food vinna mat

processed *adj* unninn: ~ food unnin matvara

procession *n* skrúðganga; *(after funeral)* líkfylgd

processor *n* gjörvi

proclaim *v* kunngera

proclamation *n* opinber yfirlýsing

procrastinate *v* fresta, skjóta á frest

procrastination *n* frestun

procure *v* útvega

prodigal *adj* eyðslusamur; *(biblical)* the ~ son glataði sonurinn

prodigality *n* eyðslusemi

produce 1 *n (product)* vara; *(agricultural)* búvara; *(offsprings)* afkomandi; 2 *v (make)* framleiða, búa til; *(create art)* skapa; *(offsprings)* geta af sér; *(play)* setja upp: ~ A Midsummer Night's Dream að setja upp Draum á Jónsmessu

produce market *n* bændamarkaður

producer *n* framleiðandi

product *n* vara

production *n* framleiðsla

productivity *n* framleiðni

profane 1 *adj* óguðlegur: ~ language guðlast; 2 *v* vanhelga

profess *v* lýsa yfir

profession *n* starf, atvinna; *(admit)* játning

professional 1 *adj* fagmannlegur, atvinnu-, atvinnumaður í: ~ basketball player atvinnumaður í körfubolta, she is very ~ hún er mjög fagmannleg; 2 *n* sérfræðingur, fagmaður, atvinnumaður

professor *n* prófessor: ~ of linguistics prófessor í málvísindum

profile *n* vangasvipur; *(online)* persónulýsing; keep a low ~ láta lítið á sér bera; high-~ politician áberandi stjórnmálamaður

profit *n* gróði, hagnaður

profitable *adj* arðbær; *(useful)* gagnlegur

profiteer *n* okrari

profound *adj* djúpur, djúpstæður

profuse *adj* gegndarlaus

profusion *n* ofgnótt

progeny *n* afkvæmi

program 1 *n comp* forrit; *(evening)* dagskrá; *(concert)* efnisskrá; *(television show)* þáttur; *(political)* stefnuskrá; 2 *v comp* forrita

progress 1 *n* framvinda: making ~ tekur framförum, miðar vel áfram; in ~ í vinnslu; 2 *v* miða áfram

progressive 1 *adj* framsækinn; *(increasing)* stigvaxandi; *(continuing)* áframhaldandi; 2 *n* framfarasinni

prohibit *v* banna

prohibited *adj* bannaður: smoking is ~ reykingar eru bannaðar

prohibition *n* bann

project 1 *n* verkefni; 2 *v (plan)* áætla; *(with projector)* varpa; *(show, e.g. feelings)* yfirfæra

projection *n (plan)* áætlun; *(forecast)* spá

projector *n* skjávarpi

pro-life *adj* andstæðingur fóstureyðinga

prolific *adj* frjór, frjósamur, afkastamikill: ~ writer afkastamikill rithöfundur

prologue *n lit* formáli

prolong *v* framlengja

prolongation *n* framlenging

prominent *adj* áberandi

promise 1 *n* loforð, heit: give a ~ gefa loforð; 2 *v* lofa, heita: I ~ not to tell ég lofa að segja ekki frá

promising *adj* efnilegur: ~ actor efnilegur leikari

promote *v (work)* veita stöðuhækkun; *(advertise)* koma á framfæri, auglýsa; *(support)* stuðla að: ~ healthy living stuðla að heilbrigðu líferni

promotion *n (at work)* stöðuhækkun;

(advertisement) kynning, auglýsing; *(support, make stronger)* efling

prompt 1 *adj* fljótur, snöggur; **2** *n* áminning; **3** *v* hvetja; *(theater)* hvísla

promptly *adv* tafarlaust, án tafar

pronoun *n ling* fornafn

pronounce *v* bera fram; *leg* lýsa yfir

pronunciation *n ling* framburður

proof *v* sönnun

prop 1 *n (support)* stoð; *(film/theater)* leikmunur; **2** *v* styðja

propaganda *n* áróður

propagate *v* æxlast *refl*

propagation *n* æxlun; *(spreading)* dreifing

propel *v* knýja

proper *adj* réttur

properly *adv* almennilega, rétt: **do it** ~ gerðu þetta almennilega

properties *n comp* eiginleikar: ~ **of a file** eiginleikar skjals

property *n* eign; *(house)* fasteign; *(land)* landareign; *chem* eiginleiki

prophecy *n* spá, spádómur

prophesy *v* spá, segja fyrir um

prophet *n* spámaður

proportion *n* hlutfall

proportional *adj* hlutfallslegur

proposal *n* uppástunga, tillaga; *(of marriage)* bónorð

propose *v* stinga upp á, leggja til; *(plan)* áforma, ætla; *(for marriage)* biðja, biðla: **she** ~**d to him** hún bað hans

proposition *n* uppástunga, tillaga

propound *v* leggja fram

proprietary *adj* eiganda-

proprietor *n* eigandi

propriety *n* velsæmi

prorogue *v* fresta

prosaic *adj* hversdagslegur

prose *n lit* prósi, óbundið mál

prosecute *v leg* lögsækja

prosecution *n leg* lögsókn

prosecutor *n leg* saksóknari

prosody *n ling* hljómfall

prospect *n (view)* útsýni; *(possibility in the future)* horfur: **good** ~**s** góðar horfur

prospective *adj* líklegur, væntanlegur

prospectus *n* kynningarbæklingur

prosper *v* blómstra

prosperity *n* velmegun

prosperous *adj* sem gengur vel: **a** ~ **business** fyrirtæki sem gengur vel

prostitute *n* vændiskona

prostitution *n* vændi

protagonist *n* aðalpersóna, söguhetja

protect *v* vernda

protected *n* friðaður: ~ **species** friðuð dýrategund

protection *n* verndun, vernd, vörn

protein *n* prótín, hvítuefni: ~ **drinks** prótíndrykkir

protest 1 *n* mótmæli; **2** *v* mótmæla; *(declare)* lýsa yfir

Protestant *n* mótmælandi: **the** ~ **Church** kirkja mótmælanda

protocol *n* siðareglur (utanríkis-þjónustunnar): **according to the** ~ samkvæmt siðareglum

proton *n chem* róteind

prototype *n* frumgerð, fyrirmynd

proud *adj* stoltur, hreykinn

proudly *adv* með stolti

prove *v* sanna; *(turn out to be)* reynast: **he** ~**d to be right** hann reyndist hafa rétt fyrir sér

proverb *n lit* málsháttur

provide *v* útvega

provided *conj* að því gefnu

provident *adj* fyrirhyggjusamur

province *n* fylki

provision *n* birgðir

provocation *n* ögrun, eggjun

provocative *adj* ögrandi, storkandi

provoke *v* ögra, espa, eggja, egna

prowess *n* kjarkur

prowl *v* laumast, læðupokast

proximate *adj (closest)* nálægasti, næsti

proximity *n* nálægð

proxy *n* umboð

prudence *n* skynsemi, hagsýni
prudent *adj* skynsamur, hagsýnn;
(careful) gætinn
prune *n* sveskja: ~ **juice** sveskjusafi
pry *v* hnýsast
psalm *n* sálmur: ~ **book** sálmabók
pseudonym *n* dulnefni
psyche *n* sál, andi
psychiatrist *n* geðlæknir
psychiatry *n* geðlækningar
psychic 1 *adj* geðrænn, sálrænn,
andlegur; *(supernatural)* dulrænn,
yfirnáttúrulegur; *(sensitive to
supernatural forces)* skyggn: **she
is** ~ hún er skyggn; **2** *n (medium)*
sjáandi, miðill
psychological *adj* sálfræðilegur,
sálfræði-
psychologist *n* sálfræðingur
psychology *n* sálfræði
psychopath *n* geðsjúklingur,
siðblindingi
psychotherapy *n* sálfræðimeðferð
ptarmigan *n zool* rjúpa
pub *n* pöbb, krá, bar, knæpa
puberty *n* kynþroskaaldur,
kynþroskaskeið
pubis *n* lífbein
public 1 *adj (open to everyone)*
almennings-: ~ **telephone** almenningssími, ~ **toilet** almenningsklósett, ~ **transportation** almenningssamgöngur; *(governmental)* opinber:
~ **building** opinber bygging, ~
servant opinber starfsmaður, ríkis-
starfsmaður; **2** *n* the ~ almenningur
public school *n* ríkisskóli
publication *n* útgáfa
publicity *n* almenn eftirtekt
publicly *adv* opinberlega
publish *v* gefa út
publisher *n* útgefandi
publishing 1 *adj* útgáfu-: ~ **house**
útgáfufyrirtæki; **2** *n* útgáfustarfsemi
pudding *n* búðingur
puddle *n* pollur
puerile *adj* barnalegur

puff 1 *n* más; **2** *v* mása, blása
puffin *n zool* lundi
pull 1 *n* tog, togkraftur; *(influence)*
ítök; **2** *v* draga
pull out *v* leggja af stað
pull through *v* komast af
pull up *v* stöðva
pullover *n* peysa
pulp *n* aldinkjöt
pulpit *n* ræðustóll; *(church)*
predikunarstóll
pulse *n* púls
puma *n zool* púma
pumice *n* vikur
pump 1 *n (air)* pumpa; *(liquids)*
dæla; **2** *v (air)* pumpa, *(liquids)*
dæla
pumpernickel *n* pumpernickel
brauð, ósætt rúgbrauð
pumpkin *n* grasker: ~ **pie** graskers-
baka, ~ **bread** graskersbrauð, ~
seeds graskersfræ
pun *n* orðaleikur
punch 1 *n (blow)* högg; *(drink)* bolla:
fruit ~ ávaxtabolla; **2** *v* slá, kýla
punctual *adj* stundvís
punctuality *n* stundvísi
punctuation *n* greinarmerkjasetning;
(symbols) greinarmerki
puncture *n* stinga gat
pungent *adj* rammur, beiskur
punish *v* refsa, straffa
punishment *n* straff, refsing
punk 1 *adj* pönk-, pönkara-; **2** *n*
pönkari
pupil *n (student)* nemandi; *(of eye)*
sjáaldur
puppet *n* brúða; *(with strings)*
strengjabrúða; *(figuratively)*
strengjabrúða
puppet show *n* brúðusýning
puppy *n zool* hvolpur
purchase 1 *v* kaupa: ~ **a new car**
kaupa nýjan bíl; **2** *n* kaup, innkaup
purchaser *n* kaupandi
pure *adj* hreinn, óblandaður; *(complete)* algjör: ~ **nonsense** algjör

vitleysa; *(not mixed)* hreinn: ~
wool hrein ull, ~ **alcohol** hreinn
vínandi
puree *n* mauk: **pea** ~ baunamauk,
corn ~ maísmauk
purely *adv* algjörlega, eingöngu,
einvörðungu: ~ **by coincidence**
fyrir algjöra tilviljun; ~ **by**
accident fyrir hreina slysni
purgative *n med* laxerandi
purgatory *n* hreinsunareldur
purge *v* hreinsa, hreinsast *refl*
purification *n* hreinsun
purify *v* hreinsa
purist *n* hreinstefnumaður; *(of lan-*
guage) málhreinsunarmaður
puritan *n* hreintrúarmaður, púritani
purity *n* hreinleiki
purple *adj (color)* fjólublár
purport *v* gefa til kynna
purpose *n* tilgangur: ~ **of visit** tilgangur ferðarinnar; **on** ~ viljandi
purse *n* (hand)taska; *(for coins)*
budda
purser *n* bryti; *(on airplanes)*
yfirflugfreyja, yfirflugþjónn
pursue *v (a person)* elta; *(happiness,*
fame) sækjast eftir; *(policy)* fylgja;
(studies) stunda

pursuit *n (of fugitive e.g.)* eftirför;
(of happiness) leit: ~ **of happiness**
leit að hamingju; *(of policy)* fylgd;
(studies) ástundun
pus *n med* gröftur
push 1 *n* ýting; **2** *v* ýta: ~ **a button**
ýta á hnapp; *(through a crowd)*
troðast; *(drugs)* selja
pusher *n (characteristic)* eigin-
hagsmunaseggur; *(drug dealer)*
eiturlyfjasali, dópsali *colloq*
push-up bra *n* brjóstahaldari með
lyftiskálum
put *v* setja, láta: ~ **together** setja
saman; *(in words)* orða; ~ **away**
ganga frá; ~ **on** fara í: ~ **on a**
sweater fara í peysu
puzzle *n (mystery)* ráðgáta; *(jigsaw)*
púsl; *(riddle)* gáta: **a crossword** ~
krossgáta
pyramid *n* píramídi
pyre *n* bálköstur
python *n zool* pýtonslanga

Q

Qatar *N* Katar
Qatari 1 *adj* katarskur; **2** *n* Katari
quack *n med* skottulæknir, fúskari
quad bike *n* fjórhjól
quadrangle *n* ferhyrningur
quadruple *n* ferfaldur
quail *n zool* kornhæna
quaint *adj* sérkennilegur, sérstakur
quake *v* skjálfa, titra
qualification *n* hæfni
qualified *adj* hæfur: **not** ~ ekki hæfur
qualify *v* vera hæfur, uppfylla skilyrði
quality *n* gæði
quandary *n* klípa
quantity *n* magn
quarantine *n* sóttkví
quarrel 1 *n* rifrildi; **2** *v* rífast, deila á
quarry *n* bráð
quarter *n* fjórðungur; *(time)* korter:
~ **past one** korter yfir eitt; *(year)*
ársfjórðungur; *(of a dollar)* tuttugu
og fimm cent; *(part of a city)* hverfi:
the Italian ~ ítalska hverfið;
(soldiers) herbúðir; *sports* ~ **final**
fjórðungsúrslit
quarterly 1 *n* ársfjórðungsrit; **2** *adv*
árfjórðungslega
quartet *n mus* kvartett
queen *n* drottning: ~ **of Denmark**
Danadrottning, ~ **of England**
Englandsdrottning
quell *v* bæla niður
quench *v* slökkva
query *n* spurning, fyrirspurn
quest *n* leit
question 1 *n* spurning; **the person
in** ~ manneskjan sem um ræðir;
out of the ~ kemur ekki til greina;

2 *v* spyrja; *(by police)* yfirheyra;
(doubt) efa: **I** ~ **your intergrety** ég
efast um heiðarleika þinn
question mark *n ling* spurning-
armerki
questionable *adj* vafasamur
questionnaire *n* spurningalisti
queue *n* röð; **2** *v* standa í biðröð
quibble *n* útúrsnúningur
quick *adj (fast)* fljótur; *(smart)* klár,
skýr
quickly *adv* fljótt
quicksand *n* kviksandur
quicksilver *n* kvikasilfur
quiet 1 *adj* hljóðlátur, lágvær; *(calm)*
rólegur; *(not talking)* þögull;
(color) mildur; **2** *n* kyrrð, ró: **in
peace and** ~ í kyrrð og ró
quietly *adv* hljóðlátlega, rólega
quinoa *n* inkanjálafræ, kínóa
quit *v* hætta; *(leave)* yfirgefa, fara frá
quite *adv (totally)* algjörlega, alveg,
gjörsamlega: **I** ~ **agree** ég er
algjörlega sammála; *(a bit)* frekar,
ansi: **you are** ~ **good at this** þú ert
ansi góð(ur) í þessu
quiver *v* skálfa
quixotic *adj* óraunhæfur
quiz *n (in school)* skyndipróf;
(game) spurningakeppni
quota *n* kvóti
quotation *n* tilvitnun; *(offer)* verðtilboð; *(market price)* markaðsverð
quotation mark *n* gæsalappir
quote *v* vitna í; *(~ a price)* gefa upp
(söluverð)

R

rabbi *n* rabbíni
rabbit *n zool* kanína
race 1 *n (speed)* keppni; *(of people)* kynþáttur; 2 *v* keppa
racial *adj* kynþátta-
racialism *n* kynþáttafordómar
racism *n* kynþáttafordómar
rack *n (for clothes)* fatahengi, fataslá; *(for luggage)* farangurshilla; ~ **of lamb** lambahryggur
racket *n sports* spaði
racquetball *n sports* veggtennis
radiance *n* ljómi
radiant *adj* geislandi
radiate *v* geisla
radiation *n* útgeislun, geislun
radiator *n* (miðstöðvar)ofn
radical *adj* róttækur
radio 1 *n* útvarp; *(for communication)* talstöð; 2 *v* útvarpa
radioactive *adj* geislavirkur
radish *n* radísa, hreðka
radius *n* radíus
raffle *n* tombóla
rag *n* tuska
rage *n* ofsi, bræði
ragout *n* ragú
raid 1 *n* áhlaup; 2 *v* gera áhlaup, gera árás
rail *n (train)* teinn, brautarteinn
railing *n* rimlagirðing; *(on stairs)* handrið
railroad *n* járnbraut: **there are no ~s in Iceland** það eru engar járnbrautir á Íslandi
railway *n* járnbraut
railway station *n* járnbrautarstöð
rain 1 *n* regn, rigning: **looks like ~** það virðist ætla að rigna; 2 *v* rigna: **it ~s every day** það rignir á hverjum degi, **it's ~ing** það rignir

rain hat *n* regnhattur
rain shower *n* regnskúr
raincoat *n* regnkápa, regnjakki, regnstakkur
rainproof *adj* regnþéttur, regnheldur
rainy *adj* rigningar-: ~ **day** rigningardagar
raise *v (lift)* lyfta; *(cause)* vekja; *(a question)* vekja máls á; *(children)* ala upp
raisin *n* rúsína
rally 1 *n (political)* fjöldafundur; *(car race)* kappakstur, rallý; 2 *v* flykkjast, fylkja; *(recover)* hressast
ram *n zool* hrútur
ramble *v* ráfa, reika um
ramp *n* rampur
rampage *n* berseksgangur: **go on a ~** ganga berserksgang
rampant *adj* hömlulaus
rampart *n* varnarveggjur
rancor *n* óvild
random *adj* af handahófi, handahófskenndur: ~ **comments** handahófskenndar athugasemdir; ~ **people** hinir og þessir
range 1 *n* röð; *(of time)* tímabil: **a long-~ forecast** langtímaspá; *(distance)* færi: **a ~ of 10 meters** tíu metra færi; 2 *v* stilla upp, raða
ranger *n (in parks)* landvörður; *(police)* lögreglumaður
rank 1 *n* staða, gráða; 2 *v* raða upp
ransack *v* leita vel, snúa á hvolf, umturna; *(robbery)* ræna: **the room was ~ed** herberginu var snúið á hvolf
ransom 1 *n* lausnargjald; 2 *v* greiða lausnargjald
rape 1 *n* nauðgun; 2 *v* nauðga: **she was ~d** henni var nauðgað

raped *adj* nauðgaður

rapeseed oil *n* repjuolía

rapid *adj* hraður, snöggur

rapidly *adv* hratt, snöggt

rapids *n* flúðir

rapist *n* nauðgari

rapport *n* samkennd

rapt *adj* hugfanginn

rapture *n* sæluvíma

rare *adj* sjaldgæfur; *(of meat)* snöggsteiktur: ~ **steak** snöggsteikt steik, ~ **meat** snöggsteikt kjöt; *(of fish)* léttsteiktur

rarely *adv* sjaldan

rascal *n* þrjótur, óþekktarormur

rash 1 *adj* fljótfær; 2 *n* útbrot

raspberry *n* hindber

rat *n zool* rotta; *expr* **I smell a ~** það er ekki allt með felldu

rate 1 *n* hlutfall; 2 *v* meta

rather *adv* frekar; ~ **than** frekar en: **I would ~ work than read** ég myndi frekar vilja vinna en að lesa

ratify *v* staðfesta

ratio *n* hlutfall

ration *n* skammtur

rational *adj* skynsamlegur: **be ~!** vertu skynsamur!

rationale *n* rökstuðningur

rationality *n* skynsemi

rationalize *v* rökstyðja, réttlæta

rattle *n* skrölta, hringla

rattlesnake *n* skröltormur

ravage *v* eyðileggja

rave *v (due to fever)* vera með óráði; *(talk highly of)* dásama; *(dance)* reifa

raven *n zool* hrafn, krummi *colloq*

ravine *n* gil, gljúfur

ravioli *n* ravíólí

raw *adj* hrár, ósoðinn: ~ **fish** hrár fiskur

ray *n* geisli

razor *n* rakhnífur; *(electric)* rakvél

razor blade *n* rakvélarblað

reach *v* ná: **I ~ed to the ceiling** ég náði upp í loft; *(hand to)* rétta

react *v* bregðast við

reaction *n* viðbragð; *phys* hvarf

reactionary *n* afturhaldsseggur

reactor *n* **nuclear ~** kjarnaofn

read 1 *adj* lesinn: **she is well ~** hún er vel lesin; 2 *v* lesa: ~ **a book** lesa bók, ~ **a thermometer** lesa á hitamæli; *(interpret)* túlka: ~ **a face** túlka svipbrigði

reader *n* lesandi; *(title)* dósent: ~ **in English** dósent í ensku; *(book)* lestrarbók

readily *adv* fúslega

reading *n* lestur, upplestur: **poetry ~** ljóðaupplestur; *(material for)* lesefni: **summer ~** sumarlesefni; *(interpretation)* skilningur; *(of thermometer, e.g.)* aflestur

ready *adj* tilbúinn

ready-made *adj* tilbúinn

reaffirm *v* ítreka

real *adj* raunverulegur, sannur

real estate *n* fasteign: ~ **agent** fasteignasali

realism *n* raunsæi; *(in literature)* raunsæisstefna, realismi

realist *n* raunsæismaður, raunsæisstefnumaður

realistic *adj (characteristic)* raunsær: **let me be ~** ég ætla að vera raunsæ(r); *(possible)* raunhæfur: **you have a ~ possibility** þú átt raunhæfan möguleika

reality *n* raunveruleiki, veruleiki

realize *v* gera sér ljóst; *(do, complete)* framkvæma

really *adv* í raun og veru; *(emphatic)* virkilega, raunverulega: **he is ~ old** hann er virkilega gamall; *(as a question)* **really?** í alvöru?, er það?

realm *n (of a king)* konungsríki; *(figuratively)* svið, vettvangur; ~ **of the dead** ríki hinna dauðu

reap *v* uppskera

reaper *n* kornskurðarmaður: **the grim ~** maðurinn með ljáinn

reappear *v* birtast aftur

rear *n* bak-, aftur-: ~ **door** bakdyr, ~
  light afturljós; *(side)* bakhlið
reason *n* ástæða, tilgangur: ~ **for**
  travel tilgangur ferðalags; *(judgement)* vit, dómgreind; **within** ~
  innan skynsamlegra marka
reasonable *adj* skynsamur; *(price, e.g.)*
  sanngjarn; *(weather)* sæmilegur; *leg*
  beyond ~ **doubt** hafið yfir skyn-
  samlegan vafa
reasonably *adv* skynsamlega
reassure *v* fullvissa
rebate *n* afsláttur
rebel 1 *n* uppreisnarmaður; **2** *v* gera
  uppreisn, mótmæla
rebellion *n* uppreisn
rebellious *adj* uppreisnargjarn
rebirth *n* endurfæðing
rebound 1 *n* endurkast; **he is on the**
  ~ hann er nýhættur í sambandi; **2** *v*
  endurkastast
rebuff 1 *n* synjun; **2** *v* synja
rebuild *v* endurbyggja, gera upp
rebuilt *adj* enduruppgerður
rebuke *v* skamma, ávíta
rebut *v* hrekja
recall 1 *n* *(of memory)* minning; *(of
  goods)* afturköllun; **2** *v* *(memory)*
  muna; *(goods)* afturkalla; *(ambassador)* kveðja heim
recapitulation *n* útdráttur, samantekt
recapture *v* endurvekja
recede *v* hörfa
receipt *n* móttaka; *(for purchase)*
  kvittun: **could I get a ~?** gæti ég
  fengið kvittun?
receive *v* taka við
receiver *n* móttakandi, viðtakandi;
  (telephone) símtól; *(radio)* viðtæki
recent *adj* nýlegur
recently *adv* nýlega
reception *n* móttaka
reception desk *n* afgreiðsluborð
receptionist *n* móttökustjóri, starfsmaður í móttöku
receptor *n* nemi
recess *v* hlé

recession *n* samdráttur, kreppa,
  efnahagslægð
recipe *n* uppskrift
recipient *n* viðtakandi, móttakandi
reciprocal *adj* gagnkvæmur
reciprocate *v* endurgjalda
recital *n* flutningur; *mus* tónleikar:
  piano ~ píanótónleikar
recitation *n* upptalning
recite *v* fara með, flytja
reckon *v* reikna; *(consider)* telja
reckoned *adj* talinn: **this book is ~
  a masterpiece** þessi bók er talin
  vera meistaraverk
reclaim *v* endurheimta
reclamation *n* endurkrafa
recluse *n* einbúi
recognition *n* viðurkenning; *(know)*
  það að þekkja: **he is beyond ~**
  hann er óþekkjanlegur
recognize *v* *(know)* þekkja; *(accept)*
  viðurkenna
recoil *v* hörfa frá
recollect *v* muna, minnast
recommend *v* mæla með: **what do
  you** ~ með hverju mælirðu?
recommendation *n* meðmæli
recompense *n* laun
reconcile *v* sætta
reconciliation *n* sættir, samkomulag
record 1 *n* *(list)* skrá; *leg (crimes)*
  sakaskrá; *(cv)* ferilsskrá; *(music)*
  (hljóm)plata; *(best result)* met:
  world ~ heimsmet; **on ~** skjalfest;
  off the ~ í trúnaði; **2** *v* skrá,
  skrásetja; *(music)* taka upp; *(a
  show)* sýna
record shop *n* tónlistarverslun
recorder *n* *mus* blokkflauta: **play the
  ~** spila á blokkflautu; *(electronic)*
  upptökutæki; *(e.g. of a book)* ritari,
  skrásetjari
recording *n* upptaka
recording studio *n* upptökustúdíó,
  hljóðver
recount 1 *n* endurtalning; **2** *v* telja
  aftur

recoup

regard 303

recoup *v* bæta, endurheimta
recover *v* fá aftur, endurheimta; *med (from disease)* ná sér: **have you ~ed yet?** ertu búin(n) að ná þér?
recovery *n* bati: **quick ~** skjótur bati
recreational *adj* til skemmtunar
recruit 1 *n* nýliði; 2 *v (more people)* ráða nýtt fólk, safna liði, endurnýja mannskapinn
recruitment *n* endurnýjun; *(to army)* herskráning
rectangle *n* rétthyrningur
rectification *n* leiðrétting
rectify *v* leiðrétta
rectum *n anat* endaþarmur
recur *v* koma upp aftur
recurrence *n* endurtekning
recurrent *adj* endurtekinn
recyclable *adj* endurvinnanlegur
recycle *v* endurvinna
recycling *n* endurvinnsla: **~ bin** endurvinnslutunna, tunna fyrir endurvinnanlegt sorp
red *adj (color)* rauður: **~ pepper** rauð paprika, **~ blood cell** rautt blóðkorn, **~ carpet** rauður dregill, **~ light** rautt ljós, **~ wine** rauðvín, **R~ Cresent** Rauði hálfmáninn, **R~ Cross** Rauði krossinn, **R~ Sea** Rauðahaf;
red currant *n* rifsber
red tape *n* skriffinnska
redeem *v* fá aftur, endurheimta
redemption *n* endurkaup; *(salvation)* björgun
redfish *n* karfi
red-handed *adj* staðinn að verki
redpoll *n* auðnutittlingur
redress *v* lagfæra
reduce *v* minnka, smækka, draga úr; **~ weight** létta; **~ prices** lækka verð
reduction *n* lækkun
redundance *n* óþarfi
redundancy *n* óþarfi
redundant *adj* óþarfur
reel *n* spóla
refer to *v* vísa í

referee *n* dómari
reference *n* tilvitnun; *(source of information)* heimild; *(list of sources)* heimildaskrá; *(for recommendation)* meðmæli; *(letter of recommendation)* meðmælabréf
reference book *n* uppsláttarrit
referendum *n* þjóðaratkvæðagreiðsla
refine *v* hreinsast; *(improve)* betrumbæta
refined *adj (oil, sugar)* hreinsaður; *(language, taste etc)* fágaður
refined sugar *n* hvítur sykur
refinery *n* hreinsunarstöð
reflect *v* endurspegla; *(thinking)* íhuga
reflection *n* endurkast, speglun; *(thinking)* íhugun
reflector *n* **safety ~** endurskinsmerki
reflex *n* viðbragð
reflexive *adj ling* afturbeygður: **~ pronoun** afturbeygt fornafn
reform 1 *n* umbót, endurbót; 2 *v* bæta, endurbæta
reformation *n* umbót; *(of religion)* siðaskipti
reformer *n* umbótasinni
refrain *v* halda aftur að sér, stilla sig um: **~ from smoking** stilla sig um að reykja
refresh *v* hressa upp á; *comp* endurhlaða
refreshing *adj* hressandi, frískandi
refreshments *n* endurnæring; *(to serve)* drykkir, veitingar
refrigeration *n* kæling
refrigerator *n* ísskápur, kæliskápur, kælir
refuge *n* skjól
refugee *n* flóttamaður: **~ camp** flóttamannabúðir
refund *n* endurgreiðsla
refusal *n* neitun, synjun
refuse *v* neita, synja
refutation *n* afsönnun
refute *v* hrekja
regal *adj* konunglegur
regard 1 *n (respect)* virðing; *(greetings)*

kveðja: **give my ~s to** ... skilaðu
kveðju til ... ; **with ~ to** viðvíkjandi; **2** v *(look at)* horfa á; *(see as)*
líta á: **I ~ you as a friend** ég lít á
þig sem vin
regarding *prep* viðvíkjandi, að því
er varðar
regenerate v endurlífga, blása nýju
lífi í
regeneration n endurreisn, endurnýjun
regime n stjórnarfyrirkomulag,
stjórn
regiment n hersveit
region n svæði
regional adj svæðisbundinn,
staðbundinn: **~ recipe** uppskrift af
svæðinu
register 1 n skrá; *(of voters)*
kjörskrá; *(in school)* kladdi; *mus*
tónsvið; **2** v skrá
registered mail n ábyrgðarpóstur
registration n skráning: **compulsory ~**
skráningarskylda, **~ form** skráning-
areyðublað, **vehicle ~ documents**
skráningarskírteini ökutækis
registry n skráning; **~ office**
manntalsskrifstofa, þjóðskrá
regret 1 n eftirsjá; **2** v sjá eftir
regular 1 adj reglulegur; *(normal)*
venjulegur, eðlilegur; **~ customer**
fastur viðskiptavinur, fastakúnni;
ling **~ verb** reglulegar sagnir; **~
hours** skrifstofutími
regularly adv reglulega
regulate v stjórna
regulation n stjórnun
regulator n stillir
rehabilitate v *(house)* endurbyggja;
(patients) endurhæfa
rehabilitation n endurnýjun; *(patients)*
endurhæfing
rehearsal n æfing
rehearse v æfa
re-heat v hita upp: **~ed** upphitaður
reign n *(time)* valdatíð; *(government)*
stjórn, yfirráð
reimburse v endurgreiða

reimbursement n endurgreiðsla
reindeer n *zool* hreindýr
reindeer lichen *flora* n hreindýramosi
reinforce v styrkja, efla
reinforcement n styrking, efling;
(more people) liðsstyrkur
reinstate v setja aftur í embætti
reinstatement n endurskipun
reiterate v ítreka
reiteration n ítrekun
reject v hafna
rejection n höfnun
rejoice v fagna
rejoinder n svar
rejuvenate v yngjast
rejuvenation n ynging
relapse v hraka
relate v tengja, tengjast *refl*
related adj skyldur
relation n tengsl, samband
relationship n samband; *(love)*
ástarsamband: **we have a ~** við
erum saman
relative 1 adj hlutfallslegur; **2** n
ættingi
relatively adv hlutfallslega; *(rather)*
frekar: **this is ~ important** þetta er
frekar mikilvægt
relatives n ættingjar: **I have ~ in
Iceland** ég á ættingja á Íslandi
relax v slappa af, slaka á
relaxation n afslöppun, slökun;
(entertainment) afþreying
relaxed adj afslappaður, slakur
relaxing adj afslappandi: **~ music**
afslappandi tónlist
release 1 n losun; *(of books, films,
records)* útgáfa; **press ~** blaða-
tilkynning; **2** v losa, sleppa;
(books, films, records) gefa út
relent v láta undan
relentless adj vægðarlaus
relevance n þýðing, mikilvægi
relevant adj viðkomandi, sem skiptir
máli; **this is not ~** þetta kemur
málinu ekki við; **how is this ~?**
hvað kemur þetta málinu við?

reliable *adj* áreiðanlegur, traustur
reliance *n* traust
relic *n* menjar, leifar: **ancient ~s** fornar menjar
relief *n* léttir; *(assistance)* aðstoð, hjálp
relieve *v* létta, lina: **~ the pain** lina þjáningarnar, **~ oneself** létta á sér
religion *n* trú, trúarbrögð
religious *adj* trúaður
religious service *n* messa
reluctance *n* tregða
reluctant *adj* tregur
rely on *v* treysta á, reiða sig á, stóla á *colloq*: **I ~ on you** ég treysti á þig
remain *v* vera eftir; *(continue)* halda áfram; **~ the same** breytast ekki
remainder *n* afgangur
remaining *adj* það sem eftir er
remains *n* leifar: **~ of an old farm** leifar af gömlum bæ
remake *n* endurgerð
remark 1 *n* ummæli; **rude ~** dónaleg athugasemd; **2** *v* segja; *(notice)* taka eftir
remarkable *adj* athyglisverður
remarry *v* giftast aftur
remedy *n* lækning; *(solution)* úrræði
remember *v* muna, muna eftir: **now I ~!** nú man ég!, **do you ~ me?** manstu eftir mér?
remembrance *n* minni
remind *v* minna á
reminder *n* áminning
reminiscence *n* endurminning
reminiscent *adj* minnir á
remission *n* fyrirgefning
remit *v* gefa eftir, láta niður falla; *(money)* senda
remittance *n* greiðsla
remorse *n* iðrun
remote *adj* fjarlægur, afskekktur
remote control *n* fjarstýring
removal *n* flutningur
remove *v* fjarlægja; *(from job)* reka
remunerate *v* launa
remuneration *n* laun, þóknun

renaissance 1 *adj* endurreisnar-; **2** *n* endurreisn: **the R~** endurreisnin; *(era)* endurreisnartímabilið
render *v* veita; *(speechless etc)* gera: **he ~ed me speechless** hann gerði mig orðlausa(n)
rendezvous *n* stefnumót; *(place for)* stefnumótastaður
renew *v* endurnýja: **I ~ed my driver's license** ég endurnýjaði ökuskírteinið mitt
renewal *n* endurnýjun, framlenging
renounce *v* afneita
renovate *v* gera upp: **the kitchen needs to be ~d** það þarf að gera upp eldhúsið
renovation *n* viðgerð: **the ~ was expensive** viðgerðin var dýr
renown *n* orðstír
renowned *adj* frægur
rent 1 *n* leiga: **for ~** til leigu, **how much is the ~?** hver er leigan?; **2** *v* leigja: **I ~ a small apartment** ég leigi litla íbúð, **~ out** leigja út
rental *adj* leigu-: **~ apartment** leiguíbúð, **~ car** bílaleigubíll
renunciation *n* afneitun
repair 1 *n* viðgerð: **shoe ~** skóviðgerð; **2** *v* gera við
repair shop *n* verkstæði
reparable *n* sem hægt er að gera við
repay *v* endurgreiða; endurgjalda: **~ a favor** endurgjalda greiða
repayment *n* endurgreiðsla
repeal *v* ógilda
repeat *v* endurtaka: **please ~ that** gætirðu endurtekið þetta?, gætirðu sagt þetta aftur?
repeated *adj* endurtekinn
repeatedly *adv* aftur og aftur
repel *v* hrekja
repellent 1 *adj* fráhrindandi; **2** *n* fæla: **insect ~** skordýrafæla
repent *v* iðrast
repentance *n* iðrun
repercussion *n* *(accident, war)* eftirköst; *(sound, water)* endurkast

repertoire *n* efnisskrá
repetition *n* endurtekning
rephrase *v* umorða
replace *v (on a shelf)* setja aftur;
  (instead of) koma í stað
replacement *n* endurnýjun; *(of an
  employee)* afleysing
replenish *v* birgja sig upp
replica *n* eftirmynd
reply 1 *n* svar; 2 *v* svara, ansa
report 1 *n* skýrsla: **annual** ~ ársskýrsla;
  school ~ einkunnaspjald; *(in a newspaper)* frásögn; 2 *v* skýra, segja frá,
  gera grein fyrir; *(to the police)* klaga,
  kæra
reporter *n* fréttamaður
repose *n* hvíld; *(calmness)* ró, kyrrð
repository *n* geymsla
represent *v* standa fyrir; *(speak for
  sby)* vera fulltrúi: **she ~s all of us**
  hún er fulltrúi okkar allra; *(theater)*
  leika: ~ **Nora** leika Nóru
representative 1 *adj* fulltrúa-; *(typical
  example)* dæmigerður; 2 *n* fulltrúi
repress *v* kúga, bæla niður
repression *n* kúgun, undirokun
reprimand *v* ávíta
reprint *v* endurprenta
reproach *v* áfellast
reproduce *v* fjölga sér, æxlast;
  (paintings) gera eftirmyndir;
  (theater) enduruppfæra
reproduction *n* æxlun, fjölgun;
  (music, sound) endursköpun;
  (painting) eftirprentun; *(movies)*
  endurgerð
reproductive *adj* æxlunar-: ~ **organs**
  æxlunarfæri
reproof *n* ávítur
reptile *n* skriðdýr
republic *n* lýðveldi
republican *n* lýðveldissinni; *(American
  politics)* repúblikani; **the R~ candidate** frambjóðandi repúblikana
repugnance *n* andstyggð
repugnant *adj* andstyggilegur,
  ógeðslegur

repulsion *n* óbeit, andúð
repulsive *adj* andstyggilegur,
  ógeðslegur
reputation *n* orðstír, mannorð
repute *v* vera álitinn
request 1 *n* beiðni; 2 *v* biðja um
require *v* þurfa, þarfnast: **the room
  ~s cleaning** það þarf að þrífa
  herbergið
required *adj* nauðsynlegur
requirement *n* þörf; *(demand)* skilyrði
requisite 1 *adj* nauðsynlegur; 2 *n*
  nauðsynjar
requisition *n* beiðni; *(demand)*
  skilyrði
rescue 1 *n* björgun; 2 *v* bjarga: ~ **from
  drowning** bjarga frá drukknun
research 1 *n* rannsóknir: **I do** ~ ég
  stunda rannsóknir; 2 *v* rannsaka;
  (academic) stunda rannsóknir,
  sinna fræðistörfum
researcher *n* fræðimaður
resemblance *n* svipur: **there is no
  ~ between them** það er enginn
  svipur með þeim
resemble *v* líkjast
reservation *n* fyrirvari; *(doubt)*
  efasemdir; *(hotel)* bókun, pöntun:
  I would like to make a ~ ég
  myndi vilja bóka herbergi; *(at restaurant)* frátekið borð: **I have a** ~
  ég á frátekið borð; *(piece of land)*
  verndarsvæði
reserve 1 *n* verndarsvæði; 2 *v* geyma;
  ~ **a table** taka frá borð
reserved *adj* frátekinn: ~ **table**
  frátekið borð
reservoir *n* vatnsgeymir; *(figurative)*
  hafsjór: ~ **of knowledge** hafsjór af
  fróðleik
reside *v* búa, eiga heima
residence *n* búseta; *(home)* heimili,
  aðsetur; *(house)* íbúðarhús
resident 1 *adj* búsettur, stað-: **a** ~
  bird staðfugl; 2 *n* íbúi
residue *n* afgangur, leifar
resign *v* segja upp

resignation *n* uppsögn
resist *v* streitast á móti, standast: **I couldn't ~** ég stóðst ekki mátið
resistance *n* andspyrna, mótspyrna
resolute *adj* ákveðinn, einbeittur
resolution *n* einbeitni, viljastyrkur; *(of a meeting)* ályktun; *(way to solve)* (úr)lausn
resolve *v (decide)* ákveða; *(parliament)* álykta; *(a crisis)* leysa: **~ a problem** leysa vandamál
resort *n* ferðamannastaður: **spa ~** baðstaður, **ski ~** skíðastaður
resound *v* hljóma
resource *n* auðlind: **natural ~s** náttúruauðlindir; *(solution)* úrræði: **this is my last ~** þetta er mín síðasta von
respect *n* virðing, heiður; *(understanding)* skilningur; **with ~ to** með tilliti til; **in some ~** að einhverju leyti
respectful *adj* kurteis
respective *adj* hver fyrir sig
respectively *n* hver um sig
respiration *n* andardráttur
respirator *n* gasgríma, *(in hospital)* öndunargríma
respiratory *adj anat* öndunar-: **~ system** öndunarkerfi, **~ tract** öndunarvegur
respire *v* draga andann
respond *v* svara, ansa
response *n* svar: **in ~ to** sem svar við
responsibility *n* ábyrgð: **take ~** bera ábyrgð
responsible *adj (has responsibilities)* ábyrgur; *(character)* áreiðanlegur
rest **1** *n* hvíld: **he needs ~** hann þarf hvíld; *(leftovers)* afgangur, rest; *mus* þögn; **2** *v* hvílast: **you need to ~** þú þarft að hvílast; *(arms on table)* hvíla
rest home *n* hvíldarheimili
restaurant *n* veitingastaður, matsölustaður: **formal ~** fínn veitingastaður

restoration *n* endurgerð, endurbygging
restore *v (return)* skila aftur; *(build)* gera upp, lagfæra
restored *adj* uppgerður, endurbyggður
restrain *v* halda í skefjum
restraint *n* aðhald
restrict *v* takmarka
restricted *adj* takmarkaður, lokaður fyrir almenningi: **~ area** lokað svæði
restriction *n* takmörkun, hömlur
restroom *n* snyrting: **ladies' ~** kvennasnyrting, **mens' ~** karlasnyrting, **where is the ~?** hvar er snyrtingin?, hvar er klósettið?
result **1** *n* niðurstaða; árangur; **2** *v* leiða til, enda með
resume *v* byrja aftur
resumé *n* ágrip
resurgence *n* endurvakning
retail **1** *n* smásala: **~ price** smásöluverð; **2** *v* selja í smásölu
retailer *n* smásali, smákaupmaður
retailing *n* smásala
retain *v* varðveita
retaliate *v* hefna sín
retaliation *n* hefnd
retard *v* hefta, hindra
retardation *n (mental)* þroskahömlun
retention *n* varðveisla
retina *n anat* sjónhimna
retinue *n* fylgdarlið
retire *v (old age)* fara á eftirlaun; *(to your room)* draga sig í hlé; *(in battle)* hörfa
retired *adj* kominn á eftirlaun: **she is ~** hún er komin á eftirlaun
retouch *v* lagfæra
retrace *v* fara yfir aftur
retread *v* sóla
retreat *v* hörfa
retrench *v* skera niður
retrenchment *n* niðurskurður
retrieve *v* endurheimta; *comp* **~ a file** endurheimta skjal
retrospect *n* **in ~** þegar litið er til baka

retrospection *n* endurminning
return *n* *(going back)* endurkoma, heimkoma; *econ (profit)* hagnaður, gróði; *(to library etc)* skil; ~ **ticket** miði báðar leiðir; **in** ~ í staðinn; **2** *v* koma aftur; *(~ a book etc)* skila; *(reward)* launa, gjalda; *(profit)* gefa af sér; ~ **to sender** endursendist
returnable *n* má skila
reveal *v* sýna, opinbera
revel *n* svallveisla
revelation *n* afhjúpun, opinberun
reveller *n* sukkari
revelry *n* sukk, svall
revenge 1 *n* hefnd; **2** *v* hefna sín
revenue *n* *econ* (ríkis)tekjur
revere *v* dýrka
reverence *n* lotning, djúp virðing
reverential *adj* virðingafullur
reverie *n* draumórar
reversal *n* viðsnúningur
reverse 1 *n* *(on a record, coin)* bakhlið; *(car)* bakkgír; *(clothing)* ranga; **2** *v* snúa við; *(car)* bakka: **drive in** ~ keyra í bakkgír; *(verdict)* ógilda
revert *v* snúa aftur
review 1 *n* upprifjun; *(of a book)* gagnrýni, ritdómur; *(of music, play)* gagnrýni; **2** *v* rifja upp: ~ **for an exam** rifja upp fyrir próf; *(a book, play)* gagnrýna: ~ **a novel** gagnrýna skáldsögu
revise *v* endurskoða
revision *n* endurskoðun; *(new edition)* endurskoðuð útgáfa
revival *n* *(from coma)* endurlífgun; *(of traditions)* endurvakning
revive *v* endurlífga
revocable *adj* afturkallanlegur
revocation *n* afturköllun, ógilding
revoke *v* afturkalla, ógilda
revolting *adj* ógeðslegur, viðbjóðslegur
revolution *n* bylting: **the French R~** franska byltingin; *(of earth)* snúningur
revolutionary *adj* byltingarkenndur
reward 1 *n* laun, umbun; *(for finding)*

fundarlaun; **2** *v* launa, verðlauna
rewind *v* spóla til baka
Reykjavik (capital of Iceland) *N* Reykjavík (höfuðborg Íslands): **I live in** ~ ég bý í Reykjavík, **are you from** ~**?** ertu frá Reykjavík?
rhetoric *n* mæskulist
rhetorical *adj* mælskufræði-; *(about style)* tilgerðarlegur; ~ **question** retorísk spurning
rheumatic 1 *adj* *med* gigtveikur; **2** *n* *med* gigtarsjúklingur
rheumatism *n* *med* gigt, gigtveiki
rhinoceros *n* *zool* nashyrningur
rhubarb *n* rabarbari: ~ **jam** rabarbarasulta, ~ **pie** rabarbarabaka
rhyme *n* rím; **nursery** ~ barnaþula
rhythm *n* taktur, hrynjandi
rhythmic *adj* taktfastur; *sports* ~ **gymnastics** nútímafimleikar
rib *n* *anat* rifbein; *(food)* rifjar; *(knitting)* garður
ribbon *n* borði
rice *n* hrísgrjón: ~ **pudding** hrísgrjónagrautur, **wild** ~ villihrísgrjón, **brown** ~ brún hrísgrjón, **basmati** ~ basmati hrísgrjón
rich *adj* *(people)* ríkur, auðugur; *(possessions)* dýrmætur; ~ **food** seðjandi matur; ~ **wine** þungt vín; ~ **voice** hljómmikil rödd
rid *v* losa, hreinsa: **be** ~ **of** vera laus við, **get** ~ **of** losna við
riddle *n* gáta, þraut
ride 1 *n* *(on bus)* ferð: **how much is the** ~**?** hvað kostar ferðin?; *(on horse)* útreiðartúr; **2** *v* *(a bus)* fara með, ferðast með; *(bicycle)* hjóla; *(horseback)* vera á hestbaki, ríða: ~ **a horse** sitja á hesti, ríða hesti
rider *n* *(on a horse)* reiðmaður; *(on a bus, in a car)* farþegi
ridge *n* fjallshryggur
ridicule *v* gera að athlægi
ridiculous *adj* fáránlegur, hlægilegur
riding *n* *(horses)* hestamennska
rifle *n* riffill

rift *n* sprunga, gjá
Riga (capital of Latvia) *N* Ríga (höfuðborg Lettlands)
right 1 *adj* réttur: **that's ~** það er rétt; *(to be right)* hafa rétt fyrir sér: **she is ~** hún hefur rétt fyrir sér; *(direction)* hægri: **to the ~** til hægri; **~-handed** rétthentur; **all ~** allt í lagi; **2** *n* það sem er rétt; *(to have permission to)* réttur: **publishing ~s** útgáfuréttur, **legal ~s** réttindi; *colloq* **Mr. R~** sá eini rétti; **3** *adv (correct)* rétt; *(straight)* beint: **go ~ home** farðu beint heim; *(exactly)* alveg: **~ in the middle** alveg í miðju; *(immediately)* strax
right now *adv* akkúrat núna, á þessari stundu
righteous *adj* réttlátur
rightly *adv* réttilega
rigid *adj* stífur, stjarfur
rigorous *adj* strangur, harður
rigor *n* harka, harðneskja; *(accuracy)* nákvæmni
rim *n* brún
rime *n* hrím
rind *n* hýði, skorpa, börkur
ring 1 *n (jewelry, circle)* hringur; *(sound from telephone)* hringing; *(sound)* hljómur; **2** *v (call)* hringja; *(bells)* hringja; *(surround)* umkringja
ring binder *n* gatamappa
ringworm *n* hringormur
rinse *v* skola
riot *n* óeirðir, uppþot: **student ~s** stúdentaóeirðir
rip *v* rífa: **it is ~ped** þetta er rifið
rip off *v* rífa af; **that's a ~!** þetta er okur!
ripe *adj* fullþroskaður: **~ fruit** fullþroskaður ávöxtur, **~ vegetables** fullþroskað grænmeti; *expr* **the time is ~ to** það er tími til kominn að
rise 1 *n (small hill)* hæð; *(increase)* hækkun; *(success)* velgengni; **2** *v* rísa: **the sun ~s at six** sólin rís klukkan sex; *(get up)* standa upp;

(increase) aukast, magnast
risk 1 *n* áhætta; **2** *v* taka áhættu
risotto *n* risottó
ritual 1 *adj* helgisiða-: **~ dance** helgisiðadans; **2** *n* siður, helgisiður
rival *n* keppinautur
rivalry *n* samkeppni
river *n* á, fljót: **~ cruise** fljótasigling, **~ boat** fljótabátur; *(of lava)* hraunstraumur
riverbank *n* árbakki
rivulet *n* lækur
roach *n* kakkalakki
road *n* vegur: **~ closed** lokaður vegur, **~ conditions** ástand vega
road map *n* (landa)kort
roam *v* reika, flækjast; *(telephone)* reika
roar *v* öskra
roast 1 *n* steik; **2** *v* steikja; *(~ coffee)* rista
roasted *adj* steiktur í ofni, ristaður
rob *v* ræna
robbed *adj* rændur: **I was ~** ég var rænd(ur)
robber *n* ræningi
robbery *n* rán: **~ band** bankarán
robe *n* skikkja; *(bath~)* sloppur
robot *n* vélmenni
rock 1 *n* grjót, berg, klettur, hamar, bjarg: **~ climbing** klettaklifur; *mus* rokk: **~ band** rokkhljómsveit, **~ and roll** rokk og ról; **2** *v (chair)* rugga; *(make music)* rokka; *(shake)* hrista
rock salmon *n* steinbítur
rock salt *n* geol gróft salt
rock slide *n* geol grjótskriða
rocket *n* eldflaug
rocket salad *n* klettasalat
rockslide *n* bergskriða
rocky *adj* óstöðugur
Rocky Mountains *N* Klettafjöll
Rococo style *n* rókókóstíll
rod *n* stafur, stöng: **fishing ~** veiðistöng
roe *n* hrogn
rogue *n* svikahrappur; *(playful)* prakkari
role *n* hlutverk

roll 1 *n* rúlla: bread ~ rúnnstykki; **2**
v rúlla, velta, veltast *refl*
roll call *n* nafnakall
rolling pin *n* kökukefli
rolling stone *n* eirðarleysingi
roly-poly *adj* þybbinn
romaine *n* romaine salat
romance *n* rómantík; *(love affair)*
ástarævintýri
Romanesque style *n* rómanskur stíll,
hringbogastíll
Romania *N* Rúmenía
Romanian 1 *adj* rúmenskur; **2** *n*
(nationality) Rúmeni; *(language)*
rúmenska
romantic *adj* rómantískur: **a ~
poet** rómantískt skáld, **a ~ place**
rómantískur staður
Romanticism *n* rómantík
Rome (capital of Italy) *N* Róm
(höfuðborg Ítalíu)
romp *n* galsi; *(person)* fjörkálfur
rood *n* kross
roof *n* þak
room *n* herbergi: ~ **number** herbergisnúmer, ~ **service** herbergisþjónusta;
(space) pláss: **is there ~ for me?**
er pláss fyrir mig?; *(opportunity)*
tækifæri
room rate *n* verð á nóttina
roommate *n* herbergisfélagi
rooster *n zool* hani
root *n* rót
rooted *adj* rótgróinn
rope *n* kaðall
rose *n* rós: ~ **water** rósavatn
rosé *n* rósavín
rosemary *n* rósmarín
rostrum *n* ræðustóll
rot *v* rotna
rotation *n* snúningur
rotisserie *adj* grill, grillstaður
rotten *adj* rotinn
rough *adj* hrjúfur; *(difficult)* erfiður:
~ **work** erfiðisvinna; *(not precise)*
grófur, lauslegur: **a ~ draft** gróft
uppkast

roughly *adv* gróflega
round 1 *adj* hringlóttur: **a ~ table**
hringlótt borð; *(planet)* hnöttóttur;
(face) kringluleitur: **she has a ~
face** hún er kringluleit í framan;
(numbers) heill: ~ **number** heil
tala; **2** *n* hringur; *(drive)* rúntur,
hringur; *(sports)* umferð; **3** *v* fara
umhverfis; *(numbers, money)*
jafna; **4** *adv* í hring, í kringum: **all
year ~** allt árið um kring; **5** *prep*
í kringum: ~ **the sun** í kringum
sólina; um: **put a scarf ~ the neck**
settu trefil um hálsinn
round about *n* hringtorg
round-the-clock *adj* allan sólarhringinn: **open ~** opið allan sólarhringinn
round-trip *adj* ferð fram og tilbaka,
ferð báðar leiðir: ~ **ticket** miði
báðar leiðir
roundup *n* smölun: ~ **of the sheep**
smölun; **go to the ~s** fara í réttir
rouse *v* vakna; *(someone else)* vekja;
(make angry) æsa upp
rout *v* reka út
route *n* leið: **en ~** á leiðinni
routine 1 *adj* hefðbundinn, vana-
bundinn; **2** *n* vani, vanagangur; **a
matter of ~** formsatriði
rove *v* flækjast
row 1 *n (on boat)* ár; *(noise)* hávaði;
(a line) röð; *(on a spreadsheet)*
lína; **2** *v* róa: ~ **a boat** róa bát;
(arguing) rífast; *(stand in line)*
standa í röð
rowan *n flora* reynir, reynitré
royal *adj* konunglegur, konungs: **the
~ palace** konungshöllin
royalty *n (king, queen, etc.)* kónga-
fólk; *(payment for art/writing)*
höfundarlaun
rub *v* nudda, nuddast *refl*, núast *refl*:
~ **off** nuddast af
rubber *n* gúmmí
rubbish *n* rusl; *(nonsense)* kjaftæði,
rugl, þvættingur

ruby *n* rúbín
rucksack *n* bakpoki
rude *adj* ókurteis, dónalegur
rudely *adv* dónalega, ókurteisislega
rudiment *n* undirstöðuatriði
rudimentary *adj* undirstöðu-: **a ~ knowledge** undirstöðuþekking
rueful *adj* sorgmæddur
ruffian *n* fantur, hrotti
rug *n* gólfteppi, motta
rugby *n sports* rugby, ruðningur
ruin 1 *n (destruction)* eyðilegging; *(old castle, etc)* rústir; **2** *v* eyðileggja
ruins *n* rústir
rule 1 *n* regla, vani: **as a ~** yfirleitt; *(by king etc)* stjórn, yfirráð; **2** *v* ráða ríkjum; *(decide)* úrskurða: **~ out** útiloka
ruler *n* þjóðhöfingi; *(for drawing)* reglustika
rum *n* romm: **~ and coke** romm í kók
rumor *n* orðrómur, kjaftasaga: **this is just a ~** þetta er bara kjaftasaga
rump *n (meat)* lendarstykki
run 1 *n* hlaup, sprettur; **2** *v* hlaupa: **~ a marathon** hlaupa maraþon; *(car, water, etc)* renna; *(machine)* vera í gangi; *(spread fast)* breiðast hratt út; *(quick visit)* skreppa, skjótast: **~ downtown** skreppa í bæinn; *(business)* reka: **I ~ a small business** ég rek lítið fyrirtæki; *(in elections)* vera í framboði; **~ across** rekast á; **~ after** hlaupa á eftir; **~ away** hlaupast á brott, **~ down** keyra á; **~ into** keyra á; **~ out of fuel** verða bensínlaus

runaway *n* flugbraut
runner *n* hlaupari; *(for errands)* sendill; *(rug)* dregill
running *n* hlaup; *(a company)* rekstur; *(a machine)* gangur
running shoes *n* hlaupaskór
running water *n* rennandi vatn
runny nose *n med* nefrennsli; **I have a ~** ég er með nefrennsli
rural *adj* sveita-: **~ area** sveit
ruse *n* klækur
rush 1 *n* flýtir, ös; **2** *v* þjóta, æða; *(~ someone)* reka á eftir: **don't ~ me!** ekki reka á eftir mér!
rush hour *n* háannatími
rusk *n* tvíbaka
Russia *N* Rússland: **I'm from ~** ég er frá Rússlandi
Russian 1 *adj* rússneskur; **2** *n (nationality)* Rússi; *(language)* rússneska: **I speak ~** ég tala rússnesku
rust 1 *n* ryð; **2** *v* ryðga
rustic *n* sveita-: **~ bread** sveitabrauð, **~ style** sveitastíll; *(rough)* grófur, óheflaður
rusty *adj* ryðgaður: **~ car** ryðgaður bíll; *(rough)* **my Icelandic is a bit ~** íslenskan mín er pínu ryðguð; *(old-fashioned)* gamaldags
rut *n* hjólfar
rutabaga *n* rófa
Rwanda *N* Rúanda
Rwandan 1 *adj* rúandskur; **2** *n (nationality)* Rúandamaður
rye *n* rúgur: **~ bread** rúgbrauð

S

Sabbath *n* sabbatsdagur
sabotage 1 *n* skemmdarverk; 2 *v*
vinna skemmdarverk, eyðileggja,
skemma
saccharin *n* sakkarín
sack 1 *n* sekkur, poki; ~ of potatoes
kartöflusekkur; *expr (get fired)* get
the ~ vera rekinn; *expr (go to bed)*
hit the ~ fara í rúmið; 2 *v (put in
sacks)* sekkja; *(rob)* ræna
sacrament *n* sakramenti
sacred *adj* heilagur
sacred music *n* kirkjutónlist
sacrilege *n* helgispjöll
sad *adj (feeling)* leiður, dapur, sorgmæddur: I feel ~ ég er leið(ur);
(film, books) sorglegur: this is a
very ~ story þetta er mjög sorgleg
saga
saddle *n (to sit in)* hnakkur; *(mountain)* hryggur, ás; *(meat)* hryggur:
~ of lamb lambahryggur
sadism *n* kvalalosti
sadly *adv* því miður: ~, I have to go
því miður verð ég að fara
sadness *n* leiði
safe *adj* öruggur, traustur, áhættulaus:
~ sex öruggt kynlíf, feel ~ vera
öruggur; be on the ~ side hafa
varann á
safely *adv* varlega: drive ~! keyrðu
varlega!
safety *n* öryggi: road ~ umferðaröryggi, ~ belt öryggisbelti,
bílbelti, ~ earmuff heyrnaskjól, ~
glasses hlífðargleraugu, ~ jacket
öryggisvesti, ~ pin öryggisnæla
saffron *n* saffran
saga *n* fornsaga: the ~s of Icelanders Íslendingasögurnar; the
legendary ~s fornaldarsögurnar

sagacious *adj* skarpskyggn
sagacity *n* skarpskyggni
sage *n (person)* spekingur; *(herb)*
salvía
Sagittarius *n astro* Bogmaðurinn
sail 1 *n (equipment)* segl: lower the
~s dragið niður seglin; 2 *v* sigla
sailboat *n* seglskúta
sailing *n* siglingar: ~ instructor
siglingakennari
sailor *n* sjómaður, háseti
saint *n* dýrlingur
salad *n* salat: ~ bar salatbar, chicken
~ kjúklingasalat
salami *n* spægipylsa
salary *n* laun: when do I get my ~?
hvenær fæ ég greidd laun?
sale *n* sala
sales *n* sala; ~ clerk afgreiðslumaður,
afgreiðslukona; ~ department
söluskrifstofa; ~ receipt strimill; ~
tax söluskattur
saliva *n* munnvatn
salmon *n* lax: farmed ~ eldislax,
smoked ~ reyktur lax
salon *n (hair)* hárgreiðslustofa; *(beauty)*
snyrtistofa; *(nail)* naglastofa;
(fashion store) tískuvöruverslun
salsa *n* salsa: hot ~ sterkt salsa, mild
~ milt salsa, spicy ~ kryddað salsa
salt *n* salt; *expr* with a grain of ~
með fyrirvara
salt container *n* saltstaukur
salted *adj* saltaður
salty *adj* salt: the popcorn is very ~
poppið er mjög salt
salutation *n* kveðja
salute *v* heilsa formlega
Salvadoran 1 *adj* salvadorskur; 2 *n
(nationality)* Salvadori
salvage *v* björgun

salvation *n* sáluhjálp

same 1 *pron* sami: **if it is the ~ to you** ef þér er sama, **the ~ thing** sami hlutur, **I'll have the ~** ég fæ það sama; **2** *adv* eins: **you look the ~** þið eruð eins, **the ~ as** alveg eins og

Samoa *N* Samóa

Samoan 1 *adj* samóskur; **2** *n (nationality)* Samóamaður

sample *n* sýnishorn

sanatorium *n* heilsuhæli

sanctify *v* helga

sanction *n (permission)* leyfi; *(formal confirmation)* staðfesting; *(punishment)* refsiaðgerðir

sanctuary *n (for peace)* griðarstaður; *(for religion)* helgidómur

sand *n* sandur

sandal *n* sandali

sandwich *n* samloka: **ham and cheese ~** samloka með skinku og osti, **veggie ~** grænmetissamloka, **turkey ~** kalkúnasamloka

sandy *adj* sendinn: **~ beach** sandströnd

sanitary napkin *n* dömubindi

Santiago (capital of Chile) *N* Santíagó (höfuðborg Síle)

sapling *n flora* ungt tré

sapphire *n* safír

Sarajevo (capital of Bosnia and Herzegovnia) *N* Sarajevó (höfuðborg Bosníu og Hersegovníu)

sarcasm *n* kaldhæðni

sardine *n* sardína

Satan *n* satan

satellite *n* gervihnöttur: **~ dish** gervihnattadiskur, **~ TV** gervihnattasjónvarp

satin *n* satín

satire *n* satíra, háðsádeila

satisfaction *n* ánægja, yndi; *(wishes, needs)* fullnæging, uppfylling

satisfied *adj* ánægður: **I'm ~ with the room** ég er ánægð(ur) með herbergið, **I'm not ~ with this** ég

er ekki ánægð(ur) með þetta

satisfy *v* þóknast, gera til geðs: **she is hard to ~** það er erfitt að gera henni til geðs; *(needs, wishes)* fullnægja, uppfylla

satisfying *adj* ánægjulegur

saturate *v* metta

saturated *adj* mettaður: **~ fat** mettuð fita

Saturday *n* laugardagur: **on ~** á laugardag, **every ~** á hverjum laugardegi, **next ~** laugardaginn í næstu viku, **this ~** nú á laugardaginn

sauce *n* sósa

saucepan *n* (skaft)pottur

saucer *n* undirskál

Saudi Arabia *N* Sádi Arabía

sauerkraut *n* súrkál

sauna *n* gufubað, sána

sausage *n* pylsa

sautéed *adj* snöggsteiktur

savage 1 *adj (wild)* villtur, frumstæður; *(cruel)* grimmur; **2** *n* frumstæður maður

save 1 *n* björgun; **2** *v* bjarga; *(protect)* vernda; *(money)* safna, spara: **~ for a trip** safna fyrir ferð

saving *n* sparnaður: **~'s account** sparireikningur; **life ~s** ævisparnaður

savior *n* bjargvættur

savor *n* bragð, keimur

savory *adj* ljúffengur

saw 1 *n* sög; **2** *v* saga

saxophone *n mus* saxófónn

say *v* segja: **can you ~ it again?** geturðu sagt þetta aftur?, **how do you ~ X in Icelandic?** hvernig segirðu X á íslensku?, **can you ~ it in English?** geturðu sagt þetta á ensku?

saying *n* orðatiltæki

scabies *n med* kláðamaur

scaffold *n (for construction)* vinnupallur; *(hanging)* aftökupallur

scald *v* skaðbrenna sig

scalding hot *adj* sjóðandi heitur

scale 1 *n (measurement)* mælikvarði; *(for weight)* vog, vigt; **2** *v (weigh)* vega

scallops *n* hörpudiskur

scalp *n* hársvörður

scalpel *n med* skurðhnífur

scampi *n* humarhali

scan *v (digitally)* skanna; *(read fast)* skima, renna yfir: ~ **through the text** renna yfir textann

scandal *n* hneyksli, skandall: **this is a ~!** þetta er hneyksli!

Scandinavia *N* Skandínavía

Scandinavian *adj* skandínavískur; ~ **countries** Norðurlönd; **in the** ~ **countries** í Skandínavíu, á Norðurlöndunum; ~ **languages** skandínavísk tungumál, norræn tungumál

scanner *n* skanni

scapegoat *n* blórabögull

scapula *n* herðablað

scar *n* ör

scare 1 *n* hræðsla, ótti; **2** *v* hræða

scared *adj* hræddur: **don't be ~** ekki vera hrædd(ur)

scarf *n (thin)* klútur; *(for winter)* trefill

scary *adj* ógnvekjandi

scatter *v (people)* tvístra; *(small things)* strá

scattered *adj* tvístraður, dreifður

scene *n (place of events)* vettvangur; *(place in a novel)* sögusvið; *(a part of a play)* atriði, sviðsmynd; *expr* **make a ~** vera með læti; **the music ~** tónlistarbransinn

scenery *n* landslag: **beautiful ~** fallegt landslag; *(theater)* leiktjöld

schedule 1 *n* áætlun; **2** *v* skrá

scheduled flight *n* áætlunarflug

schizophrenia *n med* geðklofi

schizophrenic *n* geðklofasjúklingur

schnitzel *n* snitsel

scholar *n* fræðimaður

scholarship *n* fræðimennska: **receive a ~** fá námsstyrk

school *n* skóli: **primary ~** grunnskóli, **secondary ~** menntaskóli, **high ~** menntaskóli; *(university department)* deild: **medical ~** læknadeild

school bag *n* skólataska

school book *n* skólabók

school teacher *n* kennari

sciatica *n med* settaugarbólga, þjótak

science *n* vísindi, vísindagrein: **applied ~** nytjavísindi, **social ~** félagsvísindi; **political ~** stjórnmálafræði

science fiction *n lit* vísindaskáldsaga

scientific *adj* vísindalegur

scientist *n* vísindamaður

scissors *n* skæri

scold *v* skamma

scolding *n* skammir

scone *n* skonsa

scope *n* svigrúm, umfang, svið

score *n (sports)* stig: ~ **board** stigatafla; *mus* raddskrá, partítúr: **piano ~** píanónótur

Scorpio *n astro* Sporðdrekinn

scorpion *n* sporðdreki

Scotch *n* skoti

Scotland *N* Skotland

Scottish 1 *adj* skoskur; **2** *n (nationality)* Skoti; *(language)* skoska

scramble *v (climb)* klöngrast; *(beat eggs)* hræra; *(fight)* berjast

scrambled *adj* hrærður: ~ **eggs** hrærð egg

scrape 1 *n (sound)* ískur; *(scratch)* skráma, rispa; **2** *v* skrapa, hrufla

scratch 1 *n* rispa, skráma: **its only a ~** þetta er bara skráma; **2** *v* klóra, rispa; *(sound)* ískra; *(wipe out)* þurrka út, stroka út

scratch paper *n* krassblað

scream 1 *n* öskur, óp; **2** *v* öskra, veina, æpa

screen 1 *n (TV, computer)* skjár: **computer ~** tölvuskjár; *(movie theater)* tjald; **2** *v (show a film)* sýna: **the film is ~ed at six** myndin er sýnd klukkan sex; *(~ applicants,*

etc) velja úr
screw 1 *n* skrúfa; **2** *v* skrúfa; *(betray)* svindla, plata; *(not succeed)* klúðra: **I ~ed up** ég klúðraði þessu; *slang (have sex with)* ríða
screwdriver *n* skrúfjárn
script *n (font)* letur; *(dialog for film/play)* handrit
scroll *v* skruna, skrolla
scrotum *n anat* pungur
scrutinize *v* grannskoða
scuba *n* köfunartæki: **~ diving** köfun
scuba diver *n* kafari
sculptor *n* myndhöggvari
sculpture *n* höggmynd
scurvy *n med* skyrbjúgur
sea *n* haf, sjór: **at ~** á hafi úti, **by ~** sjóleiðis, **go to ~** fara á sjóinn, **on the ~** á sjávarbotni, í fjörunni, **by the ~** við ströndina, **~ air** sjávarloft, **~ bathing** sjósund, **~ front** sjávarbakki, **~ level** sjávarmál
sea animal *n* sjávardýr
sea bass *n zool* vartari
sea bird *n zool* sjófugl
sea breeze *n* hafgola
sea kale *n* fjörukál
sea lion *n zool* sæljón
sea snails *n zool* sjávarsniglar
sea urchin *n zool* ígulker
seabed *n* sjávarbotn
seafood *n* sjávarréttur
seagull *n zool* mávur
seal *n zool* selur: **grey ~** útselur, **harbor ~** landselur, **hooded ~** blöðruselur; *(on letters, etc)* innsigli; *(to keep out cold/water)* þétting
seaman *n* sjómaður, háseti
sear *v* svíða
search 1 *n* leit: *comp* **~ engine** leitarvél; **~ party** leitarflokkur; *leg* **~ warrant** húsleitarheimild; **2** *v* leita: **I'm ~ing for ...** ég er að leita að ...
seashell *n* skel

seashore *n* strönd, fjara
seasick *adj* sjóveikur: **I think I'm getting ~** ég held að ég sé að verða sjóveik(ur)
season 1 *n (winter, summer, etc)* árstíð: **summer is my favorite ~** sumarið er uppáhaldsárstíðin mín; *(the right time for sth)* tímabil: **the soccer ~** fótboltatímabilið, **out of ~** ófáanlegur á þessum tíma; **2** *v* *(with spices)* krydda
seasonal *adj* árstíðarbundinn
seasoning *n* krydd
seat *n* sæti: **~ number** sætanúmer, **~ reservation** frátekið sæti: **I have a ~ reservation** ég á frátekið sæti
seat belt *n* bílbelti
seawall *n* sjóvarnargarður
seawater *n* sjór
seaweed *n* þang, þari
second 1 *adj* annar: **do you have a ~ pair** ertu með annað par?, **the ~ time** annað skiptið, **on the ~ floor** á annarri hæð, **~ class** annað farrými: **traveling ~ class** ferðast á öðru farrými; **2** *n (time)* sekúnda; *(serving)* ábót: **can I have a ~?** gæti ég fengið ábót?; *expr* **just a ~!** augnablik!; **3** *ord* önnur, annað: **Elisabeth the ~** Elísabet önnur; *(dates)* annar: **the ~ of December** annar desember
second opinion *n* annað álit
second thought *n* bakþankar: **I'm having ~s** ég er með bakþanka
secondary *adj (number two)* annar: **~ source** frá annarri hendi; *(small, less important)* minniháttar
second-best *adj* næstbestur
secondhand *adj* notaður: **~ clothes** notuð föt
secondhand bookstore fornbóka-verslun
secondhand store *n (clothing)* nytjamarkaður
secret 1 *adj* leynilegur; **2** *n* leyndar-mál, leyndardómur

secretary *n* ritari; *(minister)* ráðherra: ~ **of state** utanríkisráðherra; ~ **general** aðalritari
secretly *adv* í laumi
sect *n* sértrúarsöfnuður
section 1 *n* hluti, partur; *(of a text)* undirkafli; *(in newspaper)* -blað, -kálfur: **the sports** ~ íþróttablaðið; *med (operation)* skurður: **Caesarian** ~ keisaraskurður; **2** *v* sneiða, skera
sector *n* geiri: **the pubic** ~ opinberi geirinn
secular *adj* veraldlegur
secure 1 *adj* öruggur; **2** *v* tryggja
security *n* öryggi; **government securities** ríkisskuldabréf
security check *n* öryggisskoðun, vopnaleit
sedative *n med* róandi, sefandi: **give him** ~**s** gefðu honum róandi
sediment *n* botnfall, dreggjar
see *v* sjá: **I** ~ **a whale!** ég sé hval!, ~ **you later** sjáumst seinna, ~ **you soon** sjáumst bráðum aftur, **can you** ~ **it** sérðu það?; *(understand)* skilja: **I** ~ ég skil; *(talk to)* tala við: **I have to** ~ **a doctor** ég verð að tala við lækni; *(imagine)* ímynda sér; *(follow)* fylgja: ~ **him home** fylgja honum heim
seedless *adj* steinlaus: ~ **grapes** steinlaus vínber
seeds *n* fræ
seek *v* leita; *(try)* reyna; ~ **for** leitast eftir
seem *v* virðast
segment *n* partur, hluti
sei whale *n zool* sandreyður
seismograph *n geol* jarðskjálftamælir
seizure *n (a thief)* handtaka; *(of goods)* upptaka; *med* krampi; *med* **heart** ~ hjartaáfall
select 1 *adj* valinn; **2** *v* velja
selection *n (choice)* val; *(on offer)* úrval
self *n* sjálf

self-defense *n* sjálfsvörn
self-employed *adj* sjálfstætt starfandi
selfish *adj* eigingarn
selfishness *n* eigingirni
self-service *n* sjálfsafgreiðsla
self-sufficient *adj* sjálfum sér nógur
sell *v* selja: ~ **by date** síðasti söludagur
seller *n* seljandi, sölumaður
semantic *adj* merkingafræðilegur
semantics *n ling* merkingafræði
semen *n* sæði
semicolon *n ling* semíkomma
seminar *n* málstofa
semi-sweet *adj* hálf sætur
senate *n* öldungaráð; *(university)* háskólaráð
senator *n* öldungadeildarþingmaður
send *v* senda: ~ **an e-mail** senda tölvupóst, ~ **away** senda í burtu, ~ **for** senda eftir
sender *n* sendandi; *(equipment)* sendir
Senegal *N* Senegal
Senegalese *adj* senegalskur
senior 1 *adj* eldri, fullorðins-, elli-: ~ **citizen** eldri borgari, ~ **discount** afsláttur fyrir ellilífeyrisþega; **2** *n (elder)* eldri borgari; *(in high school)* efstubekkingar
sense *n* skilningarvit: **the sixth** ~ sjötta skilingarvitið;*(rationality)* skynsemi, vit; *(meaning)* merking, skilningur: **in a** ~ í vissum skilningi, **make** ~ vera skiljanlegur, **make no** ~ vera óskiljanlegur; **it doesn't make** ~ þetta er út í hött
sense of humor *n* kímnigáfa, skopskyn
senseless *adj* vitlaus, heimskulegur; *(without purpose)* tilgangslaus; *(unconscious)* meðvitundarlaus: **fall** ~ **to the ground** falla meðvitundarlaus til jarðar
sensible *adj* skynsamur
sensibly *adv* skynsamlega
sensitive *adj* viðkvæmur
sensitivity *n* viðkvæmni

sentence *n ling* setning, málsgrein;
  leg dómur: **death sentence**
  dauðadómur
Seoul (capital of South Korea) *N*
  Seoul (höfuðborg Suður-Kóreu)
separate 1 *adj* aðskilinn, aðgreindur,
  sérstakur; **2** *v* aðskilja, aðgreina;
  (from a spouse) hætta saman, skilja
separated *adj* skilinn: **we are** ~ **við**
  erum skilin (að borði og sæng)
separately *adv* hver í sínu lagi:
  could we pay ~ megum við borga
  hver í sínu lagi?; **wash** ~ þvegið sér
separation *n* aðskilnaður; *(from
  spouse)* skilnaður að borði og sæng
sepsis *n med* ígerð, sýking
September *n* september; **in** ~ **í**
  september
septic *adj med* ígerðar-
sequence *n* röð, lota, runa
sequential *adj* raðbundinn, í röð
Serbia *N* Serbía
Serbian 1 *adj* serbneskur; **2** *n*
  (nationality) Serbi; *(language)*
  serbneska
Serbo-Croat *n (language)*
  serbókróatíska
serial number *n* raðtala
series *n* sería; **television** ~
  sjónvarpsþáttaröð
serious *adj* alvarlegur
seriously *adv* alvarlega: ~ **ill**
  alvarlega veikur; *expr* **no,** ~**?** nei,
  í alvöru?
serum *n med* blóðvatn
servant *n* þjónn
serve *v (in restaurants etc)* þjóna;
  (given) bera fram: ~**d with ice
  cream** borið fram með ís; *(in
  army)* vera í hernum; *(in prison)*
  afplána
server *n* þjónn; *comp* (vef)þjónn
service *n* þjónusta: ~ **charge** þjónustugjald; *(plates etc)* borðbúnaður;
  (car) viðgerð; *(religious)* messa,
  guðsþjónusta
serving tray *n* bakki

sesame *n* sesam: ~ **seeds** sesamfræ, ~
  seed bun rúnnstykki með sesam
set 1 *n* sett, samstæða; *(TV)* tæki:
  a TV ~ sjónvarpstæki; **2** *v* setja,
  láta; ~ **the table** leggja á borðið;
  (decide) ákveða: ~ **a date** ákveða
  dagsetningu; *(a novel, film)* gerast:
  the film is ~ **in Iceland** myndin
  gerist á Íslandi
set off *v* leggja af stað
set up *v* setja upp
setting *n* umhverfi; *lit* sögusvið
settle *v* setjast að: ~ **in Iceland**
  setjast að á Íslandi; *(dust)* setjast;
  (a dispute) útkljá
settle down *v* koma sér vel fyrir
settlement *n* landnám: **the** ~ **of
  Iceland** landnám Íslands; *(colony)*
  nýlenda; *(financial)* uppgjör;
  (divorce) **a marriage** ~ kaupmáli
settler *n* landnemi: **the first** ~**s** fyrstu
  landnemarnir
setup *n* tilhögun
seven *num* sjö
seventeen *num* sautján
seventeenth *ord* sautjándi
seventh *ord* sjöundi
seventieth *ord* sjötugasti
seventy *num* sjötíu
several *pron* nokkrir: ~ **cars** nokkrir
  bílar
severe *adj* harður, strangur; *(serious)*
  alvarlegur: ~ **illness** alvarleg
  veikindi
severely *adv* alvarlega: ~ **damaged**
  alvarlega skemmdur
sew *v* sauma
sewing *n* saumaskapur
sewing machine *n* saumavél
sex *n* kyn, kynferði; *(the act)* kynlíf:
  to have ~ að stunda kynlíf, að sofa
  hjá; ~ **education** kynfræðsla; ~
  offender kynferðisbrotamaður
sexism *n* kynjamisrétti
sexual *adj* kynferðislegur: ~ **relation**
  kynferðislegt samband, ~ **inter-
  course** samfarir, ~ **discrimination**

kynjamisrétti
sexuality *n* kynhneigð
sexually *adv* kynferðislega
sexy *adj* kynþokkafullur, kynæsandi
Seychelles *n* Seychelles-eyjar
shade *n* skuggi; *(color)* litbrigði; *(for
lamp, window)* skermur
shadow *n* skuggi: **cast a ~ on** varpa
skugga á; *expr* **without a ~ of a
doubt** án nokkurs vafa
shady *adj* í skugga; *(doubtful)*
tortryggilegur
shake 1 *n* hristingur; *(drink)*
mjólkurhristingur, sjeik *colloq*;
2 *v* hrista; *(the mind)* koma úr
jafnvægi
shaker *n* staukur
shaky *adj* skjálfandi
shall *v* munu, skulu
shallot *n* skalottulaukur
shallow *adj* grunnur: **~ end**
grunna laugin; *(characteristic)*
grunnhygginn, yfirborðskenndur:
she is very ~ hún er mjög
yfirborðskennd
shaman *n* töfralæknir
shame *n* skömm; *expr* **that's a ~!**
það er leitt!; *expr* **~ on you!** þú
ættir að skammast þín!
shameful *adj* skammarlegur
shameless *adj* ósvífinn
shampoo *n* sjampó
shank *n* skanki: **a ~ of a lamb**
lambaskanki
shape 1 *n* lögun, form; *(condition)*
ástand; *(physical condition)* form:
I'm not in good ~ ég er ekki í
góðu formi; **2** *v* móta
shapka *n* loðhúfa
share 1 *n* hluti, eignarhlutur; *econ*
(in a company) hlutabréf; **2** *v* deila:
~ a room deila herbergi
shareholder *n econ* hluthafi
shark *n* hákarl: **~ steak** hákarlasteik,
~ fin hákarlauggi, **~ tail**
hákarlasporður
sharp *adj* beittur: **a ~ knife** beittur

hnífur; *(sound)* hvellur; *(smart)*
klár; *(photo)* skýr
shave *v* raka: **~ one's face** raka sig, **I
need to ~** ég þarf að raka mig
shaver *n* rakvél
shaving *n* rakstur: **~ brush** rakbursti,
~ cream raksápa
she *pron* hún
shear *v* rýja, skera
shears *n* klippur
shed 1 *n* kofi, skúr; **2** *v* hella, fella:
~ tears fella tár, **~ blood** úthella
blóði, **~ leaves** fella lauf
sheep *n zool* kind, sauður, fé; **~'s
milk cheese** kindaostur
sheep shelter *n* fjárhús
sheer *adj* einskær: **by ~ chance**
af einskærri tilviljun; *(material)*
næfurþunnur
sheet *n (for bed)* lak, rúmföt: **change
the ~s** skipta á rúminu; *(paper)*
blað, örk: **can I have a ~ of paper?**
gæti ég fengið blað?
shelf *n* hilla: **book ~** bókahilla;
geog sylla; *geog* **continental ~**
landgrunnur
shell 1 *n* skel: **clam ~** hörpuskel;
(egg~) skurn; *(for a building)*
grind; **2** *v* skelfletta
shellfish *n* skelfiskur
shelter 1 *n* skjól, skýli: **bus ~**
strætóskýli; **2** *v* skýla, *(seek ~)*
leita skjóls
sherbet *n* krapís, sorbet: **lemon
~** sítrónukrapís, **orange ~**
appelsínukrapís
sheriff *n (American)* lögreglustjóri;
(British) sýslumaður
sherry *n* sérrí: **~ glass** sérríglas
shield 1 *n* skjöldur, hlíf; **2** *n* vernda,
skýla
shield volcano *n geol* dyngja:
**Skjaldbreiður is Iceland's most
famous ~** Skjaldbreiður er þekkt-
asta dyngjan á Íslandi
shift 1 *n (change)* umskipti; *(work
schedule)* vakt: **evening ~** kvöld-

vakt; *(in cars)* gírstöng; *comp*
~ **key** hástafalykill; **2** *v* færast,
breytast; *(driving)* skipta um gír:
~ **into third gear** skipta í þriðja gír
shiitake *n* kínverskur svartsveppur
shine *v* lýsa, skína: **the sun is ~ing**
sólin skín; *(shoes etc)* pússa
shiny *adj* glansandi
ship 1 *n* skip; **2** *v* senda (með skipi)
shipping charge *n* sendingakostnaður
shipyard *n* slippur, skipasmíðastöð
shirt *n (dressy)* skyrta; *(casual)* bolur:
t-~ stuttermabolur
shish kebab *n* kjöt á teini: **chicken**
~ kjúklingur á teini, **lamb** ~
lambakjöt á teini
shivers *n* skjálfti, hrollur
shock 1 *n* högg; *(nerve)* áfall; *(elec-*
tric) raflost; **2** *v* fá á, ganga fram
af: **I'm ~ed!** ég er í sjokki!
shock absorber *n* dempari
shocking *adj* yfirgengilegur: ~
behavior yfirgengileg hegðun;
(sad) átakanlegur: ~ **news**
átakanlegar fréttir
shockproof *adj* höggþéttur
shoe 1 *n* skór: ~ **repair shop** skó-
smiður, ~ **store** skóbúð, ~ **polisher**
skóbursti, ~ **polish** skósverta; **2** *v*
járna: ~ **the horse** járna hestinn
shoehorn *n* skóhorn
shoestring *n* skóreimar
shoot *v (gun)* skjóta; *(film)* kvikmynda;
(photo) taka myndir
shop 1 *n* búð, verslun: **shoe** ~
skóbúð; *(car, machine repair)*
verkstæði; **coffee** ~ kaffihús; **2** *v*
versla, kaupa inn
shop assistant *n* afgreiðslumaður,
afgreiðslukona
shopkeeper *n* verslunareigandi
shoplifter *n* búðarhnuplari
shoplifting *n* búðarhnupl
shopping *n* innkaup: ~ **basket** inn-
kaupakarfa; ~ **cart** innkaupakerra
shopping center *n* verslunarmiðstöð
shopping street *n* verslunargata

shore *n* strönd; **on** ~ í landi; **on these**
~s í þessu landi
shore bird *n zool* vaðfugl
shore cliff *n* klettaströnd
short *adj* stuttur
short story *n lit* smásaga
shortage *n* skortur: **food** ~ matar-
skortur
shortcut *n* styttri leið
shortening *n* feiti
shortly *adv (soon)* bráðum: ~ **after**
skömmu síðar; *(with few words)* í
stuttu máli
shorts *n* stuttbuxur
shortsighted *adj* nærsýnn
short-term parking *n* skammtíma-
bílastæði
shot *n* skot; *(photo)* mynd; *(film)*
myndskeið; *(medicine)* sprauta:
get a ~ fá sprautu
shot gun *n* haglabyssa
should *v* ætti: **you** ~ **go** þú ættir að
fara; *expr* **I** ~ **think so!** það held
ég nú!
shoulder *n* öxl; *expr* ~ **to** ~ hlið við
hlið; *(road)* vegarkantur; *(meat)*
bógur: ~ **of lamb** lambabógur
shoulder blade *n* herðablað
shout 1 *n* hróp, kall; **2** *v* hrópa, kalla
shovel 1 *n* skófla; **2** *v* moka: ~ **snow**
moka snjó
show 1 *n* sýning, skemmtun; **2** *v*
sýna: **can you** ~ **me?** geturðu sýnt
mér?; *(be visible)* sjást *refl*; *(lead)*
vísa; ~ **off** monta sig af
show place *n* merkisstaður
shower *n* sturta: ~ **room** sturtu-
herbergi, **room with a** ~ herbergi
með sturtu; **rain** ~ regnskúr
show-off *n* monthani
shred 1 *n* slitur; *(tiny bit)* ögn; **2** *v*
tæta
shredder *n* tætari
shrimp *n* rækja
shrine *n* helgidómur
shrub *n* runni
shudder *v* skjálfa, titra

shush 1 *v* ussa á; **2** *interj* uss
shut *v* loka: ~ **the door** loka hurðinni; ~ **down** leggja niður; *excl* ~ **your mouth!** þegiðu!
shutter *n (on window)* gluggahleri; *(on camera)* loki
shuttle bus *n* rúta: ~ **to the airport** flugrúta
shuttle service *n* áætlunarferðir
shy *adj* feiminn; *(animals)* styggur
siblings *n* systkini
sick *adj* veikur: **car** ~ bílveikur; ~ **to one's stomach** með magaverk; *phr* **I feel** ~ mér líður illa
sick joke *n slang* andstyggilegt grín
sick leave *n* veikindafrí: **be on** ~ vera í veikindafríi
sick pay *n* sjúkradagpeningar
sickening *adj* ógeðslegur
sickness *n* veikindi, lasleiki; *(disease)* sjúkdómur; *(nausea)* ógleði; ~ **benefit** sjúkrabætur
side *n* hlið; *(team)* lið; **take** ~**s** taka afstöðu með; *(on the body)* síða; ~ **mirror** hliðarspegill; *(familial)* **on my mother's** ~ í móðurætt, **on my father's** ~ í föðurætt
side dish *n* aukaréttur
side effects *n med* aukaverkanir
sideshow *n* aukasýning
sidewalk *n* gangstétt
sideways *adv* til hliðar
Sierra Leone *N* Síerra Leóne
Sierra Leonean 1 *adj* síerralónskur; **2** *n (nationality)* Síerra Leóne-maður
sieve 1 *n* sigti; **2** *v* sigta
sift *v* sigta
sight *n* sjón, sýn: **at first** ~ við fyrstu sýn, **loose** ~ **of** missa sjónar af; **come into** ~ birtast; *(a place to see)* merkisstaður
sights *n* merkisstaðir
sightseeing *n* skoðunarferð: **do you offer any** ~? bjóðið þið upp á skoðunarferðir?
sightseeing tour *n* skoðunarferð
sign 1 *n* merki, tákn; *(traffic)* skilti:

stop ~ stöðvunarskilti; **2** *v* undirrita; *(indicate)* gefa merki um; *(in sign language)* tala táknmál
sign language *n* táknmál
signal 1 *n* merki, tákn; **2** *v* gefa merki
signature *n* undirskrift
significance *n* þýðing, merking, gildi; **person of** ~ merk persóna
significant *adj* þýðingarmikill; *(statistics)* marktækur
signpost *n* vegvísir
silage *n* súrhey
silence *n* þögn; **in** ~ þegjandi
silent *adj* þögull, hljóður
silent volcano *n* óvirkt eldfjall
silk *n* silki
silly *adj* kjánalegur, bjánalegur; *expr* **don't be** ~! láttu ekki svona!
silver *n* silfur; ~ **spoon** silfurskeið, *(coin)* silfurpeningur, *(objects)* silfurborðbúnaður
silverplate *n* silfurhúð
silversmith *n* silfursmiður
similar *adj* líkur, svipaður
similarly *adv* á sama hátt
simmer *v* láta malla
simple *adj* einfaldur: ~ **Icelandic** einföld íslenska; *(person)* venjulegur: **a** ~ **worker** venjulegur verkamaður; *(pure)* einskær, hreinn: ~ **madness** hreint brjálæði
simply *adv* einfaldlega; **dress** ~ klæða sig látlaust
simultaneous *adj* sem gerist samtímis
simultaneous interpretation *n* snartúlkun
simultaneously *adv* samtímis
sin 1 *n* synd; **2** *v* syndga
since 1 *adv* síðan; **2** *prep* síðan, frá því að: **I haven't seen him** ~ **his arrival** ég hef ekki séð hann frá því að hann kom, ~ **yesterday** síðan í gær; **3** *conj (reason)* fyrst, úr því að: ~ **you ask** fyrst þú spyrð
sincere *adj* einlægur
sincerely *adv* í einlægni; **yours** ~ virðingarfyllst

sing *v* syngja: ~ **in a choir** syngja
í kór
singe *v* sviðna
singer *n* söngvari: ~ **in a rock band**
söngvari í rokkhljómsveit
singing *n* söngur: **take** ~ **lessons**
vera í söngnámi
single *adj* einn, stakur: ~ **room** ein-
staklingsherbergi, ~ **ticket** stakur
miði; *(marital status)* einhleypur:
~ **mother** einstæð móðir, ~ **father**
einstæður faðir
single out *v* velja úr
singular 1 *adj* einstakur, sérkennilegur; *ling* eintölu-: **what is the**
~ **form for X?** hver er eintalan af
X?; **2** *n ling* eintala: **what is the** ~
of X? hver er eintalan af X?
singularly *adv* einstaklega
sink 1 *n* vaskur: **where can I find a**
~**?** hvar finn ég vask?; **2** *v* sökkva;
(voice) lækka
sinus *n (forehead)* ennishola, *(nose)*
nefhola, *(cheeks)* kinnhola:
~ **infection** ennisholubólga,
kinnholubólga
sir *n* [not used in Icelandic]: **excuse**
me, ~**!** fyrirgefðu!
siren *n* sírena
sirloin steak *n* lendarsteik, þunnasteik
sister *n* systir: **half-**~ hálfsystir, **step-**
~ stjúpsystir; *(nun)* systir
sit *v* sitja: ~ **on a chair** sitja á stól;
(sit down) setjast: ~ **down, please**
gjörið svo vel að fá ykkur sæti
site *n* staður; *(historic* ~*)* vettvangur;
(construction ~*)* lóð; *(website)*
(vef)síða: **do you have a web**~**?**
eruð þið með heimasíðu?
sitting room *n* setustofa
situated *adj* staðsettur
situation *n* ástand, aðstaða; *(place)*
staðsetning; ~ **wanted** starf óskast
six *num* sex
sixteen *num* sextán
sixteenth *ord* sextándi
sixth *ord* sjötti

sixtieth *ord* sextugasti
sixty *num* sextíu
size *n* stærð: **about the** ~ **of a** á stærð
við, **what** ~ **is this?** hvað stærð er
þetta?; *(just give number for shoe*
size) **I take** ~ **forty in shoes** ég
nota skó númer fjörutíu
skate 1 *n (for sport)* skauti; *(fish)*
skata: **fermented** ~ kæst skata; **2** *v*
sports renna sér á skautum, skauta
skateboard *n* hjólabretti
skates *n* skautar: **hockey** ~ íshokkí-
skautar: **artistic dance** ~ listdans-
skautar, **in-line** ~ línuskautar
skeleton *n* beinagrind; *expr* **a** ~ **in**
the closet fjölskylduleyndarmál
skerry *n* sker
sketch 1 *n (drawing)* skissa; *(writ-*
ing) drög; *(comic)* grínatriðið; **2**
v rissa; ~ **out a plan** koma með
grófa áætlun
skewer *v* grillteinn
skewered *adj* á teini: ~ **kebab** kebab
á teini
ski(s) 1 *n* skíði: ~ **boots** skíðaklossar,
~ **poles** skíðastafir; **2** *v* renna sér á
skíðum, skíða
ski jump *n* skíðastökk
ski lift *n* skíðalyfta
ski resort *n* skíðasvæði
skier *n* skíðamaður: ~**s' lodge**
skíðaskáli
skiing *n* skíðaíþrótt
skill *n* færni, kunnátta
skilled *adj* vanur, þjálfaður
skilled workmen *n* iðnverkamenn
skilled jobs *n* fagvinna
skillet *n* panna
skillful *adj* fær
skillfully *adv* af færni, listilega
skim milk *n* undanrenna
skin *n* skinn, húð: ~ **moisturizer**
húðkrem
skinny *adj* mjór; *(negative)* horaður
skirt *n* pils
Skopje (capital of Macedonia) *N*
Skopje (höfuðborg Makedóníu)

skull *n* höfuðkúpa
sky *n* himinn
sky blue *adj (color)* himinblár
sky diver *n* fallhlífastökkvari
skydiving *n* fallhlífastökk
skylight *n* þakgluggi
skyline *n* sjóndeildarhringur
skyrocket *n* flugeldur
skyscraper *n* skýjakljúfur
slalom *n sports* svig: **giant** ~ stórsvig,
~ **skis** svigskíði
slang *n* slangur
slash 1 *n* skurður; 2 *v* rista, skera
slate *n geol* flöguberg, skífuberg
slaw *n* cole~ hvítkálssalat
slave *n* þræll
slavery *n* þrældómur, þrælkun
slay *v* vega, drepa
sleep 1 *n* svefn; 2 *v* sofa
sleeping bag *n* svefnpoki
sleeping pills *n* svefntöflur
sleeping sickness *n* svefnsýki
sleepy *adj* syfjaður
sleet 1 *n* slydda; 2 *v* slydda: **it was**
~**ing** það var slydda
sleeve *n* ermi; *(for vinyl record)*
(plötu)umslag
slice 1 *n* sneið; 2 *v* sneiða, skera niður
sliced *adj* niðurskorinn, niðursneiddur:
~ **meats** niðursneitt kjötálegg
slide 1 *n (playground)* rennibraut;
(water) vatnsrennibraut; *(photo)*
glæra; **land**~ skriðufall; 2 *v* renna sér
slight *adj* smávægilegur, vægur: ~
fever vægur hiti
slightly *adv* svolítið, aðeins, smá; ~
overdue kominn smá yfir tímann
slim *adj* grannur, mjór; *expr* **chances**
are ~ **that ...** það eru litlar líkur til
þess að ...
slime *n* slím, leðja
sling *n med* fatli: **with the arm in a**
~ vera með höndina í fatla
slip 1 *n (receipt)* strimill; *(piece of*
paper) miði; 2 *v* renna, skrika fótur
slippers *n* inniskór
slope 1 *n* halli, brekka; 2 *v* halla

Slovak 1 *adj* slóvakískur; 2 *n*
(nationality) Slóvaki; *(language)*
slóvakíska
Slovakia *N* Slóvakía
Slovene 1 *adj* slóvenskur; 2 *n*
(nationality) Slóveni; *(language)*
slóvenska
Slovenia *N* Slóvenía
slow *adj* hægur, hægfara: *excl* ~
down! hægðu á þér!, ~ **traffic** hæg
umferð; *(mind)* tregur: **he is very** ~
hann er mjög tregur; *(time)* seinn;
(business) daufur
slowly *adv* hægt, rólega
slum *n* fátækrahverfi
slummy *adj* sóðalegur, niðurníddur
slush *n* slabb
slut *n* drusla
small *adj* lítill; *(not important)* lítil-
vægur; ~ **change** skiptimynt
small intestine *n anat* smáþarmar
small talk *n* spjall
smallpox *n med* bólusótt, stóra bóla
smaller *adj compar* minni
smart 1 *adj (clever)* gáfaður, klár;
(well-dressed) flottur, fínn, smart;
(painful) sársaukafullur; 2 *n* sviði;
3 *v* svíða, súrna
smash 1 *n* brothljóð; 2 *v* brjóta, mölva
smell 1 *n* lykt, þefur; 2 *v* finna lykt:
do you ~ **anything?** finnurðu
einhverja lykt?; *(give scent)* lykta:
you smell like a ... þú lyktar eins
og ...; *(sense)* finna á sér
smile 1 *n* bros; 2 *v* brosa
smog *n* reykur
smoke 1 *n* reykur; 2 *v* reykja
smoke detector *n* reykskynjari
smoked *adj* reyktur: ~ **meat** reykt
kjöt, ~ **bacon** reykt beikon, ~
salmon reyktur lax
smoker *n* reykingamaður
smoking *n* reykingar: **no** ~!
reykingar bannaðar!
smooth *adj* sléttur, jafn; *(soft)*
mjúkur; *(comfortable)* þægilegur,
auðveldur

smoothie *n (drink)* þeytingur: **fruit ~** ávaxtaþeytingur
smoothly *adv* mjúklega
snack *n* snarl, nasl: **~ food** snarlmatur, **~ bar** snarlbar, snakkbar
snail *n* snigill
snake *n* snákur
sneak *v* læðast *refl*, laumast *refl*
sneakers *n* íþróttaskór
snipe 1 *n zool* hrossagaukur; **2** *v* drepa úr launsátri
snob *n* snobb, *(male)* snobbaður maður, *(female)* snobbuð kona
snobbish *adj* snobbaður
snooker *n* snóker
snorkel *n* öndunarpípa
snow 1 *n* snjór: **~drift** skafrenningur, **~fall** snjókoma, **~flake** snjókorn, **~man** snjókarl, **~storm** stórhríð, **2** *v* snjóa
snow tires *n* vetrardekk
snowboard *n* snjóbretti
snowbound *adj* veðurtepptur
snowmobile *n* snjósleði, vélsleði
snowplow *n* snjóplógur
snowsuit *n* snjógalli
snow-white *adj (color)* snjóhvítur
so 1 *adv* svo: **I'm ~ tired** ég er svo þreytt(ur); *(that way)* þannig, svo; **or ~** hér um bil; **and ~ on** og svo framvegis; *(as said before)* það: **I hope ~** ég vona það; **2** *conj* svo
so what *adv* og hvað með það
soap *n* sápa
soap opera *n* sápuópera
so-called *adj* svokallaður
soccer *n sports* fótbolti: **~ game** fótboltaleikur
sociable *adj* félagslyndur
social *adj* þjóðfélagslegur, félags-
social sciences félagsvísindi
social security *n* almannatryggingar
social welfare *n* velferðarkerfi
social democrat *n* sósíaldemókrati
social worker *n* félagsráðgjafi
socialist *adj* sósíalisti, jafnaðarmaður
socially *adv* félagslega

society *n* samfélag, þjóðfélag; *(organization)* félagsskapur, samtök
sociological *adj* félagsfræðilegur, samfélagslegur
sociologist *n* félagsfræðingur
sociology *n* félagsfræði
sock *n* sokkur, leisti
socket *n (electric)* innstunga; *(lamp)* lampastæði
sod *n* torf, þaka: **~ house** torfbær
soda *n (baking ~)* matarsódi; *(drink)* sódavatn; **~ water** sódavatn; **~ pop** gos
sodium bicarbonate *n* natríum, natrón
sodium hydroxide *n* vítissódi
Sofia (capital of Bulgaria) *N* Sófía, (höfuðborg Búlgaríu)
soft *adj* mjúkur, linur: **~ cheese** mjúkir ostar
soft drink *n (soda pop)* gos
soft-boiled egg *n* linsoðið egg
softly *adv* blíðlega
software *n comp* hugbúnaður
soil *n* jarðvegur
sojourn *v* dveljast
solar *adj* sólar-
solar cell *n* sólrafall
solar energy *n* sólarorka
solar panel *n* sólpanill
solar system *n* sólkerfi
solarium *n* sólbaðstofa
sold *adj* seldur: **~ out** uppseldur
soldier *n* hermaður
sole 1 *adj* eini, einka-: **the ~ heir** einkaerfingi; **2** *n (fish)* lúða, **lemon ~** sólkoli; *(of shoe)* sóli
solely *adv* einungis
solfatara *n geol* leirhver
solicitor *n* málflutningsmaður
solid *adj* fastur, í föstu formi; *(reliable)* traustur; *(pure)* hreinn, óblandaður
solid gold *n* skíragull
solo 1 *adj* sóló-, einleiks-, einsmanns-; **2** *n* sóló, einleikur; *mus* einleikskafli; *(pilot)* sólóflug, einflug
soloist *n mus* einleikari, sólóisti
Solomon Islands *N* Salómonseyjar

solstice *n* sólstöður: **summer ~** sumarsólstöður, **winter ~** vetrarsólstöður

solution *n (to a problem)* úrlausn; *(chemical)* upplausn

solve *v* leysa, ráða

solvent *n* greiðslufær; *(chemical)* uppleysandi

Somali 1 *adj* sómalískur; **2** *n (nationality)* Sómali; *(language)* sómalíska

Somalia *N* Sómalía

some 1 *adj (a few)* nokkrir, einhverjir; *(a bit)* smá: **she gave me ~ money** hún lét mig fá smá pening; *(a few out of a group)* sumir: **~ people say** sumir segja ...; *(unknown)* einhver: **~ man called** það hringdi einhver maður; *(a bit of)* [not expressed in Icelandic]: **would you like ~ coffee?** má bjóða þér kaffi?, **take ~ bread** fáðu þér brauð; *(emphatic)* meiri: **you're ~ friend!** þú ert nú meiri vinurinn!

somebody *pron* einhver

somehow *adv* einhvern veginn; *(for some reason)* einhverra hluta vegna

someone *pron* einhver

something *pron* eitthvað: **or ~** eða eitthvað svoleiðis

sometimes *adv* stundum

somewhat *adv* dálítið, fremur, smá

somewhere *adv* einhvers staðar

son *n* sonur

son-in-law *n* tengdasonur

sonar *n med* ómsjá

song *n* lag: **sing a ~** syngja lag

songwriter *n* lagasmiður

soon *adv* bráðum: **I'm leaving ~** ég fer bráðum; *(fast)* fljótt: **as ~ as possible** eins fljótt og hægt er

soothe *v (baby)* hugga; *(pain)* lina, draga úr: **~ the pain** draga úr verkjum

soothing *adj* sefandi

sophisticated *adj* fágaður

soprano *n* sópran: **~ singer** sópransöngkona

sorbet *n* krapís

sore *adj med* aumur; *phr* **have a ~ throat** vera með hálsbólgu

sorghum *n* dúrra

sorrel *n* túnsúra

sorrow *n* sorg

sorry 1 *adj* hryggur, leiður: **I'm ~** fyrirgefðu, **I'm ~ for your loss** ég samhryggist þér; *(pitiful)* aumkunarverður, lélegur: **a ~ excuse** léleg afsökun; **2** *interj* fyrirgefðu, afsakaðu

sort 1 *n* tegund, gerð, sort; **2** *v* flokka, sortera

sorting plant *n* flokkunarstöð

so-so *adj* allt í lagi: **the food was ~** maturinn var allt í lagi, maturinn var ekkert sérstaklega góður

soul *n* sál, andi

soul music *n* sálartónlist

soulless *adj* sálarlaus, tilfinningalaus

sound 1 *adj (okay)* heilbrigður: **safe and ~** heill á húfi; *(wise)* skynsamlegur; **~ advice** hollráð; *(steady, firm)* rækilegur; **2** *n* hljóð; *mus* hljómur; **3** *adv* vært: **~ asleep** sofa vært

soup *n* súpa: **chicken ~** kjúklingasúpa, **vegetable ~** grænmetissúpa, **cream ~** rjómalögð súpa, *(Icelandic)* **meat ~** (íslensk) kjötsúpa, **split-pea ~** baunasúpa

soup bowl *n* súpudiskur

soup of the day *n* súpa dagsins: **what is the ~?** hver er súpa dagsins?, **I'll have the ~** ég ætla að fá súpu dagsins

sour *adj* súr: **~ milk** súr mjólk; *(turn)* súrna; *(figuratively)* fúll, önugur

sour cream *n* sýrður rjómi

source *n (river)* uppspretta; *(research)* heimild

source language *n* frummál: **in the ~** á frummálinu

south 1 *adj* suður-, sunnan-; **2** *n* suður; *(south Iceland)* Suðurland:

traveling around the ~ ferðast um Suðurland; **3** *adv* (í) suður, í suðurátt: **driving** ~ keyra í suður
South Africa *N* Suður-Afríka
South African 1 *adj* suður-afríkanskur; **2** *n (nationality)* Suður-Afríkani
South American 1 *adj* suður-ameríkanskur; ~ **food** suður-amerískur matur; **2** *n (nationality)* Suður-Ameríkani
South Sudan *N* Suður-Súdan
southeast 1 *adj* suðaustur-; **2** *n* suðaustur; *(southeast Iceland)* Suðausturland; **3** *adv* (í) suðaustur
southern *adj (Iceland)* sunnlenskur; *(the world)* suðrænn
souvenir *n* minjagripur: ~ **shop** minjagripaverslun
sovereign *adj* fullvalda: ~ **state** fullvalda ríki
sowing *n* sáning
soy(a) *n* soja: ~ **sauce** sojasósa, ~ **milk** sojamjólk
soybean *n* sojabaun: ~ **oil** sojaolía
spa *n* heilsulind, baðhús
space *n (to store etc.)* pláss, rými; *(cosmos)* geimur; *(between)* bil
spacebar *n comp* bilstöng: **press** ~ ýttu á bilstöngina
spacious *adj* rúmgóður: ~ **room** rúmgott herbergi
spade *n (tool)* (stungu)spaði; *(cards)* spaði
spaghetti *n* spagettí
Spain *n* Spánn
Spaniard *n* Spánverji
Spanish 1 *adj* spænskur; **2** *n (language)* spænska
spare *adj* vara-, auka-: ~ **part** varahlutur, ~ **wheel** varadekk: **I don't have a** ~ **wheel** ég er ekki með varadekk
sparkling *adj (glitter)* glitrandi; *(bubbly)* freyðandi
sparkling wine *n* freyðivín
sparrow *n* spörfugl
sparse *adj* dreifður, gisinn

spasm *n med* krampi, krampaflog
spastic *adj* spastískur
spatula *n* spaði
speak *v* tala: **do you** ~ **English?** talarðu ensku?, **I** ~ **a little Icelandic** ég tala smá íslensku, **can you** ~ **up** geturðu talað hærra?; *expr* **so to** ~ svo að segja; *expr* **strictly** ~**ing** strangt til tekið
speaker *n* mælandi; *(person giving a speech)* ræðumaður: **tonight's** ~ ræðumaður kvöldsins; **loud**~ hátalari
spear 1 *n* spjót; **2** *v* reka í gegn
special 1 *adj* sérstakur; **2** *n (at restaurant)* **today's** ~ réttur dagsins
special delivery *n* hraðsending
special needs *n* sérþarfir
specialist *n* sérfræðingur
specialize *v* sérhæfa sig
specialized *adj* sérhæfður: ~ **in X** sérhæfður í X
specially *adv* sérstaklega
specialty *n* sérgrein; *(food)* sérréttur: ~ **of the day** réttur dagsins
species *n* tegund, gerð, sort
specific *adj* sérstakur
specifically *adv* sérstaklega
specification *n* nákvæm lýsing
specify *v* tilgreina
specimen *n* eintak
spectacles *n* gleraugu
spectator *n* áhorfandi
spectrum *n* róf: **color** ~ litróf
speech *n* tal, mál; *(way to talk)* málfar; *(give a ~)* ræða
speechless *adj* orðlaus
speed *n* hraði
speed limit *n* hraðatakmörk
speed skating *n sports* skautahlaup
speedometer *n* hraðamælir
speeding *n* hraðakstur
spell 1 *n (magic)* álög; *(length of time)* tímabil, **cold** ~ kuldakast; **2** *v* stafa, stafsetja
spelling *n* stafsetning
spelt flour *n* spelti

spend *v* eyða
spending money *n* vasapeningar
sperm *n* sæði
sperm whale *n* búrhvalur
spice *n* krydd: ~ blend kryddblanda
spicy *adj* sterkur: ~ pepper sterkur
  pipar, ~ sauce sterk sósa, ~ taste
  bragðsterkur
spider *n* könguló
spider crab *n zool* trjónukrabbi
spill *v* hella niður
spin *v* snúast *refl*: the wheels ~ hjólin
  snúast; *(turn)* snúa; *(~ thread)*
  spinna
spinach *n* spínat: ~ leaves spínatblöð,
  ~ dip spínatídýfa
spinal column *n anat* hryggur,
  hryggsúla
spinal cord *n anat* mæna
spine *n anat* hryggur; *(on books)*
  kjölur
spinner *n sports* spúnn
spinning wheel *n* rokkur
spinster *n* piparkerling
spire *n* spíra
spirit *n* andi; *(energy)* kraftur;
  (mood) skap: in high ~s í góðu
  skapi; *(alcoholic drink)* brennt
  áfengi, spíri
spiritual *adj* andlegur; *(religious)*
  trúarlegur: ~ songs trúarlegir
  söngvar
spite *n* illgirni
spiteful *adj* illgjarn
spleen *n anat* milta
splinter *n* flís
split *v* kljúfa, skipta: ~ a bill skipta
  reikningi á milli sín
split peas *n* hálfbaunir, gular baunir
spoil *v (go bad)* skemma, spilla; *(by
  itself)* spillast, skemmast
spoiled *adj* skemmdur: ~ goods
  skemmdar vörur
spoken *adj* talaður
sponge *n* svampur
sponge cake *n* svampkaka
sponger *n* afæta, sníkjudýr

sponsor 1 *n* styrktaraðili,
  kostnaðarmaður; 2 *v* styrkja
spoon *n* skeið
sport *n* íþrótt
sporting goods *n* íþróttavörur: ~
  store íþróttavöruverslun
sports *n* íþróttir: ~ club íþróttafélag,
  ~ field íþróttavöllur
sports car *n* sportbíll
sportsman *n* íþróttamaður
sportswear *n* íþróttaföt
spot *n* blettur
spouse *n* maki
sprain 1 *n med* tognun; 2 *v med*
  togna: ~ one's ankle togna á ökkla
sprained *adj med* tognaður: ~ ankle
  tognaður ökkli, snúinn ökkli
spray 1 *n* úði, sprey; 2 *v* úða, spreyja
spread 1 *n (on bread)* smurálegg:
  cheese ~ smurostur; *(farmland)*
  landareign; bed~ rúmábreiða; 2 *v*
  breiðast út
spreader *n (farming)* dreifari; *(for
  bread)* smörhnífur
spreadsheet *n econ* töflureiknir
spring 1 *n (season)* vor: ~ flower
  vorblóm; *(jump)* stökk; *(of water)*
  uppspretta, hot ~ hver, laug; *(in
  mattress)* gormur, fjöður; 2 *v*
  spretta upp, stökkva
spring chicken *n* lítill kjúklingur
spring onion *n* vorlaukur
sprinkle *v (liquid)* úða; *(non-liquid)* strá
sprouts *n* spíra: soy ~ sojaspírur,
  bean ~ baunaspírur
spruce *n flora* greni; grenitré
spuds *n (potatoes)* kartöflur
spy *n* njósnari
square *n math* ferningur, ferhyrningur;
  (in a city) torg
squash *n sports* skvass; *(vegetable)*
  grasker: spaghetti ~ spagettígrasker
squeeze 1 *n* kreistingur; *(hug)* knús;
  (crowd in) þrengsli; 2 *v* kreista,
  kremja
squeezer *n* pressa: lemon ~ sítrónupressa

squid *n* smokkfiskur
squirrel *n zool* íkorni
Sri Lanka *n* Srí Lanka
Sri Lankan 1 *adj* srílanskskur; **2** *n*
  (nationality) Srí Lanka-maður
stable 1 *adj* stöðugur, í jafnvægi; **2**
  n hesthús
stack *n* drangur
stadium *n* íþróttaleikvangur
staff *n (workers)* starfsmenn; *(pole)*
  stöng, stafur
stage 1 *n (theater)* svið: ~ **manager**
  sviðsstjóri; *(for a story)* sögusvið;
  (development) stig: **first** ~ fyrsta
  stig; **2** *v* setja á svið
stagflation *n* stöðnunarverðbólga
stagnation *n* stöðnun, kyrrstaða
stain 1 *v (add color)* lita; *(make dirty)*
  flekka, ata út; *(become)* óhreinkast;
  2 *n* blettur: **tea** ~ teblettur
stain remover *n* blettahreinsir
stained glass *n* litað gler
stained-glass window *n* steindur
  gluggi
stainless *adj* flekklaus
stainless steel *n* ryðfrítt stál
stair *n* stigi, tröppur
staircase *n* stigi, tröppur
stairway *n* stigi, tröppur
stairwell *n* stigagangur
stake *n (pole)* staur, stólpi; *(money)*
  spilafé; *expr* **there is much at** ~
  það er mikið í húfi
stalagmite *n geol* dropasteinn
stale *adj (bread)* þurr; *(beer)* flatur;
  (air) þungur, vondur; *(people)*
  staðnaður
stalemate *n* pattstaða
stallion *n zool* stóðhestur
stamp *n (postage)* frímerki: ~ **collection** frímerkjasafn; *(ink ~)* stimpill;
  (with feet) stapp, tramp; **2** *v (mail)*
  frímerkja; *(~ with ink)* stimpla: ~ **a
  ticket** stimpla miða, ~ **a passport**
  að stimpla vegabréf; *(~ with feet)*
  stappa, trampa
stand *v* standa: ~ **in line** standa í röð,

~ **up** standa upp; *(tolerate)* þola; ~
back hörfa; ~ **by** standa hjá; ~ **for**
tákna; **a one-night** ~ einnar nætur
gaman
stand-alone *adj* sjálfstæður
standard 1 *adj* staðlaður; *(ordinary)*
  venjulegur: ~ **ticket** venjulegur
  miði; **2** *n* staðall
standardization *n* stöðlun
standardized *adj* staðlaður: ~ **Old
  Norse** norræna með samræmdri
  stafsetningu fornri
standby ticket *n* miði á biðlista
standing *adj* langvarandi, varanlegur:
  a ~ committee fastanefnd
stanza *n lit* erindi, vísa
staple *n* hefti
staple remover *n* tengdamamma
stapler *n* heftari
star 1 *n* stjarna: ~**-shaped** stjörnu-
  lagaður; **2** *v* stjörnumerkja; *(in a
  film)* vera í aðalhlutverki
starboard *n* stjórnborði
starch *n* sterkja, mjölvi
stardom *n* frægð
stare 1 *n* starandi augnaráð; **2** *v* stara
starfish *n zool* stjörnufiskur
starling *n zool* starri
starlit *adj* stjörnubjartur: **a ~ sky**
  stjörnubjartur himinn
starry *adj* stirndur
start 1 *n* byrjun, upphaf; **2** *v* byrja,
  hefja: ~ **working** byrja að vinna;
  (a machine) starta: ~ **a car** starta
  bíl; *(a business)* stofna, starta: ~ **a
  company** stofna fyrirtæki; **starve**
  v svelta
state 1 *n (of health etc)* ástand;
  (government) ríki: **modern ~s**
  nútíma ríki; **2** *v (say)* tjá, skýra
State Department *n* utanríkisráðuneyti
State House *n* þinghús
statement *n* staðhæfing; *(official)*
  yfirlýsing; *(to the police)* gefa
  skýrslu; *(by witness)* framburður
stateroom *n* viðhafnarsalur

station *n* stöð: **police** ~ lögreglustöð, **bus** ~ umferðarmiðstöð
stationery *n* ritföng
statistical *adj* tölfræðilegur
statistics *n* *(science)* tölfræði; *(information)* tölfræðilegar upplýsingar
statue *n* stytta, höggmynd
status *n* ástand, staða: **legal** ~ réttarstaða
statute *n* leg lög
statutory *adj* leg lögboðinn
stay 1 *n* dvöl; **2** *v* dvelja; vera: **how long are you ~ing?** hvað ætlarðu að vera lengi?, **I ~ in Hotel X** ég er á Hótel X
stay up *v* vaka
stay put *v* ekki hreyfa sig
steadily *adv* stöðugt
steady *adj* stöðugur, óbifanlegur
steak *n* steik: **beef** ~ nautasteik
steal *v* stela, hnupla
stealing *n* þjófnaður
steam 1 *n* gufa: ~ **engine** gufuvél, ~ **bath** gufubað, ~ **cooker** gufusuðupottur, ~ **iron** gufustraujárn; *expr* **run out of** ~ missa móðinn; *expr* **let off some** ~ fá útrás; **2** *v* gefa frá sér gufu; *(cooking)* gufusjóða; ~**ed vegetables** gufusoðið grænmeti
steel *n* stál
steep 1 *adj* brattur; **2** *v* trekkja: **let the tea** ~ látið teið trekkja
steer 1 *n* ungnaut; **2** *v* stýra
steering wheel *n* stýri
stem *n* *(flower)* stilkur; *(tree)* stofn; *(glass)* fótur; *(family)* ættleggur; *(language)* stofn: **word** ~ orðstofn
step 1 *n* skref: ~ **by** ~ skref fyrir skref; *(track)* fótspor; *(stairs)* trappa, þrep; **2** *v* stíga; ~ **aside** víkja; ~ **down** segja af sér; ~ **in** grípa inn í; ~ **up** herða á
stepbrother *n* stjúpbróðir
stepchild *n* stjúpbarn
stepdaughter *n* stjúpdóttir
stepfather *n* stjúpfaðir
stepmother *n* stjúpmóðir

stepsister *n* stjúpsystir
stepson *n* stjúpsonur
sterile *adj* ófrjósamur
sterilized *n* *(reproduction)* geldur, gerður ófrjór; *(cleaned of bacteria)* dauðhreinsaður
sterilizing solution *n* sáravatn
sterling *n* *(about silver)* ekta, hreinn: ~ **silver** hreint silfur
stethoscope *n* hlustunarpípa
stew *n* kássa: **beef** ~ nautakássa, **vegetable** ~ grænmetiskássa
stick 1 *n* prik, sprek, kvistur; **2** *v* stingast; *(not able to move)* festast; ~ **out** vera áberandi; ~ **around** ekki fara; ~ **together** standa saman
sticker *n* límmiði
sticking plaster *n* heftiplástur
sticky *adj* klístraður, kámugur
stiff *adj* stífur: *med* ~ **neck** stífur hnakki
still 1 *adj* kyrr, hreyfingarlaus; **2** *adv* ennþá, enn: **I'm** ~ **waiting** ég er enn að bíða; *(anyway)* samt: **I** ~ **don't want to go** ég vil samt ekki fara
still life *n* *(painting)* uppstilling
stillbirth *n* andvana fæðing
stillborn *adj* fæddur andvana
stimulate *v* örva, hvetja
stimulus *n* hvatning
sting 1 *n* stunga; *(pain)* stingur, verkur, sársauki; **2** *v* stinga, særa
stinginess *n* níska
stingy *adj* nískur
stink 1 *n* fnykur, fýla, óþefur; *expr* **raise a** ~ **about sth** gera mál úr einhverju; **2** *v* lykta illa
stir *v* hræra
stir-fry *n* snöggsteikja
stitch *n* saumur
stock *n* birgðir; *econ* *(in a company)* hlutabréf; *(origin)* ætt: **of Icelandic** ~ af íslenskum ættum; *(soup base)* soð: **chicken** ~ kjúklingasoð, **fish** ~ fiskisoð; *(tree)* trjástokkur, trjábolur; ~ **cube** súputeningur;

econ ~ **exchange** kauphöll,
verðbréfamarkaður; *econ* ~ **holder**
hlutabréfahafi; ~ **fish** skreið,
harðfiskur
Stockholm (capital of Sweden) *N*
Stokkhólmur (höfuðborg Svíþjóðar)
stockings *n* nælonsokkar
stolen *adj* stolinn
stomach *n anat* magi
stomachache *n med* magaverkur,
magakveisa: **have a** ~ vera með
magaverk
stone *n* steinn
stoned *adj* gréttur; *(with drugs)* upp-
dópaður, undir áhrifum fíkniefna
stool *n (chair)* kollur; *(bowel movement)* hægðir
stop 1 *n* stopp: **bus** ~ strætóstopp,
make a short ~ stoppa stutt; *(act
of stopping)* stöðvun, stans: ~ **sign**
stöðvunarskilti; **2** *v (stop moving)*
stöðva, stansa, stoppa; *(stop doing)*
hætta: ~ **working** hætta að vinna;
(stop from happening) hindra,
stöðva
stop by *v* líta við
stop over *v* koma við
stopcock *n* krani
stopper *n* tappi
store 1 *n* búð, verslun: **fashion** ~
tískuvöruverslun, **clothing** ~
fataverslun, **book** ~ bókabúð,
shoe ~ skóbúð, **toy** ~ leikfangabúð;
2 *v* geyma, varðveita
stork *n zool* storkur
storm *n* óveður, rok, illviðri: ~
warning stormviðvörun; **snow**~
stórhríð; **brain**~ þankahríð
stormy *adj* illviðrasamur, stormasamur
story *n* saga, frásögn
storybook *n* barnabók
stove *n* eldavél
straight 1 *adj* beinn; *(okay)* í lagi; *(honest)* hreinskilinn, hreinn og beinn;
(logical) rökréttur; *(alcoholic drink)*
óblandaður; *(sexual orientation)*
gagnkynhneigður; **2** *adv* beint:

~ **ahead** beint áfram!; *(time)* strax:
~ **away** strax
strange *adj* skrýtinn
strangely *adv* furðulega
stranger *n* ókunnur maður
straw *n* strá; *(for drinking)* rör
strawberry *n* jarðaber: ~ **ice cream**
jarðaberjaís
stream 1 *n (water)* lækur, á; *(movement)* straumur; **2** *v* streyma
street *n* gata, vegur, stræti
street children *n* útigangsbörn
streetcar *n* sporvagn
streetlight *n* ljósastaur
strength *n* styrkur
stress 1 *n (pressure)* streita, álag,
stress; *phys* spenna; *ling* áhersla:
~ **on the first syllable** áhersla á
fyrsta atkvæði; **2** *v* leggja áherslu á
stressed *adj* stressaður, áhyggjufullur
stressful *adj* streituvaldandi,
stressandi
stretch *v* teygja
stretcher *n* sjúkrabörur
strict *adj* strangur
strictly *adv* stranglega: ~ **speaking**
strangt til tekið
strike 1 *n (blow)* sláttur, högg; *(labor)*
verkfall; *(attack)* árás; **2** *v (hit)* slá;
(crash) rekast á; *(find by coincidence)*
rekast á; *(seem to be)* virðast vera,
finnast: **this** ~**s me as odd** mér finnast
þetta undarlegt; *(labor)* verkfall
striking *adj* áberandi, sláandi: ~
resemblance sláandi svipur
string *n* snæri, band; **shoe** ~**s**
(skó)reimar
string bean *n* strengjabaun
string instrument *n mus* strengja-
hljóðfæri
string orchestra *n mus* strengjasveit
string quartet *n mus* strengjakvartett
strip lightning *n* flúrljós
stripe *n* rönd
striped *adj* röndóttur
stroke 1 *n (blow)* högg, slag; *(swimming)* sundtak; *(clock)* slag; *(with*

a *brush*) (pensil)dráttur; *med* slag, heilablóðfall; **2** *v* strjúka

stroll *v* rölta, spássera

stroller *n* kerra

strong *adj* sterkur: ~ **drink** sterkur drykkur

strongly *adv* sterklega

structure *n* bygging, gerð: *ling* **sentence** ~ setningargerð; *(building)* mannvirki

struggle 1 *n* barátta; **2** *v* strita, berjast: ~ **against poverty** berjast gegn fátækt

stubborn *adj* þrjóskur

stuck *adj* fastur: **be** ~ vera fastur

stud *n* stóðhestur, graðfoli

student *n* nemandi, nemi, (háskóla) stúdent: ~ **card** stúdentaskírteini, ~ **discount** stúdentaafsláttur

studio *n* stúdíó; *(sound)* hljóðver; *(films)* kvikmyndaver; *(artist)* vinnustofa

study 1 *n* lærdómur; *(research)* rannsókn, fræðistörf: **Icelandic studies** íslensk fræði; *(subject)* fræðigrein; *(room)* lesstofa, skrifstofa; *(music)* æfing; **2** *v (student)* læra: **I'm ~ing Icelandic** ég er að læra íslensku; *(research)* rannsaka

stuff *n* dót

stuffed *n* fylltur: ~ **egg** fyllt egg; *(people)* saddur: **I'm** ~ ég er pakksaddur

stuffing *n* fylling: **turkey** ~ kalkúnafylling

stunning *adj* áhrifamikill; ~ **view** ægilega fallegt útsýni

stupid *adj* vitlaus, heimskur

sturgeon *n zool* styrja

style *n (art, fashion)* stíll; *(type)* gerð, tegund

stylist *n* stílisti

stylistic *adj* stílrænn

subject *n (topic)* efni, umræðuefni: **change the** ~ skipta um umræðuefni; *(in school)* námsgrein fræðigrein; *ling* frumlag

subject matter *n* umfjöllunarefni; *lit* yrkisefni

subjective *adj* huglægur

subjunctive *n ling* viðtengingarháttur

sublet *v* áframleigja

submarine *n* kafbátur

submit *v (give up)* gefast upp; *(~ an essay, proposal etc.)* skila: ~ **an essay** skila ritgerð

subscribe *v* vera áskrifandi

subscriber *n* áskrifandi m

subscription *n* áskrift

subsequent *adj* eftirfarandi

subsequently *adv* þar á eftir

subsidiary *n* dótturfyrirtæki

substance *n* efni

substantial *adj (strong)* sterkur; *(large)* talsverður: **a** ~ **amount of money** töluverð peningaupphæð; *(rich)* efnaður; *(real)* raunverulegur

substantially *adv (to a great extent)* talsvert, töluvert, verulega; *(essentially)* að mestu leyti, efnislega

substitute 1 *n (person)* staðgengill; *(work)* afleysingarmaður; *(food, etc)* í staðinn fyrir; **2** *v (for work)* hlaupa í skarðið, leysa af; *(for food)* nota í staðinn fyrir: **can I** ~ **X for Y?** get ég fengið X í staðinn fyrir Y?

subtitles *n* undirtitill; *(in film/movie)* þýðingartexti: **a film with** ~ textuð bíómynd

subtle *adj* hárnákvæmur; *(complicated)* flókinn

subtract *v* draga frá

subtraction *n* frádráttur

suburb *n* úthverfi

succeed *v* heppnast; *(~ in life)* ná langt; *(come after)* taka við

success *n* velgengni; *(in life)* velmegun, hagsæld; **the show was a** ~ sýningin sló í gegn

successful *adj* árangursríkur, farsæll

successfully *adv* með góðum árangri

such *pron* slíkur, þannig: ~ **is life** þannig er lífið, **and** ~ og þannig;

~ **as** eins og til dæmis; *(emphatically)* þvílíkur: ~ **an idiot!** þvílíkur asni!, ~ **a waste of time!** þvílík tímasóun!, ~ **a shame!** þvílík synd!

suck *v* sjúga, soga

Sudan *N* Súdan

Sudanese 1 *adj* súdanskur; 2 *n (nationality)* Súdani

sudden *adj* skyndilegur

suddenly *adv* skyndilega

suffer *v* þjást: ~ **from headaches** þjást af höfuðverk

suffering *n* þjáning, kvöl

sufficient *adj* nógur

sufficiently *adv* fullnægjandi

suffix *n ling* viðskeyti

sugar *n* sykur: **brown** ~ púðursykur, **cane** ~ reyrsykur, **powdered** ~ flórsykur

sugar-free *adj* sykurlaus

suggest *v* leggja til, stinga upp á; *(indicate)* gefa til kynna

suggestion *n* uppástunga, tillaga; *(indication)* merki

suicide *n* sjálfsmorð

suit 1 *n* föt: **a man's** ~ jakkaföt, **bathing** ~ sundföt; *(cards)* sort; *expr* ~ **yourself!** gerðu eins og þér sýnist!; 2 *v* henta, eiga vel við; *(clothes)* klæða: **this** ~**s you** þetta klæðir þig, þetta fer þér vel

suitable *adj* hentugur: ~ **for** hentugur fyrir

suitcase *n* ferðataska

suite *n (accomodation at hotel)* svíta, hótelíbúð; *(music)* svíta

sulphur *n chem* brennisteinn

sultana *n* kúrena, sultan rúsína

sum 1 *n* samtala, summa; *(money)* heildarupphæð; **in** ~ í stuttu máli; 2 *v* reikna, leggja saman

summarize *v* segja frá í stuttu máli

summary *n* útdráttur, ágrip

summer *n* sumar: **last** ~ síðastliðið sumar, **next** ~ næsta sumar, **the whole** ~ allt sumarið, ~ **holiday** sumarfrí, ~ **schedule** sumaráætlun,

~ **solstice** sumarjafndægur, ~ **vacation** sumarfrí

summon *v* boða, stefna

summon up *v* safna: ~ **courage** safna kjarki

sun *n* sól

sunbath *n* sólbað

sunbathe *v* vera í sólbaði

sunblock *n* sólarvörn

sunburn *n* sólbruni

Sunday *n* sunnudagur: **on** ~ á sunnudag(inn), **on** ~**s** á sunnudögum, **last** ~ síðastliðinn sunnudag

sun-dried *adj* sólþurrkaður

sunflower *n* sólblóm: ~ **oil** sólblómaolía, ~ **seeds** sólblómafræ

sunglasses *n* sólgleraugu

sunlight *n* sólskin: **in the** ~ í sólskininu

sunny *adj* sólríkur, sólbjartur: **a** ~ **day** sólbjartur dagur

sunrise *n* sólarupprás

sunroof *n* þakgluggi

sunscreen lotion *n* sólarvörn

sunset *n* sólarlag

sunshade *n* sólhlíf

sunshine *n* sólskin: **in the** ~ í sólskininu

sunstroke *n med* sólstingur

suntan lotion *n (sunscreen)* sólarvörn; *(oil)* sólarolía

super *n* frábær, stórkostlegur

superb *adj* frábær, stórkostlegur

superficial *adj* yfirborðskenndur; yfirborðs-

superintendent *n* forstöðumaður; *(police)* lögregluforingi

superior *adj* æðri, meiri, fremri

superlative 1 *adj* fremstur, efstur, frábær; 2 *n* hæstastig, hástig

supermarket *n* stórmarkaður

supernatural *adj* yfirnáttúrulegur: ~ **beings** yfirnáttúrulegar verur

superstition *n* hjátrú

superstitious *adj* hjátrúarfullur

supervision *n* stjórnun, umsjón

supper *n* kvöldmatur: **when is ~
served?** hvenær eru kvöldmatur
borinn fram?

supplement *n* viðbót, töflur:
calcium ~ kalsíumtöflur, **vitamin
~** vítamíntöflur, **mineral ~**
steinefnatöflur

supplier *n* birgðasali

supplies *n* birgðir

supply 1 *n* birgðir: **food supply**
matarbirgðir; *econ ~* **and demand**
framboð og eftirspurn; **2** *v* sjá fyrir,
útvega

support 1 *n* stoð, undirstaða; *(mental
~)* stuðningur: **you have my full ~**
ég styð þig heilshugar; *(financial)*
fjárhagsaðstoð; **2** *v* styðja; *(finan-
cially)* sjá fyrir, vinna fyrir

supporter *n* stuðningsmaður

suppose *v* gera ráð fyrir

suppository *n med* stíll

suppress *v* bæla niður, þagga

supreme *adj* æðstur, hæsti-

supreme court *n* hæstiréttur

surcharge *n* aukakostnaður

sure 1 *adj* viss, sannfærður: **are you
~?** ertu viss?; **for ~** fyrir víst; *(to
count on)* öruggur, áreiðanlegur:
a ~ friend áreiðanlegur vinur; **2**
adv (certain) auðvitað; *(okay)* allt í
lagi, jájá; **~ enough** auðvitað

surely *adv* vafalaust, áreiðanlega;
expr **slowly but ~** hægt en örugglega

surf 1 *n* brotsjór, brim; **2** *v* vera á
brimbretti; **~ the internet** vafra

surf and turf *n (food)* sjávar-og
kjötréttur;

surface *n* yfirborð

surfboard *n* brimbretti

surfing *n* brimbrettabrun

surgeon *n* skurðlæknir

surgery *n (science)* skurðlækningar;
med (operation) skurðaðgerð:
undergo ~ fara í uppskurð;
(operating room) skurðstofa

Suriname *n* Súrínam

surname *n* ættarnafn, eftirnafn:

Icelandic ~s íslensk eftirnöfn

surplus 1 *adj* afgangs-, umfram-; **~
stock** umframbirgðir; **2** *n* afgangur

surprise *n* undrun: **to my ~** mér til
mikillar undrunar; *(event)* óvæntur
atburður: **this was a ~** þetta var
óvænt

surprised *adj* hissa, undrandi

surprising *adj* óvæntur

surprisingly *adv* óvænt, furðulega:
this was ~ expensive þetta var
furðulega dýrt

surrender *v* gefast upp

surround *v* umkringja

surrounding *adj* aðliggjandi

surroundings *n* umhverfi

surveillance *n* eftirlit: **under police
~** undir eftirliti lögreglunnar

survey *n (market etc)* könnun; *geog*
landmælingar; **2** *v* kanna; *geog*
mæla út

survive *v* lifa af, komast af

sushi *n* sushi

suspect 1 *n* grunaður; **2** *v* gruna: **I ~
that he will be late** mig grunar að
hann verði seinn; *(doubt)* efa

suspicion *n* grunur; *(doubt)* efi

suspicious *adj* grunsamlegur: **he is
very ~** hann er mjög grunsamlegur;
(about one who suspects)
tortrygginn

sustain *v* halda uppi

sustainable *adj* sjálfbær: **~ development** sjálfbær þróun

sweets *n* sælgæti, nammi, gott

swab *n (with mop)* þvegill; *(with
cotton)* bómullarpinni

Swahili *n* svahílí

swallow *v* kyngja, gleypa

swamp *n* mýri, fen, votlendi

swan *n zool* svanur; *(wild)* álft

Swaziland *N* Svasíland, Swasíland

swear *v (in court)* sverja; *(in anger)*
blóta, bölva

swear words *n* blótsyrði

swearing *n* blót

sweat 1 *n* sviti; *excl* **no ~!** ekkert

mál!; **2** *v* svitna
sweater *n* peysa: **Icelandic wool** ~
lopapeysa
sweatshirt *n* íþróttapeysa
Swede *n* *(person from Sweden)* Svíi
Sweden *N* Svíþjóð
Swedish 1 *adj* sænskur; **2** *n* *(nationality)* Svíi; *(language)* sænska
sweep *v* sópa
sweet *adj* sætur: ~ **and sour sauce**
súrsæt sósa; *(pleasant)* blíður,
góður, ljúfur
sweet pepper *n* paprika
sweet water *n* ferskvatn
sweetener *n* sætuefni: **no-calorie** ~
kalóríusnautt sætuefni; **articifial** ~
gervisykur
swell 1 *n* bólga; **2** *v* bólgna
swelling *n* bólga
swim 1 *n* sund: **go for a** ~ fara í
sund; **2** *v* synda: **I** ~ **every morning** ég syndi á hverjum degi
swimming *n* sund: **No** ~! Bannað að
synda!
swimming pool *n* sundlaug: **indoor**
~ innilaug, **outdoor** ~ útilaug
swimming trunks *n* sundskýla
swimsuit *n* sundföt
swindler *n* svindlari
swing 1 *n* sveifla; *(playground)* róla;
in full ~ í fullum gangi; **2** *v* sveifla;
(on playground) róla
Swiss *adj* svissneskur: ~ **cheese**
svissneskur ostur, **the** ~ **Alps**
svissnesku Alparnir
switch 1 *n* *(light)* rofi, slökkvari;
(a change) skipti; **2** *v* *(change)*
breyta, skipta; ~ **on** kveikja á; ~ **off**
slökkva á
Switzerland *N* Sviss

swollen *adj* bólginn, þrútinn
sword *n* sverð
swordfish *n* sverðfiskur
syllable *n* *ling* atkvæði: **emphasis
on the first** ~ áhersla á fyrsta
atkvæðið
symbol *n* tákn, merki
symbolic *adj* táknrænn
symbolism *n* symbólismi, táknsæis-
stefna
symmetry *n* samræmi, samhverfa
sympathetic *adj* skilningsríkur;
(characteristic) viðkunnanlegur,
geðugur
sympathy *n* samúð
symphony *n* *mus* sinfónía
symphony orchestra sinfóníuhljómsveit: **Icelandic** ~ Sinfóníuhljómsveit Íslands
symptom *n* einkenni; *med* sjúkdóms-
einkenni
synagogue *n* synagóga, bænahús
gyðinga
syndrome *n* *med* sjúkdómsmynd
syntax *n* *ling* setningafræði
synthetic *adj* tilbúinn
synthetic material *n* gerviefni
syphilis *n* *med* sýfilis, sárasótt
Syria *N* Sýrland
Syrian *adj* sýrlenskur
syringe *n* *med* sprauta
syrup *n* síróp: **maple** ~ hlynsíróp
system *n* kerfi: **the digestive** ~
meltingarkerfið, **the school** ~
skólakerfið
systematic *adj* kerfisbundinn: ~
abuse kerfisbundin misnotkun
systematically *adv* kerfisbundið,
markvisst

T

tabasco sauce *n* tabasco sósa
table *n* borð: **kitchen** ~ eldhúsborð;
 (meal) máltíð: **dinner** ~ kvöldmáltíð;
 (numbers) tafla; ~ **of contents**
 efnisyfirlit; **bedside** ~ náttborð
table tennis *n* borðtennis
tablecloth *n* borðdúkur
tablespoon *n* matskeið: **two** ~**s of**
 sugar tvær matskeiðar af sykri
tablet *n (pill)* tafla; *(plate)* plata;
 comp spjaldtölva
tableware *n* borðbúnaður
taboo *adj* bannaður, tabú
tackle *v* fást við, glíma við; *(~ a*
 thief) grípa; *sports* tækla
tag *n* miði, merkimiði: **price** ~
 verðmiði
tail *n (dog, cat, mouse)* rófa, skott;
 (horse) tagl; *(fish)* sporður; *(cow,*
 ox, pig) hali; *(bird)* stertur, stél;
 (lamb, seal) dindill; *(airplane)* stél
tails *n (coin)* bakhlið
taillight *n* afturljós
tailor *n* klæðskeri; ~**-made** klæðskera-
 saumaður
Taiwan *N* Taívan
Taiwanese *adj* taílenskur
Tajikistan 1 *adj* tadsíkiskur; 2 *n*
 (nationality) Tadsíkistan
take *v* taka: ~ **a taxi** taka leigubíl, ~
 time taka tíma, ~ **a break** taka sér
 hlé, **it** ~**s five minutes** það tekur
 fimm mínútur, ~ **part** taka þátt;
 ~ **a nap** fá sér blund; *(bring)* fara
 með: ~ **the book to the library**
 fara með bókina á bókasafnið;
 (travel with) fara með, taka: ~ **the**
 bus fara með strætó, taka strætó;
 ~ **care!** farðu vel með þig!; *(use)*
 nota: **do you** ~ **milk or sugar?**
 notarðu mjólk eða sykur?; *(need)*

þurfa: **it** ~**s two to tango** það þarf
 tvo í tangó; *(grammar)* taka með
 sér: ~ **accusative** tekur með sér
 þolfall
take apart *v* taka í sundur
take away *v* fjarlægja, taka
take notice *v* taka eftir
take off *v (airplane)* hefja sig til flugs
take over *v* taka við
taken *adj* frátekinn, upptekinn: **the**
 seat is ~ sætið er frátekið
takeoff *n (airplane)* flugtak: **during** ~
 and landing í flugtaki og lendingu
take-out food *n* matur til að fara með
takeover *n* yfirtaka: **hostile** ~
 fjandsamleg yfirtaka
tale *n lit* frásögn, saga
talent *n* hæfileiki; *(male)* hæfileika-
 maður; *(female)* hæfileikakona
talented *adj* hæfileikaríkur
talk 1 *v* tala: **the baby doesn't** ~ **yet**
 barnið er enn ekki farið að tala;
 (discuss) tala um, ræða: **we need**
 to ~ við þurfum að ræða saman,
 we ~**ed about politics** við töluðum
 um pólitík; **2** *n* tal; *(conversation)*
 samtal, orðaskipti; **small** ~ spjall;
 (negotiations) viðræður; *(rumors)*
 orðrómur; **teenage** ~ unglingamál;
 baby ~ barnamál
tall *adj* hávaxinn
Tallinn (capital of Estonia) *N*
 Tallinn (höfuðborg Eistlands)
tallow *n* tólg
tampon *n (for menustration)*
 tíðatappi, túrtappi, bómullartappi
tan 1 *adj* gulbrúnn; **2** *n* sólbrúnka
tango *n* tangó
tangy *adj* bragðmikill
tank *n* tankur: **water** ~ vatnstankur;
 (military) skriðdreki

Tanzania *n* Tansanía
Tanzanian 1 *adj* tansanískur; **2** *n*
  (nationality) Tansani
tap *n* krani: **beer on ~** bjór á krana,
  what do you have on ~? hvað ertu
  með á krana?; *(on the shoulder)*
  bank; **wire~** símhlerun
tape *n (for paper)* límband; *(for
  recording)* spóla, kassetta, snælda;
  (police) (lögreglu)borði
tape measure *n* málband
tape recorder *n* segulbandstæki
tapestry *n* listvefnaður, veggtjald
tapioca *n* tapíókamjöl
target *n* skotmark, skotspónn
target language *n* markmál
taro *n* taró
tarragon *n* fáfnisgras
tart *adj* beiskur
tartar sauce *n* tartarasósa
task *n* verkefni
tassle *n* skúfur
taste 1 *n* bragð; *(in music, etc)* smekkur:
  good ~ góður smekkur, **bad ~**
  vondur smekkur; **2** *v* smakka,
  bragða: **this ~s good** þetta er gott
  (á bragðið), **þetta bragðast vel**
tasty *adj* bragðgóður
tattoo *n* húðflúr, tattú
Taurus *n astro* Nautið
tax 1 *n* skattur; **2** *v* skattleggja
taxation *n* skattlagning
tax-free *adj* skattfrjáls
taxi *n* leigubíll: **could you call a ~
  for me?** gætirðu hringt á leigubíl
  fyrir mig?, **~ stand** leigubílaröð,
  hail a ~ stoppa leigubíl
taxpayer *n* skattgreiðandi
T-bone steak *n* T-bone steik
tea *n* te: **~bag** tepoki, **green ~** grænt
  te, **herbal ~** jurtate
tea kettle *n* teketill
tea time *n* kaffitími
teach *v* kenna
teacher *n* kennari: **~'s desk** kennaraborð, **~'s room** kennarastofa
teaching *n* kennsla

team *n sports* lið; *(at work)* sam-
  starfshópur
tear 1 *n (from eyes)* tár; *(hole)* rifa,
  gat; **2** *v* rífa
tearoom *n* testofa
teaspoon *n* teskeið
technical *adj* tæknilegur
technician *n* tæknimaður
technique *n* tækni
technology *n* tækni: **cutting edge
  ~** nýjasta tækni, **institute of ~**
  tækniháskóli
tectonic plates *n geol* flekar jarðarinnar
teddy bear *n* bangsi
tee shirt *n* stuttermabolur
teenager *n* unglingur, táningur
teething *n* tanntaka: **she is ~** hún er
  að taka tennur
telecommunications *n* fjarskipti;
  (technology) fjarskiptatækni
telegram *n* símskeyti: **send a ~**
  senda skeyti
telephone 1 *n* sími: **do you have a
  ~?** ertu með síma?, **can I borrow
  your ~?** get ég fengið símann þinn
  lánaðan?; **2** *v* hringja
telephone bill *n* símreikningur
telephone directory *n* símaskrá
telephone number *n* símanúmer:
  what's your ~? hver er síminn
  hjá þér?
telephoto lens *n* aðdráttarlinsa
telescope *n* stjörnukíkir
television *n* sjónvarp; *(set)*
  sjónvarpstæki
tell *v* segja: **~ a story** segja sögu,
  don't ~! ekki segja frá!
teller *n (bankteller)* bankagjaldkeri
temperature *n* hitastig: **do you know
  what the ~ will be tomorrow?**
  veistu hvað hitastigið verður á
  morgun?; *med (fever)* hiti: **have a
  ~** vera með hita
temple *n (building)* musteri; *anat*
  gagnauga
temporarily *adv* tímabundið
temporary *adj* skammtíma-,
  bráðabirgða

ten *num* tíu

tenant *n* leigjandi

tend *v* hneigjast til, hætta til; **I ~ to forget** ég á það til að gleyma

tendency *n* tilhneyging

tender 1 *adj (sore)* viðkvæmur; *(soft)* mjúkur; *(kind)* blíður, ljúfur; **2** *n econ* **legal ~** gjaldmiðill

tenderloin *n* lund: **beef ~** nautalund, **pork ~** svínalund

tendon *n anat* hásin

tennis *n* tennis: **~ court** tennisvöllur, **~ elbow** *med* tennisolnbogi

tenor *n* tenór; *(singer)* tenórsöngvari

tense 1 *adj* strekktur; **2** *n ling* tíð: **present ~** nútíð, **past ~** þátíð

tension *n* spenna; *(nervous)* taugaspenna

tent *n* tjald; **~ peg** tjaldhæll

tenth *ord* tíundi

term *n (time period)* tímabil; *(school)* önn, misseri: **spring ~** vorönn, vormisseri; *(in a contract)* skilmálar; *(word)* hugtak, íðorð

terminal 1 *adj* loka-, á lokastigi: *med* **~ cancer** krabbamein á lokastigi; **2** *n* endastöð: *(airport)* flugstöð, *(bus)* umferðarmiðstöð

terminus *n* endastöð

tern *n zool* kría

terrace *n* pallur, verönd; *(sports arena)* áhorfendapallar

terrible *adj* hræðilegur, hryllilegur

terribly *adv* hræðilega

terrific *adj* æðislegur, frábær: **this is ~!** þetta er æðislegt!

territorial waters *n* landhelgi

territory *n* svæði, yfirráðasvæði

terror attack *n* hryðjuverkaárás

terrorist *n* hryðjuverkamaður

test 1 *n* próf, prófun; **2** *v* prófa, reyna

testament *n* erfðaskrá

testicles *n anat* eista; *(Icelandic specialty)* **pickled rams' ~** súrsaðir hrútspungar

testimony *n* framburður, vitnisburður

tetanus *n med* stífkrampi

Teutonic *adj* germanskur

text *n* texti

textiles *n* vefnaðarvara

texture *n* áferð

Thai *adj* tælenskur: **~ food** tælenskur matur

Thailand *N* Tæland

than *prep* heldur en, en: **he is older ~ me** hann er eldri en ég

thank *v* þakka: **give ~s** þakka fyrir sig

thank you! *phr* takk!, takk fyrir!, kærar þakkir!

that 1 *pron* þetta: **what's ~?** hvað er þetta?, **~'s all** þetta er allt og sumt; **~'s fine** það er allt í lagi; *(people)* þessi: **~ woman** þessi kona, **~ man** þessi maður, **~ one** þessi; *(relative pronoun)* sem: **the man ~ I saw** maðurinn sem ég sá; **2** *adv* svo, það: **its not ~ expensive** það er ekki svo dýrt

the *defin art* -(i)nn *masc*, -(i)n *fem*, -(i)ð *neu*: **~ man** maðurinn, **~ woman** konan, **~ child** barnið; **the ... the ...** *adv* því ... þeim mun ...: **~ older ~ better** því eldri þeim mun betri

theater *n* leikhús; *(art form)* leiklist; *(movie)* kvikmyndasalur; *med* **operating ~** skurðstofa; *(school)* **lecture ~** fyrirlestrarsalur

theft *n* þjófnaður

their *adj* þeirra: **~ son** sonur þeirra; sinn *refl*: **they talked to ~ son** þau töluðu við son sinn

theirs *pron* þeirra

them *pron* þá *masc acc*; þær *fem acc*; þau *neu acc*; þeim *masc/fem/neu dat*; þeirra *masc/fem/neu gen*

theme *n* umfjöllunarefni, þema

themselves *pron refl* sig *acc*; sér *dat*; *(emphatic)* sjálfur: **they did it ~!** þeir gerðu þetta sjálfir!

then *adv* þá: **I was young and foolish ~** ég var ungur og vitlaus þá; *(there after)* svo, þá: **first I went to a museum, ~ I went on a sight-**

seeing tour fyrst fór ég á safn og
svo fór ég í skoðunarferð
theologist *n* guðfræðingur
theology *n* guðfræði
theoretical *adj* fræðilegur
theory *n* kenning
therapeutic *n* meðferðar-, lækninga-
therapy *n* meðferð, þjálfun: *med*
  (læknis)meðferð, *psych* sálfræðimeðferð, **psycho~** sállækning,
  occupational ~ iðjuþjálfun,
  speech ~ talþjálfun
there 1 *adv (location previously
  mentioned)* þar: **I have been ~** ég
  hef verið þar; *(pointing)* þarna:
  look, over ~! sjáðu, þarna!; *(from)*
  þaðan: **I'm from ~** ég er þaðan;
  (towards) þangað: **I want to go ~**
  mig langar að fara þangað; **~ you
  are** gjörðu svo vel; **2** *interj* there,
  there svona svona; **~, I knew it!**
  sko, ég vissi það!
therefore *adv* þess vegna, þar af
  leiðandi
thermal *adj* hita-, varma-
thermal springs *n* hverir
thermal energy *n* jarðvarmaorka
thermodynamics *n* varmafræði
thermometer *n* hitamælir
thermos *n* hitabrúsi
these *pron* þessir *masc*; þessar *fem*,
  þessi *neu*: **~ bags** þessar töskur, **~
  cars** þessir bílar, **~ are my children** þetta eru börnin mín
they *pron* þeir *masc*; þær *fem*; þau
  neu: **~ are from England** þau eru
  frá Englandi
thick 1 *adj* þykkur; **2** *adv* þykkt
thickness *n* þykkt
thief *n* þjófur
thigh *n* læri: **chicken** ~ kjúklingalæri,
  turkey ~ kalkúnalæri
thin *adj* þunnur, mjór, grannur;
  (people) grannur, mjór
thing *n* hlutur, dót: **where are your
  ~s?** hvar er dótið þitt?
think *v* hugsa: **I ~ about him every**

day ég hugsa um hann á hverjum
degi; *(believe)* halda, telja: **I ~ it's
ok** ég held það sé í lagi
thinking 1 *adj* hugsandi: **~ beings**
  hugsandi menn; **2** *n* hugsun
third *ord* þriði: **~ party** þriðji aðili,
  one~ einn þriðji
thirst *n* þorsti
thirsty *adj* þyrstur: **I'm ~** ég er þyrst(ur)
thirteen *num* þrettán
thirteenth *ord* þrettándi
thirtieth *ord* þrítugasti
thirty *num* þrjátíu
this *adj* þessi *masc/fem*: **~ day**
  þessi dagur, **~ bag** þessi taska,
  ~ one þessi; þetta *neu*: **~ house**
  þetta hús, **~ is impossible!** þetta
  er ómögulegt, **what is ~?** hvað er
  þetta?
thorax *n* anat bringa
thorough *adj* ítarlegur
thoroughly *adv* ítarlega
those 1 *adj* þessir *masc*: **~ men**
  þessir menn; þessar *fem*: **~ women**
  þessar konur; þessi *neu*: **~ children** þessi börn
though 1 *adv* samt, þó; **2** *conj* þó, þó
  að, þótt; **as ~** eins og
thought *n* hugsun
thousand 1 *n* þúsund; **2** *num* þúsund
thousandth *ord* þúsundasti
thread *n* þráður, tvinni
threat *n* hótun; *(danger)* hætta: **a ~
  of rain** hætta á rigningu
threaten *v* hóta
threatening *adj* ógnandi, hættulegur
three *num* þrír *masc*: **~ chairs** þrír
  stólar; þrjár *fem*: **~ spoons** þrjár
  skeiðar; þrjú *neu*: **~ tables** þrjú
  borð
thrill 1 *n* spenna, æsingur; **2** *v* hrífa
thrilled *adj* gagntekinn, spenntur
thrilling *adj* spennandi
throat *n* anat háls: *med* **a sore ~**
  hálsbólga
thrombosis *n* med blóðtappamyndun
through 1 *adv* búinn: **are you ~?**

ertu búinn?; **hættur: they are** ~ þau
eru hætt saman; **2** *prep* (í) gegnum:
I drove ~ **the city** ég keyrði (í)
gegnum miðbæinn; *(until)* til:
open Monday ~ **Wednesday** opið
frá mánudegi til miðvikudags; **3**
adv í gegn: **get** ~ komast í gegn;
the whole night ~ alla nóttina

throughout 1 *adv* alveg, í gegn, alls
staðar; **2** *prep* *(place)* alls staðar:
~ **Iceland** um allt land; *(time)* út,
allur: ~ **the year** út árið, allt árið

throw *v* kasta, henda: ~ **a ball** kasta
bolta; ~ **out garbage** henda rusli;
~ **a party** halda veislu, halda partí;
~ **a fit** verða brjálaður

throw away *v* henda

throw up *v* kasta upp, æla, gubba

thrush *n zool* þröstur

thumb *n* þumall, þumalfingur

thunder *n* þruma: ~ **and lightning**
þrumur og eldingar

thunderstorm *n* þrumuveður

Thursday *n* fimmtudagur: **on** ~ á
fimmtudag(inn), **last** ~ síðastliðinn
fimmtudag, ~ **this week** á
fimmtudag(inn), **next** ~ fimmtudag í
næstu viku, **on** ~**s** á fimmtudögum

thus *adv* þess vegna, þar af leiðandi

thyme *n* (*herb*) tímían, *(Icelandic)*
blóðberg

thyroid *n anat* skjaldkirtill

tibia *n anat* sköflungur

tic *n med* fjörfiskur

tick *n* *(sound)* tif: **time is** ~**ing**
klukkan tifar, tíminn líður;
(insect) blóðmaur

ticket *n* miði; *(for plane)* flugmiði,
farseðill; *(entrance)* aðgöngumiði;
(for movie) bíómiði

ticket agency *n* miðasala

ticket counter *n* miðasala

tide *n* sjávarfall

tidy 1 *adj* snyrtilegur, þrifalegur; **2** *v*
laga til, gera hreint: ~ **up** laga til

tie 1 *n* *(neck)* bindi; *(bowtie)* slaufa;
sports jafntefli: ~ **game** jafntefli;

(connection) tengsl: **family** ~**s**
fjölskyldutengsl; **2** *v* binda; *sports*
jafna

tight 1 *adj* *(rope)* strekktur; *(clothing)*
þröngur: **the pants are** ~ buxurnar
eru þröngar; ~ **with money** nískur;
~ **situation** erfið staða; **2** *adv* fast;
expr **sleep** ~ sofa vært

tightly *adv* fast

tights *n* sokkabuxur

tilapia *n zool* beitarfiskur

tile *n* flís

till *prep* þangað til

time *n* tími: **free** ~ frjáls tími, **on** ~
tímalega; **at the same** ~ á sama
tíma, samtímis; **what** ~ **is it?** hvað
er klukkan?; **all the** ~ alltaf; **from**
~ **to** ~ við og við, annað slagið;
(first, second, etc) sinn, skipti: **for**
the first ~ í fyrsta sinn; **for the**
second ~ í annað skiptið

time clock *n* stimpilklukka

timer *n* tímastillir; **oven** ~ ofnklukka

timetable *n* tímaáætlun; *(school)*
stundatafla

timpani *n mus* pákur

tin *n* dós

tinfoil *n* álpappír

tiny *adj* pínulítill

tip 1 *n* *(narrow end)* oddur; *(for*
service) þjórfé: **leave a** ~ skilja
eftir þjórfé; *(for refuse)* haugur;
2 *v* *(for service)* gefa þjórfé

Tirana (capital of Albania) *N*
Tírana (höfuðborg Albaníu)

tire 1 *n* *(wheel)* deck, hjólbarði; **2** *v*
(grow weary) þreyta

tired *adj* þreyttur

tiring *adj* þreytandi

tissue *n bio* líkamsvefur; *(paper)* bréf

title *n* titill

to *prep* *(long distance)* til: ~ **Iceland**
til Íslands, ~ **Europe** til Evrópu;
(short distance) á, í: ~ **work** í
vinnuna, ~ **the store** í búðina;
(recipient) til: ~ **mom** til mömmu;
(treatment) við: **kind** ~ **me** góður

við mig; *(time)* í: **it's five ~ four** hún er fimm mínútur í fjögur; *(sport results)* gegn, á móti: **three goals ~ one** þrjú mörk á móti einu

toad *n zool* karta

toast 1 *n (drink)* skál: **let's drink a ~** við skulum skála; *(bread)* ristað brauð: **~ with cheese** ristað brauð með osti; **2** *v (with a drink)* skála; *(bread, nuts etc.)* rista: **~ed cashews** ristaðar kasjúhnetur

toaster *n* brauðrist, ristavél

tobacco *n* tóbak: **chewing ~** munntóbak, **~ plant** tóbaksplant, **~ shop** tóbaksbúð

today 1 *n* dagurinn í dag: **~'s paper** blaðið í dag; **2** *adv* í dag

toddler *n* smábarn

toe *n* tá; *expr* **from top to ~** frá hvirfli til ilja

toffee *n* karamella

tofu *n* tófú: **hard ~** stíft tófu, **soft ~** mjúkt tófú, **~ sausages** tófúpylsur, **~ allergy** *med* tófúofnæmi

together *adv* saman: **they are ~** þau eru saman; **~ with** ásamt, með

Togo *N* Tógó

toilet *n* klósett, salerni: **public ~** almenningsklósett

toilet paper *n* klósettpappír, salernispappír

toiletry *n* snyrtivörur

token *n* tákn, merki; *(in boardgame)* leikmaður

Tokyo (capital of Japan) *N* Tókíó (höfuðborg Japans)

tolerance *n* umburðarlyndi

toll *n* tollur

tomato *n* tómatur: **green ~** grænir tómatar, **~ sauce** tómatsósa, **~ juice** tómatsafi, **~ paste** tómatpúrra

tomorrow 1 *n* morgundagurinn; **2** *adv* á morgun: **day after ~** ekki á morgun heldur hinn, **see you ~!** sjáumst á morgun!; **~ morning** í fyrramálið

ton *n* tonn

tone *n* tónn

toner cartridge *n* dufthylki

Tonga *n* Tonga

tongue *n anat* tunga: **pig ~** svínatunga, **cow ~** nautatunga; *(language)* tunga, tungumál: **Icelandic ~** íslensk tunga

tonic water *n* tónik: **gin and ~** gin og tónik

tonight *adv (before midnight)* í kvöld; *(after midnight)* í nótt

tonsillitis *n med* hálskirtlabólga

tonsils *n anat* hálskirtlar

too *adv (also)* líka, einnig: **me ~!** ég líka!, **I'll have one ~** fæ ég líka; *(a lot)* of: **you talk ~ fast!** þú talar of hratt!, **~ expensive** of dýrt, **~ much** of mikið

tool *n* verkfæri, tól

toolbar *n comp* verkfærastika

tooth *n* tönn

toothache *n* tannpína: **I have a severe ~** ég er með slæma tannpínu

toothbrush *n* tannbursti: **do you have ~es?** ertu með tannbursta?

toothpaste *n* tannkrem

toothpick *n* tannstöngull: **could I have a ~?** gæti ég fengið tannstöngul?

top 1 *adj (high up)* efstur, hæstur: **on the ~ shelf** á efstu hillunni; *(speed)* hámarks-: **at ~ speed** á hámarkshraða; *(superior)* yfirburða-: **a ~ athlete** yfirburða íþróttamaður; **2** *n* toppur: **~ of a mountain** fjallstoppur, tindur; *(lid)* lok; *(on bottle)* tappi

topic *n* umfjöllunarefni, tema

torch *n* vasaljós; *(fire)* kyndill

torn *adj* rifinn

tornado *n* skýstrókur, hvirfilbylur

torrent *n* flóð

tort *n leg* skaðabótaréttur

torte *n* terta

tortilla *n* tortilla

tortoise *n zool* skjaldbaka

torture *v* pynding, misþyrming

toss *v* kasta

total 1 *adj* alger: **a ~ mess** algjör kaós; **2** *n* heild, summa; *(cost)* heildarupphæð: **what is the ~?** hver er heildarupphæðin?

total eclipse *n* almyrkvi: **~ of the sun** almyrkvi sólar, **~ of the moon** almyrkvi tungls

totally *adv* algjörlega, gjörsamlega: **this is ~ awesome!** þetta er algjörlega frábært!

touch 1 *n* snerting; *(contact)* samband: **let's keep in ~** verum í sambandi!; **2** *v* snerta, koma við: **do not ~!** ekki snerta!

touch pad *n comp* dregill

touch screen *n comp* snertiskjár

touched *adj* hrærður

touchy *adj* viðkvæmur

tough *adj* harður, seigur; *(difficult)* erfiður; *(meat)* seigur; *expr* **~ luck!** þvílík óheppni!

tour *n* ferð; *(long)* ferðalag: **~ around Iceland** ferðalag um Ísland; *(short trip)* skoðunarferð: **a guided ~** skoðunarferð (með leiðsögumanni); *(of a band)* tónleikaferðalag: **the band is on a European ~** hljómsveitin er á tónleikaferðalagi um Evrópu

tour group *n* ferðahópur

tour guide *n* leiðsögumaður

tourism *n* ferðaþjónusta, túrismi

tourist *n* ferðamaður, túristi: **~ attraction** ferðamannastaður, **~ class** annað farrými, **~ office** upplýsingaskrifstofa (fyrir ferðamenn)

tow *v* draga: **~ a car** draga bíl

tow truck *n* dráttarbíll

toward(s) *prep (movement)* í áttina að, til: **walking ~ the waterfall** ganga í áttina að fossinum; *(attitude, feelings)* gagnvart: **what are your feelings ~ me?** hverjar eru tilfinningar þínar gagnvart mér?; *(for)* fyrir: **save ~ a trip** safna fyrir ferð

towel *n* handklæði

tower *n* turn

town *n* bær: **Stykkishólmur is a beautiful ~** Stykkishólmur er fallegur bær; *(center)* miðbær: **go to ~** fara í bæinn

town hall *n* ráðhús

township *n* þorp, þéttbýliskjarni

toxic *adj* eitraður, eitur-: **~ waste** eiturefnaúrgangur

toxin *n* eitur

toy 1 *adj* leikfanga-: **a ~ gun** leikfangabyssa; **2** *n* leikfang

toy store *n* leikfangaverslun, leikfangabúð

trace 1 *n* ummerki; **2** *v* rekja

track 1 *n* slóð, stígur, troðningur; *(sports)* rás; *(railroad)* spor; **2** *v* rekja spor

track and field *n sports* frjálsar íþróttir

tracking station *n* ratsjárstöð

tractor *n* dráttarvél, traktor

trade 1 *n* verslun, viðskipti: **a fair ~** sanngjörn viðskipti; *(work)* iðn: **~ school** iðnskóli; **2** *v* stunda viðskipti; *(exchange)* skipast á: **~ cars** skiptast á bílum, **would you like to ~?** viltu skipta?;

trade gap *n econ* neikvæður vöruskiptajöfnuður

trade union *n* verkalýðsfélag

trademark *n econ* vörumerki: **registered ~** skrásett vörumerki

trader *n econ* verðbréfasali

trading *n* hlutabréfaviðskipti: *econ* **insider ~** innherjaviðskipti

tradition *n* hefð, siður: **Icelandic ~** íslenskur siður

traditional *adj* hefðbundinn: **~ Icelandic food** hefðbundinn íslenskur matur

traditionally *adv* samkvæmt venju

traffic *n* umferð: **~ accident** umferðarslys, umferðaróhapp, **~ jam** umferðaröngþveiti, **~ light** umferðarljós

trafficking *n* verslun með ólöglegan

varning; **human** ~ mansal; **drug** ~
eiturlyfjaverslun
tragedy *n* harmleikur, *colloq* tragedía:
a human ~ mannlegur harmleikur
trail *n* slóð
trailer *n* tengivagn
trailer tent *n* tjaldvagn
train *n* lest: ~ **station** lestarstöð
trained *adj* þjálfaður
trainer *n* þjálfari
training *n* þjálfun, æfing: **sports** ~
íþróttaæfing, ~ **suit** æfingagalli
trampoline *n* trampólín, fjaðurdýna
tranquility *n* ró, friður, kyrrð
tranquilizer *n* róandi lyf
transaction *n* viðskipti: **cash** ~**s**
peningaviðskipti
transcribe *n* umrita, afrita; *(pronunciation)* hljóðrita
transcript *n* afrit; *(from university)*
afrit úr námsferilsskrá
transfer 1 *n* flutningur, færsla; *(money)*
millifærsla; *(plane)* millilending;
(bus) strætóskipti; *(ticket)* skipti-
miði: **could I have a ~, please?**
gæti ég fengið skiptimiða?; **2** *v*
flytja sig, færa sig: ~ **to another department** færa sig yfir í aðra deild;
(money) millifæra; *(plane)* millilenda: **I have to ~ in Germany**
ég þarf að millilenda í Þýskalandi;
(bus) skipta um strætó
transferable *adj* framseljanlegur
transform *v* umbreytast
transformation *n* breyting, umskipti;
(e.g. by magic) hamskipti
transformer *n* straumbreytir
transfusion *n* med blóðgjöf
transit *n* flutningur; *(buses, etc.)*
samgöngur: **public** ~ almenningssamgöngur, ~ **system** samgöngu-
kerfi; **in** ~ á leiðinni
transition *n* breyting, umskipti: **a
period of** ~ umbrotatímar
translate *v* þýða: ~ **from Icelandic
to English** þýða úr íslensku á ensku
translation *n* þýðing: **a** ~ **from**

Icelandic þýðing úr íslensku
translator *n* þýðandi: **I work as a** ~
ég starfa sem þýðandi
transmission *n* *(radio, TV)* útsending;
mech (car) gírkassi
transmit *v* senda út
transparent *adj* *(see through)*
gegnsær; *(obvious)* augljós
transplant 1 *n* med ígræðsla: **liver** ~
lifrarígræðsla; **2** *v* flytja
transport 1 *n* *(people)* samgöngur;
(goods) flutningar; *(company)*
flutningafyrirtæki; **2** *v* flytja á milli
transportation *n* *(people)* samgöngur:
public ~ almenningssamgöngur;
(goods) flutningur
transvestite *n* klæðskiptingur
trap 1 *n* gildra; **2** *v* leggja gildru fyrir
trash *n* rusl, sorp, úrgangur; *slang
(people)* hyski
trash can *n* rusladallur, ruslafata
travel 1 *n* ferðalag: ~ **agency**
ferðaskrifstofa; **2** *v* ferðast: ~ **to
Iceland** ferðast til Íslands
traveler *n* ferðamaður, ferðalangur
traveler's check *n* ferðaávísun,
ferðatékki
traveling *n* ferðamennska
trawler *n* togari
tray *n* bakki: **ash~** öskubakki
treasure 1 *n* fjársjóður; **2** *v* meta mikils
treasury *n* fjármálaráðuneyti
treat 1 *n* ánægja; *expr* **my** ~! ég býð!
ég borga!; **2** *v* höndla, fara með;
(doctor) hafa til meðferðar; *(see
as)* líta á sem: ~ **it as a vacation**
líta á þetta sem sumarfrí; *(talk
about)* fjalla um
treatment *n* meðhöndlun; **alternative**
~ óhefðbundnar lækningar
treatment room *n* aðgerðastofa
treaty *n* milliríkjasamningur
tree *n* tré
trek *n* löng ganga
tremendous *adj* mjög stór, hrikalegur,
ofsalegur
tremendously *adv* ofsalega, hrikalega

trench *n* skurður, síki
trench coat *n* rykfrakki
trend *n (incline towards)* stefna, tilhneiging; *(fashion)* tíska
trespass *v* fara í leyfisleysi: **no ~ing!** bannað að fara inn á svæðið!
trial *n (test)* reynsla: **on ~** til reynslu; *leg* réttarhald
triangle *n* þríhyrningur; *mus* þríhorn
tribe *n* ættflokkur
trick 1 *n* gabb, brella; **2** *v* plata
trillion *num* trilljón
trilogy *n* þríleikur, trílógía
trim 1 *n* ástand, ásigkomulag; *(haircut)* hársnyrting; **2** *v* snyrta; *(hair)* særa
Trinidad and Tobago *N* Trínidad og Tóbagó
Trinidadian 1 *adj* trínidadískur; **2** *n (nationality)* Trínidadi
trio *n* tríó
trip 1 *n* ferð, ferðalag; *(on drugs)* víma; **2** *v* hrasa, detta
tripe *n* vömb
tripod *n* þrífótur
Tripoli (capital of Libya) *N* Trípólí (höfuðborg Líbíu)
triumph 1 *n* sigur, stórsigur; *(mood)* sigurvíma; **2** *v* sigra, vinna
trolley *n* trilla; *(for shopping)* innkaupavagn; *(for drinks on planes/trains)* veitingavagn; **~ bag** flugfreyjutaska
trombone *n mus* básúna
tropical *adj* hitabeltis-, trópískur
trot *v* skokka, trítla; *(horses)* brokka
troubadour *n* trúbadúr
trouble 1 *n* vandræði, erfiðleikar; **what's the ~?** hvað er að?; *econ* **financial ~** fjárhagserfiðleikar; **2** *v* valda áhyggjum, angra
trousers *n* buxur
trout *n* silungur
truck *n* pallbíll
true *adj* sannur: **that's not ~** það er ekki satt; *(honest)* trúr: **~ to myself** trúr sjálfum mér; *(correct)* réttur: **~**

or false rétt eða rangt
truffle *n* hallsveppur, trufflur: **chocolate ~s** súkkulaðitrufflur
truly *adv* hreinskilningslega
trumpet *n* trompet
trunk *n (tree)* trjábolur; *(body)* bolur; *(luggage)* kista; *(car)* skott; *(elephant)* rani
trunks *n (shorts for swimming)* sundskýla
trust 1 *n* traust, trúnaður; **2** *v* treysta: **I ~ you** ég treysti þér
trustee *n* fjárhaldsmaður; **board of ~s** stjórn
truth *n* sannleikur
try *v* reyna: **~ hard** reyna mikið
try on *v* máta
T-shirt *n* stuttermabolur
tsunami *n* flóðbylgja
tuba *n mus* túba
tube *n* pípa, rör; *(container)* túpa
tuber *n* hnýði
tuberculosis *n med* berklar
Tuesday *n* þriðjudagur, **on ~** á þriðjudag(inn), **last ~** síðastliðinn þriðjudag; **~ next week** á þriðjudag í næstu viku
tulip *n flora* túlipani
tumor *n med* æxli: **benign ~** góðkynja æxli, **malignant ~** illkynja æxli
tuna *n* túnfiskur: **~ salad** túnfisksalat
tune 1 *n mus* lag: **sing a ~** syngja lag; *(setting)* stilling: **out of ~** falskur, **well ~d** vel stilltur; **2** *v mus* stilla
Tunis (capital of Tunisia) *N* Túnis (höfuðborg Túnis)
Tunisia *N* Túnis
Tunisian *adj* túniskur
tunnel *n* (jarð)göng
turbot *n* sandhverfa
turbulence *n* ókyrrð
Turkey *N* Tyrkland
turkey *n* kalkúni: **roasted ~** steiktur kalkúni, **honey-glazed ~** hunangsgljáður kalkúni, **smoked ~** reyktur kalkúni
Turkish 1 *adj* tyrkneskur; **2** *n*

(nationality) Tyrki; *(language)*
tyrkneska
Turkmen 1 *adj* túrkmenskur; **2** *n*
Túrkmeni
Turkmenistan *N* Túrkmenistan
turmeric *n* túrmerik, gullinrót,
kúrkúma
turn 1 *n (circular movement)*
snúningur; *(left, right)* beygja; *phr*
it's your ~ það er komið að þér;
2 *v (in circles)* snúa, snúast; *(flip
page)* fletta; *(to left, right)* beygja:
~ **left!** beygðu til vinstri!; *(become)* verða: ~ **old** verða gamall
turn against *v* snúast á móti
turn back *v* snúa aftur
turn down *v* afþakka
turn into *v* breytast í
turn off *v* slökkva á
turn on *v* kveikja á
turn out *v* reynast
turnip *n* næpa
turnover *n* velta
turtle *n zool* skjaldbaka
tusk *n* keila
tussock *n* þúfa
tutor *n* einkakennari
tutorial *n* einkatími; **online** ~
kennslustund á vefnum
Tuvalu *n* Túvalú
TV *(abbrev for* **television***)* sjónvarp;
~ **set** sjónvarpstæki
tweezers *n* flísatöng

twelfth *ord* tólfti
twelve *num* tólf
twentieth *ord* tuttugasti
twenty *num* tuttugu; ~**four hour
service** sólarhringsafgreiðsla, opið
allan sólarhringinn
twice *adv* tvisvar, tvisvar sinnum: ~
a day tvisvar á dag
twin *n* tvíburi: ~ **beds** tvö samstæð
rúm, ~ **cities** tvíburaborgir,
samvaxnar borgir
twist 1 *n* snúningur; *(in a story)*
óvænt atburðarrás; *(yarn)* flækja;
(dance) tvist; **2** *v* snúa upp á: ~ **an
ankle** snúa upp á ökklan; *(words)*
snúa út úr; *(yarn)* flækja(st);
(dance) tvista
twist bun *n* snúður
twisted *adj* flæktur
two *num* tveir *masc*: ~ **cars** tveir bílar;
tvær *fem*: ~ **books** tvær bækur; tvö
neu: ~ **children** tvö börn; tveggja
gen: ~**door car** tveggja dyra bíll,
~**lane highway** tveggja akreina
hraðbraut
type 1 *n* tegund, gerð, sort: **what** ~
of ...? hvaða tegund af ...?; **(s)he
is not my** ~ hann/hún er ekki mín
týpa; *(letters)* leturgerð; **2** *v* vélrita
typical *adj* dæmigerður
typically *adv* venjulega

U

U.K. (*abbrev* **United Kingdom**)
Bretland, Sameinaða konungsríkið
Stóra-Bretland og Norður-Írland

U.S.A. (*abbrev* **United Stated of
America**) Bandaríkin, Bandaríki
Ameríku

Uganda *N* Úganda

Ugandan 1 *adj* úgandskur; **2** *n*
(nationality) Úgandamaður

ugly *adj* ljótur, ófríður

Ukraine *N* Úkraína

Ukrainian 1 *adj* úkraínskur; **2** *n*
(nationality) Úkraínumaður;
(language) úkraínska

ulcer *n med* sár: **gastric ~** magasár

ultimate *adj* endanlegur

ultimately *adv* að lokum, að síðustu

ultrasound *n med* ómskoðun

umbrella *n* regnhlíf

umlaut *n ling* hljóðvarp; *(on a letter)*
tvípunktur

UN (*abbrev* **United Nations**) SÞ
(Sameinuðu þjóðirnar)

unable *adj* ófær

unacceptable *adj* óásættanlegur

unbearable *adj* óþolandi

unbreakable *adj* óbrjótandi

uncanny *adj* furðulegur

uncap *v* taka lokið af

uncertain *adj* óviss: **that's ~** það
er óvíst

uncertainty *n* óvissa

uncle *n* frændi, *(father's brother)*
föðurbróðir, *(mother's brother)*
móðurbróðir

uncomfortable *adj* óþægilegur; **feel
~** líða illa

unconscious *adj* meðvitundarlaus:
she is ~ hún er meðvitundarlaus;
(without knowing) ómeðvitandi

uncooked *adj* óeldaður, ósoðinn

uncork *v* taka tappann úr: **~ the
bottle** taka tappann úr flöskunni

uncountable *adj* óteljandi

under 1 *adv* undir, niður; **2** *prep* undir

underbelly *n* kviður

underclothes *n* nærföt

underdone *adj* of lítið eldaður: **the
steak is ~** steikin er of lítið elduð

undergo *v* gangast undir, ganga í
gegnum: **~ a surgery** *med* gangast
undir aðgerð

underground *adj* neðanjarðar-:
~ music jaðartónlist; **2** *adv*
neðanjarðar; **go ~** fara í felur

underlie *v* liggja til grundvallar,
liggja að baki

underlying *adj* undirliggjandi: **~
disease** undirliggjandi sjúkdómur

underneath 1 *prep* undir; **2** *adv* fyrir
neðan

underpants *n* nærbuxur

underpass *n* göng

understand *v* skilja: **I ~ Icelandic**
ég skil íslensku, **I don't ~** ég skil
ekki

understanding *n* skilningur; *(agreement)* samkomulag: **to reach an ~**
að ná samkomulagi

understatement *n* úrdráttur

undertake *v* hefjast handa

undertaker *n* útfararstjóri

undertaking *n* viðfangsefni

underwater *adj* neðansjávar-: **~
camera** neðansjávarmyndavél

underwear *n* nærföt

undo *v (button)* hneppa frá; *(work)*
eyðileggja

undoubtedly *adv* tvímælalaust

undress *v (self)* hátta, fara úr, af-
klæðast; *(other)* klæða úr, afklæða

unemployed *adj* atvinnulaus

unemployment *n* atvinnuleysi: ~
  compensation atvinnuleysisbætur
UNESCO *abbrev* Menningar-
  málastofnun Sameinuðu þjóðanna
uneven *adj* ójafn; ~ **road surface**
  ósléttur vegur; ~ **heartbeat** *med*
  óreglulegur hjartsláttur
unexpected *adj* óvæntur
unexpectedly *adv* óvænt
unfair *adj* ósanngjarn
unfamiliar *adj* ókunnur
unfortunate *adj* óheppinn, *(not*
  good) óheppilegur: ~ **decision**
  óheppileg ákvörðun
unfortunately *adv* því miður
unfriend *v comp* taka af vinalistanum
unfriendly *adj* óvingjarnlegur
unfurnished *adj* án húsgagna
unhappiness *n* óhamingja
unhappy *adj* óhamingjusamur
unhealthy *adj* óheilbrigður; *(not*
  good for you) óhollur: ~ **food**
  óhollur matur; *(looks)* óhraustlegur
uniform *n* einkennisbúningur:
  school ~ skólabúningur
unimportant *adj* ómikilvægur
union *n (the act of)* sameining;
  (the result) samband, bandalag:
  teacher's ~ kennarasamband
unique *adj* einstæður, einstakur,
  sérstakur: **a** ~ **experience** einstök
  upplifun
unisex *adj* fyrir bæði kynin
unit *n* eining
unite *v* sameinast; *(marry)* gefa saman
united *adj* sameinaður
United Arab Emirates *N* Sameinuðu
  arabísku furstadæmin
United Kingdom *N* Bretland;
  Sameinaða konungsríkið Stóra-
  Bretland og Norður-Írland: **I'm**
  from the ~ ég er frá Bretlandi
United States of America *N*
  Bandaríkin; Bandaríki Ameríku *pl*:
  I'm from the ~ ég er frá Bandaríkjunum
universe *n* alheimurinn

university *n* háskóli: **a** ~ **degree**
  háskólagráða
unkind *adj* óvingjarnlegur
unknown *adj* óþekktur
unleaded *adj* blýlaus
unleavened *adj* gerlaus: ~ **bread**
  gerlaust brauð
unless *conj* nema
unlike **1** *adj* ólíkur, frábrugðinn; **2**
  prep ólíkt, gagnstætt
unlikely *adj* ólíklegur
unlimited *adj* ótakmarkaður: ~ **mile-**
  age ótakmarkaður kílómetrafjöldi
unload *v* losa, afferma: ~ **the car**
  afferma bílinn
unlock *v* opna, taka úr lás
unlucky *adj* óheppinn
unmarried *adj* ógiftur
unmixed *adj* óblandaður
unnecessary *adj* ónauðsynlegur
unpack *v* taka upp úr: ~ **the suitcase**
  taka upp úr töskunni
unpleasant *adj* óþægilegur, ónotalegur
unreasonable *adj* óskynsamlegur
unrefined *adj* óhreinsaður: ~ **sugar**
  óhreinsaður sykur
unripe *adj* óþroskaður: ~ **fruit**
  óþroskaðir ávextir, ~ **vegetable**
  óþroskað grænmeti
unsafe *adj* óöruggur
unsaturated *adj* ómettuð: ~ **fat**
  ómettuð fita
unscrew *v* skrúfa af: ~ **the bottle**
  skrúfa tappann af flöskunni
unstable *adj* óstöðugur
unsteady *adj* óstöðugur
unsuccessful *adj* árangurslítill
unsuccessfully *adv* árangurslaust
untidy *adj* ósnyrtilegur
until **1** *prep* til; **2** *conj* þangað til;
  not ~ ekki fyrr: **not** ~ **you go** ekki
  fyrr en þú ferð
unusual *adj* óvenjulegur
unusually *adv* óvenjulega
unwell *adj* slappur, lasinn
unwilling *adj* tregur
unwillingly *adv* treglega

unzip *v (clothing)* renna niður; *comp (file)* opna

up *adj (location)* uppi: ~ **there** þarna uppi: *(movement)* upp: **going** ~ fara upp; **to get** ~ að fara á fætur; ~ **and down** upp og niður; *expr* **it's** ~ **to you** það er undir þér komið; *expr* **what are you** ~ **to?** hvað ertu að brasa?

updated *adj* endurnýjaður, uppfærður, endurbættur

uphill *adj* upp í móti

upon *prep* á, upp á

upper *adj* efri, hærri: ~ **body** efri hluti líkamans, ~ **berth** efri koja

upset 1 *adj* í uppnámi, í ójafnvægi, vera miður sín: **he is** ~ hann er í uppnámi; **have an** ~ **stomach** fá í magann; **2** *v* raska, setja í uppnám

upside down *adv* á hvolfi

upstairs 1 *adv* upp stigann, upp: **go** ~ fara upp stigann; **2** *n* efri hæð

upwards *adv* upp, upp á við

urban *adj* borgar-

urge 1 *n* áköf löngun; **2** *v* hvetja

urgent *adj* áríðandi, mikilvægur

urinary tract infection *n med* þvagfærasýking

urine *n* þvag

URL *abbrev comp* veffang

Uruguay *N* Úrúgvæ

us *pron* okkur *acc/dat*; okkar *gen*

usage *n* notkun

USB port *n comp* USB-tengill

use *v* nota: ~ **before** notist fyrir; **for personal** ~ til einkanota

used *adj* notaður: **a** ~ **car** notaður bíll

used to *v* var vanur að: **I** ~ **to come here every day** ég var vanur að koma hingað á hverjum degi

useful *adj* gagnlegur

useless *adj* gagnslaus

user *n* notandi

username *n comp* notendanafn

usual *adj* venjulegur

usually *adv* venjulega

usury *n* okurlán

utensils *n* hnífapör

utility *n* gagn, nytsemi

utterance *n* yrðing

Uzbek *adj* úsbekskur

Uzbekistan *N* Úsbekistan

V

vacancy *n* tóm; *(room etc)* laus herbergi: **are there any ~?** ertu með
laus herbergi?, **no** ~ ekkert laust!;
(job) laus staða
vacant *adj (empty)* tómur; *(available)*
laus; *(~ mind)* andlaus
vacate *v* rýma, tæma
vacation *n* leyfi, frí: **be on** ~ vera í
fríi, **summer** ~ sumarfrí, **Christmas** ~ jólafrí, **Easter** ~ páskafrí
vaccinate *v* bólusetja: **be ~d against**
vera bólusettur gegn
vaccination *n* bólusetning
vaccine *n* bóluefni
vacuum cleaner *n* ryksuga
vagina *n anat* leggöng
vaginal infection *med* leggangasýking
valet *n* herbergisþjónn: ~ **service**
herbergisþjónusta
valid *adj* gildur: ~ **passport** gilt
vegabréf, gildur passi
validate *v* staðfesta; *leg* löggilda
valley *n* dalur
valuable *adj* verðmætur
valuables *n* verðmæti
valuation *n* verðmat
value 1 *n* virði, gildi; *(price)* verðgildi;
2 *v* meta
value-added tax (VAT) *n* virðisauka-
skattur, vaskur (VSK)
values *n (opinions)* gildismat
van *n* sendiferðabíll
vanilla *n* vanilla: ~ **bean** vanillustangir,
~ **extract** vanilludropar, ~ **ice cream**
vanilluís, ~ **sugar** vanillusykur
Vanuatu *N* Vanúatú
vapor *n* gufa, mistur
vaporize *v* gufa upp, breytast í gufu
variable 1 *adj* breytilegur, mismunandi;
2 *n* breyta
variation *n (difference)* breytileiki,

mismunur; *(versions)* tilbrigði;
(music) tilbrigði
varicose veins *n med* æðahnútar
varied *adj* margvíslegur
variety *n* fjölbreytni; *(collection)*
samansafn; *(bio)* afbrigði; *(type)*
tegund, gerð
various *adj* ýmsir: ~ **people** ýmsir
vary *v* breytast, vera mismunandi:
the size varies þetta er til í ýmsum
stærðum *(lit.:* this is available in
many different sizes)
vase *n* vasi
vast *adj (size)* mjög stór, víðáttumikill;
(knowledge) víðtækur; ~ **number
of** ... gífurlegur fjöldi ...
VAT. *See* value-added tax
Vatican City *N* Vatíkanborgríkið
vault *n* hvelfing; *(in a bank)* öryggs-
isgeymsla; **wine** ~ vínkjallari
VD. *See* veneral disease
veal *n* kálfakjöt
vegan 1 *adj* vegan-: ~ **meal** vegan-
fæði: **do you offer any ~ meals?**
ertu með eitthvað fyrir vegan fólk?;
2 *n* vegan: **I'm a vegan** ég er vegan
vegetable *n* grænmeti: ~ **stew** græn-
metisspottréttur, ~ **broth** grænmetis-
soð, ~ **garden** matjurtagarður
vegetarian 1 *adj* fyrir grænmetisætur:
~ **dish** grænmetisréttur, ~ **soup**
grænmetissúpa, ~ **menu** matseðill
fyrir grænmetisætur; **2** *n* grænmetisæta: **I'm a** ~ ég er grænmetisæta
vegetation *n* gróður
vehicle *n* farartæki
velocity *n* hraði
veil *n* blæja
vein *n* æð
velvet *n* flauel
vendor *n* söluaðili

veneral disease (VD) *n* kynsjúkdómur
Venezuela *N* Venesúela
Venezuelan 1 *adj* venesúelskur; 2 *n* Venesúelamaður
venison *n* hreindýrakjöt
venom *n* eitur
venous *adj* bláæða-
ventilator *n* loftræstitæki
venture 1 *n* áhætta; 2 *v* hætta, voga, þora; *(risk)* taka áhættu: *econ* ~ capital fund áhættufjárfestingarsjóður
venue *n* vettvangur; music ~ tónleikastaður
verb *n ling* sagnorð, sögn
verbal *adj* munnlegur, í orðum
verdict *n leg* úrskurður
vernacular *n ling* þjóðtunga
verse *n (poem)* ljóð; *(stanza)* erindi, vers; *(one line)* ljóðlína; *(Biblical)* vers
version *n* útgáfa
vertibra *n anat* hryggjarliður
vertical *adj* lóðréttur
vertigo *n med* lofthræðsla
very *adv* mjög: ~ good mjög gott, ~ much mjög mikið
veterinarian *n* dýralæknir
veto *n* neitunarvald
via *prep* um, með viðkomu í/á, í gegnum: ~ New York með viðkomu í New York
victim *n* fórnarlamb
victorious *adj* sigursæll
victory *n* sigur
video *n* vídeó: ~ camera vídeómyndavél, myndbandsupptökuvél, ~ card vídeókort, ~ game vídeóleikur, myndbandaleikur
Vienna (capital of Austria) *N* Vínarborg (höfuðborg Austurríkis)
Vietnam *N* Víetnam
Vietnamese 1 *adj* víetnamskur: ~ food víetnamskur matur; 2 *n (nationality)* Víetnami; *(language)* víetnamska
view *n (what is seen)* sýn; *(can be seen)* sjónmál, augnsýn: out of ~ úr augnsýn, úr sjónmáli; *(over)* útsýni: sea ~ sjávarútsýni, a nice ~ fallegt útsýni; *(opinion)* skoðun, sýn: political ~ pólitísk skoðun
viewer *n* áhorfandi
viewpoint *n* sjónarhorn
Viking *n* víkingur, ~ age víkingaöld, ~ ship víkingaskip
village *n* þorp
Vilnius (capital of Lithuania) *N* Viliníus (höfuðborg Lithéans)
vinaigrette *n* vinaigrette sósa
vine *n* vínviður; *(climbing)* klifurjurt
vinegar *n* edik: white wine ~ hvítvínsedik, balsamic ~ balsamik edik, apple cider ~ eplaedik
vineyard *n* vínekra
vintage 1 *adj* árgangs-: ~ wine vín af góðum árgangi; *(old)* forn-, gamaldags-: ~ clothes gamaldags föt; 2 *n* vínárgangur, vínuppskera
viola *n mus* lágfiðla, víóla
violence *n* ofbeldi
violent *adj* ofbeldisfullur
violently *adv* með ofbeldi
violin *n mus* fiðla
VIP lounge *n* vildarsalur
virgin *n* hrein mey
Virgo *n astro* Meyjan
virtually *adv* nánst, svo að segja
virtue *n* dyggð
virus *n med* veira, vírus; computer ~ tölvuveira, tölvuvírus
visa *n* vegabréfsáritun; *(credit card)* vísakort: do you take ~? tekurðu vísakort?
visible *adj* sýnilegur
vision *n* sýn
visit 1 *n* heimsókn: pay a ~ to fara í heimsókn til; 2 *v (a place)* fara til: ~ a museum fara á safn, ~ Iceland fara til Íslands; *(people)* heimsækja: ~ my relatives heimsækja ættingja, ~ friends heimsækja vini
visiting hours *n* opnunartími
visitor *n* gestur

visor *n (in cars)* skyggni
visual *adj* sjón-
vital *adj* lífsnauðsynlegur; *(lively)* fjörlegur
vitamin *n* vítamín; ~ **tablet** vítamíntafla
vocabulary *n* orðaforði
vocal *adj* tal-, radd-; *(singing)* söng-; ~ **criticism** hávær mótmæli
vodka *n* vodki: **a shot of** ~ vodkaskot
voice *n* rödd
volcanic *adj geol* eldfjalla-: ~ **activity** eldvirkni, ~ **era** eldgosatímabil, ~ **eruption** eldgos, ~ **island** eldfjallaeyja, ~ **region** eldfjallasvæði
volcano *n geol* eldfjall
volcanology *n geol* eldfjallafræði
volleyball *n (sport)* blak; *(ball)* blakbolti

voltage *n* spenna, rafspenna
volume *n (sound)* hljóðstyrkur; *(book)* bindi; *(size)* rúmmál
voluntarily *adv* sjálfviljugt
voluntary *adj* sjálfboðaliði
volunteer *n* sjálfboðaliði
vomit 1 *n* æla; **2** *v* æla, kasta upp, gubba
vote 1 *n* atkvæði; **2** *v* kjósa, greiða atkvæði
voucher *n* úttektarmiði: **lunch** ~ matarmiði
vowel *n ling* sérhljóði
vulva *n anat* píka, sköp

W

wade *v* vaða: ~ **a stream** vaða yfir læk

waders *n* bomsur

wadi *n* gil

wafer *n* ískex

waffle *n* vaffla: ~ **with jam and cream** vaffla með sultu og rjóma

waffle iron *n* vöfflujárn

wage *n* laun, kaup

wagtail *n zool* erla: **white** ~ maríuerla

waist *n* mitti

waistcoat *n* vesti

wait 1 *n* bið: **is there a long ~?** er löng bið?; **2** *v* bíða: ~ **for me!** bíddu eftir mér!

waiter *n* þjónn

waiting room *n* biðstofa

waiting list *n* biðlisti

waitress *n* þjónn, þjónustustúlka

waiver *n* afsal: **sign a** ~ skrifa undir afsal

wake *v (somebody)* vekja: **can you ~ me up at 7?** geturðu vakið mig klukkan sjö?; *(yourself)* vakna: **I ~ up at 8** ég vaknaði klukkan átta

wake-up call *n* vakning: **can I have a ~ at nine?** getið þið vakið mig klukkan níu?

Wales *N* Wales

walk *v* ganga, gönguferð; *(route)* gönguleið

walking *n* ganga: ~ **route** gönguleið, ~ **shoes** gönguskór

wall *n* veggur

wallet *n* veski

walnut 1 *adj* rauðbrúnn; **2** *n (nut)* valhneta; *(wood)* valhnotuviður

walrus *n zool* rostungur

wander *v* flækjast, reika, ráfa

want *v* vilja, langa: **I ~ to go to Iceland** mig langar að fara til

Íslands, **I ~ a beer** mig langar í bjór, **I don't ~ this** ég vil þetta ekki; *(lack)* vantar: **I ~ for nothing** mig vantar ekkert

war *n* stríð, styrjöld: ~ **memorial** stríðsminnismerki, **World ~ II** heimsstyrjöldin síðari, **the cod ~** þorskastríðið, **civil ~** borgarastyrjöld

ward *n* deild: **maternity ~** fæðingardeild, **children's ~** barnadeild

wardrobe *n* fataskápur; *(theater)* búningasafn

warehouse *n* vörugeymsla

warm *adj (day, weather)* heitur, hlýr: **it's ~ outside** það er hlýtt úti, **it's too ~ in here** það er of heitt hérna

warmer *adj* heitari, hlýrri

warmth *n* hlýja

warn *v* vara við

warning *n* viðvörun: ~ **light** viðvörunarljós, ~ **sign** viðvörunarskilti

warrant *n leg* heimild: **search ~** leitarheimild

warranty *n* ábyrgð: **under ~** (enn) í ábyrgð

Warsaw (capital of Poland) *N* Varsjá (höfuðborg Póllands)

wart *n* varta

wasabi *n* wasabi

wash 1 *n* þvottur: **hand ~** handþvottur; **2** *v* þvo: ~ **dishes** þvo upp, ~ **oneself** þvo sér, ~ **hands** þvo í höndunum

washable *adj* þvottheldur

washbasin *n* vaskur

washing *n* þvottur: ~ **line** þvottasnúra, ~ **powder** þvottaduft

washing machine *n* þvottavél

Washington, D.C. (capital of United States of America) *N*

Washington D.C. (höfuðborg
Bandaríkjanna)

washing-up *n* uppþvottur

washroom *n* baðherbergi, klósett,
snyrting

wasp *n* vespa, geitungur

waste 1 *n* sóun, eyðsla: ~ **of money**
sóun á peningum; *(garbage)* rusl,
úrgangur; *(desert)* auðn; **2** *v* sóa,
eyða; *(destroy)* eyðileggja, leggja
í auðn

wasteland *n* óbyggðir

watch 1 *n (timepiece)* úr: **do you
have a ~?** ertu með úr?; **2** *v* horfa:
~ **television** horfa á sjónvarpið, ~ **a
soccer game** horfa á fótboltaleik

watch out! *excl* passaðu þig!

watchmaker *n* úrsmiður

water *n* vatn: **bottle of ~** vatnsflaska,
sweet ~ ferskvatn; **territorial ~s**
landhelgi

water boiler *n* hraðsuðuketill

water bottle *n* vatnsflaska

water chestnut *n* vatnshneta

water faucet *n* vatnskrani

water table *n* grunnvatnsborð

watercolor *n* vatnslitur

watercress *n* vætukarsi

waterfall *n* foss

watermelon *n* vatnsmelóna

waterproof *adj* vatnsþéttur, vatns-
heldur: ~ **shoes** vatnsheldir skór

watt *n* vatt

wave 1 *n* alda, bára; **2** *v* bylgjast;
(greeting) veifa, vinka: ~ **goodbye**
vinka bless

wax *v (car, floor)* gljái, bón; **bee's ~**
vax; **ear ~** eyrnamergur

wax bean *n* vaxbaun

way *n* leið, vegur: **it's on the ~** það
er á leiðinni, **which ~?** hvaða
leið?; *(direction)* átt, leið: **go this
~** farðu í þessa átt; *expr* **by the ~**
heyrðu annars, vel á minnst

we *pron* við

weak *adj* veikburða, máttlítill,
slappur: **to be ~** að vera máttlaus,

að vera slappur; bragðlítill: ~
flavor bragðlítill

weakness *n (energy)* þróttleysi;
(willpower) veikleiki

wealth *n* auður, ríkidæmi

wealthy *adj* ríkur, auðugur

weapon *n* vopn

wear *v* vera í, klæðast: ~ **a sweater**
vera í peysu; *(carry)* vera með: ~
glasses vera með gleraugu

wear out *v* slíta

wearing *n* þreytandi

weather *n* veður: **what's the ~ like
in June?** hvernig er veðrið í júní?,
~ **forecast** veðurspá, ~ **report**
veðurfréttir

web *n* vefur: **spider ~** köngulóarvefur

webcam *n* vefmyndavél

webpage *n comp* vefsíða

website *n comp* vefsetur

webstore *n comp* netverslun

wedding *n* brúðkaup: ~ **anniversary**
brúðkaupsafmæli, ~ **cake** brúðar-
terta, ~ **present** brúðargjöf

Wednesday *n* miðvikudagur: **on
~** á miðvikudag(inn), **last ~**
síðastliðinn miðvikudag, ~ **next
week** á miðvikudaginn í næstu
viku, **on ~s** á miðvikudögum

weed *n flora* illgresi; *(slang for
marijuana)* maríúana

week *n* vika: **this ~** í þessari viku,
every ~ í hverri viku, **last ~** í
síðustu viku, **next ~** í næstu viku

weekday *n* vikudagur

weekend *n* helgi: **this ~** um helgina,
last ~ um síðustu helgi, **next ~** um
næstu helgi

weekly 1 *adj* vikulegur: **a ~ dose**
vikulegur skammtur; **2** *adv* vikulega

weigh *v* vega, vigta: ~ **a suitcase**
vikta tösku; **what do you ~?** hvað
ertu þung(ur)?

weight *n* þyngd: **maximum ~ is 20
kg** hámarksþyngd er tuttugu kíló;
lose ~ léttast

weightlifting *n* kraftlyftingar

weird *adj* skrýtinn
welcome 1 *adj* velkominn; **a ~ guest** aufúsugestur; **2** *interj* velkominn: **~ to ...** velkomin(n) til ...; *expr* **you're ~!** það var lítið!
welfare *n* velferð: **~ state** velferðarríki; **on ~** á bótum; **~ work** félagsleg aðstoð
well 1 *adj (healthy)* heilbrigður; *(good)* góður; **2** *n (water)* brunnur, uppspretta; **3** *adv* vel; **4** *interj (before an objection)* ja: **~, I don't agree** ja, ég er ekki sammála; *(before a continuation)* jæja: **~, let us begin** jæja, við skulum byrja
well-behaved *adj* kurteis, stilltur
well-being *n* vellíðan, velferð
Wellington (capital of New Zealand) *N* Wellington (höfuðborg Nýja-Sjálands)
well-known *adj* vel þekktur
wellness *n* vellíðan
wellness tourism *n* heilsutengd ferðaþjónusta
Welsh 1 *adj* velskur; **2** *n (language)* velska
west 1 *adj* vestur-; **2** *n* vestur: **in the ~** í vestri, **the wild ~** villta vestrið; **3** *adv* vestur, í vestur: **go ~** fara vestur
West Indies *N* Vestur-Indíur
western *adj* vesturlenskur, vestrænn
wet *adj* blautur, votur: **~ through** holdvotur; **~ paint** nýmálað
wetsuit *n* blautbúningur
whale *n* hvalur: **~ museum** hvalasafn, **~ watching** hvalaskoðun
what 1 *adj* hvaða: **~ street?** hvaða gata?; **2** *pron (interrogative)* hvað: **~ is that?** hvað er þetta?, **~ time is it?** hvað er klukkan?, **~ for?** til hvers?; *(relative)* það sem: **~ I saw** það sem ég sá
whatever *pron* hvað sem: **~ people say** hvað sem fólk segir
wheat *n* hveiti: **~ bread** hveitibrauð, **~ pasta** hveitipasta

wheel *n* hjól; **steering ~** stýri
wheelchair *n* hjólastóll
wheezing *n* más
whelk *n zool* beitukóngur
when 1 *pron* hvenær: **~ did you come?** hvenær komstu?; **2** *conj* þegar: **~ I was young** þegar ég var ung(ur)
whenever *conj (any time)* hvenær sem er; *(each time)* í hvert skipti sem
where *conj (location)* hvar: **~ do you stay?** hvar býrðu?; *(movement)* hvert: **~ are you going?** hvert ertu að fara?; *(relative)* þar sem: **~ I was yesterday** þar sem ég var í gær
whereas *conj (since)* þar sem; *(on the other hand)* en
wherever *conj* hvar sem er
whether *conj* hvort
whey *n* mysa
which 1 *adj* hvaða: **~ way?** í hvaða átt?; **2** *pron (of many)* hver; *(of two)* hvor: **~ of them?** hver þeirra?; *(relative)* sem: **~ we saw** sem við sáum
while 1 *n* stund: **in a ~** smá stund, **wait a ~** bíddu í smá stund; **that was a ~ ago** það er töluverður tími síðan; **2** *conj* þegar, á meðan: **~ I was in Iceland** þegar ég var á Íslandi, **~ you wait** á meðan þú bíður
whip 1 *n* svipa; **2** *v (someone)* slá, lemja; *(cream, etc)* þeyta
whipped *adj* þeyttur: **~ cream** þeyttur rjómi, **~ eggs** þeytt egg
whipping cream *n* þeytirjómi
whiskey *n* viskí
whisper 1 *n* hvísl; **2** *v* hvísla
whistle 1 *n* blístur; **2** *v* blístra
Whit Sunday *n* hvítasunnudagur
white *adj* hvítur
white bread *n* franskbrauð
white cabbage *n* hvítkál
White House *n* Hvíta húsið
white meat *n* hvítt kjöt
white sauce *n* uppstúf
white whale *n zool* mjaldur

white wine *n* hvítvín

whitebait *n (fish)* smáfiskur

whiteboard *n* tússtafla

whitefish *n* hvítur fiskur

white-water *adj* flúðir

whither *adv* hvert

whiting *n* lýsa

Whitsun *n* hvítasunna

who *pron* hver

WHO. *See* **World Health Organization**

whoever *pron* hver sem

whole 1 *adj* heill, allur: **the ~ day** allan daginn, **the ~ trip** alla ferðina; *(not refined)* ~ **rice** gróf hrísgrjón, ~ **wheat** heilhveiti; 2 *n* heild

wholesome *adj* hollur: ~ **food** hollur matur, ~ **lifestyle** hollur lífstíll

whose *pron* hvers, hver á: ~ **daughter are you?** hvers dóttir ertu?, ~ **is this?** hver á þetta?

why *adv* hvers vegna, af hverju: ~ **is that?** af hverju?, ~ **not?** af hverju ekki?

wide *adj* breiður: **a ~ river** breið á; *(covers large area)* víðfeðmur, yfirgripsmikill

widely *adv* víða: ~ **known** þekktur víða

widespread *adj* útbreiddur

widow *n* ekkja

widower *n* ekkill

width *n* vídd, breidd

wife *n* eiginkona, kona: **my ~** konan mín

wild *adj* villtur: ~ **animal** villt dýr, ~ **berries** villt ber

wildcat *n zool* villiköttur

wildlife *n zool* dýralíf

wildly *adv* tryllingslega

will 1 *n (wanting)* vilji: **he has no ~ of his own** hann hefur engan sjálfstæðan vilja; 2 *v [regular present tense]* **I ~ let you know** ég læt þig vita, **when ~ you come?** hvenær kemurðu?

willing *adj* viljugur, reiðubúinn

willingly *adv* af fúsum og frjálsum vilja

willingness *n* vilji

willow *n flora* víðir

win 1 *n* sigur; *(economic)* gróði; 2 *v* vinna, sigra; *(earn)* ávinna sér

wind 1 *n* vindur: ~ **direction** vindátt, ~ **energy** vindorka, ~ **force** vindstyrkur, ~ **speed** vindhraði; 2 *v* bugðast, hlykkjast; ~ **sth up** binda endi á; *expr* **be wound up** vera æstur

wind instrument *n mus* blásturshljóðfæri

windbreaker *n* vindjakki

windmill *n* vindmylla

window *n* gluggi: **open the ~** opna gluggann, **close the ~** loka glugganum, ~ **seat** gluggasæti

windscreen *n* framrúða

windshield *n* framrúða

windshield wiper *n* rúðuþurrkur

windsurf *v sports* fara á seglbretti

windsurfing board *n* seglbretti

windy *adj* vindasamur

wine *n* vín: **red ~** rauðvín, **white ~** hvítvín, **sparkling ~** freyðivín, **French ~** frönsk vín

wine cellar *n* vínkjallari

wine list *n* vínlisti

wineglass *n* vínglas

wing *n* vængur

winner *n* sigurvegari

winter *n* vetur: **last ~** síðastliðinn vetur, **next ~** næsta vetur, ~ **solstice** vetrarsólstöður

wipe *v* þurrka

wire *n* vír

wireless *adj* þráðlaus

wireless Internet *n comp* þráðlaust net: **do you have ~?** eruð þið með þráðlaust net?

wisdom *n* viska

wisdom tooth *n* endajaxl

wise *adj* gáfaður, klár

wish *v* óska: **I ~ you would stop**

that ég vildi óska þess að þú hættir þessu; **best** ~**es** bestu óskir!

witch n norn, galdranorn

witchcraft n galdur, svartigaldur

with prep með

withdraw v taka burt; ~ **money** taka út peninga

withdrawal n úttekt

within 1 adv að innan, inni; **2** prep (less than) innan við: ~ **one kilometer** innan við einn kílómetra; (inside) innan í, inni í

without prep án, utan: ~ **doubt** án efa

witness 1 n vitni; **2** v verða vitni að

wizard n galdramaður

wolf n zool úlfur

wolffish n zool steinbítur

woman n kona

womb n móðurlíf

women n konur: ~'s **room** kvennasnyrting, ~'s **clothing** kvenföt

wonder v undrast; (think about) velta fyrir sér: **I was** ~**ing** ég var að velta fyrir mér

wonderful adj dásamlegur, yndislegur

wood n (material) viður, tré

wooden adj tré-, viðar-: ~ **knife** smjörhnífur, ~ **spoon** tréskeið

woods n skógur

woodwind n mus tréblásturshljóðfæri

wool n ull: **Icelandic** ~ íslensk ull, lopi

woolen adj ullar-: ~ **sweater** ullarpeysa, ~ **socks** ullarsokkar, ~ **blanket** ullarteppi

woolens n ullarvörur

Worcestershire sauce n Worcestershire sósa

word n orð: ~ **order** orðaröð, ~ **play** orðaleikur

word processing n comp ritvinnsla

work 1 n (at)vinna, starf: **I'm late for** ~ ég er sein í vinnuna; (result) verk: **art**~ listaverk; **2** v vinna, starfa: **do you** ~ **here?** vinnur þú hér?; (function) virka: **this doesn't** ~ þetta virkar ekki

work out v sports stunda líkamsrækt

work permit n atvinnuleyfi

workbook n vinnubók

worker n starfsmaður; (unskilled) verkamaður

workforce n starfslið

working adj starfandi, vinnandi; **it's** ~ það virkar

working-class adj verkalýðs-

workout n sports líkamsrækt

workshop n verkstæði; (academic) málstofa

world n veröld, heimur: **the new** ~ nýi heimurinn

World Cup n sports heimsbikarinn

World Health Organization (WHO) n Alþjóðaheilbrigðismálastofnunin

worldwide 1 adj heims-; **2** adv um allan heim, á heimsvísu

worm n ormur, lirfa, maðkur: **earth**~ ánamaðkur

worried adj áhyggjufullur

worry 1 n áhyggjur; **2** v hafa áhyggjur

worrying adj hafa áhyggjur: **stop** ~! ekki hafa áhyggjur!

worse adj compar verri

worship 1 n dýrkun; **2** v dýrka, tilbiðja

worst adj superl verstur

worth adj vera virði: ~ **seeing** þess virði að sjá, **what is this** ~? hvers virði er þetta?

worthy adj verðugur

worthwhile adj ómaksins vert

would v myndi/mundi; (requests) geta, vilja: ~ **you help me?** gætirðu hjálpað mér?

wound 1 n med sár; **2** v særa

wounded adj med særður

wrap v vefja: **chicken** ~ kjúklingavefja

wrapping n umbúðir

wrestling n glíma

wrist n anat úlnliður

write v skrifa: ~ **down** skrifa niður, ~ **off** afskrifa, ~ **up** hreinskrifa

writer n (rit)höfundur

writing n skriftir; (result) ritverk

written *adj* skrifaður, ritaður
wrong 1 *adj* rangur, skakkur, vitlaus:
~ **number** skakkt númer; *expr*
what's ~? hvað er að?; **2** *adv*
rangt, skakkt, vitlaust

wrongly *adv* ranglega
www (worldwide web) *abbrev*
veraldarvefurinn

X-Y-Z

xenophobia *n* útlendingahræðsla
xerox *v* ljósrita
x-ray **1** *n med* röntgengeisli: ~ **examination** röntgenmyndataka; **2** *v* taka röntgenmynd
xylophone *n mus* sílófónn

yacht *n* snekkja, lystisnekkja
yam *n* sæt kartafla: **candied ~s** sætar kartöflur með sykurgljáa
yard *n* garður: **in the ~** í garðinum
yarn *n* garn
yarrow *n flora* vallhumall
yawn **1** *n* geispi; **2** *v* geispa
yeah! *interj* já!
year *n* ár: **happy new ~!** gleðilegt ár!, **this ~** í ár; **twenty-seven ~s old** tuttugu og sjö ára gamall
yeast *n* ger
yell *v* öskra
yellow *adj* gulur
yellow pages *n* gulu síðurnar
Yemen *N* Jemen
Yemeni *adj* jemenskur
yes *adv* já; *(answer to negative question)* jú
yesterday **1** *adv* í gær; **2** *n* gær-dagurinn; **the day before ~** í fyrradag
yet **1** *adv* enn: **not ~** ekki enn; **2** *conj* samt
Yiddish *n* jiddíska
yield *v* víkja
yoga *n* jóga
yogurt *n* jógúrt: **low fat ~** fituskert jógúrt, léttjógúrt

yolk *n* eggjarauða
you *pron* þú *sing*; þið *pl*
young *adj* ungur
your *adj* þinn
yours *pron* þinn: ~ **truly** þinn einlægi, **is this ~?** átt þú þetta?
yourself *pron* sjálfur
youth *n* æska
youth hostel *n* farfuglaheimili

Zagreb (capital of Croatia) *N* Sagreb (höfuðborg Króatíu)
Zambia *n* Sambía
zebra *n zool* sebrahestur
zero *n* núll
zest *n* **lemon ~** sítrónubörkur; *(enthusiasm)* ákafi; ~ **for life** lífslöngun; *(figuratively)* krydd: **this adds ~ to my life** þetta kryddar tilveruna
zip **1** *n* rennilás; **2** *v* að renna upp; *comp* ~ **a file** zip-skjal
zipper *n* rennilás
zodiac *n* stjörnumerki
zone **1** *n* svæði; **2** *v* skipta í svæði: ~ **as residential** skipuleggja sem íbúðasvæði
zoning *adj* svæðaskipting; *(in city planning)* borgarskipulag
zoo *n* dýragarður
zucchini *n* kúrbítur: **fried ~** steiktur kúrbítur, ~ **chips** kúrbítsflögur

Also available from Hippocrene Books

Beginner's Icelandic with 2 Audio CDs
Helga Hilmisdóttir and Jacek Kozlowski

This introductory guide is designed for both classroom use and self-study. Each of the 14 lessons opens with a dialogue about an everyday topic, followed by vocabulary lists, explanations of grammar, and exercises. Also includes Icelandic-English/English-Icelandic glossaries and two audio CDs of dialogues and vocabulary with correct pronunciation by native speakers.

$35.00pb · two audio CDs · 978-0-7818-1191-0

Dictionaries & Language Self-Study

Beginner's Danish with 2 Audio CDs
ISBN 978-0-7818-1199-6 · $35.00pb

**Danish-English/English-Danish
Dictionary & Phrasebook**
4,000 entries · ISBN 978-07818-0917-7 · $13.95pb

**Finnish-English/English-Finnish
Dictionary & Phrasebook**
5,000 entries · ISBN 0-7818-0956-8 · $14.95pb

**Norwegian-English/English-Norwegian
Dictionary & Phrasebook**
3,500 entries · ISBN 0-7818-0955-X · $14.95pb

**Norwegian-English/English-Norwegian
Practical Dictionary**
50,000 entries · ISBN 978-0-7818-1106-4 · $29.95pb

Beginner's Swedish with 2 Audio CDs
ISBN 0-7818-1157-0 · $32.00pb

Swedish-English/English-Swedish
Practical Dictionary
28,000 entries · ISBN 978-0-7818-1246-7 · $29.95pb

Swedish-English/English-Swedish
Dictionary & Phrasebook
3,000 entries · ISBN 0-7818-0903-7 · $14.95pb

Prices subject to change without prior notice. **To purchase Hippocrene Books** contact your local bookstore or visit www.hippocrenebooks.com.